Human Resource Management

Authors

DeCenzo

To order books or for customer service please,

call 1-800-CALL WILEY (225-5945).

Printed in the United States of America 10 9 8 7 6 5 4 3 2 1

Printed in the United States of America
ED-12-05-11

List of Titles

Fundamentals of Human Resource Management
by David A. DeCenzo and Stephen P. Robbins
Copyright © 2007, ISBN: 978-0-47000-794-5

Table of Contents

The first person to invent a car that runs on water…

… may be sitting right in your classroom! Every one of your students has the potential to make a difference. And realizing that potential starts right here, in your course.

When students succeed in your course—when they stay on-task and make the breakthrough that turns confusion into confidence—they are empowered to realize the possibilities for greatness that lie within each of them. We know your goal is to create an environment where students reach their full potential and experience the exhilaration of academic success that will last them a lifetime. *WileyPLUS* can help you reach that goal.

Wiley**PLUS** is an online suite of resources—including the complete text—that will help your students:

- come to class better prepared for your lectures
- get immediate feedback and context-sensitive help on assignments and quizzes
- track their progress throughout the course

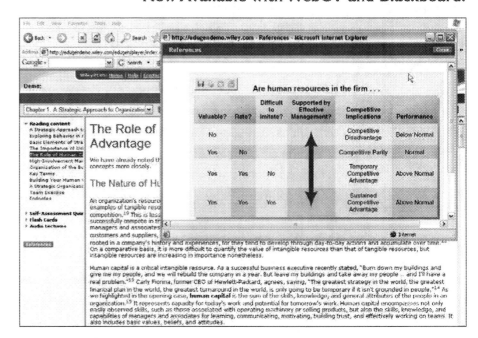

FUNDAMENTALS OF HUMAN RESOURCE MANAGEMENT

Ninth Edition

David A. DeCenzo
Coastal Carolina University
Conway, SC

Stephen P. Robbins
San Diego State University
San Diego, CA

John Wiley & Sons, Inc.

Associate Publisher	Judith Joseph
Senior Acquisitions Editor	Jayme Heffler
Associate Editor	Jennifer Conklin
Editorial Assistant	Carissa Marker
Executive Marketing Manager	Christopher Ruel
Senior Production Editor	Sandra Dumas
Senior Designer	Kevin Murphy
Media Editor	Allison Morris
Senior Illustration Editor	Sandra Rigby
Photo Manager/Photo Editor	Hilary Newman
Production Management Services	mb editorial services
Cover Photo	Per Eriksson/The Image Bank/Getty Images, Inc.

This book was typeset in 10/12 Sabon by TechBooks and printed and bound by Courier(Kendallville). The cover was printed by Courier(Kendallville).

The paper in this book was manufactured by a mill whose forest management programs include sustained yield harvesting of its timberlands. Sustained yield harvesting principles ensure that the number of trees cut each year does not exceed the amount of new growth.

This book is printed on acid-free paper. ∞

ISBN 13 978-0470-00794-5
ISBN 10 0-470-00794-X

Printed in the United States of America.

10   9   8   7   6   5   4   3   2   1

ONE

If you were to walk into a convenience store in Central Valley, California, and purchase a six-pack of Budweiser beer, would you be surprised to learn that not more than a minute after you made your purchase someone at Anheuser-Busch in St. Louis, Missouri, knew exactly what you bought? If you were familiar with BudNet technology, it probably would not surprise you at all.[1]

Anheuser-Busch's BudNet technology is dramatically changing how the beer industry operates and how employees do their jobs. Consider, for example, how Dereck Gurden, a sales representative from Sierra Beverage, one of 700 national distributors for Anheuser-Busch, spends his day. Shortly after arriving at a store in his 800-square-mile territory, Gurden quickly leaps into action with his sales tools—a hand-held computer and a cell phone—two vital parts of the BudNet technology. As he enters the store, his hand-held receives all pertinent information about the store, its inventory, previous four-week sales, and its account receivables. He inputs a variety of data, including how the products were displayed, how much of a competitor's prod-

(*Source:* © AP/Wide World Photos)

uct is available, and how it's displayed. Checking sales with inventory, he quickly determines the correct amount of product to order, using custom software, and uploads his information back to Anheuser-Busch. Gurden, like over 1000 other sales representatives who distribute Anheuser-Busch products around the United States, has simply become the source for a wealth of information about its product sales and those of its competitors.

While having such firsthand information is critical, what makes this technology so interesting is the realiza-

tion that the emphasis is more on competitive analysis than on inventory control. BudNet has been coupled with census data, community information, and other demographic information and linked to the computer networks of each store—all from the everyday work of its sales force. This is providing Anheuser-Busch with some exceptional competitive data. For example, when you purchase beer at one of these stores, Anheuser-Busch now knows what product you bought and what you paid for it, when the beer was brewed, whether the beer was warm or chilled, and whether it was available close by for a cheaper price. By having this information, as well as the competitive picture that each sales representative is recording during his or her visit, Anheuser-Busch is better able to make near real-time marketing strategy. They are also better able to determine the right promotion for any given location—based on the demographics of the area. So Anheuser-Busch's technology allows them to accurately predict what beer drinkers are buying, where they make their purchases, and when they do—store by store. It has allowed Anheuser-Busch to know, for instance, that beer sold in cans sells better in blue-collar neighborhoods, while bottles sell better in white-collar neighborhoods.[2]

The evidence suggests that BudNet is definitely helping Anheuser-Busch. During the past twenty quarters, Anheuser-Busch has had double-digit profitability, while none of its competitors have posted more than four straight quarters of such growth. And for the employees, they are enjoying the benefits such corporate gains allow!

2

Strategic Implications of a Dynamic HRM Environment

Learning Outcomes

After reading this chapter, you will be able to

1. Discuss how cultural environments affect human resource management practices.
2. Describe how technology is changing HRM.
3. Identify significant changes that have occurred in workforce composition.
4. Describe the HRM implications of a labor shortage.
5. Describe how changing skill requirements affect human resource management.
6. Explain why organizational members focus on quality and continuous improvements.
7. Describe work process engineering and its implications for HRM.
8. Identify who makes up the contingent workforce and the HRM implications.
9. Define employee involvement and list its critical components.
10. Explain the importance of ethics in an organization.

INTRODUCTION

The world of work as we know continues to rapidly change. Even as little as 25 years ago, the times were calmer than they are today. But that doesn't mean that we didn't experience change back then. On the contrary, we were, as we are today, in a state of flux. Today, however, the changes appear to be happening more rapidly.

As part of an organization, then, human resource management (HRM) must be prepared to deal with the effects of the changing world of work. This means understanding the implications of globalization, technology changes, workforce diversity, labor shortages, changing skill requirements, continuous improvement initiatives, the contingent workforce, decentralized work sites, and employee involvement. Let's look at how these changes are affecting HRM goals and practices.

UNDERSTANDING CULTURAL ENVIRONMENTS

global village

A concept in which telecommunication and transportation technologies have essentially reduced time and distance effects to produce a single worldwide community.

multinational corporations (MNCs)

Corporations with significant operations in more than one country.

Part of the rapidly changing environment organizational members face is the globalization of business. Organizations are no longer constrained by national borders. BMW, a German-owned firm, builds cars in South Carolina. Similarly, McDonald's sells hamburgers in China. Exxon, a so-called American company, receives more than three-fourths of its revenues from sales outside the United States. Toyota makes cars in Kentucky. General Motors makes cars in Brazil. And Mercedes sport utility vehicles are made in Alabama.[3] Parts for Ford Motor Company's Crown Victoria come from all over the world: Mexico (seats, windshields, and fuel tanks), Japan (shock absorbers), Spain (electronic engine controls), Germany (antilock brake systems), and England (key axle parts). These examples illustrate that the world has become a **global village**—producing and marketing goods and services worldwide. To be effective in this boundless world, organizational members need to adapt to cultures, systems, and techniques different from their own.

International businesses have been with us for a long time. For instance, Siemens, Remington, and Singer were selling their products in many countries in the nineteenth century. By the 1920s, some companies, including Fiat, Ford, Unilever, and Royal Dutch/Shell, had gone multinational. Not until the mid-1960s, however, did **multinational corporations (MNCs)** become commonplace. These corporations, which maintain significant operations in two or more countries simultaneously but are based in one home country, initiated the rapid growth in international trade. Today, companies such as Gillette, Wal-Mart, Coca-Cola, and AFLAC are among a growing number of U.S.-based firms that derive significant portions of their annual revenues from foreign operations.[4] The rise of multinational and transnational corporations[5] places new requirements on human resource managers. For instance, human resources must ensure that employees with the appropriate mix of knowledge, skills, and cultural adaptability are available to handle global assignments.

All countries have different values, morals, customs, political and economic systems, and laws. Traditional approaches to studying international business have sought to advance each of these topic areas. However, a strong case can be made that traditional business approaches need to be understood within their social context. That is, organizational success can come from a variety of practices—each of which is derived from a different business environment. For example, status is perceived differently in different countries. In France, for instance, status is often the result of factors important to the organization, such as seniority and education. This emphasis is called ascribed status. In the United States, status is more a function of what individuals have personally accomplished (achieved status). Human resource managers need to understand societal issues (such as status) that

Countries That Value Individualism and Acquiring Things	Countries That Value Collectivism, Relationships, and Concern for Others
United States	Japan
Great Britain	Colombia
Australia	Pakistan
Canada	Singapore
Netherlands	Venezuela
New Zealand	Philippines

Exhibit 1-1
Cultural Similarities

might affect operations in another country. Countries also have different laws. For instance, in the United States, laws guard against employers' taking action against employees solely on the basis of an employee's age. Not all countries have similar laws. Organizations that view the global environment from any single perspective may be too narrow and potentially problematic. A more appropriate approach is to recognize the cultural dimensions of a country's environment. Although it is not our intent here to provide the scope of cultural issues needed for an employee to go to any country, we do want to recognize that some similarities do exist (see Exhibit 1-1). Research findings allow us to group countries according to such cultural variables as status differentiation, societal uncertainty, and assertiveness.[6] These variables indicate a country's means of dealing with its people and how the people see themselves. For example, in an individualistic society like the United States, people are primarily concerned with their own family. In a collective society (the opposite of an individualistic one) like that in Japan, however, people care for all individuals who are part of their group. Thus, a strongly individualistic U.S. employee may not work well if sent to a Pacific Rim country where collectivism dominates. Accordingly, flexibility and adaptability are key components for employees going abroad. To make this a reality, human resource managers must have a thorough understanding of the culture of the areas around the globe in which they may send employees.

HRM must also develop mechanisms that will help multicultural individuals work together. As background, language, custom, or age differences become more prevalent, employee conflict is likely to increase. HRM must make every effort to acclimate different groups to each other, finding ways to build teams and thus reduce conflict.

It's important to note that not all HRM theories and practices are universally applicable to managing human resources around the world. This is especially true in countries where work values differ considerably from those in the United States. Second, human resource managers must take cultural values into account when trying to understand the behavior of people *from* different countries as well as those *in* different countries. Where possible in this text, we'll look at how U.S. HRM practices may differ in the global village.

Organizations are no longer confined to national boundaries. Now that companies can produce and market goods and services around the world, we have a global village. The global village enables companies such as McDonald's to sell products anywhere in the world—like this restaurant in China. By moving into China, McDonald's annual revenues have increased and so too has its market share. (Source: Steven Harris/Getty Images News and Sport Services)

THE CHANGING WORLD OF TECHNOLOGY

It's easy to forget that just 25 years ago, no one had a fax machine, a cellular phone, or a notebook computer. Terms we now use in our everyday vocabulary, like e-mail and Internet, were known to maybe, at best, a few hundred people. Computers often took up considerable space, quite unlike today's four-pounds or lighter laptops. Moreover, if you were to talk about networks 25 years ago, people would have assumed you were talking about ABC, CBS, or NBC—the major television networks.

The silicon chip and other advances in technology have permanently altered world economies and, as we'll show momentarily, the way people work. Digital electronics, optical data storage, more powerful and portable computers, and computers' ability to communicate with each other are changing the way information is created, stored, used, and shared. One individual who has studied these changes and predicted some of their implications is futurist Alvin Toffler. Toffler has written extensively about social change.[7] Classifying each period of social history, Toffler has argued that modern civilization has evolved over three "waves." With each wave came a new way of doing things. Some groups of people gained from the new way; others lost.

The first wave was driven by *agriculture*. Until the late nineteenth century, all economies were agrarian. For instance, in the 1890s, approximately 90 percent of people were employed in agriculture-related jobs. These individuals were typically their own bosses and were responsible for performing a variety of tasks. Their success, or failure, was contingent on how well they produced. Since the 1890s, the proportion of the population engaged in farming has consistently dropped. Now less than 5 percent of the global workforce is needed to provide our food; in the United States, it's under 3 percent.

The second wave was *industrialization*. From the late 1800s until the 1960s, most developed countries moved from agrarian societies to industrial societies. In doing so, work left the fields and moved into formal organizations. The industrial wave forever changed the lives of skilled craftsmen. No longer did they grow something or produce a product in its entirety. Instead, workers were hired into tightly structured and formal workplaces. Mass production, specialized jobs, and authority relationships became the mode of operation. It gave rise to a new group of workers—the blue-collar industrial workers—individuals paid to perform routine work that relied almost exclusively on physical stamina. By the 1950s, industrial workers had become the largest single group in every developed country. They made products such as steel, automobiles, rubber, and industrial equipment. Ironically, no class in history has ever risen faster than the blue-collar worker. And no class in history has ever fallen faster. Today, blue-collar industrial workers account for less than 30 percent of the U.S. workforce and will be less than half that in just a few years.[8] The shift since World War II has been away from manufacturing work and toward service jobs. Manufacturing jobs, as a proportion of the total civilian workforce, today are highest in Japan at just over 20 percent. In the United States, manufacturing jobs make up about 15 percent of the civilian workforce. In contrast, services make up about half of the jobs in Italy (the lowest percentage of any industrialized country) and more than three-fourths in the United States and Canada.[9]

What Is a Knowledge Worker?

Knowledge-work jobs are designed around the acquisition and application of information.

By the start of the 1970s, a new age was gaining momentum. This was based on information. Technological advancements were eliminating many low-skilled, blue-collar jobs. Moreover, the information wave was transforming society from a manufacturing focus to one of service. People were increasingly moving from jobs on the production floor to clerical, technical, and professional jobs. Job growth in the past 20 years has been in low-skilled service work (such as fast-food employees, clerks, and home health aides) and knowledge work. This latter group includes professionals such as registered nurses, accountants, teachers, lawyers, and engineers. It also includes technologists—people who work with their hands and with theoretical knowledge—commonly referred to as information technologists.[10] Computer programmers, software designers, and systems analysts are examples of jobs in this category. **Knowledge workers** as a group currently make up about a third of the U.S. workforce—individuals in jobs designed around the acquisition and application of information.

knowledge workers
Individuals whose jobs are designed around the acquisition and application of information.

Why the Emphasis on Technology?

Suppose you need information on how well your department is meeting its sales goals. Thirty years ago, you probably would have had to submit a requisition to the vice president of sales' office. The response may have taken a couple weeks, and the information would have been in whatever format the sales department dictated. Today, like the BudNet system, a few keystrokes on your computer produces that information almost instantaneously. Moreover, it will be precisely the information you want—which may be entirely different from the information one of your colleagues needs on a similar account.

Since the 1970s, U.S. companies such as General Electric, Citigroup Global Technologies, Wal-Mart, and 3M have been using automated offices, manufacturing robotics, computer-assisted design software, integrated circuits, microprocessors, and electronic meetings. Such technological advances make the organizations more productive and help them create and maintain a competitive advantage.

Technology includes any equipment, tools, or operating methods designed to make work more efficient. Technological advances integrate technology into a process for changing inputs into outputs. For example, to sell its goods or services, an organization must first transform certain inputs—labor, raw materials, and the like—into outputs. In years past, human labor performed many of these transforming operations. Technology, however, has enhanced this production process by replacing human labor with electronic and computer equipment. For instance, assembly operations at General Motors rely heavily on robotics. Robots perform repetitive tasks—such as spot welding and painting much more quickly than humans can. And the robots are not subject to health problems caused by exposure to chemicals or other hazardous materials. Technology is also making it possible to better serve customers. The banking industry, for instance, has replaced thousands of tellers with ATM machines and online banking systems.

Technological advancements also provide better, more useful information (see Technology Corner). Most cars built today, for example, have an onboard computer circuit into which a technician can plug to determine operating problems, saving mechanics countless diagnostic hours. And at Wal-Mart, technology has meant better and more timely information. Company representatives instantly obtain warehouse logistics and inventories, and as a result, Wal-Mart has increased its efficiency by more than 20 percent.

technology
Any equipment, tools, or operating methods designed to make work more efficient.

How Technology Affects HRM Practices

Technology has had a positive effect on internal operations for organizations, but it also has changed the way human resource managers work. They work and provide support in what have become integrative communication centers. By linking computers, telephones, fax machines, copiers, printers, and the like, they disseminate information more quickly. In addition, technology helps them circumvent the physical confines of working only in a specified organizational location.[11] With notebook and desktop computers, fax machines, high-speed modems, organizational intranets, and other forms of technology, organizational members can do their work anyplace, anytime in decentralized work sites.[12]

Knowing the effect of technology helps individuals better facilitate human resource plans, make decisions faster, more clearly define jobs, and strengthen communications with both the external community and employees. How? Let's look at some specific examples.

Recruiting Disseminating information to individuals is one of the most critical aspects of recruiting. Word of mouth, newspaper advertisements, college visits, and

How has technology helped this bank's customers? Those paying bills now can do so more effectively and efficiently by paying them online and avoiding writing and mailing checks. (Source: Comstock/Age Fotostock America, Inc.)

TECHNOLOGY CORNER

HRM CHANGING TIMES

A decade or so ago, finding information about any subject, let alone HRM, was a tedious task. The legwork, the time spent looking things up, and the cost were high. Today, however, all that has changed. Information is just a "click" away on the Internet. For example, the following Web addresses are just a sampling of the wealth of information available to you that may be helpful in this class and in your personal pursuits.

www.knowledgepoint.com	Provides a human resources library
www.shrm.org	A premier site containing information about all aspects of human resources, as well as the certification process for HR professionals
www.workforce.com	Provides information on workforce issues
www.eeoc.gov	The Equal Employment Opportunity Commission's Web site with case law and legal matters concerning all aspects of equal employment opportunities
www.nlrb.gov	The National Labor Relations Board's Web site providing information regarding labor and management relationships
www.osha.gov	The Occupational Safety and Health Administration's Web site providing information on health and safety issues in today's organizations
www.ebri.org	Provides information on employee benefit matters
www.diversityhotwire.com	Focuses on diversity issues in organizations
www.wfpma.com	Focuses on global/ international HRM issues

the like are being supplemented or replaced altogether by job postings on the Internet. Posting jobs on company Web sites, or through specific job-search Web sites such as careerbuilder.com and monster.com, help human resource managers reach a larger pool of potential job applicants and assist in determining if an applicant possesses some of the basic technology skills. Additionally, rather than ask for a paper copy of a résumé, many organizations are asking applicants to submit an electronic résumé—one that can be quickly scanned for "relevance" to the job in question.

Employee Selection Hiring good people is particularly challenging in technology-based organizations because they require a unique brand of technical and professional people. Employees must be smart and able to survive in the demanding cultures of today's dynamic organizations. In addition, many such "qualified" individuals are in short supply and may go wherever they like. Once applicants have been identified, HRM must carefully screen final candidates to ensure they fit well into the organization's culture. The realities of organizational life today may focus on an informal, team-spirited workplace, one in which intense pressure to complete projects quickly and on time is critical, and a 24/7 (24 hours a day, 7 days a week) work mentality dominates. HRM selection tools need to "select out" people who aren't team players and can't handle ambiguity and stress.

Training and Development Technology is also dramatically changing how human resource managers orient, train, and develop employees—including their career management. The Internet has provided HRM opportunities to deliver specific information to employees on demand, whenever the employee has the time to concentrate on the material. These training media can "send" employees to training without having to physically transport them from one location to another.

ETHICAL ISSUES IN HRM

INVASION OF PRIVACY?

Technological advances have made the process of operating an organization much easier, but technological advancements have also provided employers a means of sophisticated employee monitoring. Although most of this monitoring is designed to enhance worker productivity, it could, and has been, a source of concern over worker privacy. These advantages have also brought with them difficult questions regarding what managers have the right to know about employees and how far they can go in controlling employee behavior both on and off the job.

What can your employer find out about you and your work? You might be surprised by the answers! Consider the following:

- The mayor of Colorado Springs, Colorado, reads the electronic mail messages that city council members sent to each other from their homes. He defended his actions by saying he was making sure that their e-mail to each other was not being used to circumvent his state's "open meeting" law that requires most council business to be conducted publicly.
- The U.S. Internal Revenue Service's internal audit group monitors a computer log that shows employee access to taxpayers' accounts. This monitoring activity allows management to see what employees are doing on their computers.
- American Express has an elaborate system for monitoring telephone calls. Daily reports are provided to supervisors that detail the frequency and length of employee calls, as well as how quickly incoming calls are answered.
- Employers in several organizations require employees to wear badges at all times while on company premises. These badges contain a variety of data that allows employees to enter certain locations in the organization. Smart badges, too, can transmit where the employee is at all times!

Just how much control should a company have over the private lives of its employees? Where should an employer's rules and controls end? Does the boss have the right to dictate what you do on your own free time and in your own home? Could, in essence, your boss keep you from riding a motorcycle, skydiving, smoking, drinking alcohol, or eating junk food? Again, the answers may surprise you. What's more, employer involvement in employees' off-work lives has been going on for decades. For instance, in the early 1900s, Ford Motor Company would send social workers to employees' homes to determine whether their off-the-job habits and finances were deserving of year-end bonuses. Other firms made sure employees regularly attended church services. Today, many organizations, in their quest to control safety and health insurance costs, are once again delving into their employees' private lives.

Although controlling employees' behaviors on and off the job may appear unjust or unfair, nothing in our legal system prevents employers from engaging in these practices. Rather, the law is based on the premise that if employees don't like the rules, they have the option of quitting.

Managers, too, typically defend their actions in terms of ensuring quality, productivity, and proper employee behavior. For instance, an IRS audit of its southeastern regional offices found that 166 employees took unauthorized looks at the tax returns of friends, neighbors, and celebrities.

When does an employer's need for information about employee performance cross over the line and interfere with a worker's right to privacy?[13] Is any employer action acceptable as long as employees are notified ahead of time that they will be monitored? And what about the demarcation between monitoring work and nonwork behavior? When employees do work-related activities at home during evenings and weekends, does management's prerogative to monitor employees remain in force? What's your opinion?

Ethics and Employee Rights Electronic surveillance of employees by employers is an issue that pits an organization's desire for control against an employee's right to privacy. The development of increasingly sophisticated surveillance software only adds to the ethical dilemma of how far an organization should go in monitoring the behavior of employees who work on computers (see Ethical Issues in HRM). Today, most businesses surveyed by the American Management Association indicate they monitor employees.[14]

Motivating Knowledge Workers What challenges are unique to motivating knowledge workers in organizations? Knowledge workers appear more susceptible to distractions that can undermine their work effort and reduce their productivity. Employers often believe they must monitor what employees are doing because employees are hired to work, not to surf the Web checking stock prices, placing bets at online casinos, or shopping for presents for family or friends. Recreational on-the-job Web surfing has been said to cost a billion dollars in wasted computer resources and billions of dollars in lost work productivity annually. That's a significant cost to businesses.

Paying Employees Market Value It's becoming more difficult today for organizations to find and keep technical and professional employees. Many have implemented an extensive list of attractive incentives and benefits rarely seen by non-managerial employees in typical organizations: for instance, signing bonuses, stock options, cars, free health club memberships, full-time on-site concierges, and cell phone bill subsidies. These incentives may benefit their recipients, but they have downsides. One is the effect these rewards have on those denied them. The other is the increasing problem created by stock options. Specifically, while they look good when a firm is growing and the stock market looks favorably on the company's future, stock options can demotivate employees when conditions turn negative.

Communications The rules of communication are being rewritten as comprehensive, integrated information networks remove constraints on its uses. Employees today can communicate with any individual directly without going through channels. They can communicate instantly anytime, with anyone, anywhere (see Workplace Issues).

These open communication systems break down historical organizational communication pattern flows. They also redefine how meetings, negotiations, supervision, and water-cooler talk are conducted. For instance, virtual meetings allow people in geographically dispersed locations to meet regularly. Moreover, it's now easier

WORKPLACE ISSUES

WHAT'S THIS THING CALLED A BLOG?

Technology in communications continues to change the way many people communicate with one another. One new phenomenon is something that's called a blog—a Web log that is open for public view. While it's often been associated with expressing political viewpoints, the tool has quickly swept across corporate America—and is showing itself as both a valuable tool as well as a potential means of disaster. Let's look at this two-sided device.

On the positive side, blogs enable companies to discuss ideas among organizational members and allow consumers a means of easy feedback. It's a quick and efficient means of advertising a company's products, as well as softer, more believable public relations information. Blogs also offer opportunities for employees to discuss "good things" that are happening to them—personalizing the "faceless" company to readers.

But not all blogs are advantageous. Disgruntled employees, dissatisfied customers, and the like can also use blogs to write about anything that they don't like. For example, consider an employee who doesn't like the organization's policies and practices. Rather than discuss his discontentment with someone in the organization, he vents his frustration on a blog he's created. And as a prank, another employee posts sexually explicit short stories on a blog for all to see. Are these permissible given they were done when the employees were not at work? They more than likely are. But all organizations should have some policy on the use of blogs. For example, an employee needs to understand that company private information is not to be placed in a blog. Even putting into a blog information about what one does on the job could be providing competitive intelligence to another organization interested in finding out how a competitor designs a certain product.

Will blogging continue? Undoubtedly yes. It's simply another communications tool that organizations, and HRM, must be aware of and constantly monitor to ensure that the positive aspects of blogs are achieved.

Source: Based on D. Kirkpatrick and D. Roth, "Why There's No Escaping the Blog," *Fortune* (January 10, 2005), pp. 40–44; S. E. Needleman, "Blogging Becomes a Corporate Job: Digital Handshake?" *Wall Street Journal* (May 31, 2005), p. B-1; J. Segal, "Beware Bashing Bloggers," *HR Magazine* (June 2005), pp. 165–171; and K. Wingfield, "Blogging for Business," *Wall Street Journal* (July 20, 2005), p. A-1.

for employees in Baltimore and Singapore to covertly share company gossip than for off-line employees who work two cubicles apart.

Decentralized Work Sites For human resource managers, much of the challenge regarding decentralized work sites revolves around training managers how to establish and ensure appropriate work quality and on-time completion. Decentralized work sites remove traditional "face time," and managers' need to "control" the work must change. Instead, greater employee involvement will allow workers the discretion to make decisions that affect them. For instance, although a due date is established for the work assigned to employees, managers must recognize that home workers will work at their own pace. Instead of focusing work efforts over an eight-hour period, the individual may work two hours here, three hours at another time, and another three late at night. The emphasis, then, will be on the final product, not on the means by which it is accomplished. Work at home may also require HRM to rethink its compensation policy. Will it pay workers by the hour, on a salary basis, or by the job performed? More than likely, jobs like claims processing that can be easily quantified and standardized will earn pay for actual work done.

Skill Levels What are the skill implications of this vast spread of technology? For one, employees' job skill requirements will increase.[15] Workers will need the ability to read and comprehend software and hardware manuals, technical journals, and detailed reports. Another implication is that technology tends to level the competitive playing field.[16] It provides organizations (no matter their size or market power) with the ability to innovate, bring products to market rapidly, and respond to customer requests. Companies like E-Trade and Ameritrade, for example, allow any individual to personally trade stocks online as opposed to making similar transactions through a large brokerage house.

A Legal Concern Organizations that use technology—especially the Internet and e-mail—must address the potential for harassment, bias, discrimination, and offensive sexual behavior abuses.[17] Evidence is increasing that many employees fail to use the same constraints in electronic communications that they use in traditional work settings. As one individual noted, human resource managers "all know that they can't hang up a *Penthouse* calendar in the workplace. They all know that they can't make a racist or sexist joke in the workplace."[18] But those same people may think it's acceptable to send racist and sexist jokes via e-mail or to download pornography at work. Consider what happened at Chevron, which settled a sexual harassment lawsuit for $2.2 million because offensive e-mails—like "25 reasons why beer is better than women"—were readily circulated on the company's e-mail system. Organizations such as Citigroup and Morgan Stanley Dean Witter have also been taken to court by employees for racist e-mail proliferating on their e-mail systems.[19] As one researcher pointed out, federal law views a company's e-mail no differently than if offensive materials were circulated on a company's letterhead.[20] HRM policy must define inappropriate electronic communications, reserve the right to monitor employee Internet and e-mail usage, and specify disciplinary actions for violations.

WORKFORCE DIVERSITY

Until recently, organizations took a "melting-pot" approach to personnel diversity, assuming that people who were different would somehow automatically want to assimilate. But today's managers have found that employees do not set aside their cultural values and lifestyle preferences when they come to work. The challenge, therefore, is to make organizations more accommodating to diverse groups of

DID YOU KNOW?

INTERNATIONAL DIVERSITY

A subject of great debate in the United States focuses on the composition of our workforce and the personal characteristics of employees across organizational levels, and it's interesting to note that in comparison to other countries, the United States has made progress. For example, consider the following:

Measure	United States	Great Britain
Percent of Women Managers	37.1	11.0
Percent of Minority Managers	15.4	1.6

Source: "Management Must Set Example," *Personnel Today* (October 14, 2003), p. 3; and the U.S. Census Bureau, "Employed Civilians by Occupation, Sex, Race, and Hispanic Origin," *Statistical Abstracts of the United States* (2004–2005), p. 385.

people by addressing different lifestyles, family needs, and work styles. The melting-pot assumption is being replaced by recognition and celebration of differences. Interestingly, those who do celebrate differences are finding their organization's profits higher.[21]

The Workforce Today

Organizations that celebrate worker diversity are finding their profits higher!

workforce diversity
The varied personal characteristics that make the workforce heterogeneous.

Much workforce change is attributed to the passage of U.S. federal legislation in the 1960s prohibiting employment discrimination (see Chapter 3). Based on such laws, avenues began to open up for minority and female applicants. These two groups have since become the fastest-growing segments in the workforce, and accommodating their needs has become a vital responsibility for managers. Furthermore, during this time, birthrates in the United States began to decline. The baby boom generation had already reached its apex in terms of employment opportunities, which meant that as hiring continued, fewer baby boomers remained to choose. Also, as globalization became more pronounced, Hispanic, Asian, and other immigrants came to the United States and sought employment.

Projecting into the future is often an educated guess at best. Trying to predict the exact composition of our **workforce diversity** is no exception, even though we know it will be a heterogeneous mix of males and females; whites and people of color; homosexuals and straights, Hispanics, Asians, and Native Americans; the disabled, and the elderly. The now-aging baby boom population also has had a significant impact on the workforce. Commonly referred to as the "graying of the workforce," more individuals now want to work past "retirement" age.[22] Brought about by a need for greater income to sustain current living standards, or desire to remain active, more individuals over age 55 are expected to remain in the workforce, with more than 80 percent of the baby boom generation indicating that they expect to work past age 65. Couple this with the fact that the U.S. Congress passed the Senior Citizens' Freedom to Work Act, which eliminated the benefits penalty for those individuals on Social Security who earn more than $17,000 per year. In short, we can expect our workforce to continue to age, with 70- and 80-year-old workers no longer uncommon.

Increased participation of women and the elderly are not the only diversity issues reshaping the labor pool. Another is multiculturalism. As globalization has reduced barriers to immigration, the U.S. proportion of people of Hispanic, Asian, Pacific Island, and African origin has increased significantly over the past two

WORKPLACE ISSUES

DIVERSITY AWARENESS

The workforce is changing, and anyone insensitive to diversity issues had better stop and check his or her attitude at the door. Today, people of color, white women, and immigrants account for nearly 85 percent of our labor force. People are a company's number one asset—not the computers, not the real estate—the people. To waste people is to waste assets, and that is not only bad business, it is the kind of thinking that today, in our competitive marketplace, will put a business out of business. Management must realize that legal requirements simply are not enough to meet the needs of our changing workforce, to improve our workplace culture and environment, or to fully utilize the skills of all employees, thereby increasing a company's competitiveness. To fully maximize the contributions of African Americans and other people of color, we must commit to voluntarily focus on opportunities to foster mutual respect and understanding. This can be done by valuing our differences, which enrich our workplace, not only because it's the law, or because it's morally and ethically the right thing to do, or because it makes good business sense, but also because when we open our minds and hearts we feel better about ourselves. And decency is hard to put a price tag on.

What can companies and organizations do to facilitate diversity? Here are a few suggestions:[23]

- Enlist leadership from all levels to accomplish diversity goals.
- Identify goals, barriers, obstacles, and solutions and develop a plan to meet goals and overcome obstacles.
- Develop awareness through training, books, videos, and articles. Use outside speakers and consultants, as well as internal resources, to determine how to motivate and maximize the skills of a diverse workforce.
- Establish internally sanctioned employee support systems, networks, or groups.
- Challenge each employee to question his or her beliefs, assumptions, and traditions, and assess how they impact their relationships and decisions.
- Modify existing policies or create diversity policies and communicate them to all current and future hires.
- Hold managers accountable and reward them for developing, mentoring, or providing awareness training.
- Build in accountability through surveys and audits to measure progress as diligently as you would increasing production quotas or maintaining zero loss-time accidents. Then communicate the results and repeat the process. Continuous improvement applies to diversity as well as production.

decades. This trend will continue. Moreover, multiculturalism is not just a U.S. phenomenon. Countries such as Great Britain, Germany, and Canada are experiencing similar changes. Canada, as a case in point, has large populations of people who have recently emigrated from Hong Kong, Pakistan, Vietnam, and Middle Eastern countries. These immigrants are making Canada's population more diverse and its workforce more heterogeneous.

How Diversity Affects HRM

As organizations become more diverse, employers have been adapting their human resource practices to reflect those changes.[24] Many organizations today, such as Bank of America, have workforce diversity programs. They tend to hire, promote, and retain minorities; encourage vendor diversity; and provide diversity training for employees.[25] Some, like Coca-Cola, IBM, and Mars, actually conduct cultural audits to ensure that diversity is pervasive in the organization (see Exhibit 1-2).[26]

"Distinctive voices working together within a common culture" is one of the ways we have described how we do business at Mars. We believe that the success of our business can be enhanced by having a workforce made up of associates from many different backgrounds, much as our society and consumer base consist of a wide variety of individuals. We value the talents and contributions of our diverse workforce in reaching toward our future and in playing responsible leadership roles.

EXHIBIT 1-2
Mars Incorporated Diversity Philosophy

Source: www.mars.com/other_policies/diversity.as.

Workforce diversity requires employers to be more sensitive to the differences that each group brings to the work setting. For instance, employers may have to shift their philosophy from treating everyone alike to recognizing individual differences and responding to those differences in ways that will ensure employee retention and greater productivity. They must recognize and deal with the different values, needs, interests, and expectations of employees.[27] They must avoid any practice or action that can be interpreted as being sexist, racist, or offensive to any particular group and of course must not illegally discriminate against any employee. Employers also must find ways to assist employees in managing work/life issues.[28]

What Is a Work/Life Balance?

The typical 1960s–70s employee showed up at work Monday through Friday and did his or her job in eight- or nine-hour chunks. The workplace and hours were clearly specified. That's no longer true for a large segment of today's workforce. Employees are increasingly complaining that the line between work and nonwork time has become blurred, creating personal conflicts and stress.[29] Various forces have blurred the lines between employee work and personal lives. First, the creation of global organizations means their world never sleeps. At any time and on any day, for instance, thousands of DaimlerChrysler employees are working somewhere. The need to consult with colleagues or customers 8 or 10 time zones away means that many employees of global firms are "on-call" 24 hours a day. Second, communication technology allows employees to work at home, in their car, or on the beach in Tahiti. Many people in technical and professional jobs can work any time and from any place.[30] Third, organizations are asking employees to put in longer hours. It's not unusual for employees to work more than 45 hours a week, and some work much more than 50. Finally, fewer families have only a single breadwinner. Today's married employee is typically part of a dual-career couple.[31] This makes it increasingly difficult for married employees to find the time to fulfill commitments to home, spouse, children, parents, and friends.

Employees increasingly recognize that work is squeezing out their personal lives, and they're not happy about it. For example, recent studies suggest that employees want jobs that offer flexibility in work schedules so they can better manage work/life conflicts.[32] In addition, the next generation of employees is likely to have similar concerns.[33] A majority of college and university students say that attaining a balance between personal life and work is a primary career goal. They want "a life" as well as a job! Organizations that fail to help their people achieve

DID YOU KNOW?

WORK/LIFE ISSUES

Recent college graduates looking for jobs in the financial sector are excited about the work/life benefits that are offered with these jobs. But the benefits don't always sound as good in practice. That's because that while many financial service organizations do offer such benefits, recent new hires indicate that more than half of their supervisors expect them to work past 6 p.m. every day; with nearly 20 percent indicating that it's after 8 p.m. before they can leave. That's not the work quality these new hires were expecting.

Source: "Graduates Seek Work-Life Balance," *Employee Benefits* (April 11, 2005), p. 12.

work/life balance will find it increasingly hard to attract and retain the most capable and motivated employees.[34]

THE LABOR SUPPLY

Is skilled labor abundant in the United States? Or do we have a shortage of skilled labor? The simple answers to both of these questions is yes. Of course, simple answers neither adequately address the issue nor begin to describe how both situations (a shortage and a surplus) can exist simultaneously. Let's look at both arguments.

Do We Have a Shortage of Skilled Labor?

Responses to cyclical labor trends are difficult to predict. The world economy in the late 1990s, for instance, was generally quite robust and labor markets tight. Most employers scrambled for skilled workers to fill vacancies. Then, in 2001, most developed countries suffered an economic recession. Layoffs were widespread and the supply of skilled workers swelled. Demographic trends, conversely, are much more predictable. We currently face one that has direct implications for human resource management: Barring some unforeseeable economic or political calamity, labor shortages will continue for at least another 10 to 15 years. We'll discuss the problem using U.S. statistics, but this shortage of skilled labor is also likely to prevail in most of Europe, with its graying population and declining birthrate.

The U.S. labor shortage is a function of two factors: birthrates and labor participation rates. From the late 1960s through the late 1980s, American employers benefited from the large number of **baby boomers** (those born between 1946 and 1965) entering the workforce. Some boomers have already retired early. The problem becomes severe around 2010, when the major exodus of boomers from the workplace is in full force—anticipating that nearly 6 million jobs will be unfilled.[35] And this shortage will encompass most industries, including health care, government, construction, engineering, finance, energy, and information technology. Importantly, despite continued increases in immigration, workforce entrants from foreign countries will do little to correct the supply shortage. Moreover, repercussions from the terrorist attacks of September 11, 2001, in the United States could potentially reduce this immigration, further compounding the skilled labor shortage.

baby boomers
Individuals born between 1946 and 1965.

By 2010, nearly 6 million jobs will be unfilled in the United States.

In times of labor shortage, good wages and benefits aren't always enough to hire and keep skilled employees. Human resource managers need sophisticated recruitment and retention strategies and need to understand human behavior.[36] In tight labor markets, managers who don't understand human behavior and fail to treat their employees properly, risk having no one to manage!

Why Do Organizations Lay Off During Shortages?

At one time, in corporate America, organizations followed a relatively simple "rule": In good times you hire employees; in bad times, you fire them.[37] Since the late 1980s, that rule no longer holds true, at least for most of the world's largest companies. Throughout the past decade, most Fortune 500 companies made significant cuts in their overall staff. Thousands of employees have been cut by organizations such as IBM, AT&T, Boeing, and Sears. This **downsizing** phenomenon is not going on just in the United States. Jobs are being eliminated in almost all industrialized nations.[38]

downsizing
An activity in an organization aimed at creating greater efficiency by eliminating certain jobs.

Why this trend for downsizing? Organizations are attempting to increase their flexibility to better respond to change. Quality-emphasis programs are creating flatter structures and redesigning work to increase efficiency. The result is a need for fewer employees. Are we implying that big companies are disappearing? Absolutely not! They are changing how they operate. Big isn't necessarily inefficient. Companies such as PepsiCo and Home Depot manage to blend large size with agility by dividing their organization into smaller, more flexible units.

Downsizing as a strategy is here to stay. It's part of a larger goal of balancing staff to meet changing needs. When organizations become overstaffed, they will likely cut jobs. At the same time, they are likely to increase staff if doing so adds value to the organization. A better term for this organizational action, then, might be **rightsizing**. Rightsizing involves linking staffing levels to organizational goals.[39] Rightsizing promotes greater use of outside firms for providing necessary products and services—called **outsourcing**—in an effort to remain flexible and responsive to the ever-changing work environment.

How Do Organizations Balance Labor Supply?

Thousands of organizations in the global village have decided they could save money and increase their flexibility by converting many jobs into temporary or part-time positions, giving rise to what is commonly referred to as the **contingent workforce** (see Exhibit 1-3).[40] Today, temporary workers can be found in secretarial, nursing, accounting, assembly-line, legal, dentistry, computer programming, engineering, marketing, and even senior management positions.

Why the organizational emphasis on contingent employees? Organizations facing a rapidly changing environment must be ready to adjust rapidly. Having too many permanent full-time employees limits management's ability to react.[41] For

rightsizing
Linking employee needs to organizational strategy.

outsourcing
Sending work "outside" the organization to be done by individuals not employed full time with the organization.

contingent workforce
The part-time, temporary, and contract workers used by organizations to fill peak staffing needs or perform work not done by core employees.

EXHIBIT 1-3
The Contingent Workforce

Part-Time Employees	Part-time employees are those employees who work fewer than 40 hours a week. Generally, part-timers are afforded few, if any, employee benefits. Part-time employees are generally a good source of employees for organizations to staff their peak hours. For example, the bank staff that expects its heaviest clientele between 10 a.m. and 2 p.m. may bring in part-time tellers for those four hours. Part-time employees may also be a function of job sharing, where two employees split one full-time job.
Temporary Employees	Temporary employees, like part-timers, are generally employed during peak production periods. Temporary workers also act as fill-ins when some employees are off work for an extended time. For example, a secretarial position may be filled using a "temp" while the secretary is off work during his 12-week unpaid leave of absence for the birth of his daughter. Temporary workers create a fixed cost to an employer for labor "used" during a specified period.
Contract Workers	Contract workers, subcontractors, and consultants (who may be referred to as freelance individuals) are hired by organizations to work on specific projects. These workers, typically highly skilled, perform certain duties for an organization. Often their fee is set in the contract and is paid when the organization receives particular deliverables. Organizations use contract workers because their labor cost is fixed and they incur none of the costs associated with a full-time employee population. Additionally, some contract arrangements may exist because the contractor can provide virtually the same good or service in a more efficient manner.

EXHIBIT 1-4
Are Layoffs Justified?

(*Source:* DILBERT: © Scott Adams/Dist. by United Features Syndicate, Inc.)

example, an organization that faces significantly decreased revenues during an economic downturn may have to cut staff. Deciding whom to lay off and how layoffs will effect productivity and the organization is extremely complex in organizations with a large permanent workforce (see Exhibit 1-4). On the other hand, organizations that rely heavily on contingent workers have greater flexibility because workers can be easily added or taken off as needed. In addition, staffing shortages, opportunities to capitalize on new markets, obtaining someone who possesses a special skill for a particular project, and the like all point to a need for the organization to rapidly adjust its staffing level.[42]

Issues Contingent Workers Create for HRM

Temporaries and the flexibility they foster present special challenges for human resource managers. Each contingent worker may need to be treated differently in terms of practices and policies. Human resource managers must also make sure that contingent workers do not perceive themselves as second-class workers. Because they often do not receive many of the amenities—such as health and paid-leave benefits—that full-time **core employees** do (see Exhibit 1-5), contingent workers may tend to view their work as not critically important. Accordingly, they may be less loyal, committed to the organization, or motivated on the job than are permanent workers. That tendency may be especially relevant to individuals forced to join the temporary workforce. Today's human resource managers must recognize their responsibility to motivate their entire workforce—full-time and temporary employees—and to build their commitment to doing good work!

Additionally, when an organization makes its strategic decision to employ a sizable portion of its workforce from the contingency ranks, other HRM issues come to the forefront. These include having these "virtual" employees available when needed, providing scheduling options that meet their needs, and making decisions about whether benefits will be offered to the contingent workforce. No organization can make the transition to a contingent workforce without sufficient planning. As such, when these strategic decisions are made, HRM must be an active partner in the discussions. After all, it is HRM's responsibility to locate these temporary workers and bring them into the organization. Just as employment has played an integral role in recruiting full-time employees, so too will it play a major part in securing needed just-in-time talent.

As temporary workers are brought in, HRM will also have the responsibility of quickly adapting them to the organization. Although orientation for full-time employees is more detailed, the contingent workforce, nonetheless, must be made aware of the organization's personality. Along this line, too, some training may be required. Even a network analyst brought in to work on a specific intranet problem must quickly be brought up to speed on the organization's unique system.

HRM must also give some thought to how it will effectively attract quality temporaries. As this becomes more prominent in business, there will be significant competition for the "good" talent. Accordingly, HRM must reexamine its

core employees
An organization's full-time employee population.

Exhibit 1-5
Employee vs. Independent Contractor

One issue that arises in hiring contingent workers revolves around the definition of an employee. This distinction is important because it has federal income, Social Security, and Medicare tax implications for the organization. Although the debate continues as to what precisely an employee is versus an independent contractor, below are Internal Revenue Service (IRS) guidelines for making this determination that generally focus on three major categories—behavioral control, financial control, and the relationships of the parties. Remember, these are only guidelines, not "absolutes" from the IRS.

An individual is an employee if

* The employee receives extensive instruction on how to do the work; such as where and when it is done, what tools to use, where to purchase supplies, and what assistants one may use in the work. (Behavioral)
* The employee receives training on required procedures and methods the organization uses. (Behavioral)
* The employee receives benefits such as insurance, pension, or paid leave. (Relationship of the Parties)
* Implications for HRM:
  * Employer must withhold income tax and the employee's portion of Social Security and Medicare taxes.
  * Employer must pay unemployment taxes on an employee's wages.

An individual may be an independent contractor if

* An individual schedules his or her own work schedule and receives little to no instruction on how the work is done. (Behavioral)
* One does not receive reimbursement for some or all business expenses. (Financial)
* An individual can realize a profit or loss from his or her work. (Financial)
* One is not eligible for any employee benefits from the organization. (Relationship of the Parties)
* Implications for HRM:
  * Employer must give independent contractors a form 1099-MISC reporting what monies have been paid to the individual.
  * Employer should have a written document indicating that the individual is an independent contractor and what is expected by both parties.

Source: Internal Revenue Service, "Independent Contractor or Employee . . ." www.irs.gov (July 2003).

The late W. Edwards Deming, a statistician from Wyoming, has been credited with helping Japanese industries make a significant turnaround following World War II primarily by using statistical methods to improve quality. He also recognized a need for extensive employee training, team work, and strong supplier relationships.
(Source: © AP/Wide World Photos)

compensation philosophy. If temporaries are employed solely as a cost-cutting measure, the pay and benefits offered to contingent workers might differ from those offered to other workers hired part-time as a result of restructuring and work process engineering. HRM, then, must discover specifically what these employees want. Is it flexibility in scheduling, autonomy, or the control over one's career destiny that such situations afford that attracts them? Or is it just bad luck, and they are forced into this situation?

Finally, HRM must be prepared to deal with potential conflicts between core and contingent workers. The core employees may become envious of the higher pay rates and flexibility in scheduling that the contingent workers receive. In the total compensation package, which includes benefits, core employees might earn substantially more money, but these employees may not immediately include the "in-kind" pay (their benefits) in the rate of pay received. For example, paying a training consultant $4,000 for presenting a two-day skills-training program might cause some conflict with core HRM trainers, although the HRM trainer may not have the time or resources to develop such a program. If the consultant offers 20 of these two-day programs over the year, earning $80,000 in consulting fees, a $50,000-a-year company trainer might take offense. Consequently, HRM must ensure that its communication programs anticipate some of these potential conflicts and address them before they become detrimental to the organization—or worse, provide an incentive for core employees to leave!

CONTINUOUS IMPROVEMENT PROGRAMS

A quality revolution continues in both the private and the public sectors. The generic terms that describe this revolution are **quality management** or **continuous improvement**. The revolution was inspired by a small group of quality experts—individuals such as Joseph Juran and the late W. Edwards Deming.[43] For our discussion, we'll focus our attention primarily on Deming's work.

An American who found few managers in the United States interested in his ideas, Deming went to Japan in 1950 and began advising many top Japanese managers on ways to improve their production effectiveness. Central to his management methods was the use of statistics to analyze variability in production processes. A well-managed organization, according to Deming, was one in which statistical control reduced variability and resulted in uniform quality and predictable quantity of output. Deming developed a 14-point program for transforming organizations.[44] Today, Deming's original program has been expanded into a philosophy of management driven by customer needs and expectations[45] (see Exhibit 1-6). Quality management expands the term *customer* beyond the traditional definition to include everyone involved with the organization—either internally or externally—encompassing employees and suppliers as well as the people who buy the organization's products or services. The objective is to create an organization committed to continuous improvement or, as the Japanese call it, *kaizen*[46]—one that leads to achieving an effective and lean workplace.[47]

Work Process Engineering

Although continuous improvement methods are useful innovations in many organizations, they generally focus on incremental change. Such action—a constant and permanent search to make things better—is intuitively appealing. Many organizations, however, operate in an environment of rapid and dynamic change. As the elements around them change so quickly, a continuous improvement process may keep them behind the times.

The problem with a focus on continuous improvements is that it may provide a false sense of security. It may make employers feel as if they are actively doing something positive, which is somewhat true. Unfortunately, ongoing incremental change may allow employers to avoid facing up to the possibility that

quality management
Organizational commitment to continuous process of improvement that expands the definition of *customer* to include everyone involved in the organization.

continuous improvement
Organizational commitment to constantly improving quality of products or services.

kaizen
The Japanese term for an organization's commitment to continuous improvement.

---

1 Intense focus on the *customer*. The customer includes not only outsiders who buy the organization's products or services but also internal customers (such as shipping or accounts payable personnel) who interact with and serve others in the organization.

2 Concern for *continuous improvement*. Continuous improvement is a commitment to never being satisfied. "Very good" is not good enough. Quality can always be improved.

3 Improvement in the *quality of everything* the organization does. Continuous improvement uses a broad definition of quality. It relates not only to the final product but also to how the organization handles deliveries, how rapidly it responds to complaints, how politely the phones are answered, and the like.

4 Accurate *measurement*. Continuous improvement uses statistical techniques to measure every critical variable in the organization's operations. These are compared against standards, or benchmarks, to identify problems, trace them to their roots, and eliminate their causes.

5 *Empowerment of employees*. Continuous improvement involves the people on the line in the improvement process. Teams are widely used in continuous improvement programs as empowerment vehicles for finding and solving problems.

EXHIBIT 1-6
Components of Continuous Improvement

work process engineering
Radical, quantum change in an organization.

what the organization may really need is radical or quantum change, referred to as **work process engineering.**[48] Continuous change may also make employers feel as if they are taking progressive action while, at the same time, avoiding quantum changes that will threaten organizational members. The incremental approach of continuous improvement, then, may be today's version of rearranging the deck chairs on the *Titanic.*

How HRM Can Support Improvement Programs

HRM plays an important role in implementing continuous improvement programs. Whenever an organization embarks on any improvement effort, it introduces change into the organization. As such, organization development efforts dominate.

Specifically, HRM must prepare individuals for the change. This requires clear and extensive communications of why the change will occur, what is expected, and its effects on employees. Improvement efforts may change work patterns, operations, and even reporting relationships. HRM must be ready to help affected employees overcome barriers that may result in resistance to change, that is, overcome the fear dimension often associated with change.

HRM must be ready to help affected employees overcome barriers to change.

Looking for better ways of working often results in new ways of doing things. Consequently, HRM must be prepared to train employees in these new processes and help them attain new skills levels that may be associated with the improved operations.

How HRM Assists in Work Process Engineering

If we accept the premise that work process engineering will change how we do business, it stands to reason that our employees will be directly affected. As such, the gains work process engineering offers will not occur unless we address the people issues.

First of all, work process engineering may leave employees, at least the survivors, confused and angry. Although a preferred method of "change" would involve employees throughout the process, we need to recognize that work process engineering may leave some of our employees frustrated and unsure of what to expect. Longtime work relationships may be severed, and stress levels may be magnified. Accordingly, HRM must have mechanisms in place to give employees appropriate answers and direction for what to expect, as well as assistance in dealing with conflicts that may permeate the organization.

Although the emotional aspect is difficult to resolve, work process engineering will generate its benefits only if HRM trains its employee population. Whether it's a new process, a technology enhancement, working in teams, or adding decision-making authority, employees will need new skills. Consequently, HRM must be ready to offer the skills training necessary in the "new" organization. Even the best process will fail if employees lack the requisite skills to perform as the process task dictates.

Furthermore, as many components of the organization are redefined, so too will be many HRM activities that affect employees. For example, if redesigned work practices change employee compensation packages (for example, bonus/incentive pay), employees need to know. Likewise, they must understand performance standards and how employees will be evaluated.

EMPLOYEE INVOLVEMENT

Whenever significant changes occur in an organization, subsequent changes in work methods must also occur. With respect to work process engineering and continuous improvements, many companies today require their employees to do

What makes Tom Brady, quarterback of the New England Patriots, so successful? Is it his ability to go onto the field and make the plays? That's part of it, but football is a team effort. To make the team successful, it requires the efforts of many individuals—coaches, specialized position players, and a field general (the quarterback) who becomes one of the team's biggest cheerleaders! (*Source:* Tom Brady/Getty Images, Inc.)

more, faster, and better, with less. Involving employees means different things to different organizations and people, but by and large for today's workers to be successful, a few necessary employee involvement concepts appear to be accepted. These are delegation, participative management, work teams, goal setting, and employer training—the empowering of employees! Let's elaborate on these a bit.

How Organizations Involve Employees

Succeeding when facing multiple tasks, often on multiple projects, requires more employees at all levels to delegate some activities and responsibilities to other organizational members. This means that employees need certain amounts of authority to make decisions that directly affect their work. Even though *delegation* was once perceived as something that managers did with lower levels of management, delegation is required at all levels of the organization—in essence, peer delegation, or using influence without authority!

In addition to taking on more responsibilities, employees will be expected to make decisions without benefit of tried-and-true past decisions. Because all these employees become part of the process, the need is greater for them to contribute to the decision-making process. In most organizations, the days of autocratic management are over. To facilitate customer demands and fulfill corporate expectations, today's employees must be more involved. Group decision making gives these employees more input into the processes and greater access to needed information. Such actions are also consistent with work environments that require increased creativity and innovation.

Another phenomenon of involving employees is an emphasis on work teams. The bureaucratic structure of yesterday—where clear lines of authority existed and the chain of command was paramount—is not appropriate for many of today's companies. Workers from different specializations in an organization increasingly must work together to successfully complete complex projects. As such, traditional work areas have given way to more team effort, building and capitalizing on the various skills and backgrounds that each member brings to the team. Consider, for example, what kind of group it takes to put together a symphony. One musician could not possibly play all the various instruments at one time. Accordingly, to blend the music of the orchestra, symphonies have string sections, brass instruments, percussion, and the like. At times, however, a musician may cross over these boundaries, like the trombonist who also plays the piano. These work teams, then, are driven by the tasks at hand. Involving employees allows them to focus on the job goals. With greater freedom, employees are in a better position to develop the means to achieve the desired ends.

Tomorrow's organizations will have a major emphasis on teams.

Employee Involvement Implications for HRM

We have addressed some components of employee involvement; for an organization, however, addressing them is not enough. Useful employee involvement requires demonstrated leadership, as well as supportive management. Additionally, employees need training, and that's where HRM can make a valuable contribution. Employees expected to delegate, to have decisions participatively handled, to work in teams, or to set goals cannot do so unless they know and understand what they are to do. Empowering employees requires extensive training in all aspects of the job. Workers may need to understand new job design processes. They may need training in interpersonal skills to make participative management and work teams function properly. We can anticipate much more involvement from HRM in all parts of the organization.

A LOOK AT ETHICS

Ethics
A set of rules or principles that defines right and wrong conduct.

Ethics commonly refers to a set of rules or principles that define right and wrong conduct.[49] Right or wrong behavior, though, may be difficult to determine. Most recognize that something illegal is also unethical, but what about the questionable "legal" areas? Our literature has been filled with organizational practices at companies such as WorldCom, Enron, and ImClone. What executives at these companies did may be questionable, or even illegal, but the larger issue is what implications have such actions created? For many, these corporate scandals have created a lack of trust for management.[50] People are questioning how such unethical actions could have gone unnoticed if proper controls were in place in the organization. Moreover, the public is now examining the unethical cultures pervasive in these organizations.

Understanding ethics may be difficult, depending on your view of the topic (see Learning an HRM Skill—Guidelines for Acting Ethically, p. 28). People who lack a strong moral sense, however, are much less likely to do wrong if they feel constrained by rules, policies, job descriptions, or strong cultural norms that discourage such behaviors. For example, someone in your class has stolen the final exam and is selling a copy for $50. You need to do well on this exam or risk failing the course. You expect some classmates have bought copies—and that could affect any possibility of the exam being curved by the professor. Do you buy a copy because you fear that without it you'll be disadvantaged, do you refuse to buy a copy and try your best, or do you report your knowledge to your instructor?

The example of the final exam illustrates how ambiguity about what is ethical can be a problem for managers. Codes of ethics are an increasingly popular tool for attempting to reduce that ambiguity.[51] A **code of ethics** is a formal document that states an organization's primary values and the ethical rules it expects managers and operative employees to follow. Ideally, these codes should be specific enough to guide organizational personnel in what they are supposed to do yet loose enough to allow for freedom of judgment.

code of ethics
A formal document that states an organization's primary values and the ethical rules it expects organizational members to follow.

In isolation, ethics codes are unlikely to be much more than window dressing; Enron had a code of ethics statement. Their effectiveness depends heavily on whether management supports them, ingrains them into the corporate culture, and how individuals who break the codes are treated.[52] If all managers, including those in HRM, consider ethics important, regularly reaffirms their content, follow the rules themselves, and publicly reprimand rule breakers, ethics codes can supply a strong foundation for an effective corporate ethics program.[53]

SUMMARY

(This summary relates to the Learning Outcomes identified on page 3.) After having read this chapter you can

1. **Discuss how cultural environments affect HRM practices.** Globalization is creating a situation where HRM must search for mobile and skilled employees who can succeed at their jobs in a foreign land. These employees must, therefore, understand the host country's language, culture, and customs.
2. **Describe how technology is changing HRM.** Technology is having a major impact on HRM. It's giving all employees instant access to information and changing the skill requirements of employees. Technological changes have required HRM to address or change its practices when it deals with such activities as recruiting and selecting employees, motivating and paying individuals, training and developing employees, and in legal and ethical matters.
3. **Identify significant changes in workforce composition.** The workforce composition has changed considerably over the past 35 years. Once characterized as having a dominant number of white males, the workforce of the new millennium is comprised of a mixture of women, minorities, immigrants, and white males.

4. **Describe the HRM implications of a labor shortage.** It is estimated that there will be a shortage of skilled labor in the United States over the next 10–15 years. The primary reasons for this shortage are birthrates and labor participation rates. For HRM, the labor shortage means that human resource managers will need sophisticated recruitment and retention strategies and will need to understand human behavior.

5. **Describe how changing skill requirements affect HRM.** Changing skill requirements require HRM to provide extensive employee training. This training can be in the form of remedial help for those who have skill deficiencies or specialized training dealing with technology changes.

6. **Explain why organizational members focus on quality and continuous improvements.** Organizational members focus on quality and continuous improvements for several reasons: today's educated consumers demand it, and quality improvements have become strategic initiatives in the organization. HRM is instrumental in quality initiatives by preparing employees to deal with the change and training them in new techniques.

7. **Describe work process engineering and its implications for HRM.** Continuous incremental improvements focus on enhancing the quality of a current work process. Work process engineering focuses on major or radical change in the organization.

8. **Identify who makes up the contingent workforce and its HRM implications.** The contingent workforce includes part-time, temporary, consultant, and contract workers who provide as-needed services to organizations. The HRM implications of a contingent workforce include attracting and retaining skilled contingent workers, adjusting to their special needs, and managing any conflict that may arise between core and contingent workers.

9. **Define employee involvement and list its critical components.** Employee involvement can be best defined as giving each worker more control over his or her job. To do this requires delegation, participative management, work teams, goal setting, and employee training. If handled properly, involving employees should lead to developing more productive employees who are more loyal and committed to the organization.

10. **Explain the importance of ethics in an organization.** Ethics refers to rules or principles that define right or wrong conduct. Given organizational practices of the early 2000s, ethics has become a focal point of proper organizational citizenship.

DEMONSTRATING COMPREHENSION: *Questions for Review*

1. How has the global village contributed to the need for diversity awareness in our organizations?
2. Describe the workforce shifts in types of jobs during the past 100 years. What implications have these shifts created for today's human resource managers?
3. Which groups will comprise the greatest influx into the U.S. workforce over the next 10 years? What will be the HRM effect of these groups?
4. How can human resource managers help employees deal with work/life issues?
5. What is a knowledge worker? What HRM changes can be expected in dealing with knowledge workers with respect to recruiting, selection, motivation, and work/life issues?
6. Explain the increased popularity of continuous improvements and work process engineering in the past 20 years.
7. What is the purpose of a continuous improvement program? What role does HRM play in assisting continuing improvements?
8. What are the necessary ingredients for a successful empowerment program?
9. What are ethics and why are they important for organizations?

VISUAL SUMMARY

CHAPTER 1: STRATEGIC IMPLICATIONS OF A DYNAMIC HRM ENVIRONMENT

1   Understanding Cultural Environments

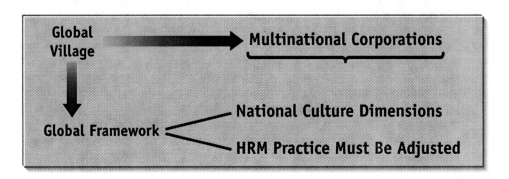

Global Village → Multinational Corporations

Global Village ↓ Global Framework

Global Framework — National Culture Dimensions

Global Framework — HRM Practice Must Be Adjusted

2   The Changing World of Technology

Knowledge Workers
People who acquire and apply information

HRM Implications of Technology

- Recruiting
- Employee selection
- Training and development
- Motivation of workers
- Paying employees market value
- Communications
- Decentralized work sites
- Skill levels
- Legal issues

3   Workforce Diversity

Who Are Our Workers?

- Males
- Females
- Whites
- People of Color
- Homosexuals
- Straights
- National Origin
- Disabled
- Elderly

Work/Life Balance
Balancing work and personal lives

4 Labor Supply

A Labor Shortage?

→ Downsizing   Rightsizing   Outsourcing

Population/Social Trends:
• Refocus of early retirement

Core Employees

Contingent Workers

? Employee or independent contractor?

5 Continuous Improvement Programs

1 **Quality Management**—continuously improving or, as the Japanese call it, *kaizen*
2 **Work Process Engineering**—radical change

6 Employee Involvement

• **Delegation**—having the authority to make decisions in one's job.
• **Work teams**—workers of various specializations who work together in an organization.
• Employee involvement requires demonstrated leadership and supportive management.

7 Ethics

A set of rules that defines right or wrong behavior

Code of Ethics—formal document that states an organization's values and the ethical rules it expects employees to follow

KEY TERMS

baby boomers
code of ethics
contingent
   workforce
continuous
   improvement
core employees

downsizing
ethics
global village
kaizen
knowledge
   workers

multinational
   corporation
outsourcing
quality
   management
rightsizing

technology
workforce
   diversity
work process
   engineering

CROSSWORD COMPREHENSION

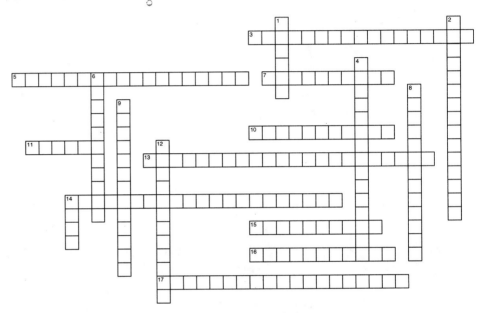

ACROSS

3. an organizational commitment to continuous improvement
5. the varied personal characteristics that exist in the workplace today
7. any equipment, tools, or operating methods designed to make work more efficient
10. having work done by people external to the organization
11. a set of rules that define right or wrong conduct
13. radical, quantum change in an organization
14. an organizational commitment to constantly improving the quality of goods and services produced
15. an organizational activity in which greater efficiency is created by eliminating jobs
16. individuals born between 1946 and 1965
17. the classification of part-time, temporary, and contract workers used by an organization

DOWN

1. the Japanese term for an organization's commitment to continuous improvement
2. an individual whose job is designed around acquisition and application of information
4. balancing a career with one's personal life
6. linking employee needs to organizational strategy
8. a corporation with significant operations in more than one country
9. producing goods and services worldwide
12. a formal organizational document that states the rules employees are expected to follow
14. the organization's full-time employee population

HRM Workshop

LINKING CONCEPTS TO PRACTICE: *Discussion Questions*

1. How can HRM ensure that it is properly preparing the organization for dealing in the global village?
2. "Workforce diversity is nothing new. We need only look back to the early 1900s when thousands of immigrants came to the United States, understand how we handled them, and then implement similar practices again." Do you agree or disagree with the statement? Explain.
3. What can HRM do to help ensure the highest ethics in an organization?

4. Discuss the implications of hiring contingent workers from both the organizational and contingent worker perspective.
5. Training organizational members how to be coaches and how to empower employees will be a major HRM activity in the next decade. Do you agree or disagree with this statement? Explain.

DEVELOPING DIAGNOSTIC AND ANALYTICAL SKILLS

Case 1-A: WORK/LIFE BALANCE AT BAXTER

Many a CEO of a Fortune 100 company thinks nothing of working 70+ hours a week or spending several days a week out of town meeting with customers, suppliers, or other company executives. Workaholic tendencies are assumed to come with the job. Not so for Harry M. Jansen Kraemer Jr., former chairman and CEO of Baxter International, one of the world's largest producers of medical products. Kraemer believed that while work is important, one's family is more important.[54]

On any given workday, you might have found Kraemer staying home to take care of his infant son. Or you may have seen him taking his daughter to school or coaching her softball team after school. Moreover, you rarely found Kraemer in his office later than 6:00 p.m. And he wouldn't accept work-related calls after hours—because that was family time. But don't interpret this by perceiving that Kraemer wasn't working. He worked hard—sometimes even upward of 80 hours per week. But he did so at his own pace that didn't interfere with important family matters.

What Kraemer created was an example for employees to live by. One employee, for example, David Olson, a Web designer at Baxter lived nearly 50 miles from the company, worked at home every Friday and every other Thursday. In doing so, he was with his family more. Olson believed that he "gets more work done at home because no one is stopping by his office," and he's no longer distracted by home matters. Other employees in the company have similar beliefs.

Was this work/life balance that Kraemer implemented at Baxter beneficial? That answer depends on how one defines *benefic-*

ial. Consider that work/life balance is a value that Baxter corporate officers hold and have ingrained into the corporate culture, and that because this was implemented over a decade ago, Baxter has hit earnings targets every quarter. They've also nearly doubled their profit goal, with revenues and profits rising at double digit rates, employment has grown to more than 48,000 employees, and the company has successfully acquired five major companies. Based on these performance measures, you could say that Kraemer's plan was successful. In addition, by allowing employees to alter their work schedules and work at home, the organization has been able to attract top-notch employees, who in turn have generated greater productivity for the company.

Questions:

1. What role, if any, does work/life balance play in the success of an organization? Explain.
2. How does diversity in an organization affect the organization's work/life balance? What ethical considerations exist that may drive the organization to be more work/life balanced?
3. Do you believe the balanced work/life plan at Baxter would work as well if the CEO was not one of its primary supporters? Explain your position.
4. What role does human resources play in making sure work/life practices are effective? Describe.

Case Application 1-B: TEAM FUN!

Team Fun Kenny and Norton Bell founded TEAM FUN!, a sporting goods and equipment store and manufacturer, 10 years ago. Kenny and Norton had always been sports enthusiasts. As stellar athletes through high school and college, these twin brothers knew they wanted to open a business that catered to the leisure sporting industry.

Shortly after graduating from college, they presented to a bank the business plan they had developed as part of their small-business

entrepreneurial course. They were given a loan, and with $15,000 they had saved between them, they started the company. Initially, they were the only two employees.

Within the first six months of business, Kenny and Norton added three employees to help deal with a new contract they had just won. By the end of their first year, the company had more than $300,000 in revenues and six employees.

Kenny and Norton were pleased with their initial success, but they anticipated more competitors and knew they had to diversify their product lines. As they did, it became apparent that they needed to add a couple of locations to better serve their growing customer base, as well as hire more people to meet customer demand.

They now have 125 employees, 3 suburban branches, and annual revenues approaching $10 million. Overlooking their LAGOON, where employees try out new water gear (kayaks, swim fins, wet suits, racing suits, goggles), Norton says to Kenny, "Maybe we are getting too old for this. I got the prototype for the new soccer gear, and the labeling looks funny to me." Kenny frowns. Norton continues, "Some funny language. Maybe two. Looks like Spanish. *Agua* is water, right?"

Kenny slugs Norton's shoulder. "Si!"

Norton says, "Maybe French or German for the other. Why would SideKick do that? We've been doing business for 10 years."

Kenny scratches his head. "I dunno. Lots of things going on around here that I don't understand. Carlos asked me if we could make a corner of the lunchroom into a babysitting place. Said we'd be work/life friendly. We've always been that, right?" They head outside to the GREEN, their golf supply area, and pass a few people who smile and nod. Kenny comments, "I don't even know everyone who works here anymore. Edna in personnel asked me about an insurance file claim on Jane Edwards from her optometrist. I don't even know who Jane is or why we have vision insurance. Edna talked about 'human resources issues.'"

Norton offers, "Last week I played racquetball with Keith." Kenny frowns and Norton goes on, "Sure, you know Keith. He runs that football recleater operation in Springfield. He was bragging about their strategic new human resources manager."

Kenny picks up the new TEAM TigerPutter at the sign, TRY THIS OUT. "This golf club is a strategic advantage. What is a strategic human resource?"

Questions:

1. Is TEAM FUN! affected by globalization? If so, how?
2. What other major workforce issues are evident in this case?
3. Do you believe that TEAM FUN! needs a human resources professional? Explain your answer to Kenny and Norton.

WORKING WITH A TEAM: *Understanding Diversity Issues*

Workforce diversity has become a major issue for managers. Although similarities are common among individuals, obvious differences do exist. A means of identifying some of those differences is getting to know individuals from diverse groups. For this exercise, you will need to contact people from a different country. If you don't know any, the office of your college responsible for coordinating international students can give you a list of names. Interview at least three people to ask such questions as

1. What country do you come from?
2. What is your first language?
3. Describe your country's culture in terms of, for example, form of government, emphasis on individuals versus

groups, roles of women in the workforce, benefits provided to employees, and how employees are treated.

4. What were the greatest difficulties in adapting to this new culture?
5. What advice would you give me if I had an HRM position in your country?

In groups of three to five class members, discuss your findings. Are there similarities in what each of you found? If so, what are they? Are there differences? Describe them. What implications for managing in the global village has this exercise generated for you and your group?

LEARNING AN HRM SKILL *Guidelines for Acting Ethically*

About the skill: Making ethical choices can be difficult for human resource managers. Obeying the law is mandatory, but acting ethically goes beyond mere compliance with the law. It means acting responsibly in those "gray" areas where right and wrong are not defined. What can you do to enhance your abilities in acting ethically? We offer some guidelines.

1. *Know your organization's policy on ethics.* Company policies on ethics, if they exist, describe what the organization perceives as ethical behavior and what it expects you to do. This policy will help you clarify what is permissible and what discretion you will have. This becomes your code of ethics to follow!

2. *Understand the ethics policy.* Just having the policy in your hand does not guarantee that it will achieve what it is intended to. You need to fully understand it. Behaving ethically is rarely a cut-and-dried process, but the policy can

act as a guide by which you will act in the organization. Even if no policy exists, you can take several steps before you deal with a difficult situation.

3. *Think before you act.* Ask yourself, "Why am I going to do what I'm about to do? What led up to the problem? What is my true intention in taking this action? Is my reason valid, or are ulterior motives behind it—such as demonstrating organizational loyalty? Will my action injure someone? Would I disclose to my boss or my family what I'm going to do?" Remember, it's your behavior and your actions. Make sure that you are not doing something that will jeopardize your role as a manager, your organization, or your reputation.

4. *Ask yourself what-if questions.* When you think about why you are going to do something, ask yourself what-if questions. The following questions may help you shape

your actions. "What if I make the wrong decision? What will happen to me? to my job?" "What if my actions were described, in detail, on the local TV news or in the newspaper? Would it bother or embarrass me or those around me?" "What if I get caught doing something unethical? Am I prepared to deal with the consequences?"

5. *Seek opinions from others.* If you must do something major, about which you are uncertain, ask for advice from other managers. Maybe they have been in a similar situation and can give you the benefit of their experience. Or maybe they can just listen and act as a sounding board for you.

6. *Do what you truly believe is right.* You have a conscience, and you are responsible for your behavior. Whatever you do, if you truly believe it was the right action to take, then what others say or what the "Monday-morning quarterbacks" say is immaterial. Be true to your own internal ethical standards. Ask yourself: "Can I live with what I've done?"

ENHANCING YOUR COMMUNICATION SKILLS

1. Visit a human resource management department (or you may want to visit a company's Web site). Research information on this organization in terms of human resource activities. For instance, if the organization has a job posting Web site, visit it and critique its usefulness to you.

2. Provide a two- to three-page write up on a technology-based organization (for example, Amazon.com, Dell, Varsitybooks.com) and the effect of technology on the human resource aspects of the business. Emphasize the way the business has had to change its HRM practices to accommodate technology changes, and the benefits that have accrued or that are anticipated.

3. Develop a report on the pros and cons of the work/life conflict. Prepare your report from either the organization's or the person's perspective. [Note: This would make a good debate if one individual takes the organization's perceptive and one person takes the individual's perspective.]

TWO

"Good morning staff," said Chris Hernandez, senior vice president of HRM. "It's time once again for us to take a look at where we've been, and what issues need addressing as we continue to support this organization's strategic directions. Even though we meet biweekly to discuss day-to-day activities, I feel it's necessary for us to have these planning sessions to reassess how we are helping this organization achieve its goals. So, now that you have settled in, let me start by giving you my 'state-of-HRM' recap.

"We have been providing a first-class service to this organization. Over the past couple of years, we have worked hard to put in place many of the programs that have truly aided this company and supported its strategic direction. For example, our work/life balance program has been credited with cutting recruiting costs by more than 30 percent annually since the program began, and reducing turnover by more than 11 percent per year. We were also one of the first in the area to implement a detailed policy on employee monitoring—keeping informed on employee activities. But a policy alone wouldn't suffice. We effectively enlightened each employee of this organization about the policy and what is unacceptable behavior. We've implemented an applicant tracking system—our entire application process is now electronic. We've helped design online interactive training programs that support senior management's continuous improvement program, and continue to take a lead role in supporting the training that's necessary to ensure the organization has the right people for the right jobs. And let me remind you of these findings just released by our president. Through these efforts, productivity has improved

(*Source:* Tanya Constantine/Photodisc/Getty Images, Inc.)

more than 15 percent in the past 12 months. Much of this productivity increase has been attributable to our realization that the organization as we know it is in a constant state of change—and we must be at the forefront of those changes in helping everyone adapt.

"Let's also continue to remember the legislation that we face. Each day we make decisions that may be reviewed or questioned by people external to our organization. We must ensure that our HRM practices do not adversely affect any one group. We must give all employees an equal chance to realize their potential and fulfill their career dreams. When that happens, the organization can only benefit. But we can do this only by continuing to have in place effective HRM practices.

"Beyond the legal arena is the ethical one. We know all too well the problems organizations have had the past few years as a result of ethics breaches. We will continue to take the lead in this organization to promote ethical behaviors, ethical practices, and will work with senior management to ensure that ethical standards become part of this organization's culture.

"We must begin preparations to deal with a variety of HRM-related issues making their way into corporate America. For example, increases in minimum wages, continuation of the globalization of the workforce, treatment of applicants who smoke or are obese, blogging, and spirituality at work are all on the horizon. As we've done before, we will be at the forefront of these issues for this organization, and prepare recommendations for our executives on how we believe each of these should be handled.

"Thank you for your wonderful years of service to HR and this organization."

Fundamentals of HRM

Learning Outcomes

After reading this chapter, you will be able to

1. Explain what we mean by *human resource management.*

2. Describe the importance of human resource management.

3. Identify the primary external influences affecting human resource management.

4. Characterize how management practices affect human resource management.

5. Discuss the effect of labor unions on human resource management.

6. Outline the components and the goals of the staffing, training, and development functions of human resource management.

7. List the components and goals of the motivation and maintenance functions.

8. Outline the major activities in the employment, training and development, compensation and benefits, and employee relations departments of human resource management.

9. Explain how human resource management practices differ in small businesses and in international settings.

INTRODUCTION

People, not buildings, make a company successful.

When you reflect for a moment on Chris Hernandez's comments, it is important to note that achieving organizational goals cannot be done without human resources. What is Sprint without its employees? A lot of buildings, expensive equipment, and some impressive bank balances. Similarly, if you removed the employees from such varied organizations as the Philadelphia Eagles, Microsoft, Jet Blue Airlines, or the American Red Cross, what would you have left? Not much. People—not buildings, equipment, or brand names—make a company.

This point is one that many of us take for granted. When you think about the millions of organizations that provide us with goods and services, any one or more of which will probably employ you during your lifetime, how often do you explicitly consider that these organizations depend on people to make them operate? Only under unusual circumstances, such as when you are put on hold for too long on a company's toll-free customer-service line or when a major corporation is sued for a discriminatory HRM practice, do you recognize the important role that employees play in making organizations work. But how did these people come to be employees in their organizations? How were they selected? Why do they come to work on a regular basis? How do they know what to do on their jobs? How does management know if the employees are performing adequately? And if they are not, what can be done about it? Will today's employees be adequately

DID YOU KNOW?

A MANAGEMENT RECAP

HRM does not exist in isolation. Rather, it is a subset of the field of management. For those who desire a quick review of management, please read on.

Management is the process of efficiently achieving the objectives of the organization with and through people. To achieve its objective, management typically requires the coordination of several vital components that we call functions. The primary functions of management that are required are **planning** (e.g., establishing goals), **organizing** (i.e., determining what activities need to be completed to accomplish those goals), **leading** (i.e., ensuring that the right people are on the job with appropriate skills, and motivating them to levels of high productivity), and **controlling** (i.e., monitoring activities to ensure that goals are met). When these four functions operate in a coordinated fashion, we can say that the organization is heading in the correct direction toward achieving its objectives. Common to any effort to achieve objectives are three elements: goals, limited resources, and people.

In any discussion of management, one must recognize the importance of setting goals. Goals are necessary because activities undertaken in an organization must be directed toward some end. For instance, your goal in taking this class is to build a foundation of understanding

HRM and obviously to pass the class. There is considerable truth in the observation, "If you don't know where you are going, any road will take you there." The established goals may not be explicit, but where there are no goals, there is no need for managers.

Limited resources are a fact of organizational life. Economic resources, by definition, are scarce; therefore, the manager is responsible for their allocation. This requires not only that managers be effective in achieving the established goals but that they be efficient in doing so. Managers, then, are concerned with the attainment of goals, which makes them effective, and with the best allocation of scarce resources, which makes them efficient.

The need for two or more people is the third and last requisite for management. It is with and through people that managers perform their work. Daniel Defoe's legendary Robinson Crusoe could not become a manager until Friday's arrival.

In summary, managers are those who work with and through other people, allocating resources, in the effort to achieve goals. They perform their tasks through four critical activities—planning, organizing, leading, and controlling.

Source: For a comprehensive overview of management, see Stephen P. Robbins and David A. DeCenzo, *Fundamentals of Management,* 5th ed. (Upper Saddle River, NJ: Prentice Hall, 2006), ch. 1. It is also worth noting that changes in the world of work reveal that these work functions may no longer be just the purview of managers but instead part of every worker's job responsibility.

prepared for the technologically advanced work the organization will require of them in the years ahead? What happens in an organization if a union is present?

These are some of the many questions whose answers lie at the foundations of HRM. But, as we saw in Chapter 1, answers to these questions are affected by elements outside any organization's control. Make no mistake, the global village is changing the strategic nature of organizations, including HRM. For example, consider the shifting of jobs worldwide. Given the technology available for customer service, where the phone is answered makes no difference to the customer. Realistically, it's always 9-to-5 somewhere in the world. Routing customer service calls to different countries in different time zones can enable a company to provide 24/7 service without having to pay premium wages for work after "normal work hours."

We will discuss various elements as a set of activities to be accomplished by individuals, whether actual members or service providers for an organization. Regardless of the doer, certain actions must take place—actions that serve as the fundamentals of HRM. Yet the field of HRM cannot exist in isolation. Rather, it's part of the larger field of management (see Did You Know?).

WHY IS HRM IMPORTANT TO AN ORGANIZATION?

Prior to the mid-1960s, personnel departments in organizations were often perceived as the "health and happiness" crews.[1] Their primary job activities involved planning company picnics, scheduling vacations, enrolling workers for health-care coverage, and planning retirement parties. That has changed during the past three-plus decades.

Federal and state laws have placed on employers many new requirements concerning hiring and employment practices. Jobs have also changed. They have become more technical and require employees with greater skills. Furthermore, job boundaries are becoming blurred. In the past, a worker performed a job in a specific department, working on particular job tasks with others who did similar jobs. Today's workers are just as likely, however, to find themselves working on project teams with various people from across the organization. Others may do the majority of their work at home and rarely see any of their co-workers. And, of course, global competition has increased the importance of improving workforce productivity and looking globally for the best-qualified workers. Thus, organizations need HRM specialists trained in psychology, sociology, organization and work design, and law.

Federal legislation requires organizations to hire the best-qualified candidate without regard to race, religion, color, sex, disability, or national origin—and someone must ensure that this is done. Employees need to be trained to function effectively within the organization—and again, someone must oversee this as well as the continuing personal development of each employee. Someone must ensure that these employees maintain their productive affiliation with the organization. The work environment must be structured to encourage worker retention while simultaneously attracting new applicants. Of course, the "someones" we refer to, those primarily responsible for carrying out these activities, are human resource professionals.

Today, professionals in human resources are important elements in the success of any organization. Their jobs require a new level of sophistication. Not surprisingly, their status in some organizations has also been elevated. Even the name has changed. Although the terms *personnel* and *human resource management* are frequently used interchangeably, it is important to note that the two connote quite different aspects. The human resource department head, once a single individual heading the personnel function, today may be a senior vice president sitting on executive boards and participating in the development of the overall organizational strategy.

management
The process of efficiently completing activities with and through other people.

planning
A management function focusing on setting organizational goals and objectives.

organizing
A management function that deals with determining what jobs are to be done, by whom, where decisions are to be made, and how to group employees.

leading
Management function concerned with directing the work of others.

controlling
Management function concerned with monitoring activities to ensure goals are met.

What makes Starbucks so successful? The answer is often simple—it's the people. From day one, Starbucks employees know exactly what's expected of them and how they are vital to the success of the busness. As Starbucks says, it puts people before products. No wonder Starbucks is regarded as one of the "most admired companies."
(*Source:* © AP/Wide World Photos)

The Strategic Nature

Many companies today recognize the importance of people in meeting their goals. HRM must therefore balance two primary responsibilities: assisting the organization in it strategic direction and representing and advocating for the organization's employees. Clearly, HRM has a significant role in today's organization.[2] HRM must be forward thinking. HRM must not simply react to what "management" states. Rather, HRM must take the lead in assisting management with the "people" component of the organization. Moreover, organization's employees can assist in gaining and maintaining a competitive advantage. Attracting and keeping such employees requires HRM policies and practices that such employees desire. Being a strategic partner also involves supporting the business strategy. This means working with line management in analyzing organizational designs, the culture, and performance systems, and recommending and implementing changes where necessary.

HRM must also serve the organization by determining lowest-cost strategies to its HRM practices. It must look for ways to reduce personnel costs and find more effective means of offering employee amenities. Today's HR function needs to be as concerned with the total costs of an organization's human resources as it is with the employees themselves. As such, HRM needs to take whatever steps it can to demonstrate its return on investment dollars spent by the organization for human resource activities—determining the value added that HRM brings to the organization.[3]

HRM Certification

Many colleges and universities are also helping prepare HRM professionals by offering concentrations and majors in the discipline in addition to an accreditation process for HRM professionals. The Society for Human Resource Management offers opportunities for individuals to distinguish themselves in the field by achieving a level of proficiency predetermined by the Human Resource Certification Institute as necessary for successful handling of human resource management affairs (see Learning an HRM Skill at the end of this chapter).

HRM is a function of every manager's job, not just those who work in human resources.

HRM is the part of the organization concerned with the "people" dimension. HRM can be viewed in one of two ways. First, HRM is a staff or support function in the organization. Its role is to provide assistance in HRM matters to line employees, or those directly involved in producing the organization's goods and services. Second, HRM is a function of every manager's job. Whether or not one works in a formal HRM department, the fact remains that to effectively manage employees all managers must handle the activities we'll describe in this book. That's important to keep in mind!

Every organization is comprised of people. Acquiring their services, developing their skills, motivating them to high levels of performance, and ensuring that they maintain their commitment to the organization are essential to achieving organizational objectives. This is true regardless of the type of organization—government, business, education, health, recreation, or social action. Hiring and keeping good people is critical to the success of every organization.

To look at HRM more specifically, we propose that it consists of four basic functions: (1) staffing, (2) training and development, (3) motivation, and (4) maintenance. In less academic terms, we might say that HRM is made up of four activities: (1) hiring people, (2) preparing them, (3) stimulating them, and (4) keeping them.

When one attempts to piece together an approach for HRM, many variations and themes may exist.[4] However, when we begin to focus on HRM activities as subsets of the four functions, a clearer picture arises (see Exhibit 2-1). Let's take a closer look at each component.

EXHIBIT 2-1
Human Resource Management:
Primary Activities

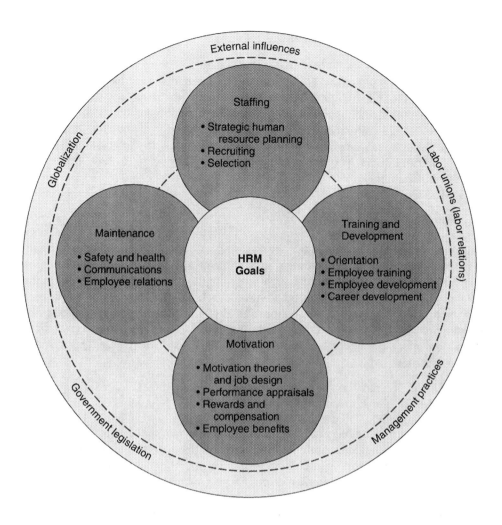

Exhibit 2-1
Human Resource Management: Primary Activities

HOW EXTERNAL INFLUENCES AFFECT HRM

The four HRM activities are highly affected by what occurs outside the organization. It is important to recognize these environmental influences, because any activity undertaken in each of the HRM processes is directly or indirectly affected by these external elements. For example, when a company downsizes (sometimes referred to as rightsizing) its workforce, does it lay off workers by seniority? If so, are an inordinate number of minority employees affected?

Although any attempt to identify specific influences may prove insufficient, we can categorize them into four general areas: the dynamic environment, governmental legislation, labor unions, and current management practice.

TECHNOLOGY CORNER

HRM BASICS

Some of the more routine HRM applications can be computerized to assist HRM members in becoming more efficient in their daily duties. Here is an application that can be purchased off the shelf and used immediately:

HR Consultant in a Box: A software package that provides numerous forms and policies for use in HR functions. These include forms such as job-offer letters, applicant ratings, attitude surveys, and exit interviews forms.

Available at hrconsultantinabox.com ($99.95).

The HRM Strategic Environment

It has been stated that the only constant during our lifetimes is change (and paying taxes!). We must therefore prepare ourselves for events that have a significant effect on our lives. HRM is no different. Many events help shape our field. Some of the more obvious include globalization, technology, workforce diversity, changing skill requirements, continuous improvement, work process engineering, decentralized work sites, teams, employee involvement, and ethics. If these sound familiar to you, congratulations, you are reading carefully. They were, in fact, the topics presented in Chapter 1.

Governmental Legislation

Today, employees who want to take several weeks of unpaid leave to be with their newborn children and return to their jobs without any loss of seniority have an easier time making the request. Although some employers may think such an application negatively affects work flow, government legislation has given employees the right to take this leave. Laws supporting this and other employer actions are important to the HRM process. Listed in Exhibit 2-2 are laws that have had a tremendous effect on HRM in organizations. We'll explore this critical area in depth in Chapter 3.

Labor Unions

Labor unions were founded and exist today to assist workers in dealing with the management of an organization. As the certified third-party representative, the union acts on behalf of its members to secure wages, hours, and other terms and conditions of employment. Another critical aspect of unions is that they promote and foster what is called a *grievance procedure,* or a specified process for resolving differences between workers and management. In many instances, this process alone constrains management from making unilateral decisions. For instance, a current HRM issue is the debate over employers' ability to terminate employees whenever they want. When a union is present and HRM practices are spelled out in a negotiated agreement, employers cannot fire for unjustified reasons. Because of the complexities involved in operating with unionization and the special laws that pertain to it, we will defer that discussion until Chapter 14, when we will explore the unique world of labor relations and collective bargaining.

Management Thought

management thought
Early theories of management that promoted today's HRM operations.

scientific management
A set of principles designed to enhance worker productivity.

The last area of external influence is current **management thought.** Since the inception of the first personnel departments, management practices have played a major role in promoting today's HRM operations. Much of the emphasis has come from some of the early and highly regarded management theorists. Four individuals specifically are regarded as the forerunners of HRM support: Frederick Taylor, Hugo Munsterberg, Mary Parker Follet, and Elton Mayo.

Frederick Taylor, often regarded as the father of **scientific management,** developed a set of principles to enhance worker productivity. By systematically studying each job and detailing methods to attain higher productivity levels, Taylor's work offered the first sense of today's human resource practices. For instance, Taylor advocated that workers needed appropriate job training and should be screened according to their ability to do the job (a forerunner of skill-based hiring). Hugo Munsterberg and his associates suggested improved methods of employment testing, training, performance evaluations, and job efficiency. Mary Parker Follet, a social philosopher, advocated people-oriented organizations. Her writings focused

Year Enacted	Legislation	Focus of Legislation
1866	Civil Rights Act	prohibits discrimination based on race
1931	Davis-Bacon Act	requires paying prevailing wage rates
1935	Wagner Act	legitimized unions
1938	Fair Labor Standards Act	requires premium pay rates for overtime
1947	Taft-Hartley Act	balanced union power
1959	Landrum-Griffin Act	requires financial disclosure for unions
1963	Equal Pay Act	requires equal pay for equal jobs
1964	Civil Rights Act	prohibits discrimination
1967	Age Discrimination in Employment Act	adds age to protected group status
1970	Occupational Safety and Health Act	protects workers from workplace hazards
1974	Privacy Act	permits employees to review personnel files
1974	Employee Retirement Income and Security Act	protects employee retirement funds
1976	Health Maintenance Organization Act	requires alternative health insurance coverage
1978	Mandatory Retirement Act	raises mandatory retirement age from 65 to 70; uncapped in 1986
1986	Immigration Reform and Control Act	requires verification of citizenship or legal status in the United States
1986	Consolidated Omnibus Budget Reconciliation Act	provides for benefit continuation when laid off
1988	Employment Polygraph Protection Act	prohibits use of polygraphs in most HRM practices
1989	Plant Closing Bill	requires employers to give advance notice to affected employees
1990	Americans with Disabilities Act	prohibits discrimination against those with disabilities
1991	Civil Rights Act	overturns several Supreme Court cases concerning discrimination
1993	Family and Medical Leave Act	permits employees to take unpaid leave for family matters
2002	Sarbanes-Oxley Act	establishes requirements for proper financial recordkeeping for public companies as well as penalties for noncompliance

Exhibit 2-2
Relevant Laws Affecting HRM Practices

on groups, as opposed to individuals in the organization. Thus, Follet's theory was a forerunner of today's teamwork concept and group cohesiveness. But probably the biggest advancement in HRM came from the works of Elton Mayo and his famous Hawthorne studies.

The **Hawthorne studies,** so named because they were conducted at the Hawthorne Plant of Western Electric just outside of Chicago, ran for nearly a decade beginning in the late 1920s. They gave rise to what today is called the human relations movement. The researchers found that informal work groups had a significant effect on worker performance. Group standards and sentiments were more important determinants of a worker's output than the wage incentive plan. Results of the Hawthorne studies justified many of the paternalistic programs that human resource managers have instituted in their organizations. The advent of employee benefit offerings, safe and healthy working conditions, and the concern of every manager for human relations stem directly from the work of Mayo and his associates at Hawthorne.[5]

Hawthorne studies

A series of studies that provided new insights into group behavior.

What effect does the informal work group have on these workers' productivity? According to the Hawthorne studies, a significant amount. In fact, this classic research, which paved the way to the human relations movement, showed management that group standards and employee sentiments were the most important determinants of employee productivity— even more so than pay! (Source: Javier Pierini/Photodisc/Getty Images, Inc.)

staffing function
Activities in HRM concerned with seeking and hiring qualified employees.

In today's organizations, we can see the influence of management practice affecting HRM in a variety of ways. Motivation techniques cited in management literature, as well as W. Edwards Deming's influence on continuous improvement programs to enhance productivity, have made their way into HRM activities. Writers such as Tom Peters and Peter Drucker emphasize giving employees a say in what affects their work, teams, and work process engineering. Implementing these will ultimately require the assistance of HRM professionals.

Now that you have a brief picture of the external influences affecting this field, let's turn our attention to the functions and activities within HRM. It's important to recognize, too, that in some organizations that lack formal human resource management departments, these functions will be the responsibility of each line manager. In fact, in most cases, line managers will always have this responsibility whether a formal human resources department exists or not. When formal HRM departments exist, those working in human resources are generally responsible for assisting the line manager in these activities. In other cases, however, senior management may have decided that such activities, although supportive of line management, will be more effective if handled in a more centralized fashion in the human resource department. For ease of clarity, we'll discuss the following functions as if they are the responsibility of those working in HRM.

STAFFING FUNCTION ACTIVITIES

Although recruiting is frequently perceived as the initial step in the **staffing function,** it has prerequisites. Specifically, before the first job candidate is sought, the HR specialist must embark on employment planning. This area alone has probably fostered the most change in human resource departments during the past 30 years. We can no longer hire individuals haphazardly. We must have a well-defined reason for needing individuals who possess specific skills, knowledge, and abilities directly likened to specific jobs. No longer does the HR manager exist in total darkness, or for that matter, in a reactive mode. Not until the organization's mission and strategy have been fully developed can human resource managers begin to determine human resource needs.[6]

Specifically, when an organization plans strategically, it determines its goals and objectives for a given period of time. These goals and objectives often lead to structural changes in the organization; that is, these changes foster changes in job requirements, reporting relationships, how individuals are grouped, and the like. As such, these new or revised structures bring with them a host of pivotal jobs. It is these jobs that HRM must be prepared to fill.[7]

As these jobs are analyzed, specific skills, knowledge, and abilities are identified that the job applicant must possess to succeed. This aspect cannot be understated, for herein lies much of the responsibility and success of HRM.[8] Through the job analysis process, HRM identifies the essential qualifications for a particular job. This is sound business acumen, for these jobs are critically linked to the strategic direction of the company. It is also well within the stated guidelines of major employment legislation. Additionally, almost all activities involved in HRM revolve around an accurate description of the job. One cannot successfully recruit without knowledge of the critical skills required, nor can one appropriately set performance standards and pay rates or invoke disciplinary procedures fairly without this understanding. Once these critical competencies have been identified, the recruiting process begins. Armed with information from employment planning, we can begin to focus on our prospective candidates. When involved in recruiting, HR specialists should attempt to achieve two goals, to obtain an adequate pool of applicants, thereby giving line managers more choices, and simultaneously provide enough information about the job to head off unqualified applicants. Recruiting, then, becomes an activity designed to locate potentially good applicants, conditioned by the recruiting effort's constraints, the job market, and the need to reach members of underrepresented groups such as minorities and women.

Once applications have come in, it is time to begin the selection phase. Selection, too, has a dual focus. It attempts to thin out the large set of applications that arrived during the recruiting phase and to select an applicant who will be successful on the job. To achieve this goal, many companies use a variety of steps to assess the applicants. The candidate who successfully completes all steps is typically offered the job, but that is only half of the equation. HRM must also ensure that the good prospect accepts a job offer. Accordingly, HRM must communicate a variety of information to the applicant, such as the organization culture, what is expected of employees, and any other information that is pertinent to the candidate's decision-making process.

The completed selection process ends the staffing function. The goals, then, of the staffing function are to locate competent employees and bring them into the organization. When this goal has been reached, HRM focuses its attention on the employee's training and development.

The goal of recruiting is to give enough information about the job to attract a large number of qualified applicants and simultaneously discourage the unqualified from applying.

Goals of the Training and Development Function

Whenever HRM embarks on the hiring process, it attempts to search and secure the "best" possible candidate. And while HRM professionals pride themselves on being able to determine those who are qualified versus those who are not, the fact remains that few, if any, new employees can truly come into an organization and immediately become fully functioning, 100 percent performers. First, employees need to adapt to their new surroundings. Socialization is a means of bringing about this adaptation. While it may begin informally in the late stages of the hiring process, the thrust of socialization continues for many months after the individual begins working. During this time, the focus is on orienting the new employee to the rules, regulations, and goals of the organization, department, and work unit. Then, as the employee becomes more comfortable with his or her surroundings, more intense training begins.

Reflection over the past few decades tells us that depending on the job, employees often take months to adjust to their new organizations and positions. Does that imply that HRM has not hired properly or the staffing function goals were not met? On the contrary, it indicates that intricacies and peculiarities involved in each organization's positions result in jobs being tailored to adequately meet organizational needs. Accordingly, HRM plays an important role in shaping this reformulation of new employees so that within a short time they, too, will be fully productive. To accomplish this, HRM typically embarks on four areas in the training and development phase: employee training, employee development, organization development, and career development. It is important to note that employee and career development are more employee centered, whereas employee training is designed to promote competency in the new job. Organization development, on the other hand, focuses on systemwide changes. While each area has a unique focus, all four are critical to the success of the training and development phase. We have summarized these four in Exhibit 2-3.

At the conclusion of the **training and development function**, HRM attempts to reach the goal of having competent, adapted employees who possess the up-to-date skills, knowledge, and abilities needed to perform their current jobs more successfully. If that is attained, HRM turns its attention to finding ways to motivate these individuals to exert high energy levels.

training and development function
Activities in HRM concerned with assisting employees to develop up-to-date skills, knowledge, and abilities.

EXHIBIT 2-3
Training and Development Activities

Employee Training	Employee training is designed to assist employees in acquiring better skills for their current job. The focus of employee training is on current job-skill requirements.
Employee Development	Employee development is designed to help the organization ensure that it has the necessary talent internally for meeting future human resource needs. The focus of employee development is on a future position within the organization for which the employee requires additional competencies.
Career Development	Career development programs are designed to assist employees in advancing their work lives. The focus of career development is to provide the necessary information and assessment in helping employees realize their career goals. However, career development is the responsibility of the individual, not the organization.
Organization Development	Organization development deals with facilitating systemwide changes in the organization. The focus of organization development is to change the attitudes and values of employees according to new organizational strategic directions.

The Motivation Function

motivation function

Activities in HRM concerned with helping employees exert at high energy levels.

The **motivation function** is one of the most important yet probably the least understood aspects of the HRM process. Human behavior is complex, and trying to figure out what motivates various employees has long been a concern of behavioral scientists. However, research has given us some important insights into employee motivation.

First of all, one must begin to think of motivation as a multifaceted process—one with individual, managerial, and organizational implications. Motivation is not just what the employee exhibits, but a collection of environmental issues surrounding the job.[9] It has been proposed that one's performance in an organization is a function of two factors: ability and willingness to do the job.[10] Thus, from a performance perspective, employees need the appropriate skills and abilities to adequately do the job. This should be ensured in the first two phases of HRM by correctly defining the requirements of the job, matching applicants to those requirements, and training the new employee in how to do the job.[11] But another concern is the job design itself. If jobs are poorly designed, inadequately laid out, or improperly described, employees will perform below their capabilities. Consequently, HRM must ask has the latest technology been provided to permit maximum work efficiency? Is the office setting appropriate (properly lit and adequately ventilated, for example) for the job? Are the necessary tools readily available for employee use? For example, imagine an employee who spends considerable time each day developing product designs. This employee, however, lacks ready access to a computer-aided design (CAD) software program or a powerful enough computer system to run it. Compared to another employee who does have access to such technology, the first individual is going to be less productive. Indeed, office automation and industrial engineering techniques must be incorporated into the job design. Without such planning, the best intentions of organizational members to motivate employees may be lost or significantly reduced.

Additionally, many organizations today recognize that motivating employees also requires a level of respect between management and the workers. This respect can be seen as involving employees in decisions that affect them, listening to employees, and implementing their suggestions where appropriate.

The next step in the motivation process is to set performance standards for each employee. While no easy task, managers must be sure that the performance evaluation system is designed to provide feedback to employees regarding their past performance, while simultaneously addressing any performance weaknesses the employee may have. A link should be established between employee compensation and performance: the compensation and benefit activity in the organization should be adapted to and coordinated with a pay-for-performance plan.[12]

Throughout the activities required in the motivation function, the efforts all focus on one primary goal: to have those competent and adapted employees, with up-to-date skills, knowledge, and abilities, exerting high energy levels. Once that is achieved, it is time to turn the HRM focus to the maintenance function.

How Important Is the Maintenance Function?

The last phase of the HRM process is called the **maintenance function**. As the name implies, this phase puts into place activities that will help retain productive employees. When one considers how employee job loyalty has declined in the past decade, it's not difficult to see the importance of maintaining employee commitment.[13] To do so requires some basic common sense and some creativity. HRM must ensure a safe and healthy working environment; caring for employees' well-being has a major effect on their commitment. HRM must also realize that any problem an employee faces in his or her personal life will ultimately be brought into the workplace. This calls for employee assistance programs, such as programs that help individuals deal with stressful life situations. Such programs provide many benefits to the organization while helping the affected employee.

In addition to protecting employees' welfare, HRM must operate appropriate **communications programs** in the organization. Such programs help employees know what is occurring around them and provide a place to vent frustrations. Employee relations programs should ensure that employees are kept well informed—through such things as the company's intranet, bulletin boards, town hall meetings, or teleconferencing—and foster an environment where employee voices are heard. Time and effort expended in this phase help HRM achieve its ultimate goal of having competent employees who have adapted to the organization's culture with up-to-date skills, knowledge, and abilities, who exert high energy levels, and who are now willing to maintain their commitment and loyalty to the company. This process is difficult to implement and maintain, but the rewards should be such that the effort placed in such endeavors is warranted.

maintenance function
Activities in HRM concerned with maintaining employees' commitment and loyalty to the organization.

communications programs
HRM programs designed to provide information to employees.

TRANSLATING HRM FUNCTIONS INTO PRACTICE

The areas of HRM can take numerous characteristics. Describing the various permutations and combinations goes well beyond the scope of this book. Realize, too, that more than half of all HR departments also offer administrative services to the organization. These might include operating the company's credit union, making childcare arrangements, providing security, or operating in-house medical or food services.[14] Yet in spite of the different configurations, in a typical nonunion HRM department, we generally find four distinct areas: (1) employment, (2) training and development, (3) compensation/benefits, and (4) employee relations. Usually reporting to a vice president of human resources, managers in these four areas have specific responsibilities. Exhibit 2-4 is a simplified organizational representation of HRM areas, with some typical job titles and a sampling of what these job incumbents earn.[15]

Employment

The main thrust of the employment function is to promote staffing activities. Working in conjunction with position control specialists (in compensation, in benefits, or in a comptroller's office), the employment department embarks on the

EXHIBIT 2-4
Sample HRM Organizational Chart, Sample Activities, and Selected Salaries

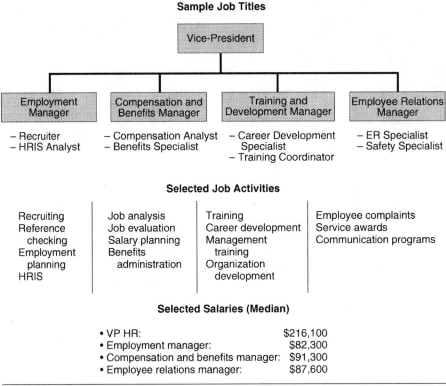

Sample Job Titles

Vice-President

Employment Manager	Compensation and Benefits Manager	Training and Development Manager	Employee Relations Manager
– Recruiter – HRIS Analyst	– Compensation Analyst – Benefits Specialist	– Career Development Specialist – Training Coordinator	– ER Specialist – Safety Specialist

Selected Job Activities

Recruiting
Reference
   checking
Employment
   planning
HRIS
	Job analysis
	Job evaluation
	Salary planning
	Benefits
	   administration
		Training
		Career development
		Management
		   training
		Organization
		   development
			Employee complaints
			Service awards
			Communication programs

Selected Salaries (Median)

- VP HR: $216,100
- Employment manager: $82,300
- Compensation and benefits manager: $91,300
- Employee relations manager: $87,600

Source: Society for Human Resource Management, *Spectra Personnel* (October 2000), pp. 1–16; and J. Vocino, "HR Feels Pinch of Economic Slowdown," *HR Magazine* (November 2002), p. 39.

process of recruiting new employees.[16] This means correctly advertising the job to attract those with appropriate knowledge and abilities. After sorting through résumés or applications (whether manually or on a computer), the employment specialist usually conducts the weeding out of applicants who fail to meet the job's requirements. The remaining applications and résumés are then typically forwarded to the line area for its review. After her review, the line manager may then instruct the employment specialist to interview the selected candidates. In many cases, this initial interview is another step in the hiring process. Understanding what the line manager desires in an employee, the employment specialist begins to further filter down the list of prospective candidates. During this phase, candidates who appear to "fit" the line area's need typically are scheduled to meet with the line manager for another interview.

It is important to note that the employment specialist's role is not to make the hiring decision but to coordinate the effort with line management. Once the line area has selected its candidate, the employment specialist usually makes the job offer and handles the routine paperwork associated with hiring an employee.

Training and Development

The training and development section of an organization is often responsible for helping employees maximize their potential. Their focus is to enhance employees' personal qualities that lead to greater organizational productivity. More important, training and development members are often better known as the organization's internal change agents. (We'll look at this topic in more detail in Chapter 8.) These change agents, or organizational development specialists, help organization members cope with change in many forms. It can be a cultural change where top management changes the philosophy, values, and ways of operating. For instance, changing from a production focus of producing whatever the company wants and selling it to the public, to a marketing focus whereby the company produces and sells contingent on consumer demand, requires a new organizational orientation. A change in the organization's structure can result in layoffs, new job assignments, team involvement, and the like, and again require new orientations for organizational members. We may also see changes in procedures or policies where employees must be informed and taught to deal with such occurrences. For instance, a growing concern of companies has been to implement policies to address an ethical violation. Employees must understand what constitutes an ethics violation. Training and education often is the best form of prevention. Training and development may also include career development activities and employee counseling to help people make better choices about their careers and to achieve their desired goals.

One employee benefit organizations have been providing is the on-site health club. Companies have found that giving employees a place to reduce their stress and enhance their overall well-being helps attract and retain employees. (Source: © AP/Wide World Photos)

Compensation and Benefits

Work in compensation and benefits[17] is often described as dealing with the most objective areas of a subjective field. As the name implies, compensation and benefits is concerned with paying employees and administering their benefits package. These tasks are by no means easy ones. First of all, job salaries are not paid on a whim; rather, dollar values assigned to positions often come from elaborate investigations and analyses. These investigations run the gamut of simple, logical job rankings (that is, the position of company president should pay more than the position of maintenance engineer) to extensive analyses. Once these analyses are finished, job ratings are statistically compared to determine the job's relative worth to the company. External factors such as market conditions, limited supply of potential workers, and the like may affect the overall range of job worth. Further analysis ensures internal equity in the compensation system. This means that as job rates are set, they are determined on such dimensions as skill, job responsibility, effort, and accountability—not by personal characteristics that may be suspect under employment law.

DID YOU KNOW?

GLOBAL LABOR COSTS

How much of a difference is there among countries in terms of labor costs for employers? Most everyone has heard the concern that U.S. jobs are heading "overseas," where the cost of labor is cheaper. How much cheaper? Consider this.

The average hourly wage cost (total hourly wages plus benefit costs per hour of work) for U.S. employers for factory workers is $21.11. And though the U.S. cost only rose approximately 4 percent in 2003 dollars, as compared to over 12 percent for foreign factory workers, the difference may startle you. On average, the total hourly labor cost to employees in 30 foreign industrialized nations (excluding the United States) was $14.22,

nearly 33 percent less. But that number may not be totally indicative of the debate. The following chart may bring some things to a better light:

Country	Average per Hourly Labor Cost
United States	$21.11
Average of 30 foreign industrialized countries	$14.22
Mexico	$ 2.48
China	$ 0.64

Could these "averages" be a leading cause of job shift in the United States?

Source: P. Coy, "Just How Cheap Is Chinese Labor?" *Business Week* (December 13, 2004), p. 46.

On the benefits side of the equation, much change has occurred over the past decade. As benefit offerings to employees have become significantly more costly, the benefits administrator (who may also have the title of risk manager) has the responsibility of piecing together a benefits package that meets employee needs and is cost-effective to the organization. As such, much effort is expended searching for lower-cost products, like health or workers' compensation insurance, while concurrently maintaining or improving quality. Additionally, various new products are often reviewed, such as flexible benefits programs and utilization reviews, to help in benefit cost containment. But benefits should not be viewed solely from a cost-containment perspective. Benefits are of a strategic nature in that they help attract and retain high-quality employees.[18]

The benefits administrator also serves as the resource information officer to employees regarding their benefits. This information may be provided through a variety of methods, including a company's intranet. Activities include helping employees prepare for their retirement, looking for various payout options, keeping abreast of recent tax law changes, or helping executives with their perquisites.[19] This is a great deal of responsibility, but also highly visible in the organization.

Employee Relations

employee relations function

Activities in HRM concerned with effective communications among organizational members.

The final phase in our scheme of HRM operations is the **employee relations function**. Employee relations (ER) has several major responsibilities. Before we go further, however, we must differentiate between employee relations and labor relations. The two are structurally similar, but labor relations involves dealing with labor unions. As such, because other laws apply, some employee relations techniques may not be applicable. For instance, in a unionized setting, a specific grievance procedure might be detailed in the labor-management contract, and might involve the union, management, and the allegedly wronged employee. In a nonunion environment, a similar procedure might exist or the grievance might be handled one on one. These may be subtle differences, but labor relations requires a different set of competencies and understanding.

In the nonunion setting, however, we see employee relations specialists performing many tasks. As mentioned earlier, one of their key responsibilities is to ensure that open communications permeates the organization.[20] This entails fostering an environment where employees talk directly to supervisors and settle any differences that may arise. If needed, employee relations representatives intervene to assist in achieving a fair and equitable solution. ER specialists are also intermediaries in helping employees understand the rules. Their primary goal is to ensure that policies and procedures are enforced properly, and to permit a wronged employee a forum to obtain relief. As part of this role, too, comes the disciplinary process. These representatives see that appropriate disciplinary sanctions are used consistently throughout the organization.

What is the purpose of HRM communications? HRM communications programs are designed to keep employees abreast of what is happening in the organization and knowledgeable of the policies and procedures affecting them. Whereas public relations departments keep the public informed of what an organization does, HRM communications focus on the internal constituents—the employees. Communication programs help increase employee loyalty and commitment by building into the corporate culture a systematic means of free-flowing, timely, and accurate information by which employees better perceive that the organization values them.[21] Such a system builds trust and openness among organizational members that helps withstand even the sharing of "bad news."

Building effective HRM communications programs involves a few fundamental elements. These include top management commitment, effective upward communication, determining what is to be communicated, allowing for feedback, and information sources. Let's look at each of these.

Top Management Commitment Before any organization can develop and implement an internal organizational communications program, it must have the backing, support, and "blessing" of the CEO. Employees must see any activity designed to facilitate work environments as being endorsed by the company's top management. These programs then receive priority and are viewed as significant components of the corporate culture. Just as it is critical for employees to see top management supporting communications, so, too, they must see communications operating effectively at all levels. Effective communications does not just imply that top management sends information down throughout the company. It also implies that information flows upward as well and laterally to other areas in the organization.[22]

Effective Upward Communication The upward flow of communication is particularly noteworthy because often the employees, the ones closest to the work, may have vital information that top management should know. For instance, let's take a situation that occurs in HRM. We've recognized the ever-changing nature of this field. Legislation at any level—federal, state, or local—may add new HRM requirements for the organization. Unless top management is made aware of the implications of these requirements severe repercussions could occur. Thus, that information must filter up in the company.

A similar point could easily be made for any part of an organization. And in keeping with the spirit of employee empowerment,[23] as employees are more involved in making decisions that affect them, that information must be communicated up the ladder. Furthermore, it's important for top management to monitor the pulse of the organization regarding how employees view working for the company. Whether that information is obtained from walking around the premises, through formal employee suggestions, or through employee satisfaction/morale surveys, such information is crucial. In fact, on the latter point, advances in technology have allowed some employee satisfaction measures to be captured in almost real time at significantly reduced costs.[24] At IBM, for instance, such surveys are online, making them easier for the employees to use, more expedient in their analysis, and more timely for company use.

Determining What to Communicate At the extreme, if every piece of information that exists in our organizations were communicated, no work would ever get done; people would be spending their entire days on information overload. Employees, while wanting to be informed, generally are not concerned with every piece of information, like who just retired, or was promoted, or what community group was given a donation yesterday. Rather, employees need *pertinent* information—addressing what employees should know to do their jobs. This typically includes where the business is going (strategic goals), current sales/service/production outcomes, new product or service lines, and human resource policy changes.

One means of determining what to communicate is through a "what-if, so-what" test. When deciding the priority of the information to be shared, HR managers should ask themselves What if this information is not shared? (See Ethical Issues in HRM.) Will employees be able to do their jobs as well as if it were shared? Will they be disadvantaged in some way by not knowing? If employees will not be affected one way or the other, then that may not be a priority item. Next, the so-what test: Will employees care about the information? Or will they see it as an overload of meaningless information? If the latter is the case, then that, too, is not priority information. That's not to say this information may never be exchanged; it only means that it's not important for employees to get the information immediately.

ETHICAL ISSUES IN HRM

PURPOSELY DISTORTING INFORMATION

The idea of withholding information is an issue for all HRM managers. Read the following two scenarios and think about what ethical dilemmas those in HRM might face relating to the intentional distortion of information.

Scenario 1:   At the president's monthly executive staff meeting, you were informed of the past quarter's revenue figures. Moreover, you also were informed that the organization is going to more than double its quarterly expected numbers, and the value of your company's stock will likely surge. Your organization has a bonus plan that shares profits with employees. But this profit sharing is based solely on management's discretion and follow no systematic formula. If word gets out that profits are outstanding, employees might expect larger bonuses. The executive committee wants to share about half of the windfall with employees, reinvest most of the rest into capital equipment, and save some for less favorable times. Your staff and several employees from a cross-section of departments are meeting with you

tomorrow to begin the process of making profit-sharing decisions for the year. What do you tell them?

Scenario 2:   An employee asks you about a rumor she's heard that some HR activities may be outsourced to a company in Des Moines, Iowa. You know the rumor to be true, but you'd rather not let the information out just yet. You're fearful that it could hurt departmental morale and lead to premature resignations. What do you say to your employee?

These two scenarios illustrate dilemmas that HRM managers may face relating to evading the truth, distorting facts, or lying to others. And here's something else that makes the situation even more problematic: it might not always be in a manager's best interest or that of his or her unit to provide full and complete information. Keeping communications fuzzy can cut down on questions, permit faster decision making, minimize objections, reduce opposition, make it easier to deny one's earlier statements, preserve the freedom to change one's mind, permit one to say "no" diplomatically, help avoid confrontation and anxiety, and provide other benefits that work to the advantage of the individual.

Is it unethical to purposely distort communications to get a favorable outcome? What about "little white lies" that don't really hurt anybody? Are these ethical? What guidelines could you suggest for those in HRM who want guidance in deciding whether distorting information is ethical or unethical?

Allowing for Feedback We cannot assume that our communication efforts are achieving their goals. Consequently, we must develop into the system a means of assessing the flow of information and for fostering employee feedback. How that information is generated may differ from organization to organization. For some, it may be a casual word-of-mouth assessment. Others may use employee surveys to capture data, or provide a suggestion box for comments, or institute a formalized and systematic communications audit program.

Irrespective of how that information is gathered, employees must be involved. Otherwise, not only will measurement of communications program effectiveness be difficult, but you may also give the perception that employee commitment is unnecessary.

www.wiley.com/college/decenzo
What Would You Do?
EXPERIENCE: Writing Personnel Policies

Information Sources HRM communications should serve as a conduit in promoting effective communications throughout the organization. Although HRM plays an important role in bringing this to fruition, they are neither the only nor the main source of information. For that, we turn to one's immediate supervisor. If successful programs can be linked to the immediate supervisor, then HRM must ensure that these individuals are trained in how to communicate properly. Even a health insurance premium change, if implemented, would likely result in questions for one's supervisor. Thus, HRM must make every effort to empower these supervisors with accurate data to deal with the "frontline" questions.[25]

In addition to the communications role, the employee relations department is responsible for additional assignments. Typically in such a department, recruiting, employment, and turnover statistics are collected, tabulated, and written up in the company's affirmative action plan documentation. This material is updated frequently and made available to employees on request. Part of their responsibility is to ensure safe and healthy work sites. This may range from casual work inspections to operating nursing stations and coordinating employee-assistance programs. However involved, the premise is the same—to focus on those aspects that help make an employee committed and loyal to the organization through fair and equitable treatment, and by listening to employees.

Last, there is the festive side of employee relations. This department is typically responsible for company outings, company athletic teams, and recreational and recognition programs. Whatever they do under this domain, the goal remains having programs that benefit the workers and their families and make them feel part of a community.

Does HRM Really Matter?

Is an organization better off with a properly functioning HRM department? Intuitively, most individuals would say yes, but intuition alone may not suffice in these days of cost-saving searches. Intuition aside, the Watson Wyatt's Human Capital Index (HCI) emphatically states that a fully functioning HR department does make a difference.[26]

The HCI continuing study in North American and European companies, indicates that good-quality HRM services improved both the financial well-being of an organization and shareholder value. The companies studied by Watson Wyatt indicated that over a five-year period quality HRM "provided a 59 percent total return to shareholders . . . as compared to 11 percent return for companies with weaker HR practices."[27] In other words, organizations that spend the money to have quality HR programs perform better than those who don't. Accordingly, there is no chicken-and-egg syndrome here. It's not that HR practices are improved when financially viable, but rather by investing in HR up front, the financials followed.

Practices that go into superior HR services include rewarding productive work, creating a flexible, work-friendly environment, properly recruiting and retaining quality workers, effective communications. Many of the practices sometimes viewed as the latest HRM "fad," such as 360-degree appraisals (see Chapter 10), were not inherently problematic. Rather, they were implemented without a clear reason for implementation and without a link to the organization's strategic mission. As such, they lost their true potential benefits.

What does the HCI study tell us about HRM? Simply put, offer quality services to employees—but only after you confirm a direct linkage of those services to the overall strategy of the organization!

Conclusion

Although we have presented four generic areas of HRM, we would be remiss not to recognize the changing nature of HRM in today's organizations. As organizations change structures (to reflect global competition and the like), movement has been away from centralized functional areas toward more self-contained units. In companies where strategic business units or market-driven units dominate,[28] an HRM professional may be assigned to these units to handle all the HRM operations. While a headquarters HRM staff remains to coordinate the activities, the HRM representative is expected to perform all the HR functions. Accordingly, the movement toward generalist positions in HRM appears to be on the rise.

shared services

Sharing HRM activities among geographically dispersed divisions.

Another trend is also closely aligned with the generalist-versus-specialist discussion. That trend is called **shared services**.[29] Large organizations that are geographically dispersed are finding it more cost-effective to share their HRM services among the divisions.[30] For example, at Ford, shared HRM services enabled the company to cut its workforce from 14,000 to approximately 3,000 employees, supporting more than 300,000 Ford employees worldwide. And at General Electric, shared services enabled the company to reduce its HR staff by 75 percent and provide more cost-effective, high-quality HR services.[31]

Under shared services, each location is staffed by a few generalists who handle routine local matters such as recruiting, policy implementation, grievances, and employee training. Specialized services such as organization development and compensation and benefits are handled by a centralized staff. Each location, then, shares these services offered by the centralized unit and uses only what is necessary for the division. As such, each location receives as-needed specialized care without the cost of full-time staff.

One last area must be addressed about the changing nature of HRM. In some organizations, top management has made a decision to outsource some, if not all, of the work HRM professionals once handled.[32] For example, private staffing agencies may perform the recruiting and selection activities, with several consulting firms providing training programs, and yet another financial organization handling the majority of a company's benefits administration. It is our contention that when much of HRM is outsourced, managers and employees still need to understand the basic HRM issues and activities. So, whether the activities we describe in this book fall to you or to another company employee, or to someone external to your organization, you need some familiarity with these fundamental HRM practices.

HRM IN AN ENTREPRENEURIAL ENTERPRISE

The discussion about the four departments of HRM refers to situations with resources sufficient for functional expertise to exist. However, such is not always the case. Take, for instance, the entrepreneurial enterprise and the small business operation. In these organizations, the owner-manager often is responsible for and may perform these activities. In other situations, small-business human resource departments are staffed with one individual and possibly a full-time secretary. Accordingly, such individuals are forced, by design, to be HRM generalists. Irrespective of the unit's size, the same activities are required in small businesses, but on a smaller scale. These small-business HRM managers must properly perform the four HRM functions and achieve the same goals that a larger department achieves. The main difference is that they are doing the work themselves without benefit of a specialized staff. There may be a tendency to use outside consultants to assist in or perform all HRM activities. For instance, benefit administration may be beyond the capability of the small businessperson. In that case, benefit administration may need to be contracted out. HRM in a small business requires that individuals keep current in the field and legal issues. For example, the Family and Medical Leave Act of 1993 is applicable to those organizations that have 50 or more employees. Accordingly, the small business may be exempt from some laws affecting employment practices. Being aware of this information can save the small business time and money. Before we begin to pity this small-business HRM manager, let's look at the potential benefits from such an arrangement. Often, these individuals feel less constrained in their jobs. That is, the bureaucratic hierarchy that typically accompanies larger organizations is often absent in the small business. Furthermore, some small-business HRM managers use this arrangement to their advantage. For instance, a selling point to attract a good applicant might be the freedom from rigid structure the small-business opportunity offers, as well as the opportunity to share in the success of the business.

HRM in a Global Village

As a business grows from regional to national to international size, the HRM function must take on a new and broader perspective.[33] As a national company expands overseas, first with a sales operation, then to production facilities and fully expanded operations or to international joint ventures, the human resource function must adapt to a changing and far more complex environment.[34]

All basic functions of domestic HRM become more complex when the organization's employees are located around the world, and additional HRM activities often are necessary that would be considered invasions of employee privacy in domestic operations. This is necessary partially because of the increased vulnerability and risk of terrorism American executives sometimes experience abroad.

When a corporation sends its American employees overseas, that corporation takes on responsibilities that add to the basic HRM functions. For example, the staffing and training and development functions take on greater emphasis.[35] Not only are organizations concerned about selecting the best employee for the job, they must also be aware of the entire family's needs. Why? Many individuals who take international assignments fail because their spouse or family can't adjust to the new environment. Furthermore, the relocation and orientation process before departure may take months of foreign language training and should involve not just the employee but the employee's entire family. Details must be provided for such as work visas, travel, safety, household moving arrangements, taxes, and family issues such as the children's schooling, medical care, and housing.[36] Administrative services for the expatriate employees also must be available once they are placed in their overseas posts. All these additional functions make international HRM a very costly undertaking.

Running a multinational corporation takes a lot of energy and planning. Companies such as Costco need to ensure that their HRM practices are proper in whatever part of the world they operate. Here, Costco in Mexico needs to ensure that its policies and practices comply with the laws, social mores, and cultural aspects of the Mexican people. (Source: Larah Martone/Bloomberg News/Landov LLC)

HR and Corporate Ethics

We'll close this chapter by revisiting the topic of ethics. This time we're not defining ethics but rather discussing HRM's role in ensuring that ethics exist in an organization and are adhered to.

One of the primary changes related to corporate management scandals in the early years of the new millenium has been legislation signed into law in July 2002 by President Bush.[37] That legislation, called the Sarbanes-Oxley Act, establishes procedures for public companies regarding how they handle and report their financial picture. The legislation also established penalties for noncompliance. For example, Sarbanes-Oxley requires the following:[38]

- Top management (the CEO and chief financial officer [CFO]) must personally certify the organization's financial reports;
- The organization must have in place procedures and guidelines for audit committees.
- CEOs and CFOs must reimburse the organization for bonuses and stock options when required by restatement of corporate profits; and
- Personal loans or lines of credit for executives are now prohibited.

The noncompliance penalty of Sarbanes-Oxley is catching executives' attention. Failure to comply with the requirements stipulated under Sarbanes-Oxley—such as falsely stating corporate financial—can result in the executive being fined up to $1 million and imprisoned for up to 10 years.[39] Moreover, if the executive's action is determined to be willful, both the fine and the jail time can be doubled. What does any of this have to do with HRM?

Although Sarbanes-Oxley does not specifically identify HRM activities in the law, it does require items generally under HRM responsibility. For example, the act provides protection for employees who report executive wrongdoing (whistle-blowing). HRM must create that environment where employees can come forward with their allegation without fear of reprisal from the employer. This critical employee relations aspect is not limited solely to whistleblowing under Sarbanes-Oxley but the act does require that companies have mechanisms in place where the complaint can be received and investigated. As a result, many companies are creating "organizational ombuds," HR professionals who will offer confidential help for employees and "handle potentially unethical or illegal behavior" in the organization.[40] In some organizations, this job is called the corporate ethicist.

HRM also has other responsibilities. As keepers of corporate policies and employee documents, HRM must make sure that employees know about corporate ethics policies and train employees and supervisors on how to act ethically in organizations. Furthermore, given the added responsibility that Sarbanes-Oxley places on CEOs and CFOs, HR must, when involved in hiring for either of these positions, provide the needed leadership to ensure that the individual hired understands compliance issues.

The bottom line is that corporate greed and unethical behavior must be stopped. Employees and other stakeholders demand it. Although regulations signed into law attempt to legislate "proper" behavior, legislation alone cannot work. HRM must work with senior executives to establish the moral fabric of the organization, ensuring that it becomes part of the standard operating procedures of the enterprise.[41]

SUMMARY

(This summary relates to the Learning Outcomes identified on page 31.) After having read this chapter you can

1. **Explain what is meant by the term** *human resource management.* HRM is comprised of the staffing, development, motivation, and maintenance functions. Each of these functions, however, is affected by external influences.

2. **Describe the importance of human resource management.** HRM is responsible for the people dimension of the organization. It is responsible for hiring competent people, training them, helping them perform at high levels, and providing mechanisms to ensure that these employees maintain their productive affiliation with the organization.

3. **Identify the primary external environmental influences affecting human resource management.** External environmental influences are factors that affect HRM functions. They include the dynamic environment of HRM, government legislation, labor unions, and management thought.

4. **Characterize how management practices affect human resource management.** Management practices affect HRM in various ways. As new ideas or practices develop in the field, they typically have HRM implications. Accordingly, once these practices are implemented, they typically require support from HRM to operate successfully.

5. **Discuss the effect of labor unions on human resource management.** Labor unions affect HRM practices in a variety of ways. If a union exists, HRM takes on a different focus—one of labor relations as opposed to employee relations. Additionally, what occurs in the unionized sector frequently affects the activities in nonunion organizations.

6. **Outline the components and goals of the staffing, training, and development functions.** The components of the staffing function include strategic human resource planning, recruiting, and selection. The goal of the staffing function is to locate and secure competent employees. The training and development function includes orientation, employee training, employee development, organization development, and career development. The goal of the development function is to adapt competent workers to the organization and help them obtain up-to-date skills, knowledge, and abilities for their job responsibilities.

7. **List the components and goals of the motivation and maintenance functions of human resource management.** The components of the motivation function include motivation theories, appropriate job design, reward and incentive systems, compensation, and benefits. The goal of the motivation function is to provide competent, adapted employees who have up-to-date skills, knowledge, and abilities with an environment that encourages them to exert high energy levels. The components of the maintenance function include safety and health issues and employee communications. The goal of the maintenance function is to help competent, adapted employees with up-to-date skills, knowledge, and abilities and exerting high energy levels maintain their commitment and loyalty to the organization.

8. **Outline the major activities in the employment, training and development, compensation and benefits, and employee relations departments of human resource management.** The departments of employment, training and development, compensation and benefits, and employee relations support the components of the staffing, training and development, motivation, and maintenance functions, respectively.

9. **Explain how human resource management practices differ in small businesses and in an international setting.** In large HRM operations, individuals perform functions according to their specialization. Small-business HRM practitioners may instead be the only individuals in the operation and thus must operate as HRM generalists. In an international setting, HRM functions become more complex and typically require additional activities associated with staffing and training and development.

DEMONSTRATING COMPREHENSION: *Questions for Review*

1. Contrast management, personnel, and HRM.
2. Explain the purpose of HRM in an organization.
3. What activities are involved in the staffing function of HRM?
4. Explain the goals of the training and development function of HRM.
5. Describe the primary goals of the motivation function of HRM.
6. In what ways can HRM meet its goals of the maintenance function?
7. What role does HRM play in the strategic direction of an organization?
8. How does HRM affect all managers?

KEY TERMS

communications programs	leading	motivation function	shared services
controlling	maintenance function	organizing	staffing function
employee relations function	management	planning	training and development function
Hawthorne studies	management thought	scientific management	

VISUAL SUMMARY

CHAPTER 2: FUNDAMENTALS OF HRM

1 **Why Is HRM Important to an Organization?**

Focus on the Strategic Nature of HR

Specialized Skills Are Needed to Do an Effective Job in HRM

The HRM Functions

- **Staffing**—finding people
- **Training and Development**—training employees
- **Motivation**—getting employees to exert high energy levels
- **Maintenance**—keeping employees

External Influences on HRM

The strategic, dynamic environment of HRM

Governmental legislation

HRM

Current management thought and practice

Labor unions

2 How Are HRM Functions Translated into Practice?

- **Employment**—activities surrounding the staffing and selection function
- **Training and Development**—helps employees and the organization achieve greater productivity
- **Compensation Are Benefits**—paying employees and administering benefits packages
- **Employee Relations**—ensuring open **communication** exists for all employees

Effective **communication** programs involve:
- Top management commitment
- Effective upward communication
- Determining what to communicate
- Allowing for feedback
- Accurate information sources

3 HRM in an Entrepreneurial Enterprise

Owner/Entrepreneur

Runs the business   Often handles HRM activities

If HR exists that person is a generalist, handling all HR activities

4 HRM in a Global Village

- Recognizing the complexities of the global village
- Properly preparing employees for international assignments

5 HRM and Corporate Ethics

Sarbanes–Oxley Act—states how public companies are to handle and report their financial picture

CROSSWORD COMPREHENSION

ACROSS

2. function in HRM concerned with helping employees update their skills
6. HRM activities concerned with effective communications among organizational members
8. determining what jobs are to be done and by whom
9. function in HRM concerned with helping employees exert high energy levels
10. programs designed to provide information to employees
11. setting organizational goals
12. monitoring activities to ensure goals are met

DOWN

1. process of efficiently completing activities with and through other people
3. function in HRM concerned with keeping employees committed and loyal to the organization
4. directing the work of others
5. early theories promoting today's HRM operations
7. sharing HRM activities among geographically dispersed divisions

HRM WORKSHOP

LINKING CONCEPTS TO PRACTICE: *Discussion Questions*

1. "Motivation is the primary responsibility of line managers. HRM's role in motivating organizational employees is limited to providing programs that equip line managers with means of motivating their employees." Do you agree or disagree with the statement? Explain your position.

2. You have been offered two positions in HRM. One is a generalist position in a smaller business, and one is a recruiting position in a large corporation. Which of the two jobs do you believe will give you more involvement in a variety of HRM activities? Defend your answer.

3. "Globalization had led us to the realization that workers are interchangeable between countries so long as language issues are resolved." Do you agree or disagree with this statement? Explain your position.

4. "Employers only need to provide employees with enough information so they can effectively and efficiently get their jobs done. Beyond that, employees don't have a need to know." Do you agree or disagree with the statement? Defend your answer.

DEVELOPING DIAGNOSTIC AND ANALYTICAL SKILLS

Case 2-A: NINE-TO-FIVE NO MORE

Talk with nearly any HR manager in a company of considerable size, and they will tell you one thing. To make HR function smoothly, employees need to know what the policies are and how they are to be followed. For without such policies there can only be chaos; out of that chaos can only come serious organizational problems. Well, somebody apparently forgot to tell Greg Strakosch, CEO of TechTarget, a Needham, Massachusetts–based interactive media company, that policies need to be written and strictly followed.[42]

Strakosch leads an organization of more than 400 employees in the high-tech media field. These employees are located in three primary locations—Needham, San Francisco, and New York. What makes TechTarget so unique is that employees are permitted to come and go as they please. TechTarget's management has implemented no attendance policies, nor offers employees sick leave benefits. Rather, as a general rule, the company believes in hiring the best employees in the market, and then giving them the freedom and autonomy to do their jobs. Simply stated, this means leaving them alone. Thus, if someone works better from 4 p.m. until midnight, so be it. But they must remain available to others should they need to be contacted—availability by e-mail, cell phone, and the like. Yet if they need time off during the day to attend a child's school event or some other personal issue, they take it. No questions asked—ever.

But don't assume that this "freedom" is risk-free. It carries with it significant responsibilities. Employees at TechTarget are given quarterly goals that they must meet. While it's true how and when employees complete this work is up to them, failure to meet targets is not acceptable. Should that happen, the employee is terminated.

Does TechTarget's "autonomy" work? For the most part, the answer is yes. While employees have the freedom to work when they want to, employees in the company report they often spend more than 50 hours per week on job-related activities. But they do so in a way that's convenient to them—which is translating into success for the business. During its seven years of operation, company revenues have risen sevenfold, and 2005 revenues are up well over 50 percent from the previous year. Maybe there's something to be said about giving employees their freedom!

Questions:

1. What is your reaction to this "no attendance" plan implemented at TechTarget? Do you believe it's too simplistic? Defend your position.
2. Do you believe that such an employee policy as described in the case can succeed in other companies? Why or why not?
3. What special HRM conditions must exist for such a plan to work? Explain. How do you believe these conditions relate to employee motivation?

Case Application 2-B: TEAM FUN!

Team Fun

Kenny and Norton own TEAM FUN!, a medium-sized company that manufactures and sells sporting goods and equipment. They are watching a CROSSKATES video about cross-country roller skates in the LOUNGE. Norton says, "I don't know. This stuff looks dangerous! What do you think? Remember that bungee-jumping thing we tried?"

Kenny responds, "Edna was out a long time with that knee problem. She sure is a good sport. Keith said we were lucky not to get sued for that. Do you think employees could sue us if they are hurt on product-test assignments?"

"Let's ask Tony," Norton suggests. "That guy you hired as—what did you call him—director of human resources?"

Kenny smiles broadly, "Yep. He sure seems to be busy. He's pulled together all that paperwork for insurance and retirement that Edna used to handle and named her compensation and benefits manager."

"He wants to send Joe and Eric to a supervisor's school for work scheduling, job team assignments, and project management," Norton adds. "He started those picnics by the LAGOON for people to talk about work conditions and issues."

Kenny asks, "Do you think we should let him hire a full-time secretary? I thought Edna could do that, but Tony said she has a full plate. Did you tell him to do that employee bulletin board he tacked into the Web site?"

Norton shakes his head no.

"Me neither," Kenny muses. "Wonder why he did that? Guess we'd better talk to him."

Questions:

1. Which of the functional HR processes can be identified in Tony's area?
2. Identify the environmental influences important to TEAM FUN!
3. How do its HR functional areas line up with the overall HR process?
4. Does Tony need to do anything else to set up a strategic HR function?

WORKING WITH A TEAM: *Making a Layoff Decision*

Every manager, at some point in his or her career, is likely to face the difficult task of managing laying off employees. Assume that you are the human resource director of a 720-member technology company. You have been notified by top management that you must permanently reduce your staff by two individuals. Below are some data about your five employees.

Shawana Johnson: African American female, age 36. Shawana has been employed with your company for five years, all in HRM. Her evaluations over the past three years have been outstanding, above average, and outstanding. Shawana has an MBA from a top-25 business school. She has been on short-term disability the past few weeks because of the birth of her second child and is expected to return to work in twenty weeks.

Greg Oates: White male, age 49. Greg has been with you for four months and has 11 years of experience in the company in systems management. He has a degree in computer science and master's degrees in accounting information systems. He's also a CPA. Greg's evaluations over the past three years in the systems department have been average, but he did save the company $150,000 on a suggestion he made to use electronic time sheets.

Carlos Rodriques: Hispanic male, age 31. Carlos has been with the company almost four years. His evaluations over the past three years in your department have been outstanding. He is committed to getting the job done and devotes whatever it takes. He has also shown initiative by taking job assignments that no one else wanted. Carlos has been instrumental in starting up your benefits administration intranet for employees.

Cathy Williams: White female, age 35. Cathy has been with your company seven years. Four years ago, Cathy was in an automobile accident while traveling on business to a customer's location. As a result of the accident, she was disabled and is wheelchair-bound. Rumors have it that she is about to receive several million dollars from the insurance company of the driver who hit her. Her performance the past two years has been above average. She has a bachelor's degree in human resource management and a master's degree in human development. Cathy specializes in training, career, and organization development activities.

Rodney Smith: African American male, age 43. Rodney just completed his joint MBA and law program and recently passed the bar exam. He has been with your department four years. His evaluations have been good to above average. Five years ago, Rodney won a lawsuit against your company for discriminating against him in a promotion to a supervisory position. Rumors have it that now, with his new degree, Rodney is actively pursuing another job outside the company.

Given these five brief descriptions, make a recommendation to your boss in which two employees will be laid off. Discuss any other options you might suggest to meet the requirement of downsizing by two employees without resorting to layoffs. Discuss what you will do to (1) assist the two individuals who have been let go and (2) assist the remaining three employees. Then, in a group of three to five students, seek consensus on the questions posed above. Be prepared to defend your actions.

LEARNING AN HRM SKILL: *HR Certification*

What skills and competencies lead to successful HRM performance? Although it is extremely difficult to pinpoint exactly what competencies will serve you best when dealing with the uncertainties of human behavior, we can turn to the certifying body in HRM for answers. Specifically, the Human Resources Certification Institute (HRCI) suggests that certified HR practitioners must have exposure to and an understanding in six specific areas of the field.[43] These include strategic management, workforce planning and employment, human resource development, compensation and benefits, employee and labor relations, and occupational health, safety, and security. Let's briefly look at each one, and relate these specifically to the part of this book where they are addressed.

Strategic Management: As a subset of management, HRM practitioners must understand how laws are made, the strategic planning process, environmental analyses, social responsibility, and creativity; as well as how HRM contributes to the overall success of the organization. Specific references in this text: Chapters 1, 2, 3, 4, and 5.

Workplace Planning and Employment: HRM practitioners require an understanding of why and how jobs are filled and the various methods of recruiting candidates. Emphasis in this area is on understanding various staffing means and making good decisions about job candidates that use valid and reliable measures and are within the legal parameters. Interviewing technique is also a major component of this knowledge area. Specific references in this text: Chapters 3, 4, 6, and 7.

Human Resource Development: Employees, to be successful in an organization, must be trained and developed in the latest technologies and skills relevant to their current and future jobs. This means an understanding of adult learning methodologies, relating training efforts to organizational goals, and evaluating the effort. Specific references in this text: Chapters 8 and 9.

Compensation and Benefits: One of the chief reasons people work is to fulfill needs. One major need is compensation and benefits, probably the most expensive with respect to the employment relationship. The HRM practitioner must understand the intricacies involved in establishing a cost-effective compensation and benefits package. Specific references in this text: Chapters 10, 11, and 12.

Employee and Labor Relations: Working with employees requires an understanding of what makes employees function. Satisfying monetary needs alone will not have a lasting impact. Employees need to be kept informed and have way to raise suggestions or complaints. When the case involves unionized workers, the HRM/labor relations practitioner must understand the various laws that affect the labor-management work relationship. Specific references in this text: Chapters 1 and 14.

Occupational Health, Safety, and Security: A basic human need to feel safe in the workplace. This means freedom from physical and emotional harm. Mechanisms must be in place to provide a safe work environment for employees. Programs must permit employees to seek assistance for those things affecting their work and personal lives. Specific references in this text: Chapters 1 and 13.

If you intend to specialize in HRM and may be interested in taking the certification examination, we invite you to visit the Society of Human Resource Management's Web site at www.hrci.org. You can access information about the exam, sign up for a testing date, or even take the exam online.

ENHANCING YOUR COMMUNICATION SKILLS

1. Visit an HRM department, either on or off campus. During your meeting, ask an HRM representative what he or she does on the job. Focus specifically on the person's job title and key job responsibilities and why he or she is in HRM. After your appointment, provide a three- to five-page summary of the interview, highlighting how the information will help you better understand HRM practices.
2. Discuss how you believe the Hawthorne studies have influenced HRM. Find three examples of HRM applications that can be linked to these studies. What benefits have these applications provided to the organization?
3. Go to the Society of Human Resource Management's Web site at www.shrm.org. Research the process one must follow to prepare for the Human Resource Certification Exam and what certification means.

THREE

Imagine living in a world where you have a strong desire to work, a set of skills that you know would add value to an organization, and the motivation to prove you can succeed. But you also have a serious disability that you believe is frightening potential employers off. It's not that people don't want to employ your services, but you feel it's your responsibility to tell the recruiter that you are frequently sick, need to see a doctor often, and periodically may miss considerable time. You know you're not a slacker; after all, your disabilities were brought on by injuries you received while serving your country during a time of war. What do you do to maintain some level of consistent employment? If you're one of the several thousand affected individuals who are in the New York City area, you turn to Diversity Services.[1]

Originally founded in 1996, Diversity Services is an employment agency that works with a variety of organizations to fulfill critical employee needs as well as assist them in their diversity staffing. While there are numerous employment agencies in the area, Diversity Services is the only agency in the United States that "makes accommodations necessary to include persons with disabilities." Under the direction of Stacey Strother, its president, Diversity Services has grown revenues significantly over the past decade—increasing from $2.6 million in 2000 to $7.8 million in 2004—and has helped place more than

(*Source:* Walter Hodges/Getty Images, Inc.)

2000 workers, many who are disabled, in such areas as office support, legal, financial services, information technology, and medical services.

What makes Diversity Services unique is how they assist both the employer and the employee. For instance, if an employee is sent to a job and for some medical reason cannot show up for work, Diversity Services immediately replaces that worker with another qualified, prescreened individual who is capable of immediately taking over where the other employee left off. Accordingly, employers know that employing someone from Diversity Services will not interfere with work flow should the employee need to be off from the job for an extended period of time. From the employee side, the benefits are equally amazing. Diversity Services continues to pay the affected employee his or her salary—even though they are "not working." As such, employees recognized that they are cared for and that Diversity Services is truly looking out after their best interests.

Can an organization marry the ethical values of work ethics with the success and drive needed to run a successful organization? In Diversity Services' case, the answer is clear: Yes it can! And in doing so, a valuable service is offered to organizations in the New York City area. But more important, a valuable segment of society is given the opportunity to show exactly what it is capable of doing.

Equal Employment Opportunity

Learning Outcomes

After reading this chapter, you will be able to

1. Identify the groups protected under the Civil Rights Act of 1964, Title VII.

2. Discuss the importance of the Equal Employment Opportunities Act of 1972.

3. Describe affirmative action plans.

4. Define the terms *adverse impact, adverse treatment,* and *protected group members.*

5. Identify the important components of the Americans with Disabilities Act of 1990.

6. Explain the coverage of the Family and Medical Leave Act of 1993.

7. Discuss how a business can protect itself from discrimination charges.

8. Specify the HRM importance of *Griggs v. Duke Power.*

9. Define what constitutes sexual harassment in today's organizations.

10. Discuss the term *glass ceiling.*

INTRODUCTION

What do Domino's, Aon, Federal Express, Burger King, and Target stores have in common? Each has been singled out for practices that allegedly discriminated against minorities, women, or the disabled. In the last chapter, we briefly introduced the concept of government legislation as it affects employment practices. In this chapter, we will explore this critical influence to provide an understanding of the legislation. Why? Because it is a fact of doing business. Almost every U.S. organization, both public and private, must abide by the guidelines established in the 1964 Civil Rights Act, its subsequent amendment (1972), and other federal laws governing employment practices. The importance of such legislation cannot be overstated, as these laws permeate all organizational HRM functions.

Keep in mind that although our discussion will be limited to federal employment legislation, state or municipal laws may go beyond what the federal government requires. For example, by late 2005, 16 states and hundreds of municipalities viewed sexual orientation as a "protected class."[2] While it is impossible to cover all of these laws, HRM managers must know and understand what additional requirements they face. Interestingly, approximately 16 countries around the globe have national laws that protect gays, lesbians, and bisexuals from employment discrimination.[3] It's also important to note that many companies have voluntarily implemented policies to protect employees on the basis of sexual orientation. These include such companies as Wal-Mart, Microsoft, Nike, and MetLife.[4]

LAWS AFFECTING DISCRIMINATORY PRACTICES

The beginning of equal employment opportunity is usually attributed to passage of the 1964 Civil Rights Act. Even though the activities we will explore in this chapter are rooted in this 1964 act, equal employment's beginning actually goes back more than 100 years. For instance, Section 1981 of Title 42 of the U.S. Code, referred to as the **Civil Rights Act of 1866**, coupled with the Fourteenth Amendment to the Constitution (1868), prohibited discrimination on the basis of race, sex, and national origin. Although these earlier actions have been overshadowed by the 1964 act, they've gained prominence in years past as being the laws that white male workers could use to support claims of reverse discrimination. In such cases, white males used the Civil Rights Act of 1866 and the Fourteenth Amendment to support their argument that minorities received special treatment in employment decisions that placed them at a disadvantage. Under the Civil Rights Act of 1866, employees could sue for racial discrimination.[5] As a result of this act, individuals could also seek punitive and compensatory damages under Section 1981, in addition to the awarding of back pay.[6] However, in 1989, a Supreme Court ruling limited Section 1981 use in discrimination suits in that the law does not cover racial discrimination after a person has been hired.[7] We'll look more at reverse discrimination in our discussion of relevant Supreme Court decisions.

Although earlier attempts were rudimentary in promoting fair employment practices among workers, not until the 1960s was earnest emphasis placed on achieving such a goal. Let's turn our attention, then, to the landmark piece of employment legislation, the Civil Rights Act of 1964.

Civil Rights Act of 1866
Federal law that prohibited discrimination based on race.

No single piece of legislation has had a greater effect on reducing employment discrimination than the Civil Rights Act of 1964.

The Importance of the Civil Rights Act of 1964

No single piece of legislation in the 1960s had a greater effect on reducing employment discrimination than the Civil Rights Act of 1964. It was divided into parts called *titles*—each dealing with a particular facet of discrimination. On college campuses, you may have heard about

Title IX issues, usually in the context of what a university spends on both men's and women's sports programs. For HRM purposes, however, **Title VII** is especially relevant.

Title VII prohibits discrimination in hiring, compensation, terms, conditions, or privileges of employment based on race, religion, color, sex, or national origin. Title VII also prohibits retaliation against an individual who files a charge of discrimination, participates in an investigation, or opposes any unlawful practice. Most organizations, both public and private, are bound by the law. The law, however, specifies compliance based on the number of employees in the organization. Essentially, as originally passed in 1964, any organization with 25 or more employees (amended to 15 or more in 1972) is covered. This minimum number of employees serves as a means of protecting, or removing from the law, small, family-owned businesses.[8] The organizations initially covered by the EEO regulations, however, found compliance confusing.

Organizations faced relatively new requirements, but detailed guidelines for compliance were lacking. Days of purposefully excluding certain individuals significantly decreased, yet practices like testing applicants appeared to create the same effect. In an attempt to clarify this procedure, several cases were challenged in the Supreme Court. The outcomes of these cases indicated that any action that had the effect of keeping certain groups of people out of particular jobs was illegal, unless the company could show why a practice was required. The implication of these decisions, for example, was that a company could not hire a maintenance employee using an aptitude test and a high-school diploma requirement unless those criteria could be shown to be directly relevant to the job. In one of these cases, *Griggs v. Duke Power Company* (1971), the company was unable to show job relatedness. Griggs, an applicant for a maintenance job, demonstrated that the power company's tests and degree requirements were unrelated to performance of the job in question. The decision in the *Griggs* case, though, did not mean that specific selection criteria couldn't be used. For instance, in the case of *Washington v. Davis* (1967),[9] the Supreme Court upheld the use of aptitude tests. In this case, Davis applied for a position as a metropolitan Washington, D.C., police officer. The police force required all applicants to pass a comprehensive aptitude test. The Supreme Court held that the test measured necessary competencies required to be successful as a police officer.

Even though we began to better understand what Congress meant in the writing of Title VII, something was clearly lacking—enforcement mechanisms. By 1972, after realizing that the Civil Rights Act left much to interpretation, Congress passed an amendment to the act called the **Equal Employment Opportunity Act (EEOA)**. This act provided a series of amendments to Title VII.[10] Probably the greatest consequence of the EEOA was the granting of enforcement powers to the **Equal Employment Opportunity Commission (EEOC)**. The EEOC could effectively prohibit all forms of employment discrimination based on race, religion, color, sex, or national origin. The EEOC could file civil suits against organizations if unable to secure an acceptable resolution of discrimination charges within 120 days. (Individuals may also file suit themselves if the EEOC declines to sue.) In addition, the EEOA also expanded Title VII coverage to include employees of state and local governments, employees of educational institutions, and employees of labor organizations—as we mentioned earlier, those with 15 or more employees or members.

Title VII, as it exists today, stipulates that organizations must do more than just discontinue discriminatory practices, they must actively recruit and give preference to minority group members in employment decisions. This action is commonly referred to as **affirmative action**.

Affirmative Action Plans

Affirmative action programs are instituted by an organization to correct past injustices in an employment process. The four primary reasons for these plans are as follows:

Title VII
The most prominent piece of legislation regarding HRM, it states the illegality of discriminating against individuals based on race, religion, color, sex, or national origin.

Griggs v. Duke Power Company
Landmark Supreme Court decision stating that tests must fairly measure the knowledge or skills required for a job.

Equal Employment Opportunity Act (EEOA)
Granted enforcement powers to the Equal Employment Opportunity Commission.

Equal Employment Opportunity Commission (EEOC)
The arm of the federal government empowered to handle discrimination in employment cases.

affirmative action
A practice in organizations that goes beyond discontinuance of discriminatory practices to include actively seeking, hiring, and promoting minority group members and women.

Does this employee need a high school diploma to do his job? According to the Griggs v. Duke Power *case, if the organization cannot show how having a high school diploma relates directly to successful performance on the job, then a high school diploma cannot be required. To do so could be discriminatory.* (Source: © AP/Wide World Photos)

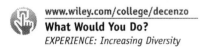
www.wiley.com/college/decenzo
What Would You Do?
EXPERIENCE: *Increasing Diversity*

adverse (disparate) impact
A consequence of an employment practice that results in a greater rejection rate for a minority group than for the majority group in the occupation.

- Affirmative action programs reflect the 1972 premise that white males made up the majority of workers in our companies.
- U.S. companies were in the early 1970s still growing and could accommodate more workers.
- As a matter of public policy and decency, minorities should be hired to correct past prejudice that kept them out.
- "Legal and social coercion [were] necessary to bring about the change."[11]

What do these reasons imply about affirmative action programs? Affirmative action means that an organization must take certain steps to show that it is not discriminating. For example, the organization must analyze the demographics of its current workforce. Similarly, the organization must analyze the composition of the community from which it recruits. If the workforce resembles the community for all jobs classifications, then the organization may be demonstrating that its affirmative action program is working. If, however, there are differences, affirmative action also implies that the organization will establish goals and timetables for correcting the imbalance and have specific plans for recruiting and retaining protected group members.

Coordinating an EEO program creates certain issues. First of all, the company must know what the job requires in terms of skills, knowledge, and abilities. Candidates are then evaluated on how well they meet the essential elements of the job. Candidates who meet these criteria are essentially qualified, meaning that they should be successful performers of the job. Nowhere under EEO does the federal government require organizations to hire unqualified workers. They must actively search for qualified minorities by recruiting from places like predominantly African American or women's colleges but need not necessarily hire these individuals under this process. However, as a result of affirmative action programs, an organization should be able to show significant improvements in hiring and promoting women and minorities or justify why external factors prohibited them from achieving their affirmative action goals.

Over the past decade, there has been a backlash against affirmative actions programs.[12] Much of the criticism has focused on the realization that affirmative action bases employment decisions on group membership rather than individual performance. This giving certain groups of individuals (by race, sex, age) preference tugs at the heart of fair employment. As the argument goes, if it was wrong 50 years ago to give white males preference for employment, why is it right today to give other individuals preference simply because they possess certain traits? Despite some movement in a few states to eliminate affirmative action plans, and debate in the U.S. Congress, affirmative action plans still exist. And it appears that they will be around for some time.[13]

Irrespective of the controversy surrounding affirmative action plans, throughout much of this discussion we have addressed practices designed to ensure equal employment opportunity for all individuals. But how do we know if equal employment programs are not operating properly? The answer to that question may lie in the concept of **adverse (disparate) impact**.

Adverse Impact Adverse impact can be described as any employment consequence that discriminates against employees who are members of a protected group. Protected status categories include race, color, religion, national origin, citizenship status, sex, age 40 and above, pregnancy-related medical conditions, disability, and Vietnam-era veteran military status.

For an example of an adverse impact, we can look at the height and weight requirements police departments around the country had many years ago. The height requirement was frequently 5'10" or greater. As such, many women and certain nationalities were unable to become police officers. Because the average height of these individuals was shorter than that of males, using this height requirement significantly reduced job opportunities for them. The concept of adverse impact, then, results from a seemingly neutral, even unintentional consequence of an employment practice.[14]

Another issue differs from adverse impact but follows a similar logic. This is called **adverse (disparate) treatment**. Adverse treatment occurs when a member of a protected group receives less favorable outcomes in an employment decision than a nonprotected group member. For example, if a protected group member is more often evaluated as performing poorly or receives fewer organizational rewards, adverse treatment may have occurred.

The Civil Rights Act of 1964 led the way to change how HRM would function. As the years progressed, other amendments and legislation were passed that extended equal employment opportunity practices to diverse groups. Let's take a look at the more critical of these laws summarized in Exhibit 3-1.

adverse (disparate) treatment
An employment situation where protected group members receive treatment different from other employees in matters such as performance evaluations and promotions.

EXHIBIT 3-1
Summary of Primary Federal Laws Affecting Discrimination

Civil Rights Act of 1964	Title VII prohibits employment discrimination in hiring, compensation, and terms, conditions, or privileges of employment based on race, religion, color, sex, or national origin.
Executive Order (E.O.) 11246	Prohibits discrimination on the basis of race, religion, color, and national origin, by federal agencies as well as those working under federal contracts.
Executive Order 11375	Added sex-based discrimination to E.O. 11246.
Age Discrimination in Employment Act of 1967	Protects employees 40–65 years of age from discrimination. Later amended to age 70 (1978), then amended (1986) to eliminate the upper age limit altogether.
Executive Order 11478	Amends part of E.O. 11246, states practices in the federal government must be based on merit; also prohibits discrimination based on political affiliation, marital status, or physical handicap.
Equal Employment Opportunity Act of 1972	Granted the enforcement powers for the EEOC.
Age Discrimination in Employment Act of 1978	Increased mandatory retirement age from 65 to 70. Later amended (1986) to eliminate upper age limit.
Pregnancy Discrimination Act of 1978	Affords EEO protection to pregnant workers and requires pregnancy to be treated like any other disability.
Americans with Disabilities Act of 1990	Prohibits discrimination against an essentially qualified individual, and requires enterprises to reasonably accommodate individuals.
Civil Rights Act of 1991	Nullified selected Supreme Court decisions. Reinstates burden of proof by employer. Allows for punitive and compensatory damages through jury trials.
Family and Medical Leave Act of 1993	Permits employees in organizations of 50 or more workers to take up to 12 weeks of unpaid leave for family or medical reasons each year.

What Other Laws Affect Discrimination Practices?

In addition to the Civil Rights Act of 1964, other laws and presidential orders equally affect HRM practices. Specifically, we'll address the Age Discrimination in Employment Act of 1967 (amended in 1978 and 1986), the Pregnancy Discrimination Act of 1978, the Americans with Disabilities Act of 1990, the Family and Medical Leave Act of 1993, and Executive Orders 11246, 11375, and 11478.

Age Discrimination in Employment Act (ADEA)

This act prohibits arbitrary age discrimination, particularly among those over age 40.

Age Discrimination in Employment Act of 1967
The **Age Discrimination in Employment Act (ADEA)** of 1967 prohibited the widespread practice of requiring workers to retire at age 65.[15] It gave protected-group status to individuals between the ages of 40 and 65. Since 1967, this act has been amended twice—once in 1978, which raised the mandatory retirement age to 70, and again in 1986, where the upper age limit was removed altogether. As a result, anyone over age 39 is covered by the ADEA. Organizations with 20 or more employees, state and local governments, employment agencies, and labor organizations are covered by the ADEA.[16]

Of course, there are and have been exceptions to this law. For instance, employees such as commercial pilots may be required to leave their current positions because of strict job requirements. That is, pilots may not captain a commercial airplane on reaching the age of 60. Why age 60? At that age, the Federal Aviation Agency believes that medical research indicates a potential lack or significant decline in the skills necessary to handle an emergency. Thus, using age 60 as the determining factor, airlines may remove a pilot at that age for public safety reasons. But that does not mean that they must leave the organization. Should a 60-year-old pilot decide to be a flight engineer or even an airport ticket agent, and if an opening exists, the individual may apply for the job. Failure to allow their retiring pilots to do so is in violation of ADEA.

In applying this act to the workplace, a four-pronged test is typically used to determine if age discrimination has occurred. This test involves proving that one is "a member of a protected group, that adverse employment action was taken, the individual was replaced by a [younger] worker, and the individual was qualified for the job."[17] For example, assume that in an organization's attempt to cut salary costs, it lays off senior employees. Yet instead of leaving the jobs unfilled, the organization hires recent college graduates who are paid significantly less. This action may be risky and may lead to a charge of discrimination. Should the organization be found guilty of age discrimination, punitive damages up to double the compensatory amount may be awarded by the courts.

As a final note to the ADEA, it's important to recognize that age discrimination cases may extend beyond employment issues. One area of concern involves pension benefits for older workers. In 1990, the ADEA was amended by the Older Workers Benefit Protection Act to prohibit organizations from excluding employee benefits for older workers. However, the law does permit benefit reduction based on age so long as the cost of benefits paid by the organization is the same for older as it is for younger employees.[18] We'll look at employee benefits in greater detail in Chapter 12.

Pregnancy Discrimination Act of 1978

Law prohibiting discrimination based on pregnancy.

The Pregnancy Discrimination Act of 1978
The **Pregnancy Discrimination Act of 1978** (supplemented by various state laws) prohibits discrimination based on pregnancy. Under the law, companies may not terminate a female employee for being pregnant, refuse to make a positive employment decision based on one's pregnancy, or deny insurance coverage to the woman. The law also requires organizations to offer the employee a reasonable period of time off from work. Although no specific time frames are given, the pregnancy leave is typically 6 to 10 weeks. At the end of this leave, the worker is entitled to return to work. If the exact job she left is unavailable, a similar one must be provided.

It is interesting to note that this law is highly contingent on other benefits the company offers. Should the organization not offer health or disability-related benefits such as sick leave to its employees, it is exempt from this law. However, any type of health or disability insurance offered, no matter how much or how little, requires compliance. For instance, if a company offers a benefit covering 40 percent of the costs associated with any short-term disability, then it must include pregnancy in that coverage.

The Americans with Disabilities Act of 1990
The **Americans with Disabilities Act of 1990 (ADA)** extends employment protection to most forms of disability status, including those afflicted with AIDS.[19] It's important, however, to recognize that ADA doesn't protect all forms of disability. For example, some psychiatric disabilities (like pyromania and kleptomania) may disqualify an individual from employment. And while some mental illness advocates have raised concerns, the EEOC and some courts have held that the employer not accountable in these special cases.[20] In addition to the extended coverage, companies are further required to make **reasonable accommodations** to provide a qualified individual access to the job.[21] A company may also be required to provide necessary technology so that an individual can do his or her job. For example, suppose a worker is legally blind. If special "reading" equipment is available and could assist this individual in doing the job, then the company must provide it if that accommodation does not present an undue hardship.[22]

The ADA extends its coverage to private companies and all public service organizations. Compliance with ADA was phased in over four years, with full compliance for companies with 15 or more employees effective July 26, 1994. As a final note on this act, it's important to mention that contagious diseases, including HIV and AIDS, are considered conditions of being disabled. In advancing the decision in the 1987 Supreme Court case of *Aline v. Nassau County*, the ADA views contagious diseases as any other medical disability. With respect to AIDS, exceptions can be implemented, but most of these are rare. In restaurants, for example, the individual may simply be assigned other duties, rather than terminated. Under this law, you must treat the AIDS worker in the same way you would treat a worker suffering from cancer, and all job actions must be based on job requirements.

The Family and Medical Leave Act of 1993
The **Family and Medical Leave Act of 1993 (FMLA)** provides employees in organizations[23] employing 50 or more workers within a 75-mile radius of the organization the opportunity to take up to 12 weeks of unpaid leave in a 12-month period for family matters (like childbirth or adoption, or for their own illness or to care for a sick family member).[24] To be eligible for these benefits, an employee must have worked for an employer for a total of 12 months (not necessarily consecutively) and must have worked for the organization at least 1,250 hours in the past 12 months. These employees are generally guaranteed their current job, or one equal to it, on their return. If, however, an organization can show that it will suffer significant economic damage by having a "key" employee out on FMLA leave, the organization may deny the leave.[25] A key employee is generally a salaried employee among the top 10 percent of wage earners in the organization. The organization, however, must notify an employee who requests the leave that he or she is considered a "key" employee and that although the employee will have an opportunity to return to the same job, the organization cannot guarantee it.

During this period of unpaid leave, employees retain their employer-offered health insurance coverage (see Exhibit 3-2). Nearly 80 percent of all U.S. workers are covered under FMLA. The act, while providing a benefit to employees, has, however, created some hardships for organizations. These hardships stem from compliance with the law as well as the administrative complexity in processing FMLA matters.[26]

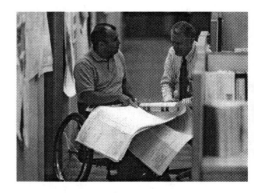

Years ago, an employee in a wheelchair may have had difficulty obtaining employment. However, with the passage of the Americans with Disabilities Act of 1990, employees such as this cannot be discriminated against simply because of the disability. Disabled employees have therefore become productive members of today's organizations. (Source: Lonnie Duka/Index Stock)

Americans with Disabilities Act of 1990
Extends EEO coverage to include most forms of disability, requires employers to make reasonable accommodations, and eliminates post-job-offer medical exams.

reasonable accommodations
Providing the necessary technology to enable affected individuals to do a job.

Family and Medical Leave Act of 1993
Federal legislation that provides employees up to 12 weeks of unpaid leave each year to care for family members or for their own medical reasons.

EXHIBIT 3-2
Family and Medical Act

www.wiley.com/college/decenzo
What Would You Do?
EXPERIENCE: ADA, FMLA, and Worker's Compensation

Your Rights
under the
Family and Medical Leave Act of 1993

FMLA requires covered employers to provide up to 12 weeks of unpaid, job-protected leave to "eligible" employees for certain family and medical reasons. Employees are eligible if they have worked for their employer for at least one year, and for 1,250 hours over the previous 12 months, and if there are at least 50 employees within 75 miles. The FMLA permits employees to take leave on an intermittent basis or to work a reduced schedule under certain circumstances.

Reasons for Taking Leave:

Unpaid leave must be granted for any of the following reasons:
• to care for the employee's child after birth, or placement for adoption or foster care;
• to care for the employee's spouse, son or daughter, or parent who has a serious health condition; or
• for a serious health condition that makes the employee unable to perform the employee's job.

At the employee's or employer's option, certain kinds of *paid* leave may be substituted for unpaid leave.

Advance Notice and Medical Certification:

The employee may be required to provide advance leave notice and medical certification. Taking of leave may be denied if requirements are not met.

• The employee ordinarily must provide 30 days advance notice when the leave is "foreseeable."
• An employer may require medical certification to support a request for leave because of a serious health condition, and may require second or third opinions (at the employer's expense) and a fitness for duty report to return to work.

Job Benefits and Protection:

• For the duration of FMLA leave, the employer must maintain the employee's health coverage under any "group health plan."

• Upon return from FMLA leave, most employees must be restored to their original or equivalent positions with equivalent pay, benefits, and other employment terms.
• The use of FMLA leave cannot result in the loss of any employment benefit that accrued prior to the start of an employee's leave.

Unlawful Acts by Employers:

FMLA makes it unlawful for any employer to:
• interfere with, restrain, or deny the exercise of any right provided under FMLA:
• discharge or discriminate against any person for opposing any practice made unlawful by FMLA or for involvement in any proceeding under or relating to FMLA

Enforcement:

• The U.S. Department of Labor is authorized to investigate and resolve complaints of violations.
• An eligible employee !nay bring a civil action against an employer for violations.

FMLA does not affect any Federal or State law prohibiting discrimination, or supersede any State or local law or collective bargaining agreement which provides greater family or medical leave rights.

For Additional Information:

If you have access to the Internet visit our FMLA website: **http://www.dol.gov/esa/whd/fmla**. To locate your nearest Wage-Hour Office, telephone our Wage-Hour toll-free information and help line at 1-866-4USWAGE (1-866-487-9243): a customer service representative is available to assist you with referral information from 8am to 5pm **in your time zone**; or log onto our Home Page at **http://www.wagehour.dol.gov**.

U.S. Department of Labor
Employment Standards Administration
Wage and Hour Division
Washington, D.C. 20210

WH Publication 1420
Revised August 2001

*U.S. GOVERNMENT PRINTING OFFICE 2001-476-344/49051

Relevant Executive Orders In 1965, President Lyndon Johnson issued Executive Order 11246, which prohibited discrimination on the basis of race, religion, color, or national origin by federal agencies as well as by contractors and subcontractors who worked under federal contracts. This was followed by Executive Order 11375, which added sex-based discrimination to the above criteria. In 1969, President Richard Nixon issued Executive Order 11478 to supersede part of Executive Order 11246. It stated that employment practices in the federal government must be based on merit and must prohibit discrimination based on race, color, religion, sex, national origin, political affiliation, marital status, or physical disability.

These orders cover all organizations with contracts of $10,000 or more with the federal government. Additionally, those organizations with 50 or more employees and/or $50,000 in federal grants must have a written active affirmative action program. The Office of Federal Contract Compliance Program (OFCCP) administers the order's provisions and provides technical assistance. We'll return to the OFCCP shortly when we discuss the enforcement aspects of equal employment opportunities.

TECHNOLOGY CORNER

DEALING WITH THE LEGAL SIDE OF HRM

A variety of software and Internet-based applications have been created to help organizations deal with many of the legal issues in HRM. The following are a few highlights of these applications.

■ *LexisNexis Bookstore* (bookstore.lexis.com/bookstore). This software-based material offers a comprehensive guide in how to set up and meet compliance requirements. Prices for software vary depending on topic chosen.

■ *Preventing Sexual Harassment* (New Media Learning: www.newmedialearning.com). This software program permits customization to more properly reflect an organization's issues. Software includes "test" questions to reinforce concepts on the software. Feedback on these test questions is immediate. The software program costs vary depending on the number of site licenses granted.

The Civil Rights Act of 1991

The **Civil Rights Act of 1991** was one of the most hotly debated civil rights laws since the 1964 act. The impetus for this legislation stemmed from Supreme Court decisions in the late 1980s that diminished the effect of the Griggs decision. Proponents of the 1964 legislation quickly banded together in an attempt to issue new legislation aimed at restoring the provisions lost in these Supreme Court rulings.

The Civil Rights Act of 1991 prohibits discrimination on the basis of race and prohibits racial harassment on the job; returns the burden of proof that discrimination did not occur back to the employer; reinforces the illegality of employers who make hiring, firing, or promoting decisions on the basis of race, ethnicity, sex, or religion; and permits women and religious minorities to seek punitive damages in intentional discriminatory claims. Additionally, this act also included the Glass Ceiling Act—establishing the Glass Ceiling Commission, whose purpose is to study a variety of management practices in organizations.

What impact did this legislation have on employers? The issue dealing with punitive damages may prove to be the most drastic change. For the first time, individuals claiming they have been intentionally discriminated against may sue for damages. The amount of these compensatory and punitive charges, however, is prorated based on number of employees in the organization.[27]

Civil Rights Act of 1991
Employment discrimination law that nullified selected Supreme Court decisions. Reinstated burden of proof by the employer, and allowed for punitive and compensatory damage through jury trials.

GUARDING AGAINST DISCRIMINATION PRACTICES

The number of laws and regulations make it critical for HRM to implement nondiscriminatory practices. Although it is hoped that senior management has established an organizational culture that encourages equal employment opportunity, discrimination does happen. Recall from our earlier discussion that employment discrimination may stem from a decision based on factors other than those relevant to the job. Should that occur frequently, the organization may face charges that it discriminates against some members of a protected group (see Did You Know?). Determining what constitutes discrimination, however, typically requires more than one individual being adversely affected.

Determining Potential Discriminatory Practices

To determine if discrimination possibly occurred, one of four tests can be used: the 4/5ths rule, restricted policies, geographic comparisons, and the McDonnell-Douglas Test. Remember, however, that each of these tests is simply an indicator that risky practices may have occurred. It is up to some judicial body to make the final determination.

DID YOU KNOW?

IS A PROBLEM BREWING?

Often, HR managers react to an event or, in the case of a discrimination charge, a legal matter. Although they often have policies in place on how to handle such events, a more fundamental question arises. That is, are there signs that something is brewing? The answer is often yes—if one is keyed in on what's happening in the organization.

For instance, one might expect a problem ahead if:

- large numbers of employees (often individuals who share something in common—a personal characteristic, the same supervisor, etc.) ask for their personnel files;

- significant increases are witnessed in the use of the company's complaint procedure;
- a union campaign has just failed; and
- employees are using blogs to bash the organization.

Though each of the above items might not always indicate a legal action is forthcoming, it should tell HR that there is a potential problem and they need to look into it. Being a bit proactive—investigating things before they reach a fever pitch—is often the best defense one may have.

Source: J. Harmon, "Identifying and Preventing Class Actions," *Workforce Management* (August 2004), available online at www.workforce.com/section/03/article/23/81/53.html; and M. T. Johnson, "The Car Wreck You Can Stop," *Workforce Management* (December 2003), pp. 18–20.

4/5ths rule

A rough indicator of discrimination, this rule requires that the number of minority members a company hires must equal at least 80 percent of the majority members in the population hired.

The 4/5ths Rule One of the first measures of determining potentially discriminatory practices is a rule of thumb called the **4/5ths rule**. Issued by the EEOC in its Uniform Guidelines on Employee Selection Procedures, the 4/5ths rule helps assess whether an adverse impact has occurred. Of course, the 4/5ths rule is not a definition of discrimination. It is, however, a quick analysis to helps assess HR practices in an organization. Moreover, in applying the 4/5ths rule, the Supreme Court ruled in *Connecticut v. Teal* (1984) that decisions in each step of the selection process must conform to the 4/5ths rule.[28]

To see how the 4/5ths rule works, suppose we have two pools of applicants for jobs as management information systems analysts. Our applicants' backgrounds reflect the following: 40 applicants are classified in the majority and 15 applicants are classified as members of minority populations.[29] After we test and interview, we hire 22 majority and 8 minority members. Is the organization in compliance? Exhibit 3-3 provides the analysis. In this case, we find that the company is in compliance; that is, the ratio of minority to majority members is

EXHIBIT 3-3
Applying the 4/5ths Rule

IN COMPLIANCE						
Majority Group (Maj) = 40 applicants			**Minority Group (Min) = 15 applicants**			
ITEM	**NUMBER**	**PERCENT**	**ITEM**	**NUMBER**	**PERCENT**	**%MIN/%MAJ**
Passed test	30	75%	Passed test	11	73%	73%/75% = 97%
Passed interview	22	73%	Passed interview	8	72%	72%/73% = 98%
Hired	22	100%	Hired	8	100%	100%/100% = 100%
Analysis	22/40 =	55%	Analysis	8/15 =	53%	
Ratio of minority/majority 53%/55% = 96%						

NOT IN COMPLIANCE						
Majority Group (Maj) = 40 applicants			**Minority Group (Min) = 15 applicants**			
ITEM	**NUMBER**	**PERCENT**	**ITEM**	**NUMBER**	**PERCENT**	**%MIN/%MAJ**
Passed test	30	75%	Passed test	11	73%	73%/75% = 97%
Passed interview	22	86%	Passed interview	4	36%	36%/86% = 41%
Hired	26	100%	Hired	4	100%	100%/100% = 100%
Analysis	26/40 =	65%	Analysis	4/15 =	26%	
Ratio of minority/majority 26%/65% = 40%						

80 percent or greater (the 4/5ths rule). Accordingly, even though fewer minority members were hired, no apparent discrimination has occurred. Exhibit 3-3 also shows the analysis of an organization not in compliance.

Remember, whenever the 4/5ths rule is violated, it indicates only that discrimination may have occurred. Many factors can enter in the picture. Should the analysis show that the percentage is less than 80 percent, more elaborate statistical testing must confirm or deny adverse impact. For instance, if Company A finds a way to keep most minority group members from applying in the first place, it need hire only a few of them to meet its 4/5ths measure. Conversely, if Company B actively seeks numerous minority-group applicants and hires more than Company A, it still may not meet the 4/5ths rule.

Restricted Policy A *restricted policy* infraction occurs whenever an enterprise's HRM activities exclude a class of individuals. For instance, assume a company is restructuring and laying off an excessive number of employees over age 40. Simultaneously, however, the company is recruiting for selected positions on college campuses only. Because of economic difficulties, this company wants to keep salaries low by hiring people just entering the workforce. Those over age 39 who were making higher salaries are not given the opportunity to even apply for these new jobs. These actions may indicate a restricted policy. That is, through its hiring practice (intentional or not), a class of individuals (in this case, those protected by age discrimination legislation) has been excluded from consideration.

Geographical Comparisons A third means of supporting discriminatory claims is through the use of a geographic comparison. In this instance, the characteristics of the potential qualified pool of applicants in an organization's hiring market are compared to the characteristics of its employees. If the organization has a proper mix of individuals at all levels in the organization that reflects its recruiting market, then the company is in compliance. Additionally, that compliance may assist in fostering diversity in the organization. The key factor here is the qualified pool according to varying geographic areas.

McDonnell-Douglas Test Named for the *McDonnell-Douglas Corp. v. Green* 1973 Supreme Court case,[30] this test provides a means of establishing a solid case.[31] Four components must exist:[32]

1. The individual is a member of a protected group.
2. The individual applied for a job for which he or she was qualified.
3. The individual was rejected.
4. The enterprise, after rejecting this applicant, continued to seek other applicants with similar qualifications.

McDonnell-Douglas Corp. v. Green
Supreme Court case that led to a four-part test used to determine if discrimination has occurred.

If these four conditions are met, an allegation of discrimination is supported. It is up to the company to refute the evidence by providing a reason for such action. Should that explanation be acceptable to an investigating body, the protected group member must then prove that the company's reason is inappropriate. If any of the preceding four tests are met, the company might find itself having to defend its practices. In the next section, we'll explain how an enterprise can do that.

Responding to an EEO Charge

If HRM practices have adverse impact in an organization, the employer has a few remedies for dealing with valid allegations. First, the employer should discontinue the practice. Only after careful study should the practice, or a modified version, be reinstated. However, even if enough evidence exists, an employer may choose to defend its practices. Generally, three defenses can be used when confronted with an allegation. These are job relatedness or business necessity; bona fide occupational qualifications; and seniority systems.

Business Necessity An organization has the right to operate in a safe and efficient manner. This includes business necessities without which organizational survival could be threatened. A major portion of business necessity involves job-relatedness factors, or having the right to expect employees to perform successfully. Employees are expected to possess the skills, knowledge, and abilities required to perform the essential elements of the job. Job-relatedness criteria are substantiated through the validation process. We'll return to this topic in Chapter 7.

bona fide occupational qualification (BFOQ)

Job requirements that are "reasonably necessary to meet the normal operations of that business or enterprise."

Bona Fide Occupational Qualifications The second defense against discriminatory charges is a **bona fide occupational qualification (BFOQ)**. Under Title VII, a BFOQ was permitted where such requirements were "reasonably necessary to meet the normal operation of that business or enterprise." As originally worded, BFOQs could be used only to support sex discrimination. Today, BFOQ coverage is extended to other categories covered. BFOQs cannot, however, be used in cases of race or color.

It is important to note that while BFOQs are "legal" exceptions to Title VII, they are narrowly defined. Simply using a BFOQ as the response to a charge of discrimination is not enough; it must be directly related to the job. Let's look at some examples.

Just a few decades ago, airlines used BFOQs as a primary reason for hiring female flight attendants. The airlines' position was that most of their passengers were male and preferred to see stewardesses. The courts, however, did not hold the same view. As a result, it is now common to see both sexes as flight attendants. Using gender as a job criterion is difficult to prove. Even the classic washroom attendant case has seen a change: many fine restaurants have members of the opposite sex working in washroom facilities. However, under certain circumstances gender as a BFOQ has been supported. In some health-care jobs, gender may be used as a determining factor to "protect the privacy interests of patients, clients, or customers."[33]

A religious BFOQ may have similar results. Religion may be used as a differentiating factor in ordaining a church minister, but a faculty member doesn't have to be Catholic to teach at a Jesuit college. An organization under certain circumstances may refuse to hire individuals whose religious observances fall on days that the enterprise normally operates. And if the organization demonstrates that it cannot reasonably accommodate these religious observances, then a BFOQ may be permissible.[34] But it's becoming harder to demonstrate an inability to make a reasonable accommodation.[35] For example, pizza delivery establishments cannot refuse to hire, or terminate, an employee who has facial hair—like that in the Hindu tradition. HRM managers must understand that some "traditional" policies may have to change to reflect religious diversity in the workforce. For instance, a policy that prohibits employees who have customer contact from having beards may be a violation of the Civil Rights Act. Accordingly, the company may have to change its policy to accommodate religious traditions.[36]

Why does the Age Discrimination in Employment Act permit certain exceptions, like requiring commercial airlines pilots to retire on reaching their 60th birthday? The rationale focuses on the potential for a pilot's skills to lessen after age 60. That, coupled with concern for air safety of traveling passengers, has resulted in an exception to the law. (Source: Bernard van Berg/Iconica/Getty Images, Inc.)

In terms of national origin, BFOQs have become rarer. However, if an organization can show that a foreign accent or the inability to communicate effectively "materially interferes with the individual ability to perform" the job, then nationality can be used as a BFOQ.[37]

Our last area of BFOQ is age. With subsequent amendments to the Age Discrimination in Employment Act, age BFOQs are hard to support. As we mentioned in our discussion of age discrimination, age can sometimes be used as a determining factor. However, aside from pilots and a select few key management executives in an organization, age as a BFOQ is limited.

Seniority Systems Finally, the organization's bona fide seniority system can serve as a defense against discrimination charges. So long as employment decisions such as layoffs stem from a well-established and consistently applied seniority system, decisions that may adversely affect protected group members may be permissible. However, an organization using seniority as a defense must be able to demonstrate the "appropriateness" of its system.

Although means are available for organizations to defend themselves, the best approach revolves around job-relatedness. BFOQ and seniority defenses are often subject to great scrutiny and at times, are limited in their use.

SELECTED RELEVANT SUPREME COURT CASES

In addition to the laws affecting discriminatory practices, HRM practitioners must be aware of decisions rendered in the Supreme Court. Many of these cases help further define HRM practices or indicate permissible activities. Although it is impossible to discuss every applicable Supreme Court case, we have chosen a few of the more critical ones for what they have meant to the field.

Cases Concerning Discrimination

Let's return to one of the most important legal rulings affecting selection procedures. In the 1971 *Griggs v. Duke Power Company* decision, the U.S. Supreme Court adopted the interpretive guidelines set out under Title VII: tests must fairly measure the knowledge and skills required in a job in order not to discriminate unfairly against minorities. This action single-handedly made invalid any employment test or diploma requirement that disqualified African Americans at a substantially higher rate than whites (even unintentionally) if this differentiation could not be proved job related. Such action was said to create an adverse (disparate) impact.[38]

The *Griggs* decision had even wider implications. It made illegal most intelligence and conceptual tests used in hiring without direct empirical evidence that the tests employed were valid. This crucial decision placed the burden of proof on the employer, who must provide adequate support that any test used did not discriminate on the basis of non–job-related characteristics. For example, if an employer requires all applicants to take an IQ test, and test results factor in the hiring decision, the employer must prove that individuals with higher scores will outperform on the job those individuals with lower scores. Nothing in the Court's decision, however, precludes the use of testing or measuring procedures. What it did was to place the burden of proof on management to demonstrate, if challenged, that the tests used provided a reasonable measure of job performance.

Although companies began a process of validating these tests, requiring all job applicants to take them raised further questions. In 1975, the Supreme Court decision in the case of ***Albemarle Paper Company v. Moody*** clarified the methodological requirements for using and validating tests in selection.[39] In the case, four African American employees challenged their employer's use of tests for selecting candidates from the unskilled labor pool for promotion into skilled jobs. The Court endorsed the EEOC guidelines by noting that Albemarle's selection methodology was defective because

- The tests had not been used solely for jobs on which they had previously been validated.
- The tests were not validated for upper-level jobs alone but were also used for entry-level jobs.
- Subjective supervisory ratings were used for validating the tests, but the ratings had not been done with care.
- The tests had been validated on a group of job-experienced white workers, whereas the tests were given to young, inexperienced, and often nonwhite candidates.

Albemarle Paper Company v. Moody
Supreme Court case that clarified the requirements for using and validating tests in selection processes.

EXHIBIT 3-4
Summary of Selected Supreme Court Cases Affecting EEO

CASE	RULING
Griggs v. Duke Power (1971)	Tests must fairly measure the knowledge or skills required for a job; also validity of tests.
Albemarle Paper Company v. Moody (1975)	Clarified requirements for using and validating test in selection.
Washington v. Davis (1976)	Job-related tests are permissible for screening applicants.
Connecticut v. Teal (1984)	Requires all steps in a selection process to meet the 4/5ths rule.
Firefighters Local 1784 v. Stotts (1984)	Layoffs are permitted by seniority despite effects it may have on minority employees.
Wyant v. Jackson Board of Education (1986)	Layoffs of white workers to establish racial or ethnic balances are illegal; however, reaffirmed the use of affirmative action plans to correct racial imbalance.
United States v. Paradise (1986)	Quotas may be used to correct significant racial discrimination practices.
Sheetmetal Workers Local 24 v. EEOC (1987)	Racial preference could be used in layoff decisions only for those who had been subjected to previous race discrimination.
Johnson v. Santa Clara County Transportation Agency (1987)	Reaffirmed the use of preferential treatment based on gender to overcome problems in existing affirmative action plans.

Wards Cove Packing Company v. Atonio

A notable Supreme Court case that had the effect of potentially undermining two decades of gains made in equal employment opportunities.

In addition to these two landmark cases, other Supreme Court rulings have effected HRM practices. We have identified some of the more important ones and their results in Exhibit 3-4. During the late 1980s, however, we began to see a significant change in the Supreme Court's perception of EEO. One of the most notable cases during this period was **Wards Cove Packing Company v. Atonio** (1989).[40] Wards Cove operates two primary salmon canneries in Alaska. The issue in this case stemmed from different hiring practices for two types of jobs. Noncannery jobs viewed as unskilled positions were predominately filled by nonwhites (Filipinos and native Alaskans). On the other hand, cannery jobs, seen as skilled administrative/engineering positions, were held by a predominately white group. Based on the ruling handed down in *Griggs v. Duke Power,* an adverse (disparate) impact could be shown by the use of statistics (the 4/5ths rule). However, in the decision, the Court ruled that statistics alone could not support evidence of discrimination. Consequently, the burden of proof shifted from the employer to the individual employee.

The *Wards Cove* decision had the effect of potentially undermining two decades of gains made in equal employment opportunities. This case could have struck a significant blow to affirmative action. Despite that potential, businesses appeared unwilling to significantly deviate from the affirmative action plans developed over the years. Of course, it's now a moot point, as the Civil Rights Bill of 1991 nullified many of these Supreme Court rulings.

Cases Concerning Reverse Discrimination

Affirmative action programs are necessary to ensure continued employment possibilities for minorities and women. Programs to foster the careers of these two groups have grown over the decades. But while this voluntary action may have been needed to correct past abuses, what about the white male—who at some point is becoming a minority in the workforce? Some white males believe that affirmative action plans work against them, leading to charges of **reverse discrimination**. Although reverse discrimination cases exist, two specific cases of reverse discrimination have been noteworthy: *Bakke* and *Weber*.

In 1978, the Supreme Court handed down its decision in the case of *Bakke v. The Regents of the University of California at Davis Medical School*.[41] Allen Bakke applied to the Davis Medical School for one of 100 first-year seats. At that time, U.C. Davis had a self-imposed quota system to promote its affirmative action plan: that is, of the 100 first-year seats, 16 were set aside for minority applicants. Bakke's charge stemmed from those 16 reserved seats. His credentials were not as good as those gaining access to the first 84 seats, but were better than those of minorities targeted for the reserved seats. The issue that finally reached the Supreme Court was, could an institution impose its own quota to correct past imbalances between whites and minorities? The Supreme Court ruled that the school could not set aside those seats, for doing so resulted in "favoring one race over another." Consequently, Bakke was permitted to enter Davis Medical School.

The Supreme Court's decision in the case of the *United Steelworkers of America v. Weber* (1979) appeared to have important implications for organizational training and development practices and for the larger issue of reverse discrimination.[42] In 1974, Kaiser Aluminum and the United Steelworkers Union set up a temporary training program for higher-paying skilled trade jobs, such as electrician and repairer, at a Kaiser plant in Louisiana. Brian Weber, a white employee at the plant who was not selected for the training program, sued on the grounds that he had been illegally discriminated against. He argued that African Americans with less seniority were selected over him to attend the training due solely to their race. The question facing the Court was whether it is fair to discriminate against whites to help African Americans who have been longtime victims of discrimination. The justices said that Kaiser could choose to give special job preference to African Americans without fear of being harassed by reverse discrimination suits brought by other employees. The ruling was an endorsement of voluntary affirmative action efforts—goals and timetables for bringing an organization's minority and female workforce up to the percentages they represent in the available labor pool.

Despite the press coverage that both cases received, many questions remained unanswered. Just how far was a company permitted to go regarding preferential treatment (see Ethical Issues in HRM)? In subsequent cases, more information became available. In 1984, the Supreme Court ruled in *Firefighters Local 1784 v. Stotts*[43] that when facing a layoff situation, affirmative action may not take precedence over a seniority system: that is, the last in (often minorities) may be the first to go. This decision was further reinforced in *Wyant v. Jackson Board of Education* (1986),[44] when the Supreme Court ruled that a collective bargaining agreement giving preferential treatment to preserve minority jobs in the event of a layoff was illegal. On the contrary, in *Johnson v. Santa Clara County Transportation* (1987) the Supreme Court did permit affirmative action goals to correct worker imbalances as long as the rights of nonminorities were protected. This ruling had an effect of potentially reducing reverse discrimination claims.

The implications of these cases may be somewhat confusing. The conclusion one needs to draw from these is that *any HRM practice may be challenged by anyone*. HRM must be able to defend its practices if necessary and explain the basis and the parameters on which the decisions were made. Failure to document or to base the decisions on business necessities may lead to serious challenges to the action taken.

reverse discrimination
A claim made by white males that minority candidates are given preferential treatment in employment decisions.

Failure to document decisions on business necessity may lead to serious challenges.

ETHICAL ISSUES IN HRM

English-Only Rules

Can an organization require its employees to speak only English on the job? The answer is an unquestionable "maybe." At issue here are several items. On one hand, employers have identified the need to have a common language spoken at the work site. Employers must be able to communicate effectively with all employees, especially when safety or productive efficiency matters are at stake.[45] This, they claim, is a business necessity. Consequently, if it is a valid job requirement, the practice could be permitted. Furthermore, an employer's desire to have one language may stem from the fact that some workers may use bilingual capabilities to harass and insult other workers in a language they could not understand. With today's ever-increasing concern with protecting employees, especially women, from hostile environments, English-only rules serve as one means of reasonable care.

A counterpoint to this English-only rule firmly rests with the workforce diversity issue. Workers in today's organizations come from all nationalities and speak different languages. More than 30 million workers in the United States speak a language other than English. What about these individuals' desire to speak their language, communicate effectively with their peers, and maintain their cultural heritage? To them, English-only rules are discriminatory in terms of national origin in that they create an adverse impact for non–English-speaking individuals.[46]

Should employers be permitted to require that only English be spoken in the workplace? What if it is necessary for successful performance or to prevent a safety or health hazard? Should the Supreme Court view this as a discriminatory practice, or render a decision that would create a single, nationwide standard on English-only? What do you think about this issue?

ENFORCING EQUAL OPPORTUNITY EMPLOYMENT

Two U.S. government agencies are primarily responsible for enforcing equal employment opportunity laws. They are the Equal Employment Opportunity Commission (EEOC) and the Office of Federal Contract Compliance Programs (OFCCP).

The Role of the EEOC

Any charge leveled against an enterprise regarding discrimination based on race, religion, color, sex, national origin, age, qualified disabilities, or wages due to gender falls under the jurisdiction of the EEOC.[47] That is, the EEOC is the enforcement arm for Title VII of the 1964 Civil Rights Act, the Equal Pay Act,[48] the Age Discrimination in Employment Act, the Vocational Rehabilitation Act of 1973, the Americans with Disabilities Act,[49] and the Civil Rights Act of 1991. The EEOC requires that charges typically be filed within 180 days of an alleged incident,[50] and that these charges be written and sworn under oath. Once the charges have been filed, the EEOC may progress (if necessary) through a five-step process:[51]

1. The EEOC will notify the organization of the charge within 10 days of its filing and then begin to investigate the charge to determine if the complaint is valid. The company may simply settle the case here, and the process stops.
2. The EEOC will notify the organization in writing of its findings within 120 days. If the charge is unfounded, the EEOC's process stops, the individual is notified of the outcome, and informs the individual that he or she may still file charges against the company in civil court (called a right-to-sue notice). The individual has 90 days on receipt of the right-to-sue notice to file his or her suit.
3. If there is justification to the charge, the EEOC will attempt to correct the problem through informal meetings with the employer. Again, the company, recognizing that discrimination may have occurred, may settle the case at this point.
4. If the informal process is unsuccessful, the EEOC will begin a formal settlement meeting between the individual and the organization (called a *mediation meeting*). The emphasis here is to reach a voluntary agreement between the parties.
5. Should Step 3 fail, the EEOC may file charges in court.

It's important to note that while acting as the enforcement arm of Title VII, the EEOC has the power to investigate claims, but it has no power to force organizations to cooperate.

The EEOC is staffed by five presidentially appointed commissioners and staff counsels. It is generally well known that the EEOC is quite under-staffed in its attempt to handle more than 84,000 cases each year.[52] And as a result, thousands of cases have been backlogged.[53] Consequently, the EEOC began prioritizing cases in the mid-1990s, attempting to spend more time on cases that initially appear to have merit. Furthermore, its enforcement plans are prioritized, with cases that "raise issues appropriate for widespread or class relief" receiving the highest priority.[54] But even then, the EEOC may decide not to file suit. If conciliation efforts are unsuccessful, the EEOC may simply issue a "right-to-sue" letter to the complainant and reallocate its resources on other cases. Under these new EEOC directions, it's more important than ever for HRM to investigate the complaints internally, communicate openly with the EEOC regarding the priority level of the complaint, and even seek alternative means to resolve the dispute with the individual.

The EEOC prioritizes its cases to spend more time on those that have the greatest significance.

The relief that the EEOC tries to achieve for the individual is regulated by Title VII. If the allegation is substantiated, the EEOC attempts to make the indi-vidual whole. That is, under the law, the EEOC attempts to obtain lost wages or back pay, job reinstatement, and other rightfully due employment factors (for example, seniority or benefits). The individual may also recover attorney fees. However, if the discrimination was intentional, other damages may be awarded. Under no circumstances may the enterprise retaliate against an individual filing charges—whether or not the person remains employed by the organization. The EEOC monitors that no further adverse action against that individual occurs.

Office of Federal Contract Compliance Program (OFCCP)

In support of Executive Order 11246, the OFCCP enforces the provisions of this order (as amended), as well as Section 503 of the Vocational Rehabilitation Act of 1973 and the Vietnam Veterans Readjustment Act of 1974.[55] Provisions of the OFCCP apply to any organizations, including universities, that have a federal con-tract or act as a subcontractor on a federal project. The OFCCP operates within the U.S. Department of Labor. Similar to the EEOC, the OFCCP investigates alle-gations of discriminatory practices and follows a similar process in determining and rectifying wrongful actions. One notable difference is that the OFCCP has the power to cancel an enterprise's contract with the federal government if the orga-nization fails to comply with EEO laws.

HRM IN A GLOBAL ENVIRONMENT

Does HRM face the same laws globally? In other words, are the laws presented above the same throughout the world? The simple answer to that question is unequivocally no. Unfortunately, there are not enough pages in this text to ade-quately cover the laws affecting HRM in any given country. What we can do, however, is highlight some of the differences and suggest that you need to know the laws and regulations that apply in your locale. To illustrate how laws and reg-ulations shape HRM practices, we can highlight some primary legislation that influences HRM practices in Canada, Mexico, Australia, and Germany.

Canadian laws pertaining to HRM practices closely parallel those in the United States. The Canadian Human Rights Act provides federal legislation that prohibits discrimination on the basis of race, religion, age, marital status, sex, physical or mental disability, or national origin. This act governs practices through-out the country. Canada's HRM environment, however, differs somewhat from that in the United States in that more lawmaking is done at the provincial level in Canada. For example, discrimination on the basis of language is prohibited nowhere in Canada except Quebec.

In Mexico, employees are more likely to be unionized than they are in the United States. Labor matters are governed by the Mexican Federal Labor Law. One law regarding hiring states that an employer has 28 days to evaluate a new employee's work performance. After that period, the employee is granted job security, and termination is quite difficult and expensive. Infractions of the Mexican Federal Labor Law are subject to severe penalties, including criminal action. This means that high fines and even jail sentences can be imposed on employers who fail to pay, for example, the minimum wage.

Australia's discrimination laws were not enacted until the 1980s. The laws that do exist, however, generally apply to discrimination and affirmative action for women. Yet gender opportunities for women in Australia appear to lag behind those in the United States. In Australia, however, a significant proportion of the workforce is unionized. The higher percentage of unionized workers has placed increased importance on industrial relations specialists in Australia and reduced the control of line managers over workplace labor issues. However, in 1997 Australia overhauled its industrial labor relations laws with the objective of increasing productivity and reducing union power. The Workplace Relations Bill gives employers greater flexibility to negotiate directly with employees on pay, hours, and benefits. It also simplifies regulation of labor–management relations.

The goal of representative participation is to redistribute power within an organization, putting labor on a more equal footing with the interests of management and stockholders.

Our final country, Germany, is similar to most Western European countries when it comes to HRM practices. Legislation requires companies to practice representative participation. The goal of representative participation is to redistribute power within the organization, putting labor on a more equal footing with the interests of management and stockholders. The two most common forms that representative participation takes are work councils and board representatives. *Work councils* link employees with management. They are groups of nominated or elected employees who must be consulted when management makes decisions involving personnel. *Board representatives* are employees who sit on a company's board of directors and represent the interest of the firm's employees.

CURRENT ISSUES IN EMPLOYMENT LAW

EEO today continues to address two important issues affecting female employees. These are harassment in the workplace—primarily sexual in nature—and the glass-ceiling initiative. Let's take a closer look at both of these.

What Is Sexual Harassment?

Sexual harassment is a serious issue in both public- and private-sector organizations. More than 13,000 complaints are filed with the EEOC each year; 15% of these are filed by males.[56] Settlements in some of these cases incurred substantial litigation costs to the companies. It is possibly the single biggest financial risk facing companies today, and results in a more than 30 percent decrease in a company's stock price.[57] At Mitsubishi, for example, the company paid out more than $34 million to 300 women for the rampant sexual harassment to which they were exposed.[58] But it's more than just jury awards. Sexual harassment results in millions lost in absenteeism, low productivity, and turnover.[59] Sexual harassment, furthermore, is not just a U.S. phenomenon. It's a global issue. For instance, sexual harassment charges have been filed against employers in such countries as Japan, Australia, the Netherlands, Belgium, New Zealand, Sweden, Ireland, and Mexico.[60] Discussions of sexual harassment cases often focus on the large court awards, but employers have other concerns. Sexual harassment creates an unpleasant work environment for organization members and undermines their ability to perform their job. But just what is sexual harassment?

Sexual harassment can be regarded as any unwanted activity of a sexual nature that affects an individual's employment. It can occur between members of the opposite or of the same sex, between organization employees or employees and nonemployees.[61] Although such an activity was generally protected under Title VII (sex discrimination) in the United States, in recent years this problem has gained more recognition. By most accounts, prior to the mid-1980s this problem was generally viewed as an isolated incident, with the individual committing the act being solely responsible (if at all) for his or her actions.[62] By the beginning of the new millennium, however, charges of sexual harassment appeared in the headlines on an almost regular basis.

Much of the problem associated with sexual harassment is determining what constitutes this illegal behavior.[63] In 1993, the EEOC cited three situations in which sexual harassment can occur. These are instances where verbal or physical conduct toward an individual

1. creates an intimidating, offensive, or hostile environment;
2. unreasonably interferes with an individual's work; or
3. adversely affects an employee's employment opportunities.

For many organizations, the offensive or hostile environment issue is problematic.[64] Just what constitutes such an environment? Challenging hostile environment situations gained much support from the Supreme Court case of *Meritor Savings Bank v. Vinson*.[65] This case stemmed from a situation in which Ms. Vinson initially refused the sexual advances of her boss. However, out of fear of reprisal, she ultimately conceded. According to court records, it did not stop there. Vinson's boss continued to hassle Vinson, subjecting her to severe hostility, which affected her job.[66] In addition to supporting hostile environment claims, the *Meritor* case also identified employer liability: That is, in sexual harassment cases, an organization can be held liable for sexual harassment actions by its managers, employees, and even customers![67]

Although the *Meritor* case has implications for organizations, how do organizational members determine if something is offensive? For instance, does sexually explicit language in the office create a hostile environment? How about off-color jokes? Pictures of women totally undressed? The answer is: It could! It depends on the people in the organization and the environment in which they work. The point here is that we all must be attuned to what makes fellow employees uncomfortable—and if we don't know, we should ask! Organizational success in the new millennium will in part reflect how sensitive each employee is toward others in the company. DuPont corporate culture and diversity programs, for example, are designed to eliminate sexual harassment through awareness and respect for all individuals.[68] This means understanding one another and, most important, respecting others' rights. Similar programs exist at FedEx, General Mills, and Levi-Strauss.

If sexual harassment carries potential costs to the organization, what can a company do to protect itself (see Learning an HRM Skill, p. 86)?[69] The courts want to know two things: did the organization know about, or should it have known about, the alleged behavior; and what did management do to stop it?[70] The judgments and awards against organizations today indicate even greater need for management to educate all employees on sexual harassment matters and have mechanisms available to monitor employees. Furthermore, "victims" no longer have to prove that their psychological well-being is seriously affected. The Supreme Court ruled in 1993 in the case of *Harris v. Forklift Systems, Inc.*, that victims need not suffer substantial mental distress to merit a jury award. Furthermore, in June 1998, the Supreme Court ruled that sexual harassment may have occurred even if the employee had not experienced any "negative" job repercussions. In this case, Kimberly Ellerth, a marketing assistant at Burlington Industries, filed harassment charges against her boss

sexual harassment
Anything of a sexual nature that creates a condition of employment, an employment consequence, or a hostile or offensive environment.

Is what you see in the picture sexual harassment? Perhaps. If the employee believes his supervisor's action interferes with his work and he has asked for the offensive behavior to stop and it hasn't, then he may be experiencing sexual harassment. Actions like this may be part of the reason why more than 20 percent of all working women have reported instances of sexual harassment at work. (Source: Thomas Schmidt/Getty Images, Inc.)

DID YOU KNOW?

MACKENZIE V. MILLER: THE FINAL WORDS

Several years back, during the height of TV's comedy show *Seinfeld,* a sexual harassment case made its way through the courts. In the case of *Jerold Mackenzie v. Miller Brewing,* Mackenzie allegedly made inappropriate comments to a female employee based on something he heard on an episode of *Seinfeld.* In investigating the case, Miller officials determined that Mackenzie acted inappropriately and his actions constituted sexual harassment. Consequently, acting in what they believed was good faith, Mackenzie was fired. But Mackenzie challenged his firing, filing suit for wrongful termination. At the end of his trial, a jury found in his favor and awarded him over $26 million—$6.2 million in compensatory damages and an additional $18 million for punitive damages. As a result of this decision, many simply asked, does an alleged harasser have rights, too? While the answer is obviously yes, this was not the end of the story.

Appealing the lower court's decision, Miller Brewing demonstrated that they had done what was expected of them given the circumstances they faced. The Wisconsin Appellate Court agreed and overturned the decision. But even this doesn't end the story.

Although the appellate court's decision stood, Mackenzie filed suit against his attorney for malpractice—citing that his lawyer made mistakes on his case and did not give him a true opportunity to settle the original case for $3 million when offered by Miller. In June 2003, Mackenzie and his attorney's malpractice insurer settled their dispute by offering Mackenzie $625,000—which he accepted.

Sources: Mackenzie v. Miller Brewing Company, Wisc Ct. App. (February 22, 2000); and C. Spivak and D. Bice, "Seinfeld Suit Punch Line: $625,000," *Milwaukee Journal Sentinel* (June 8, 2003), available online at www.jsonline.com/news/metro/jun03/146469.asp.

because he "touched her, suggested she wear shorter skirts, and told her during a business trip that he could make her job 'very hard or very easy.'" When Ellerth refused, the harasser never "punished" her. In fact, Kimberly even received a promotion during the time the harassment was ongoing. The Supreme Court's decision in this case indicates that "harassment is defined by the ugly behavior of the manager, not by what happened to the worker subsequently."[71]

Finally, whenever involved in a sexual harassment matter one must remember that the harasser may have rights, too.[72] (see Did You Know?) This means that no action should be taken against someone until a thorough investigation has been conducted. Furthermore, the results of the investigation should be reviewed by an independent and objective individual before any action against the alleged harasser is taken. Even then, the harasser should have an opportunity to respond to the allegation and a disciplinary hearing if desired. Additionally, an avenue for appeal should also exist for the alleged harasser, heard by someone in a higher level of management who is not associated with the case.

Are Women Reaching the Top of Organizations?

In decades past, many jobs were formally viewed as being male- or female-oriented. For example, positions such as librarian, nurse, and elementary schoolteacher were considered typical jobs for women; by contrast, police officers, truck drivers, and top management positions were regarded as the domain of men. Historically, this attitude resulted in the traditional female-oriented jobs paying significantly less than the male-oriented positions. This differentiation led to concerns over gender-based pay systems, commonly referred to as the **comparable worth** issue. For instance, a nurse may be judged to have a comparable job to that of a police officer. Both must be trained, both are licensed to practice, both work under stressful conditions, and both must exhibit high levels of effort. But they are not typically paid the same; male-dominated jobs have traditionally been paid more than female-oriented jobs. Under comparable worth, estimates of the importance of each job are used in determining and equating pay structures. The 1963 Equal Pay Act requires that workers doing essentially the same work must initially be paid the

comparable worth

Equal pay for jobs similar in skills, responsibility, working conditions, and effort.

WORKPLACE ISSUES

IF IT'S OFFENSIVE . . .

Sexually explicit language. Sexual joking. Sexually suggestive remarks. Inappropriate touching. Displaying a questionable pin-up photo or drawing. Some employees would find some or all behaviors on that list offensive. The fact that some people are offended by some or all of the above can place those actions squarely under the heading of "sexual harassment."

Although offering or demanding sexual favors in return for rewards in the workplace clearly qualifies as sexual harassment or sex discrimination, a harder-to-recognize kind of harassment is defined by the EEOC. Such conduct "has the purpose or effect of unreasonably interfering with another employee's job performance or creating an intimidating, hostile or offensive work environment." Title VII of the 1964 Civil Rights Act prohibits sexual harassment. Any behavior that may be perceived as harassment is prohibited. Suppose someone is told that keeping his or her job, or receiving a raise or plum assignment, depends on submitting to sexual advances or granting sexual favors; that's sexual harassment, pure and simple.

If it happens to you, report it immediately—to the ethics hot line, to your supervisor, or to another supervisor. The reverse situation—offering sexual favors for a job, an assignment, or a raise—can also be sexual harassment. When an employee gains job advantages in exchange for sex, it's discrimination against other employees, and that's illegal conduct as well. Everyone loses.

A hostile work environment is one where sexual conduct between co-workers is offensive to either one of them or to an observer, and that may include the actions on our list above. Sexual harassment can have negative effects on employees and on the company. It can lead to reduced productivity. An employee trapped in work areas where sexual harassment is tolerated is under stress and becomes less productive. Customers may gain an unfavorable impression of the company's professionalism if they see harassment being tolerated. Supervisors or co-workers can report sexual harassment they observe, resulting in an investigation and discipline of those involved. Knowing what is and what is not acceptable and being sensitive to others' feelings is extremely important.

But what if you believe you are being harassed? A word to the offender might be enough. That person may be unaware of your sensitivity to the behavior. If that doesn't work, report the behavior to your supervisor or another manager, to labor or employee relations, or to the president of the company if you have to.

Education and training play an important role in cultivating an environment free of harassment.[73] Managers throughout many companies have received training in identifying and eliminating sexual harassment problems. Additional training in larger organizations is usually offered by human resources. Some people may fear that their complaints will be ignored or that reporting an incident will become a negative in their work record. Neither is the case. Companies should take all complaints of sexual harassment seriously and investigate each thoroughly and discreetly.[74] Both sides are considered, and disciplinary action is often taken against proven violators, as well as those who make false accusations.

same wage (later wage differences may exist due to performance, seniority, merit systems, and the like). The act, however, is not directly applicable to comparable worth. Comparable worth proponents want to take the Equal Pay Act one step further. Under such an arrangement, factors present in each job (for example, skills, responsibilities, working conditions, effort) are evaluated. A pay structure is based solely on the presence of such factors on the job. The result is that dissimilar jobs equivalent in terms of skills, knowledge, and abilities are paid similarly.

The point of the comparable worth issue revolves around the economic worth of jobs to employers. If jobs are similar, even though they involve different occupations, why shouldn't they be paid the same? The concern here is one of pay disparities: women still earn less than men. While the disparity is lessening, the fact remains that despite significant progress in affirmative action for women, many may have reached a plateau in their organization. That is, laws may prohibit organizations from keeping qualified women out of high-paying positions, but a "glass ceiling" appears to be holding them down.

The **glass ceiling** description reflects why women and minorities aren't more widely represented at the top of today's organizations. The glass ceiling is not, however, synonymous with classic discrimination. Rather, according to the Glass Ceiling Commission, it indicates "institutional and psychological practices, and the limited advancement and mobility of men and women of diverse racial and ethnic

glass ceiling
The invisible barrier that blocks females and minorities from ascending into upper levels of an organization.

backgrounds."[75] It appears that despite significant gains by minorities and women in entry to organizations, women hold less than 16 percent of senior management positions.[76] Although the percentage is low, around the globe it's even worse. For example, in Europe, women hold approximately 5 percent of the top slots; in Japan and Germany, fewer than 3 percent of women are top executives.[77]

To begin to correct this invisible barrier, the OFCCP is expanding its audit compliance reviews. In these reviews, the auditors look to see if government contractors do indeed have training and development programs operating to provide career growth to the affected groups. Should these be lacking, the OFCCP may take legal action to ensure compliance. For example, an audit of the Coca-Cola Company revealed several violations. Consequently, Coca-Cola, while admitting no wrongdoing, made several internal changes to improve the career opportunities of both women and minorities.[78] Beyond those organizations covered under the OFCCP, several are implementing policies and changing the organization's culture to enhance opportunities for women and minorities.[79] With such practices over the past few years, for example, more than 7 million women are now in "full-time executive, administrative, or managerial positions."[80] Similar progress for minorities has been noted, too.[81]

SUMMARY

(This summary relates to the Learning Outcomes identified on page 59.) After having read this chapter you can now

1. **Identify the groups protected under the Civil Rights Act of 1964, Title VII.** The Equal Employment Opportunity Act of 1972 is an important amendment to the Civil Rights Act of 1964, as it granted the EEOC enforcement powers to police the provisions of the act. The Civil Rights Act of 1964, Title VII, gives individuals protection on the basis of race, color, religion, sex, and national origin. In addition to those protected under the 1964 act, amendments to the act, as well as subsequent legislation, give protection to the disabled, veterans, and individuals over age 40. In addition, state laws may supplement this list and include categories such as marital status.

2. **Discuss the importance of the Equal Employment Opportunity Act of 1972.** The Equal Employment Opportunity Act of 1972 is an important amendment to the Civil Rights Act of 1964 as it granted the EEOC enforcement powers to police the provisions of the act.

3. **Describe affirmative action plans.** Affirmative action plans are good-faith efforts by organizations to actively recruit and hire protected group members and show measurable results. Such plans are voluntary actions by an organization.

4. **Define what is meant by the terms *adverse impact, adverse treatment,* and *protected group members*.** An adverse impact is any consequence of employment that results in a disparate rate of selection, promotion, or termination of protected group members. Adverse treatment occurs when members of a protected group receive different treatment than other employees. A protected group member is any individual who is afforded protection under discrimination laws.

5. **Identify the important components of the Americans with Disabilities Act of 1990.** The Americans with Disabilities Act of 1990 provides employment protection for individuals who have qualified disabilities. The act also requires organizations to make reasonable accommodations to provide qualified individuals access to the job.

6. **Explain the coverage of the Family and Medical Leave Act of 1993.** The Family and Medical Leave Act grants up to 12 weeks of unpaid leave for family or medical matters. Fetal protection laws were overturned because they created an adverse impact for women.

7. **Discuss how a business can protect itself from discrimination charges.** A business can protect itself from discrimination charges first by having HRM practices that do not adversely affect protected groups, through supported claims of job relatedness, bona fide occupational qualifications, or a valid seniority system.

8. **Specify the HRM importance of the *Griggs v. Duke Power* case.** *Griggs v. Duke Power* was one of the most important Supreme Court rulings that pertain to EEO. Based on this case, items used to screen applicants had to be related to the job. Additionally, post-*Griggs*, the burden was on the employer to prove discrimination did not occur.

9. **Define what constitutes sexual harassment in today's organizations.** Sexual harassment is a serious problem existing in today's enterprises. Sexual harassment is defined as any verbal or physical conduct toward an individual that (1) creates an intimidating, offensive, or hostile environment; (2) unreasonably interferes with an individual's work; or (3) adversely affects an employee's employment opportunities.

10. **Discuss what is meant by the term *glass ceiling*.** The glass ceiling is an invisible barrier existing in today's organizations that keeps minorities and women from ascending to higher employment levels in the workplace.

DEMONSTRATING COMPREHENSION: *Questions for Review*

1. What is the Civil Rights Act of 1964 and whom does it protect?
2. What are the *Griggs v. Duke Power* implications for HRM?
3. What is an adverse impact? How does it differ from adverse treatment?
4. What is meant by reasonable accommodation as it pertains to the Americans with Disabilities Act of 1990?
5. What is "business necessity" as it applies to equal employment opportunity?
6. How can HRM provide supporting documentation for business necessity?
7. In what ways do employment laws differ in a global environment?
8. Identify and explain how organizations can use BFOQs or seniority systems to defend charges of discrimination.
9. What is sexual harassment? Identify and describe the three elements that may constitute sexual harassment.
10. What are the arguments for a glass ceiling existing in today's organizations?

KEY TERMS

adverse (disparate) impact

adverse (disparate) treatment

affirmative action

Age Discrimination in Employment Act (ADEA)

Albemarle Paper Company v. Moody

Americans with Disabilities Act of 1990

bona fide occupational qualification (BFOQ)

Civil Rights Act of 1866

Civil Rights Act of 1991

comparable worth

Equal Employment Opportunity Act

Equal Employment Opportunity Commission

Family and Medical Leave Act of 1993

4/5ths rule

glass ceiling

Griggs v. Duke Power Company

McDonnell-Douglas Corp. v. Green

Pregnancy Discrimination Act of 1978

reasonable accommodation

reverse discrimination

sexual harassment

Title VII

Wards Cove Packing Company v. Atonio

VISUAL SUMMARY

CHAPTER 3: EQUAL EMPLOYMENT OPPORTUNITY

1 Laws Affecting Discriminatory Practices

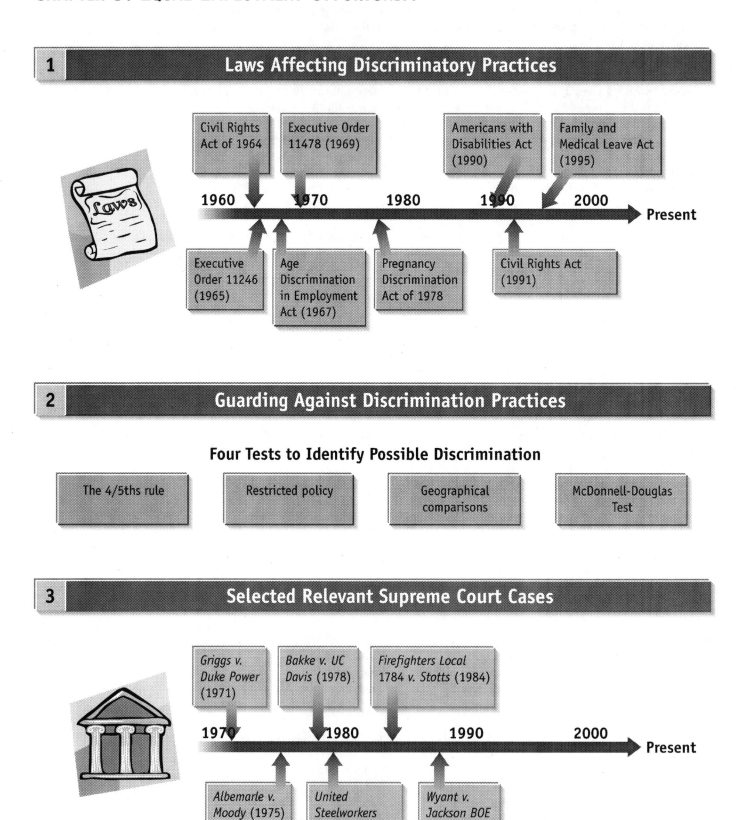

Civil Rights Act of 1964

Executive Order 11478 (1969)

Americans with Disabilities Act (1990)

Family and Medical Leave Act (1995)

1960   1970   1980   1990   2000   Present

Executive Order 11246 (1965)

Age Discrimination in Employment Act (1967)

Pregnancy Discrimination Act of 1978

Civil Rights Act (1991)

2 Guarding Against Discrimination Practices

Four Tests to Identify Possible Discrimination

The 4/5ths rule

Restricted policy

Geographical comparisons

McDonnell-Douglas Test

3 Selected Relevant Supreme Court Cases

Griggs v. Duke Power (1971)

Bakke v. UC Davis (1978)

Firefighters Local 1784 v. Stotts (1984)

1970   1980   1990   2000   Present

Albemarle v. Moody (1975)

United Steelworkers v. Weber (1979)

Wyant v. Jackson BOE

4   Enforcing Equal Employment Opportunity

Equal Employment Opportunity Commission (EEOC)	Office of Federal Contract Compliance Programs (OFCCP)

Four-Step Process Followed by EEOC and OFCCP to Pursue Charges that Are Filed

1. EEOC will notify the company within 10 days of filing and begin investigation
2. EEOC notifies in writing within 120 days
   - if unfounded, process stops
   - if founded, EEOC tries to resolve
3. If informal process is unsuccessful, EEOC begins formal settlement meeting (mediation)
4. If unsuccessful, EEOC may file charges in court

5   HRM in a Global Environment

- HRM laws differ throughout the world.
- Know the local laws that apply.

6   Current Issues in Employment Law

- **Sexual Harassment**—any unwanted behavior of a sexual nature that affects an individual's employment
- **The Glass Ceiling**—institutional and psychological practices that limit the advancement and mobility of men and women of diverse racial and ethnic backgrounds

CROSSWORD COMPREHENSION

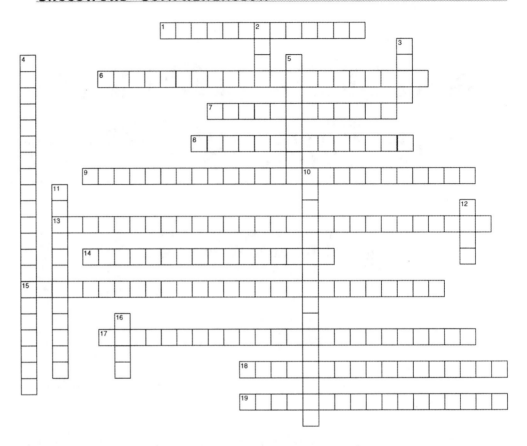

ACROSS

1. a consequence of an employment practice that results in a greater rejection rate for minority group members
6. a claim made by white males that minority candidates are given preferential treatment in employment decisions
7. equal pay for similar jobs
8. a practice in an organization to actively seek, hire, and promote minority group members
9. law prohibiting discrimination against a woman who is carrying a child
13. Supreme Court case that clarified the requirements for using and validating tests in the selection process
14. an employment situation where protected group members receive treatment different from other employees
15. the act that extended EEO coverage to the disabled
17. providing the necessary technology to enable affected individuals to do a job
18. landmark Supreme Court decision stating that tests must fairly measure the knowledge or skills required for a job
19. anything of a sexual nature that creates a hostile work environment

DOWN

2. the arm of the federal government empowered to handle discrimination cases
3. job requirements that are reasonably necessary to meet the normal operations of the business
4. the act that provides employees up to 12 weeks of unpaid leave each year to care for their own illness or that of a family member
5. most prominent piece of legislation stating the illegality of discriminating against individuals based on race, religion, color, sex, or national origin

10. Supreme Court case that led to a four-part test used to determine if discrimination has occurred
11. the invisible barrier that blocks females and minorities from ascending into upper levels of an organization
12. the act that prohibits age discrimination
16. the act that granted enforcement powers to the EEOC

HRM WORKSHOP

LINKING CONCEPTS TO PRACTICE: *Discussion Questions*

1. "Affirmative action does not work. When you're hired under an affirmative action program, you're automatically labeled as such and are rarely recognized for the value that you can bring to an organization." Do you agree or disagree with the statement? Defend your position.

2. Given that the white male is becoming a "minority" in the workplace, white males should be afforded affirmative action protection. Do you agree or disagree with this? Explain your rationale.

3. "If all organizations would hire based solely on the ability to do the job, there would be no need for equal employment opportunity laws." Do you agree or disagree? Defend your position.

4. "Sexual harassment occurs between two people only. The company should not be held liable for the actions of a few wayward supervisors." Do you agree or disagree with this statement? Explain.

DEVELOPING DIAGNOSTIC AND ANALYTICAL SKILLS

Case Application 3-A: WHEN OVERSIGHT FAILS

What's in a job? For most workers, jobs entail specific and routine work activities. These work activities generally take place on the employer's premise where many different people come together to achieve certain goals. There should be, however, one common element to all work activities—whatever occurs in the office should be related to organizational efforts. Every once in a while, though, this concept evades some employers. When it does, it may be a costly lesson for the organization. Consider the lesson learned at Federal Express regarding an incident that happened in FedEx's Middletown, Pennsylvania, facility.[82]

Marion Shaub worked for FedEx at its Middletown facility. At the time of her employment, Shaub was the only female tractor-trailer driver who worked for FedEx in this facility. Although being the only female in this often male-dominated job brought about some gentle kidding, the jokes and actions by fellow employees gradually turned ugly. Shaub was often subjected to antifemale comments and questioned as to why she wanted to work a man's job. Shaub tried to ignore the comments directed toward her, but they became more pronounced and mean-spirited. Although she was attempting to do her job to the best of her abilities, the comments got nastier. She eventually saw them as threats against her. And that's where, in Shaub's mind, the line had been crossed.

Shaub reported to her supervisor that the "guys" were creating a threatening work environment for her. She had hoped that her male supervisor would speak to fellow employees and have such abuse stopped. But it didn't work out that way. Instead, after filing her complaint, Shaub was subjected to even more abuse, this time including the sabotage of the brakes of her truck. Moreover, as a general rule, when a package is over a certain weight, two FedEx employees are expected to handle the carton. When Shaub had such a package, she found that no one would help her.

To Shaub's dismay, FedEx officials in the Middletown facility did nothing to stop the harassment. Her complaints and requests for help fell on deaf ears. Finally, in desperation, she filed a suit against FedEx for sex discrimination and retaliation.

Under federal discrimination laws, it's the employer's responsibility to ensure that the workplace is safe and free from any form of discrimination. Regardless of employees' background, gender, age, and the like, individuals are not to be treated differently. But when discrimination occurs and management does little or nothing about it, the organization can be held liable.

For FedEx, Shaub's experiences proved a painful lesson. After conducting an investigation and finding her accusations to be factual, the EEOC awarded Shaub more than $3 million. This included monies for her lost wages, for the pain and suffering she endured, and $2.5 million in punitive damages as punishment because FedEx didn't protect her civil rights as an employee.

Questions:

1. Where do you believe HR failed Marion Shaub in this case? Explain.
2. What do you believe FedEx must do differently to ensure that such an event does not occur again?
3. What effect on (a) corporate image and (b) attracting female employees to the organization do you believe this case has had on FedEx? Describe.

Case Application 3-B: TEAM FUN!

Team Fun

Tony, the new director of human resources, and Edna, the compensation and benefits manager, are hanging employment legislation posters in RETREAT, the TEAM FUN! employee cafeteria. Edna offers, "I remember some woman who applied for a job to advertise men's baseball gear and sued when she didn't get the job. The EEOC said she had no case. A couple of years ago, we moved Fred from fitness demos to stock management because he couldn't do the treadmill or lift the big weights anymore. There was talk about an age discrimination case because he was 57, but that never went anywhere."

Tony asks, "Do you realize that all of the warehouse workers are male and all the RETREAT workers are female?"

Edna replies, "What's your point?" Tony waves his hand at the EEOC information they have displayed. Edna shrugs, "This is the best job I ever had. If you ask anyone else who works here, they will say the same thing."

Questions:

1. What is the probable defense for the baseball gear job (BFOQ, 4/5ths rule, glass ceiling)? Explain.
2. Why didn't Fred's age discrimination case go anywhere?
3. Is TEAM FUN! open to discrimination charges in other areas?
4. What should be done to protect TEAM FUN! from discrimination charges?

WORKING WITH A TEAM: *What's Your Perception?*

Could these situations demonstrate sexual harassment or prohibitive behaviors? Answer *true* or *false* to each question. Make whatever assumptions you need to make to form your opinion. Form into groups of three or four students and discuss each of your responses. Where differences exist, come to some consensus on the situation. Then, you can look at the footnote for suggested responses.[83]

1. A female supervisor frequently praises the work of a highly competent male employee.
2. A male employee prominently posts a centerfold from a female pornographic magazine.
3. A female employee voluntarily accepts a date with her male supervisor.
4. A male employee is given favored work assignments in exchange for arranging dates for his boss.
5. A female employee is offered a job promotion in exchange for sex.
6. A client pressures a female salesperson for dates and sexual favors in exchange for a large purchase.
7. A female requests that her male assistant stay in her hotel room to save on expenses while out of town at a conference and holds acceptance as a job condition for continued employment.
8. A male has asked two female co-workers to stop embarrassing him by telling jokes of a sexual nature and sharing their sexual fantasies, but they continue, telling him a "real man wouldn't be embarrassed."
9. Although he has shared with his co-worker that rubbing his shoulders and arms, calling him "Babe" in front of his co-workers, and pinching him is offensive, she continues to touch him in a way that makes him feel uncomfortable.
10. Al tells Marge an offensive joke, but when Marge says "Al, I don't appreciate your nasty jokes," Al responds, "I'm sorry, Marge, you're right, I shouldn't have told that one at work."

LEARNING AN HRM SKILL: *Investigating a Harassment Complaint*

About the skill: Harassment, sexual or otherwise, is a major issue for today's organizations. Given the rulings at all court levels, organizations can and should limit their liability. Below are recommended nine steps.

1. *Issue a sexual harassment policy describing what constitutes harassment and what is inappropriate behavior.* Just stating that harassment is unacceptable at your organization is not enough. This policy must identify specific unacceptable behaviors. The more explicit these identifications, the less chance of misinterpretation later on.
2. *Institute a procedure (or link to an existing one) to investigate harassment charges.* Employees, as well as the courts, need to understand what avenue is available for an employee to levy a complaint. This, too, should be clearly stated in the policy and widely disseminated to employees.
3. *Inform all employees of the sexual harassment policy.* Educate employees (via training) about the policy and how it

will be enforced. Don't assume that the policy will convey the information simply because it is a policy. It must be effectively communicated to all employees. Some training may be required to help in this understanding.

4. *Train management personnel in how to deal with harassment charges and in what responsibility they have to the individual and the organization.* Poor supervisory practices in this area can expose the company to tremendous liability. Managers must be trained in how to recognize signs of harassment and where to go to help the victim. Because of the magnitude of the issue, a manager's performance evaluation should reinforce this competency.
5. *Investigate all harassment charges immediately.* All means *all*—even those that you suspect are invalid. You must give each charge of harassment your attention and investigate it by searching for clues, witnesses, and so on. Investigating

the charge is also consistent with our societal view of justice. Remember, the alleged harasser also has rights. These, too, must be protected by giving the individual the opportunity to respond. You may also have an objective party review the data before implementing your decision.

6. *Take corrective action as necessary.* Discipline the harassers and "make whole" the harassed individual. If the charge can be substantiated, you must take corrective action, up to dismissing the individual. If the punishment does not fit the crime, you may be reinforcing or condoning the behavior. The harassed individual should also be given whatever was taken away. For example, if the sexual behavior led to an individual's resignation, making the person whole would mean reinstatement, with full back pay and benefits.

7. *Continue to follow up on the matter to ensure that no further harassment occurs or that retaliation does not occur.* One concern individuals have in coming forward with sexual harassment charges is the possibility of retaliation against them—especially if the harasser has been disciplined. Continue to observe what affects these individuals through follow-up conversations with them.

8. *Periodically review turnover records to determine if a potential problem may be arising.* (This may be EEO audits, exit interviews, and the like.) A wealth of information at your disposal may offer indications of problems. For example, if only minorities are resigning in a particular department, that may indicate that a serious problem exists. Pay attention to your regular reports and search for trends that may be indicated.

9. *Don't forget to privately recognize individuals who bring these matters forward.* Without their courageous effort, the organization might have faced with tremendous liability. These individuals took a risk in coming forward. You should show your appreciation for that risk. Besides, if others know that such risk is worthwhile, they may feel more comfortable in coming to you when any type of problem exists.

ENHANCING YOUR COMMUNICATION SKILLS

1. Several Supreme Court cases relating to sexual harassment were decided in the early 2000s. Visit the Supreme Court's Web site (www.supremecourtus.gov) and research these cases. Then provide a three- to five-page write-up regarding the implications these cases had for same-sex harassment, responsibilities of management in sexual harassment matters, and the determination of harassment even when an implied threat is not carried out.

2. Contact your local EEO office (may be called Human Rights Commission or Fair Employment Practice Agencies). Determine what equal employment opportunity laws exist in your state that go beyond those required under federal law. Provide a two- to three-page write-up of your findings.

3. Visit your college's EEO/Affirmative Action officer. Find out what specific EEO requirements on your campus affect students, faculty, and staff in matters such as recruiting, promotion, sexual harassment, and so on. Provide a two- to three-page write up of your findings.

FOUR

Should an employee of any company, large or small, feel obligated to inform a manager about an inter-workplace relationship? Can an employee be safely terminated from his or her job for having a romantic relationship with a co-worker? And how discreet should the romance of two co-workers be kept to maintain a professional working environment? While thinking about your answers to these questions, consider this brief story about Robert Barbee.[1]

A few years ago, Barbee was a well-respected national sales manager for Household Automotive Finance Corporation in California. However, Barbee was fired soon after the company found out that he was dating Melanie Tomita, another salesperson within the company.

The firing caused many legal battles between Barbee and the company, taken up in the California courts. According to Barbee, this relationship did not jeopardize Household Automotive Finance, seeing that Tomita was not directly supervised by Barbee and they worked in different locations. He also argued that their relationship was kept completely outside of their working environment.

(*Source:* Image Source Limited/Index Stock)

However, the California appeals court sided against Barbee in November 2004, declaring that such a relationship was likely to create conflicts of interest. While Barbee is currently employed by another company, and has since married Tomita, this case brought up a major ethical issue that cannot be forgotten. Does firing an employee on such grounds violate this employee's right to privacy?

Many would respond yes to this question. However, there is also some truth that dating within the workplace has provided many managers with obstacles for maintaining professionalism in their company. Managers fear legal issues as seen with Barbee, fear facing charges of sexual harassment, and also see this type of dating as a threat to a company's productivity. However, though many managers may disapprove, most companies do not have written restrictions on employee/employee dating. Rather, most employees are simply forbidden from working on the same team as their significant other.

Workplace romance is becoming a common occurrence, and therefore, many companies cannot afford to avoid the issue. A number of polls across the United States have showed an increase in managerial disproval of such affairs. In fact, the numbers from the Society for Human Resource Management show that bosses are taking more penalizing stances in cases now than they were even as few as five years ago—55 percent of 581 companies surveyed in 2001 feel that an employee who mismanaged a workplace romance should be transferred, a 13 percent increase from a 1998 study; 35 percent of surveyed companies reported that employees engaging in such romances should be terminated, an 8 percent increase in numbers from the 1998 survey.

Many employers have found office relationships to be inevitable and have subsequently established ways to handle such occurrences. While internal workplace relationships may be hard to balance, it certainly can be done. Essentially, maturity and professionalism are the key components in separating work from romance. If the relationship with a co-worker fails, the employees need to be mature enough to face each other day after day, be able to work together, and maintain a professional attitude.

Employee Rights and HR Communications

Learning Outcomes

After reading this chapter, you will be able to

1. Explain the intent of the Privacy Act of 1974, the Drug-Free Workplace Act of 1988, and the Polygraph Protection Act of 1988 and their effects on HRM.

2. Describe the provisions of the Worker Adjustment and Retraining Notification Act of 1988.

3. Identify the pros and cons of employee drug testing.

4. Explain why honesty tests are used in hiring.

5. Discuss the implications of the employment-at-will doctrine and identify the five exceptions to it.

6. Define discipline and the contingency factors that determine the severity of discipline.

7. Describe the general guidelines for administering discipline.

8. Describe the purpose of the employee handbook and explain what information should be included in the handbook.

9. Discuss the critical components of an effective suggestion program.

10. Identify characteristics of workplace spirituality.

11. Identify how employee counseling can assist a poorly performing employee.

Introduction

Employee rights has become one of the more important issues for human resource management. Individuals are guaranteed certain rights based on amendments to the U.S. Constitution. For instance, the Fourth Amendment prohibits illegal searches and seizures by the government or its agents. However, this does not exclude those outside the government, like businesses, from such an activity. Are employers all-powerful in this arena? No! In fact, in more situations—such as terminating an employee or maintaining health files on employees for insurance purposes—such organizational practices may be more constrained. Consequently, various laws and Supreme Court rulings are establishing guidelines for employers dealing with employee privacy and other matters. Let's turn to these laws.

Employee Rights Legislation and Its HRM Implications

Over the past few decades, federal laws have given specific protection to employees. These laws are the Privacy Act of 1974, the Drug-Free Workplace Act of 1988, the Employee Polygraph Protection Act of 1988, and the Worker Adjustment and Retraining Notification Act of 1988. Let's briefly explore each of these.

The Privacy Act of 1974: HRM Requirements

When an organization begins the hiring process, it typically establishes a personnel file for that person. The file is maintained throughout a person's employment. Any pertinent information, like the completed application, letters of recommendation, performance evaluations, or disciplinary warnings, is kept in the file. Originally, the contents of these files often were known only to those who had access to them—usually managers and HRM personnel. The **Privacy Act of 1974** sought to change that imbalance of information. This act, applicable to only federal government agencies, requires that an employee's personnel file be open for inspection.[2] This means that employees are permitted to review their files periodically to ensure that the information contained within is accurate. The Privacy Act also gives these federal employees the right to review letters of recommendation written on their behalf.

Even though this act applies solely to federal workers, it provided impetus for state legislatures to pass similar laws governing employees of state- and private-sector enterprises. This legislation is often more comprehensive and includes protection regarding how employers disseminate information on past and current employees. For HRM, a key question is how employees should be given access to their files. Although the information contained within rightfully may be open for inspection, certain restrictions must be addressed. First, any information the employee has waived his or her right to review must be kept separate. For instance, job applicants often waive their right to see letters of recommendation written for them. When that happens, human resources is not obligated to make that information available to the employee. Second, an employee can't simply demand to immediately see his or her file; there is typically a 24-hour turnaround time. Consequently, organizations frequently establish special review procedures. For example, whether the employee can review the file alone or only in the presence of an HRM representative is up to each organization. In either case, personnel files generally are not permitted to leave the HRM area. And although an

Privacy Act of 1974

Requires federal government agencies to make available information in an individual's personnel file.

individual may take notes about the file's contents, copying the file often is not permitted.

The increasing use of computers in HRM has complicated the issue of file reviews. Because much of this information is now stored in computerized employee data systems, access has been further constrained. Yet although computerization of HRM files is a more complicated system, appropriate access to this information should not be any different from a paper file; employees still have a right to see the information about themselves, regardless of where it is kept. Gaining entry into computerized information, however, can be a more time-consuming process. Many times, such access requires certain security clearances to special screens—clearance not available to everyone. However, as technology continues to improve, HRM will be better able to implement procedures to give employees access, while simultaneously protecting the integrity of the system.

Companies are also being held accountable to the **Fair Credit Reporting Act of 1971,** an extension to the Privacy Act. In many organizations, the employment process includes a credit check on the applicant. The purpose of such checks is to obtain information about the individual's "character, general reputation," and various other personal characteristics. Typically, companies can obtain this information by two approaches. The first is through a credit reporting agency, similar to when you apply for a loan. In this instance, the employer is required to notify the individual that a credit report is being obtained. However, if an applicant is rejected based on information in the report, the individual must be provided a copy of the credit report, as well as a means for appealing the accuracy of the findings. The second type of credit report is obtained through a third-party investigation. Under this arrangement, not only is one's credit checked, but people known to the applicant are interviewed regarding the applicant's lifestyle, spending habits, and character. For an organization to use this type of approach, the applicant must be informed of the process in writing and, as with the credit report, must be notified of the report's details if the information is used to negatively affect an employment decision. Keep in mind, however, that how the information is used must be job relevant. If, for example, an organization denies employment to an individual who once filed for bankruptcy, and this information has no bearing on the individual's ability to do the job, the organization may be opening itself up to a challenge in the courts.

Fair Credit Reporting Act of 1971
Requires an employer to notify job candidates of its intent to check into their credit.

Credit report information used in employment decisions must be job relevant.

The Drug-Free Workplace Act of 1988 and HRM

The **Drug-Free Workplace Act of 1988** was passed to help keep the problem of substance abuse from entering the workplace. Under the act, government agencies, federal contractors, and those receiving federal funds ($25,000 or more) are required to actively pursue a drug-free environment. In addition, the act requires employees who hold certain jobs in companies regulated by the Department of Transportation (DOT) and the Nuclear Regulatory Commission to be subjected to drug tests. For example, long-haul truck drivers, regulated by the DOT, are required to take drug tests.

Other stipulations address organizations covered under this act. For example, the enterprise must establish its drug-free work environment policy and disseminate it to its employees. This policy must spell out employee expectations in terms of being substance free and infraction penalties. In addition, the organization must provide substance-abuse awareness programs to its employees.

No doubt this act has created difficulties for organizations. To comply with the act, they must obtain information about their employees. The whole issue of

Drug-Free Workplace Act of 1988
Requires specific government-related groups to ensure that their workplace is drug free.

Can an organization use a polygraph in its HRM activities? Generally speaking, no. However, under certain circumstances (like assisting in resolving an employee theft when a chief suspect has been identified) and for certain jobs (like those involving security), they can and do. (*Source:* Robert E. Daemmrich/Stone/Getty Images)

Polygraph Protection Act of 1988

Prohibits the use of lie detectors in screening all job applicants.

Worker Adjustment and Retraining Notification (WARN) Act of 1988

Specifies for employers notification requirements when closing down a plant or laying off large numbers of workers.

drug testing in today's companies is a major one, and we'll come back to its applications later in this chapter.

The Polygraph Protection Act of 1988

As a criminal investigation analyst applicant for the Federal Bureau of Investigation (FBI), you are asked to submit to a polygraph test as a condition of employment. Unsure of what will transpire, you agree to be tested. During the examination, you are asked if you have ever used Ecstasy. You respond that you never have, but the polygraph records that you are not telling the truth. Because suspicion of illegal substance use is grounds for disqualification from the job, you are removed from consideration. Can this organization use the polygraph information against you? If the job involves security operations, it can!

However, the **Polygraph Protection Act of 1988** prohibits employers in the private sector from using polygraph tests (often referred to as lie-detector tests) in all employment decisions.[3] Based on the law, companies may no longer use these tests to screen all job applicants.[4] The act was passed because polygraphs were used inappropriately. In general, polygraph tests have been found to have little job-related value, which makes their effectiveness questionable.[5] However, the Employee Polygraph Protection Act did not eliminate their use in organizations altogether. The law permits their use, for example, when theft occurs in the organization, but this process is regulated, too. The polygraph cannot be used in a "witch hunt." For example, the Employee Polygraph Protection Act prohibits employers with a theft in the organization from testing all employees in an attempt to determine the guilty party. However, if an investigation into the theft points to a particular employee, then the employer can ask that employee to submit to a polygraph. Even in this case, however, the employee has the right to refuse to take a polygraph test without fear of retaliation from the employer. And in cases in which one does submit to the test, the employee must receive, in advance, a list of questions that will be asked. Futhermore, the employee has the right to challenge the results if he or she believes the test was inappropriately administered. Exhibit 4-1 contains the Department of Labor's Notice of Polygraph Testing explaining employee rights.

The Worker Adjustment and Retraining Notification Act of 1988 and HRM

Early in the new millennium, many companies either closed a business unit, sold the company, or laid off hundreds of employees. Can a business do this without notifying employees? No![6] The **Worker Adjustment and Retraining Notification (WARN) Act of 1988**,[7] sometimes called the Plant Closing Bill, places specific requirements on employers considering significant changes in staffing levels. Under WARN, an organization employing 100 or more individuals must notify workers 60 days in advance if it is going to close its facility or lay off 50 or more individuals.[8] Should a company fail to provide this advance notice, the penalty is to pay employees a sum of money equal to salary and benefits for each day notification was not given (up to 60 days).[9] However, the law does recognize that under certain circumstances, advance notice may be impossible. Assume, for example, a company is having financial difficulties and is seeking to raise money to keep the organization afloat. If they fail and subsequently file for bankruptcy, WARN would not apply.

Plant closings, similar to the employee rights issues raised previously, continue to pose problems for human resource management. These laws have created specific guidelines for organizations to follow. None precludes the enterprise from doing what is necessary. Rather, the laws exist to ensure that whatever action the organization takes, it also protects employee rights. A summary of these laws is presented in Exhibit 4-2.

EXHIBIT 4-1
Employee Polygraph Protection Act Notification

U.S. DEPARTMENT OF LABOR
EMPLOYMENT STANDARDS ADMINISTRATION

Wage and Hour Division
Washington, D.C. 20210

NOTICE

EMPLOYEE POLYGRAPH PROTECTION ACT

The Employee Polygraph Protection Act prohibits most private employers from using lie detector tests either for pre-employment screening or during the course of employment.

Prohibitions

Employers are generally prohibited from requiring or requesting any employee or job applicant to take a lie detector test, and from discharging, disciplining, or discriminating against an employee or prospective employee for refusing to take a test or for exercising other rights under the Act.

Exemptions*

Federal, State and local governments are not affected by the law. Also, the law does not apply to tests given by the Federal Government to certain private individuals engaged in national security-related activities.

The Act permits *polygraph* (a kind of lie detector) tests to be administered in the private sector, subject to restrictions, to certain prospective employees of security service firms (armored car, alarm, and guard), and of pharmaceutical manufacturers, distributors and dispensers.

The Act also permits polygraph testing, subject to restrictions, of certain employees of private firms who are reasonably suspected of involvement in a workplace incident (theft, embezzlement, etc.) that resulted in economic loss to the employer.

Examinee Rights

Where polygraph tests are permitted, they are subject to numerous strict standards concerning the conduct and length of the test. Examinees have a number of specific rights, including the right to a written notice before testing, the right to refuse or discontinue a test, and the right not to have test results disclosed to unauthorized persons.

Enforcement

The Secretary of Labor may bring court actions to restrain violations and assess civil penalties up to $10,000 against violators. Employees or job applicants may also bring their own court actions.

Additional Information

Additional information may be obtained, and complaints of violations may be filed, at local offices of the Wage and Hour Division, which are listed in the telephone directory under U.S. Government, Department of Labor, Employment Standards Administration.

THE LAW REQUIRES EMPLOYERS TO DISPLAY THIS POSTER WHERE EMPLOYEES AND JOB APPLICANTS CAN READILY SEE IT.

*The law does not preempt any provision of any State or local law or any collective bargaining agreement which is more restrictive with respect to lie detector tests.

U.S. DEPARTMENT OF LABOR
EMPLOYMENT STANDARDS ADMINISTRATION

Wage and Hour Division
Washington, D.C. 20210

WH Publication 1462
September 1988

EXHIBIT 4-2
*Summary of Laws Affecting
Employee Rights*

LAW	EFFECT
Fair Credit Reporting Act	Requires employers to notify individuals that credit information is being gathered and may be used in the employment decision.
Privacy Act	Requires government agencies to make information in their personnel files available to employees.
Drug-Free Workplace Act	Requires government agencies, federal contractors, and those who receive government monies to take steps to ensure that their workplace is drug free.
Employee Polygraph Protection Act	Prohibits the use of lie-detector tests in screening all job applicants. Permits their use under certain circumstances.
Worker Adjustment and Retraining Notification Act	Requires employers with 100 or more employees contemplating closing a facility or laying off 50 or more employees to give 60 days' notice of the pending action.

CURRENT ISSUES REGARDING EMPLOYEE RIGHTS

Recently, emphasis has been placed on curtailing specific employer practices, as well as addressing what employees may rightfully expect from their organizations. These basic issues are drug testing, honesty tests, employee monitoring and workplace security, and workplace romance.

Drug Testing

Previously in our discussion of the Drug-Free Workplace Act, we mentioned the legislation applicable to certain organizations. However, the severity of substance abuse in our organizations has prompted many organizations not covered by this 1988 act to voluntarily begin drug testing. Why? It is estimated that a sizable percentage of the U.S. workforce may be abusing some substance (such as drugs or alcohol).[10] Moreover, nearly half of all on-the-job injuries and work-related deaths are attributed to substance abuse. And if that weren't enough, it is estimated that employee substance abuse costs U.S. companies more than $100 billion annually in increased health-care costs, lost productivity, and workplace accidents.[11] Making this matter worse are the companies found on the Internet offering "drug-free" urine or other products such as shampoo "guaranteed" to help one pass a drug test.[12]

As a result of the numbers, many private employers began to implement programs to curb substance-related problems in their organizations.[13] For instance, Home Depot and Motorola test all current employees as well as job applicants. In fact, walk into any Home Depot and you'll see prominently displayed at the entrance a sign that says something to the effect that "the employees of this store are drug free. Applicants who cannot pass a drug screening test should not apply." Drug testing is designed to identify the abusers, either to help them overcome their problem (current employees) or avoid hiring them in the first place (applicants). In this arena, many issues arise. For example, what happens if an individual refuses to take the drug test? What happens if the test is positive? Let's look at some possible answers.

A major concern for opponents of drug testing is how the process works and how the information will be used. **Drug testing** in today's organizations should be conducted to eliminate illegal substance use in the workplace, not to catch those using them. For instance, drug testing may make better sense when there is a reason to suspect substance abuse or after a work-related accident. Although many might say that the same outcome is achieved, it's the process, and how employees view the process, that matters. In some organizations, individuals who refuse the drug test may be terminated immediately. Although this treatment appears harsh, the ill effect of employing a substance abuser is perceived as too great. But what if that person took the drug test and failed it? Many organizations place these individuals into a rehabilitation program with the intent to help them. However, if they don't accept the help, or later fail another test, they can be terminated.

Applicants, on the other hand, present a different story. If an applicant tests positive for substance abuse, that applicant generally drops from consideration. The company's liability begins and ends there—they are not required to offer those applicants any help. But that needn't imply that applicants can't "straighten out" and try again. It is recommended that employers conduct applicant drug testing only after a conditional job offer is made. That is, the job offer is contingent on the applicant passing a drug test. Why a drug test at this stage? To properly administer the test requires information about one's health and medication record. Posing such questions before making a conditional offer may violate the Americans with Disabilities Act.

From all indications, drug testing can lessen the effects of drugs and alcohol on job-related activities: lower productivity, higher absenteeism, and job-related accidents.[14] (See Did you know?) Nonetheless, until individuals believe that the tests are administered properly and employees' dignity is respected, criticism of drug testing is likely to continue. In many instances, drug tests gave a false reading or the specimen was improperly handled. Many results may be false—that is, attributed to legitimate medication or the food one eats.[15] To help with this concern, companies are moving toward more precise tests—ones that involve no body fluids and some that involve computers.[16]

As we move forward in drug-testing methodologies, the process should continue to improve. However, we must not forget individuals' rights—especially to privacy. Most employees recognize why companies must drug test but expect to be treated

drug testing
The process of testing applicants/employees to determine if they are using illicit substances.

DID YOU KNOW?

WHY ORGANIZATIONS DRUG TEST

Over two-thirds of all U.S. organizations use some form of drug testing—either as a preemployment requirement, a random testing of current employees, or a required test after a workplace accident has happened. Why are companies likely to do this? Consider the following statistics. Substance abusers are:

- 10 times more likely to miss work;
- 5 times more likely to file a workers' compensation claim;
- 3.6 times more likely to be involved in a work-related accident;
- 33% less productive than nonusers; and
- costing U.S. corporations nearly $100 billion annually from the above.

Utilizing tests that are administered using urine, blood, or hair samples, organizations most commonly look for such substances as marijuana, alcohol, amphetamines, cocaine, opiates such as heroin, and phencyclidine (PCP). Depending on the situation, organizations may also test for such substances as Valium, Ecstasy, LSD, and certain inhalants.

Source: K. Blumberg, "Critical Components of Workplace Drug Testing," *SHRM White paper* (July 2004), available online at www.shrm.org/hrresources/whitepapers_published/CMS_009212.asp.

humanely in the process; they also want safeguards built into the process to challenge false tests. And if a problem appears, many may want help, not punishment. Organizations can take several steps to create this positive atmosphere, and this is where HRM comes into play. HRM must issue its policies on substance abuse and communicate them to every employee. The policies must state what is prohibited, under what conditions an individual will be tested, consequences of failing the test, and how testing will be handled. Making clear what is expected, as well as what the company intends to do, can reduce the emotional aspect of this process. Where such policies exist, questions of legality and employee privacy issues are reduced.

Honesty Tests

honesty test

A specialized question-and-answer test designed to assess one's honesty.

Honesty tests typically focus on two areas: theft and substance abuse.

How would you respond to the question: How often do you tell the truth? All the time? Sorry, we can't hire you because everyone has stretched the truth at some point in life. So you must be lying, and therefore are not the honest employee we desire. Most of the time? Sorry again! We can't afford to hire someone who may not have the highest ethical standards. Sound like a catch-22? Welcome to the world of **honesty tests** (sometimes referred to as integrity tests). Although polygraph testing has been significantly curtailed in the hiring process, employers have found another mechanism that supposedly provides similar information.

These integrity tests mostly entice applicants to provide information about themselves that otherwise would be hard to obtain. They tend to focus on two particular areas, theft and drug use, but are not simply indicators of what has happened; typically, they assess an applicant's past dishonest behavior and that individual's attitude toward dishonesty. One would anticipate that applicants would try to answer these questions to avoid "being caught," or would even lie; however, research findings suggest otherwise. That is, individuals frequently perceive that being dishonest may be okay as long as you are truthful about your dishonesty. As such, applicants may discuss questions in such a way that the tests do reveal the information intended. These tests frequently are designed with multiple questions covering similar topic areas, to assess consistency. If consistency in response is lacking, the test may indicate that an individual is being dishonest.[17]

The effectiveness of these tests, coupled with their lower costs than other types of investigations, have prompted companies to use them in their selection process. In fact, an estimated several thousand organizations are using some variation of honesty tests to screen applicants, testing several million individuals each year.[18] Surprisingly, however, companies using these tests seldom reveal that they do. The large use of these tests has provoked questions about their validity and their potential for adverse impact. Research to date is promising. Although instances have been recorded that indicate that individuals have been wrongly misclassified as dishonest, other studies have indicated that they do not create an adverse impact against protected group members.[19] Based on the evidence, our conclusion is that these tests may be useful for providing more information about applicants but should not be used as the sole criterion in the hiring decision.

Whistle-Blowing

Over the past few years, more emphasis has been placed on companies being good corporate citizens. Incidents like those that occurred at Enron have fueled interest in the area. One aspect of being responsible to the community at large is permitting employees to challenge management's practice without fear of retaliation. This challenge is often referred to as whistle-blowing.

Whistle-blowing occurs when an employee reports the organization to an outside agency for what the employee believes is an illegal or unethical practice. In the past, these employees were often subjected to severe punishment for doing what they believed was right.[20]

Although federal legislation is generally lacking for most employers (the Sarbanes-Oxley Act covers employees of public corporations and a federal law passed in 1989 covers public employees), state laws may be available in some jurisdictions. However, the extent of these laws and how much protection they afford differ greatly. Many firms have voluntarily adopted policies to permit employees to identify problem areas. The thrust of these policies is to have an established procedure whereby employees can safely raise concerns and the company can take corrective action.

It is also important to note that passage of the Sarbanes-Oxley Act (see Chapter 2) gave employees protection for whistle-blowing activities if they perceive company wrongdoing. So long as the employee reasonably believes that some inappropriate or fraudulent activities exist in the organization, they are protected from employer retaliation. This is true whether the allegation is correct or not.[21]

whistle-blowing
A situation in which an employee notifies authorities of wrongdoing in an organization.

Employee Monitoring and Workplace Security

Technology, enhanced in part by improvements in computers, has made some wonderful improvements in our work environment. It has allowed us to be more productive; to work smarter, not harder; and to bring about efficiencies in organizations impossible two decades ago. It has also provided a means of **employee monitoring**—what some would call spying on employees![22]

Workplace security has become a critical issue for employers. Workplace security can be defined as actions on behalf of an employer to ensure that the employer's interests are protected: that is, workplace security focuses on protecting the employer's property and its trade business.[23] Without a doubt, employers must protect themselves. Employee theft, revealing trade secrets to competition, or using the company's customer database for personal gain could damage the company. But how far can this protection extend? Shouldn't we consider employees' rights, too? Yes, but how do we create that balance?[24]

Consider what happened to Callie Johnson. Arriving at work one morning, Callie noticed her boss reading her e-mail. Although company managers verbally stated that e-mail messages were private, the company's written policy was different. Her employer contended that it owned the system and accordingly had the right to see what was going on. And it was right! In fact, employers can even film you in the restroom. But whatever employers deem fair game, they should explain for employees in a company policy.[25]

Part of the problem here goes back to the balance of security. Abuses by some employees—for instance, employees using the company's computer system for gambling purposes, running their own businesses, playing computer games, or pursuing personal matters—have resulted in companies implementing a more "policing" role.[26] This can extend, too, to Internet sites, ensuring that employees are not logging on to adult-oriented Web sites.[27]

As employee-monitoring issues become more noticeable, keep a few things in mind: Employers, as long as they have a policy regarding how employees are monitored, will continue to check on employee behavior.[28] Specifically targeted for this monitoring are system computers, e-mail, and the telephone. In fact, it's estimated most large companies and more than 20 percent of small and mid-sized employers monitor their employees' e-mail and Internet usage.[29] In companies such as Gateway, Continental Airlines, and UPS, employees are continually told that they may be monitored. Undoubtedly, the debate regarding the necessity of this action

employee monitoring
An activity whereby the company keeps informed of its employees' activities.

Be careful; someone is watching. With technology enhancements, companies can monitor many employee activities. Although some may feel this is intrusive, safety and liability issues almost mandate that employers ensure a safe and proper work environment. (*Source:* Spencer Grant/PhotoEdit)

EXHIBIT 4-3
When Workplace Romance Exists

OUTCOMES	PERCENT
No Problems Witnessed	55%
Long-Term Relationship Resulted	19%
Work Disruption Occurred	17%
Someone's Reputation Damaged	5%
One or Both Employees Fired	3%
One or Both Employees Reprimanded	1%

Source: Survey results presented in "Workplace Romance Works Out for Many People, Polls Show," © 2003, *Seattle Times.* Distributed by Knight Ridder/Tribune Business News (February 14, 2003).

will continue. Nonetheless, only when employees understand what the company expects and how it will gather its information will their rights be safeguarded.

Workplace Romance

workplace romance
A personal relationship that develops at work.

The focus on **workplace romance** in our companies today is a direct result of potential discrimination or sexual harassment issues facing our organizations.[30] The work environment has long been a place to develop romantic interests; many individuals have met their mates or significant others through work or organizational contacts.[31] In fact, it is estimated that upward of 70 percent of all employees have had some type of workplace romance.[32] But it has also been a source of problems—especially when the romance ends bitterly. In several cases, following a bitter break-up, one of the individuals filed suit charging retaliation. The majority of executives and HR managers simply prefer to ban all workplace romances.[33]

Exhibit 4-3 lists some outcomes of workplace romances.

What if your significant other is now your boss? Most organizations would find that situation unacceptable.

But what happens when this organization-based love reaches another plateau? What if your significant other is now your boss or has moved on to work for a competitor? Many organizations find such situations unacceptable[34] and try to avoid possible conflicts of interest.

To do so, many issue policies and guidelines—called consensual relationship contracts—on how relationships at work may exist. Those that have policies often offer training to employees on how to manage workplace romances.

THE EMPLOYMENT-AT-WILL DOCTRINE

employment-at-will doctrine
Nineteenth-century common law that permitted employers to discipline or discharge employees at their discretion.

The concept of the **employment-at-will doctrine** is rooted in nineteenth-century common law, which permitted employers to discipline or discharge employees at their discretion. The doctrine seeks to equalize the playing field. If employees can resign at any time they want, why shouldn't an employer have a similar right?

Under the employment-at-will doctrine, an employer can dismiss an employee "for good cause, for no cause, or even for a cause morally wrong, without being guilty of a legal wrong."[35] Of course, even then, you can't fire on the basis of race, religion, sex, national origin, age, or disability. Although this doctrine has existed for more than 100 years, the courts, labor unions, and legislation have attempted to lessen its use.[36] In these instances, jobs are likened to private property. That is, individuals have a right to these jobs unless the organization has specified otherwise. Employees today are challenging the legality of their discharge more frequently. When firing without cause occurs, employees may seek the assistance of the courts to address their wrongful discharge. Most states permit employees to sue their employers if they believe their termination was unjust. These suits contend that through some action on the part of the employer, exceptions to the employment-at-will doctrine exist.

Exceptions to the Doctrine

Although employment-at-will thrives in contemporary organizations, five exceptions can support a wrongful discharge suit: contractual relationship, statutory considerations, public policy violation, implied contracts, and breach of good faith.[37] Let's take a closer look at these.

Contractual Relationship A contractual relationship exists when employers and employees have a legal agreement regarding how employee issues are handled. Under such contractual arrangements, discharge may occur only if it is based on just cause. Where a distinct definition of just cause does not exist, just cause can be shown under guidelines derived from labor arbitration of collective-bargaining relationships (we'll look at discipline in labor-management relationships in Chapter 14):

- Was there adequate warning of consequences of the worker's behavior?
- Are the rules reasonable and related to safe and efficient operations of the business?
- Before discipline was rendered, did a fair investigation of the violation occur?
- Did the investigation yield definite proof of worker activity and wrongdoing?
- Have similar occurrences, both prior and subsequent to this event, been handled in the same way and without discrimination?
- Was the penalty in line with the seriousness of the offense and in reason with the worker's past employment record?[38]

Statutory Considerations In addition to this contractual relationship, federal legislation may play a key role. Discrimination laws such as those discussed in the previous chapter may further constrain an employer's use of at-will terminations. For example, an organization cannot terminate an individual based on his or her age just because such action would save the company some money.

Public Policy Violation Another exception to the employment-at-will doctrine is the public policy violation. Under this exception, an employee cannot be terminated for failing to obey an order from an employer that can be construed as an illegal activity. Should an employee refuse to offer a bribe to a public official to increase the likelihood of the organization obtaining a contract, that employee is protected. Furthermore, employers cannot retaliate against an employee for exercising his or her rights (like serving on a jury). Accordingly, employees cannot be justifiably discharged for exercising their rights in accordance with societal laws and statutes.

Implied Employment Contract The fourth exception to the doctrine is the **implied employment contract**. An implied contract is any verbal or written statement made by members of the organization that suggests organizational guarantees or promises about continued employment.[39] These implied contracts, when they exist, typically take place during employment interviews or are included in an employee handbook. We'll look at employee handbooks late in this chapter.

implied employment contract
Any organizational guarantee or promise about job security.

One of the earlier cases reaffirming implied contracts was *Toussaint v. Blue Cross and Blue Shield of Michigan*.[40] In this case, Toussaint claimed that he was discharged for unjust causes by the organization. He asserted that he was told he'd have a job in the company until he reached retirement age of 65 so long as he did his job. The employee's handbook also clearly reinforced this tenure with statements reflective of discharge for just cause. Even if just cause arose, the discharge could occur only after several disciplinary steps. We'll look at the topic of discipline in the next section. In this case, the court determined that the discharge was improper because the organization implied the permanence of his position.

The issue of implied contracts is changing how HRM operates in several of its functions. For instance, interviewers are increasingly cautious, avoiding anything that could conjure up a contract. Something as innocent as discussing an annual salary may cause problems, for such a comment implies at least 12 months on the job. To avoid this, salaries are often communicated in terms of the amount of pay for each pay period. Many organizations, because management wants to maintain employment-at-will, have disclaimers such as "This handbook is not a contract of employment," or "Employment in the organization is at the will of the employer," on the covers of their employee handbooks and manuals to reinforce their employment-at-will policy. Yet caution is warranted, as a supervisor's statements may override the printed words.

Breach of Good Faith The final exception to the employment-at-will doctrine is the breach of good faith. Although this is the most difficult of the exceptions to prove, in some situations an employer may breach a promise. In one noteworthy case, an individual employed more than 25 years by the National Cash Register Company (NCR) was terminated shortly after completing a major deal with a customer.[41] The employee claimed that he was fired to eliminate NCR's liability to pay him his sales commission. The court ruled that this individual acted in good faith in selling the company's product and reasonably expected his commission. Although NCR had an employment-at-will arrangement with its employees, the court held that his dismissal and their failure to pay commissions were breaches of good faith.

www.wiley.com/college/decenzo
What Would You Do?
EXPERIENCE: Employee Rights

DISCIPLINE AND EMPLOYEE RIGHTS

The exceptions to the employment-at-will doctrine may lead you to think that employers cannot terminate employees or are significantly limited in their action. That's not the point of the discussion. Rather, where exceptions exist, so too may a requirement that such an employment action follow a specific process. That process, and how it works, are embedded in the topic we call discipline.

What Is Discipline?

discipline

A condition in the organization when employees conduct themselves in accordance with the organization's rules and standards of acceptable behavior.

Discipline refers to a condition in the organization where employees conduct themselves in accordance with the organization's rules and standards of acceptable behavior. For the most part, employees discipline themselves by conforming to what is considered proper behavior because they believe it is the reasonable thing to do. Once they know what is expected of them, and assuming they find these standards or rules reasonable, they seek to meet those expectations.[42]

But not all employees will accept the responsibility of self-discipline. Some do not accept the norms of responsible employee behavior (see Workplace Issues). These employees, then, require some degree of extrinsic disciplinary action. We will address this need to impose extrinsic disciplinary action in the following sections.

Factors to Consider When Disciplining

Before we review disciplinary guidelines, we should look at major factors to consider if we are to have fair and equitable disciplinary practices.[43] The following seven contingency factors can help us analyze a discipline problem.

1. *Seriousness of the Problem.* How severe is the problem? As noted previously, dishonesty is usually considered a more serious infraction than reporting to work 20 minutes late.[44]

WORKPLACE ISSUES

MANAGERS SHOULD BE PREPARED BEFORE DISCIPLINING EMPLOYEES

In a perfect world, there would be no disciplining, no policies or procedures to misinterpret or ignore. Each employee would check his or her own work and contribute ways to cut costs, reduce waste, and improve quality and service to both internal and external customers. Lunch hours would never exceed agreed-on limits, and no personal business or phone calls would be conducted on company time or with company resources, equipment, or personnel. No one would blame computers, equipment, managers, the company, or "someone else" for work not completed or completed late or incorrectly. Managers would involve, train, and listen to employees, building teamwork through empowerment and trust. In a perfect world!

In a slightly less perfect but more exciting and challenging world, managers occasionally must discipline employees. Dealing with the effects of the mistakes and masking anger, resentment, disappointment, and disgust to create teaching moments can test even the most patient manager. The challenge is to keep employees focused on their behavior and how to correct or improve it, not on how they're being treated. Following these guidelines should help:

- *Cool off, but don't wait too long.* Even though you might like to ignore the problem and hope that it will go away, don't kid yourself. Any problem has a tendency to escalate from a minor to a major issue. It's not worth it. Become comfortable with positively confronting situations, mutually identifying problems, and agreeing on solutions and follow-up plans. Failing to address issues undermines your credibility and ability to do what you are paid to do: manage.
- *Think before you speak.* Stay calm. It may be tempting to sound off, but how you handle it may be as important

as the issue. Your goal should be to correct the situation, not to further impede the working relationship. You may wish to ask the employee to consider possible solutions and bring one or two to the meeting if appropriate.

- *Always discipline in private, one on one.* Consider using a conference room if added privacy is needed.
- *Follow company disciplinary procedures to ensure fairness and consistency.* If in doubt, take the time to check with the policy manual, your boss, or a personnel officer first. If you don't, you may be the next person in line to be disciplined for not following procedures.
- *Be prepared to hear a variety of both imaginative and worn-out excuses.* These can range from "I was stuck in traffic" to "Somebody made that up" to "The other department takes one-hour-45-minute lunches" to "Everybody else does it."
- *Prepare to avoid nervousness.* No one likes to discipline, but it's part of the job. Before the meeting, think about possible objections or issues. Rehearse in your mind, outline your comments—whatever it takes to resolve the issue in a win-win manner.
- *Prepare by comparing the actual to the desired situation.* State what action is necessary, why it is necessary, and its impact.
- *Clarify expectations and contingencies for specific actions and timetables.* Make sure that the employee understands by asking for a summarization—something beyond just a grunt of agreement.
- *Ask employees for feedback.* How can you best help or support them in making the necessary changes? What suggestions do they have? How can problems be prevented in the future?
- *Let it go.* There is no need to ignore employees, stare at them, or use any other of a variety of cruel and unusual (and immature) punishments.

Imagine an environment that tolerated no mistakes because it tolerated no risks, no changes, no tests. A less-than-perfect world looks good after all.

2. *Duration of the Problem.* Have there been other discipline problems in the past, and over how long a time span? The violation does not take place in a vacuum. A first occurrence is usually viewed differently from a third or fourth offense.

3. *Frequency and Nature of the Problem.* Is the current problem part of an emerging or continuing pattern of disciplinary infractions? We are concerned with not only the duration but also the pattern of the problem. Continual infractions may require a different type of discipline from that applied to isolated instances of misconduct. They may also point out a situation that demands far more severe discipline to prevent a minor problem from becoming a major one.

4. *Extenuating Factors.* Do extenuating circumstances relate to the problem? The student who fails to turn in her term paper by the deadline because of the death of her grandfather is likely to have her violation assessed more leniently than will her peer who missed the deadline because he overslept.

5. *Degree of Socialization.* To what extent has management made an earlier effort to educate the person causing the problem about the existing rules and procedures and the consequences of violations? Discipline severity must reflect the degree of knowledge that the violator holds of the organization's standards of acceptable behavior. In contrast to the previous item, the new employee is less likely to have been socialized to these standards than the 20-year veteran. Additionally, the organization with formalized, written rules governing employee conduct is more justified in aggressively enforcing violations of these rules than is the organization whose rules are informal or vague.

6. *History of the Organization's Discipline Practices.* How have similar infractions been dealt with in the past within the department? Within the entire organization? Has there been consistency in the application of discipline procedures? Equitable treatment of employees must take into consideration precedents within the unit where the infraction occurs, as well as previous disciplinary actions taken in other units within the organization. Equity demands consistency against some relevant benchmark.

7. *Management Backing.* If employees decide to take their case to a higher level in management, will you have reasonable evidence to justify your decision? Should the employee challenge your disciplinary action, you need data to back up the necessity and equity of your action and to feel confident that management will support your decision. No disciplinary action is likely to carry much weight if violators believe that they can usually challenge and successfully override their manager's decision.

How can these seven items help? Consider the many reasons why we might discipline an employee. With little difficulty, we could list several dozen or more infractions that management might believe require disciplinary action. For simplicity's sake, we have classified the most frequent violations into four categories: attendance, on-the-job behaviors, dishonesty, and outside activities. We've listed them and potential infractions in Exhibit 4-4. However, these infractions may be minor or serious given the situation or the industry in which one works. For example, while concealing defective work in a hand-power-tool assembly line may be viewed as minor, the same action in an aerospace manufacturing plant is more serious. Furthermore, recurrence and severity of the infraction will play a role. For instance, employees who experience their first minor offense might generally expect a minor reprimand. A second offense might result in a more stringent reprimand, and so forth. In contrast, the first occurrence of a serious offense might mean not being allowed to return to work, the length of time being dependent on the circumstances surrounding the violation.

Disciplinary Guidelines

All human resource managers should be aware of disciplinary guidelines. In this section, we briefly describe them.

■ *Make Disciplinary Action Corrective Rather Than Punitive.* The object of disciplinary action is not to deal out punishment. The object is to correct an employee's undesirable behavior. Punishment may be a necessary means to that end, but one should never lose sight of the eventual objective.

■ *Make Disciplinary Action Progressive.* Although the appropriate disciplinary action may vary depending on the situation, it is generally desirable

EXHIBIT 4-4
Specific Disciplinary Problems

TYPE OF PROBLEM	INFRACTION
Attendance	Tardiness
	Unexcused absence
	Leaving without permission
On-the-job behaviors	Malicious destruction of organizational property
	Gross insubordination
	Carrying a concealed weapon
	Attacking another employee with intent to seriously harm
	Intoxicated on the job/substance abuse
	Sexually harassing another employee
	Failure to obey safety rules
	Defective work
	Failure to report accidents
	Loafing
	Gambling on the job
	Fighting
	Horseplay
Dishonesty	Stealing
	Deliberate falsification of employment record
	Clock-punching another's timecard
	Concealing defective work
	Subversive activity
Outside activities	Unauthorized strike activity
	Outside criminal activities
	Wage garnishment
	Working for a competing company

for discipline to be progressive. Only for the most serious violations will an employee be dismissed after a first offense. Typically, progressive disciplinary action begins with a verbal warning and proceeds through a written warning, suspension, and, only in the most serious cases, dismissal. More on this in a moment.

■ *Follow the "Hot-Stove" Rule.* Administering discipline can be viewed as analogous to touching a hot stove (hence, the **hot-stove rule**).[45] Although both are painful to the recipient, the analogy goes further. When you touch a hot stove, you have an immediate response; the burn you receive is instantaneous, leaving no question of cause and effect. You have ample warning; you know what happens if you touch a red-hot stove. Furthermore, the result is consistent: every time you touch a hot stove, you get burned. Finally, the result is impersonal; regardless of who you are, if you touch a hot stove, you will get burned. The comparison between touching a hot stove and administering discipline should be apparent, but let us briefly expand on each of the four points in the analogy.

hot-stove rule
Discipline, like the consequences of touching a hot stove, should be immediate, provide ample warning, be consistent, and be impersonal.

The impact of a disciplinary action fades as the time between the infraction and the penalty's implementation lengthens. The more quickly the discipline follows the offense, the more likely the employee is to associate the discipline with the offense rather than with the manager imposing the discipline. As a result, it is best that the disciplinary process begin as soon as possible after the violation is noticed. Of course, this desire for immediacy should not result in undue haste. If all the facts are not in, managers may invoke a temporary suspension, pending a final decision in the case. The manager has an obligation to give advance warning prior to initiating formal disciplinary action. This means the employee must be aware of the organization's rules and accept its standards of behavior. Disciplinary action is more likely to seem fair to employees when they have clear

Can you imagine placing your hand atop this stove? Clearly, if you did, you'd get burned. That's precisely the analogy used for disciplining employees. They have ample warning that it's hot, every time they touch it they'll get burned—and it doesn't make a difference who touches the stove, it will burn anyone regardless of who they are. (*Source:* PhotoDisc, Inc./Getty Images)

warning that a given violation will lead to discipline and what that discipline will be.

Fair employee treatment also demands that disciplinary action be consistent.[46] When rule violations are enforced in an inconsistent manner, the rules lose their impact. Morale will decline and employees will question the competence of management. Productivity will suffer as a result of employee insecurity and anxiety. All employees want to know the limits of permissible behavior, and they look to their managers' actions for such feedback. If, for example, Barbara is reprimanded today for an action that she took last week, for which nothing was said, these limits become blurry. Similarly, if Bill and Marty are both goofing off at their desks and Bill is reprimanded while Marty is not, Bill is likely to question the fairness of the action. The point, then, is that discipline should be consistent. This need not result in treating everyone exactly alike, because that ignores the contingency factors we discussed earlier, but it does put the responsibility on management to clearly justify disciplinary actions that may appear inconsistent to employees.

The last guideline that flows from the hot-stove rule is to keep the discipline impersonal. Penalties should be connected with a given violation, not with the personality of the violator.[47] That is, discipline should be directed at what employees have done, not the employees themselves. As a manager, you should make it clear that you are avoiding personal judgments about the employee's character. You are penalizing the rule violation, not the individual, and all employees committing the violation can expect to be penalized. Furthermore, once the penalty has been imposed, you as manager must make every effort to forget the incident; you should attempt to treat the employee in the same manner as you did prior to the infraction.

A final point needs to be made, and it revolves around whether an employee can be represented in a meeting where he or she may be subject to disciplinary action. Though one of the protections unions offer is the opportunity to have a union representative present in such a meeting, that same protection has been afforded to nonunion employees, too. Based on a U.S. Supreme Court case of *NLRB v. J. Weingarten, Inc.,* nonunion employees were permitted to have a fellow employee or other individual represent them at a disciplinary meeting. But in 2004 this changed. Based on a National Labor Relations Board decision, *Weingarten* rights no longer apply outside the union setting. But that's not to say that a nonunion employee cannot be represented. It's up to the company—although they are not obligated under law to do so, they may choose to allow a representative if they want.[48]

Disciplinary Actions

As mentioned earlier, discipline generally follows a typical sequence of four steps: written verbal warning, written warning, suspension, and dismissal[49] (see Exhibit 4-5). Let's briefly review these four steps.

EXHIBIT 4-5
The Progressive Discipline Process

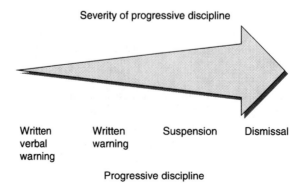

Severity of progressive discipline

Written verbal warning   Written warning   Suspension   Dismissal

Progressive discipline

Written Verbal Warning The mildest form of discipline is the written verbal warning. Yes, the term is correct. A **written verbal warning** is a temporary record of a reprimand that is placed in the manager's file on the employee. This written verbal warning should state the purpose, date, and outcome of the interview with the employee. This, in fact, is what differentiates the written verbal warning from the verbal warning. Because of the need to document this step in the process, the verbal warning must be put into writing. The difference, however, is that this warning remains in the hands of the manager; that is, it is not forwarded to HRM for inclusion in the employee's personnel file.

The written verbal reprimand is best achieved when completed in a private and informal environment. The manager should begin by clearly informing the employee of the rule that has been violated and the problem that this infraction has caused. For instance, if the employee has been late several times, the manager would reiterate the organization's rule that employees are to be at their desks by 8 A.M., and then proceed to give specific evidence of how violating this rule has increased work for others and lowered departmental morale. After the problem has been made clear, the manager should then allow the employee to respond. Is he aware of the problem? Are there extenuating circumstances that justify his behavior? What does he plan to do to correct his behavior?

After the employee has been given the opportunity to make his case, the manager must determine if the employee has proposed an adequate solution to the problem. If not, the manager should direct the discussion toward helping the employee figure out ways to prevent the trouble from recurring. Once a solution has been agreed on, the manager should ensure that the employee understands what, if any, follow-up action will be taken if the problem recurs.

If the written verbal warning is effective, further disciplinary action can be avoided. If the employee fails to improve, the manager will need to consider more severe action.

Written Warning The second step in the progressive discipline process is the **written warning**. In effect, it is the first formal stage of the disciplinary procedure. This is because the written warning becomes part of the employee's official personnel file. This is achieved by not only giving the warning to the employee but sending a copy to HRM to be inserted in the employee's permanent record. In all other ways, however, the procedure for writing the warning is the same as the written verbal warning; that is, the employee is advised in private of the violation, its effects, and potential consequences of future violations. The only difference is that the discussion concludes with the employee being told that a formal written warning will be issued. Then the manager writes up the warning, stating the problem, the rule that has been violated, any acknowledgment by the employee to correct her behavior, and the consequences from a recurrence of the deviant behavior, and sends it to HRM.

Suspension A **suspension** or layoff would be the next disciplinary step, usually taken only if the prior steps have been implemented without the desired outcome. Exceptions—where suspension is given without any prior verbal or written warning—occasionally occur if the infraction is of a serious nature.

A suspension may be for one day or several weeks; disciplinary layoffs in excess of a month are rare. Some organizations skip this step completely because it can have negative consequences for both the company and the employee. From the organization's perspective, a suspension means the loss of the employee for the layoff period. If the person has unique skills or is a vital part of a complex process, her loss during the suspension period can severely affect her department or the organization's performance if a suitable replacement cannot be located. From the

written verbal warning
Temporary record that a verbal reprimand has been given to an employee.

written warning
First formal step of the disciplinary process.

suspension
A period of time off from work as a result of a disciplinary process.

employee's standpoint, a suspension can result in the employee returning in a more unpleasant and negative frame of mind than before the layoff.

Why would management consider suspending employees as a disciplinary measure? A short layoff is potentially a rude awakening to problem employees. It may convince them that management is serious and may move them to accept responsibility for following the organization's rules.

dismissal

A disciplinary action that results in the termination of an employee.

Dismissal Management's ultimate disciplinary punishment is dismissing the problem employee. **Dismissal** should be used only for the most serious offenses. Yet it may be the only feasible alternative when an employee's behavior seriously interferes with a department or the organization's operation.

A dismissal decision should be given long and hard consideration. Almost all individuals find being fired from a job is an emotional trauma. When employees have been with the organization for many years, dismissal can make it difficult to obtain new employment or may require the individual to undergo extensive retraining. In addition, management should consider the possibility that a dismissed employee will take legal action to fight the decision.[50] Recent court cases indicate that juries are cautiously building a list of conditions under which employees may not be lawfully discharged.

EMPLOYEES AND SPIRITUALITY

What do organizations like Southwest Airlines, Tom's of Maine, Herman Miller, or Hewlett-Packard have in common? Among other characteristics, they are among a growing number of organizations that have embraced workplace spirituality.

workplace spirituality

The recognition that people have an inner life that nourishes and is nourished by meaningful work that takes place in the context of an organizational community.

Workplace spirituality is not about organized religious practices.[51] It's not about theology or about one's spiritual leader. Rather, **workplace spirituality** is about recognizing that employees have an inner life that nourishes and is nourished by meaningful work that takes place in the context of an organizational community.[52] Organizations that promote a spiritual culture recognize that employees have both a mind and a spirit, seek to find meaning and purpose in their work, and desire to connect with other employees and be part of a community.

Why the Emphasis on Spirituality in Today's Organizations?

Historical models of management had no room for spirituality.[53] These models typically focused on organizations that were efficiently run without feelings toward others. Similarly, concern about an employee's inner life had no role in managing organizations. But just as we've now come to realize that the study of emotions improves our understanding of how and why people act the way they do in organizations, an awareness of spirituality can help one better understand employee work behavior in the twenty-first century organization.

What Does a Spiritual Organization Look Like?

The concept of spirituality draws on the ethics, values, motivation, work/life balance, and leadership elements of an organization. Spiritual organization are concerned with helping employees develop and reach their full potential. They are also concerned with addressing problems created by work/life conflicts.

What differentiates spiritual organizations from their nonspiritual counterparts? Although research is fairly new in this arena, several characteristics tend to be associated with the spiritual organization.[54] We've listed them in Exhibit 4-6.

Though workplace spirituality has generated some interest in many organizations, it is not without its critics. Those who argue against spirituality in organizations

CHARACTERISTIC	DESCRIPTION
Strong Sense of Purpose	Organizational members knowing why the organization exists and what it values.
Focus on Individual Development	Employees are valuable and need to be nurtured to make them grow. This also includes a sense of job security.
Trust and Openness	Organizational member relationships are characterized by mutual trust, honesty, and openness.
Employee Empowerment	Letting employees make work-related decisions that affect them; highlighted by a strong sense of delegation of authority.
Toleration of Employee Expression	Allowing employees to be themselves, to express their moods and feelings without guilt or fear or reprimand.

EXHIBIT 4-6
Characteristics of a Spiritual Organization

typically focus on two issues. First is the question of legitimacy. Specifically, do organizations have the right to impose spiritual values on their employees? Second is the question of economics. Are spirituality and profits compatible? Let's briefly look at these issues.

There is clearly the potential for an emphasis on spirituality to make some employees uneasy. Critics have argued that organizations have no business imposing spiritual values on employees. This criticism is undoubtedly valid when spirituality is defined as bringing religion and God into the workplace.[55] However, the criticism appears less stinging when the goal is limited to helping employees find meaning in their work lives.

The issue of whether spirituality and profits are compatible objectives is certainly relevant for anyone in business. The evidence, though limited, indicates that the two objectives may be very compatible. Several studies show that the organizations that have introduced spirituality into workplace have witnessed improved productivity, reduced turnover, greater employee satisfaction, and increased organizational commitment.[56]

HRM and Spirituality

Ironically, introducing spirituality into the organization is nothing new for HR. In actuality, many of the areas that HRM addresses, and has done so for many years, are many of the same things that support spirituality.[57] For instance, matters such as work/life balances, proper selection of employees, setting performance goals, and rewarding people for the work they do are all components of making the organization more "spiritual." In fact, as you review the characteristics of a spiritual organization, in every case HRM is either the leader in making such things happen or is the vehicle by which the organization helps employees understand their responsibilities and offers the requisite training to make things happen. In the end, it's HRM that will make the workplace a supportive work environment, where communication abounds and employees feel free to express themselves.

EMPLOYEE COUNSELING

Whenever an employee exhibits work behaviors inconsistent with the work environment (that is, fighting, stealing, unexcused absences, and so forth) or is unable to perform the job satisfactorily, a manager must intervene. In many cases, this

employee counseling

A process whereby employees are guided in overcoming performance problems.

is done through a process called **employee counseling.** But before any intervention can begin, it is imperative for the manager to identify the problem. If as managers we realize that the performance problem is ability related, our emphasis becomes one of facilitating training and development efforts.[58] This type of intervention, then, is more closely aligned to mentoring or coaching (see Chapter 8). However, when the performance problem is desire related, where the unwillingness is either voluntary or involuntary, employee counseling is the next logical approach.[59]

Although employee counseling processes differ, some fundamental steps apply when counseling an employee. As a prerequisite, a manager must have good listening skills. The purpose of employee counseling is to uncover the reason for the poor performance, a response that must be elicited from the employee. A manager who dominates the meeting by talking may destroy the benefits of an effective counseling session.

In employee counseling, the manager must attack the inappropriate behavior, not the person. Although at times they appear difficult to separate, we must deal with only objective performance data. For instance, telling an employee he or she is a poor worker is only asking for emotions to run high and for confrontation to arise. Instead, stating that he or she has been late four times this past month, which has caused a backlog of shipping receivables, is better understood and dealt with. In doing so, the manager is dealing with performance-related behaviors. Accordingly, the manager and the employee are in a better position to deal with the problem as adults.

The manager must probe to determine why the performance is not acceptable. It is important to note that the manager is not attempting to be a psychologist; he or she is interested only in the behaviors that affect performance. If the problem is personal, under no circumstances should the manager attempt to "fix" it. Rather, the well-informed manager who recognizes a personal problem will refer the employee to an appropriate place in or outside the organization (such as the company's employee assistance program, which we'll look at in Chapter 13). Irrespective of where the problem lies, the manager must ensure that the employee accepts the problem. Until the employee has such an understanding, little hope exists for its correction. When the employee accepts the problem, the manager should work with the employee to find ways to correct it. At this point, the manager may offer whatever possible assistance. Assistance aside, the employee must understand that it is his or her sole responsibility to make the change; failure to do so will result in disciplinary procedures.

USING EMPLOYEE COMMUNICATIONS TO ENHANCE EMPLOYEE RIGHTS

During the first few days employees are hired, organizations provide them with a lot of information. In fact, some informing may start during the hiring process. Although employees may appear to absorb a lot, we must recognize that stating information once isn't enough. There's often too much for the employee to comprehend, especially during the excitement of the first days on the job. Consequently, we provide a permanent reference guide. This reference guide for employees is called the *employee handbook*.

Why Use an Employee Handbook?

employee handbook

A booklet describing important aspects of employment an employee needs to know.

An **employee handbook**, when developed properly, serves both employees and the employer. A well-designed handbook gives employees a central information source for such useful information as what the company is about, its history, and employee benefits. The handbook, then, gives employees an opportunity to learn about the company and what the company provides for them and to understand the information at their own pace. Such a readily available resource helps ensure quicker and easier answers to questions that may arise over such benefits as vacation accrual, matching contributions, and vesting.[60] The employee handbook also serves as an easy reference guide for employees whenever it is warranted. Employee handbooks also generate some other benefits. They can assist in creating an atmosphere in which employees become more productive members of the organization and increase their commitment and loyalty to the organization.[61] By being thorough in its coverage, an employee handbook will address various HRM policies and work rules, which set the parameters within which employees are expected to perform. For example, the handbook may discuss discipline and discharge procedures and a means of redressing disciplinary action should the employee believe that it was administered unfairly. The handbook, then, serves to ensure that any HRM policy will be fair, equitable, and consistently applied.

Employers, too, can benefit from using an employee handbook. In addition to any benefits accrued from having a more committed and loyal workforce, handbooks are tools to educate, inform, and guide employees in the organization. But a word of caution is in order. In our earlier discussion in this chapter on employment-at-will, we addressed the issue of implied contracts. Recall that an implied contract is anything expressed, orally or in writing, that may be perceived by the individual to mean that she or he can't be terminated. For example, telling an employee that as long as her performance is satisfactory, she will have a job until retirement, could be construed as an implied contract. Over the years, the courts have ruled that various statements made in employee handbooks may be binding on the company. To prevent this from occurring, many legal advocates and HRM researchers recommend a careful choice of words in the handbook, and a disclaimer. We have reproduced a disclaimer from one business in Exhibit 4-7.

It is important to note that an employee handbook is of little use if employees don't read it. To facilitate that goal, we recommend that first of all, the handbook should be pertinent to employees' needs. Handbooks filled with seemingly unnecessary information or unclear wording or excessive verbiage may diminish meeting this goal. Consequently, employers should, through feedback mechanisms, assess how useful employees find the employee handbook information, gather their input, and make modifications where necessary. HRM should not assume that once developed and disseminated to employees, the employee handbook is final. Rather, it should be updated and refined on a continuous basis. Contemporary employers are finding that putting the employee handbook on the company's intranet is an effective way of making the materials available to employees.[62] Updates, too, can be handled expeditiously. But the traditional loose-leaf binder system is still functional and readily allows for corrections, updates, and additions.

The handbook should also be well organized to make it easy to find the needed information. Just as this book has a table of contents and an index to help you find specific information more quickly, so too should the employee handbook. HRM must remember that the handbook will be helpful to employees only if it is easy to use.

This handbook is not a contract, expressed or implied, guaranteeing employment for any specific duration. Although [the company] hopes that your employment relationship with us will be long term, either you or the company may terminate this relationship at any time, for any reason, with or without cause or notice.

EXHIBIT 4-7
A Sample Employee Handbook Disclaimer

ETHICAL ISSUES IN HRM

COMPLETE INFORMATION

Effective communication in organizations is built on the premise of conveying only appropriate and accurate information. Organization members deserve the respect and dignity that factual information can deliver. But at what point is it best to withhold information from employees?

In Chapter 1, we addressed a so-what test: if it really matters to individuals, the information should be conveyed. But reality tells us that even factual information can, at times, be difficult to deliver and may best be withheld for various reasons. For example, confidentiality is a must in matters that personally affect employees. Assume, then, that one of your employees has just told you that he has Hodgkin's lymphoma, a treatable form of lymph node cancer. Consequently, he may be absent frequently at times, especially during his chemotherapy treatments. Yet he doesn't anticipate his attendance to be a problem, nor will it directly affect his work. After all, many of his duties involve direct computer work, so he can work at home and forward the data electronically to the appropriate people.

On several occasions, the employee has either called in sick or has had to leave early because he felt ill. Your employees are beginning to suspect something is wrong and have come to you for information. Rumors are going around that the employee might be HIV-positive, and that is causing quite a stir. You simply and politely decline to discuss an employee's issues with other employees. However, some of them think that you are giving this employee preferential treatment. You know if they only knew what was going on they'd understand, but you can't disclose the nature of the illness. On the other hand, perceived continued favoritism will surely be disruptive in your department. What do you do? Should the employees hear the whole story? What if it is affecting their work? What's your opinion?

Using Information Technology for Employee Communications

Information technology has radically changed how individuals in organizations communicate. For example, employees can have more complete information to make faster decisions and more opportunities to collaborate and share information (see Ethical Issues in HRM). In addition, information technology has made people in organizations fully accessible 24 hours a day, 7 days a week, regardless of where they are. Employees needn't be at their desk with their computer turned on to communicate with others in the organization. Three developments in information technology appear to have the most significant effect on current organizational communication: networked computer systems, wireless capabilities, and knowledge management systems.

Networked Communication In a networked computer system, an organization links its computers together through compatible hardware and software, creating an integrated organizational network. Organizational members communicate with each other and tap into information whether they're down the hall, across town, or anyplace around the globe. Although the mechanics of how network systems work are beyond the scope of this book, we'll address some of its communication applications. These include e-mail, instant messaging, voice mail, fax, electronic data interchange, intranets and extranets, and the talking Internet.

E-mail, the instantaneous transmission of messages between computers, stores messages at the receiver's computer to be read at the receiver's convenience. E-mail is fast and cheap and can send the same message to many people at the same time. It's a quick and convenient way for organizational members to share information and communicate. E-mail messages may also contain attached files that give the receiver a copy of a document.

Organizational members who find e-mail slow and cumbersome may also use *instant messaging (IM).* This interactive real-time communication takes place among computer users who are logged onto the computer network at the same time. IM first became popular among teens and preteens who wanted to communicate with their friends online. Now it's moving to the workplace. IM avoids waiting around for a colleague to read e-mail. Information is communicated instantaneously. However, instant messaging has a couple of drawbacks. It requires groups of users to log onto the organization's computer network at the same time, which leaves the network open to security breaches.

A *voice-mail* system digitizes a spoken massage, transmits it over the network, and stores the message on a disk for the receiver to retrieve later.[63] This capability transmits spoken information even though a receiver may not be physically present to hear it. Receivers can choose to save the message for future use, delete it, or route it to other parties.

Facsimile or fax machines transmit documents containing both text and graphics over ordinary telephone lines. A sending fax machine scans and digitizes the document. A receiving fax machine reads the scanned information and prints it out. Information that is best viewed in printed form can be easily and quickly shared by organizational members.

Meetings—one-on-one, team, divisional, or organization-wide—have always been one way to share information. The limitations of technology used to dictate that meetings take place among people in the same physical location. But that's no longer the case. *Teleconferencing* allows a group of people to confer simultaneously using telephone or e-mail group communications software. If meeting participants can see each other over video screens, the simultaneous conference is called *videoconferencing*. Work groups, large and small, that might be in different locations, can use these communication network tools to collaborate and share information. Doing so is often much less expensive than the cost of bringing members together from several locations.

Networked computer systems have allowed the development of organizational intranets and extranets. An *intranet* is an organizational communication network that uses Internet technology but is accessible only by organizational employees. Many organizations are using intranets as ways for employees to share information and collaborate on documents and projects—as well as access company policy manuals and employee specific materials such as employee benefits—from different locations.[64] An *extranet* is an organizational communication network that uses Internet technology and allows authorized users inside the organization to communicate with certain outsiders such as customers or vendors. Most of the large auto manufacturers, for example, have extranets that allow faster and more convenient communication with dealers.

Finally, the Internet now supports voice communication. Popular Web sites such as Yahoo! let users chat verbally with each other. America Online has introduced a Web browser that lets users click on a button to talk to others. Similarly, companies are moving to intranet-based voice communications. For instance, the New Jersey offices of Merrill Lynch have installed 6,500 Internet phones for employees to use in conference calls or for instant messaging communication.[65]

Wireless Communications Communication possibilities for an employee in a networked world are exciting, but the real potential is yet to come. Networked computer systems require organizations and organizational members to be connected by wires. Wireless communication relies on signals sent through air or space with no physical connection, using such devices as microwave signals, satellites, radio waves and radio antennas, or infrared light rays. Wireless smart phones, notebook computers, and other pocket communication devices have spawned a whole new way for managers to "keep in touch." Globally, millions of users have wireless technology that allows them to send and receive information from anywhere. One result: employees no longer need be at their desks with their computers plugged in and turned on to communicate with others in the organization. As technology continues to improve in this area, we'll see more organizational members using wireless communication as a way to collaborate and share information.[66]

complaint procedure
A formalized procedure in an organization through which an employee seeks to resolve a work problem.

Complaint Procedures An organization's **complaint procedure** is designed to permit employees to question actions that have occurred in the company and to seek the company's assistance in correcting the problem. For example, if the employee believes her boss has inappropriately evaluated her performance, or believes the boss's behavior is counterproductive, a complaint process allows her information to be heard. That's important, if for no other reason than to keep disgruntled employees from venting their complaints about the organization on the Internet.[67]

Complaints are typically investigated and decisions made regarding the validity of the alleged wrongdoings under the direction of employee relations specialists.

Complaint procedures implemented in nonunionized organizations are called by a variety of titles. Irrespective of their names, most follow a set pattern. Given the structure of HRM laid out in Chapter 2, a nonunionized complaint procedure may consist of the following. We have graphically portrayed these steps in Exhibit 4-8.

1. *Employee–supervisor.* This is generally regarded as the initial step to resolve an employee problem. Here, the employee tries to address the issue with her supervisor, seeking some resolution. If the issue is resolved here, nothing further need be done. Accordingly, this is considered an informal step in the process. Furthermore, depending on the problem, this step may be skipped altogether, should the employee fear retaliation from the supervisor.

2. *Employee–employer relations.* Failing the satisfaction desired in Step 1, the employee files the complaint with the employee-relations representative. As part of his or her job, the ER representative investigates the matter, including gathering information from both parties, and makes a recommendation for resolution. Although this is the first formal step, the employee may continue upward should she find the recommended solution unsatisfactory.

3. *Employee–department head.* If employee relations fails to correct the problem, or if the employee wishes to further exercise her rights, the next step in the complaint procedure is to meet with the area manager. Once again, there will follow an investigation and a decision. It is important to note, however, that if employee relations found no validity in the individual's charge, they are not responsible for continuing to assist the employee.

EXHIBIT 4-8
A Sample Complaint Procedure in a Nonunionized Work Environment

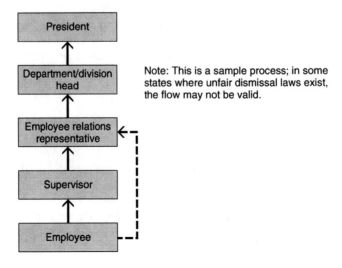

Note: This is a sample process; in some states where unfair dismissal laws exist, the flow may not be valid.

EXHIBIT 4-9
Suggestive Suggestions

(Source: ©2003 United Features Syndicate, Inc.)

4. *Employee–president.* The final step in the process involves taking the issue to the president. Generally, although employee rights may be protected under various state laws, the president's decision is final.

Inasmuch as this is a generic portrayal of a complaint process, it is important to recognize that this serves as the foundation of an internal complaint procedure. Keep in mind that more levels of management could be included in the picture. In any case, however, employees must be notified that this is how the company resolves employee complaints. And this communication should occur initially during orientation, appear in employee handbooks, and be posted throughout the company.

Finally, we mentioned that this process is generally useful in nonunionized settings. Why is it not in a unionized company? The answer to that question lies in the various labor laws unique to labor-management relationships. The complaint procedure, called a *grievance procedure,* is unique enough for us to discuss it as part of the *collective bargaining process* (Chapter 15).

Why Companies Support Suggestion Programs

Similar to the complaint procedure, a **suggestion program** allows employees to tell management what they are doing right and what they are doing wrong, at least from an employee's point of view.[68] In many companies, management welcomes such suggestions in conjunction with continuous improvement processes and employee involvement.

Although employees value the "reward," the most important aspect of a suggestion program is for individuals to witness management action. That is, whether the suggestion is useful or not, employers must recognize employees who submit suggestions and inform them of their outcome.[69] Even if the idea isn't appropriate for the company, employees still should be told management's decision (see Exhibit 4-9). Failure to do so will more than likely decrease employees' willingness to make suggestions. And if the suggestion is good, in the spirit of employee communication, not only should they be rewarded, but their input should be recognized on the company's intranet or broadcast in some other communication medium.[70]

suggestion program
A process that allows employees to tell management how they perceive the organization is doing.

SUMMARY

(This summary relates to the Learning Outcomes identified on page 89.)
After having read this chapter you can

1. **Explain the intent of the Privacy Act of 1974, the Drug-Free Workplace Act of 1988, and the Polygraph Protection Act of 1988 and their effect on HRM.** The Privacy Act of 1974 was intended to require government agencies to make available to employees information contained in their personnel files.

Subsequent state laws have afforded the same ability to nongovernment agencies. HRM must ensure that policies exist and are disseminated to employees regarding access to their personnel files. The Drug-Free Workplace Act of 1988 required government agencies, federal contractors, and those who receive more than $25,000 in government money to take various steps to ensure that their workplace is drug free. Nongovernment agencies with less than $25,000 in government grants are exempt from this law. The Polygraph Protection Act of 1988 prohibits the use of lie-detector tests in screening all job applicants. The act, however, does permit selective use of polygraphs under specific circumstances.

2. **Describe the provisions of the Worker Adjustment and Retraining Notification Act of 1988.** The Worker Adjustment and Retraining Notification Act of 1988 requires employers with 100 or more employees contemplating closing a facility or laying off 50 or more workers to provide 60 days' advance notice of the action.

3. **Identify the pros and cons of employee drug testing.** Drug testing is a contemporary issue facing many organizations. The problems associated with substance abuse in our society, and our organizations specifically, lead companies to test employees. The costs in terms of lost productivity and the like support such action. On the other hand, however, comes the issue of privacy. Does the company truly have the right to know what employees do on their own time? Additionally, drug test validity as well as proper procedures are often cited as reasons for not testing.

4. **Explain why honesty tests are used in hiring.** Honesty testing in hiring has been used to capture the information now unavailable from a polygraph in screening applicants. Many companies use these question-and-answer tests to obtain information on one's potential to steal from the company, as well as to determine whether an employee has stolen before. Validity of honesty tests has some support, and their use as an additional selection device appears reasonable.

5. **Discuss the implications of the employment-at-will doctrine and identify the five exceptions to the doctrine.** The employment-at-will doctrine permits employers to fire employees for any reason, justified or not. Although based on nineteenth-century common law, exceptions to employment-at-will have curtailed employers' use of the doctrine. The five exceptions to the employment-at-will doctrine are contractual relationships, statutory considerations, public policy violations, implied employment contracts, and breach of good faith by the employer.

6. **Define discipline and the contingency factors that determine the severity of discipline.** Discipline is a condition in the organization when employees conduct themselves in accordance with the organization's rules and standards of acceptable behavior. Whether to impose discipline and with what severity should reflect factors such as problem seriousness, problem duration, problem frequency and nature, the employee's work history, extenuating circumstances, degree of orientation, history of the organization's discipline practices, implications for other employees, and management backing.

7. **Describe the general guidelines for administering discipline.** General guidelines in administering discipline include making disciplinary actions corrective, making disciplinary actions progressive, and following the hot-stove rule—be immediate, provide ample warning, be consistent, and be impersonal.

8. **Describe the purpose of the employee handbook and explain what information should be included in the handbook.** The employee handbook provides one central source of organizational information for employees regarding the company and its HRM policies. Although employee handbooks

differ, most include introductory comments about the organization, and information employees need to know about the workplace, their benefits, and employee responsibility.

9. **Discuss the critical components of an effective suggestion program.** A critical component of an organizational suggestion program is the recognition that employees' suggestions will be heard. Failure to pay attention to employees' suggestions may decrease the value of the program to them.

10. **Identify the characteristics of workplace spirituality.** The characteristics of workplace spirituality are a strong sense of purpose, focus on individual development, trust and openness, employee empowerment, and toleration of employee expression.

11. **Identify how employee counseling can assist a poorly performing employee.** Employee counseling can help the employee make behavior changes. It is an effort to correct performance declines and to take corrective action before more serious disciplinary action is taken.

DEMONSTRATING COMPREHENSION: *Questions for Review*

1. What should an organization do to make employees' personnel files available to them?
2. Describe the pros and cons of giving workers advance notice of a major layoff or plant closing.
3. What are the pros and cons of using honesty tests to screen job applicants?
4. What is employment-at-will? How does it affect employees? Employers?
5. Explain the potential advantages and disadvantages of having organizational policies that deal with workplace romance.
6. Define positive discipline.
7. Describe how positive discipline differs from the traditional disciplinary process.
8. How does the employee handbook serve as a communications vehicle?
9. What is the hot-stove rule?
10. Describe why workplace spirituality is an important element in an organization.

KEY TERMS

complaint procedure
discipline
dismissal
Drug-Free Workplace Act of 1988
drug testing
employee counseling
employee handbook
employee monitoring

employment-at-will doctrine
Fair Credit Reporting Act of 1971
honesty test
hot-stove rule
implied employment contract
Polygraph Protection Act of 1988

Privacy Act of 1974
suggestion program
suspension
whistle-blowing
Worker Adjustment and Retraining Notification (WARN) Act of 1988

workplace romance
workplace spirituality
written verbal warning
written warning

VISUAL SUMMARY

CHAPTER 4: EMPLOYEE RIGHTS AND HR COMMUNICATIONS

1 Employee Rights and Legislation

Fair Credit Reporting Act of 1971—requires an organization to notify an applicant if failure to hire is due to a credit problem

Privacy Act of 1974—allows employees to view their personal files

Drug-Free Workplace Act of 1988—attempts to keep organizations free of illicit drugs

197[0] — 1980 — 1990 — 2000 — Present

Polygraph Protection Act of 1988—prohibits companies from using lie-detector tests in hiring decisions

Worker Adjustment and Retraining Notification Act of 1988—requires organizations to give notice of major layoffs or plant closings

2 Current Issues Regarding Employee Rights

- Drug testing
- Honesty tests
- Whistle-blowing
- Employee monitoring
- Workplace romance

3 The Role of Employment-at-Will Doctrine

Exceptions to Employment-at-Will
- Contractual relationship
- Statutory considerations
- Public policy violation
- Implied employment contract
- Breach of good faith

116

4 Discipline and Employee Rights

Discipline—a condition where employees conduct themselves according to the organization's rules and standards of behavior

Factors to Consider in Analyzing Discipline Problems
- Seriousness of problem
- Duration of problem
- Frequency and nature of problem
- Extenuating factors
- Degree of socialization
- History of organization's discipline practices
- Management backing

Disciplinary Guidelines
- Make disciplinary action corrective, not punitive
- Make disciplinary action progressive
- Follow hot-stove rule

Progression of Disciplinary Actions

Written verbal warning ▶ Written warning ▶ Suspension ▶ Dismissal

5 Employee Counseling

- When performance problem is not a training issue
- Offer employee what assistance is needed to correct problem

6 Using Employee Communication to Enhance Employee Rights

Employee Handbook—provides employees with a central source of crucial information

Technology (e.g., intranets, email) to assist in employee communication

Spirituality

117

CROSSWORD COMPREHENSION

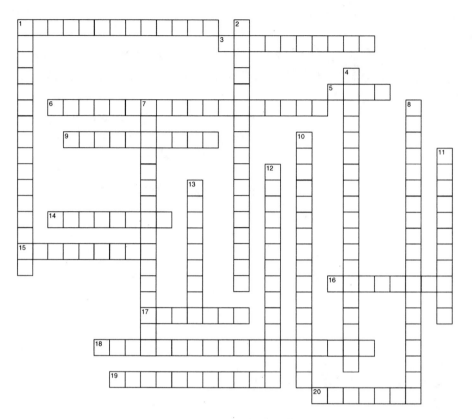

ACROSS

1. a temporary record that a reprimand has been given to an employee
2. a period of time off from work as a result of the disciplinary process
5. act specifying for employers the notification requirements when closing a plant or laying off large numbers of workers
6. a process whereby employees are guided in overcoming performance problems
9. a condition in the organization when employees conduct themselves in accordance with the organization's rules and standards of acceptable behavior
14. workplace act requiring specific government groups to ensure that their workplace is free of illicit substances
15. a formalized process in an organization through which an employee seeks to resolve a work problem
16. rule of discipline which states that it should be immediate, provide ample warning, and be impersonal
17. type of employment contract that guarantees or promises job security
18. an activity whereby the company keeps informed of its employees' activities
19. process of testing applicants to determine if they are using illicit substances
20. the first formal step in the disciplinary process

DOWN

1. a personal relationship that develops at work
2. a process that allows employees to tell management how they perceive the organization is doing
4. act requiring employees to notify job applicants of its intent to check into their credit background
7. doctrine that permits employers to discipline or discharge employees at their discretion
8. act prohibiting the use of lie detectors in screening job applicants

10. a document describing important aspects of employment an employee needs to know
11. a specialized question-and-answer test designed to assess one's truthfulness
12. a situation in which an employee notifies authorities of wrongdoing in an organization
13. a disciplinary action that results in the termination of an employee

HRM Workshop

LINKING CONCEPTS TO PRACTICE: *Discussion Questions*

1. "Employees should not be permitted to see their personnel files. Allowing them access to review the file constrains realistic observations by managers. Accordingly, as long as the information is not used against an employee, these files should be off limits. Do you agree or disagree with the statement? Explain.

2. "The goals of 'consistency' and having the punishment 'fit the crime' are incompatible with just-cause termination." Do you agree or disagree with the statement? Explain.

3. Do you believe drug testing is necessary for most organizations? Why or why not? Defend your position.

4. "Whistle-blowers who go outside the organization to correct abuses in the company should be disciplined for insubordination." Do you agree or disagree? Defend your position.

5. If you were a human resource manager would you implement a suggestion system? Why or why not?

DEVELOPING DIAGNOSTIC AND ANALYTICAL SKILLS

Case Application 4-A: OFF-THE-JOB BEHAVIORS

Balancing the realities of protecting the organization and the rights of employees, both in and out of work, has become a major focal point to contemporary human resource managers. For example, by everyone's account, Peter Oiler was an outstanding employee. Oiler, a truck driver for Winn-Dixie Stores and a 20-year employee, had an impeccable and unblemished work record.[71] He was punctual, trustworthy, and an exceptionally productive employee. Most co-workers viewed him as an asset to the organization. But none of that appeared to matter when Oiler was fired. The reason: Oiler was a cross-dresser. On his own time, Oiler changed his persona, becoming Donna, complete with wearing women's clothing, a wig, and makeup. Frequently out in public with his wife—in restaurants, at church—Donna maintained a dignified public appearance, bothering no one, and simply going on with his personal life as he chose.

Management at Winn-Dixie, however, saw things differently. Shortly after learning of the cross-dressing behavior, Oiler was fired. This happened in spite of the realization that his out-of-work behavior had absolutely no adverse effect on his job performance. Rather, Winn-Dixie's position was that if he was seen in public by someone who recognized him as a Winn-Dixie employee, the company's image could be damaged.

Oiler sued the company for wrongfully terminating him on the basis of sex discrimination. He claimed that what happened to him was nothing more than him "not conforming to gender stereotype as a man." During the trial, records reinforced that there was not one shred of evidence that any of Oiler's out-of-

work activities affecting his ability to work. Nonetheless, the court ruled in Winn-Dixie's favor, citing that there are no federal or state laws that protect the rights of "transgendered" employees.

Although Winn-Dixie won at the trial, they experienced an aftermath that they were not expecting. Many co-workers rallied behind Oiler, wondering that if the company could do this to him, what might they do next? Certainly people understood that a company can fire anyone for any legal reason, but how much latitude should a company have in defining a "legal" reason? Could they fire an employee who drinks alcohol outside of work, views an "inappropriate" movie, or visits adult Web sites? What if one is arrested? Does that result in an automatic termination? The answer is, they could. But if and when they do there are consequences to this employer action. In such cases, companies have found that terminating an employee for outside-of-work activities brings them negative publicity, lowers employee morale, and increases employee turnover.

Questions:

1. Do you believe Oiler's employee rights were violated? Explain your position.
2. What do you see as the consequences of organizations that punish employees for certain off-the-job behaviors? Explain.
3. Would you consider Winn-Dixie an organization that exhibits characteristics of workplace spirituality? Defend your position.

Case Application 4-B: TEAM FUN!

Team Fun

Tony, the new director of human resources, Joe, the general manager, and Ray, the comptroller, are in conference (in the HUDDLE) about an inventory problem with Kenny and Norton, the owners of TEAM FUN!, a sporting goods manufacturer and retail outlet. They see Roberto, an employee who works in the manufacturing plant, walk past the HUDDLE, bragging about his self-appointed "bonus" and stock shelves of uniforms. He just bought a new expensive car. During the past few months, the uniform production and sales count has been low. The problem could be bad material and quality control from the material source, or problems with the machine operators in the production process, an accounting error, or something else. At news of Roberto's comment, Kenny explodes, "I can't believe Roberto stole all those uniforms! Maybe he just borrowed them."

Norton says, "Maybe he isn't involved in this at all. What about Chris and that other guy we hired?"

"Get all three of them in here to talk about it," Kenny responds. "Can we do a lie-detector test on them? Let's do that today."

Tony adds, "We can do a polygraph on all the employees in the warehouse. And while we are working on security measures, I think we should institute drug testing for all employees who demo equipment. And what do the two of you think about getting smart cards for everyone?"

Kenny thinks. "I hate this stuff. If we do anything, everyone will be grouchy for a couple of months and no work will get done. We'd have to change our name to TEAM NOFUN!"

Norton frowns in agreement and adds, "What's a smart card?"

Tony says, "Let me see your employee discipline policy. I couldn't find one in the employee manual. Consistent discipline should get good reactions. Everyone knows what's expected and what's out of bounds."

Kenny and Norton both stare at him and say, "What?"

Questions:

1. Inform Kenny and Norton about the pros and cons of a polygraph test. Is Tony's suggestion legal?
2. Is drug testing legal at TEAM FUN!? What policies should be instituted regarding drug testing?
3. Outline the general guidelines for administering discipline for Kenny and Norton.
4. Should the employee handbook have a section on employee discipline? Why?
5. What organizational culture issues are relevant to this discussion?

WORKING WITH A TEAM: *Dealing in Gray Areas*

Below are several scenarios and several alternatives. After reading each scenario, select the alternative you think best handles the situation. After completing the exercise, discuss your selections with a group of four to five students. Note where you agree on an alternative and where you differ. Where differences exist, describe the differences. Finally, as a group, reach consensus on an alternative.

■ A co-worker, Brad, invites you to share a pizza for lunch on the outside picnic tables the company recently installed. After eating pizza, Brad lights a marijuana cigarette and asks if you would like your own or a share of his. Although you know that having or consuming drugs at the work site is a violation of policy and law, you must decide whether to
  a. Inform Brad's supervisor, safety coordinator, or human resource manager of the incident.
  b. Tell Brad he shouldn't smoke dope at work and encourage him to seek help such as the employee assistance program in the human resource department.
  c. Say nothing, excuse yourself, and hope that when Brad returns to work, his reflexes aren't slowed, mental powers and perceptions aren't lessened, or that he won't become more forgetful and injure himself or someone else.
  d. Join Brad in prohibited behavior.
  e. Other (specify).

■ You are completing an honesty test for a potential employer. The question, "Have you ever knowingly stolen any item from an employer," is a tough one because you remember the time when you were working as a cashier in a grocery store and at break you and other cashiers would eat pieces of fruit that did not meet quality requirements of store policy. You would
  a. Check yes.
  b. Check no, rationalizing fruit consumption as an employee benefit.
  c. Reconsider working for a company that asks such questions on tests.
  d. Other (specify).

■ A co-worker shares that she recently logged into the database, printed the customer mailing list, then sold it to various list subscribers for her "petty cash fund," since she didn't get the raise increase she deserved. You
  a. Tell a human resources staff member.
  b. Tell other co-workers.
  c. Wish she hadn't told you and say nothing.
  d. Other (specify).

■ You know that a co-worker uses, sells, and distributes drugs to other co-workers. You
  a. Tell human resources.
  b. Call the company security or the local police.
  c. Leave an anonymous message.
  d. Other (specify).

In addition to considering these situations from the employee view, in your group, consider management's perspective—that is, how management can lower the probability that these types of questionable employee behaviors would occur at work, and what actions management would like their employees to take if faced with any of these scenarios.

LEARNING AN HRM SKILL: *Guidelines for Counseling Employees*

About the skill: Counseling employees involves activities that go beyond disciplinary actions. No one set procedure addresses counseling employees, but we offer the following nine guidelines that you should consider following when faced with the need to counsel an employee.[72]

1. *Document all problem performance behaviors.* Document specific job behaviors such as absenteeism, lateness, and poor quality, in terms of dates, times, and what happened. This provides you with objective data.

2. *Deal with the employee objectively, fairly, and equitably.* Treat each employee similarly. That means that one should not be counseled for something that another person did, and nothing was mentioned. Issues discussed should focus on performance behaviors.

3. *Confront job performance issues only.* Your main focus is on what affects performance. Even though it may be a personal problem, you should not try to psychoanalyze the individual. Leave that to the trained specialists! You can, however, address how these behaviors are affecting the employee's job performance.

4. *Offer assistance to help the employee.* Just pointing the finger at an employee serves little useful purpose. If the employee could "fix" the problem alone, he or she probably would have. Help might be needed—yours and the organization's. Offer this assistance where possible.

5. *Expect the employee to resist the feedback and become defensive.* It is human nature to dislike constructive or negative feedback. Expect that the individual will be uncomfortable with the discussion. Make every effort, however, to keep the meeting calm such that the message can get across. Documentation, fairness, focusing on job behaviors, and offering assistance help reduce this defensiveness.

6. *Make sure the employee owns up to the problem.* All things said, the problem is not yours; it's the employee's. The employee needs to take responsibility for his or her behavior and begin to look for ways to correct the problems.

7. *Develop an action plan to correct performance.* Once the employee has taken responsibility for the problem, develop a plan of action designed to correct the problem. Be specific as to what the employee must do (for example, what is expected and when it is expected), and what resources you are willing to commit to assist.

8. *Identify outcomes for failing to correct problems.* You're there to help, not carry a poor performer forever. Inform the employee what the consequences will be if he or she does not follow the action plan.

9. *Monitor and control progress.* Evaluate the employee's progress. Provide frequent feedback on what you're observing. Reinforce good efforts.

ENHANCING YOUR COMMUNICATION SKILLS

1. Develop a two- to three-page report on how drug testing and drug information programs at work may discourage the sale and use of drugs in the workplace.

2. Conduct some research on employee monitoring. In a three- to five-page writeup, describe ways that employers can monitor on-site employee behaviors. In your research, cite the benefits and drawbacks for companies from implementing such a practice.

3. In two to three pages, develop arguments for and against using honesty tests in hiring.

FIVE

What do organizations like Coca-Cola, Proctor & Gamble, McDonald's, Walgreens, and Quest Diagnostics have in common? Each of these organizations has gone through a succession planning effort in replacing their chief executive officer (CEO). But none of them have approached the transition like that at Quest Diagnostics, the Teterboro, New Jersey–based medical testing company, where CEO Kenneth W. Freeman spent five years grooming his successor.[1]

Back in 1999, Freeman, then chairman and CEO, recognized that at some point in time he'd be leaving the company. Not wanting to wait until the last moment or face uncertainty should anything happen to him unexpectedly, Freeman set out to find a successor. But what made the Quest Diagnostics succession planning unique was that Freeman was determined to groom the individual over a period of years, making sure that when the time came, that person would be well positioned to take the helm of the company, being able to proverbially hit the ground running and

(*Source:* Todd France)

move the organization forward. Interestingly, Freeman also recognized that the new CEO must be different than him, needing instead a scientific background that would allow Quest Diagnostics to capitalize in the medical testing and technology markets where growth was targeted.

To begin the process, Freeman put the 200 Quest Diagnostics executives through several day-long programs designed to challenge their abilities and allow them to demonstrate how well they might be prepared for the CEO's position. Freeman was not looking for perfection during this "testing" period, but he was focusing heavily on demonstrated leadership skills and the ability and willingness to develop in those areas that needed improvement.

Throughout this process one person stood out among his peers. That was Surya N. Mohapatra. Freemen recognized that he was smart, very focused, and could multitask exceptionally well. And Mohapatra had the scientific background that Freeman felt would be needed to lead the company in the next decade. This was not meant to say that Mohapatra had everything he would need to become the next CEO.

To help in this arena, Freeman quickly began turning over authority and decision-making power to Mohapatra. He needed to demonstrate that he did have the necessary skills to run the company. Mohapatra spoke frequently about his leadership style and how it would need to be adjusted to be the CEO. He was also given a variety of assignments to help him develop these skills. For example, one of Mohapatra's weaknesses was his ability to speak in a public forum. As such, Freeman continually gave him opportunities to speak in front of a lot of people, gave him time to assimilate himself with Quest Diagnostics board of directors, and had him make numerous formal presentations. In the end, Mohapatra rose to the challenge and effectively developed his public speaking skills.

What makes this succession grooming all the more interesting is that Mohapatra is actually a year older than Freeman. Having two people relatively the same age, one serving as a mentor to another, is somewhat unusual. But in the Quest Diagnostics case, this didn't prove to be a barrier as both Freeman and Mohapatra developed a bond of trust that served them and the organization well. It also served well in the transition of CEO powers from Freeman to Mohapatra as Freeman stepped aside in May 2004 and Mohapatra became the new chairman and CEO of the company.

Human Resource Planning and Job Analysis

Learning Outcomes

After reading this chapter, you will be able to

1. Describe the importance of human resource planning.
2. Define the steps involved in the human resource planning process.
3. Explain what human resource information systems are used for.
4. Define the term *job analysis*.
5. Identify the six general techniques for obtaining job analysis information.
6. Describe the steps involved in conducting the job analysis.
7. Explain job descriptions, job specifications, and job evaluations.
8. Describe how job analysis permeates all aspects of HRM.

INTRODUCTION

Kenneth W. Freeman realized that changes do occur in organizations. But adapting to these changes requires all organizational members to understand where the organization is going and to support what the enterprise is about to do. Individuals like Freeman understand that before you can depart on a journey, you have to know your destination. Just think about the last time you took a vacation. For example, if you live in Frostburg, Maryland, and decide to go to a Florida beach for two weeks in the summer, you need to decide specifically what beach—Daytona or Fort Lauderdale—you want to go to and the best route you can take. In an elementary form, this is what planning is all about—knowing where you are going and how you are going to get there. The same holds true for human resource management.

human resource planning
Process of determining an organization's human resource needs.

Whenever an organization is in the process of determining its human resource needs, it is engaged in a process we call **human resource planning.** Human resource planning is one of the most important elements in a successful HRM program, because it is a process by which an organization ensures that it has the right number and kinds of people, at the right place, at the right time, capable of effectively and efficiently completing those tasks that will help the organization achieve its overall strategic objectives.[2] Employment planning, then, ultimately translates the organization's overall goals into the number and types of workers needed to meet those goals.[3] Without clear-cut planning, and a direct linkage to the organization's strategic direction, estimations of an organization's human resource needs are reduced to mere guesswork.

This means that employment planning cannot exist in isolation. It must be linked to the organization's overall strategy.[4] Just a few decades ago, outside of possibly the firm's top executives, few employees in a typical firm really knew about the company's long-range objectives. The strategic efforts were often no more than an educated guess in determining the organization's direction. But things are different today. Aggressive domestic and global competition, for instance, have made strategic planning virtually mandatory. Although it's not our intention to go into every detail of the strategic planning process in this chapter, senior HRM officials need to understand it because they're playing a more vital role in the strategic process.[5] Let's look at a fundamental strategic planning process in an organization.

mission statement
A brief statement of the reason an organization is in business.

AN ORGANIZATIONAL FRAMEWORK

The strategic planning process in an organization is both long and continuous.[6] At the beginning of the process, the organization's main emphasis is to determine what business it is in. This is commonly referred to as developing the **mission statement.** Defining the organization's mission forces key decision makers to identify the scope of its products or services carefully.[7] For example, *Fast Company,* a business magazine, established its mission and set its sights "to chronicle the epic changes sweeping across business and to equip readers with the ideas, tool, and tactics that they need to thrive."[8]

Why are Home Depot stores the size they are? Why do they sell more than 50,000 different products? Answers to these and many other questions are rooted in the company's mission statement— to be, in part, the world's largest home improvement retailer. (Source: Scott Olson/Getty Images News and Sport Services)

Why is the mission statement important? It's the foundation on which every decision in the organization should be made. Take, for instance, a part of Home Depot's mission statement—to be the world's largest home improvement retailer. The mission statement clarifies for all organizational members what exactly the company is about. For example, Home Depot's decision to expand into Canada and Mexico, to build stores that average 100,000 square feet, as well as to stock upward of 50,000 products are decisions within the boundaries set by the mission.[9] However, these same managers would know that any effort to expand the company's product lines to include food products is inconsistent with the mission. This discussion is not meant to say that mission statements are written in stone; at any time, after careful study and deliberation, they can be changed. For example, the March of Dimes was originally created to facilitate the cure of infantile paralysis (polio). When polio was essentially eradicated in the 1950s, the organization redefined its mission as seeking cures for children's diseases. Nonetheless, the need to specifically define an organization's line of business is critical to its survival.

After reaching agreement on what business the company is in and who its consumers are, senior management then begins to set strategic goals.[10] During this phase, these managers define objectives for the company for the next 5 to 20 years. These objectives are broad statements that establish targets the organization will achieve. After these goals are set, the next step in the strategic planning process begins—the corporate assessment. During this phase, a company begins to analyze its goals, its current strategies, its external environment, its strengths and weaknesses, and its opportunities and threats, in terms of whether they can be achieved with the current organizational resources. Commonly referred to as a "gap or **SWOT** (strengths, weaknesses, opportunities, and threats) **analysis,**" the company begins to look at what skills, knowledge, and abilities are available internally, and where shortages in terms of people skills or equipment may exist (see Ethical Issues in HRM).

SWOT analysis
A process for determining an organization's strengths, weaknesses, opportunities, and threats.

ETHICAL ISSUES IN HRM

COMPETITIVE INTELLIGENCE

One of the fastest-growing areas of a SWOT analysis is competitive intelligence.[11] It seeks basic information about competitors: Who are they? What are they doing? How will what they are doing affect us? Many who study competitive intelligence suggest that most of the competitor-related information an organization needs to make crucial strategic decisions is available and accessible to the public.[12] In other words, competitive intelligence isn't organizational espionage. Advertisements, promotional materials, press releases, reports filed with government agencies, annual reports, want ads, newspaper reports, information on the Internet, and industry studies are readily accessible sources of information. Specific information on an industry and associated organizations is increasingly available through electronic databases. Managers can literally tap into a wealth of competitive information by purchasing access to databases sold by companies such as Nexus and Knight-Ridder—or obtained free through information on corporate or the Securities and Exchange Commission Web sites. Trade shows and the debriefing of your own sales staff can be good sources of information on competitors. Many organizations even regularly buy competitors' products and ask their own employees to evaluate them to learn about new technical innovations.[13]

The techniques and sources listed can reveal various issues and concerns that can affect an organization, but in a global business environment, environmental scanning and obtaining competitive intelligence are more complex. Because global scanning must gather information from around the world, many of the previously mentioned information sources may be too limited. One means of overcoming this difficulty is for management to subscribe to news services that review newspapers and magazines from

around the globe and provide summaries to client companies. But even with the best information available, sometimes "intelligence" is overlooked. At AT&T, for instance, company officials' failure to truly understand the ins and outs of the cable industry led to the company abandoning its goal to deliver digital services over cable lines. AT&T officials were forced to sell off its AT&T Broadband division—giving up on their nearly five-year venture.

Most individuals do understand the difference between what is legal and what's not. That's not the issue. Rather, while some competitive intelligence activities may be legal, are they ethical? Consider the following scenarios:

1. You obtain copies of lawsuits and civil cases that have been filed against a competitor. Although the information is public, you use some of the surprising findings against your competitor in bidding for a job.
2. You pretend to be a journalist who's writing a story about the company. You call company officials and seek responses to some specific questions regarding the company's plans for the future. You use this information in designing a strategy to better compete with this company.
3. You apply for a job with one of your competitors. During the interview you ask specific questions about the company and its direction. You report what you've learned back to your employer.
4. You dig through a competitor's trash and find some sensitive correspondence about a new product release. You use this information to launch your competing product before your competitor's.
5. You purchase some stock in your competitor's company so that you'll receive the annual report and other company information. You use this information to your advantage in developing your marketing plan.

Which, if any, of these actions are unethical? Defend your position. What ethical guidelines would you suggest for competitive intelligence activities? Explain.

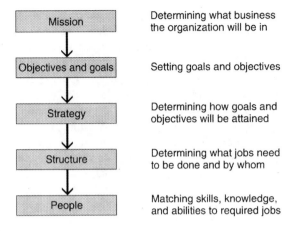

Mission	Determining what business the organization will be in
Objectives and goals	Setting goals and objectives
Strategy	Determining how goals and objectives will be attained
Structure	Determining what jobs need to be done and by whom
People	Matching skills, knowledge, and abilities to required jobs

strengths

An organization's best attributes and abilities.

core competency

Organizational strengths that represent unique skills or resources.

weaknesses

Resources an organization lacks or activities it does poorly.

This analysis forces management to recognize that every organization, no matter how large and powerful, is constrained in some way by the resources and skills it has available. An automobile manufacturer such as Ferrari cannot start making minivans simply because its management sees opportunities in that market. Ferrari does not have the resources to successfully compete against the likes of DaimlerChrysler, Ford, Toyota, and Nissan. On the other hand, Renault and a Peugeot Fiat partnership can, and they may begin expanding their European markets by selling minivans in North America.

The SWOT analysis should lead to a clear assessment of the organization's internal resources—such as capital, worker skills, patents, and the like. It should also indicate organizational departmental abilities, such as training and development, marketing, accounting, human resources, research and development, and management information systems. An organization's best attributes and abilities are called its **strengths**. And any of those strengths that represent unique skills or resources that can determine the organization's competitive edge are called its **core competency**. On the other hand, those resources an organization lacks or activities the firm does poorly are its **weaknesses**. This SWOT analysis phase of the strategic planning process cannot be overstated; it serves as the link between the organization's goals and ensuring that the company can meet its objectives—that is, establishes the direction of the company through strategic planning.

The company must determine what jobs need to be done and how many and what types of workers will be required. In management terminology, we call this *organizing*. Thus, establishing the structure of the organization assists in determining the skills, knowledge, and abilities required of jobholders. Only at this point do we begin to look at people to meet these criteria. And that's where HRM comes into play an integral role. To determine what skills are needed, HRM conducts a job analysis. Exhibit 5-1 is a simplistic graphic representation of this process. The key message in Exhibit 5-1 is that all jobs in the organization ultimately must be tied to the company's mission and strategic direction. Unless jobs can be linked to the organization's strategic goals, these goals become a moving target. It's no wonder, then, that employment planning has become more critical in organizations. Let's look at how human resource planning operates within the strategic planning process.

LINKING ORGANIZATIONAL STRATEGY TO HUMAN RESOURCE PLANNING

To ensure that appropriate personnel are available to meet the requirements set during the strategic planning process, human resource managers engage in employment planning. The purpose of this planning effort is to determine what HRM requirements exist for current and future supplies and demands for workers.[14] For example, if a company has set as one of its goals to expand its production capabilities over the next five years, such action will require that skilled employees be available to handle the jobs. After this assessment, employment planning matches the supplies and demands for labor, supporting the people component.

Assessing Current Human Resources

Assessing current human resources begins by developing a profile of the organization's current employees. This internal analysis includes information about the workers and the skills they currently possess. In an era of sophisticated computer systems, it is not too difficult for most organizations to generate an effective and detailed human resources inventory report. The input to this report would be derived from forms completed by employees and checked by supervisors. Such reports would include a complete list of all employees by name, education, training, prior employment, current position, performance ratings, salary level, languages spoken, capabilities, and specialized skills. For example, if internal translators were needed for suppliers, customers, or employee assistance, a contact list could be developed.

From a planning viewpoint, this input is valuable in determining what skills are currently available in the organization. The inventory serves as a guide for supporting new organizational pursuits or in altering the organization's strategic direction. This report also has value in other HRM activities, such as selecting individuals for training and development, promotion, and transfers. The completed profile of the human resources inventory can also provide crucial information for identifying current or future threats to the organization's ability to successfully meets its goals. For example, the organization can use the information from the inventory to identify specific variables that may have a particular relationship to training needs, productivity improvements, and succession planning. A characteristic like technical obsolescence, or workers not trained to function with new computer requirements, can, if it begins to permeate the entire organization, adversely affect the organization's performance.

Identifying these employees and their skills is important, but one must also recognize that keeping them in the organization is crucial. With less employee loyalty in existence in today's organizations, HRM must find ways to ensure that employees are retained. Frequently called employee retention, HRM must lead the way to help managers understand that they play a critical role in retaining workers, that their actions can go a long way to either stimulate or reduce employee turnover.[15] That's because it's estimated that about three-fourths of the reasons employees quit their jobs and leave organizations are within the control of managers, such as being honest with employees, giving them challenging work, and recognizing them for their performance.[16]

Human Resource Information Systems To assist in the HR inventory, organizations have implemented a **human resource information system (HRIS)**. The HRIS (sometimes referred to as a human resource management system [HRMS]) is designed to quickly fulfill the HRM informational needs of the organization. The HRIS is a database system that keeps important information about employees in a central and accessible location—even information on the global workforce. When such information is required, the data can be retrieved and used to facilitate employment planning decisions. Its technical potential permits the organization to track most information about employees and jobs and to retrieve that information when needed. In many cases, this information can help an organization gain a competitive advantage (see SWOT analysis discussed earlier in this chapter).[17] An HRIS may also be used to help track EEO data.[18]

How well trained are these workers for tomorrow's work? That's a question HRM must assess, as its answers will affect the need for human resources. HRM must ensure that employees are properly prepared to do the work needed so that organizational performance does not falter. (Source: Manchan/Photodisc/Getty Images, Inc.)

human resource information system (HRIS)
A computerized system that assists in the processing of HRM information.

HRISs have grown significantly in popularity in the past two decades.[19] This is essentially due to the recognition that management needs timely information on its people; moreover, new technological breakthroughs have significantly cut the cost of these systems.[20] Additionally, HRISs are now more user-friendly and provide quick and responsive reports—especially when linked to the organization's management information system. Moreover, systems today can streamline certain HRM processes, such as having employees select their employee benefits online during a period called open enrollment.[21]

At a time when quick analysis of an organization's human resources is critical, the HRIS is filling a void in the human resource planning process. With information readily available, organizations are in a better position to quickly move forward in achieving their organizational goals.[22] Additionally, the HRIS is useful in other aspects of human resource management, providing data support for compensation and benefits programs, as well as providing a necessary link to corporate payroll.[23]

Succession Planning In addition to the computerized HRIS system, some organizations also generate a separate management inventory report. This report, typically called a **replacement chart**, covers individuals in middle to upper-level management positions. In an effort to facilitate succession planning[24]—ensuring that another individual is ready to move into a position of higher responsibility—the replacement chart highlights those positions that may become vacant in the near future due to retirements, promotions, transfers, resignations, or death of the incumbent.[25] Not only is this useful for planning purposes, research suggests that in organizations where succession planning efforts occur, employee morale is increased by 25 percent.[26]

Against this list of positions is placed the individual manager's skills inventory to determine if there is sufficient managerial talent to cover potential future vacancies. This "readiness" chart gives management an indication of time frames for succession, as well as helping spot any skill shortages.[27] Should skill shortages exist, HRM can either recruit new employees or intensify employee development efforts (see Chapter 8). At Intel, for example, succession starts shortly after an individual is hired. Employees marked for promotions are coached on management activities and are extensively trained to assume positions of greater responsibility.[28]

Replacement charts look similar to traditional organizational charts. With the incumbents listed in their positions, those individuals targeted for replacement are listed beneath with the expected time in which they will be prepared to take on the needed responsibility. We have provided a sample replacement chart in Exhibit 5-2.

replacement chart
HRM organizational charts indicating positions that may become vacant in the near future and the individuals who may fill the vacancies.

EXHIBIT 5-2
Sample Replacement Chart

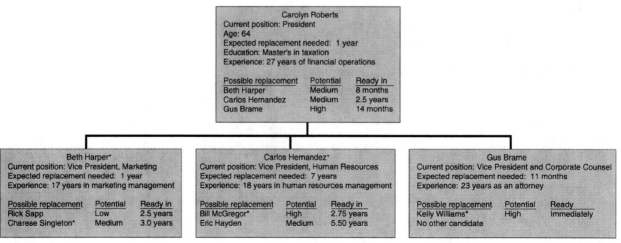

* Denotes minority

Determining the Demand for Labor

Once an assessment of the organization's current human resources situation has been made and the future direction of the organization has been considered, it's time to develop a projection of future human resource needs. This means performing a year-by-year analysis for every significant job level and type. In effect, the result is a human resource inventory covering specified years into the future. These pro forma inventories obviously must be comprehensive and therefore complex. Organizations usually require a diverse mix of people. That's because employees are not perfectly substitutable for one another within an organization. For example, a shortage of actuaries in an insurance company cannot be offset by transferring employees from the purchasing area where there is an oversupply. Accurate estimates of future demands in both qualitative and quantitative terms require more information than to determine that, for example, in the next 24 months, we will have to hire another 85 individuals. Instead, it is necessary to know what types of employees, in terms of skills, knowledge, and abilities, are required. Remember, these skills, knowledge, and abilities are determined based on the jobs required to meet the strategic direction of the organization. Accordingly, our forecasting methods must allow for the recognition of specific job needs as well as the total number of vacancies.

Predicting the Future Labor Supply

Estimating changes in internal supply requires HRM to look at those factors that can either increase or decrease its employee base. As previously noted in the discussion on estimating demand, forecasting of supply must also concern itself with the micro, or unit, level. For example, if one individual in Department X is transferred to a position in Department Y, and an individual in Department Y is transferred to a position in Department X, the net effect on the organization is zero. However, if only one individual is initially involved—say, promoted and sent to another location in the company—only through effective human resource planning can a competent replacement will be available to fill the position vacated by the departing employee. An increase in the supply of any unit's human resources can come from a combination of four sources: new hires, contingent workers, transfers in, or individuals returning from leaves. The task of predicting these new inputs can range from simple to complex.[29]

Forecasting methods must allow for the recognition of specific jobs as well as the total number of vacancies.

Decreases in the internal supply can come about through retirements, dismissals, transfers out of the unit, layoffs, voluntary quits, sabbaticals, prolonged illnesses, or deaths. Some of these occurrences are obviously easier to predict than others. The easiest to forecast are retirements, assuming that employees typically retire after a certain length of service and the fact that most organizations require some advance notice of one's retirement intent. Given a history of the organization, HRM can predict with some accuracy how many retirements will occur over a given time period. Remember, however, that retirement, for the most part, is voluntary. Under the Age Discrimination in Employment Act, an organization cannot force most employees to retire.

At the other extreme, voluntary quits, prolonged illnesses, and deaths are difficult to predict—if not impossible. Deaths of employees are the most difficult to forecast because they are often unexpected. Although Southwest Airlines or Nokia can use probability statistics to estimate the number of deaths that will occur among its employee population, such techniques are useless for forecasting in small organizations or estimating the exact positions that will be affected in large ones. Voluntary quits can also be predicted by utilizing probabilities when the population size is large. In a company like Microsoft, managers can estimate the approximate number of voluntary quits during any given year. In a department consisting of two or three workers, however, probability estimation is essentially meaningless. Weak predictive ability in small units is unfortunate, too, because voluntary quits typically have the greatest impact on such units.

In between the extremes—transfers, layoffs, sabbaticals, and dismissals— forecasts within reasonable limits of accuracy can be made. All four of these types of action are controllable by management—that is, they are either initiated by management or are within management's veto prerogative—and so each type can be reasonably predicted. Of the four, transfers out of a unit, such as lateral moves, demotions, or promotions, are the most difficult to predict because they depend on openings in other units. Layoffs are more controllable and anticipated by management, especially in the short run. Sabbaticals, too, are reasonably easy to forecast, since most organizations' sabbatical policies require a reasonable lead time between request and initiation of the leave.

Dismissals based on inadequate job performance can usually be forecasted with the same method as voluntary quits, using probabilities where large numbers of employees are involved. Additionally, performance evaluation reports are usually a reliable source for isolating the number of individuals whose employment might have to be terminated at a particular point in time due to unsatisfactory work performance.

Where Will We Find Workers?

The previous discussion on supply considered internal factors. We will now review those factors outside the organization that influence the supply of available workers. Recent graduates from schools and colleges expand the supply of available human resources. This market is vast and includes high-school and college graduates, as well as those who received highly specialized training through an alternative supplier of job skills training. Entrants to the workforce from sources other than schools may also include men and women seeking full or part-time work, students seeking work to pay for their education or support themselves while in school, employees returning from military service, job seekers who have been recently laid off, and so on. Migration into a community may also increase the number of individuals seeking employment opportunities and accordingly represent another source for the organization to consider as potential additions to its labor supply.

It should be noted that consideration of only these previously identified supply sources tends to understate the potential labor supply because many people can be retrained through formal or on-the-job training. Therefore, the potential supply can differ from what one might conclude by looking only at the obvious sources of supply. For example, with a minimal amount of training, a journalist can become qualified to perform the tasks of a book editor; thus, an organization having difficulty securing individuals with skills and experience in book editing should consider those candidates who have had recent journalism or similar experience and are interested in being editors. In similar fashion, the potential supply for many other jobs can be expanded.

Matching Labor Demand and Supply

The objective of employment planning is to bring together the forecasts of future demand for workers and the supply for human resources, both current and future. The result of this effort is to pinpoint shortages both in number and in kind; to highlight areas where overstaffing may exist (now or in the near future); and to keep abreast of the opportunities existing in the labor market to hire qualified employees—either to satisfy current needs or to stockpile potential candidates for the future.

Special attention must be paid to determining shortages. Should an organization find that the demand for human resources will increase in the future, it must hire or contract with additional staff or transfer people within the organization, or both, to balance the numbers, skills, mix, and quality of its human resources. An often overlooked action, but one that may be necessary because of inadequate availability of human resources, is to change the organization's objectives. Just as inadequate financial resources can restrict the growth and opportunities available to an organization, the unavailability of the right types of employees can also act as such a constraint, even leading to changing the organization's objectives.

When dealing with employment planning, another outcome is also likely: the existence of an oversupply. When this happens, HRM must undertake some difficult steps to sever these people from the organization—a process referred to as *decruitment.*

Corporate strategic and employment planning are two critically linked processes; one cannot survive without the other. Accordingly, to perform both properly requires a blending of activities. We have portrayed these linkages in Exhibit 5-3.

Clarke and Associates, a strategic management services company, has a client with a 65 percent turnover of sales professionals over the past 18 months. An analysis of the resignations indicated that the average length of stay has been only nine months. Perplexed by this dilemma and the resulting loss to productivity and revenue, consultants from Clarke recommended an investigation to find out why such high turnover levels exist.

The complex investigation partly involved contacting most of the individuals who resigned to ask them why they quit. Responses indicated that what they were hired to do often differed from what they were required to do. The actual work required different skills and aptitudes. Feeling frustrated and bored, and not wanting to jeopardize their career records, they quit. Unfortunately, the company's training costs these past three years had run approximately 300 percent over budget. When one senior manager was asked what made it so difficult to properly match the job requirements with people skills, she had no answer. No one in the organization had taken the time to find out what the jobs were all about. In other words, the job analysis process was lacking.

The day of going to work for a company and remaining there for the next 40 years is rare. Most companies, like PepsiCo, have had to cut employees at times to change the direction of the company and make it profitable again. Although it's not the easiest of HR tasks to undertake, downsizing is a natural phenomenon in contemporary organizations. (Source: Mario Tama/Getty Images News and Sport Services)

EXHIBIT 5-3
Employment Planning and the Strategic Planning Process

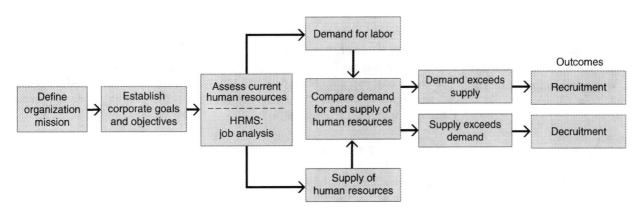

JOB ANALYSIS

job analysis
Provides information about jobs currently being done and the knowledge, skills, and abilities that individuals need to perform the jobs adequately.

A **job analysis** is a systematic exploration of the activities within a job. It is a technical procedure used to define a job's duties, responsibilities, and account-abilities. This analysis "involves the identification and description of what is happening on the job . . . accurately and precisely identifying the required tasks, the knowledge, and the skills necessary for performing them, and the conditions under which they must be performed."[30] Let's explore how this can be achieved.

Job Analysis Methods

The basic methods by which HRM can determine job elements and the essential knowledge, skills, and abilities for successful performance include the following:

observation method
A job analysis technique in which data are gathered by watching employees work.

Observation Method Using the **observation method**, a job analyst watches employees directly or reviews films of workers on the job. Although the observation method provides firsthand information, workers rarely function most efficiently when they are being watched, and thus distortions in the job analysis can occur. This method also requires that the entire range of activities be observable, which is possible with some jobs, but impossible for many—for example, most managerial jobs.

individual interview method
Meeting with an employee to determine what his or her job entails.

Individual Interview Method The **individual interview method** assembles a team of job incumbents for extensive individual interviews. The results of these interviews are combined into a single job analysis. This method is effective for assessing what a job entails. Involving employees in the job analysis is essential.

group interview method
Meeting with a number of employees to collectively determine what their jobs entail.

Group Interview Method The **group interview method** is similar to the individual interview method except that job incumbents are interviewed simultaneously. Accuracy is increased in assessing jobs, but group dynamics may hinder its effectiveness.

structured questionnaire method
A specifically designed questionnaire on which employees rate tasks they perform in their jobs.

Structured Questionnaire Method The **structured questionnaire method** gives workers a specifically designed questionnaire on which they check or rate items they perform in their job from a long list of possible task items. This technique is excellent for gathering information about jobs. However, exceptions to a job may be overlooked, and opportunity may be lacking to ask follow-up questions or to clarify the information received.

technical conference method
A job analysis technique that involves extensive input from the employee's supervisor.

Technical Conference Method The **technical conference method** uses supervisors with extensive knowledge of the job, frequently called subject matter experts. Here, specific job characteristics are obtained from the experts. Although a good data-gathering method, it often overlooks the incumbent workers' perceptions about what they do on their job.[31]

diary method
A job analysis method requiring job incumbents to record their daily activities.

Diary Method The **diary method** requires job incumbents to record their daily activities. This is the most time consuming of the job analysis methods and may extend over long periods of time—all adding to its cost.

These six methods are not mutually exclusive; nor is one method universally superior. Even obtaining job information from incumbents can create a problem,

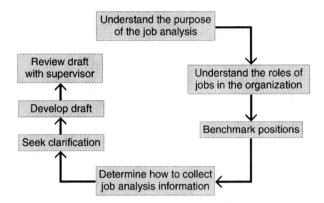

EXHIBIT 5-4
Steps in a Job Analysis

especially if these individuals describe what they think they should be doing rather than what they actually do. The best results, then, are usually achieved with some combination of methods—with information provided by individual employees, their immediate supervisors, a professional analyst, or an unobtrusive source such as filmed observations.

There are several steps involved in conducting the job analysis. We've listed them in Exhibit 5-4 (see also Learning an HRM Skill, p. 144)

Structured Job Analyses Techniques

Now that we realize that job analysis data can be collected in several ways, and that we can follow a process to do the work, let us consider other notable job analysis processes. These are the Department of Labor's Job Analysis Process and the Position Analysis Questionnaire.

The Department of Labor's Job Analysis Process
The *Department of Labor's Job Analysis Process* describes what a worker does by having someone observe and interview the employee. This information is standardized and cataloged into three general functions that exist in all jobs: data, people, and things (see Exhibit 5-5). An employment interviewer, for example, might analyze data, speak to people, and handle things; the job would be coded 2, 6, 7. Exhibit 5-6 shows the listing for the employment interviewer's position. Key elements have been similarly coded for thousands of job titles listed in the *O*Net Online,*

WORK FUNCTIONS		
DATA	**PEOPLE**	**THINGS**
0 Synthesizing	0 Mentoring	0 Setting up
1 Coordinating	1 Negotiating	1 Precision working
2 Analyzing	2 Instructing	2 Operating-controlling
3 Compiling	3 Supervision	3 Driving-operating
4 Computing	4 Diverting	4 Manipulating
5 Copying	5 Persuading	5 Tending
6 Comparing	6 Speaking-signaling	6 Feeding-offbearing
	7 Serving	7 Handling
	8 Taking instructions-helping	

EXHIBIT 5-5
Department of Labor Job Analysis Process

Source: U.S. Department of Labor, *Dictionary of Occupational Titles,* 4th ed. revised (Washington, DC: Government Printing Office, 1997), p. xix.

EXHIBIT 5-6
Excerpts from a Department of Labor Job Narrative

(O*Net 21508) Employment Interviewer

Regular evaluation of employee job skills is an important part of the job for interviewers working in temporary help services companies. Initially, interviewers evaluate or test new employees' skills to determine their abilities and weaknesses. The results are kept on file and referred to when filling job orders. In some cases, the company trains employees to improve their skills, so interviewers periodically reevaluate or retest employees to identify any new skills they may have developed.

The duties of employment interviewers in job service centers differ somewhat from those in personnel supply firms because applicants may lack marketable skills. An employment interviewer reviews these forms and asks the applicant about the type of job sought and salary range desired.

Applicants may also need help identifying the kind of work for which they are best suited. The employment interviewer evaluates the applicant's qualifications and either chooses an appropriate occupation or class of occupations or refers the applicant for vocational testing. After identifying an appropriate job type, the employment interviewer searches the file of job orders seeking a possible job match and refers the applicant to the employer if a match is found. If no match is found, the interviewer shows the applicant how to use listings of available jobs.

Besides helping individuals find jobs, employment interviewers help firms fill job openings. The services they provide depend on the company or type of agency they work for and the clientele it serves.

A private industry employment interviewer must also be a salesperson. Counselors pool together a group of qualified applicants and try to sell them to many different companies. Often a consultant will call a company that has never been a client with the aim of filling their employment needs. Maintaining good relations with employers is an important part of the employment interviewer's job because this helps assure a steady flow of job orders. Being prepared to fill an opening quickly with a qualified applicant impresses employers most and keeps them as clients.

Source: Bureau of Labor Statistics, U.S. Department of Labor, *Occupational Outlook Handbook, 2004–2005 Edition,* Human Resources, Training, and Labor Relations Managers and Specialists, on the Internet at www.bls.gov/oco/ocos021.htm (February 27, 2004).

which is readily available online (see Technology Corner). Use of this service may significantly reduce HRM's burden of gathering information on jobs for its organization. Additionally, the DOL job codes are supplemented with a detailed narrative that tells us the jobholder's main functions, with whom the jobholder speaks, and which things are handled. The DOL technique allows managers to

TECHNOLOGY CORNER

EMPLOYEE DATABASE REQUIREMENTS

Technology has enhanced our ability to obtain information on job requirements and build databases of employee skills and job requirements and provided alternatives to massive, expensive systems. Here are some opportunities technology offers to HRM practitioners.

O*Net OnLine: Online database (www.onetcenter. org) providing information on "critical information on essential elements of job performance." This site provides information on worker charac-

teristics, worker requirements, experience requirements, occupational requirements, occupation characteristics, and occupation specific information. O*Net replaces the Department of Labor's *Dictionary of Occupational Titles.* Materials can be accessed free on the Internet. Requires Adobe software.

SOAR: Part of the Job Accommodation Network (JAN), www.jan.wvu.edu, which specializes in providing information on job accommodations. SOAR (Searchable Online Accommodation Resource) is "designed to let users explore various accommodation options for persons with disabilities in the work setting (www.jan.wvu.edu/soar/ index.html). This is a free service.

DATA	PEOPLE	THINGS
1. Comparing	1a. Taking instruction	1a. Handling
	1b. Serving	1b. Feeding/off-bearing
		1c. Tending
2. Copying	2. Exchanging information	2a. Manipulating
		2b. Operating/controlling
		2c. Driving/controlling
3a. Computing	3a. Coaching	3a. Precision work
3b. Compiling	3b. Persuading	3b. Setting up
	3c. Diverting	
4. Analyzing	4a. Consulting	
	4b. Instructing	
	4c. Treating	
5a. Innovating	5. Supervising	
5b. Coordinating		
6. Synthesizing	6. Negotiating	
	7. Mentoring	

EXHIBIT 5-7
Fine's Functional Job Analysis (FJA) Scale

Source: S. A. Fine, *Functional Job Analysis Scales: A Desk Aid* (Kalamazoo, MI: W.E. Upjohn Institute for Employment Research, 1973). Used with permission.

group jobs into job families that require similar kinds of worker behavior. Candidates for these jobs, therefore, should hold similar worker skills.

A variation of the Department of Labor's methodology was developed by a U.S. Employment Service employee, Sidney Fine. Fine developed a process that further described those items listed by the DOL, called the Functional Job Analysis (FJA) (see Exhibit 5-7). The FJA provides a more accurate picture of what the jobholder does.[32]

Position Analysis Questionnaire Developed by researchers at Purdue University, the **Position Analysis Questionnaire (PAQ)** generates job requirement information applicable to all types of jobs. In contrast to the DOL approach, the PAQ presents a more quantitative and finely tuned description of jobs. The PAQ procedure involves "194 elements that are grouped within six major divisions and 28 sections"[33] (see Exhibit 5-8).

The PAQ allows HRM to scientifically and quantitatively group interrelated job elements into job dimensions. This, in turn, should allow jobs to be compared

Position Analysis Questionnaire (PAQ)

A job analysis technique that rates jobs on elements in six activity categories.

CATEGORY	NUMBER OF JOB ELEMENTS
1. *Information input* Where and how does the worker get the information he or she uses on the job?	35
2. *Mental processes* What reasoning, decision making, planning, etc., are involved in the job?	14
3. *Work output* What physical activities does the worker perform and what tools or devices are used?	49
4. *Relationships with other people* What relationships with other people are required in the job?	36
5. *Job context* In what physical and social contexts is the work performed?	19
6. *Other job characteristics* What special attributes exist on this job (e.g., schedule, responsibilities, pay)?	41

EXHIBIT 5-8
PAQ Categories and Their Number of Job Elements

Source: Reprinted with permission from the Position Analysis Questionnaire, Copyright 1969, Purdue Research Foundation.

with each other. However, research on the PAQ's usefulness is suspect. For the most part, it appears more applicable to higher-level, professional jobs.

Purpose of Job Analysis

No matter what method you use to gather data, the information amassed and written down from the conceptual, analytical job analysis process generates three tangible outcomes: job descriptions, job specifications, and job evaluation. Let's look at them more closely.

job description
A statement indicating what a job entails.

Job Descriptions A **job description** is a written statement of what the jobholder does, how it is done, under what conditions, and why. It should accurately portray job content, environment, and conditions of employment. A common format for a job description includes the job title, the duties to be performed, the distinguishing characteristics of the job, environmental conditions, and the authority and responsibilities of the jobholder. An example of a job description for a benefits manager is provided in Exhibit 5-9.

When we discuss employee recruitment, selection, and performance appraisal we will find that the job description acts as an important resource

EXHIBIT 5-9
Example of a Job Description

Job Title: Benefits Manager	**Occupational code:** 166.167.018
Reports to: Director, Human Resources	**Job No.** 1207
Supervises: Staff of three	**Date:** February 2003

Environmental Conditions: None

Functions: Manages employee benefits program for organization

Duties and Responsibilities:

- Plans and directs implementation and administration of benefits programs designed to insure employees against loss of income due to illness, injury, layoff, or retirement;
- Directs preparation and distribution of written and verbal information to inform employees of benefits programs, such as insurance and pension plans, paid time off, bonus pay, and special employer sponsored activities;
- Analyzes existing benefits policies of organization, and prevailing practices among similar organizations, to establish competitive benefits programs;
- Evaluates services, coverage, and options available through insurance and investment companies, to determine programs best meeting needs of organization;
- Plans modification of existing benefits programs, utilizing knowledge of laws concerning employee insurance coverage, and agreements with labor unions, to ensure compliance with legal requirements;
- Recommends benefits plan changes to management; notifies employees and labor union representatives of changes in benefits programs;
- Directs performance of clerical functions, such as updating records and processing insurance claims;
- May interview, select, hire, and train employees.

Job Characteristics:

- Successful incumbent will have knowledge of policies and practices involved in personnel/human resource management functions—including recruitment, selection, training, and promotion regulations and procedures; compensation and benefits packages; labor relations and negotiations strategies; and human resource information systems.
- Excellent written and verbal communications skills as well as deductive and inductive reasoning skills are critical.

Source: Adapted from Bureau of Labor Statistics, U.S. Department of Labor, Occupational Outlook Handbook, 2002–03 Edition, Human Resources, Training, and Labor Relations Managers and Specialists, on the Internet at www.bls.gov/oco/ocos021.htm (visited September 14, 2003).

for (1) describing the job to potential candidates (either verbally by recruiters and interviewers or in written advertisements), (2) guiding newly hired employees in what they are specifically expected to do, and (3) providing a point of comparison in appraising whether the actual activities of a job incumbent align with the stated duties. Furthermore, under the Americans with Disabilities Act, job descriptions have taken on an added emphasis in identifying essential job functions.

Job Specifications The **job specification** states the minimum acceptable qualifications that the incumbent must possess to perform the job successfully. Based on information acquired through job analysis, the job specification identifies pertinent knowledge, skills, education, experience, certification, and abilities. Individuals possessing the personal characteristics identified in the job specification should perform the job more effectively than those lacking these personal characteristics.[34] The job specification, therefore, is an important tool for keeping the selector's attention on the list of necessary qualifications and assisting in determining whether candidates are essentially qualified.

job specification
Statements indicating the minimal acceptable qualifications incumbents must possess to successfully perform the essential elements of their jobs.

Job Evaluations In addition to providing data for job descriptions and specifications, job analysis also provides valuable information for making job comparisons. If an organization is to have an equitable compensation program, jobs that have similar demands in terms of skills, knowledge, and abilities should be placed in common compensation groups. **Job evaluation** contributes by specifying the relative value of each job in the organization, which makes it an important part of compensation administration, as will be discussed in detail in Chapter 11. In the meantime, keep in mind that job evaluation relies on data generated from job analysis.

job evaluation
Specifies the relative value of each job in the organization.

The Multifaceted Nature of Job Analysis

One of the overriding questions about job analysis is whether it is conducted properly, if at all. The answer to this question varies, depending on the organization. Generally, most organizations do conduct some type of job analysis. This job analysis, however, extends beyond meeting the federal equal employment opportunity requirement. Almost everything that HRM does relates directly to the job analysis process (see Exhibit 5-10).[35] Organizations frequently cite recruiting, selection, compensation, and performance appraisal as activities directly affected by the job analysis, among others. The job analysis process assists employee training and career development by identifying necessary skills, knowledge, and abilities.

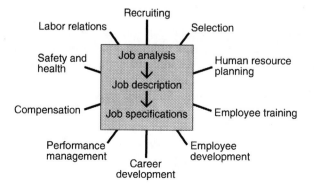

EXHIBIT 5-10
The Multifaceted Nature of the Job Analysis

Traditional job analysis may not accurately reflect what workers in some organizations do. For example, at the Toyota Avalon Plant in Kentucky, employees are grouped in work teams. Because these workers manage themselves, they need a different set of skills. The flexibility needed to achieve their team goals isn't always reflected in traditional job analysis processes. (Source: © AP/Wide World Photos)

job morphing
Readjusting skills to match job requirements.

Where deficiencies exist, training and development efforts can help. Job analysis also aids in determining safety and health requirements and labor relations processes. Accordingly, the often lengthy and complex job analysis process cannot be overlooked.

We cannot overemphasize the importance of job analysis, as it permeates most of an organization's activities. If an organization doesn't do its job analysis well, it probably doesn't perform many of its human resource activities well. If employees in the organization understand human resource activities, they should understand the fundamental importance of job analysis. The job analysis, then, is the starting point of sound HRM. Without knowing what the job entails, the HRM activities covered in the following chapters may be merely an effort in futility.

Job Analysis and the Changing World of Work

We leave this chapter with a few words, revisiting the changing world of work and the importance of employment planning. Globalization, quality initiatives, telecommuting, and teams, for example, are requiring organizations to rethink job components. When jobs are designed around individuals, job descriptions frequently clarify employee roles. Jobs today often go beyond individual efforts, however, requiring the activities and collaboration of a team.

To be effective, teams need to be flexible and continually making adjustments. Effective work teams require competent individuals. Team members must have the relevant technical skills and abilities to achieve the desired corporate goals and the personal characteristics required to achieve excellence while working well with others. These same individuals must also be capable of readjusting their work skills—called **job morphing**—to fit the needs of the team. It's important not to overlook personal characteristics. Not everyone who is technically competent has the skills to work well as a team member. Accordingly, employment planning requires finding team members who possess both technical and interpersonal skills. As such, team members must have excellent communication skills. Team members must be able to convey readily and clearly understood messages to each other. This includes nonverbal as well as spoken messages. Good communication is also characterized by a healthy dose of feedback from team members and management. This helps guide team members and correct misunderstandings. Team members must be able to quickly and efficiently share ideas and feelings.

SUMMARY

(This summary relates to the Learning Outcomes identified on page 123.)
After reading this chapter, you can

1. **Describe the importance of human resource planning.** Employment planning is the process by which an organization ensures that it has the right number and kinds of people capable of effectively and efficiently completing tasks that directly support the company's mission and strategic goals.
2. **Define the steps involved in the human resource planning process.** The steps in the employment planning process include mission formulating, establishing corporate goals and objectives, assessing current human resources, estimating supplies and demand for labor, and matching demand with current supplies of labor. The two outcomes of this process are recruitment and decruitment.

3. **Explain what human resource information systems are used for.** A human resource information system is useful for quickly fulfilling HRM information needs by tracking employee information and having that information readily available when needed.

4. **Define the term *job analysis*.** Job analysis is a systematic exploration of the activities surrounding and within a job. It defines the job's duties, responsibilities, and accountabilities.

5. **Identify the six general techniques for obtaining job analysis information.** The six general techniques for obtaining job information are observation method, individual interview method, group interview method, structured questionnaire method, technical conference method, and diary method.

6. **Describe the steps involved in conducting a job analysis.** The steps involved in conducting a job analysis include: (1) understanding the purpose of conducting the job analysis, (2) understanding the role of jobs in the organization, (3) benchmarking positions, (4) determining how to collect job analysis information, (5) seeking clarification wherever necessary, (6) developing the first draft of the job description, and (7) reviewing the draft with the job supervisor.

7. **Explain job descriptions, job specifications, and job evaluations.** Job descriptions are written statements of what the jobholder does (duties and responsibilities), job specifications identify the personal characteristics required to perform successfully on the job, and job evaluation uses job analysis information to establish a compensation system.

8. **Describe how job analysis permeates all aspects of HRM.** Job analysis permeates all aspects of HRM in that almost everything that HRM does relates directly to the job analysis process. Recruiting, selection, compensation, performance appraising, employee training and career activities, and safety and health requirements, for example, are affected by the job analysis, which identifies necessary skills, knowledge, and abilities.

DEMONSTRATING COMPREHENSION: *Questions for Review*

1. Define human resource planning. Why is it important to organizations?
2. What is involved in the human resource planning process?
3. How can an organization increase its human resource supply?
4. What is a job analysis?
5. Identify the advantages and disadvantages of the observation, structured questionnaire, and diary job analysis methods.
6. Explain the terms *job description, job specification,* and *job evaluation.*
7. Describe the human resource planning implications when an organization is downsizing.

KEY TERMS

core competency
diary method
group interview
  method
human resource
  information
  system (HRIS)
human resource
  planning

individual
  interview
  method
job analysis
job description
job evaluation
job morphing
job specification
mission
  statement

observation
  method
Position Analysis
  Questionnaire
  (PAQ)
replacement chart
strengths
structured
  questionnaire
  method

SWOT analysis
technical
  conference
  method
weaknesses

VISUAL SUMMARY

CHAPTER 5: HUMAN RESOURCE PLANNING AND JOB ANALYSIS

1   An Organizational Framework

Mission → **Strategy** → **Structure** → **People**

Strategy → **SWOT Analysis** → **Competitive Intelligence**

2   Linking Organizational Strategy to Human Resource Planning

- Assess and identify the current human resources
    1. Employee skills
    2. The Human Resource Information System—HRIS
    3. Succession planning
- Identify the demand for labor
- Forecast the supply of labor
- Match supply and demand for labor
    1. Rightsizing
    2. Outsourcing

3   What Is Job Analysis?

Job Analysis—a systematic exploration of the activities in a job

Conducted by

Department of Labor's Job Analysis Process
Position Analysis Questionnaire (PAQ)

Job Analysis Methods
- Observation
- Individual interview
- Group interview
- Structured questionnaire
- Technical conference
- Diary method

4 — Purpose of Job Analysis

- **Job Description**—states what the jobholder does
- **Job Specification**—states minimum acceptable qualifications to perform job successfully
- **Job Evaluation**—specifies the relative value of each job in the organization

5 — The Multifaceted Nature of Job Analysis

CROSSWORD COMPREHENSION

ACROSS

3. readjusting skills to match job requirements
11. a job analysis technique that rates jobs on elements in six activity categories
12. a job analysis method in which one meets with an employee to determine what his or her job entails
15. an organization's best attributes and abilities
16. organizational strengths that represent unique skills or resources
17. a job analysis method requiring job incumbents to record their daily activities
19. a statement indicating what a job entails

DOWN

1. a job analysis method in which one uses an instrument to rate tasks employees perform
2. a job analysis method in which data are gathered by watching employees work
4. a device that indicates positions that may become vacant in the near future and the individuals who may fill those vacancies
5. a process that specifies the relative value of each job in the organization
6. a process for determining an organization's strengths, weaknesses, opportunities, and threats
7. a statement indicating the minimal acceptable qualifications incumbents must possess to be successful job performers
8. resources an organization lacks or activities it does poorly
9. process of determining an organization's personnel needs
10. a job analysis method that involves extensive input from the employee's supervisor
13. a job analysis method in which one meets with a number of employees to collectively determine what their jobs entail

14. providing information about jobs in terms of skills, knowledge, and abilities
18. a computerized system that assists in the processing of HRM information

HRM WORKSHOP

LINKING CONCEPTS TO PRACTICE: *Discussion Questions*

1. "More emphasis should be placed on the external supply of employees for meeting future needs because these employees bring new blood into the organization. This results in more innovative and creative ideas." Do you agree or disagree with this statement? Explain your response.

2. "Job analysis is just another burden placed on organizations through EEO legislation." Do you agree or disagree with this statement? Defend your position.

3. "Although systematic in nature, a job description is still at best a subjective process." Build arguments for and against this statement.

4. "Permanent layoffs should occur only as a last resort. Cutting staff affects morale, and ultimately the organization falters more. Organizations also have a social responsibility to their employees and owe it to them to find alternative ways to cut costs." Do you agree or disagree with the statement? Defend your position.

DEVELOPING DIAGNOSTIC AND ANALYTICAL SKILLS

Case Application 5-A: MS WOES

There was a time in the software development world when there was one and only one major employer that most desired—Microsoft. As the market leader, Microsoft made it a primary goal to recruit and hire the best and brightest talent in the market. They would be swamped at college fairs with one applicant after another who wanted to work for the premiere software company. Filling vacancies was easy—put out an ad that Microsoft was hiring and get them in—and as such, the human resource planning process was rather simplistic. Venturing into new markets was not a problem—most everyone in the field wanted to work for the company. After all, it was Microsoft that made more millionaires out of its employees than any other company ever![36]

But this is changing. The best and brightest that have been hired are now leaving the company in droves. Unexpected resignations of key people are starting to cause some concern in the company. Companies like Google and eBay are raiding Microsoft to hire away this talent pool. As a result, managers, marketing experts, and creative software developers are jumping ship. Many are upset about the internal infighting that occurs in the organization, as well as the compensation and benefits cuts they've experienced. And if that wasn't bad enough, the one stable element of Microsoft has been its stock options and stock price. Lately, both of these have been lagging. As a result, employee morale is low.

Clearly Microsoft won't go away. But as it moves into new markets, it needs to ensure that it will have the necessary talent available. But unless some visible corporate changes are made, meeting the demand for new employees may be a major constraint the company faces.

Questions:

1. Describe the human resource planning implications for Microsoft in terms of the SWOT analysis.

2. In your opinion, could these dramatic resignations have been predicted by Microsoft management? Defend your position.

3. Using Exhibit 5-1, describe the strategic implications from the outflow of creative talent at Microsoft.

Case Application 5-B: TEAM FUN!

Team Fun

Tony has been director of human resources at TEAM FUN!, a sporting goods manufacturer and retailer, for three months. He is constantly amazed that the company does so well, considering that everything is so loose. Nothing is documented about job roles and responsibilities. People apparently have been hired because Kenny and Norton, the owners and founders, liked them or their relatives. Tony is lunching with Mary, a friend from college who now manages the human resource function for a large financial investor. Tony tells Mary, "I don't know if I should quit or what. They both got mad at me last week when I suggested smart cards for security. The employee handbook looks like a scrapbook from their kids' high school football days . . . no, *their* high school football days. No one has job descriptions. I don't get it. Everyone likes working there. The job does get done. Am I the one with the problem?"

Mary replies, "Couldn't be you! It does sound like a great place to work. Has it grown fast in the past few years?"

"Unbelievably," Tony says. "It had 25 employees 5 years ago, now we have nearly 150."

"That's probably part of it," Mary answers. "Remember how Dr. Smith said in his class that you could get by without a formal human resource structure up to about 100 employees?"

"Yeah. That was a great class! I met my wife in that class! We did lots of team exercises and projects," Tony sighs.

Mary nods. "Anyway, maybe you could begin with writing your own job description. That would be a start."

"Then I could talk about formal job evaluation processes." Tony cheers up. "That's a great idea. Have you used QUICKHR, the new software tool?"

Mary shakes her head. "No, but a package is a good idea. What's your current HRIS like?" Tony laughs until he can't catch his breath. Mary continues, "Okay. That's another place you could start."

Questions:

1. Help Tony write his job description.
2. What techniques should he use to gather data?
3. How should he conduct the job analysis?
4. What should he say to Kenny and Norton to ensure their buy-in on this project?
5. How will job descriptions change the organization?
6. Give Tony some pointers on software packages and HRIS.

WORKING WITH A TEAM: *Job Analysis Information*

Research the technical and people skills and conceptual knowledge required to perform a human resources manager's tasks effectively. Describe your findings and compare them with the results of members of your group.

You may obtain samples directly from a company's manager, with permission; interview a human resources manager; or use Web sites such as www.hrq.com and www.shrm.org. Discuss what values will be important for the human resources manager to personally possess and how these will be demonstrated in that role.

Finally, based on the information you've obtained, write a brief description of the job. What challenges did you experience in reaching consensus on job responsibilities and in choosing the correct words for inclusion in the job description?

LEARNING AN HRM SKILL: *Conducting the Job Analysis*

About the skill: Because the job analysis is the cornerstone of HRM activities, it's important to understand how the activity is performed. We suggest the following steps in conducting a job analysis (an elaboration of Exhibit 5-4).

1. *Understand the purpose of conducting the job analysis.* Before embarking on a job analysis, one must understand the nature and purpose of conducting the investigation. Recognize that job analyses serve a vital purpose in such HRM activities as recruiting, training, setting performance standards, evaluating performance, and compensation. In fact, nearly every activity in HRM revolves around the job analysis.
2. *Understand the role of jobs and values in the organization.* Every job in the organization should have a purpose. Before conducting the job analysis, one must understand the job's link to the organization's strategic direction. In essence, one must answer why the job is needed. If an answer cannot be determined, then maybe the job is unnecessary.
3. *Benchmark positions.* In a large organization, it would be impossible to evaluate every job at one time. Accordingly, by involving employees and seeking their input, selected jobs can be chosen based on how well they represent other, similar jobs in the organization. This information, then, serves as a starting point in later analysis of other positions.
4. *Determine how you want to collect job analysis information.* Proper planning at this stage permits you to collect the desired data in the most effective and efficient manner. This means developing a process for collecting data. Several methods should be combined, such as structured questionnaires, group interviews, and technical conferences. Select the ones that best meet your job analysis goals and timetables.
5. *Seek clarification, wherever necessary.* When the job analyst doesn't entirely understand some of the information collected, it's time to seek clarification from those who possess the critical information. This may include the employee and the supervisor. Clearly understanding and comprehending the information will make the next step in the job analysis process—writing the job description—easier and more productive.
6. *Develop the first draft of the job description.* Although job descriptions follow no specific format, most include certain elements. Specifically, a job description contains the job title, a summary sentence of the job's main activities, the job's level of authority and accountability, performance requirements, and working conditions. The last paragraph of the job description typically includes the job specifications, or those personal characteristics the job incumbent should possess to be successful on the job.
7. *Review draft with the job supervisor.* Ultimately, the supervisor of the position being analyzed should approve the job description. Review comments from the supervisor can assist in determining a final job description document. When the description is an accurate reflection, the supervisor should sign off, or approve the document.

Enhancing Your Communication Skills

1. Develop a two- to three-page response to the following statement: "Formal employment planning activities reduce flexibility and may hinder success." Present both sides of the argument and include supporting data. Conclude your paper by defending and supporting one of the two arguments you've presented.

2. Over the past few years we've witnessed a few mega-mergers of organizations such as DaimlerBenz and Chrysler or Travelers Insurance and Citicorp. These organizations have used mergers as a growth strategy. But with mergers comes the potential duplication of personnel. Describe what you believe to be mergers' benefits and potential drawbacks to the employment planning process.

3. Select a job (or position in an organization) in which you have an interest. Visit the O*Net OnLine Web site (www.onetcenter.org) and locate all relevant information about the position. Write a two- to three-page analysis of what the job entails, highlighting the job description and job specification data.

SIX

How do you handle the challenging task of filling all vacancies in your organization—especially as it expands dramatically over the years? That's a simple question if you're Kip Tindell or Garrett Boone, founders of The Container Store. They simply turn every aspect of the operations into a recruiting frenzy.[1]

In 1978, Tindell and Boone opened their first Container Store in Dallas, Texas. As two inspired entrepreneurs, they dreamed of the day that they would expand operations in their quest to have stores across the United States. But they knew that if they did succeed, they would have the daunting task of hiring good-quality employees and finding ways to ensure that they stayed. What they embarked on is simply amazing. They've turned their best customers into their most loyal employees.

It is the responsibility of every employee from Tindell and Boone on down to recruit employees. In fact, the store goes upward of a year before it needs to place an advertisement

(*Source:* Kathryn Adams/Getty Images News and Sport Services)

that the organization is hiring. That's because as customers enter the store, a sales associate is trained to talk up the benefits of working for The Container Store and all that the company offers. And if the individual applies and is hired, the sales associate is given a $500 reward for their recruiting efforts ($250 if the person is hired on a part-time basis). Not a bad reward for simply enjoying and doing one's job!

By 2005, The Container Store has recruited more than 2,500 employees. Over a third of them have come from employee referrals and customer contacts. But recruiting is only half of the equation. Tindell and Boone know that they don't want to be recruiting over and over again for the same positions; they want to keep the successful and loyal employees. By offering outstanding benefits and continuous training to help employees grow their skills (and advocate the business), The Container Store has one of the best turnover ratios in the industry. Whereas similar stores have annual turnover upward of 70 percent, The Container Store has a full-time turnover just under 10 percent a year and less than 35 percent for part-timers. That's a magnificent record for a company that started with a $35,000 investment and now has revenues approaching $400 million annually.

Worry about finding the next qualified applicant? No way at The Container Store! That's because their 2,500-plus employees are always looking for the next best associate! What better way to recruit than by those closest to the jobs that are being done?

146

Recruiting

Learning Outcomes

After reading this chapter, you will be able to

1. Define the term *recruiting*.
2. Identify the dual goals of recruiting.
3. Explain what constrains human resource managers in determining recruiting sources.
4. Identify the principal sources involved in recruiting employees.
5. Describe the advantages and disadvantages of employee referrals.
6. Identify three important variables that affect response rates to job advertisements.
7. Explain what distinguishes a public employment agency from a private employment agency.
8. Describe the benefits of online recruiting.
9. Explain the concept of employee leasing and the organizational benefits of such an arrangement.

147

INTRODUCTION

Successful employment planning is designed to identify an organization's human resource needs. Once these needs are known, an organization will want to meet them. The next step in staffing, then—assuming, of course, that demand for certain skills, knowledge, and abilities is greater than the current supply—is recruiting. The company must acquire the people necessary to ensure the continued operation of the organization. **Recruiting** is the process of discovering potential candidates for actual or anticipated organizational vacancies. Or, from another perspective, it is a linking activity that brings together those with jobs to fill and those seeking jobs.

In this chapter, we'll explore the activities surrounding looking for employees. We'll look at the fundamental activities surrounding the recruiting process and provide insight and guidance in preparing a résumé and cover letter that may enhance your own chances of making it through this first step of the hiring process.

recruiting
The process of seeking sources for job candidates.

RECRUITING GOALS

An effective recruiting process requires a significant pool of candidates to choose from—and the more diversity within that group the better. Achieving a satisfactory pool of candidates, however, may not be easy, especially in a tight labor market. The first goal of recruiting, then, is to communicate the position in such a way that job seekers respond. Why? The more applications received, the better the recruiter's chances for finding an individual who is best suited to the job requirements.[2]

Simultaneously, however, the recruiter must provide enough information about the job that unqualified applicants can select themselves out of job candidacy. For instance, when Ben & Jerry's was searching for a new CEO several years ago, someone with a conservative political view and a classical, bureaucratic perspective on management would not have wanted to apply because that individual wouldn't fit the company's renowned countercultural ways. Why is having potential applicants remove themselves from the applicant pool important to human resource management? Typically, the company acknowledges applications received. That acknowledgment costs time and money. Then there are the application reviews and a second letter to send, this time rejecting failed applications. Again, this incurs some costs. A good recruiting program should attract the qualified and discourage the unqualified. Meeting this dual objective will minimize the cost of processing unqualified candidates.

The more applications received, the better the recruiter's chances of finding an individual best suited to the job requirements.

Factors That Affect Recruiting Efforts

Although all organizations will, at one time or another, engage in recruiting activities, some do so more than others. Obviously, size is one factor; an organization with 100,000 employees must recruit continually. So, too, must fast-food firms, smaller service organizations, and firms that pay lower wages. Certain other variables will also influence the extent of recruiting.[3] Employment conditions in the local community influence how much recruiting takes place. The effectiveness of past recruiting efforts will show itself in the organization's historical ability to locate and keep people who perform well. Working conditions and salary and benefit packages also influence turnover and, therefore, the need for future recruiting. Organizations not growing, or those actually declining, may find little need to recruit. On the other hand, growing organizations such as Home Depot, Pfizer, or FedEx will find recruitment a major human resource activity.[4]

DID YOU KNOW?

SOMETHING FOR EVERYONE

Read almost any business publication and you'll probably find something about the shortage of skilled workers in the United States and abroad. Competition, accordingly, is enhanced to recruit the best and the brightest of the applicant pool. But is treating everyone alike a means of putting an organization's best foot forward? Some research is suggesting not.

Consider that in today's organizations four distinct groups (or generations) are being sought. These include those classified as traditional workers, Baby Boomers, Generation Xers, and Generation Yers. A plain vanilla ad attempting to be all-encompassing simply won't reach its intended target—all potential qualified workers. As such, the organization must tailor its advertisements to address what each group may be interested in—something that reaches accord with their values and core beliefs. For instance, consider the following:

What Do Groups Look For?

- Traditionalists look for the history of the organization and the opportunity to work part-time.
- Baby Boomers are interested in the market leadership of the organization and the image it has.
- Generation Xers respond better to flexible work policies and programs designed to permit work/life balance.
- Generation Yers look for organizations that are technologically advanced and companies that are good stewards of the environment.

Source: G. Kovary and A. Buahene, "Recruiting the Four Generations," *Canadian HR Reporter* (May 23, 2005). Available online at www.hrreporter.com.

Recruitment efforts are a challenge, even in these growing companies. Recall in Chapter 1 the discussion of skill shortages. Quality workers are becoming harder to locate. Unemployment in the new millennium, although fluctuating, is still relatively low. Therefore, HRM must develop new strategies to locate and hire individuals possessing the skills the company needs.

Constraints on Recruiting Efforts

The ideal recruitment effort might bring in a satisfactory number of qualified applicants who want the job, but certain realities cannot be ignored. For example, a pool of qualified applicants may not include the best candidates, or the best candidate may not want to work for the organization. These and other **constraints on recruiting efforts** limit human resource recruiters' freedom to recruit and select a candidate of their choice. However, let us narrow our focus to five specific constraints.

Organization Image We noted that a prospective candidate may not be interested in pursuing job opportunities in the particular organization. The image of the organization, therefore, can be a potential constraint. A poor image may limit its attraction to applicants. Many college graduates know, for example, that those in the top spots at Disney earn excellent salaries, receive excellent benefits, and are greatly respected in their communities. Among most college graduates, Disney generally has a positive image. The hope of having a shot at one of its top jobs, being in the spotlight, and having a position of power means Disney has little trouble attracting college graduates into entry-level positions. But some graduates have negative or, more specifically, pessimistic views of some organizations. In certain communities, local firms have a reputation for being in a declining industry; engaging in practices that result in a polluted environment, poor-quality products, and unsafe working conditions; or being indifferent to employees' needs. Such reputations can and do reduce these organizations' abilities to attract the best personnel available.

constraints on recruiting efforts
Factors that can limit recruiting outcomes.

How important is corporate image? Just ask the HR people at Disney. It's critical for the organization to continue to attract and hire the best talent they can. By being recognized as a fun place to work, Disney finds that its image helps attract and retain good employees—which is a hallmark of their success (Source: Brad Barket/Getty/Images News and Sport Services)

Job Attractiveness If the position to be filled is an unattractive job, recruiting a large and qualified pool of applicants will be difficult. In recent years, for instance, many employers have been complaining about the difficulty of finding suitably qualified individuals for manual labor positions. In a job market where unemployment rates are low, and where a wide range of opportunities creates competition for these workers, a shortage results.[5] Moreover, jobs viewed as boring, hazardous, anxiety creating, low paying, or lacking in promotion potential seldom attract a qualified pool of applicants. Even during economic slumps, people have refused to take many of these jobs.

Internal Organizational Policies Internal organizational policies, such as "promote from within wherever possible," may give priority to individuals inside the organization. Such policies, when followed, typically ensure that all positions, other than the lowest-level entry positions, will be filled from within the ranks. Although this looks good once one is hired, it may reduce the number of applications.

Government Influence The government's influence in the recruiting process should not be overlooked. An employer can no longer seek out preferred individuals based on non–job-related factors such as physical appearance, sex, or religious background. An airline that wants to hire only attractive females for flight attendant positions will find itself breaking the law if comparably qualified male candidates are rejected on the basis of gender—or female candidates are rejected on the basis of age (see Diversity Issues in HRM).

DIVERSITY ISSUES IN HRM

JOB ADVERTISEMENTS AND EEO

Recall from Chapter 3 the discussion of adverse impact. In essence, an adverse impact occurs when protected group members are treated differently from others. Although most organizations will state that they are an equal employment opportunity employer, sometimes their actions may indicate differently. For instance, the following vignettes reflect job advertisements that ended up in the hands of the EEOC.[6]

- A newspaper advertisement for a cashier in a grocery store: "Applicant must be young and energetic . . . and be required to stand for long periods of time."
- An advertisement from an advertising firm: "Young-thinking, 'new wave' progressive advertising firm has openings for entry level graphic artist with no more than three years' experience."
- An advertisement for a part-time laundromat employee: "Opening for a person seeking to supplement pension . . . retired persons preferred."

What's potentially wrong with these ads? Let's take a look. In the first ad, the word *young* indicated a preference for someone under age 40. Therefore, those 40 and older might be deterred from applying for the job. The second ad, although not as clear-cut as the language in the first advertisement, implies that older workers might not be "young thinking." Furthermore, "with no more than three years' experience" also points to someone younger.

The third ad is somewhat unique. Indicating a retirement preference might be viewed as acceptable, but retirement usually comes after age 55 and more likely closer to age 65. Thus, although the ad focuses on older workers, individuals age 40 to 55 (or 65) might be excluded from this recruiting pool. Accordingly, an adverse impact may be occurring.

The primary lesson from these vignettes should be that, although we may hold ourselves as an equal opportunity employer, our choice of words in our communication to the public may indicate otherwise. Whatever we communicate in HR, we must make sure that the language is proper.

What do you think of situations like this?

Recruiting Costs The last constraint, but certainly not lowest in priority, centers on recruiting costs. Recruiting efforts are expensive—costing as much as $10,500 per position being filled.[7] Sometimes budget restrictions put a time limit on searches. Accordingly, when an organization considers various recruiting sources, it considers effectiveness, like maximizing its recruiting travel budget by first interviewing employees using conference calls or through video-conferencing.

RECRUITING: A GLOBAL PERSPECTIVE

The first step in recruiting for overseas positions, as always, is to define the relevant labor market. For international positions, however, that market is the whole world.[8] Organizations must decide if they want to send an American overseas, recruit in the host country, or ignore nationality and do a global search for the best person available. It's important to make a proper choice; the cost of failure in an international assignment can run several hundred thousands of dollars.[9]

This basic decision depends partly on the type of occupation and its requirements, as well as the stage of national and cultural development of the overseas operations. Although production, office, and clerical occupations are rarely filled beyond a local labor market, executive and sometimes scientific, engineering, or professional managerial candidates may be sought in national or international markets. If the organization is searching for someone with extensive company experience to launch a technical product in a new target country, it will probably want a home-country national. This approach often serves when a new foreign subsidiary is being established and headquarters wants to control all strategic decisions, but the plan requires technical expertise and experience. It is also appropriate where there is a lack of qualified host-country nationals in the workforce.

Other situations might benefit more from hiring a **host-country national** (HCN), assuming this is a choice. For an uncomplicated consumer product, wise corporate strategy may let each foreign subsidiary acquire its own distinct national identity.[10] Clothing has different styles of merchandising, and an HCN may have a better feel for the best way to market the sweaters or jeans of an international manufacturer.

Sometimes the choice may not be entirely left to the corporation. In some countries, including most African nations, local laws control how many **expatriates** a corporation can send. The law may establish ratios, such as that 20 HCNs must be employed for every American granted working papers. Using HCNs eliminates language problems and avoids problems of expatriate adjustment and the high cost of training and relocating an expatriate with a family. It also minimizes one of the chief reasons international assignments fail—the family's inability to adjust to their new surroundings. Even if companies pay premiums to lure the best local applicants away from other companies, employee-related costs are significantly lower than with sending an American overseas. In countries with tense political environments, an HCN is less visible and can somewhat insulate the U.S. corporation from hostilities and possible terrorism.

The third option, recruiting regardless of nationality, develops an international executive cadre with a truly global perspective. On a large scale, this type of recruiting may reduce managers' national identification with particular organizational units. For example, automobile manufacturers may develop a Taiwanese parts plant, Mexican assembly operations, and a U.S. marketing team, creating internal status difficulties through its different treatment of each country's employees.

host-country national (HCN)
A citizen of the host country hired by an organization based in another country.

expatriate
An individual who lives and works in a country of which he or she is not a citizen.

Global companies like Unilever, which headquarters in the Netherlands, must take great care when sending expatriates onto foreign soil to work. Despite many benefits, if the assignment proves unsuccessful, the HRM cost to Unilever could reach several hundred thousand dollars. Accordingly, Unilever must go to great lengths to ensure that the expatriate has all the necessary tools to succeed in the foreign assignment. (Source: AFP/Getty Images News and Sport Services)

internal search

A promotion-from-within concept.

RECRUITING SOURCES

Recruiting is more likely to achieve its objectives if recruiting sources reflect the type of position to be filled. For example, an ad in the business employment section of the *Wall Street Journal* is more likely to be read by a manager seeking an executive position in the $150,000- to $225,000-a-year bracket than by an automobile assembly-line worker seeking employment. Similarly, an interviewer trying to fill a management-training position who visits a two-year vocational school in search of a college graduate with undergraduate courses in engineering and a master's degree in business administration is looking for the right person in the wrong place. Moreover, the Internet is rewriting all the rules. Jobs at all levels can be advertised on the Internet and potentially reach literally millions of people.

Certain recruiting sources are more effective than others for filling certain types of jobs. As we review each source in the following sections, we will emphasize their strengths and weaknesses in attempting to attract lower-level and managerial-level personnel.

The Internal Search

Many large organizations attempt to develop their own low-level employees for higher positions. These promotions can occur through an **internal search** of current employees who have bid for the job, been identified through the organization's human resource management system, or even been referred by a fellow employee. The promote-from-within-wherever-possible policy has advantages:

- It is good public relations.
- It builds morale.
- It encourages good individuals who are ambitious.
- It improves the probability of a good selection, because information on the individual's performance is readily available.
- It is less costly than going outside to recruit.
- Those chosen internally already know the organization.
- When carefully planned, promoting from within can also act as a training device for developing middle- and top-level managers.

There can be distinct disadvantages, however, to using internal sources. They could be dysfunctional if the organization uses less-qualified internal sources only because they are there, when excellent candidates are available on the outside. However, an individual from the outside, in contrast with someone already employed in the organization, may appear more attractive because the recruiter is unaware of the outsider's faults. Internal searches also may generate infighting among rival candidates for promotion and decrease morale levels of those not selected.

The organization should also avoid excessive inbreeding. Occasional new blood can broaden current ideas, knowledge, and enthusiasm, and productively question the "we've-always-done-it-that-way" mentality. As noted in the discussion of human resource inventories in Chapter 5, the organization's HRM files should provide information as to which employees might be considered for positions opening up within the organization. Most organizations can generate lists from computer databases of individuals who have the desirable characteristics to potentially fill the vacant position.

In many organizations, it is standard procedure to post any new job openings and to allow any current employee to apply for the position. This action, too, receives favorable marks from the EEOC. The posting notification can be communicated on a central "positions open" bulletin board in the plants or offices, in the weekly or monthly organization newsletter, or, in some cases, in a specially prepared posting sheet from human resources outlining those positions currently available. Even if current employees are not interested in the position, they can pass these notices on to other individuals who may seek employment within the organization—the employee referral.

Employee Referrals and Recommendations

One of the better sources for individuals who will perform effectively on the job is a recommendation from a current employee. Why? Because employees rarely recommend someone unless they believe the individual can perform adequately. Such a recommendation reflects on the recommender, and when someone's reputation is at stake, we can expect the recommendation to reflect considered judgment. **Employee referrals** also may receive more accurate information about their potential jobs. The recommender often gives the applicant more realistic information about the job than could be conveyed through employment agencies or newspaper advertisements. This information reduces unrealistic expectations and increases job survival. As a result of these preselection factors, employee referrals tend to be more acceptable applicants, to be more likely to accept an offer, and, once employed, to have a higher job survival rate. Additionally, employee referrals are an excellent means of locating potential employees in those hard-to-fill positions.[11] For example, difficulty in finding certain IT professionals, computer programmers, engineers, or nurses with specific skills has prompted some organizations to turn to their employees for assistance. Many of these organizations include a reward if an employee referral candidate is hired for these specifically identified hard-to-fill positions. Referral bonuses of $10,000 or more are not unusual in these fields.[12] In doing so, both the organization and the employee benefit; the employee receives a monetary reward and the organization receives a qualified candidate without the major expense of an extensive recruiting search.

employee referral
A recommendation from a current employee regarding a job applicant.

Employee referrals are an excellent means of locating potential employees for hard-to-fill positions.

There are, of course, some potentially negative features of employee referral. For one, recommenders may confuse friendship with job performance competence. Individuals often like to have their friends join them at their place of employment for social and even economic reasons; for example, they may be able to share rides to and from work. As a result, a current employee may recommend a friend for a position without unbiased consideration to the friend's job-related competence. Employee referrals may also lead to nepotism, that is, hiring individuals related to persons already employed by the organization. Although such actions may not necessarily align with the objective of hiring the most qualified applicant, interest in the organization and loyalty to it may be long-term advantages. Finally, employee referrals may also minimize an organization's desire to add diversity to the workplace.

Employee referrals do, however, appear to have universal application. Lower-level and managerial-level positions can be, and often are, filled by the recommendation of a current employee. Higher-level positions, however, are more likely to be referred by a professional acquaintance rather than a close friend. Jobs that require specialized expertise and where employees participate in professional organizations often produce acquaintances between current employees and individuals they think would make an excellent contribution to the organization.

External Searches

In addition to looking internally for candidates, organizations often open up recruiting efforts to the external community. These efforts include advertisements (including Internet postings), employment agencies, schools, colleges and universities, professional organizations, and unsolicited applicants.

Advertisements Sign outside a construction location: "Now Hiring—Framers." Newspaper advertisement: "Telemarketing Sales. We are looking for someone who wants to assume responsibility and wishes to become part of the fast-growing cellular telephone business. No previous sales experience required. Salary to $45,000. For appointment, call Mrs. Brown: 1-800-555-0075." More sophisticated Internet job search engines can provide us with a richness of data about the job and the company and link us to several other web sites that provide additional information, like that of Vault (see vault.com).

Most of us have seen these kinds of advertisements. When an organization wishes to tell the public it has a vacancy, advertisement is one of the most popular methods used. The type of job often determines where the advertisement is placed. Although it is not uncommon to see blue-collar jobs listed on placards outside plant gates, we would be surprised to find a vice presidency listed similarly. The higher the position in the organization, the more specialized the skills, or the shorter the supply of that resource in the labor force, the more widely dispersed the advertisement is likely to be. The search for a top executive might include advertisements in national publications—perhaps the *Wall Street Journal* or the *New York Times*—or be posted on executive-search firm Web sites.[13] On the other hand, advertisements of lower-level jobs usually appear in local daily newspapers, regional trade journals, or on broad-based Internet job sites.

Three important variables influence the response rate to advertisements: identification of the organization, labor market conditions, and the degree to which the advertisement includes specific requirements. Some organizations place a **blind-box ad,** one that includes no specific identification of the organization. Respondents are asked to reply to a post office box number or to an employment firm acting as an agent between the applicant and the organization. Large organizations with a national reputation seldom use blind advertisements to fill lower-level positions; however, when the organization does not wish to publicize the fact that it is seeking to fill an internal position, or when it seeks to recruit for a position where there is a soon-to-be-removed incumbent, a blind-box advertisement may be appropriate.

Although blind ads can assist HRM in finding qualified applicants, many individuals may be reluctant to answer them. Obviously, there is the fear, sometimes justified, that the advertisement has been placed by the organization in which the individual is currently employed. Also, the organization itself is frequently a key determinant of whether the individual is interested; therefore, potential candidates may be reluctant to reply. Such advertisements also have a bad reputation because some organizations place ads when no position exists to test the supply of workers in the community, to build a backlog of applicants, or to identify those current employees who are interested in finding a new position. Others place ads to satisfy affirmative action requirements when the final decision, for the greater part, has already been made.

The job analysis process is the basic source for ad information (see Learning an HRM Skill, p. 168). The ad can focus on descriptive elements of the job (job description) or on the applicant (job specification), a choice that often affects the number of replies received. If, for example, you are willing to sift through 1,000 or more responses, you might place a national ad in the *Los Angeles Times,* the *Chicago Tribune,* a regional newspaper's employment section, or on a Web site like Monster.com (see Exhibit 6-1). However, an advertisement in these locations that looks like Exhibit 6-2 might attract fewer than a dozen replies.

As you can see, Exhibit 6-1 uses more applicant-centered criteria to describe the successful candidate. Most individuals perceive themselves as having confidence and seeking high income. More important, how can an employer measure these qualities? The response rate should therefore be high. In contrast, Exhibit 6-2 calls for precise abilities and experience.

blind-box ad

An advertisement that does not identify the advertising organization.

EXHIBIT 6-1
Advertisement with General Information

US-NY-NEW YORK-HR Generalist - Recruiter

Status: Full-Time, Employee   **Salary:** from 50,000.00 per year   **Reference Code:** 294-036310

Job Location: NEW YORK 10028

Arts non-profit currently seeking an HR Generalist with a concentration in recruitment.

Qualifications:

Arts non-profit currently seeking an HR Generalist with a concentration in recruiting. This position requires a variety of generalist/administrative human resources functions in areas such as recruitment, employee relations, training and development, and benefits administration. Candidate must be comfortable working with management and staff on relevant corporate personnel practices, policies, and procedures. Prior recruiting experience is a must! Candidate must be a strategic and analytical thinker and thrive in a fast-paced environment. Excellent benefits offered. Salary commensurate with experience.

OfficeTeam is the world's leader in specialized administrative staffing offering job opportunities from Executive and Administrative Assistants to Office Managers, and Receptionists. We have the resources, experience and expertise to select companies and temporary to full-time positions that match your skills and career goals. We provide one of the industry's most progressive training, benefits-and-compensation packages. OfficeTeam is an Equal Opportunity Employer.

EXHIBIT 6-2
Advertisement with Specific Information

A2Z Development Center, an **Amazon.com** company, is very excited to announce its newest development center in Phoenix, Arizona!

This center is focused on developing cutting-edge solutions to stretch the frontiers of e-commerce. Our Engineering team uses their creative talents and new and innovative technologies to help merchants get their products online for the first time, and continue to develop solutions that allow them to succeed in the e-commerce arena.

What's in it for me?

As a **Software Development Engineer** on the team you will be responsible for full life cycle software development including design, deployment, integration, testing and maintenance of software applications. Specifically, you will:

- Design, write and test new software programs.
- Enhance existing applications by analyzing and identifying areas for modification.
- Maintain applications by identifying and correcting software defects.
- Develop and implement new software applications.
- Create technical specifications, documentation and test plans.
- Consult clients and colleagues concerning maintenance and performance of software applications.

Our Ideal Candidate:

- A Bachelor's degree, or higher, in Computer Science, or related discipline.
- Real, practical experience designing and delivering enterprise-grade solutions using Java and large-scale relational databases.
- Experience solving complex software problems in an object-oriented way.
- Strong analytical and problem solving skills.
- Experience with e-commerce integration, web services and any of the following technologies: J2EE, XML, XSLT, SOAP, JDBC.

Amazon.com

Work hard. Have fun. Make history.

Employment Agencies We will describe three forms of employment agencies: public or state agencies, private employment agencies, and management consulting firms. The major difference between them is the type of clientele served. All states provide a public employment service. The main function of these agencies is closely tied to unemployment benefits because some states supply benefits only to individuals registered with their state employment agency. Accordingly, most public agencies tend to attract and list individuals who are unskilled or have had minimum training. This, of course, does not reflect on the agency's competence, but rather reflects on the image of public agencies. Prospective applicants tend to think state agencies have few high-skilled jobs, and employers tend to see such agencies as having few high-skilled applicants. The result is a self-fulfilling prophecy; that is, few high-skilled individuals place their names with public agencies, and, similarly, few employers seeking individuals with high skills list their vacancies or inquire about applicants at state agencies.

Yet this image may not always be the case. For example, a nationwide computer network at the Employment Security Commission acts as a clearinghouse for professional-level jobs. In this case, a public agency may be a good source for such applicants.

How do private employment agencies, which charge for their services, compete with state agencies that give their services away? They must do something different, or at least given that impression. The major difference between public and private employment agencies is their image; that is, private agencies are believed to offer positions and applicants of a higher caliber. Private agencies may also provide a more complete line of services. They may advertise the position, screen applicants against the criteria specified by the employer, and provide a guarantee covering six months or a year as protection to the employer should the applicant not perform satisfactorily. The private employment agency's fee can be totally absorbed by either the employer or the employee, or it can be split. The alternative chosen usually depends on demand and supply in the community involved.

The third agency source consists of management consulting, **executive search,** or "headhunter" firms. Agencies of this type—such as Korn/Ferry International in New York, Heidrick & Struggles in Chicago, and international Odgers Ray & Berndtson—are actually specialized private employment agencies. They specialize in middle-level and top-level executive placement, as well as hard-to-fill positions such as actuaries or IT specialists. For example, Hewlett Packard has partnered with Recruitsoft to assist the organization in "increasing the quality of global hires, and increase retention rates."[14] In addition to the level at which they recruit, the features that distinguish executive search agencies from most private employment agencies are their fees, their nationwide contacts, and the thoroughness of their investigations. In searching for an individual of vice-president caliber, whose compensation package may far exceed $250,000 a year, the potential employer may be willing to pay a high fee to locate exactly the right individual to fill the vacancy: up to 35 percent of the executive's first-year salary is not unusual as a charge for finding and recruiting the individual.

Executive search firms canvass their contacts and do preliminary screening. They seek out highly effective executives who have the right skills, can adjust to the organization, and most important, are willing to consider new challenges and opportunities. Possibly such individuals are frustrated by their inability to move up quickly in their current organization, or they recently may have been bypassed for a major promotion. The executive search firm can act as a buffer for screening candidates and, at the same time, keep the prospective employer anonymous. In the final stages, senior executives in the prospective firm can move into the negotiations and determine the degree of mutual interest.

executive search firm
Private employment agency specializing in middle- and top-management placements.

When hiring an executive for an organization, many companies turn to executive search firms for their network and other capabilities. Firms such as Odgers Ray & Berndtson provide access to quality executive candidates beyond that of many organizations acting alone. (Source: Reproduced with pemission of Odgers, Ray & Berndtson.)

Schools, Colleges, and Universities Educational institutions at all levels offer opportunities for recruiting recent graduates. Most educational institutions operate placement services where prospective employers can review credentials and interview graduates. Most also allow employers to see a prospective employee's performance through cooperative arrangements and internships. Whether the job requires a high-school diploma, specific vocational training, or a bachelor's, master's, or doctoral degree, educational institutions are an excellent source of potential employees.

High schools or vocational-technical schools can provide lower-level applicants, business or secretarial schools can provide administrative staff personnel, and two- and four-year colleges and graduate schools can provide professional and managerial-level personnel. Although educational institutions are usually viewed as sources for inexperienced entrants to the workforce, it is not uncommon to find individuals with considerable work experience using an educational institution's placement service. They may be workers who have recently returned to school to upgrade their skills or former graduates interested in pursuing other opportunities.

Professional Organizations Many professional organizations, including labor unions, operate placement services for the benefit of their members. Professional organizations serving such varied occupations as industrial engineering, psychology, accounting, legal, and academics publish rosters of job vacancies and distribute these lists to members. It is also common practice to provide placement facilities at regional and national meetings where individuals looking for employment and companies looking for employees can find each other—building a network of employment opportunities.

Professional organizations, however, can also apply sanctions to control the labor supply in their discipline. For example, although the law stipulates that unions cannot require employers to hire only union members, the mechanisms for ensuring that unions do not break this law are poorly enforced. As a result, it is not unusual for labor unions to control supply through their apprenticeship programs and through their labor agreements with employers. Of course, this tactic is not limited merely to blue-collar trade unions. In professional organizations where the organization placement service is the focal point for locating prospective employers, and where certain qualifications are necessary to become a member (such as special educational attainment or professional certification or license), the professional organization can significantly influence and control the supply of prospective applicants.

Unsolicited Applicants Unsolicited applications, whether they reach the employer by letter, e-mail, telephone, or in person, constitute a source of prospective applicants. Although the number of unsolicited applicants depends on economic conditions, the organization's image, and the job seeker's perception of the types of jobs that might be available, this source does provide an excellent supply of stockpiled applicants. Even if the company has no current openings, the application can be kept on file for later needs. Unsolicited applications made by unemployed individuals, however, generally have a short life. Those individuals who have adequate skills and who would be prime candidates for a position in the organization if a position were currently available usually find employment with some other organization that does have an opening. However, in times of economic stagnation, excellent prospects are often unable to locate the type of job they desire and may stay actively looking in the job market for many months.

Online Recruiting

Newspaper advertisements and employment agencies may be on their way to extinction as primary sources for conveying information about job openings and finding job candidates, thanks to Internet recruiting. Most companies, both large

EXHIBIT 6-3
Electronic Recruiting

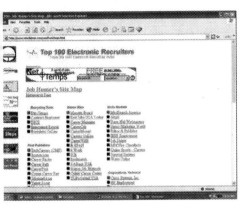

websumés
Web pages that are used as résumés.

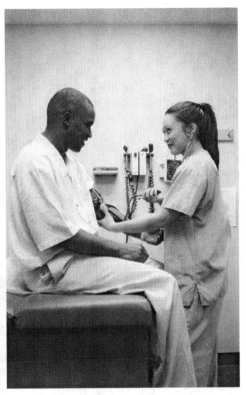

Is this nurse a full-time employee of the hospital or an individual assigned to the hospital on a temporary basis? In contemporary organizations one simply doesn't know. Temporary workers today can include nurses, computer programmers, accountants, librarians, and, yes, administrative assistants. (*Source:* Andersen Ross/Photodisc Red/Getty Images, Inc.)

and small, use the Internet to recruit new employees by adding a recruitment section to their Web site.[15] Those organizations planning to do a lot of Internet recruiting often develop dedicated sites specifically designed for recruitment. They have the typical information you might find in an employment advertisement, qualifications sought, experience required, benefits provided, but they also showcase the organization's products, services, corporate philosophy, and mission statement. This information should increase the quality of applicants, as those whose values don't mesh with the organization should self-select themselves out. It's important to note, however, that the goals of recruiting should not be forgotten simply because of the use of technology. That is, it's in the best interest of the organization to continue to provide as much job description information as possible so the unqualified do not apply. Why? Studies indicate that nearly 80 percent of all résumés submitted are inappropriate for the position.[16] But fortunately, that does not always result in severe inefficiencies for employers. Thanks to the use of technology and key word searches, most of the unqualified applicants receive their "no thank you" responses directly from the computer—without a human ever having to get involved.[17] The best designed of those Web sites include an online response form, so applicants need not send a separate résumé by mail, e-mail, or fax. Applicants fill in a résumé page and click the "submit" button. Cisco Systems, for example, receives nearly all of its résumés electronically.[18]

Facilitating the growth of Internet recruitment are commercial job-posting services that provide essentially electronic classified ads.[19] We've listed the Web site for the 100 most popular of these, by category, in Exhibit 6-3.

Aggressive job candidates are also using the Internet. They set up their own Web pages—frequently called **websumés**—to "sell" their job candidacy. When they learn of a possible job opening, they encourage potential employers to "check me out at my Web site." There, applicants have standard résumé information, supporting documentation, and sometimes a video where they introduce themselves to potential employers. These same websumés are also frequently searched by recruiting firms that scan the Internet in search of viable job candidates.

Internet recruiting provides a low-cost means for most businesses to gain unprecedented access to potential employees worldwide even for senior-level executives.[20] For example, a job posted online for the San Francisco–based Joie de Vivre Hospitality organization cost $50. Had company officials used the more traditional local paper advertisement, the same ad would have cost $2,000.[21] It's also a way to increase diversity and find people with unique talents.[22] For example, job-posting services create subgroup categories for employers looking to find bilingual workers, female attorneys, or African American engineers.

Finally, Internet recruiting won't be merely the choice of those looking to fill high-tech jobs. As computer prices fall, access costs to the Internet decrease, and the majority of working people become comfortable with the Internet, online recruiting will be used for all kinds of nontechnical jobs—from those paying thousands of dollars a week to those paying $7 an hour.

Recruitment Alternatives

Much of the previous discussion on recruiting sources implies that these efforts are designed to locate and hire full-time, permanent employees. However, economic realities, coupled with management trends such as rightsizing, have created a slightly different focus. More companies today are hiring temporary help (including retirees), leasing employees, and using independent contractors. Remember, however, our discussion in Chapter 1 that temporary or contingent workers may also raise some legal issue for employers—especially over the question about whether or not an individual is in fact an employee.[23]

Temporary Help Services Organizations such as Kelly Services and Accountemps supply temporary employees. Temporary employees are particularly valuable in meeting short-term fluctuations in HRM needs.[24] Although traditionally developed in office administration, temporary staffing services have expanded to a broad range of skills. It is now possible, for example, to hire temporary nurses, computer programmers, accountants, librarians, drafting technicians, administrative assistants—even CEOs.

In addition to specific temporary help services, another quality source of temporary workers is older workers, those who have already retired or have been displaced by rightsizing in many companies.[25] An aging workforce and some individuals' desire to retire earlier have created skill deficiencies in some disciplines. Older workers bring those skills back to the job. The reasons older workers continue to work vary,[26] but they bring several advantages: flexibility in scheduling, low absenteeism, high motivation, and mentoring abilities for younger workers."[27]

Employee Leasing Whereas temporary employees come into an organization for a specific short-term project, **leased employees** typically remain with an organization for longer times. Under a leasing arrangement, individuals work for the leasing firm.[28] When an organization needs specific employee skills, it contracts with the leasing firm to provide trained employees. For example, consider Robert Half International. As a leasing firm, Robert Half has on its staff fully trained accountants ready to meet an organization's accounting needs. If tax season requires additional tax accountants, Robert Half can supply them; the same holds true for other accounting areas. One reason for leasing's popularity is cost. The acquiring organization pays a flat fee for the employees. The company is not directly responsible for the benefit or other costs, such as Social Security payments, it would incur for a full-time employee. Furthermore, when the project is over, employees return to the leasing company, thus eliminating any cost associated with layoffs or discharge.

Leased employees are also well trained. They are screened by the leasing firm, trained appropriately, and often go to organizations with an unconditional guarantee. Thus, if an individual doesn't work out, the company receives a new employee or makes arrangements to have its fee returned. There are also benefits from the employee's point of view. Some of today's workers prefer more flexibility in their lives. Working with a leasing company and being sent out at various times allow these workers to work when they want, for the length of time they desire.

Our discussion in Chapter 1 regarding professional employee organizations (PEOs) is precisely what employee leasing is about. As more organizations—especially smaller ones—move toward PEOs, we can expect the trend of employee leasing to increase significantly.[29] When that happens, the effort organizational members expend on recruiting will drop significantly.

Independent Contractors Another means of recruiting is the use of independent contractors. Often referred to as consultants, independent contractors are taking on a new meaning. Companies may hire independent contractors to do specific work at a location on or off the company's premises. For instance, claims processing or medical and legal transcription activities can easily be done at home and routinely forwarded to the employer. The continuing growth of personal computers, fax machines, and voice mail ensures that home work is timely.

Independent contractor arrangements benefit both the organization and the individual. Because the worker is not an employee, the company saves costs

leased employees
Individuals hired by one firm and sent to work in another for a specific time.

www.wiley.com/college/decenzo
What Would You Do?
EXPERIENCE: Recruiting

WORKPLACE ISSUES

"BEST PRACTICE" IDEAS APPLICABLE TO RECRUITMENT AND HIRING[30]

What are the EEOC-recognized best practices for private-sector organizations? Below are examples of what the "best of the best" do when recruiting.

- Establish a policy for recruitment and hiring, including criteria, procedures, responsible individuals, and applicability of diversity and affirmative action.
- Engage in short-term and long-term strategic planning.
- Identify the applicable barriers to equal employment opportunity.
- Ensure a communication network notifying interested persons of opportunities, including advertising within the organization and, where applicable, not only with the general media, but with media aimed at minority people, disabled people, older people, and women.
- Communicate the competencies, skills, and abilities required for available positions.
- Communicate about family-friendly and work-friendly programs.
- Where transportation is an issue, consider arrangements with the local transit authority.

- Participate in career and job fairs and open houses.
- Work with professional associations, civic associations, and educational institutions with attractive numbers of minorities, women, persons with disabilities, and/or older persons to recruit.
- Use recruiter, referral, and search firms with instructions to present diverse candidate pools to expand search networks.
- Partner with organizations that have missions to serve targeted groups.
- Use internship, work/study, co-op, and scholarship programs to attract interested persons and to develop interested and qualified candidates.
- Develop and support educational programs and become more involved with educational institutions that can refer a more diverse talent pool.
- Ensure that personnel involved in recruitment and hiring are well trained in their equal employment opportunity responsibilities.
- Explore community involvement options so the company's higher profile may attract more interested persons.
- Eliminate practices that exclude or present barriers to minorities, women, people with disabilities, older people, or any individual.
- Include progress in equal employment opportunity recruitment and hiring as factors in management evaluation.

associated with full- or part-time personnel, such as Social Security taxes and workers' compensation premiums. Additionally, such opportunity is also a means of keeping good individuals associated with your company. Suppose an employee wants to work but also to be at home when the kids are home. Allowing the individual to work at home, on his or her time, can be a win-win solution to the problem.

MEETING THE ORGANIZATION

So far in this chapter we've introduced you to organizational recruiting activities. When recruiters decide to hire employees, they often announce the job in some format. Seeing that announcement, and recognizing a potential match between what you can offer and what the organization wants, you need to throw your hat into the hiring ring.

Applying for a job is one of the more stressful situations you will face.[31] Generally, you have no specific guidelines to follow to guarantee you success. However, several tips may increase your chances of finding employment. Even though obtaining a job interview should be one of your major goals in the hiring process, being offered an interview opportunity requires hard work. Your current job is, in fact, obtaining a job.

Competition for most good jobs is fierce—even in times of low unemployment. You can't afford to wait until the last minute; your job hunt must start well

TECHNOLOGY CORNER

CREATING A RÉSUMÉ

Recruiting in organizations has two certainties: résumés and the need to track them.[32] Software on the market today can help in both of these areas—from helping someone design an effective résumé to helping the organization track applicant information.[33]

Resume Maker: Resume Maker (Individual Software, $29.95 students; $49.95 others, www.resumemaker.com) provides sample résumé designs, recommended résumé phrases (key words), and sample cover letters. Resume Maker also allows you to develop and submit an electronic résumé to several career Web sites, such as Monster.com. You can also develop a Web page of your résumé with Resume Maker.

Trak-It Applicant: A very easy-to-use applicant tracking system that helps you trim recruiting expenses by reducing the clerical costs of job application processing. Trak-It Applicant allows you to effortlessly generate standard letters, produce EEO reports, and analyze the costs and statistics of recruiting. Because applicants can be searched for by skill, school, past employer, or anything else for that matter, you can find the right candidate fast. Over 100 Standard Reports are included, as well as a Custom Report Writer. Pricing may vary, and the software is available at www.applicant-tracking-software.com/recruit.htm.

in advance of when you plan to start work. So, for college seniors who plan to graduate in May, starting in the fall has two advantages. First, it shows that you are taking an interest in your career and that you are planning. Not waiting until the last minute to begin reflects favorably on you. Second, starting in the fall coincides with many companies' recruiting cycles. If you wait until March to begin the process, some job openings are likely to already have been filled. For specific information regarding the company recruiting cycles in your area, visit your college's career development center.

Preparing Your Résumé

All job applicants need to circulate information that reflects positively on their strengths and to send that information to prospective employers in a format that is understandable and consistent with the organization's hiring practices. In most instances, this requires a résumé (see Technology Corner).

No matter who you are or where you are in your career, you should have a current résumé. Your résumé is typically a recruiter's primary information source in determining whether to grant you an interview. Therefore, your résumé must be a sales tool; it must give key information that supports your candidacy, highlights your strengths, and differentiates you from other job applicants. Include anything positive that distinguishes you from other applicants. Information to include is shown in Exhibit 6-4. Note that volunteer or community service, for example, shows that you are well rounded, committed to your community, and willing to help others.

It's important to pinpoint a few key themes regarding résumés that may seem like common sense but are frequently ignored. First, if you are making a paper copy of your résumé, it must be printed on a quality printer. The font style should be easy to read (for example, Courier or Times New Roman type fonts). Avoid any style that may be hard on the eyes, such as a script or italic font. A recruiter who must review 100 or more résumés a day will look more favorably at those that make the job easier.

It is also important to note that many companies today rely on computer software for making the first pass through résumés. Each résumé is scanned for specific information such as key job elements, experience, work history, education, or

EXHIBIT 6-4
A Sample Résumé

Shane Reynolds
1820 North Avenue
Bentonville, AR 72712

CAREER OBJECTIVE: Seeking employment in an investment firm that provides a challenging opportunity to combine exceptional interpersonal and computer skills.

EDUCATION: University of Arkansas
B.S., Business Economics and Computer Science (May 2007)

EXPERIENCE: University of Arkansas
9/2003 to present Campus Bookstore, Assistant Bookkeeper
Primary Duties: Responsible for coordinating book purchases with academic departments; placing orders with publishers; invoicing, receiving inventory, pricing, and stocking shelves. Supervised four student employees. Managed annual budget of $55,000.

9/2005 to 12/2005 Student Intern
Wal-Mart Corporation
Primary Duties: Worked on team responsible for developing and maintaining a product tracking system for Southwest region. Presented concept to regional management and began process of implementation. Cited for outstanding work on the internship.

SPECIAL SKILLS:
- Experienced in C++ and Java, Microsoft Excel and Word, Netscape, dBase, and PowerPoint presentation software.
- Fluent in speaking and writing Chinese.
- Certified in CPR.

SERVICE ACTIVITIES:
- Secretary/Treasurer, Student Government Association
- President, Computer Science Club
- Volunteer, Meals-on-Wheels

REFERENCES: Available on request.

---

technical expertise. This has created two important aspects for résumé writers to remember. First, the computer matches key words in a job description. Thus, in creating a résumé, use standard job description phraseology. Second, use a font the scanner can easily read. If it can't, your résumé may be put in the rejection file. Copy your résumé on good-quality white or off-white paper (no off-the-wall colors). This suggestion may be inappropriate for certain types of jobs—such as a creative artist position—but these are exceptions. You can't go wrong using a 20-pound bond paper with about 20 percent cotton content. By all means, don't send standard duplicating paper—it may look as if you are mass-mailing résumés (even if you are).

Some Final Remarks

Much of what we stated in the last few paragraphs also holds true if you are producing an electronic résumé. Ads and Internet recruiting sites usually specify whether an electronic résumé is required. In spite of all the technology improvements that come about, do not forget about a tried-and-true means of gaining access into an organization—networking. It still ranks as one of the best means of learning about jobs.[34]

Finally, regardless of whether your résumé is on paper or electronic, make sure it is carefully proofread. The résumé is your only representation to the recruiter, and a sloppy one can be deadly. If it contains misspelled words or is grammatically incorrect, your chances for an interview will be significantly reduced. Proofread your résumé several times, and if possible, let others proof-read it.

SUMMARY

(This summary relates to the Learning Outcomes identified on page 147.)
After reading this chapter, you can

1. **Define the term** *recruiting*. Recruiting is discovering potential applicants for actual or anticipated organizational vacancies. It involves seeking viable job candidates.
2. **Identify the dual goals of recruiting.** The two goals of recruiting are to generate a large pool of applicants and to provide enough information for individuals to self-select out of the process.
3. **Explain constraints human resource managers face in determining recruiting sources.** Influences that constrain HRM in determining recruiting sources include image of the organization, attractiveness and nature of the job, internal policies, government requirements, and the recruiting budget.
4. **Identify the principal sources for recruiting employees.** The principal sources for recruiting employees include internal search, advertisements, employee referrals/recommendations, employment agencies, temporary leasing services, schools, colleges, universities, professional organizations, the Internet (or online recruiting), and casual or unsolicited applicants. Employee leasing, temporary employees, and independent contractors continue to be good sources of employees.
5. **Describe the advantages and disadvantages of employee referrals.** The advantages of employee referrals include access to individuals who possess specific skills, having job applicants with more complete job and organization information, and a universal application to all levels in the organization. The disadvantages of employee referrals include the potential of confusing friendship with job performance, the potential for nepotism, and a potential for minimizing the organization's desire to add diversity to the organization's employee mix.
6. **Identify three important variables that affect response rates to job advertisements.** The three important variables are identification of the organization, labor market conditions, and the degree to which specific requirements are included in the advertisement.
7. **Explain what distinguishes a public employment agency from a private employment agency.** The major difference between public and private employment agencies often lies in their image. Private employment agencies are believed to offer positions and applicants of a higher caliber. Private agencies may also provide a more complete line of services in that they advertise the position, screen applicants against the criteria specified by the employer, and provide a guarantee covering six months or a year as protection to the employer should the applicant not perform satisfactorily. Public employment agencies are more closely linked to unemployment benefits. Accordingly, the image of most public agencies (not completely accurate) is that they tend to attract and list individuals who are unskilled or have had minimum training.
8. **Describe the benefits of online recruiting.** Internet recruiting provides businesses with low-cost and unprecedented access to potential employees worldwide. Online recruiting also helps increase diversity and find people with unique talents.

VISUAL SUMMARY

CHAPTER 6: RECRUITING

1   Recruiting Goals

- Find a large, diverse job-candidate pool
- Help unqualified candidates self-select out of candidacy

Barriers to Recruiting Success

- Image of the organization
- Attractiveness of job
- Internal/Organizational policies
- Government influence
- Recruiting costs

2   Recruiting from a Global Perspective

Three Approaches to Recruiting for International Positions

- Host-country national (HCN)
- Expatriates
- Recruiting regardless of nationality

164

3 Recruiting Sources

1 **Internal Search**
2 **Employee Referrals/Recommendations**

3 **External Searches**
- Advertisement
- Employment agencies
- Schools, colleges, and universities
- Professional organizations
- Unsolicited applicants
- Internet recruiting

4 **Alternatives**
- Temporary help services
- Employee leasing
- Independent contractors

4 Getting into the Organization

- **Getting a Job Is a Full-time Activity**
- **Start Early**
- **Prepare Your Résumé**

Shane Reynolds
1820 North Avenue
Bentonville, AR 72712

CAREER OBJECTIVE:	Seeking employment in an investment firm that provides a challenging opportunity to combine exceptional interpersonal and computer skills.
EDUCATION:	University of Arkansas B.S., Business Economics and Computer Science (May 2007)
EXPERIENCE: 9/2003 to present	University of Arkansas Campus Bookstore, Assistant Bookkeeper *Primary Duties:* Responsible for coordinating book purchases with academic departments; placing orders with publishers; invoicing, receiving inventory, pricing and stocking shelves. Supervised four student employees. Managed annual budget of $55,000.
9/2005 to 12/2005	Student Intern Wal-Mart Corporation *Primary Duties:* Worked on team responsible for developing and maintaining a product tracking system for Southwest region. Presented concept to regional management and began process of implementation. Cited for outstanding work on the internship.
SPECIAL SKILLS:	• Experienced in C++ and Java, Microsoft Excel and Word, Netscape, dBase, and PowerPoint presentation software. • Fluent in speaking and writing Chinese. • Certified in CPR.
SERVICE ACTIVITIES:	• Secretary/Treasurer, Student Government Association • President, Computer Science Club • Volunteer, Meals-on-Wheels
REFERENCES:	Available on request.

9. **Explain the concept of employee leasing and the organizational benefits of such an arrangement.** Employee leasing refers to when individuals employed in an organization actually work for the leasing firm. One reason for leasing's popularity is cost. The acquiring organization pays a flat fee for the employees and is not responsible for benefits or other costs, such as Social Security payments, it would incur for a full-time employee.

DEMONSTRATING COMPREHENSION: *Questions for Review*

1. What is the "dual objective" of recruiting?
2. Identify and describe factors that influence the degree to which an organization will engage in recruiting.
3. What specific constraints might prevent an HR manager from hiring the best candidate?
4. Present the advantages and disadvantages of recruiting through an internal search.
5. What are the pros and cons of using employee referrals for recruiting workers?
6. Describe the differences one may encounter when recruiting globally.
7. What are the advantages and disadvantages of having a websumé?

KEY TERMS

blind-box ad	employee	host-country	recruiting
constraints on	referrals	national (HCN)	websumés
recruiting	executive search	internal search	
efforts	expatriates	leased employees	

CROSSWORD COMPREHENSION

ACROSS

1. a recommendation from a current employee regarding a job applicant
3. a promotion-from-within concept
6. a private employment firm that specializes in middle- and top-management placements
7. a citizen of the home country hired by an organization based in another country

8. an individual who lives and works in a country of which he or she is not a citizen
9. advertisements that do not identify the advertising organization
10. Web pages that are used as résumés

DOWN

2. individuals hired by one firm and sent to work in another firm for a specified period of time
4. factors that limit recruiting outcomes
5. the process of seeking sources for job candidates

HRM Workshop

LINKING CONCEPTS TO PRACTICE: Discussion Questions

1. "A job advertisement that generates 1,000 responses is always better than one that gets 20 responses." Build an argument supporting this statement and an argument against this statement.
2. "An organization should follow a promote-from-within policy." Do you agree or disagree with this statement? Explain.
3. When you go looking for a job after graduation, what sources do you expect to use? Why?
4. "The emphasis on leased or temporary employees in an organization will only lead to a decrease in employee morale. These employees come in, do their jobs, then leave it up to the full-timers to handle the details." Build an argument supporting this statement, and an argument against this statement.

DEVELOPING DIAGNOSTIC AND ANALYTICAL SKILLS

Case Application 6-A: PRIORITY STAFFING

Imagine you work for a large global company in human resources. You are faced with some special staffing needs for a few of the departments that you serve. You know that the people you're looking for must be well trained and able to do the job immediately. So when staffing gets tough like this, you frequently turn to temporary staffing agencies for assistance. But today's challenge is a bit more complex. You need an administrative assistant who is fluent in Spanish for one of the executives visiting from Spain. You also have a project for which you are providing HRM support that will require someone who is well versed in Hindi and its customs. And your manufacturing vice president is asking for your help as she's preparing for a visit from a Korean client who doesn't speak English. What do you do? If you're in the New York area, the answer is simple. You contact Deborah Wainstein, founder of Priority Staffing Solutions, and ask for help.[35]

Priority Staffing Solutions is a temporary staffing agency in New York. Founded in 1999 by Wainstein, the organization provides multilingual temporary workers to organizations in the New York City area. Employing 15 full-time individuals and more than 500 part-time employees, the company places nearly 70 temporary employees daily as administrative assistants, computer graphics specialists, word processing operators, and legal office support staff. Serving the needs of approximately 80

clients—such organizations as Revlon and RCN Corporation—Priority Staffing Solutions offers their clients "cost-effective strategies while distinguishing and responding to the ever-changing needs of each individual organization."

For Wainstein, her service is a wonderful help to her client organizations. She's helped them staff for peak periods or find that special skill needed for special projects. Through her service she's also assisted her clients in saving some HR-related costs—such as those associated with recruiting. In return, she's distinguished her company as a leading multilingual temporary staffing agency, resulting in the company generating several million in annual revenues.

Questions:

1. What role does a temporary staffing agency like Priority Staffing Solutions play in the recruiting efforts of an organization?
2. Does a surplus or a shortage of workers play a role in how organizations recruit? Discuss.
3. How does an organization like Priority Staffing Solutions assist in filling "hard-to-recruit" jobs? Explain.
4. What effect on an organization's image do you believe there is from using a firm like Priority Staffing Solutions? Defend your position.

Case Application 6-B: TEAM FUN!

Team Fun

Kenny and Norton, owners of TEAM FUN!, a sporting goods manufacturer and retailer, are in the OFFICE, looking at the model of their organization on the wall. Norton comments, "I think it's great that your daughter, Gloria, is getting married again. And I agree that we should give Bobby, your new son-in-law, a manager job at a branch. But we have all the branch managers we need."

Kenny grins. "I think this would be a great time to open a Florida store. They could live there; run the place in the summer. We go down there in the winter and make sure everything is going fine. It will be great."

Norton groans. "Maybe. Hey, Tony!" he yells to the director of human resources, who is walking by. "Come in here for a minute. We need to hire 20–30 people in the Fort Myers, Florida, area to work in our new branch. How long will it take you to get that together?"

Meanwhile, Kenny picks up the phone. "Ray, remember that mall area by the new golf course in Punta Gorda we played last year? Find out if we can lease 30,000–40,000 square feet of it by. . . ." He puts his hand over the receiver and looks at Tony. "How long 'til you get the people?"

Tony gulps and says, "Six months, probably. Who do I take from here?"

Kenny continues on the phone with Ray, the comptroller, "By . . . what is this, June? By September–October 1. That gives us about 60 to 90 days to redo the inside. We can open TEAM FUN! SOUTH in time for a Christmas rush! Sure. Sure. Whatever you need. Get back to me." He hangs up, obviously well pleased.

As Tony slumps into a side chair, Norton says to him, "Now that you did all those job descriptions, I'm amazed you think it will take five months. We know lots of people along the Gulf Coast. Let me find you some names." He and Kenny both paw through a huge Rolodex and laugh at certain names and memories as they pull cards for Tony.

Tony sighs, "Good thing I've got that intern starting next week."

Questions:
(You are Tony's intern.)

1. Make a recruiting plan for TEAM FUN! Identify at least four principal recruiting sources for the new store. Be sure to discuss the pros and cons of each of your suggestions.
2. Recommend to Tony which of the four sources should get top priority. Defend your decision.

WORKING WITH A TEAM: *A Question of Effective Recruiting*

Tommy Ford is an impatient, results-oriented, innovative, hard-working, focused entrepreneur. He likes working with aggressive, highly creative, skilled, focused team players who are flexible, change driven, informed, cutting-edge professionals much like himself in work ethic but from diverse groups. He believes that professionals with varied backgrounds contribute to better solutions and creativity. He wants only those who are as committed as he is to growing a company that produces the industry standard and benchmark in intranet and software technology. That means being willing to work 60 to 90 hours a week at High-5-Tech if the project requires, and dedication to and passion for customers, the firm, and the project team.

Ford may start people out with salaries slightly below industry average, but he rewards performance and tenure. He's reputed to double a salary when a developer exceeds expectations. He also contributes his company's stock to the employees' benefit package, subject to their length of employment. At the current rate, a person might retire a millionaire if he or she can withstand the pace.

Interested? Discuss why or why not, comparing responses with your paired team member. Also, here are some guiding questions for you and your partner to consider:

1. What Web sites would you use if you were interested in an international job?
2. Would you consider being an expatriate; why or why not?

LEARNING AN HRM SKILL: *Writing a Job Advertisement*

About the skill: How do you persuade individuals to pay attention to your job opening? Interest them in your organization? Give them enough information so that those who are not qualified do not respond? The answer to these questions lies in the job advertisement.[36] The more effective your advertisement, the more likely you will achieve the dual goal of recruiting.

1. *Tell enough about the job.* Provide enough information about the job so that potential applicants can determine whether they are interested or qualified.
2. *Give relevant information about the job.* Provide a job title and a description of job duties. This information should be drawn directly from the job description.
3. *List the minimum qualities a successful job incumbent needs.* Include specific requirements a job incumbent must

possess. This may reflect educational levels, prior experience, and specific competencies or skills. Again, much of this information should be readily available from the job-specification component of the job description.

4. *Be specific about unique aspects of the job.* Disclose any pertinent information the job applicant should know. For example, if the job requires extensive traveling, state so, as well as experience on specific equipment, technology applications, and so forth.
5. *Check the advertisement for correctness.* Make sure the advertisement is properly written, contains no grammatical or punctuation errors, and is easy to read. Whenever possible, avoid jargon and abbreviations that may be confusing. Review each word to ensure that no terms used may be deemed inappropriate or potentially create an adverse impact.

ENHANCING YOUR COMMUNICATION SKILLS

1. Using the job description of the benefits manager from Exhibit 5-9 (Chapter 5, p. 136), write a job advertisement for this position to be placed in a national newspaper such as the *Wall Street Journal*.

2. Develop a two- to three-page response to the following question: What are the pluses and minuses for an organization that uses temporary employees as a pool from which to select permanent employees? Are there pluses from the employee's standpoint?

3. Visit three different online job-recruiting sites (as listed in Exhibit 6-3, p. 158). Describe the similarities and differences you noticed among the three. Which job site did you prefer? Explain why.

SEVEN

Reality in many cases is stranger than fiction. And when it comes to employment selection, some things are just remarkable. That's because anyone who's ever worked in the screening process—especially when interviewing job candidates—typically has some fascinating stories to tell. Consider the following questions posed or comments made by interviewees during actual interviews.[1]

- Do you know of any companies where I could get a job I would like better than this one?
- I'm quitting my present job because I hate to work hard.
- I don't think I'm capable of doing this job, but I sure would like the money.
- I think what would help this organization would be if it had a more creative side to it.
- My résumé might look like I'm a job hopper. But I want you to know that I never left any of these jobs voluntarily.
- I don't believe that anyone in my former organizations was as gifted as I was.

- Did you know my uncle is president of a competing organization?
- What job am I applying for anyway?
- I'm leaving my present job because my manager is a jerk; all managers are jerks.
- A candidate expressed her interest in the position but only if her boyfriend liked the company and the hiring manager. She then asked if she could go get her boyfriend, who was waiting outside.
- When asked how he'd improve sales in the company (he was applying for a sales position), the candidate got up, walked out of the room, and was never seen again.
- After being complimented on the candidate's choice of college and GPA, the candidate remarked that he really didn't go to that college—just thought he'd say so to get the company's attention.
- One candidate arrived at the airport for the start of his interview. As he got off the plane, he said it was too cold to live and work in that city, and immediately left to find a return flight.

Wouldn't it be nice if making determinations about candidates were this clear-cut? It sure would make things easier! How about the applicant who is impeccably dressed for the interview, handles questions exceptionally well, and has a good bit of experience? The organization is a rather conservative one, where proper business attire is the status quo. The candidate, however, has multiple facial piercings, visible tattoos, or has dyed his or her hair some color you simply are not sure about. Now what?

Of course, these are exaggerations. HR practitioners usually do not have clear-cut situations that allow them to make quick, decisive decisions about a candidate. Making selection determinations is often difficult. Yet all selection activities exist for the purpose of making effective selection decisions—seeking to predict which job applicants will be successful job performers if hired.

Foundations of Selection

Learning Outcomes

After reading this chapter, you will be able to

1. Describe the selection process.
2. Identify the primary purpose of selection activities.
3. Discuss why organizations use application forms.
4. Explain the primary purposes of performance simulation tests.
5. Discuss the problems associated with job interviews and means of correcting them.
6. Specify the organizational benefits derived from realistic job previews.
7. Explain the purpose of background investigations.
8. List three types of validity.
9. Explain how validity is determined.

INTRODUCTION

A recent international business graduate went on her first interview in a organization with significant operations on four continents.[2] Not knowing what to expect, she prepared as best she could. She was exquisitely dressed in a new navy pinstriped suit and carried her new black leather briefcase. As she entered the human resource management office, she encountered two doors. On the first door was "International Business Majors." On the second was "All Other Majors." She entered door one, which opened up to two more doors. On door one was "3.55 or Better GPA"; door two, "All Other GPAs." Having a 3.78 GPA, she once again entered door one, and found herself facing yet two more choices. Door one stated, "Fluent in three languages," and door two, "Fluent in two or fewer languages." Because her education did not require language proficiency and she was fluent in only one language, she went through door two. Upon opening the door, she found a box with preprinted letters saying, "Your qualifications did not meet the expectations of the job. Thanks for considering our organization. Please exit to the right."

Of course no selection activity is this clear-cut. Successful selection activities entail a lot of careful planning and careful thought. The selection process is composed of steps, each of which provides decision makers with information that will help them predict whether an applicant will be a successful job performer.[3] One way to conceptualize this is to think of each step as a higher hurdle in a race. The applicant able to clear all the hurdles wins the race and the job offer.

THE SELECTION PROCESS

Selection activities follow a standard pattern, beginning with an initial screening interview and concluding with the final employment decision. The selection process typically consists of eight steps: (1) initial screening interview, (2) completing the application form, (3) employment tests, (4) comprehensive interview, (5) background investigation, (6) conditional job offer, (7) medical or physical examination, and (8) permanent job offer. Each step represents a decision point requiring some affirmative feedback for the process to continue. Each step in the process seeks to expand the organization's knowledge about the applicant's background, abilities, and motivation, and it increases the information decision makers use to make their predictions and final choice. However, some steps may be omitted if they do not yield useful data, or if the cost of the step is unwarranted. Applicants should also be advised of any specific screening, such as credit checks, reference checking, and drug tests. The flow of these activities is depicted in Exhibit 7-1. Let's take a closer look at each.

Initial Screening

initial screening
The first step in the selection process whereby job inquiries are sorted.

As a culmination of our recruiting efforts, we initiate a preliminary review of potentially acceptable candidates. This **initial screening** is, in effect, a two-step procedure: (1) screening inquiries and (2) screening interviews.

If our recruiting effort has been successful, we will have a pool of potential applicants. We can eliminate some of these respondents based on the job description and job specification. Perhaps candidates lack adequate or appropriate experience, or adequate or appropriate education. Other red flags include gaps in the applicant's job history, many brief jobs, or numerous courses and seminars instead of appropriate education.

The screening interview is also an excellent opportunity for HRM to describe the job in enough detail so the candidates can consider if they are really serious about applying. Sharing job description information frequently encourages the

EXHIBIT 7-1
The Selection Process

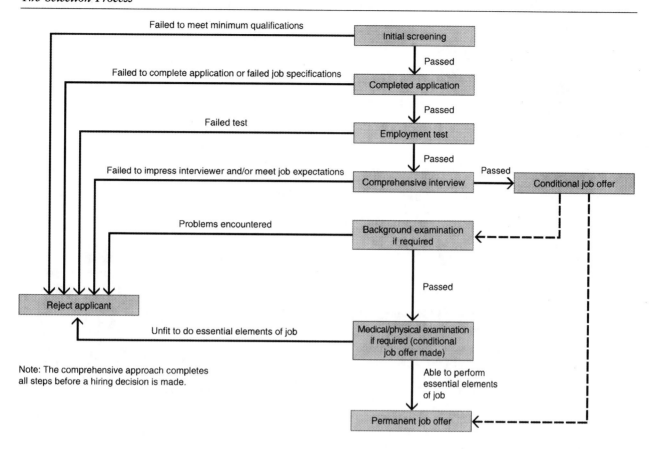

Note: The comprehensive approach completes
all steps before a hiring decision is made.

unqualified or marginally qualified to voluntarily withdraw from candidacy with a minimum of cost to the applicant or the organization. Conference call interviews or videoconferencing can help minimize costs during screening interviews.

Another important point during the initial screening phase is to identify a salary range. Most workers are concerned about their salaries, and even if a job opening sounds exciting, a low salary may drive away excellent talent. During this phase, if proper HRM activities have been conducted, you should not need to mask salary data.

Completing the Application Form

Once the initial screening is completed, applicants are asked to complete the organization's **application form.** This may require only the applicant's name, address, and telephone number. Some organizations, on the other hand, may want a more comprehensive employment profile. In general terms, the application form gives a job-performance-related synopsis of applicants' adult life, their skills, and their accomplishments (see Diversity Issues in HRM).

Applications obtain information the company wants. Completing the application also serves as another hurdle; that is, if the job requires following directions and the individual fails to do so on the application, that is a job-related reason for rejection. Last, applications require a signature attesting to the truthfulness of the information given and giving permission to check references. If, at a later point, the company finds out the information is false, it can justify immediate dismissal.

application form
Company-specific employment form used to generate specific information the company wants.

DIVERSITY ISSUES IN HRM

EMPLOYER'S GUIDE TO APPLICATION FORMS AND INTERVIEWS UNDER
THE SASKATCHEWAN HUMAN RIGHTS CODE

Inquiries Before Hiring	Okay	Don't Ask
1. Address	Okay to ask about current and previous addresses in Canada and how long applicant stayed there.	Don't ask about foreign addresses which would indicate national origin.
2. Birthplace, nationality, ancestry, place of origin	**After hiring,** may ask for birth certificate.	Don't make any inquiry about place of birth or national origin. That includes asking about the national origin of relatives or asking for a birth certificate or baptismal certificate.
3. Photographs	**After hiring,** okay to ask for photos if needed.	**Before hiring,** don't ask for photo.
4. Religion	**After hiring,** may ask about religion to determine when leave of absence may be required for the observance of religious holidays.	**Before hiring,** don't ask anything that would identify religious affiliation. That includes asking for a pastor's recommendation or reference.
5. Citizenship	May ask if applicant is legally entitled to work in Canada.	Don't ask about applicant's citizenship status—it could reveal applicant's nationality, ancestry, or place of origin. That includes questions about proof of citizenship or the date citizenship was received.
6. Education	Okay to ask about schools where education was obtained and about foreign language skills.	Don't ask about the religious or racial affiliation of educational institutions.
7. Relatives	**After hiring,** may ask for a contact name in case of emergency.	**Before hiring,** don't ask questions that would require someone to reveal their marital or family status.
8. Organization	Okay to ask about clubs and organizations that would reveal a person's affiliation based on race, disability, sexual orientation, etc., **as long as** applicants are told, "You may decline to list organizations which would indicate your religion, race, etc."	
9. Work schedule	May ask applicants whether they are able to work the required schedule. If applicants are not able to work the required schedule because of religious practices or family needs, the employer must determine if accommodation is possible.	
10. Sex		On the application form don't ask about the sex of the applicant.

(continued)

11. Age	Okay to ask if the applicant is younger than the minimum age or older than the maximum age required by employment law.	**Before hiring**, don't ask for any record (like a birth certificate) or other information that would reveal the applicant's age.
12. Marital status	Although you can't ask about an applicant's marital status, if the job requires it, you **can ask** if the applicant is willing to travel or be transferred.	Don't ask if applicant is single, married, remarried, engaged, divorced, separated, widowed, living common-law. Don't ask a woman for her birth name.
13. Family status	May ask if applicant is able to work the required schedule. If she can't because of family needs, the employer must try to accommodate her.	Don't ask about the number of children or other dependents. Don't ask about child-care arrangements. Don't ask applicant whether she is breastfeeding, using birth control, or plans to have children.
14. Disability	The following questions should be asked: (i) Do you have a disability which will affect your ability to perform any of the functions of the job for which you have applied?	Don't ask about disabilities or health problems except as set out in the adjacent column.
	If the answer to the above is yes then ask: (ii) what functions can you not perform and what accommodations could be made which would allow you to do the work adequately?	Don't ask if applicant has ever had previous work injuries or made a claim for workers' compensation.
15. Height and weight		Don't ask unless it can be shown they are essential to the performance of the job.
16. Sexual orientation		Don't ask about applicant's sexual orientation.
17. Receipt of public assistance		Don't ask if applicant is receiving assistance under *The Saskatchewan Assistance Act* (welfare) or *The Saskatchewan Income Plan Act*.

18. Drug testing is generally prohibited by human rights legislation. After a job offer has been made, testing may be acceptable in exceptional circumstances that must be justified by the employer in accordance with criteria established by the Supreme Court of Canada, otherwise drug testing is not allowed under *The Saskatchewan Human Rights Code*. If an employee has a drug-related disability, employers may be required to accommodate.

What's your opinion of this? Perhaps it is surprising that this is not based on U.S. EEO laws. Many of the practices we've discussed regarding employment discrimination are quickly becoming a global phenomenon.

Source: The Saskatchewan Human Rights Commission (2001).

Key Issues The Civil Rights Acts of 1964 and 1991 and subsequent amendments, executive orders, court rulings, and other legislation have made it illegal to discriminate on the basis of sex, race, color, religion, national origin, disability, and age. The only major exceptions to these guidelines involving age, sex, and religion are cases where these criteria are bona fide occupational qualifications (BFOQ). Many items that traditionally appeared on application forms—religion, age, marital status, occupation of spouse, number and ages of children, and hobbies—were not demonstrably job-related.[4] The onus is now on management to demonstrate that information supplied by applicants is job related, and items that fail that test should be omitted.

In addition to these changes in application forms, one important aspect has been added. Applications typically include a statement giving the employer the right to dismiss an employee for falsifying information. They also typically indicate that employment is at the will of either party (the employer or the employee can end the work relationship) and that the employee understands that employment is not guaranteed. Furthermore, the applicant gives the company permission to obtain previous work history. Of course, an applicant has the right not to sign the application. In that event, however, one's application may be removed from consideration.

weighted application forms

A special type of application form that uses relevant applicant information to determine the likelihood of job success.

Weighted Application Forms Weighted application forms offer excellent potential in helping recruiters differentiate between potentially successful and unsuccessful job performers.[5] To create such an instrument, individual form items, such as years of schooling, months on last job, salary data for all previous jobs, and military experience, are validated against performance and turnover measures and given appropriate weights. Let's assume, for example, that HRM is interested in developing a weighted application form that would predict which applicants for the job of accountant, if hired, would stay with the company. They would select from their files the application forms from each of two groups of previously hired accountants—a group that had short tenure with the organization (adjusters who stayed, say, less than one year), and a group with long tenure (say, five years or more). These old application forms would be screened item by item to determine how employees in each group responded. In this way, management would discover items that differentiate the groups and weight them relative to how well they differentiate applicants. If, for example, 80 percent of the long-tenure group had a college degree, possession of a college degree might have a weight of 4. But if 30 percent of the long-tenure group had prior experience in a major accounting firm, compared to percent of the short-tenured, this item might have a weight of only 1. Note, of course, that this procedure would have to be done for every job in the organization and balanced against the factors of those that do not fall into the majority category; that is, although 80 percent of the long-tenure individuals had a college degree, we would need to factor into our weighting scheme those who had a college degree and were successful on the job, but had only short tenure with the company.

Items that predict long tenure for an accountant might be totally different from items that predict long tenure for an engineer or even an financial analyst. However, improvements in sophisticated computer software may make the task of developing applications for each job more manageable.

Successful Applications The application form, as noted earlier, has had wide success in selection for diverse jobs. For instance, the hotel industry has found application form analysis valuable. In one study, seven items on the application were highly predictive of successful performance as measured by job tenure.[6] Evidence that the application form provides relevant information for predicting job success is well supported across a broad range of jobs. Care must be taken to ensure that application items are validated for each job. Also, since their predictive ability may change over time, the items must be continuously reviewed and updated. Finally, management should be aware of the possibility that the application information given is erroneous. A background investigation can verify most data.

Employment Tests

Organizations historically relied to a considerable extent on intelligence, aptitude, ability, and interest tests to provide major input to the selection process. Even handwriting analysis (graphology) and honesty tests (see Chapter 4) have been used in attempts to learn more about the candidate—information that supposedly leads to more effective selection.[7]

In the 1970s and early 1980s, reliance on traditional written tests for selection purposes decreased significantly. This was attributed to legal rulings that required employers to justify as job-related any test they used. Given the historical difficulty and costs in substantiating this relationship, some organizations merely eliminated employment testing as a selection device.

Since the mid-1980s, however, that trend has reversed. It is estimated that more than 60 percent of all organizations use some type of employment test today.[8] These organizations recognized that scrapping employment tests was equivalent to throwing the baby out with the bath water. They realized that some tests are quite helpful in predicting who will be successful on the job.[9] Literally hundreds of tests can serve as selection tools. They can measure intellect, spatial ability, perception skills, mechanical comprehension, motor ability, or personality traits.[10] It is not the purpose of this text to review each of these test categories; that is generally the province of books in applied industrial psychology. However, a basic understanding of a few test types can be beneficial for HRM practitioners.

Performance Simulation Tests To avoid criticism and potential liability from using psychological, aptitude, and other types of written tests, interest has been increasing in **performance simulation tests**. The single identifying characteristic of these tests is that they require the applicant to engage in specific behaviors necessary for doing the job successfully. As a result, performance simulation tests should more easily meet the requirement of job relatedness because they are made up of actual job behaviors rather than surrogates.

> **performance simulation tests**
> Work sampling and assessment centers evaluation abilities in actual job activities.

Work Sampling Work sampling creates a miniature replica of a job. Applicants demonstrate that they possess the necessary talents by actually doing the tasks. Carefully devised work samples based on job analysis data determine the knowledge, skills, and abilities needed for each job. Then, each work sample element is matched with a corresponding job performance element. For example, a work sample for a customer service representative at Wachovia Bank may involve keyboard computation: the applicant makes computations during a customer transaction. At Lowe's, a potential check-out clerk is screened for a job to scan the prices of your purchases quickly and accurately. Most go through a similar work-sampling session where supervisors demonstrate how to scan accurately, ensuring that the product did indeed ring up. Then the candidate is given an opportunity to show that he or she can handle the job. Work sampling, then, reflects hands-on experience.

> **work sampling**
> A selection device requiring the job applicant to actually perform a small segment of the job.

The advantages of work sampling over traditional pencil-and-paper tests should be obvious. Because work samples are essentially identical to job content, work sampling should be a better predictor of short-term performance and should minimize discrimination. Additionally, the nature of their content and the methods used to determine content help well-constructed work sample tests easily meet EEOC

DID YOU KNOW?

REMEMBERING EEO

How can something so innocent and with such a good reason end up so problematic? That's probably something the management team at Volvo is wondering. What appeared to be a great idea has now cost them some money—40,000 kronors (or about $5,000 in U.S. dollars).

At issue in this instance is a job requirement at Volvo that stated the following: "For safety reasons and to prevent injuries, employees must be between 5 feet 4 inches and 6 feet 5 inches to work on the conveyor belt" at the company's assembly plant in Goteborg, Sweden. Those who applied and were not within this height range were ulti-

mately denied employment opportunity. That's what happened to one 5-foot-3-inch female applicant. As a result, she filed a complaint with the Equal Opportunity ombudsman—and won her case! Why? Because the requirement had a consequence of an adverse impact based on gender.

But that's not to say that all individuals, irrespective of height, are eligible for these assembly line jobs at Volvo's plant. Rather, each individual will have to be evaluated to determine if they can successfully do the job—a physical condition that must be met in terms of the individual's ability to reach and his or her muscle strength—rather than simply height.

Source: M. Karen, "Volvo Convicted of Gender Discrimination," *Yahoo Financial News* (September 21, 2005).

How can an organization like Lowe's ensure that it has the right person handling the check-out counter? Using work sampling as part of the selection process, the organization can determine which candidate has the requisite skills to perform the job. (*Source:* © AP/Wide World Photos)

assessment center

A facility where performance simulation tests are administered. These include a series of exercises used for selection, development, and performance appraisals.

comprehensive interview

A selection device used to obtain in-depth information about a candidate.

job-related requirements. The main disadvantage is the difficulty in developing good work samples for each job. Furthermore, work sampling is not applicable to all levels of the organization. Its difficulty in use for managerial jobs lies in creating a work sample test that can address the full range of managerial activities.

Assessment Centers A more elaborate set of performance simulation tests, specifically designed to evaluate a candidate's managerial potential, is administered in **assessment centers**. Assessment centers use procedures that incorporate group and individual exercises. Applicants go through a series of these exercises and are appraised by line executives, practicing supervisors, and/or trained psychologists as to how well they perform. As with work sampling, these exercises are designed to simulate the work of managers and so tend to be accurate predictors of later job performance. In some cases, however, the assessment center also includes traditional personality and aptitude tests.[11]

Testing in a Global Arena Many of the standard selection techniques described in this text do not easily transfer to international situations. When recruiting and employing host-country nationals, typical American testing works in some countries but not in others. For example, handwriting or graphology tests, sometimes used in the United States, are frequently used in France. In Great Britain, most psychological tests such as graphology, polygraph, and honesty tests are rarely used in employment.[12] Accordingly, whenever American corporations prepare to do business abroad, their practices must adapt to the cultures and regulations of the country in which they will operate.

Comprehensive Interviews

Applicants who pass the initial screening, application form, and required tests typically receive a **comprehensive interview**. The applicant may be interviewed by HRM interviewers, senior managers within the organization, a potential supervisor, potential colleagues, or some or all of these. In fact, in a company like Disney, applicants are interviewed by numerous individuals.

The comprehensive interview is designed to probe areas not easily addressed by the application form or tests, such as assessing one's motivation, values, ability to work under pressure, and ability to "fit in" with the organization.[13] Fit cannot be overstated. Ironically, in many cases, employees are typically hired based on their competencies and how likely they are to be successful performers. The majority that fail do so because they cannot fit within the organization's culture. Accordingly, skills and aptitudes may get candidates in the door, how well they adapt to the organization frequently determines how long they'll stay.[14]

Interview Effectiveness A common question arises whenever we discuss interviews: Are interviews effective for gathering accurate information from which selection decisions can be made?[15] The interview has proven an almost universal selection tool—one that can take numerous forms.[16] It can be a one-on-one encounter between the interviewer and the applicant (the traditional interview) or involve several individuals who interview an applicant at once (the panel interview). Interviews can follow a predetermined pattern that identifies both questions and expected responses (a situational interview). The interview can also be designed to create a difficult environment in which the applicant is "put to the test" to assess his or her confidence levels. This is frequently referred to as the stress interview (see Ethical Issues in HRM).

Interviews may vary, but few people secure jobs without one or more. This is extremely interesting, given that the interview's validity as a selection tool has been subject to considerable debate. Let's look at research findings regarding interviews.[17]

ETHICAL ISSUES IN HRM

THE STRESS INTERVIEW

Your interview day has finally arrived. You are all dressed up to make that lasting first impression. You finally meet Ms. Prince; she shakes your hand firmly and invites you to be comfortable. Your interview has started! This is the moment you've waited for.

The first few moments appear mundane enough. The questions to this point, in fact, seem easy. Your confidence is growing. That little voice in your head keeps telling you that you are doing fine—just keep going. Suddenly, the questions become tougher. Ms. Prince leans back and asks about why you want to leave your current job—the one you've been in for only 18 months. As you explain that you wish to leave for personal reasons, she begins to probe more. Her smile is gone. Her body language changes. All right, you think, be honest. You tell Ms. Prince that you want to leave because you think your boss is unethical and you don't want your reputation tarnished through association with this individual. You've already had several public disagreements with your boss, and you're tired of dealing with the situation. Ms. Prince looks at you and replies: "If you ask me, that's not a valid reason for wanting to leave. It appears to me that you should be more assertive about the situation. Are you sure you're confident enough and have what it takes to make it in this company?" How dare she talk to you that way! Who does she think she is? You respond with an angry tone in your voice. And guess what, you've just fallen victim to one of the tricks of the interviewing business—the stress interview.

Stress interviews are becoming more common in today's business.[18] Every job produces stress, and every worker has an occasional horrendous day, so stress interviews become predictors of how you may react at work under less-than-favorable conditions. Interviewers want to observe how you'll react under pressure—as well as your values and ethics in stressful conditions.[19] Those who demonstrate the resolve and strength to handle stress indicate a level of professionalism and confidence, the characteristics being assessed. Individuals who react to the pressure interview in a more positive manner indicate that they should be more able to handle day-to-day irritations at work. Those who don't, well . . .

On the other hand, these are staged events. Interviewers deliberately lead applicants into a false sense of security—the comfortable interaction—then they abruptly change. They attack, and it's usually a personal affront that picks on a weakness they've uncovered about the applicant. It's possibly humiliating; at the very least it's demeaning.

So, should we use stress interviews? Should interviewers be permitted to assess professionalism and confidence and how one reacts to the everyday nuisances of work by putting applicants into a confrontational scenario? Does becoming angry in an interview when pressured indicate one's propensity toward violence under work stress? Should HRM advocate the use of an activity that could possibly slip out of control? What's your opinion?

Unfortunately for recruiters, interview situations are rarely cut and dried. Many factors enter into the deliberation in determining if a candidate is a good fit for the organization. Although interviews are typically part of every job search, summaries of research on interviewing have concluded that the interview is expensive, inefficient, and often not job related. These conclusions (see Exhibit 7-2), generated over the past few decades, still hold today. Let's elaborate on a few of them.

Seeing the candidate's résumé, application form, possible test scores, or appraisals of other interviewers may introduce interviewer bias.[20] In such cases, the interviewer no longer relies on data gained in the interview alone. Data received prior to the interview creates an image of the applicant. Much of the early part of the interview, then, becomes an exercise wherein the interviewer compares the actual applicant with the image formed earlier. In addition to interviewer bias, and directly related to the applicant's actions, is impression management. **Impression management** refers to one's attempt to project an image that will result in a favorable outcome.[21] Thus, if an applicant can say or do something the interviewer approves of, that person may be viewed more favorably for the position.[22] For example, suppose you find out that the interviewer values workers who can work seven days a week, 12-plus hours a day, if needed. Accordingly, you make statements of being a workaholic, which conform to this interviewer's values and may create a positive impression.

impression management

Influencing performance evaluations by portraying an image desired by the appraiser.

EXHIBIT 7-2
Conclusions About Interviewing

A review of the research has generated the following conclusions about interviews:

* Prior knowledge about the applicant can bias the interviewer's evaluation.
* The interviewer often holds a stereotype of what represents a "good" applicant.
* The interviewer often tends to favor applicants who share his or her own attitudes.
* The order in which applicants are interviewed often influences evaluations.
* The order in which information is elicited influences evaluations.
* Negative information is given unduly high weight.
* The interviewer may make a decision as to the applicant's suitability in the first few minutes of the interview.
* The interviewer may forget much of the interview's content within minutes after its conclusion.
* Structured and well-organized interviews are more reliable.
* The interview is most valid in determining an applicant's organizational fit, level of motivation, and interpersonal skills.

Source: See Charles Foster and Lynn Godkin, "Employment Selection in Health Care: The Case for Structured Interviewing," *Health Care Management Review* (Winter 1998), p. 46; Cynthia Kay Stevens, "Effects of Preinterview Beliefs on Applicants' Reactions to Campus Interviews." *Academy of Management Journal*, vol. 40, no. 4 (August 1997), pp. 947–966; Baker and Spier, p. 87; and Dipboye, Chapter 1.

Interviewers often have remarkably short and inaccurate memories. In one study of an interview simulation, a 20-minute videotape of a selection interview was played for a group of 40 interviewers. Following this, the interviewers were given a 20-question test. Although the questions were straightforward and factual, the average number of wrong answers was 10. The researchers concluded that even in a short interview, the average interviewer remembers only half of the information. However, taking notes during an interview has been shown to reduce memory loss. Note-taking—albeit possibly disconcerting for the interviewee—helps retain accurate information and develop a clearer understanding of the applicant's fit by allowing follow-up questions.[23]

It is also believed that the interview offers the greatest value as a selection device in determining an applicant's organizational fit, level of motivation, and interpersonal skills. This is particularly true of senior management positions. Accordingly, candidates for these positions often go through many extensive interviews with executive recruiters, company executives, and even board members before a final decision is made. Similarly, where teams hire their own members, often each team member interviews the applicant. One final issue about interviews revolves around when the interviewer actually makes the decision. Early studies indicated that interviewers made their choice to hire or not hire a candidate within the first few minutes of the interview. That belief was widely held, but subsequent research does not support these findings.[24] In fact, initial impressions may have little effect, unless that is the only information available for an interviewer to use.

What sense can we make of these issues raised about interviews? And where might interviews be most appropriate? If interviews will continue to have a place in the selection decision, they appear to be more appropriate for high-turnover jobs and less routine ones like middle- and upper-level managerial positions. In nonroutine activities, especially senior managerial positions, failure (as measured by voluntary terminations) is more frequently caused by a poor fit between the individual and the organization than by lack of competence on the part of the individual. Interviewing can be useful, therefore, when it emphasizes the candidate's ability to fit into the organization rather than specific technical skills.

behavioral interview

Observing job candidates not only for what they say but for how they behave.

The Behavioral Interview One last modification to interviews that is becoming popular in contemporary organizations is the **behavioral** or situation **interview.**[25] In this type of interview, candidates are observed not only for what they say but for how they fit the identified dimensions or competencies of the position.

Organizations have found that past performance in similar environments and situations is a much better indicator of future success than any other factor. If the available position is analyzed and its competencies identified, then, through obtaining real-life examples in questioning how the candidate has dealt with these situations in the past, the organization can see whether the candidate has the necessary qualities and behaviors to succeed in their organizational environment. Candidates are presented with situations—often complex problems that may sometimes involve role playing—and they are to either discuss how they have dealt with this in the past, using relevant examples, or how they would go about dealing with this, if it is a role-play situation. This type of interview can also provide an opportunity for interviewers to see how a potential employee will behave and how they react under stress—especially if that is one of the necessary competencies identified with success at that position. Proponents of behavioral interviewing indicate such a process is much more indicative of a candidate's performance than simply having the candidate tell the interviewer what he or she has done. In fact, research in this area indicates that behavioral interviews are nearly eight times more effective for predicting successful job performance.[26]

Realistic Job Previews The primary purpose of any selection device is to identify individuals who will be effective performers. But it is also in an interviewer's best interest to find good prospects, hire them, and have them stay in the organization. Therefore, part of selection should be concerned with reducing voluntary turnover and its associated costs. One device to achieve that goal is the **realistic job preview (RJP)**.[27] A realistic job preview may include brochures, films, plant tours, work sampling, or merely a short script made up of realistic statements that accurately portray the job. The key element in RJP is that unfavorable as well as favorable information about the job is shared.[28] Although the RJP is not normally treated as a selection device, it should take place during the interview. Also, because it has demonstrated effectiveness as a method for increasing job survival among new employees, we've included it here.

Every applicant acquires during the selection process a set of expectations about the organization and about the specific job the applicant is hoping to be offered. It is not unusual for these expectations to be excessively inflated as a result of receiving almost uniformly positive information about the organization and job during recruitment and selection activities. Evidence suggests, however, that interviewers may be erring by giving applicants only favorable information. More specifically, research leads us to conclude that applicants who receive a realistic job preview (as well as a realistic preview of the organization) hold lower and more realistic expectations about the job they will be doing and are better prepared for coping with the job and its frustrating elements.[29] Realistic job previews also appear to work best for jobs that are more attractive to the individual, resulting in lower turnover rates. Most studies demonstrate that giving candidates a realistic job preview before offering them the job reduces turnover without lowering acceptance rates. Of course, exposing an applicant to RJP may also result in the hiring of a more committed individual.

Background Investigation

The next step in the process is to undertake a **background investigation** of applicants who appear to offer potential as employees. Background investigations, or reference checks, are intended to verify that information on the application form is correct and accurate information.[30] This can include contacting former employers to confirm the candidate's work record and to obtain their appraisal of his or her performance, contacting other job-related and personal references, verifying educational accomplishments, verifying an individual's legal status to work in the United States (via the Employment Eligibility Verification, I-9 Form;

realistic job preview (RJP)
A selection device that allows job candidates to learn negative as well as positive information about the job and organization.

background investigation
The process of verifying information job candidates provide.

DID YOU KNOW?

INTERVIEW QUESTIONS

Individuals who fairly infrequently interview job candidates often ask for guiding questions; that is, what they should ask to assess certain areas that are relevant to the job. Though questions may vary, here are some guiding questions that you might find useful and where they are appropriate.

- Assessing Integrity
    - In what business situations do you feel honesty would be inappropriate?
    - What would you do if your boss asked you to do something unethical?
- Assessing Personality
    - What kinds of people bother you? Why?
    - Describe a situation in which you had to take risk.
    - What motivates you most?
    - What does your employer owe to you?
- Past Mistakes
    - The last time you were criticized, how did you deal with it?
    - If you could change one decision you made in the past year, what would it be and why?
- Describe a situation where you blew it, and what you did to correct the problem.
- Assessing Problem-Solving Ability
    - What is the most difficult decision you had to make, and why?
    - If you could change anything in the world, what would it be?
    - Your colleague is talking to you about a problem and needs help. Your boss has just handed you a report with a lot of questions and needs it returned in the next hour. Your assistant tells you a customer is on the phone with a complaint. What do you do to handle these three things happening simultaneously?

Again, remember that asking the questions is the easy part. Listening to the responses and making sense of what is said is the critical part. You need to know what you're looking for and how what is said relates to successful performance on the job.

Source: Questions were adapted from Ceridian Abstracts, "General Interview Questions," (2005), available online at www.ceridian.com/www/content/10/12455/12487/12903/12909/041305_customer_query.htm.

see Exhibit 7-3), checking credit references and criminal records, and even using third-party investigators to do the background check.[31] Why do this? Documentation supports the premise that a good predictor of an individual's future behavior is his or her past behavior, as well as that many—in some studies nearly half—of all applicants exaggerate their backgrounds or experiences.[32] Although behavior indicators are important, organizations need to be aware of *negligent hiring* liability.

Negligent hiring occurs when an employer has failed to properly investigate an employee's background and that employee is later involved in wrongful conduct.[33] Negligent hiring assumes that a proper background check would have uncovered information about the candidate and the candidate would not have been hired. For instance, any individual who works with children—in a school or day care, for instance—must not have been accused or convicted of abusing children. An organization that fails to check if a candidate has a record and hires the individual, opens itself up to a negligent-hiring lawsuit. If the employee is ever involved in some wrongful conduct involving children, the organization can be held liable for its failure to properly hire.

Common sense dictates that HRM find out as much as possible about its applicants before the final hiring decision is made. Failure to do so can have a detrimental effect on the organization, both in cost and morale. Obtaining needed information may be difficult, especially when there may be a question about invading privacy. In the past, many organizational policies stated that any request for information about a past employee be sent to HRM. Then, HRM typically verified only employment dates and positions held. Why? Companies that wanted to stay away from being sued by a previous employee simply verified "the facts."[34] Some of that has changed.

EXHIBIT 7-3
Employment Eligibility Verification Form (I-9)

U.S. Department of Justice   OMB No. 1115-0136
Immigration and Naturalization Service   **Employment Eligibility Verification**

Please read instructions carefully before completing this form. The instructions must be available during completion of this form. ANTI-DISCRIMINATION NOTICE: It is illegal to discriminate against work eligible individuals. Employers CANNOT specify which document(s) they will accept from an employee. The refusal to hire an individual because of a future expiration date may also constitute illegal discrimination.

Section 1. Employee Information and Verification. To be completed and signed by employee at the time employment begins.

Print Name: Last	First	Middle Initial	Maiden Name

Address (Street Name and Number)	Apt. #	Date of Birth (month/day/year)

City	State	Zip Code	Social Security #

I am aware that federal law provides for imprisonment and/or fines for false statements or use of false documents in connection with the completion of this form.	I attest, under penalty of perjury, that I am (check one of the following): ☐ A citizen or national of the United States ☐ A Lawful Permanent Resident (Alien # A_____) ☐ An alien authorized to work until ___/___/___ (Alien # or Admission #)_____

Employee's Signature	Date (month/day/year)

Preparer and/or Translator Certification. *(To be completed and signed if Section 1 is prepared by a person other than the employee.) I attest, under penalty of perjury, that I have assisted in the completion of this form and that to the best of my knowledge the information is true and correct.*

Preparer's/Translator's Signature	Print Name

Address (Street Name and Number, City, State, Zip Code)	Date (month/day/year)

Section 2. Employer Review and Verification. To be completed and signed by employer. Examine one document from List A OR examine one document from List B and one from List C, as listed on the reverse of this form, and record the title, number and expiration date, if any, of the document(s)

List A	OR	List B	AND	List C
Document title:_____		_____		_____
Issuing authority:_____		_____		_____
Document #: _____		_____		_____
Expiration Date (if any): ___/___/___		___/___/___		___/___/___
Document #: _____				
Expiration Date (if any): ___/___/___				

CERTIFICATION – I attest, under penalty of perjury, that I have examined the document(s) presented by the above-named employee, that the above-listed document(s) appear to be genuine and to relate to the employee named, that the employee began employment on (month/day/year) ___/___/___ and that to the best of my knowledge the employee is eligible to work in the United States. (State employment agencies may omit the date the employee began employment.)

Signature of Employer or Authorized Representative	Print Name	Title

Business or Organization Name	Address (Street Name and Number, City, State, Zip Code)	Date (month/day/year)

Section 3. Updating and Reverification. To be completed and signed by employer.

A. New Name (If applicable)	B. Date of rehire (month/day/year) (If applicable)

C. If employee's previous grant of work authorization has expired, provide the information below for the document that establishes current employment eligibility.

Document Title:_____   Document #:_____   Expiration Date (if any):___/___/___

I attest, under penalty of perjury, that to the best of my knowledge, this employee is eligible to work in the United States, and if the employee presented document(s), the document(s) I have examined appear to be genuine and to relate to the individual.

Signature of Employer or Authorized Representative	Date (month/day/year)

Form I-9 (Rev. 11-21-91)N Page 2

qualified privilege
The ability for organizations to speak candidly to one another about employees.

Based on a concept of **qualified privilege,** some courts have ruled that employers must be able to talk to one another about employees. Additionally, about half of the states have laws that protect employers from "good-faith references." Accordingly, these discussions may be legal and may not invade one's right to privacy so long as the discussion is a legitimate concern for the business—and in some cases if the applicant has authorized the background investigation. For example, had a Midwest hospital learned that one of its anesthesiologist applicants lost his license in three states for substance abuse, it clearly would not have hired him. The information given, however, cannot be discriminatory, retaliate against a former employee, or "disclose confidential facts that constitute an invasion of privacy."[35]

Two methods apply to background investigations: internal and external investigations. In the internal investigation, HRM undertakes the task of questioning former employers, personal references, and possibly credit sources. Although this is a viable, well-used option, unless the investigation process is handled thoroughly, little useful information may be found. On the other hand, the external investigation typically involves using a reference-checking firm. Despite the greater cost associated with this investigation, such firms have a better track record of gathering pertinent information, as well as being better informed on privacy rights issues. However it is done, documentation is the important element. Should an employer be called on to justify what has or has not been found, supporting documentation is invaluable.

Conditional Job Offers

conditional job offer
A tentative job offer that becomes permanent after certain conditions are met.

If a job applicant has passed each step of the selection process so far, a **conditional job offer** is usually made. Conditional job offers typically come from an HRM representative (we'll revisit this momentarily). In essence, the conditional job offer implies that if everything checks out—such as passing a certain medical, physical, or substance abuse test—the conditional nature of the job offer will be removed and the offer will be permanent.

Medical/Physical Examination

medical/physical examination
An examination to determine an applicant's physical fitness for essential job performance.

The next-to-last step in the selection process may consist of having the applicant take a **medical/physical examination.** Physical exams can only be used as a selection device to screen out individuals who are unable to physically comply with the requirements of a job. For example, firefighters must perform activities that require a certain physical condition. Whether it is climbing a ladder, lugging a water-filled four-inch hose, or carrying an injured victim, these individuals must demonstrate that they are fit for the job. Jobs that require certain physical characteristics, then, may entail a job-related physical examination. However, this includes a small proportion of jobs today. A company must show that any required medical clearance is job-related. Failure to do so may result in the physical examination creating an adverse impact. Also, the company must keep in mind the Americans with Disabilities Act. Thus, even a valid physical examination may be required only after a conditional job offer. Having a physical disability may not be enough to exclude an individual from the job; companies, as we mentioned in Chapter 3, may be required to make reasonable accommodations for these individuals. Remember, however, that in doing so a company must show that the reasoning behind this exclusion is job related.

Aside from its use as a screening tool, the physical exam may also show that minimum standards of health exist to enroll in company health and life insurance programs. Additionally, a company may use this exam to provide base data in case of an employee's future claim of injury on the job. This occurs, however, after one has been hired. In both cases, the exam is paid for by the employer.

One last event fits appropriately under medical examination: the drug test. As we discussed in Chapter 4, many companies require applicants to submit to a drug test. Where in this process that test occurs is somewhat immaterial; the fact remains that failing an employment drug test may be grounds for rejecting an applicant.

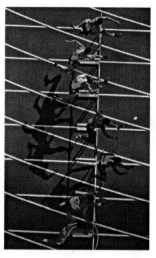

The selection process can be likened to a hurdle race. Similar to these runners, those who fail to clear a hurdle are out of the race. In selection, the hurdles involve tests, interviews, reference checks, and the like. (Source: Michael Steele/Getty Images, Inc.)

Job Offers

Individuals who perform successfully in the preceding steps are now considered eligible to receive the employment offer. Who makes the final employment depends on several factors. For administrative purposes (processing salary forms, maintaining EEO statistics, ensuring a statement exists that asserts that employment is not guaranteed, etc.), the offer typically is made by an HRM representative. But that individual's role should be only administrative. The actual hiring decision should be made by the manager in the department where the vacancy exists. First, the applicant will eventually work for this manager, which necessitates a good fit between boss and employee. Second, if the decision is faulty, the hiring manager has no one else to blame. Remember—as we mentioned in Chapter 6—finalists not hired deserve the courtesy of prompt notification.

The Comprehensive Approach

We have presented the general selection process as being comprised of multiple hurdles—beginning with a screening interview and culminating with a final selection decision. This discrete selection process is designed so that tripping over any hurdle puts one out of the race. This approach, however, may not be the most effective selection procedure for every job. If, for example, the application form shows that the candidate has only two years of relevant experience, but the job specification requires five, the candidate is rejected. Yet in many jobs, positive factors can counterbalance negative factors. Poor performance on a written test, for example, may be offset by several years of relevant job experience. This suggests that sometimes it may be advantageous to do comprehensive rather than discrete selection. In **comprehensive selection**, all applicants complete every step of the selection process, and the final decision is based on a comprehensive evaluation of the results from all stages.

The comprehensive approach overcomes the major disadvantage of the discrete method (eliminating potentially good employees simply because they receive an acceptable but low evaluation at one selection step). The comprehensive method is more realistic. It recognizes that most applicants have weaknesses as well as strengths. But it is also more costly because all applicants must go through all the screening hurdles. Additionally, the method consumes more of management's time and can demoralize many applicants by building up hope. Yet in those instances where job success relies on many qualities, and where finding candidates who are strong on all qualities is unlikely, the comprehensive approach is probably preferable to the typical discrete method.

No matter which approach you use or which steps you take, one critical aspect must be present: the devices used must measure job-related factors. That is, these devices must indicate how one would perform on the job. That's critical for business success, and it's necessary to defend and respond to an allegation that the hiring practices are discriminatory (see Workplace Issues).

comprehensive selection
Applying all steps in the selection process before rendering a decision about a job candidate.

WORKPLACE ISSUES

AVOIDING HIRING MISTAKES

As an owner or manager, it may seem like your rights to hire, interview, retain, and terminate employees are diminishing. Learning too little too late is a continuing frustration and challenge as managers and entrepreneurs seek to work within legal limitations to obtain information about possible candidates. For example, a manager recently hired a seemingly outstanding applicant only to have the newly hired department head resign one week later after realizing his inability to fulfill the job's expectations. On closer investigation, it seemed the candidate had projected the right experience and credentials on paper—not falsifying, but embellishing in the name of a competitive job market.

In fact, the résumé and cover letter were the best the manager had seen, thanks to the candidate's outside professional assistance. Résumé writers may help project images on paper to secure employment, but it takes more than illusions to keep a job. Implying or exaggerating accomplishments is not only poor judgment; it's bad business.

As managers and entrepreneurs, we make hiring mistakes. We may not detect some situations, such as an exaggerated résumé, but we can prevent others by knowing our rights as employers—not only what we cannot do but what we can do. Here are some suggestions.

- Prior to interviewing applicants, update and prepare a list of job requirements, duties, and responsibilities so that you and the applicant will understand the expectations of the position. After all, the longer a position is open and the more desperate you are to fill it, the more likely you are to make the position fit the candidate—any candidate.
- Don't panic. Hire a temporary, contract or subcontract out some of the work, or ask others to assist during the transition rather than hiring the wrong person.
- Ask appropriate questions: What are your long- and short-range goals? Why are you interested in this position? What do you consider your greatest strengths and weaknesses? Why should I hire you? In what specific ways do you think you can make a contribution to the company? Do you have plans for continuing education?
- Before you extend an offer, check references, including several supervisors or managers, even with an exemplary interview and seemingly perfect matched background. Although many companies allow only human resources to provide information about former employees and you can gain little information, check references, including education references. The answer to the question, "Would you rehire this individual?" may not provide all you need to know, but it's a start.
- Obtain applicants' permission to check references with a signed release form saying that they agree to your calling their references to ask about their background and work performance. Ask for former supervisors or managers, and if the applicant cannot provide them as references, ask why not.
- Don't depend on letters that provide only partial information. Call and talk with someone, ask open-ended questions, and listen for content as well as hesitation and inflections. If you do not feel adept, ask your personnel or human resources manager to check references or hire a consultant or reference-checking service.
- Sample questions to ask those you wish to check references with include one or more of the following: Why didn't you persuade him or her to stay? How well did he or she take criticism or suggestions given in his or her last performance appraisal process? Go over the part of the résumé that relates to the reference and ask for comments.
- Avoid questions that indirectly or directly identify age; physical characteristics, such as height, weight, hair or eye color; religious affiliation; marital and family status; medical history; work absenteeism due to illness or physical limitations; or child- or adult-care obligations.

The process may take time, effort, and patience to match the right person to the right job, but consider the alternative: the dismissal process.

Now It's Up to the Candidate

If the organization selection process has been effective in differentiating between those individuals who will make successful employees and those who will not, the selection decision is now in the hands of the applicant. What can management do at this stage to increase the probability that the individual will accept an offer? Assuming that the organization has not lost sight of the process of selection's dual objective—evaluation and a good fit—we can expect that the potential employee has a solid understanding of the job being offered and what it would be like to work for the organization. Yet it might be of interest at this point to review what we know about how people choose a job. This subject—job choice—represents selection from the perspective of the potential employee rather than the organization.

Research indicates that people gravitate toward jobs compatible with their personal orientation. Individuals appear to move toward matching their work with their personality. Social individuals lean toward jobs in clinical psychology, foreign service, social work, and the like. Investigative individuals are compatible with jobs in biology, mathematics, and oceanography. Careers in management, law, and public relations appeal to enterprising individuals. This approach to matching people and jobs suggests that management can expect a greater proportion of acceptances if it has properly matched the candidate's personality to the job and to the organization, making the good fit.

Not surprisingly, most job choice studies indicate that an individual's perception of the company's attractiveness is important.[36] People want to work where their expectations are positive and where they believe their goals can be achieved. This, coupled with conclusions from previous research, should encourage management to ensure that those to whom they make offers can see the job's compatibility with their personality and goals.

Before we leave this last step in the selection process, what about those applicants to whom we did not make an offer? We believe that those involved in the selection process should carefully consider how they treat rejected candidates. What we communicate and how we communicate will have a central bearing on the image rejected candidates have of our organization. And that image may be carried for a lifetime. The young college graduate rejected for a position by a major computer manufacturer may a decade later be the influential decision maker for his or her current employer's computer purchases. The image formed many years earlier may play a key part in the decision.

SELECTION FOR SELF-MANAGED TEAMS

Much of the discussion about selection devices thus far has assumed that HRM has responsibility for the selection process. Today, however, that may not always be the case. Companies such as Perdue Farms (the chicken company of Frank Perdue), General Mills, Corning, Motherwear, Toyota, and Federal Express are more team oriented, and they empower their employees to take responsibility for the day-to-day functions in their areas. Accordingly, these employees may now work without direct supervision and take on the administrative responsibilities once performed by their supervisor. One aspect of this change has been a more active role in hiring their co-workers.[37]

Consider a time when you took a course that required a group project. How was your team formed? Did the professor assign you to a group, or were you permitted to form the group yourself? If you selected your own group, what did you look for in a potential group member? Other students who shared your values in finishing work on time and of high quality? Those who you knew would pull their own weight and not let one or two in the group do all of the work? Well, that's the same premise behind self-managed work-team selection. In any organization, a critical link to success is how well employees perform their jobs. It is also understood that when those jobs require the interaction of several individuals, or a team, coming together as a unified unit takes time. The length of that time, however, is a function of how the team views its goals and priorities and how open and trusting group members are. A good way to begin this team-building is to have the "personalities" involved actually making the hiring decision.[38]

Workers empowered to hire their co-workers bring to the selection process varied experiences and backgrounds. This better enables them to assess applicants' skills in their field of expertise.[39] They want to hire people they can count on to perform their duties and not let the others down. This means that they focus their attention on the job duties required and on the special skills and qualifications necessary for success. Although a more objective evaluation may result, that's not

Is the physical part of the selection process for firefighters job relevant? Should firefighter candidates be expected to lift objects, connect a fire hose in a certain amount of time, and the like? For those who test firefighter candidates, the answer is simple: yes. The physical demands of the job require firefighters to perform numerous activities, many times while under stress. Therefore, we call these selection activities content valid. (Source: David McNew/Getty Images, Inc.)

to say that self-managed work teams are without problems. If these workers are unfamiliar with proper interviewing techniques or the legal ramifications of their hiring decisions, they too, could experience many of the difficulties often associated with interviews.

KEY ELEMENTS FOR SUCCESSFUL PREDICTORS

We are concerned with selection activities that can help us predict which applicants will perform satisfactorily on the job. In this section we explore the concepts of reliability, validity, and cut scores. For illustration purposes, we will emphasize these elements as they relate to employment tests, but they are relevant to any selection device.

Reliability

reliability

A selection device's consistency of measurement.

For any predictor to be useful, the scores it generates must possess an acceptable level of **reliability** or consistency of measurement. This means that the applicant's performance on any given selection device should produce consistent scores each time the device is used.[40] For example, measuring your height every day with a wooden yardstick would yield highly reliable results, but using an elastic tape measure would probably produce considerable disparity between measurements. Your height does not change; the variability reflects the unreliable measuring device.

Similarly, if an organization uses tests to provide input to the selection decision, the tests must give consistent results. If the test is reliable, any single individual's scores should remain fairly stable over time, assuming that the characteristic it is measuring remains stable. An individual's intelligence, for example, is generally a stable characteristic, and if we give applicants an IQ test, we should expect that someone who scores 110 in March would score close to 110 if tested again in July. If, in July, the same applicant scored 85, the reliability of the test would be highly questionable. On the other hand, if we were measuring an attitude or a mood, we would expect different scores on the measure, because attitudes and moods change.

Validity

validity

The proven relationship of a selection device to relevant criterion.

High reliability may mean little if the selection device has low **validity**, that is, if the measures obtained do not relate to a relevant criterion such as job performance. For example, just because a test score is consistent is no indication that it is measuring important characteristics related to job behavior. It must also differentiate between satisfactory and unsatisfactory performance on the job. We should be aware of three specific types of validity: content, construct, and criterion related.

content validity

The degree to which test content, as a sample, represents all situations that could have been included, such as a typing test for a clerk typist.

Content Validity Content validity is the degree to which test content or questions about job tasks, as a sample, represent situations on the job. All candidates for that job receive the same test or questions so applicants can be properly compared. A simple example of a content-valid test is a typing test for a word-processing position. Such a test can approximate the work; the applicant can be given a typical sample of typing, on which his or her performance can be evaluated. Assuming that the tasks on the test, or the questions about tasks, constitute an accurate sample of the tasks on the job (ordinarily a dubious assumption at best), the test is content valid.[41]

construct validity

The degree to which a particular trait relates to successful job performance, as in IQ tests.

Construct Validity Construct validity is the degree to which a test measures a particular trait related to successful performance on the job.[42] These traits are usually abstract in nature, such as the measure of intelligence, and are called *constructs*. Construct validity is complex and difficult. In fact, it is the most difficult type of validity to prove because you are dealing with abstract measures.

Criterion-Related Validity Criterion-related validity is the degree to which a particular selection device accurately predicts the level of performance or important elements of work behavior. This validation strategy shows the relationship between some predictor (test score, for example) and a criterion, job performance (say, production output or managerial effectiveness). To establish criterion-related validity, either of two approaches can be used: **predictive validity** or **concurrent validity**.

To give a test *predictive validity*, an organization would administer the test (with an unknown validity) to all prospective applicants. The test scores would not be used at this time; rather, applicants would be hired as a result of successfully completing the entire selection process. At some prescribed date, usually at least a year after being hired, the applicants' job performance would be evaluated by their supervisors. The evaluation ratings would then be compared with the initial test scores, which have been stored in a file over the period. At that time, an analysis would assess any relationship between test scores (the predictors) and performance evaluation (the measure of success on the job, or the criterion). If no clear relationship exists, the test may have to be revised. However, if the organization found statistically that employees who scored below some predetermined score, called a **cut score** (determined in the analysis), were unsuccessful performers, management could appropriately state that any future applicants scoring below the cut score would be ineligible for employment. Unsuccessful performers would be handled like any other employee who has experienced poor evaluations: training, transfer, discipline, or discharge.

The *concurrent validity* method validates tests using current employees as subjects. These employees take a proposed selection test experimentally. Their scores are immediately analyzed, revealing a relationship between their test scores and existing performance appraisal data. Again, if a relationship appears between test scores and performance, a valid test has been found.

Predictive validity is the preferred choice. Its advantage over concurrent validity is that it is demonstrated by using actual job applicants, whereas concurrent validity focuses on current employees. These validation strategies are similar, with the exception of who they test and the time that elapses between gathering of predictor and criterion information (see Exhibit 7-4).

criterion-related validity

The degree to which a particular selection device accurately predicts the important elements of work behavior, as in the relationship between a test score and job performance.

predictive validity

Validating tests by using prospective applicants as the study group.

concurrent validity

Validating tests by using current employees as the study group.

cut score

A scoring point below which applicants are rejected.

EXHIBIT 7-4
Predictive vs. Concurrent Validation

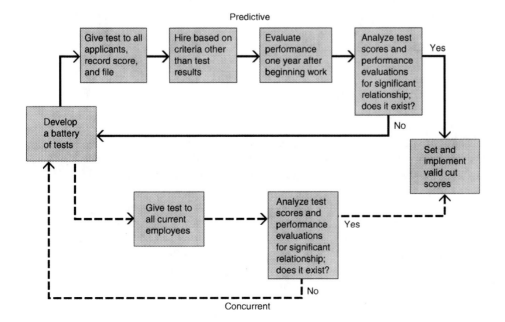

Although the costs associated with each method are drastically different, predictive validation strategies should be used if possible. Concurrent validity, although better than no validity at all, leaves many questions to be answered.[43] Its usefulness has been challenged on the premise that current employees know the jobs already and that a learning process takes place. Thus, similarity may be lessened between the current employee and the applicant.

Validity Analysis

Correlation coefficients used to demonstrate the statistical relationships existing between an individual's test score and his or her job performance are called *validity coefficients*. The correlation analysis procedure can result in a coefficient ranging from -1 to $+1$ in magnitude. The closer the validity coefficient is to the extreme (1), the more accurate the test;[44] that is, the test is a good predictor of job performance. For instance, individuals who score higher on the test have a greater probability of succeeding at their jobs than those who score lower. Based on this relationship, this test appears to be valid. When we have a valid test as determined by our correlation analysis, we may then identify the test score that distinguishes between successful and unsuccessful performers (the cut score).

Cut Scores and Their Impact on Hiring

In this discussion, we have referred to test scores and their ability to predict successful job performance. By using our statistical analyses, we generate a scoring point, the cut score, below which applicants are rejected.[45] However, existing conditions (such as applicant availability) may cause an organization to change the cut score. If cut scores do change, what impact will this have on hiring applicants who will be successful on the job? Let us review again the positive relationship we found in our validity correlation analysis. We have reproduced the main elements in the graph in Exhibit 7-5. Let us assume that after our analysis, we determined that our cut score should be 70. At this cut score, we have shown that the majority of applicants who scored above 70 have a greater probability of being successful performers on the job, the majority scoring below 70, unsuccessful performers. If we change our cut score, however, we alter the number of applicants in these categories. For example, suppose the organization faces a "buyer's market" for particular positions. The many potential applicants permit the organization to be selective. In a situation such as this, the organization may choose to hire only those applicants who meet the most extreme criteria. To achieve this goal, the organization increases its cut score to 98. By increasing the cut score from 70 to 98, the organization has rejected all but two candidates (areas A and B in Exhibit 7-5). However, many potentially successful job performers also would be rejected (individuals shown in area C). Here the organization has become more selective and has put more faith in the test than is reasonable. If, out of 100 applicants only two were hired, we could say that the selection ratio (the ratio of number hired to the number of applicants) is 2 percent. A 2 percent selection ratio means that the organization is highly particular about who is hired.

Lowering the cut score also has an effect. Using the same diagram, let us lower our cut score to 50 and see what results. We have graphically portrayed this in Exhibit 7-6. By lowering the cut score from 70 to 50, we increase our number of eligible hires who have a greater probability of being successful on the job (area D). At the same time, however, we have also made eligible more applicants who could be unsuccessful on the job (area E). Although using a hiring

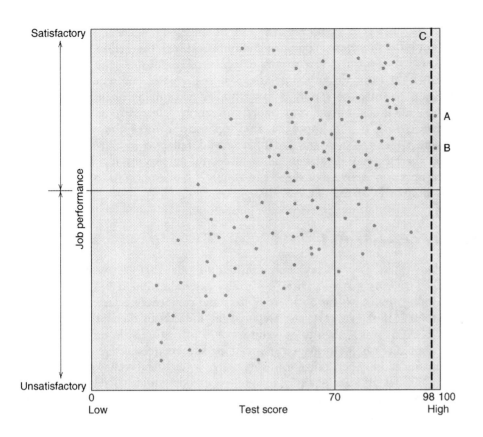

EXHIBIT 7-5
Validity Correlation Analysis After Cut Score Is Raised

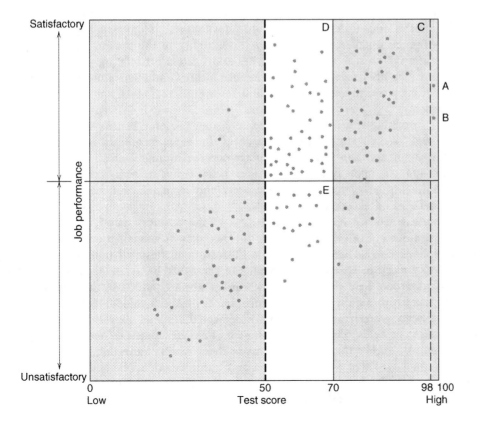

EXHIBIT 7-6
Validity Correlation Analysis After Cut Score Is Lowered

process that offers a greater likelihood of engaging unsuccessful performers seems not to make sense, conditions may necessitate the action. Labor market conditions may lead to a low supply of potential applicants who possess particular skills. For example, in some cities, finding a good computer modeler may be difficult. Because the supply is low, coupled with many openings, companies may hire individuals on the spot (more commonly referred to as an *open-house recruiting effort*). In this approach, the organization hires almost all the applicants who appear to have the skills needed (as reflected in a score of 50), puts them on the job, and filters out the unsuccessful employees at a later date. This may not appear effective, but the organization is banking on the addition of individuals in area D of Exhibit 7-6.

Validity Generalization

In the late 1970s, two researchers published a model that supported a phenomenon called *validity generalization*.[46] Validity generalization refers to a test valid for screening applicants for a variety of jobs and performance factors across many occupations.[47] For example, the Department of Labor's General Aptitude Test Battery (GATB) was shown to be valid for 500 jobs studied in terms of the test's ability to predict job performance and training success irrespective of race.[48] What distinguishes validity generalization is its use of a statistical technique called *meta-analysis*.[49] Through meta-analysis, researchers can determine correlations that may exist among numerous variables, and correct or adjust for any variances that may exist in predictor-criterion relationships.

SELECTION FROM A GLOBAL PERSPECTIVE

The selection criteria for international assignments are broader in scope than those for domestic selection. To illustrate the point, in addition to such factors as technical expertise and leadership ability, an international assignment requires greater attention to personality and especially to flexibility in the design. The individual must have an interest in working overseas and a talent for relating well to all types of people. The ability to relate to different cultures and environments, a sensitivity to different management styles, and a supportive family are often selection requirements.[50]

Not surprisingly, many corporations consider personal factors of maturity and age, as well as the "family situation factor," far more important in their international assignments than in domestic placements. Although not all expatriates are married, many human resource managers believe that marital stability reduces a person's likelihood of returning home early and in many countries enhances the individual's social acceptability.

American women have been successful in the business world, and it is unacceptable in our culture to discriminate on the basis of gender in employment, but organizations know that some Middle Eastern countries will not grant working papers to American women executives. On the other hand, in Asia, where common wisdom has held that women executives are less effective, the opposite has proven true! Although few Asian women are at or above middle-management levels, American women are often highly respected because they have risen to be experts in their fields. Thus, past reluctance to assign women to overseas positions where culture rather than law once made them rare is vanishing, and American women are more often working in Asia and Latin America. Not only may the candidate's gender be considered, but also the social acceptability of single parents, unmarried partners, and blended families.

© 2000 Randy Glasbergen. www.glasbergen.com

EXHIBIT 7-7
The Interview

"Unfortunately, you are overqualified. However, your résumé is full of misspelled words and grammatical errors so that tips the scales back in your favor."

In addition, personal factors such as health, background, and education may be considered in international placements. In fact, the ideal candidate for many corporations is an older couple in good health, with no young children at home and a long and stable marital history. These factors would play no role in domestic assignments.

FINAL THOUGHTS: EXCELLING AT THE INTERVIEW

In the previous chapter we discussed some important elements of making your résumé look good to secure an interview. Interviews play a critical role in determining whether you are hired. Up to now, all the recruiter has seen is your well-polished cover letter and résumé (see Exhibit 7-7). Remember, however, few individuals get a job without an interview. No matter how qualified you are for a position, if you perform poorly in the interview, you're not likely to be hired!

Interviews are popular because they help the recruiter determine if you are a good fit for the organization, in terms of your level of motivation and interpersonal skills.[51] The following suggestions can help you make your interview experience a successful one.

First, do some homework. Search for the company on the Internet (or visit your library) and find as much information on it as possible. Develop a solid grounding in the company, its history, markets, financial situation—and the industry in which it competes.

The night before the interview, get a good night's rest. As you prepare for the interview, keep in mind that your appearance will make your first impression. Dress appropriately. Incorrect attire can result in a negative impression. Arrive early, about 15 minutes ahead of your scheduled interview. It's better for you to wait than to chance having the unexpected, like a traffic jam, make you late. Arriving early also gives you an opportunity to survey the office environment and gather clues about the organization. Pay attention to the waiting room layout, the formality of the receptionist, and anything else that can give you insights into the organization.[52]

Now's your chance. What you do and say in the next 15 to 30 minutes will have a tremendous impact on whether you get the job. The more preparation you do, the more you anticipate interview question topics, the better you'll do. Interviewing for a job can be nerve-racking. But with a little advanced work on your part, you can succeed. (Source: AJA Productions/The Image Bank/Getty Images)

As you meet the recruiter, give him or her a firm handshake. Make good eye contact and maintain it throughout the interview. Remember, let your body language augment the good impression you want an interviewer to pick up. Sit erect and maintain good posture. Although likely nervous, try your best to relax. Recruiters know that you'll be anxious, and a good one will try to put you at ease. Being prepared for an interview can also help build your confidence and reduce the nervousness. You can start building that confidence by reviewing a set of questions most frequently asked by interviewers, usually available at your college career center. Develop rough responses to these questions beforehand. This will lessen the likelihood that you'll be asked a question that catches you off guard. Our best advice, however, is to be yourself. Don't go into an interview with a prepared text and recite it from memory. Have an idea of what you would like to say, but don't rely on verbatim responses. Experienced interviewers will see through this over-preparedness and likely downgrade their evaluation of you.

If possible, go through several practice interviews.[53] Universities often have career days on campus, when recruiters from companies visit to interview students. Take advantage of them. Even if a job doesn't fit what you want, the practice will help you become more skilled at dealing with interviews. You can also practice with family, friends, career counselors, student groups, or your faculty adviser.

When the interview ends, thank the interviewer for his or her time and for this opportunity to talk about your qualifications, but don't think that selling yourself stops there. Send an immediate thank-you letter to the recruiter for taking the time to interview you and giving you the opportunity to discuss your job candidacy. This little act of courtesy has a positive effect—use it to your advantage.

SUMMARY

(This summary relates to the Learning Outcomes identified on page 171.)
After reading this chapter, you can

1. **Describe the selection process.** The selection process includes the following: initial screening interview, completion of the application form, employment tests, comprehensive interview, background investigation, conditional job offer, physical or medical examination, and the permanent job offer. In the discrete selection process, each step acts as a stand-alone predictor—failing to pass any of these discrete steps means disqualification from the job. In the comprehensive approach, candidates go through most of the steps before a final decision about them is rendered.

2. **Identify the primary purpose of selection activities.** Selection devices provide managers with information that helps them predict whether an applicant will prove a successful job performer. Selection activities primarily predict which job applicant will be successful if hired. During the selection process, candidates also learn about the job and organization. Proper selection can minimize the costs of replacement and training, reduce legal challenges, and result in a more productive workforce.

3. **Discuss why organizations use application forms.** The application form is effective for acquiring hard biographical data that can ultimately be verified.

4. **Explain the primary purposes of performance simulation tests.** Performance simulation tests require the applicant to engage in specific behaviors demonstrated to be job related. Work sampling and the assessment center,

which are performance simulations, receive high marks for their predictive capability.

5. **Discuss the problems associated with job interviews and means of correcting them.** Interviews consistently achieve low marks for reliability and validity. These, however, are more the result of interviewer problems than problems with the interview. Interviewing validity can be enhanced by using a structured process.

6. **Specify the organizational benefits derived from realistic job previews.** Realistic job previews reduce turnover by giving the applicant both favorable and unfavorable information about the job.

7. **Explain the purpose of background investigations.** Background investigations are valuable when they verify hard data from the application; they tend, however, to offer little practical value as a predictive selection device.

8. **List three types of validity.** The three validation strategies are content, construct, and criterion-related validity.

9. **Explain how validity is determined.** Validity is determined either by discovering the extent to which a test represents actual job content, or through statistical analyses that relate the test used to an important job-related trait or to performance on the job.

DEMONSTRATING COMPREHENSION: *Questions for Review*

1. Describe the eight-step selection process.
2. What is meant by a "reliable and valid" selection process?
3. What is a legal employee selection process? How does that differ from an illegal one?
4. What is a weighted application form? How does it work?
5. Contrast work samples with the assessment center.
6. What are the major problems of the interview as a selection device? What can HRM do to reduce some of these problems?
7. What effect should a realistic job preview have on a new hire's attitude and behavior?
8. Why should HRM conduct a background investigation?
9. Define the concepts of reliability and validity. What are the three types of validity? Why are we concerned about reliability and validity?

KEY TERMS

application form
assessment center
background
  investigation
behavioral interview
comprehensive
  interview
comprehensive
  selection
concurrent validity

conditional job offer
construct validity
content validity
criterion-related validity
cut score
impression management
initial screening
medical/physical exam
performance simulation
  tests

predictive validity
qualified privilege
realistic job preview
  (RJP)
reliability
validity
weighted application
  form
work sampling

VISUAL SUMMARY

CHAPTER 7: FOUNDATIONS OF SELECTION

1   The Selection Process

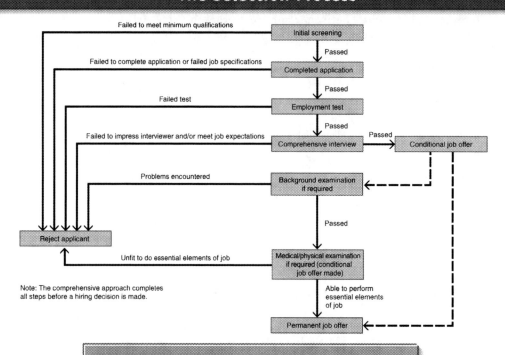

Failed to meet minimum qualifications — Initial screening

Passed

Failed to complete application or failed job specifications — Completed application

Passed

Failed test — Employment test

Passed

Failed to impress interviewer and/or meet job expectations — Comprehensive interview — Passed — Conditional job offer

Problems encountered — Background examination if required

Reject applicant

Passed

Unfit to do essential elements of job — Medical/physical examination if required (conditional job offer made)

Note: The comprehensive approach completes all steps before a hiring decision is made.

Able to perform essential elements of job

Permanent job offer

The Selection Process
- Discrete Approach—candidates are eliminated as they pass through the hurdles of the selection process
- Comprehensive Approach—all candidates go through all the hurdles

Some Key Ideas Concerning Interviews

Effectiveness of Interviews
- More appropriate for high-turnover jobs
- Most effective when they are structured and measure job-related factors
- Most valuable when they are used to assess level of motivation and interpersonal skills

Realistic Job Preview
provides a candidate with both favorable and unfavorable information about a job

Behavioral Interviews
- Observing candidate not only for what they say but how they behave
- See how a candidate will react

Stress Interview

196

2 Key Elements for Successful Predictions

Reliability—consistency of measure
Validity—measuring job-related factors
Content validity—the degree to which the content of the test represents the situation on the job
Construct validity—the degree to which a test measures a particular trait
Criterion-related validity—the degree to which a selection device predicts the level of performance
Predictive
Concurrent
Predictive
Give test to all applicants, record score, and file
Hire based on criteria other than test results
Evaluate performance one year after beginning work
Analyze test scores and performance evaluations for significant relationship; does it exist?
Yes
No
Develop a battery of tests
Set and implement valid cut scores
Give test to all current employees
Analyze test scores and performance evaluations for significant relationship; does it exist?
Yes
No
Concurrent
The Validity Analysis
Correlation coefficients of +1 to −1—predictor of job performance
Cut score—a point at which an applicant scoring lower is rejected

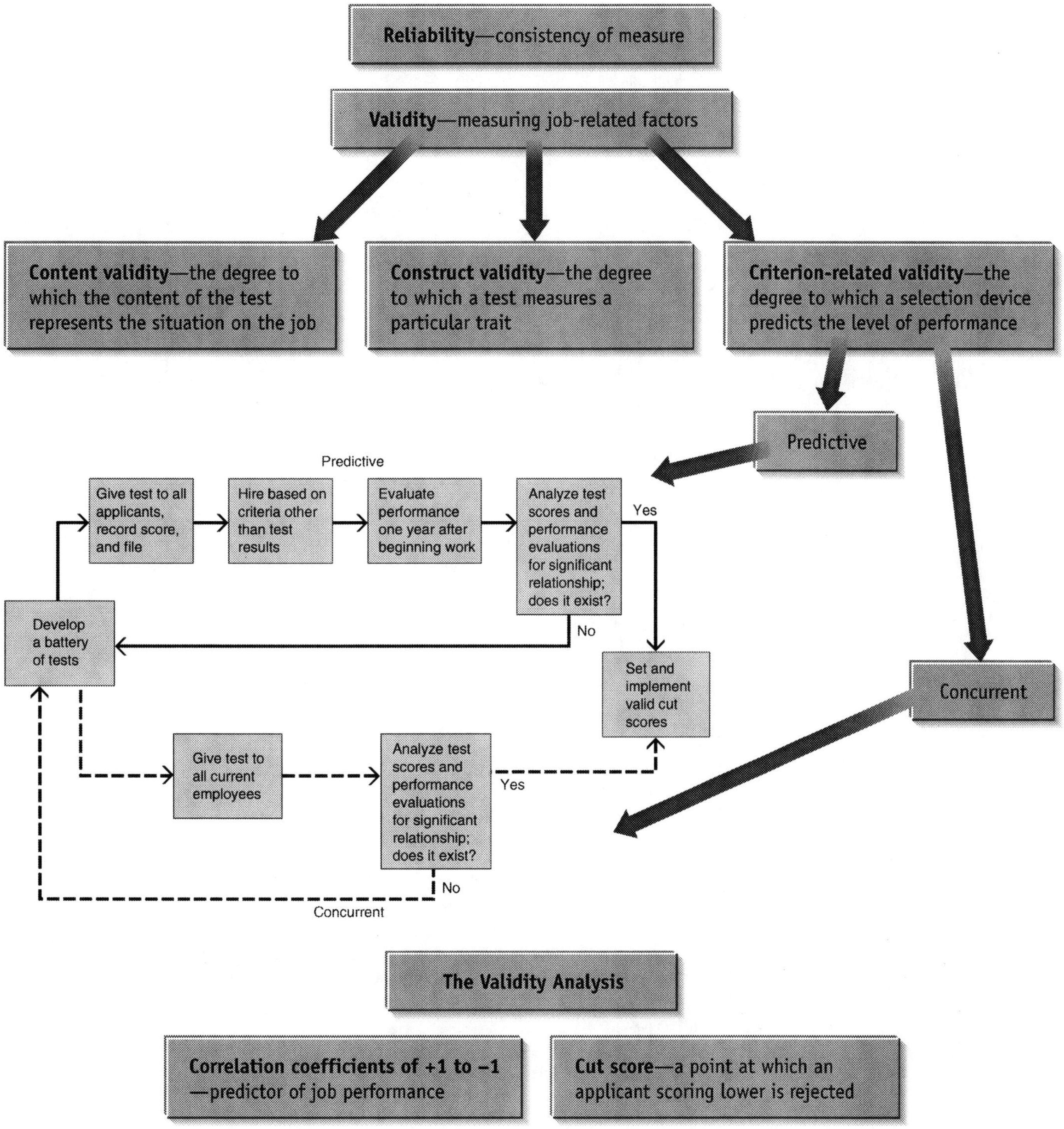

CROSSWORD COMPREHENSION

ACROSS

4. influencing performance evaluations by portraying an image desired by the appraiser
5. company-specific employment document used to generate specific information the company wants about someone applying for a job
7. a tentative job offer that becomes permanent after certain matters are finalized
9. a scoring point below which applicants are rejected
14. a type of validity that shows the degree to which a particular trait relates to successful job performance
15. the first step in the selection process whereby job inquiries are sorted
16. an examination to determine an applicant's fitness for essential job performance
17. observing job candidates not only for what they say but how they behave in an interview
18. a type of validity that shows the degree to which a particular selection device accurately predicts the important elements of work behavior
19. a selection device's consistency of measurement
20. a work sampling and assessment center evaluation
21. a special type of application form that uses relevant applicant information to determine the likelihood of job success
22. validating tests by using current employees as the study group

DOWN

1. a selection device that allows job candidates to learn negative as well as positive information about the job
2. applying all steps in the selection process before rendering a decision about a job candidate
3. the proven relationship of a selection device to relevant criteria
6. the ability of organizations to speak candidly to one another about employees
8. a selection device requiring the job applicant to actually perform a small segment of a job
9. a selection device used to obtain in-depth information about a candidate
10. a type of validity that shows the degree to which the test represents all situations that could be included in a job
11. the process of verifying information job candidates provide
12. validating tests by using prospective applicants as the study group
13. a facility where performance simulation tests are administered

HRM WORKSHOP

LINKING CONCEPTS TO PRACTICE: *Discussion Questions*

1. What do you think of realistic job previews? Would you be more likely to choose a position where recruiters emphasized only the positive aspects of the job?

2. "Because of the law regarding employment questions, application forms provide limited information. Accordingly, they should not be used." Do you agree or disagree with this statement? Explain.

3. "Even though interviews have been widely criticized, they are heavily used." Discuss why this selection device still rates highly although we know it can provide unreliable information.

4. "When hiring a member of a team, each team member should have equal say in who is hired." Do you agree or disagree? Explain.

DEVELOPING DIAGNOSTIC AND ANALYTICAL SKILLS

Case Application 7A: TIMING OF THE JOB OFFER

Does it make a difference when a job offer is made? For many, the answer may be no, but then, in HRM things are rarely cut and dried. Consider the events that took place in early 2005 at American Airlines.[54]

In their quest to add flight attendants to their organization, company officials began a major recruiting effort. To deal with the numbers they anticipated, American representatives spent considerable time screening applicants through extensive phone interviews. Those who passed this initial screening were invited to Dallas, American's headquarters, for group and individual interviews. For expediency's sake and for competitive reasons, successful candidates were then given a conditional job offer—conditioned on passing a drug test, a background investigation, and a medical exam. These individuals were then taken to the company's on-site medical facility, where they were asked to complete a personal history questionnaire and give a blood sample. Shortly thereafter, the results were available, and three individuals had a questionable blood test result. After discussing the matter with them, American officials learned that the three were HIV+. Consequently, the company withdrew the conditional offer. As a result, the three applicants sued.

At issue from the American's perspective was that the three individuals did not fully disclose their medical situation on the questionnaire—thus they lied on their "application." American held that the conditional job offer was just that—conditional. They hadn't completed the entire hiring process—like the background check—and only after all relevant information is in do they actually make a real or permanent job offer. They also cited that employment law requires individuals to be honest in disclosing their medical conditions—which in this case the individuals did not. The first court to look at this matter agreed and dismissed the case in favor of American.

But the three individuals persevered. They appealed, and on appeal the court ruled that American had, in fact, made a real job offer, then fired them for reasons that violate the Americans with Disabilities Act. In its decision, the appellate court said that a conditional offer should be made only after all nonmedical factors have been evaluated. In this case, American had not done everything prior to requesting the medical examination, thus they did not follow the standard hiring process they had in place. As a result, the lower court's decision was overturned and the case was permitted to go to trial.

Questions:

1. Do you believe American Airlines has the right to rescind a conditional job offer? Why?

2. Is the fact that they did not follow their standard hiring process a problem here? Explain.

3. Do you believe American Airlines has the right to not hire someone who is HIV+? Defend your position.

4. If you were the judge at the trial, given the facts presented above, who would you rule in favor of—American or the three individuals? Why?

Case Application 7-B: TEAM FUN!

Team Fun

Tony, director of human resources for TEAM FUN!, a sporting goods manufacturer and retailer, is meeting with Kenny and Norton, the owners and founders. He is ready to go to south Florida to select people for the new store opening there in a few months.

Tony: "We had over a thousand people interested in the newspaper ad: 200 for the sales representatives; 300 for the stockroom people; 200 for the cashiers; 100 for cleanup; and 500 for manager. We need to pre-screen some of these people. I thought I'd go down for only two weeks to hire everyone."

Kenny: "That's a great response! Wonder if they have all heard about us? Bobby [Kenny's son-in-law, who will manage the operation] can go down week after next. I think he should hire the managers. That should take a load off you. And just pick the best few out of the rest to talk to."

Norton: "What about all that EEO stuff that Tony has been telling us about? Do we have to keep records of all these inquiries?"

Tony: "We do need an applicant pool profile. I can do that when I go there for the selection process. Could we agree on a few guidelines for me, to cut the numbers down to size?"

Kenny: "Sure. Put some ideas together. We'll go over it tomorrow."

Tony: "I thought some performance simulation tests would be a good idea, especially for the cashiers and the salespeople. Maybe lifting and stacking for the stockroom, too."

Norton: "Sure. Put some tests together. We'll go over them tomorrow."

Tony: "What about drug testing and background checks?"

Kenny and Norton both glare at him until he walks out of the room.

Questions:

You are Tony's intern. Help him prepare for the meeting with Kenny and Norton tomorrow.

1. Devise a screening mechanism for each job category.
2. What kinds of performance simulation tests would be appropriate?
3. Set up an interview protocol for each job category.
4. Should Bobby select the managers himself? Should Bobby select all the other employees?
5. If you want Tony to try again with background checks and drug testing, prepare a carefully worded statement for him to present to Kenny and Norton. If you think these steps are undesirable, explain your position.

WORKING WITH A TEAM: *Preparing for the Interview*

Using the job description you developed for the benefits manager (Chapter 5) and the ad you wrote (Chapter 6), develop a list of interview questions you'd ask of job candidates. In groups of two or three, compare your interview questions and reach consensus on the questions you'd ask. Based on those questions, develop a list of evaluation metrics (how you'll evaluate candidate responses). Share your team's responses with other teams in the class.

What similarities and differences did you note? If time permits, you may want to have a mock interview. One of you play the role of the interviewer, one the job candidate, and one the observer. Ask the candidate your questions and evaluate the information obtained. The observer's job is to critique the interview. When you are finished, change roles and redo the mock interview.

LEARNING AN HRM SKILL: *Becoming an Effective Interviewer*

About the skill: If you are interviewing prospective job candidates, whether as an HRM recruiter or in any other capacity, we can offer several suggestions for improving interview effectiveness.

Steps in Practicing the Skill:

1. *Review the job description and job specification.* Reviewing pertinent information about the job provides valuable information about on what you will assess the candidate. Furthermore, relevant job requirements help eliminate interview bias.

2. *Prepare a structured set of questions to ask all applicants for the job.* A set of prepared questions ensures that the information you wish to elicit is attainable. Furthermore, if you ask them all similar questions, you can better compare candidates' answers against a common base.

3. *Before meeting a candidate, review his or her application form and résumé.* Doing so helps you create a complete picture of the candidate in terms of what the résumé or application says and what the job requires. You will also begin to identify areas to explore in the interview. That is, areas not clearly defined on the résumé or application but essential for the job will become a focal point of your discussion with the candidate.

4. *Open the interview by putting the applicant at ease and by providing a brief preview of the topics to be discussed.* Interviews are stressful for job candidates. By opening with small talk (for example, the weather) you give the candidate time to adjust to the interview setting. Providing a preview of topics to come gives the candidate an agenda with which to begin framing his or her responses to your questions.

5. *Ask your questions and listen carefully to the applicant's answers.* Select follow-up questions that naturally flow from the answers given. Focus on the responses as they relate to information you need to ensure that the candidate meets your job requirements. Any uncertainty you may still have requires a follow-up question to probe further for the information.

6. *Close the interview by telling the applicant what is going to happen next.* Applicants are anxious about the status of your hiring decision. Be honest with the candidate regarding others who will be interviewed and the remaining steps in the hiring process. If you plan to make a decision in two weeks or so, let the candidate know what you intend to do. In addition, tell the applicant how you will let him or her know about your decision.

7. *Write your evaluation of the applicant while the interview is still fresh in your mind.* Don't wait until the end of your day, after interviewing several candidates, to write your analysis of a candidate. Memory can fail you. The sooner you complete your write-up after an interview, the better chance you have for accurately recording what occurred in the interview.

ENHANCING YOUR COMMUNICATION SKILLS

1. Develop a two- to three-page response to the following statement: "Graphology as a selection criterion is not a valid selection device. Accordingly, it should not be used in determining whether or not to hire a job candidate." Present both sides of the argument and include supporting data. Conclude your paper by defending and supporting one of the two arguments you've presented.

2. Visit your college's career center and obtain a copy of the 50 most frequently asked interview questions. Reviewing the questions, which ones do you believe would pose the greatest difficulty for you? Which ones would be easier for you? In a two- to three-page write up, discuss *why* the questions you've identified would be diffi-

cult for you, and what you can do to help overcome this difficulty.

3. Search the Internet for software packages that can assist HRM in the selection process. Identify three different software packages that can be purchased by the public. State the benefits of the software package to the HRM practitioner and the costs associated with purchasing the product. Based on your limited search, which of the three software packages would you recommend? Write a two-page memo to your boss requesting permission to purchase your selected software. Remember to include in your memo a comparison of the software packages and the reasons for your recommendation.

EIGHT

Anyone running a successful company understands that for employees to be effective, communications must be outstanding. There really are no exceptions to this rule. But what happens when communications are in one language and the employees speak predominantly another language? If you are the management team at Chipotle Mexican Grill, you do what you must do—train employees to speak the language.[1]

Chipotle is a Mexican food chain that is 90 percent owned by McDonald's Corporation. On the job, Chipotle employees frequently make customized burritos and other Mexican food in front of the customers. Being unable to speak the customers' language is clearly a barrier—one that effects all aspects of the business. But rather than complain, Chipotle management decided to take some action. Employees in nearly all of their 425 restaurants are provided language train-

(*Source:* Tim Boyle/Getty Images, Inc.)

ing. Given that the majority of employees are fluent in Spanish but speak little English, employees are frequently invited to be part of the company's on-site English class. With eight trainers in the corporation who teach managers in the locations how to teach English to their employees, Chipotle employees are gaining greater English language skills—which are carrying over into their personal lives.

For the most part, Chipotle management doesn't appear to be that out of the ordinary. They, like many organizations today, are recognizing the importance of diversity in their workplace and how to best create a positive work environment. What's unique at Chipotle is that they are endorsing different cultures and using the training function to help workers achieve greater work performance. What they are finding, too, is that such training is having a wonderful effect on many parts of the business. How so? Consider the following.

Because of their actions, Chipotle's turnover is approximately one-third the industry's average in the fast-food business. Accordingly, this language training is helping build employee loyalty—and giving their employees greater self-confidence. In return, the employees are maintaining their loyalty to the company. Additionally, because they are better able to understand corporate communications, things like company policies or work procedures are not being misinterpreted.

All in all, that's a win-win situation for everyone involved. Todos en todo que sea ganar-ganan para cada uno implicado.

Socializing, Orienting, and Developing Employees

Learning Outcomes

After reading this chapter, you will be able to

1. Define *socialization*.
2. Identify the three stages of employee socialization.
3. Identify the key personnel involved in orientation.
4. Explain why employee training is important.
5. Define *training*.
6. Describe how training needs evolve.
7. Discuss the term *organizational development* and the role of the change agent.
8. Explain the term *learning organization*.
9. Describe the methods and criteria involved in evaluating training programs.
10. Explain issues critical to international training and development.

INTRODUCTION

When we talk about socializing, orienting, and developing employees, we refer to a process of helping new employees adapt to their new organizations and work responsibilities. These programs are designed to help employees fully understand what working is about in the organization and help them become fully productive as soon as possible. In essence, it's about learning the ropes! When employees better understand and accept behaviors the organization views as desirable, likelihood increases that each employee will attain his or her goals.

In this chapter, we'll explore the arena of socializing, orienting, and developing employees. We'll first look at the socialization process and what organizations should do when employees first join them. We'll then explore training and later development efforts designed to ensure a supply of highly skilled employees.

THE OUTSIDER–INSIDER PASSAGE

socialization

A process of adaption that takes place as individuals attempt to learn the values and norms of work roles.

When we talk about **socialization**, we are talking about a process of adaptation. In the context of organizations, the term refers to all passages employees undergo. For instance, when you begin a new job, accept a lateral transfer, or are promoted, you must make adjustments. You adapt to a new environment—different work activities, a new boss, a different and most likely diverse group of co-workers, and probably a different set of standards for what constitutes successful performance. Although we recognize that this socialization will go on throughout people's careers—within an organization as well as between organizations—the most profound adjustment occurs when one makes the first move into an organization: the move from being an outsider to being an insider. The following discussion, therefore, is limited to the outsider–insider passage, or, more appropriately, organization–entry socialization. This an important topic for HRM. FedEx, for example, learned that their extensive turnover related directly to experiences employees had on their first few days on the job.[2]

Socialization

Think back to your first day in college. What feelings did you experience? Anxiety over new expectations? Uncertainty over what was to come? Excitement at being on your own and experiencing new things? Fear based on everything friends said about how tough college courses were? Stress over what classes to take and with which professors? You probably experienced many of these—and maybe much more. Entry into a job is no different. Organizations can assist in the adjustment process if a few matters are understood. We'll call these the assumptions of employee socialization.

Assumptions of Employee Socialization

Loneliness and a feeling of isolation are not unusual for new employees—they need special attention to put them at ease.

Several assumptions underlie the process of socialization: (1) socialization strongly influences employee performance and organizational stability; (2) new members suffer from anxiety; (3) socialization does not occur in a vacuum; and (4) individuals adjust to new situations in remarkably similar ways. Let's look a little closer at each of these assumptions.[3]

Socialization Strongly Influences Employee Performance and Organizational Stability Your work performance depends to a considerable degree on knowing what you should or should not do. Understanding the right way to do a job indicates proper socialization. Furthermore, appraisal of your performance includes how well you fit into the organization. Can you get along with your co-workers? Do you have acceptable work habits? Do you demonstrate the right attitude and present appropriate behaviors? These qualities differ among jobs and organizations. For instance, on some jobs you will be evaluated higher if you are aggressive and outwardly indicate that you are ambitious. On others, or in other organizations, such an approach might be evaluated negatively. As a result, proper socialization becomes a significant factor in influencing both your actual job performance and how others perceive it.

Organizational Stability Also Increases Through Socialization When, over many years, jobs are filled and vacated with a minimum of disruption, the organization will be more stable.[4] Its objectives transfer more smoothly between generations. Loyalty and commitment to the organization should be easier to maintain because the organization's philosophy and objectives appear consistent over time. Given that most managers value high employee performance and organizational stability, the proper socialization of employees should be important.

New Members Suffer from Anxiety The outsider–insider passage produces anxiety. Stress is high because the new member feels a lack of identification—if not with the work itself, certainly with a new superior, new co-workers, a new work location, and new rules and regulations. Loneliness and a feeling of isolation are not unusual. This anxiety state has at least two implications. First, new employees need special attention to put them at ease. This usually means providing adequate information to reduce uncertainty and ambiguity. Second, tension can be positive in that it often motivates individuals to learn the values and norms of their newly assumed role as quickly as possible. The new member is usually anxious about the new role but motivated to learn the ropes and rapidly become an accepted member of the organization.

Socialization Does Not Occur in a Vacuum Learning associated with socialization goes beyond comprehending the formal job description and the expectations of human resources people or managers. Socialization is influenced by subtle and less subtle statements and behaviors offered up by colleagues, management, employees, clients, and other people with whom new members come in contact.

Individuals Adjust to New Situations in Remarkably Similar Ways This holds true even though the content and type of adjustments may vary. For instance, as pointed out previously, anxiety is high at entry and the new member usually wants to reduce that anxiety quickly. Information obtained during recruitment and selection is always incomplete and usually distorted. New employees, therefore, must alter their understanding of their role to fit more complete information once they are on the job. Adjustments take time—every new member goes through a settling-in period that tends to follow a relatively standard pattern.

The Socialization Process

Socialization can be conceptualized as a process made up of three stages: pre-arrival, encounter, and metamorphosis.[5] The first stage encompasses learning the new employee has gained before joining the organization. In the second stage, the new employee gains clearer understanding of the organization and deals with the realization that the expectations and reality may differ. The third stage involves lasting change. Here, new employees become fully trained in their jobs, perform successfully, and fit in with the values and norms of co-workers.[6] These three stages ultimately affect new employees' productivity on the job, their commitment to the organization's goals, and their decision to remain with

How does this individual adjust to her new job? Research tells us that every individual new to an organization goes through the outsider–insider passage, a time of adjusting to the organization and learning what to do and what not to do. (Source: Reza Estakhrian/ Stone/Getty Images, Inc.)

EXHIBIT 8-1
A Socialization Process

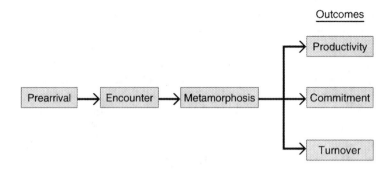

prearrival stage

This socialization process stage recognizes that individuals arrive in an organization with a set of organizational values, attitudes, and expectations.

encounter stage

The socialization stage where individuals confront the possible dichotomy between their organizational expectations and reality.

metamorphosis stage

The socialization stage during which the new employee must work out inconsistencies discovered during the encounter stage.

the organization.[7] Exhibit 8-1 is a graphic representation of the socialization process.

The **prearrival stage** explicitly recognizes that each individual arrives with a set of organizational values, attitudes, and expectations. These may cover both the work to be done and the organization. In many jobs, particularly high-skilled and managerial jobs, new members will have considerable prior socialization in training and in school.[8] Part of teaching business students is to socialize them to what business is like, what to expect in a business career, and what kind of attitudes professors believe will lead to successful assimilation in an organization. Prearrival socialization, however, goes beyond the specific job. Most organizations use the selection process to inform prospective employees about the organization as a whole. In addition, of course, selection interviews also help ensure including the right type of employee—those who will fit the organization's culture.

On entry into the organization, new members enter the **encounter stage**. Here, individuals confront the possible dichotomy between their expectations about jobs, co-workers, supervisors, and the organization in general and reality. If expectations prove to have been more or less accurate, the encounter state merely reaffirms perceptions generated earlier. However, this is not always the case. Where expectations and reality differ, new employees must be socialized to detach them from their previous assumptions and replace these with the organization's pivotal standards.[9] Socialization, however, cannot solve all expectation differences. At the extreme, some new members may become totally disillusioned with the actualities of their jobs and resign. Proper selection, including realistic job previews, can significantly reduce this.

Finally, the new member must work out any problems discovered during the encounter stage. This may mean going through changes—hence this is called the **metamorphosis stage**. But what is a desirable metamorphosis? Metamorphosis is complete—as is socialization—when new members become comfortable with the organization and their work teams. They internalize co-worker and organization norms, and they understand and accept these norms.[10] New members will feel accepted by their peers as trusted and valued individuals. They will feel competent to complete their jobs successfully. They will understand the organizational system—not only their own tasks but the rules, procedures, and informally accepted practices as well. Finally, they will know how they will be evaluated. That is, they've gained an understanding of what criteria will be used to measure and appraise their work. They'll know what is expected of them and what constitutes a good job. Consequently, as Exhibit 8-1 shows, successful metamorphosis should have a positive effect on new employees' productivity and the employee's commitment to the organization, and should reduce the likelihood that the employee will leave the organization any time soon.[11]

If HRM recognizes that certain assumptions hold for new employees entering an organization and that they typically follow a three-staged socialization process, they can develop a program to begin helping these employees adapt to the organization. Let's turn our attention, then, to this aspect of organizational life—socializing our new employees through the new-employee orientation process.

THE PURPOSE OF NEW-EMPLOYEE ORIENTATION

New-employee **orientation** covers the activities involved in introducing a new employee to the organization and to the individuals in his or her work unit. It expands on information received during the recruitment and selection stages and helps reduce the initial anxiety we all feel when beginning a new job.[12] For example, an orientation program should familiarize the new member with the organization's objectives, history, philosophy, procedures, and rules; communicate relevant HRM policies such as work hours, pay procedures, overtime requirements, and company benefits; review the specific duties and responsibilities of the new member's job; provide a tour of the organization's physical facilities; and introduce the employee to his or her manager and co-workers.[13]

Who is responsible for orienting the new employee? This can be done by either the new employee's supervisor, the people in HRM, through computer-based programs, or some combination thereof. In many medium-sized and most large organizations, HRM takes charge of explaining such matters as overall organizational policies and employee benefits. In other medium-sized and most small firms, new employees will receive their entire orientation from their supervisor or be exposed to an orientation program on the company's intranet.[14] Of course, the new employee's orientation may not be formal at all. For instance, in many small organizations, orientation may mean the new member reports to her supervisor, who then assigns her to another employee who introduces her to her co-workers. This may be followed by a quick tour of the facilities, after which the new employee is shown to her desk and work begins.

We contend that new-employee orientation requires much more. For instance, in today's dynamic organizations, new employees must understand the organization's culture.

orientation
Activities that introduce new employees to the organization and their work units.

Learning the Organization's Culture

We know that every individual has what psychologists have termed personality, a set of relatively permanent and stable traits. When we describe someone as warm, innovative, relaxed, or conservative, we are describing personality traits. An organization, too, has a personality, which we call the organization's culture. What do we specifically mean by **organization culture**? We refer to a system of shared meaning.[15] Just as tribal cultures have totems and taboos that dictate how each member should act toward fellow members and outsiders, organizations have cultures that govern how their members should behave.[16] Every organization, over time, evolves stories, rituals, material symbols, and language.[17] These shared values determine, in large part, what employees see and how they respond to their world.[18]

An employee who has been properly socialized to the organization's culture, then, has learned how work is done, what matters, and which work-related behaviors and perspectives are or are not acceptable and desirable. In most cases, this involves input from many individuals.

organization culture
The system of sharing meaning within the organization that determines how employees act.

An employee who has been properly socialized to the organization's culture knows what is acceptable behavior and what is not.

The CEO's Role in Orientation

Prior to the mid-1980s, new-employee orientation operated, if at all, without input from the company's executive management. That began to change, in part when management consultants advocated making senior management more accessible to employees. Many senior managers have become highly visible in their organizations, meeting and greeting employees and listening to employee concerns. At the same time, managers talk about the company—where it is going and how—in management terminology, *visioning*. As more successful companies have been cited in business literature for their leaders' involvement with the workforce, one question arises. If this connection works well for existing employees, what would it do for employees joining the organization? The answer appears to be a lot.

One of the more stressful aspects of starting a new job is the thought of entering the unknown. Although conditions at a previous organization may have made you leave—like lack of upward mobility—at least you knew what you had. But starting a new job is frightening. You may wonder if you made the right choice. Having the CEO present from day one, addressing new employees, helps allay those fears. The CEO's first responsibility is to welcome new employees aboard and talk to them about what a good job choice they made.[19] In fact, this segment of new-employee orientation can be likened to a cheerleading pep rally. The CEO is in a position to inspire new employees by talking about what it is like to work for the organization. In addition, the CEO can begin to discuss what really matters in the company—an indoctrination to the organization's culture.

When a CEO is present, the company shows that it truly cares for its employees. Employee satisfaction concepts are sometimes thrown around an organization to such an extent that they become nothing more than lip service to the idea.[20] But this senior company official's presence validates that the company really is concerned—the CEO's commitment to making the first day special is evidenced by his or her presence. When scheduling conflicts arise, some companies use previously prepared videos or other electronic means of carrying the same message.

HRM's Role in Orientation

In our introductory comments we stated that the orientation function can be performed by HRM, line management, or a combination of the two. Despite a preference for a combination strategy, we contend that HRM plays a major coordinating role in new-employee orientation, which ensures that the appropriate components are in place. In addition, HRM also serves as a participant in the program. Consequently, we should recognize what HRM must do. For example, in our discussion of making the job offer (Chapter 7), we emphasized that the offer should come from human resources to better coordinate administrative activities surrounding a new hire. The same holds true for new-employee orientation. Depending on the recruiting, a systematic schedule should guide employee entry into a company.

As job offers are made and accepted, HRM should instruct the new employee when to report to work. However, before the employee formally arrives, HRM must be prepared to handle some of the more routine needs of these individuals; for example, new employees typically have a long list of questions about benefits. More proactive organizations, such as AT&T, prepare a package for new employees. This package generally focuses on important decisions a new employee must make—choice of health insurance, institutions for direct deposit of paychecks, and tax-withholding information. When HRM provides this information a few weeks before new hires start work, they have ample time to make a proper choice—quite possibly one affected by a working spouse's options. Furthermore, forms often require information that few employees keep with them—for example, Social Security numbers of family members and medical histories. Accordingly, having that information before the new-employee orientation session saves time.

HRM's second concern involves its role as a participant in the process. Most new employees' exposure to the organization thus far has been with HRM, but after the hiring process is over, HRM quickly drops out of the picture unless there is a problem. Therefore, HRM must spend some orientation time addressing what assistance it can offer to employees in the future. This point cannot be minimized. If HRM provides an array of services such as career guidance, benefit administration, or employee training, HRM cannot become complacent. They must let these new employees know what else HRM can do for them in the future, particularly if many HRM services may be contracted out by departments, thereby lessening HRM's effect in the organization.[21]

EMPLOYEE TRAINING

Every organization needs well-adjusted, trained, and experienced people to perform its activities. As jobs in today's dynamic organizations have become more complex, the importance of employee education has increased. On the whole, for example, planes don't cause airline accidents, people do. Nearly three-quarters of collisions, crashes, and other airline mishaps result from pilot or air traffic controller errors or inadequate maintenance. Weather and structural failures typically account for the remaining accidents.[22] We cite these statistics to illustrate the importance of training in the airline industry. These maintenance and human errors could be prevented or significantly reduced by better employee training.

Employee training is a learning experience: it seeks a relatively permanent change in employees that their improves job performance. Thus, training involves changing skills, knowledge, attitudes, or behavior.[23] This may mean changing what employees know, how they work, or their attitudes toward their jobs, co-workers, managers, and the organization. It has been estimated, for instance, that U.S. business firms alone spend billions of dollars each a year on formal courses and training programs to develop workers' skills.[24] Managers, possibly with HRM assistance, decide when employees need training and what form that training should take (see Diversity Issues in HRM).

For our purposes, we will differentiate between **employee training** and **employee development** for one particular reason: Although both are similar in learning methods, their time frames differ. Training is more present-day oriented; it focuses on individuals' current jobs, enhancing those specific skills and abilities to immediately perform their jobs. For example, suppose you enter the job market during your senior year of college, pursuing a job as a marketing

employee training
Present-oriented training that focuses on individuals' current jobs.

employee development
Future-oriented training that focuses on employee personal growth.

DIVERSITY ISSUES IN HRM

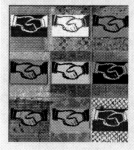

TRAINING AND EEO

Much of our previous discussions of equal employment opportunity (EEO) have centered on the selection process. Undoubtedly, equal employment opportunities are most prevalent in the hiring process, but EEO's application to training cannot be overlooked. Remember that our definition of adverse impact includes any HRM activity that adversely affects protected group members in hiring, firing, and promoting. So how does training fall into the EEO realms?[25] Let's take a brief look.

Training programs may be required for promotions, job bidding (especially in unionized jobs), or salary increases. Regarding any of these, the organization must ensure that training selection criteria relate to the job. Furthermore, equal training opportunities must exist for all employees. Failure at something as simple as informing all employees of the schedule of training programs could raise suspicions regarding how fair the training programs are.

Organizations should also pay close attention to training completion rates. If more protected group members fail to pass training programs than "majority group" members, this might indicate dissimilarities in the training offered. Once again, organizations should monitor these activities and perform periodic audits to ensure full compliance with EEO regulations.

What type of training is this pilot receiving? We'd classify it as vestibule training, training that occurs in a flight simulator. Such training can be highly cost-effective. Computer programming allows trainers to present scenarios for pilots to handle that could be difficult or dangerous to replicate in a real aircraft. Make a mistake in the simulator, and you start over. Make a mistake at 35,000 feet, and starting over may not be an option. (Source: Alvis Upitis/Getty Images, Inc.)

representative. Despite your degree in marketing, you will need some training. Specifically, you'll need to learn the company's policies and practices, product information, and other pertinent selling practices. This, by definition, is job-specific training, or training designed to make you more effective in your current job.

Employee development, on the other hand, generally focuses on future jobs in the organization. As your job and career progress, you'll need new skills and abilities. For example, if you become a sales territory manager, the skills you need to perform that job may be quite different from those you used to sell products. Now you must supervise sales representatives and develop a broad-based knowledge of marketing and specific management competencies in communication skills, evaluating employee performance, and disciplining problem individuals. As you are groomed for positions of greater responsibility, employee development efforts can help prepare you for that day.

Determining Training Needs

Determining training needs typically involves generating answers to several questions (see Exhibit 8-2).[26] Recall from Chapter 5 that these types of questions demonstrate the close link between employment planning and determining training needs. Based on our determination of the organization's needs, the work to be done, and the skills necessary to complete this work, our training programs should follow naturally. Once we identify where deficiencies lie, we have a grasp of the extent and nature of our training needs.

The leading questions in Exhibit 8-2 suggest the kinds of signals that can warn a manager when training may be necessary. The more obvious ones relate directly to productivity. Indications that job performance is declining may include production decreases, lower quality, more accidents, and higher scrap or rejection rates. Any of these outcomes might suggest that worker skills need to be fine-tuned. Of course, we are assuming that the employee's performance decline is in no way related to lack of effort. Managers, too, must also recognize that a constantly evolving workplace may require training. Changes imposed on employees as a result of job redesign or a technological breakthrough also require training.

A word of caution on training, however: If deficiencies in performance occur, it doesn't necessarily follow that the manager should take corrective action. It is important to put training into perspective. Training may be costly, and it should not be viewed as a cure-all for what ails the organization. Rather, judge training by its contribution to performance, where performance is a function of skills, abilities, motivation, and the opportunity to perform. Managers must also compare the value received from performance increases attributable to training with the costs that training incurred.[27]

Once it has been determined that training is necessary, training goals must be established. Management should explicitly state its desired results for each

EXHIBIT 8-2
Determining Training Needs

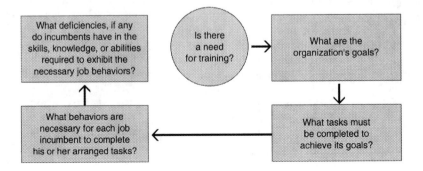

On-the-Job Training Methods	
Job rotation	Lateral transfers allow employees to work at different jobs. Provides good exposure to a variety of tasks.
Understudy assignments	Working with a seasoned veteran, coach, or mentor provides support and encouragement from an experienced worker. In the trades industry, this may also be an apprenticeship.
Off-the-Job Training Methods	
Classroom lectures	Lectures convey specific technical, interpersonal, or problem-solving skills.
Films and videos	Media productions explicitly demonstrate technical skills not easily presented by other training methods.
Simulation exercises	Learning a job by actually performing the work (or its simulation). May include case analyses, experiential exercises, role playing, and group interaction.
Vestibule training	Learning tasks on the same equipment that one actually will use on the job but in a simulated work environment.

EXHIBIT 8-3
Typical Training Methods

employee.[28] It is not adequate to say we want change in employee knowledge, skills, attitudes, or behavior, we must clarify what is to change and by how much. These goals should be tangible, verifiable, timely, and measurable.[29] They should be clear to both the supervisor and the employee. For instance, a firefighter might be expected to jump from a moving fire truck traveling at 15 miles per hour, successfully hook up a four-inch hose to a hydrant, and turn on the hydrant, all in less than 40 seconds. Such explicit goals ensure that both the supervisor and the employee know what is expected from the training effort.

Training Methods

Many different types of training methods are available.[30] For the most part, however, we can classify them as on-the-job or off-the-job training. We have summarized the more popular training methods in Exhibit 8-3.

EMPLOYEE DEVELOPMENT

Employee development, as mentioned earlier, is more future oriented and more concerned with education than employee job-specific training. By education we mean that employee development activities attempt to instill sound reasoning processes—to enhance one's ability to understand and interpret knowledge—rather than imparting a body of facts or teaching a specific set of motor skills. Development, therefore, focuses more on the employee's personal growth.[31] Successful employees prepared for positions of greater responsibility have analytical, human, conceptual, and specialized skills. They think and understand. Training per se cannot overcome an individual's inability to understand cause-and-effect relationships, to synthesize from experience, to visualize relationships, or to think logically. As a result, we suggest that employee development be predominantly an education process rather than a training process.

Consider one critical component of employee development: all employees, regardless of level, can be developed. Historically, development was reserved for potential management personnel. Although it is critical for individuals to be trained in specific skills related to managing—planning, organizing, leading, controlling, and decision making—time has taught us that nonmanagerial employees need these skills as well. The use of work teams, reductions in supervisory roles,

www.wiley.com/college/decenzo
What Would You Do?
EXPERIENCE: Employee Orientation Programs

allowing workers to participate in setting job goals, and a greater emphasis on quality and customers have changed the way we view employee development. Accordingly, organizations now require new employee skills, knowledge, and abilities. Thus, as we go through the next few pages, note that the methods used to develop employees in general are the same as those used to develop future management talent.

Employee Development Methods

Some development of an individual's abilities can take place on the job (see Workplace Issues, p. 218). We will review several methods, three popular on-the-job techniques (job rotation, assistant-to positions, and committee assignments) and three off-the-job methods (lecture courses and seminars, simulation exercises, and outdoor training).

job rotation

Moving employees horizontally or vertically to expand their skills, knowledge, or abilities.

Job Rotation Job rotation involves moving employees to various positions in the organization in an effort to expand their skills, knowledge, and abilities. Job rotation can be either horizontal or vertical. Vertical rotation is nothing more than promoting a worker into a new position. In this chapter, we will emphasize the horizontal dimension of job rotation, also known as a short-term lateral transfer.

Job rotation represents an excellent method for broadening an individual's exposure to company operations and for turning a specialist into a generalist. In addition to increasing the individual's experience and allowing him or her to absorb new information, it can reduce boredom and stimulate the development of new ideas. It can also provide opportunities for a more comprehensive and reliable evaluation of the employee by his or her supervisors.

Assistant-To Positions Employees with demonstrated potential sometimes work under a seasoned and successful manager, often in different areas of the organization. Working as staff assistants, or in some cases, serving on special boards, these individuals perform many duties under the watchful eye of a supportive coach (see Workplace Issues, p. 218). In doing so, these employees experience a wide variety of management activities and are groomed for assuming the duties of the next higher level.

Committee Assignment Committee assignments can allow the employee to share in decision making, to learn by watching others, and to investigate specific organizational problems. Temporary committees often act as a taskforce to delve into a particular problem, ascertain alternative solutions, and recommend a solution. These temporary assignments can be both interesting and rewarding to the employee's growth. Appointment to permanent committees increases the employee's exposure to other members of the organization, broadens his or her understanding, and provides an opportunity to grow and make recommendations under the scrutiny of other committee members.

In addition to the above on-the-job techniques, employees benefit from off-the-job development. We will briefly discuss three of the more popular means: lecture courses and seminars, simulations, and outdoor training.

Lecture Courses and Seminars Traditional forms of instruction revolve around formal lecture courses and seminars. These help individuals acquire knowledge and develop their conceptual and analytical abilities. Many organizations offer these in-house, through outside vendors, or both.

Technology however, is allowing for significant improvements in the training field. A growing trend at companies is to provide lecture courses and seminars through distance learning. Digitized computer technology allows a facilitator to give a lecture in one location that is simultaneously transmitted over fiber-optic cables to several other locations.

Over the past few years, we've witnessed an expansion of lecture courses and seminars for organizational members. Some have returned to college classes, some for credit toward a degree; others have taken continuing education courses. Either way, employees are taking the responsibility to advance their skills, knowledge, and abilities in an effort to enhance their value-addedness to their current or future employer.

Simulations Simulations, as cited in Exhibit 8-3, are a training technique. While critical in training employees on actual work experiences, simulations are probably even more popular for employee development.[32] The more widely used simulation exercises include case studies, decision games, and role plays.

Employee development through case-study analysis was popularized at the Harvard Graduate School of Business. Taken from the actual experiences of organizations, these cases represent attempts to describe, as accurately as possible, real problems that managers have faced. Trainees study the cases to determine problems, analyze causes, develop alternative solutions, select what they believe to be the best solution, and implement it. Case studies can provide stimulating discussions among participants, as well as excellent opportunities for individuals to defend their analytical and judgmental abilities. It appears to be a rather effective method for improving decision-making abilities within the constraints of limited information.

Simulated decision games and role-playing exercises put individuals in the role of acting out supervisory problems. Simulations, frequently played on a computer program, provide opportunities for individuals to make decisions and witness the implications of their decisions for other segments of the organization. Airlines, for instance, find that simulations are a much more cost-effective means of training pilots—especially in potentially dangerous situations. And poor decisions typically have no worse effects on the learner than the need to explain why the choice was not a good one. Role playing allows participants to act out problems and deal with real people. Participants are assigned roles and are asked to react to one another as they would have to do in their managerial jobs.

The advantages of simulation exercises are the opportunities to attempt to "create an environment" similar to real situations managers face, without high costs for poor outcomes. Of course, the disadvantages are the reverse of this: it is difficult to duplicate the pressures and realities of actual decision making on the job, and individuals often act differently in real-life situations than they do in a simulated exercise.

Outdoor Training A trend in employee development has been the use of outdoor (sometimes referred to as wilderness or survival) training. The primary focus of such training is to teach trainees the importance of working together, of coming together as a team.[33] Outdoor training typically involves some major emotional and physical challenge. This could be white-water rafting, mountain climbing, paintball games, or surviving a week in the "jungle." The purpose of such training is to see how employees react to the difficulties that nature presents to them. Do they face these dangers alone? Do they freak out? Or are they controlled and successful in achieving their goal? The reality is that today's business environment does not permit employees to stand alone. This has reinforced the importance of working closely with one another, building trusting relationships, and succeeding as a member of a group. Companies such as Asea Brown Boveri and DaimlerChrysler spend millions each year in their outdoor training efforts.[34]

simulation
Any artificial environment that attempts to closely mirror an actual condition.

www.wiley.com/college/decenzo
What Would You Do?
EXPERIENCE: Training and Development

ORGANIZATION DEVELOPMENT

organization development (OD)

The part of HRM that addresses systemwide change in the organization.

Although our discussion so far has related to the people side of business, it is important to recognize that organizations change from time to time. Changes with respect to continuous improvements, diversity, and work process engineering require the organization to move forward through a process we call **organization development (OD)**. OD has taken on a renewed importance today. Brought about by continuous-improvement goals, many organizations have drastically changed the way they do business.[35]

No matter what role OD takes in an organization, it requires facilitation by an individual well versed in organization dynamics. In HRM terms, we call this person a **change agent**. Change agents are responsible for fostering the environment in which change can occur, working with the affected employees to help them adapt to the change. Change agents may be either internal employees, often associated with the training and development function of HRM, or external consultants. Before we discuss specific aspects of organization development, let's look at this phenomenon we call change.

change agent

Individual responsible for fostering the change effort and assisting employees in adapting to changes.

What Is Change?

Change usually affects four areas: the organization's systems, its technology, its processes, and its people. No matter what the change, or how minor it may appear, understanding its effect is paramount for it to be supported and lasting.[36] OD comes into play with efforts designed to support the business's strategic direction. For instance, if work processes change, people need to learn new production methods and procedures and maybe new skills. OD becomes instrumental in bringing about the change. How so? The effects of change become organizational culture issues. Accordingly, OD efforts help ensure that all

DID YOU KNOW?

TRAINING EXPENDITURES

How much do United States and Canadian organizations spend annually for employee training and development activities? Where are these training efforts focused? And how do North American training expenditures compare to those in other industrialized nations? Let's take a look at some of the data.

Organizations in the United States and Canada have some of the highest per employee expenditures anywhere on the globe—although that ultimate honor goes to organizations in Australia and New Zealand. In the United States, employers spend, on average, approximately $1,135 per employee on training. That's 2.34 percent of their total payroll costs. In Canada, the investment is $824 per employee, which represents 1.55 percent of total payroll. In both of these countries, the top four training areas are alike—the highest training expenditures go to (1) skills training, (2) management/supervisory development training, (3) information technology skills training, and (4) procedures training. In these two countries, approxi-

mately 77 percent of all employees receive some formal training each year. In contrast, more than 90 percent of the employees in Australia and New Zealand receive training each year. In Asia, training costs average about 3 percent of payroll.

Whereas specific numbers show some differences, what's more important is that in all industrialized nations, the employer training expenditures are increasing and are expected to continue to increase over the next decade. That's a clear indication that globally, employers recognize the importance of training and development activities and the effect they have on assisting organizational members in achieving their performance goals.

Source: Data from U. Vu, "$824 to Train Isn't Enough, Conference Board Says," *Canadian HR Reporter* (July 18, 2005), available online at www.hrreporter.com; "ASTD Reveals Snapshot of International Training Trends," *Industrial and Commercial Training*, Vol. 33, Issue 6/7 (2001), pp. 274–275; and ASTD, "ASTD Highlights International Training Trends in Its 2002 International Comparisons Report" (June 3, 2002), available online at www.astd.org/NR/rdonlyres/C290E926-F089-4CB4-9FB2-22E266FCD241/0/ICRreport.pdf.

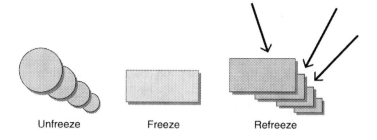

EXHIBIT 8-4
Lewin's Change Process

organizational members support the new culture and assist in bringing the new culture to fruition.

We often use two metaphors to clarify the change process.[37] The *calm waters metaphor* envisions the organization as a large ship crossing a calm sea. The ship's captain and crew know exactly where they are going because they have made the trip many times before. Change surfaces as the occasional storm, a brief distraction in an otherwise calm and predictable trip. The *white-water rapids metaphor* pictures the organization as a small raft navigating a raging river with uninterrupted white-water rapids. Aboard the raft are a half dozen people who have never worked together before, who are totally unfamiliar with the river, who are unsure of their eventual destination, and who, as if things weren't bad enough, are traveling in the pitch-dark of night. In the white-water rapids metaphor, change is a natural state, and managing change is a continual process.

These two metaphors present widely differing approaches to understanding and responding to change. Let's take a closer look at each one.

The Calm Waters Metaphor

Until recently, the calm waters metaphor dominated the thinking of practicing managers and academics. The prevailing model for handling change in calm waters is best illustrated in Kurt Lewin's three-step description of the change process (see Exhibit 8-4).[38]

According to Lewin, successful change requires unfreezing the status quo, changing to a new state, and refreezing the new change to make it permanent. The status quo can be considered an equilibrium state. Unfreezing, necessary to move from this equilibrium, is achieved in one of three ways:

- The driving forces, which direct behavior away from the status quo, can be increased.
- The restraining forces, which hinder movement from the existing equilibrium, can be decreased.
- The two approaches can be combined.

After unfreezing, the change itself can be implemented. However, the mere introduction of change does not ensure that it will take hold. The new situation, therefore, needs to be refrozen so that it can be sustained over time. Without this last step, the change will likely be short-lived, and employees will revert to the previous equilibrium state. The objective of refreezing, then, is to stabilize the new situation by balancing the driving and restraining forces.

Note how Lewin's three-step process treats change as a break in the organization's equilibrium state. The status quo has been disturbed, and change is necessary to establish a new equilibrium state.[39] This view might have been appropriate to the relatively calm environment that most organizations faced in the 1950s, 1960s, and early 1970s, but the calm waters metaphor is an increasingly obsolete description of the kind of seas managers now navigate.

The White-Water Rapids Metaphor

This metaphor takes into consideration the fact that environments are both uncertain and dynamic. To understand

The uncertainty surrounding change in a dynamic environment is significant. Just as white-water rafters deal with continuously changing water currents, organizational members facing rapid and uncertain change must adjust quickly and react properly to unexpected events. (Source: Javier Pierini/Digital Vision/Getty Images, Inc.)

what managing change while negotiating uninterrupted rapids might be like, imagine attending a college in which courses vary in length. When you sign up, you don't know whether a course will last for 2 weeks or 30 weeks. Furthermore, the instructor can end a course at any time, with no prior warning. If that isn't bad enough, the length of the class session changes each time—sometimes 20 minutes, other times 3 hours—and the time of the next class meeting is set by the instructor during the previous class. Oh, yes: The exams are unannounced; you must be ready for a test at any time. To succeed in this college, you would have to be incredibly flexible and able to respond quickly to every changing condition. Students too structured or slow on their feet would not survive.

A growing number of organizational members are accepting that their job is much like what a student would face in such a college. The stability and predictability of calm waters do not exist. Disruptions in the status quo are not occasional and temporary, followed by a return to calm waters. Many of today's employees never get out of the rapids. They face constant change, bordering on chaos. These individuals must play a game they have never played before, governed by rules created as the game progresses.[40]

Is the white-water rapids metaphor merely an overstatement? No! Take the case of General Motors.[41] In the intensely competitive automotive manufacturing business, a company must be prepared for any possibility. Cars are being surpassed by sport utility vehicles. Gasoline engines are still the fury of environmentalists who desire a more environment-friendly source of power for vehicles. Government regulators demand ever-increasing gasoline mileage. Customers want new and unique styles more frequently. Competition in the industry is fierce. While GM focuses on "big" competitors, new entrants into the marketplace—such as Hyundai and Kia—pick away at market share. GM, to succeed, must change and continuously improve and revamp everything that they do! As one of GM's Advanced Portfolio Exploration Group (APEX) members stated, "Change takes guts. It takes imagination. It takes commitment." All necessary ingredients for dealing with the chaotic world of business!

OD Methods

We know that most organizational change that employees experience happens not by chance, but often by a concerted effort to alter some aspect of the organization. Whatever happens—in terms of structure or technology—however, ultimately affects organizational members. Organization development assists organizational members with planned change.

Organization Development *Organization development* facilitates long-term organization-wide changes. Its focus is to constructively change attitudes and values among organizational members so that they can more readily adapt to and be more effective in achieving the new directions of the organization.[42] When they plan OD efforts, organization leaders, in essence, attempt to change the organization's culture.[43] However, one fundamental issue of OD is its reliance on employee participation to foster an environment of open communication and trust.[44] Persons involved in OD efforts acknowledge that change can create stress for employees. Therefore, OD attempts to involve organizational members in changes that will affect their jobs and seeks their input about how the innovation is affecting them.

OD Techniques Any organizational activity that assists with implementing planned change can be viewed as an OD technique (see Ethical Issues in HRM). However, the more popular OD efforts in organizations rely heavily on group

ETHICAL ISSUES IN HRM

OD INTERVENTION

Organization development interventions often produce positive change results. Interventions that rely on participation of organizational members can create openness and trust among co-workers and respect for others. Interventions can also help employees understand that the organization wants to promote risk taking and empowerment. "Living" these characteristics can lead to better organizational performance.

However, a change agent involved in an OD effort imposes his or her value system on those involved in the intervention, especially when the intervention addresses co-worker mistrust. The change agent may deal with this problem by bringing all affected parties together to openly discuss their perceptions of the dilemma.

Although many change agents are well versed in OD practices, sometimes they walk a fine line between success and failure. To resolve personal problems in the workplace, participants must disclose private, and often sensitive information. An individual can refuse to divulge such information, but doing so may carry negative ramifications. For example, it could lead to lower performance appraisals, fewer pay increases, or the perception that the employee is not a team player.

On the other hand, active participation can cause employees to speak their minds, which also carries risks. For instance, imagine that an employee questions a manager's competence. This employee fully believes the manager's behavior is detrimental to the work unit, but his or her reward for being open and honest could be retaliation from the boss. Although, at the time, the manager might appear receptive to the feedback, he or she may retaliate later. In either case—participation or not—employees could be hurt. Even though the intent was to help overcome worker mistrust, the result may be more back stabbing, more hurt feelings, and more mistrust.

Do you think that co-workers can be too open and honest under this type of OD intervention? What do you think a change agent can do to ensure that employees' rights will be protected?

---

interactions and cooperation. These include survey feedback, process consultation, team building, and intergroup development.

Survey feedback efforts assess employee attitudes about and perceptions of the change they are encountering. Employees generally respond to a set of specific questions regarding how they view organizational aspects such as decision making, leadership, communication effectiveness, and satisfaction with their jobs, coworkers, and management.[45] The data the change agent obtains help clarify problems that employees may be facing. The change agent can consider actions to remedy the problems.

In *process consultation,* outside consultants help organizational members perceive, understand, and act on process events.[46] These might include, for example, workflow, informal relationships among unit members, and formal communications channels. It is important to recognize that consultants give organizational members insight into what is going on, but they are not there to solve problems. Rather, they coach managers in diagnosing interpersonal processes that need improvement. If organizational members, with consultants' help, cannot solve the problem, consultants will often help organizational members locate experts who do have the requisite knowledge (see Workplace Issues).

Organizations are made up of individuals working together to achieve some goals. Because organizational members frequently must interact with peers, a primary function of OD is to help them become a team. Team building helps work groups set goals, develop positive interpersonal relationships, and clarify the role and responsibilities of each team member. There may be no need to address each area because the group may be in agreement and understand what is expected of it. Team building's primary focus is to increase each member's trust and openness toward one another.[47]

Whereas team building focuses on helping a work group become more cohesive, **intergroup development** attempts to achieve cohesion among different work

survey feedback
Assessment of employees' perceptions and attitudes regarding their jobs and organization.

One of the fundamental issues behind OD is the need to foster an environment of communication and trust.

intergroup development
Helping members of various groups become a cohesive team.

WORKPLACE ISSUES

PLAYING COACH

Increasingly, managers must assume the role of coach. In fact, some organizations officially have changed the title from manager to coach. Changing titles doesn't change abilities, but with training and practice, managers—by whatever name—can learn to coach and counsel their employees more effectively.[48]

Change toward teamwork, empowerment, and managing by influence makes acquiring such skills imperative for the success of both corporations and their employees. Coaching and counseling improves efficiency and productivity and prevents situations from escalating, while enhancing job satisfaction and confidence when attitude or performance problems occur. Some managers suffer from the ostrich syndrome—hiding their heads in the sand in hopes that the problem or employee will go away. Too pressed for time, afraid that they may give the wrong advice and be blamed for it, or just not having any solutions for a particular situation, managers may avoid counseling or coaching.

But as managers, we must accept coaching and counseling as a part of our jobs, however uncomfortable we may be. We must provide employees with regular feedback about their performances, not just at appraisal time. We must provide appropriate ongoing training, support, and encouragement; view them as partners in the process; give credit when deserved; and provide information about the company and its goals, as well as their role, responsibilities, and expectations in meeting them.

If your employees feel blocked from career opportunities or dissatisfied with their jobs, need help setting priorities, or are stressed, burned out, and insecure, your counseling skills will be tested. Employees may not tell you initially that they have a problem, but they will give you an assortment of clues such as missed deadlines, absenteeism, and decreased quality and productivity. They may show less initiative or interest or become irritable or withdrawn. Your job is to find out why their attitude or performance is waning; could it be that they were not recognized for some work or they are frustrated because of a lack of time, training, or feedback? After all, most employees believe that their managers either can or should read minds.

Maybe it's time to reassess what's happening. For example, have you as a manager taken time to explain expectations, directions, and priorities? Have you removed obstacles and reinforced performance? When it's time to practice your new coaching/counseling insights, carefully plan what you will say in advance, then allow enough time without distractions or interruptions to discuss how the situation affects performance, to listen without becoming defensive, and to obtain enough information to develop an action plan of improvement. Invite the employee to propose solutions or alternatives. Be prepared to have a follow-up session to review progress and reinforce improvements.

Sometimes even the best coaches and counselors must cut their losses if performance continues to decline, which may call for more severe measures, such as probation, demotion, transfer, termination, or disciplinary action, if alternatives such as transfer, retraining, or job restructuring are impossible. On the optimistic side, however, if the coaching or counseling session is effective, everybody wins—the company, employee, and manager. Attitude or performance improves, communication lines up, and both managers and employees can build on the situation.

You should consider the alternatives—not saying anything, not taking action—but not too long. The problem may persist, even if the opportunity to fill the job doesn't.

---

groups. That is, intergroup development attempts to change attitudes, stereotypes, and perceptions that one group may have toward another group. Doing so can build better coordination among the various groups.

A Special OD Case: The Learning Organization

learning organization

An organization that values continued learning and believes a competitive advantage can be derived from it.

The concept of a learning organization describes a significant organizational mindset or philosophy. A **learning organization** has the capacity to continuously adapt and change because all members take an active role in identifying and resolving work-related issues.[49] In a learning organization, employees practice knowledge management by continually acquiring and sharing new knowledge and willingly apply that knowledge in making decisions or performing their work.

In a learning organization, it's critical for members to share information and collaborate on work activities throughout the entire organization—across different functional specialties and even at different organizational levels. Employees are free to work together and collaborate in doing the organization's work the best way they can and to learn from each other. This need to collaborate also tends to make teams an important feature of a learning organization. Employees work on activities in teams and make decisions about doing their work or resolving issues. Empowered employees and teams have little need for "bosses" to direct and control them. Instead, traditional managers serve as facilitators, supporters, and advocates for employee teams.

Learning can't take place without information. For a learning organization to learn, information must be shared among members; that is, organizational employees must engage in knowledge management. This means sharing information openly, in a timely manner, and as accurately as possible. The learning organization environment is conducive to open communication and extensive information sharing.

Leadership plays an important role as an organization moves to become a learning organization. One most important leader function is to facilitate creation of a shared vision for the organization's future and keep organizational members working toward that vision. In addition, leaders should support and encourage the collaborative environment critical to learning. Without strong and committed leadership throughout the organization, it would be extremely difficult to be a learning organization.

Finally, the organizational culture is an important aspect of being a learning organization. A learning organization's culture is one in which everyone agrees on a shared vision and recognizes the inherent interrelationships among the organization's processes, activities, functions, and external environment. There is a strong sense of community, caring for each other, and trust. In a learning organization, employees feel free to openly communicate, share, experiment, and learn without fear of criticism or punishment.

If you delve deeply into many of the learning organization's characteristics you may notice something startling. Many of these elements are parts of a fully functioning, effective HRM system in an organization.

EVALUATING TRAINING AND DEVELOPMENT EFFECTIVENESS

Any training or development implemented in an organization effort must be cost-effective. That is, the benefits gained must outweigh the costs of the learning experience. Only analyzing such programs determines effectiveness. It is not enough to merely assume that any training an organization offers is effective; we must develop substantive data to determine whether our training effort is achieving its goals—that is, if it's correcting the deficiencies in skills, knowledge, or attitudes we assessed as needing attention. Note, too, that training and development programs are expensive—in the billions of dollars annually in the United States alone. The costs incurred alone justify evaluating the effectiveness.

Evaluating Training Programs

It is easy to generate a new training program, but if the training effort is not evaluated, any employee training efforts can be rationalized. Sadly, research indicates that nearly half of all training programs are not measured against any substantive outcome, such as employee retention, satisfaction, or productivity.[50] It would be nice, however, if all companies could boast the returns on investments in training that Neil Huffman Auto Group executives do; they claim they receive $230 in increased productivity for every dollar spent on training.[51] Such a claim is valueless unless training is properly evaluated.

Can training pay off? We will never know unless we evaluate the training effort. At Neil Huffman Auto Group in Louisville, Kentucky, they believe training is truly valuable and that for every dollar they spend in training they receive a $230 increase in productivity. That's an outstanding return on investment from training dollars. (*Source:* Andersen Ross/Photodisc/Getty Images, Inc.)

The following approach for evaluating training programs is probably generalizable across organizations: Several managers, representatives from HRM, and a group of workers who have recently completed a training program are asked for their opinions. If the comments are generally positive, the program may receive a favorable evaluation and it will continue until someone decides, for whatever reason, it should be eliminated or replaced.

The reactions of participants or managers, though easy to acquire, are the least valid; their opinions are heavily influenced by factors that may have little to do with the training's effectiveness: difficulty, entertainment value, or the personality characteristics of the instructor. Trainees' reactions to the training may, in fact, provide feedback on how worthwhile the participants viewed the training.[52] Beyond general reactions, however, training must also be evaluated in terms of how much the participants learned, how well they use their new skills on the job (did their behavior change?) and whether the training program achieved its desired results (reduced turnover, increased customer service, etc.).[53]

Performance-Based Evaluation Measures

We'll explore three popular methods of evaluating training programs. These are the post-training performance method, the pre–post-training performance method, and the pre–post-training performance with control group method.

post-training performance method

Evaluating training programs based on how well employees can perform their jobs after training.

Post-Training Performance Method The first approach is the **post-training performance method**. Participants' performance is measured after attending a training program to determine if behavioral changes have been made. For example, assume we provide a week-long seminar for HRM recruiters on structured interviewing techniques. We follow up one month later with each participant to see if, in fact, attendees use the techniques addressed in the program and how. If changes did occur, we may attribute them to the training, but we cannot emphatically state that the change in behavior related directly to the training. Other factors, like reading a current HRM journal or attending a local Society of Human Resource Management presentation, may have also influenced the change. Accordingly, the post-training performance method may overstate training benefits.

pre–post-training performance method

Evaluating training programs based on the difference in performance before and after training.

Pre–Post-Training Performance Method In the **pre–post-training performance method**, each participant is evaluated prior to training and rated on actual job performance. After instruction—of which the evaluator has been kept unaware—is completed, the employee is reevaluated. As with the post-training performance method, the increase is assumed to be attributable to the instruction. However, in contrast to the post-training performance method, the pre–post-performance method deals directly with job behavior.

pre–post-training performance with control group method

Evaluating training by comparing pre- and post-training results with individuals.

Pre–Post-Training Performance with Control Group Method The most sophisticated evaluative approach is the **pre–post-training performance with control group method**. Two groups are established and evaluated on actual job performance. Members of the control group work on the job but do not undergo instruction, but the experimental group does. At the conclusion of training, the two groups are reevaluated. If the training is really effective, the experimental group's performance will have improved and will perform substantially better than the control group. This approach attempts to correct for factors, other than the instruction program, that influence job performance.

Despite numerous methods for evaluating training and development programs, these three appear to be the most widely recognized. Furthermore, the latter two methods are preferred because they provide a stronger measure of behavioral change directly attributable to the training effort.

INTERNATIONAL TRAINING AND DEVELOPMENT ISSUES

Important components of international human resource management include both cross-cultural training and a clear understanding of the overseas assignment as part of a manager's development.[54]

Cross-Cultural Training

Cross-cultural training is necessary for expatriate managers and their families before, during, and after foreign assignments.[55] It is crucial to remember that when the expatriates arrive, they are the foreigners, not the host population. Before the employee and family relocate to the overseas post, they need to absorb much cultural and practical background. Language training is essential for everyone in the family.

Although English is the dominant business language worldwide, relying on English puts the expatriate at a disadvantage. The expatriate will be unable to read trade journals and newspapers, which contain useful business information, and must rely on translators, which at best only slow down discussions and at worst lose things in the process. Even if an expatriate manager is not fluent, a willingness to try communicating in the local language makes a good impression on the business community—unlike the insistence that all conversation be in English. Foreign-language proficiency is also vital for family members to establish a social network and accomplish the everyday tasks of maintaining a household. Americans may be able to go to the produce market and point at what they recognize on display, but if the shop has unfamiliar meats or vegetables, it helps to be able to ask what each item is, and it's even better to understand the answers!

Cross-cultural training is, of course, much more than language training. It should provide an appreciation of the new culture, including details of its history and folklore, economy, politics (both internal and its relations with the United States), religion, social climate, and business practices.[56] It is easy to recognize that religion is highly important in daily life in the Middle East, but knowledge of the region's history and an understanding of the specific practices and beliefs is important to avoid inadvertently insulting business associates or social contacts.

All this training can be carried out through a variety of techniques. Language skills are often provided through classes and recordings, whereas cultural training utilizes many different tools. Lectures, reading materials, video recordings, and movies are useful for background information, but cultural sensitivity is more often taught through role playing, simulations, and meetings with former international assignees and natives of the countries now living in the United States.

After the overseas assignment has ended and the employee has returned, more training is required for the entire family. All family members must reacclimate to life in the United States. The family faces changes in the extended family, friends, and local events that have occurred in their absence. Teenagers find reentry particularly difficult, as they are ignorant of the most recent jargon and the latest trends, but often are more sophisticated and mature than their local friends. The employee also must adjust to organizational changes, including the inevitable promotions, transfers, and resignations that have taken place during his or her absence. Returnees are anxious to know where they fit in, or if they have been gone for so long that they are no longer on a career path.

Development

The current global business environment makes the overseas assignment a vital component in developing top-level executives. However, this is currently truer in Europe and Japan than in the United States. Many American managers return with broader experiences, having been relatively independent of headquarters. Particularly, mid-level managers experience greater responsibilities than others at their level and frequently acquire greater sensitivity and flexibility to alternative ways of doing things. Unfortunately they are often ignored and untapped after their return.

It is vital for the organization to make the overseas assignment part of a career development program.[57] In the absence of such a developmental program, two negative consequences often occur. First, the recently returned manager who is largely ignored or underutilized becomes frustrated and leaves the organization. This is extremely costly, losing the investment in developing this individual and the talent that will likely be recruited by a competitor, either at home or overseas.

Second, when overseas returnees are regularly underutilized or leave out of frustration, other potential expatriates become reluctant to accept overseas posts, inhibiting the organization's staffing ability. When the overseas assignment is completed, the organization has four basic options. First, the expatriate may be assigned to a domestic position, beginning the repatriation process. Hopefully, this new assignment will build on some of the newly acquired skills and perspectives. Second, the return may be temporary, with the goal of preparing for another overseas assignment. This might be the case where a manager has successfully opened a new sales territory and is being asked to repeat that success in another region. Third, the expatriate may seek retirement, either in the United States or in the country in which she or he spent the past few years. Finally, employment may be terminated, either because the organization has no suitable openings or because the individual has found opportunities elsewhere.

All of these options involve substantial expenses or a loss in human investment. A well-thought-out and organized program of employee development can make overseas assignments a part of the comprehensive international human resource management program.

SUMMARY

(This summary relates to the Learning Outcomes identified on page 203.) After having read this chapter, you can

1. **Define** *socialization.* Socialization is a process of adaptation. Organization-entry socialization refers to the adaptation that takes place when an individual passes from outside the organization to the role of an inside member.
2. **Identify the three stages of employee socialization.** The three stages of employee socialization are the prearrival, the encounter, and the metamorphosis states.
3. **Identify the key personnel involved in orientation.** The key people in orientation are the CEO and HRM representatives. The CEO welcomes the new employees, reaffirms their choice of joining the company, and discusses the organization's goals and objectives while conveying information about the organization's culture. Each function in HRM has a specific role in orientation to discuss what employee services they can offer in the future.
4. **Explain why employee training is important.** Employee training has become increasingly important as jobs have become more sophisticated and influenced by technological and corporate changes.

5. **Define *training*.** Training is a learning experience that seeks a relatively permanent change in individuals that will improve their ability to perform on the job.

6. **Describe how training needs evolve.** An organization's training needs will evolve from seeking answers to these questions: (a) What are the organization's goals? (b) What tasks must be completed to achieve these goals? (c) What behaviors are necessary for each job incumbent to complete his or her assigned tasks? and (d) What deficiencies, if any, do incumbents have in the skills, knowledge, or attitudes required to perform the necessary behaviors?

7. **Discuss the term *organizational development* and the role of the change agent.** Organization development is the process of effecting change in the organization. This change is facilitated through the efforts of a change agent.

8. **Explain the term *learning organization*.** A learning organization continuously adapts and changes because all members take an active role in identifying and resolving work-related issues. In a learning organization, employees practice knowledge management by continually acquiring and sharing new knowledge, which they willingly apply.

9. **Describe the methods and criteria involved in evaluating training programs.** Training programs can be evaluated by post-training performance, pre–post-training performance, or pre–post-training performance with control group methods. The evaluation focuses on trainee reaction, what learning took place, and how appropriate the training was to the job.

10. **Explain issues critical to international training and development.** International issues in training and development include cross-cultural training, language training, and economic-issues training.

DEMONSTRATING COMPREHENSION: *Questions for Review*

1. How can a socialization process benefit an organization?
2. What benefits can socialization provide for the new employee?
3. Describe the role HRM plays in orientation.
4. Explain the CEO/senior management's role in orientation.
5. What kinds of signals can warn a manager that employee training may be necessary?
6. Why is evaluation of training effectiveness necessary?
7. Why is cultural training critical for employees embarking on an overseas assignment?
8. Describe how selection and training are related.
9. Describe how socialization and training are related.

KEY TERMS

change agent	learning	orientation	pre–post-training
employee	organization	post-training	performance
development	metamorphosis	performance	with control
employee training	stage	method	group
encounter stage	organization	prearrival stage	simulations
intergroup	culture	pre–post-training	socialization
development	organization	performance	survey feedback
job rotation	development	method	
	(OD)		

VISUAL SUMMARY

CHAPTER 8: SOCIALIZING, ORIENTING, AND DEVELOPING EMPLOYEES

1 | The Outsider–Insider Passage

Organization–Entry Socialization—getting acclimated to the new organization

Three Stages of Socialization

Prearrival Stage
Employees join an organization with a set of values, attitudes and expectations.

→

Encounter Stage
Employees confront differences between their expectations of the job and the realities of it.

→

Metamorphosis Stage
Employees make necessary changes to reconcile encounter–stage differences.

2 | Purpose of New Employee Orientation

- Learn the culture
- Understand the organization's vision

Role of HRM
- Handles administrative aspects of a new employee starting a job
- "Sells" HRM services to new employees

3 | Employee Training

Preparing employees to do current job more effectively

What deficiencies, if any do incumbents have in the skills, knowledge, or abilities required to exhibit the necessary job behaviors?

Is there a need for training? →

What are the organization's goals?

What behaviors are necessary for each job incumbent to complete his or her arranged tasks?

←

What tasks must be completed to achieve its goals?

4 | Employee Development

Preparing employees for jobs of greater responsibility in the organization

Development Methods

On-the-Job
- Job rotation
- Assistant-to position
- Committee assignment

Off-the-Job
- Lecture course and seminars
- Simulation
- Outdoor training

5   Organization Development

Change Agent—a person who is responsible for fostering an environment where change can take place

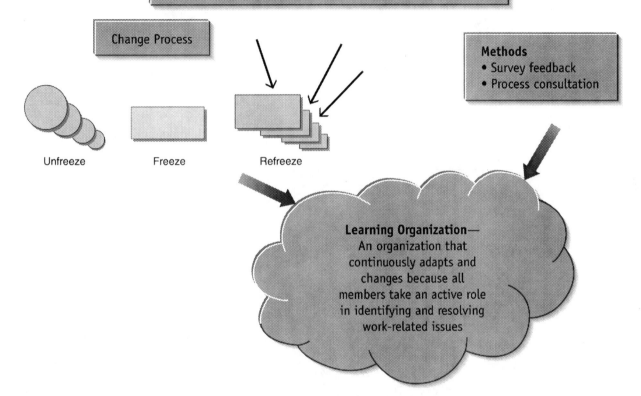

Change Process

Unfreeze   Freeze   Refreeze

Methods
- Survey feedback
- Process consultation

Learning Organization—
An organization that continuously adapts and changes because all members take an active role in identifying and resolving work-related issues

6   Evaluating Training and Development Effectiveness

Performance-Based Evaluation Measures
- Post-training performance method
- Pre–post-training performance method
- Pre–post-training performance with control group method

7   International Training and Development Issues

- Language training
- Training in local cultural/business practices
- Overseas assignments—part of a career development program

CROSSWORD COMPREHENSION

ACROSS

1. the part of HRM that addresses systemwide changes in the organization
4. assessment of employees' perceptions and attitudes regarding their jobs and organization
7. a method of training evaluation based on how well employees can perform their jobs after training
9. categories of individuals who are used in training evaluation but who do not undergo the instruction the experimental group did
12. the system of shared meaning within the organization that determines how employees act
13. moving employees horizontally or vertically to expand their skills, knowledge, or abilities
14. the stage of recognizing that a new employee comes to an organization with a set of values, expectations, and attitudes
15. type of organization that values continued education and believes a competitive advantage can be derived from it
16. a method of training based on the difference between performance before and after the training
17. present-oriented education that focuses on an individual's current job

DOWN

1. activities that introduce new employees to the organization
2. future-oriented education that focuses on employee personal growth
3. the stage where a new employee confronts the possible dichotomy between their organizational expectations and reality
5. an individual responsible for fostering an organization's change effort
6. a process of adaptation when a new employee learns the norms of the organization
8. any artificial environment that attempts to closely mirror an actual condition
10. type of development that helps members of various groups become a cohesive team
11. a stage during which the new employee must work out inconsistencies between organizational expectations and reality

HRM WORKSHOP

LINKING CONCEPTS TO PRACTICE: *Discussion Questions*

1. "Proper selection is a substitute for socialization." Do you agree or disagree with this statement? Explain.
2. Describe what a socialization program might look like if management desired employees who were innovative and individualistic?
3. Training programs are frequently the first items eliminated when management wants to cut costs. Why do you believe this occurs?

4. Explain the effects a learning organization may have on employees in today's organizations. What are the HRM implications of these effects?

DEVELOPING DIAGNOSTIC AND ANALYTICAL SKILLS

Case Application 8-A: DELIVERING AT UPS

Imagine you're responsible for moving much of nearly 145 million packages each day. How are you going to do it? At UPS, the answer is relatively simple—you rely on stringent rules, regulations, and procedures. That means such things as recognizing how to carry your keys, how to honk as one approaches a delivery location, to how many steps one takes each second. It's rigidity based on some sound industrial engineering measurements designed to produce the most effective and efficient outcomes. Everyone knows what's expected, and one simply does his or her job correctly. After all, rules are rules, and they are meant to be followed. While for the most part he agrees, Mark Colvard, UPS manager in San Roman, California, recognized that doing so may not always be the best approach. As Colvard states, his past was to focus on the numbers, the bottom line. Today, however, he realizes that to make the numbers he needs his people—and accordingly, he must think about what's in their best interests. Colvard, and many UPS managers before him, learned this at the company's Community Internship Program.

UPS founder James Casey realized that many of the managers in his organization had no idea of what poverty and inequality was. This sheltered perspective made it more difficult for these managers to deal with the diversity in their workforce. As such, Casey believed that if UPS was going to be most effective, it had to learn about and live with societal elements that were foreign to most of them. That did not mean, however, relaxing the rigid rules of UPS. Rather, it meant fitting the rigid rules to the diversity of the organization.[58]

To accomplish this, the Community Internship Program (CIP), founded in 1968, was designed to place 50 UPS senior managers each year in low-income communities in New York City, Chicago, Chattanooga, TN, McAllen, TX, or San Francisco, CA. During this 30-day internship, these UPS managers lived among the area's poorest residents. They may serve meals to the homeless, build homes, counsel recovering addicts, fix bikes in a community center, tutor individuals in

prison, or aid migrant farmers. They spend time in the community attempting to find workable solutions to transportation, housing, education, or healthcare problems. But most of all, the CIP was designed to develop the UPS manager's ability to listen and be empathetic toward their employees. For example, Colvard had a situation several years ago where he had to make a hard decision. One of his drivers needed some time off work to care for an ill family member. Under the rules that applied to this worker, he was not eligible for the leave. But Colvard made the decision to give the employee some time off—even though other drivers had an issue with the action Colvard took. But Colvard never second-guessed what he did. He knew, based on his experience with CIP, that the employee was not going to show up at work anyway. Why complicate the problem and ultimately lose a productive worker? Even though Colvard took some flack over the two weeks the driver was out, the driver returned to work very appreciative of what Colvard had done. Colvard retained a valuable employee.

What the CIP program does, in essence, is develop another aspect of UPS managers. Although the process and procedure training is thorough, UPS leaders realized that managers need to be sensitive to needs of today's workers. By developing employees in this manner, UPS is reinforcing a culture of what is important and gives its members the necessary tools to walk the walk. As one UPS manager stated, the program "made me a better person and a better manager. I've never been exposed to anything like it in my life."

Questions:

1. How does the CIP at UPS foster a culture in the organization?
2. What role can human resources play in ensuring success for this internship program?
3. Identify how you would evaluate the CIP program to demonstrate that it's beneficial to the manager and the organization.

Case Application 8-B: TEAM FUN!

Team Fun

Kenny and Norton, owners of a sporting goods manufacturing and retail operation, are meeting with Tony, director of human resources, and Bobby, the manager of a new store. Twenty-five employees have just been hired, and the new store in south Florida is scheduled to open in a month. Norton thunders, "No way am I going to bring all those socialist bozos up here for a week! What's the matter with you! Why did you hire a bunch of socialists?"

Kenny calms him, "He said to socialize them, not that they were socialists. But why should they come here for a party? We should go to south Florida! And I think an opening party is a great idea. Bobby, that's your idea, right?"

Bobby smiles, and Tony says, "I don't mean party. I mean get them used to the way things run at TEAM FUN! They need to know the rules, what's expected of them, how to treat the customers and each other, that sort of thing."

Kenny asks, "What did you do when you interviewed them? I thought they'd know what to expect from day one."

Norton adds, "I know as soon as I meet someone if they should work at TEAM FUN! Anyway, people just all work out or quit right away—first day, usually. New people just start one day, follow someone around for a week, and then they are fine."

Tony looks helplessly at both of them until Norton finally says, "Oh, I get it. There is no one down there for a new person to follow around. Everyone will be new!" Tony nods his head. So does Kenny. Norton continues, "That's still a lot of airfare. I thought you said they were mostly family people. Do we have to bring all their kids and dogs up here, too? Find another way."

Kenny offers, "Dogs don't usually like to fly. I don't know. Remember that video we did for Christmas last year? Ginny followed everyone around at work for a few minutes with her video camera. I think I'm the only one who watched the whole thing. Most everyone only watched their part and the rest of the crew they worked with. Tony, could we send the video to Florida with a few key people to run everyone through their paces a week or so before we open? Would that be socialization?"

Norton frowns, "We just started working when we opened this store. What's the big deal?"

Tony says, "That was just the two of you, and you'd known each other all your lives." Norton looks at him skeptically. "So?"

Questions:

1. Explain to Kenny and Norton why employee socialization is necessary (or not necessary) for the new TEAM FUN! store.
2. What orientation activities do you recommend? Who should be involved?
3. What training needs should they consider?

WORKING WITH A TEAM: *Orienting Employees*

Identify, call, and ask a human resource manager at your college or university, employer, a nonprofit organization, or a company, if you may observe part or all of an upcoming orientation or training program as a part of a class assignment.

1. Summarize your orientation experience in a one- or two-page report, then share your experience with your class or team.
2. What guidelines, policies, or standards did your organization practice regarding orientation?
3. Discuss your responses with your team. What similarities or differences did you find?

LEARNING AN HRM SKILL: *Coaching Employees*

About the skill: Effective managers are increasingly described as coaches rather than bosses. Just like coaches, they're expected to provide instruction, guidance, advice, and encouragement to help team members improve their job performance.

Steps in the Coaching Skill.

1. *Analyze ways to improve the team's performance and capabilities.* A coach looks for opportunities for team members to expand their capabilities and improve performance. We recommend the following coaching behaviors. Observe your team members' behavior on a day-to-day basis. Ask questions of them: Why do you do a task this way? Can it be improved? What other approaches might work? Show genuine interest in team members as individuals, not merely as employees. Respect them individually. Listen to each employee.

2. *Create a supportive climate.* It's the coach's responsibility to reduce barriers to development and to facilitate a climate that encourages personal performance improvement. Create a climate that contributes to a free and open exchange of ideas. Offer help and assistance. Give guidance and advice when asked. Encourage your team. Be positive and upbeat. Don't use threats. Ask "What did we learn from this that can help us in the future?" Reduce obstacles. Assure team members that you value their contribution to the team's goals. Take personal responsibility for the outcome, but don't rob team members of their full responsibility. Validate the team members' efforts when they succeed. Point to what was missing when they fail. Never blame team members for poor results.

3. *Influence team members to change their behavior.* The ultimate test of coaching effectiveness is whether an

employee's performance improves. You must encourage ongoing growth and development. Recognize and reward small improvements and treat coaching as a way of helping employees continually work toward improvement. Use a collaborative style by allowing team members to participate in identifying and choosing among improvement ideas. Break difficult tasks down into simpler ones. Model the qualities you expect from your team. If you want openness, dedication, commitment, and responsibility from your team members, you must demonstrate these qualities yourself.

ENHANCING YOUR COMMUNICATION SKILLS

1. Do a search of articles on learning organizations. Summarize in a two- to three-page article how organizations become learning organizations and what benefits a learning organization provides for a company.

2. Write a two-page discussion of training program development costs. Discuss how companies may find ways to make training programs more cost effective.

3. Write a two-page summary of the type of organization culture you would prefer to work in. In your discussion, describe how you anticipate locating such an organization with the type of preferred culture you identified.

NINE

"Will you still want me, will you still need me when I'm 64?" Recognize this? They are words to a song popularized by the Beatles in the 1960s. But they may also be words uttered by many employees across the globe in the new millennium. That's certainly true of Robert Christensen of Johnston, Iowa.[1]

Christensen began his career nearly 40 years ago as a broadcaster in his family's radio and cable television station. Arriving at work at 4 a.m. to prepare for the broadcast, Christensen worked the 6 a.m. to 1 p.m. radio shift. After going off air, he spent the next several hours traveling around the town visiting potential clients, attempting to sell them advertising. And if long days weren't enough, on Fridays and Saturdays he spent his time doing play-by-play announcing of high school sports. This rough and enduring schedule lasted for years, when after 23 years in the business the family decided to sell the company. Too young to retire and needing something to do, Christensen decided to move to Des Moines and start a new career—one in sales where he could use his experiences. He landed a job with Champion Company, the oldest funeral supply company in the United States.

For nearly 20 years, Christensen excelled at his job. He sold embalming fluid and other funeral supplies to funeral homes. It was a hectic

(Source: Steve Skjold/Alamy Images)

job, but one that he flourished in. As one of 34 sales representatives of the company, Christensen was always one of the company's top sales executives. He had command of his products, had built a wonderful relationship with his customers, and had everything under control in his southeast South Dakota and eastern Nebraska territory. But in 1999, his world began to change. Due to economic pressures and increased competition, Champion decided to downsize. They cut the sales staff from 34 to 8 representatives.

While Christensen was one of the lucky eight to remain, what followed began to be a nightmare. His territory expanded significantly, from this southeast Dakota and eastern Nebraska territory to one that included seven states. Here he was, nearing 60 years of age, driving some 60,000 miles a year. Yet as a dedicated employee and in the interest of serving his customers, Christensen didn't complain—he simply kept doing his job as effectively as he could. After all, he still had a good job—unlike 26 of his former peers. But that, too, changed in late 2002, when on a Friday evening, Christensen and the other sales executives got a page that their positions were being eliminated—the company had de-cided to cut costs further, all sales would be handled through telemarketing. Needless to say, that's not the kind of message anyone wants to get—let alone someone in the twilight of his or her career.

Upset, Christensen began pondering what to do. He knew he had excellent skills, but would a company hire a 60-year-old employee? How did he start looking for a job? And whom should he contact? Using the services of a career counselor, Christensen realized that he had the answer readily available to him—look deeply into his sphere of influence. He recalled countless conversations with the president of a client organization, Hamilton Funeral Home. The president enjoyed dealing with Christensen because he found him compassionate, caring, and skilled. He knew the funeral home business from all angles and had a wonderful way of dealing with people. It wasn't long after the two had talked that Christensen started his new career at Hamilton as an advanced planning counselor—someone who works with families in making funeral arrangements for their loved ones.

Managing Careers

Learning Outcomes

After reading this chapter, you will be able to

1. Explain who is responsible for managing careers.

2. Describe the term *career*.

3. Discuss the focus of careers for both organizations and individuals.

4. Describe how career development and employee development differ.

5. Explain why career development is valuable to organizations.

6. Identify the five traditional stages involved in a career.

7. List the Holland vocational preferences.

8. Describe the implications of personality typologies and jobs.

9. Identify several suggestions that you can use to manage your career more effectively.

Was Robert Christensen one of the lucky ones, finding a new career at age 60? Some may say so, but as his counselor mentioned, it was more of what he did throughout his career. He kept his skills up to date, he kept networks alive, and he never lost sight of the need to treat others with respect and dignity. When it was time for that respect to be returned to him, it did so quickly.

INTRODUCTION

Career development is important to us all. We know that people sometimes have difficulties achieving their career goals. This reflects the new and unexpected complexities managers now confront in their efforts to mobilize and manage their employees. The historical beliefs that every employee would jump at the chance for a promotion, that competent people will somehow emerge within the organization to fill vacancies, and that a valuable employee will always be a valuable employee are no longer true. Lifestyles, too, are changing. We are increasingly aware of employees' different needs and aspirations. HRM representatives, to have competent and motivated people to fill the organization's future needs, should be increasingly concerned with matching employee career needs with the organization's requirements.

It's important to note that although career development has been an important topic in HRM-related courses for several decades, we have witnessed some drastic changes over the past 20 years. Years ago, career development programs were designed to assist employees in advancing their work lives. HRM provided information and assessments to help employees realize their career goals. Career development helped organizations attract and retain highly talented personnel. But those days are all but disappearing in today's dynamic work environment—and so too are jobs as we have known them for the past several decades.[2] Downsizing, restructuring, work process engineering, globalization, contingent workers, and so forth have drawn us to one significant conclusion about managing careers: You, the individual, are responsible for your career.[3] It's not the organization's obligation! Sadly, millions of employees have learned this the hard way over the past few years.[4] Therefore, you must be prepared to do whatever is necessary to advance your career.

You, not the organization, are responsible for managing your career!

What, if any, responsibility does the organization have for career development under the "new rules" in today's contemporary organization? The organization's responsibility is to build employee self-reliance and help employees maintain their marketability through continual learning.[5] The essence of a contemporary career development program is providing support so employees can continually add to their skills, abilities, and knowledge. This support includes

- *Communicating clearly the organization's goals and future strategies.* When people know where the organization is headed, they're better able to develop a personal plan to share in that future.
- *Creating growth opportunities.* Employees should have opportunities for new, interesting, and professionally challenging work experiences.
- *Offering financial assistance.* The organization should offer tuition reimbursement to help employees keep current.
- *Providing the time for employees to learn.* Organizations should be generous in providing paid time off from work for off-the-job training. Additionally, workloads should not be so demanding that they preclude employees from having the time to develop new skills, abilities, and knowledge.

In this chapter we'll review some of the basics of career development, and HRM's current role in offering assistance. Throughout the chapter, remember that it's up to you to manage your career. If you don't, chances are no one else will!

WHAT IS A CAREER?

The term *career* has numerous meanings. In popular usage it can mean advancement ("He's moving up in his career"), a profession ("She's chosen a career in medicine"), or stability over time (career military).[6] For our purposes, we define career as "the pattern of work-related experiences that span the course of a person's life."[7] Using this definition, it is apparent that we all have or will have careers. The concept is as relevant to transient, unskilled laborers as it is to engineers and physicians. For our purposes, therefore, any work, paid or unpaid, pursued over an extended time, can constitute a career. In addition to formal job work, careers can include schoolwork, homemaking, or volunteer work. Furthermore, career success is defined not only objectively, in terms of promotion, but also subjectively, in terms of satisfaction.

career
The sequence of positions that a person has held over his or her life.

Individual versus Organizational Perspective

The study of careers takes on a different orientation, depending on whether it is viewed from the perspective of the organization or of the individual. A key question in career development, then, is, "With whose interests are we concerned?" From an organizational or HRM viewpoint, career development involves tracking career paths and developing career ladders.[8] HRM seeks information to direct and to monitor the progress of special groups of employees, and to ensure that capable professional, managerial, and technical talent will be available to meet the organization's needs. Career development from the organization's perspective is also called *organizational career planning*.

In contrast, individual career development, or career planning, focuses on assisting individuals to identify their major goals and how to achieve them. Note that the latter case focuses entirely on the individual and includes his or her life outside the organization, as well as inside. So, while organizational career development looks at individuals filling the needs of the organization, individual career development addresses each individual's personal work career and other lifestyle issues. For instance, an excellent employee, assisted in better understanding his or her needs and aspirations through interest inventories, life-planning analysis, and counseling, may even decide to leave the organization if it becomes apparent that career aspirations can be best achieved outside the employing organization. Employee expectations today are different from employee expectations a generation ago. Sex-role stereotypes are crumbling as people are less restricted by gender-specific occupations. Additionally, our lifestyles are more varied, with, for example, more dual-career couples, more single parents in the workplace, and overall, a richness of diversity.[9] Both individual and organizational career approaches have value. However, because the primary focus of HRM is the organization's interest in careers, we will primarily emphasize this area. At the end of the chapter we will take a special look at how you can better manage your career.

Career Development versus Employee Development

Given our discussions in Chapter 8 on employee development, you may be wondering what, if any, differences there are between career development and employee development. These topics have a common element, but they have one distinct difference—the time frame.

Career development looks at the long-term career effectiveness and success of organizational personnel. By contrast, the kinds of development discussed in Chapter 8 focused on work effectiveness or performance in the immediate or intermediate time frames. These two concepts are closely linked; employee training and development should be compatible with an individual's career development in the organization. But a successful career program, in attempting to match individual abilities and aspirations with the needs of the organization, should develop people for the long-term needs of the organization and address the dynamic changes that will take place over time.

Career Development: Value for the Organization

Assuming that an organization already provides extensive employee development programs, why should it need to consider a career development program as well? A long-term career focus should increase the organization's effectiveness in managing its human resources. More specifically, several positive results can accrue from a well-designed career development program. We'll examine them.

Needed Talent Will Be Available Career development efforts are consistent with and a natural extension of strategic and employment planning. Changing staff requirements over the intermediate and long term should be identified when the company sets long-term goals and objectives. Working with individual employees to help them align their needs and aspirations with those of the organization will increase the probability that the right people will be available to meet the organization's changing staffing requirements.

The Organization's Ability to Attract and Retain Talented Employees Improves Outstanding employees will always be scarce and competition to secure their services considerable. Such individuals may prefer employers who demonstrate a concern for employees' futures. These people may exhibit greater loyalty and commitment to an organization that offers career advice.[10] Importantly, career development appears to be a natural response to the rising concern by employees for the quality of work life and personal life planning. As more individuals seek jobs that offer challenge, responsibility, and opportunities for advancement, realistic career planning becomes increasingly necessary. Additionally, social values have changed so that fewer members of the workforce consider their work in isolation. Their work must be compatible with their personal and family interests and commitments. Again, career development should result in a better individual–organization match for employees and thus lead to less turnover.[11]

Minorities and Women Have Comparable Opportunities for Growth and Development As discussed in previous chapters, equal employment opportunity legislation and affirmative action programs have demanded that minority groups and women receive opportunities for growth and development that will prepare them for greater responsibilities within the organization. The fair employment movement has served as a catalyst to career development programs targeted for these special groups. Recent legislation, such as the Americans with Disabilities Act, offers an even greater organizational career challenge. Furthermore, courts frequently look at an organization's career development efforts with these groups when ruling on discrimination suits.

Reduced Employee Frustration Although the workforce educational level has risen, so, too, have occupational aspirations. However, as periods of economic stagnation increase organizations' efforts to reduce costs they also reduce opportunities. This has increased frustration in employees who often see a significant disparity between aspirations and actual opportunities. When organizations downsize to cut costs, employee career paths, career tracks, and career ladders often collapse. Career counseling can produce realistic, rather than raised, employee expectations.

Enhanced Cultural Diversity The workforce in the next decade will continue to reflect a more varied combination of race, nationality, gender, and values in the organization. Effective organizational career development provides access to all levels of the organization for more employees. Extended career opportunities make cultural diversity, and the appreciation of it, an organizational reality.

Organizational Goodwill If employees think their employing organizations care about their long-term well-being, they tend to respond in kind by projecting positive images of the organization into other areas of their lives (for example, through volunteer work in the community). For instance, Gary works for a cellular phone company. He also coaches clinic soccer with other parents in the community. When he expresses trust of the company, because of their expressed career interest, his friends might have a better perception of the overall operations of the organization.

Gary Marshall likes his job with a large cellular carrier. That positive attitude extends to his outside activities as he interacts with those in his community. Hearing how Gary views the company promotes goodwill for the company throughout the area. (Source: Zoran Milich/Masterfile)

Career Development: Value for the Individual

Effective career development is also important for the individual. In fact, as we've previously mentioned, it is more important today than ever. Changing definitions of careers and success have expanded, the value of individual career development programs. Career success may no longer be measured merely by an employee's income or hierarchical level in an organization. It may now include using one's skills and abilities to face expanded challenges, or having greater responsibilities and increased autonomy in one's chosen profession. Contemporary workers, seeking more than salary and security from their jobs, want intrinsic career development, or "psychic income," too. They want interesting and meaningful work, such as that derived from a sense of being the architect of one's own career.

Careers are both external and internal. The **external career** involves properties or qualities of an occupation or an organization.[12] For example, think of a career in business as a person's sequence of jobs or positions: undergraduate degree in business; sales representative for a construction supply house; graduate training in business; district manager in a do-it-yourself hardware chain; president of a small housing inspection and appraisal firm; retirement. External careers may also be characterized by career ladders within a particular organization (employment recruiter, employment manager, HRM director, vice president HRM).

The individual career encompasses a variety of individual aspects or themes: accumulation of external symbols of success or advancement (bigger office with each promotion); threshold definition of occupational types (that is, physicians have careers, dogcatchers have jobs); long-term commitment to a particular occupational field (that is, career soldier); a series of work-related positions; and work-related attitudes and behaviors.[13]

Careers are indeed the pattern of work-related experiences that span the course of a person's life, but we must understand that both personal relationships and family concerns are also of intrinsic value to employees. Subjective and objective elements, then, are necessary components of a theoretical perspective that captures the complexity of career.[14] Success can thus be defined in external terms. For example, if after five years at the same company you are promoted, and Chris, a colleague hired the same day you were for the same type of job, has not yet been promoted, you may view yourself as more successful than Chris. The external definition also states that a certified public accountant is more successful than a dogcatcher. However, if you consider the subjective, internal valuation of success, the story may be different. A dogcatcher who defines his job as protecting children and others in the community from danger, who goes home proud at night because he has successfully

external career
Attributes related to an occupation's properties or qualities.

and compassionately captured stray dogs that day, is successful in his career. Compare that to a CPA who works only to buy a new sports car so she can escape from the drudgery of her day-to-day office life of dealing with clients, accounting forms, and automated systems. Is she more or less successful than the dogcatcher?

This differentiation of internal from external is important to the manager who wants to motivate employees. Different employees may respond to different motivational tools. For instance, Danny is working for you as a consultant, looking to earn enough money to purchase a time-share in a condo in Florida. Diane, your newest software developer, joined the company with the expectation that within four years she will have obtained a master's degree and be in a supervisory position in the company. Would they respond equally to the opportunity to be trained in interpersonal skills? Would both of them be as likely to accept (or reject) a transfer to another city? Probably not, because they have different motivations. Thus, we can say that internal and external career events may be parallel but result in different outcomes. We have displayed these events in Exhibit 9-1, which discusses them in the context of career stages, the topic discussed in the next section.

mentoring or coaching
Actively guiding another individual.

Making it in an organization takes a lot of hard work, being at the right place at the right time, and possibly a little luck. One way of helping bring each of these to fruition is to have a mentor. A mentor is a personal coach in the organization who assists the "next generation" of leaders in learning the organizational ropes. (Source: Creatas/Age Fotostock America, Inc.)

Mentoring and Coaching

It has become increasingly clear over the years that employees who aspire to higher management levels in organizations often need the assistance and advocacy of someone higher up in the organization. These career progressions often require the favor of the dominant in-group, which sets corporate goals, priorities, and standards.[15]

When a senior employee takes an active role in guiding another individual, we refer to this activity as **mentoring or coaching.** Just as baseball coaches observe, analyze, and attempt to improve the performance of their athletes, "coaches" on the job can do the same. The effective coach, whether on the diamond or in the corporate hierarchy, gives guidance through direction, advice, criticism, and suggestions in an attempt to aid the employee's growth.[16] These individuals offer to assist certain junior employees by providing a support system.[17] This system, in part, is likened to the passing of the proverbial baton—that is, the senior employee shares his or her experiences with the protegé, providing guidance on how to make it in the organization.[18] Accordingly, in organizations such as Wal-Mart that promote from within, employees who aspire to succeed must have the corporate support system in their favor.[19] This support system, guided by a mentor, vouches for the candidate, answers for the candidate in the highest circles within the organization, makes appropriate introductions, and advises and guides the candidate on how to effectively move through the system.[20]

The technique of senior employees coaching individuals has the advantages of learning by doing, particularly the opportunities for high interaction and rapid feedback on performance. Unfortunately, its two strongest disadvantages are (1) its tendencies to perpetuate the current styles and practices in the organization and (2) its heavy reliance on the coach's ability to be a good teacher. Just as we recognize that not all excellent Hall of Fame baseball players make outstanding baseball coaches, we cannot expect all excellent employees to be effective coaches. An individual can become an excellent performer without necessarily possessing the knack of creating a proper learning environment for others to do the same; thus, the effectiveness of this technique relies on the ability of the coach. Coaching of employees can occur at any level and can be most effective when the two individuals have no type of reporting relationship but share other similarities in their perspectives.[21] In some cases, mentors are current

EXHIBIT 9-1
Internal and External Events and Career Stages

STAGE	EXTERNAL EVENT	INTERNAL EVENT
Exploration	Advice and examples of relatives, teachers, friends, and coaches Actual successes and failures in school, sport, and hobbies Actual choice of educational path—vocational school, college, major, professional school	Development of self-image, what one might be, what sort of work would be fun Self-assessment of own talents and limitations Development of ambitions, goals, motives, dreams Tentative choices and commitments, changes
Establishment	Explicit search for a job Acceptance of a job Induction and orientation Assignment to further training or first job Acquiring visible job and organizational membership trappings (ID card, parking sticker, uniform, organizational manual) First job assignment, meeting the boss and co-workers Learning period, indoctrination period of full performance—"doing the job"	Shock of entering the "real world" Insecurity around new tasks of interviewing, applying, being tested, facing being turned down Making a real choice: to take a job or not, which job; first commitment Fear of being tested for the first time under *real* conditions and found out to be a fraud Reality shock—what the work is really like, doing the "dirty work" Forming a career strategy, how to make it—working hard, finding mentors, conforming to an organization, making a contribution This is real, what one is doing matters Feeling of success or failure—going uphill, either challenging or exhausting Decision to leave organization if outlook isn't positive Feeling of being accepted fully by the organization, having made it—satisfaction of seeing "my project"
Mid-Career	Leveling off, transfer, and/or promotion Entering a period of maximum productivity Becoming more of a teacher/mentor than a learner Explicit signs from boss and co-workers that one's progress has plateaued	Period of settling in or new ambitions based on self-assessment More feeling of security, relaxation, but danger of leveling off and stagnation Threat from younger, better trained, more energetic, and ambitious persons—"Am I too old for my job?" Thoughts of new possibilities and challenges—"What do I really want to do?" Working through mid-life crisis toward greater acceptance of oneself and others "Is it time to give up on my dreams? Should I settle for what I have?"
Late Career	Job assignments drawing primarily on maturity of judgment More jobs involving teaching others	Psychological preparation for retirement Deceleration in momentum Finding new sources of self-improvement off the job, new sources of job satisfaction through teaching others
Decline	Formal preparation for retirement Retirement rituals	Learning to accept a reduced role and less responsibility Learning to live a less structured life New accommodations to family and community

Source: Adapted from John Van Maanen and Edgar H. Schein, "Career Development," in *Improving Life at Work*, eds. J. Richard Hackman and J. Lloyd Suttle (Santa Monica, CA: Goodyear, 1977), pp. 55–57; and D. Levinson, *The Seasons of a Man's Life* (New York: Ballantine Books, 1986).

co-workers[22] or, in the case of some reverse mentoring programs, people external to the organization. In fact, co-worker mentoring has been found to be extremely effective in organizations—more so than the traditional mentoring relationship.[23]

ETHICAL ISSUES IN HRM

Special Mentoring Programs for Women and Minorities

We have witnessed many recent discussions regarding how more women and minorities can break through the glass ceiling. Data suggests these groups are underrepresented at the top echelons of organizations. Several reasons for this have been well documented. One centers on the issue of mentoring.

Finding or convincing a mentor to support you is rarely easy. In fact, more often than not, a mentor approaches you to begin the relationship. In the past, many mentors were white males, and women and minorities found it difficult to gain their favor simply because mentors preferred someone more like them.

Constantly changing workforce composition, employment legislation, and changing societal views of women and minorities in the workplace have increased mentoring relationships for this group. But the concept is not, as yet, fully ingrained in the minds and hearts of some managers. Consequently, organizations have developed special mentoring programs for women and minorities—formalizing a practice that typically naturally evolved. In some respects, this may be the best way at this time to help further advance these two groups. The prevalence of the glass ceiling dilemma attests to that. On the other hand, can a mentoring relationship be forced and regulated? The crux of these relationships is for an individual to become close to his or her protegé in an effort to further the career. Won't forcing together two individuals lead to a constrained relationship?[24] Given the degree of potential conflict between the two, more harm than good for the protegé's career may result.

Should women and minorities receive special treatment in the mentoring relationship by having organizational policies dictating who will mentor and how? Should special guidelines ensure that mentoring for women and minorities occurs? And what about the white male? Is he being left out? What do you think?

Recall from Chapter 3 our discussion of the glass ceiling. A main reason for its existence is that women previously had few role models at top levels in the organization who could help them through the system.[25] There is no excuse for this situation, but there may be some explanation. Mentors sometimes select their protegés on the basis of seeing themselves, in their younger years, in the employee.[26] Because men rarely can identify with younger women, many appeared unwilling to play the part of their mentor (see Ethical Issues in HRM). Of course, women have battled their way into the inner circle of organizational power with some visible success. Additionally, organizations are beginning to explore ways of advocating cross-gender mentoring. This revolves around identifying the problems associated with such an arrangement,[27] deciding how to handle problems effectively, and providing organizational support.[28]

Traditional Career Stages

One traditional way to analyze and discuss careers is to consider them in stages or steps.[29] Progress from a beginning point through growth and decline phases to a termination point is typical in one's work life. Most of us begin to form our careers during our early school years. Our careers begin to wind down as we reach retirement age. We can identify five career stages typical for most adults, regardless of occupation: exploration, establishment, mid-career, late career, and decline. These stages are portrayed in Exhibit 9-2. The age ranges for each stage in Exhibit 9-2 are intended *only* to show general guidelines. Although this model may be too simplistic for some individuals pursuing certain careers, the key is to give primary attention to the stages rather than the age categories. For instance, someone who makes a dramatic change in career to undertake a completely different line of work at age 45 will have many of the same establishment-stage concerns as someone starting at age 25. On the

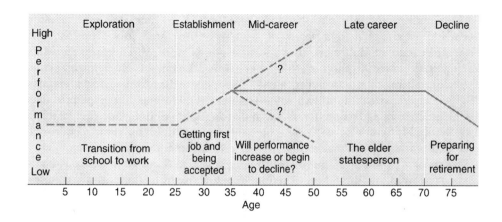

EXHIBIT 9-2
Career Stages

other hand, if the 45-year-old started working at 25, he or she now has 20 years of experience, as well as interests and expectations that differ from those of a peer just starting a career at middle age. Of course, if the 45-year-old individual is a newly admitted college student who starts college once her children have grown, she will have more in common—regarding career stages—with the 23-year-old sitting next to her than she will with the 45-year-old full professor teaching the class. So, don't get hung up on the age generalizations in Exhibit 9-2. They are simply points of reference.

Exploration

We make many critical choices about our careers before we enter the workforce for pay. What we hear from our relatives, teachers, and friends; what we see on television, in the movies, or on the Internet helps us narrow our career choices, lead us in certain directions. Certainly, family careers, interests, and aspirations and our financial resources are heavy factors in determining our perception of what careers are available or what schools, colleges, or universities we might consider.

The **exploration period** ends for most of us as we make the transition from formal education programs to work. This stage has the least relevance to organizations because it occurs prior to employment. It is, of course, not irrelevant. During the exploration period we develop many expectations about our career, many of them unrealistic. Such expectations may lie dormant for years and then pop up later to frustrate both employee and employer.

Successful career exploration strategies involve trying a lot of potential fields to see what you like or don't like. The college internships and cooperative education programs are excellent exploration tools to help you see your future co-workers firsthand and to do, day in and day out, a "real" job. Some successful internships lead to job offers. From a career stage perspective, any internship that helps you realize that you're bored to death with the work is also a successful one. In the exploration stage, we form our attitudes toward work (doing homework, meeting deadlines, taking or avoiding shortcuts, attendance), and our dominant social relationship patterns (easygoing, domineering, indifferent, likable, obnoxious). Therefore, exploration is preparation for work.

exploration period
A career stage that usually ends in the mid-twenties as one makes the transition from school to work.

Establishment

The **establishment period** begins with the search for work and includes accepting your first job, being accepted by your peers, learning the job, and gaining the first tangible evidence of success or failure in the real world. It begins with uncertainties and anxieties, and is indeed dominated by two problems: finding a niche and making your mark.

establishment period
A career stage in which one begins to search for work and finds a first job.

When you establish your career, you are trying to find your niche and make your mark.

Finding the right job takes time for many of us. In fact, you may know a 37-year-old who has held a series of seemingly unrelated jobs (for instance, after high school, clerk in a sporting goods store, three years; navy, six years; police dispatcher, four years; small business owner, three years; long-distance truck driver, now). This person has looked for a niche—or attempted to establish one—for nearly 20 years! Many people may not change as frequently as the individual above, but your first real job probably won't be with the company from which you retire. Thorough career exploration helps make this part of establishment an easier step.

The second problem of the establishment stage, making your mark, is characterized by making mistakes, learning from those mistakes, and assuming increased responsibilities. Individuals in this stage have yet to reach their peak productivity, though, and they rarely receive work assignments that carry great power or high status. As shown in Exhibit 9-2, this stage is experienced as "going uphill." The career takes a lot of time and energy, and often engenders a sense of growth, of expectation, or anticipation, such as a hiker feels when approaching a crest, waiting to see what lies on the other side. And, just as a hiker "takes" a hill when she stands at the crest, the establishment stage has ended when you "arrive" (make your mark). Of course, at this time you're considered a seasoned veteran. Consequently, you're now responsible for your own mistakes.

Mid-Career

mid-career stage

A career stage marked by continuous improvement in performance, leveling off in performance, or beginning deterioration of performance.

Many people do not face their first severe career dilemmas until they reach the **mid-career stage**. Here, individuals may continue their prior improvements in performance, level off, or begin to deteriorate. Therefore, although remaining productive at work after you're seasoned is a major challenge of this career stage, the pattern ceases to be as clear as it was for exploration and establishment. Some employees reach their early goals and go on to even greater heights. For instance, a worker who wants to be the vice president of HRM by the time he's 35 to 40 years old might want to be CEO by the time he's 55 to 60, if he has achieved the prior goal. Continued growth and high performance are not the only successful outcomes at this stage. Maintenance, or holding onto what you have, is another possible outcome of the mid-career stage. These employees are plateaued, not failed. **Plateaued mid-career** employees can be highly productive.[30] They are technically competent—even though some may not be as ambitious and aggressive as the climbers. They may be satisfied to contribute a sufficient amount of time and energy to the organization to meet production commitments; they also may be easier to manage than someone who wants more. These employees are not deadwood but good, reliable employees and "solid citizens." An example would be the same HRM vice president who decides at 45 to not go for the next promotion, but to enjoy other aspects of his life more—pursuing his hobbies—while still performing well on the job.

plateaued mid-career

Stagnation in one's current job.

The third option for mid-career deals with the employee whose performance begins to deteriorate. This stage for this kind of employee is characterized by loss of both interest and productivity at work. Organizations are often limited to relegating such individuals to less conspicuous jobs, reprimanding them, demoting them, or severing them from the organization altogether. The same HRM vice president could become less productive if, by 46, he realizes that he will never be CEO and tries to "wait it out" for 13 years until he can take early retirement. Fortunately, some affected individuals can be reenergized by moving them to another position in the organization. This can boost their morale and their productivity (see Workplace Issues).

Late Career

Those who continue to grow through the mid-career stage often experience the **late-career stage** as a pleasant time with the luxury to relax a bit and enjoy playing the part of the elder statesperson, rest on one's laurels, and bask in the respect of less experienced employees. Late-career individuals frequently escape expectations of outdoing their previous performance. Their value to the organization typically lies heavily in their judgment, built up over many years and through varied experiences. They can teach others based on the knowledge they have gained.

Those who have stagnated or deteriorated during the previous stage, on the other hand, often realize in the late career that they will not have an everlasting impact or change the world as they once thought. Employees who decline in mid-career may fear for their jobs. It is a time when individuals recognize that they have decreased work mobility and may be locked into their current job. One begins to look forward to retirement and opportunities for doing something different. Mere plateauing is no more negative than it was during mid-career. In fact, it is expected at late career. The marketing vice president who didn't make it to executive vice president might begin delegating more to her next in line. Life off the job is likely to carry far greater importance than it did in earlier years, as time and energy, once directed to work, are now being redirected to family, friends, and hobbies.

> **late-career stage**
> A career stage in which individuals are no longer learning about their jobs nor expected to outdo levels of performance from previous years.

Decline (Late Stage)

The **decline or late stage** in one's career is difficult for just about everyone, but ironically is probably hardest on those who have had continued successes in the earlier stages. After decades of continued achievements and high levels of performance, the

> **decline or late stage**
> The final stage in one's career, usually marked by retirement.

DID YOU KNOW?

WHERE ARE THE JOBS?

Many individuals who are at the beginning of a career search often ask the $64,000 question: where are the jobs? What's popular today, when the greatest employee needs are different than they were a generation ago—different even than a decade ago. And although having a solid foundation of communications, technology, and people skills is critical, even these skills need to be focused on where the demand for jobs exists.

So in what field are these jobs—and which ones are slowly, and significantly declining? Let's look at what the research is telling us about specific jobs.

Jobs That Are Declining	Jobs That Are In Demand
■ sewing machine operators	■ college professors
■ word processors	■ managers
■ telephone operators	■ software engineers
■ travel agents	■ management consultants
■ title examiners	■ artists and designers

As you may see, many of the jobs that are in demand

are professional jobs. In a similar study, *Fortune* magazine published the Bureau of Labor Statistics' 20 fastest-growing professional jobs (many of which are included in the broad categories of jobs that are in demand). Among them are:

- environmental engineers
- network and datacom analysts
- personal financial advisors
- software engineers
- media specialists
- emergency management specialists
- compensation and benefits specialists
- training and development specialists
- marketing and sales managers
- social workers
- lawyers
- public relations specialists

The interesting item about these professions is that each requires higher education degrees and often specific certifications. Furthermore, each is also a field that is constantly changing, which necessitates ongoing education throughout one's career.

Source: Based on information found in P. Coy, "The Future of Work," *Business Week,* (March 22, 2004), pp. 50–52; and A. Fisher, "Hot Careers for the Next Ten Years," *Fortune* (March 21, 2005), p. 131.

time has come for retirement. These individuals step out of the limelight and relinquish a major component of their identity. For those who have seen their performance deteriorate over the years, it may be a pleasant time; the frustrations associated with work are left behind. For the plateaued, it is probably an easier transition to other life activities.

Adjustments, of course, must be made, whether one is leaving a sparkling career or a hopeless job. The structure and regimentation that work provided is gone. Work responsibilities are generally fewer. It is a challenging stage for anyone to confront.

However, as we live longer, healthier lives, coupled with laws removing age-related retirement requirements, 62, 65, or 67 ceases to be a meaningful retirement age demand. Some individuals shift their emphasis to other work—either paid or volunteer. Often, the key element in this decision is financial security. Those who have adequate funds to maintain their lifestyles in retirement are more likely to engage in activities that they desire. Unfortunately, those less financially secure may be unable to retire when they want, or find that they have to seek gainful employment in some capacity to supplement their retirement income.

CAREER CHOICES AND PREFERENCES

The best career choice offers the best match between what you want and what you need. Good career choice outcomes for any of us should produce a series of positions that give us an opportunity for good performance, make us want to maintain our commitment to the field, and give us high work satisfaction. A good career match, then, lets us develop a positive self-concept and to do work that we think is important.[31] Let's look at some of the existing research that can help you discover which careers may provide the best match for your skills.

Holland Vocational Preferences

Holland vocational preferences model

Represents an individual occupational personality as it relates to vocational themes.

One of the most widely used approaches to guide career choices is the **Holland vocational preferences model**.[32] This theory consists of three major components. First, Holland found that people have varying occupational preferences; we do not all like to do the same things. Second, his research demonstrates that if you do a job you think is important, you will be a more productive employee. Personality of workers may be matched to typical work environments where that can occur. Third, you will have more in common with people who have similar interest patterns and less in common with those who don't. For instance, Karen hates her job; she thinks it is boring to waste her time packing and unpacking trucks on the shipping dock of a manufacturing firm and would rather be working with people in the recruiting area. Pat, on the other hand, enjoys the routine of her work; she likes the daily rhythm and the serenity of loading and unloading the warehouse. Karen and Pat feel differently about the same job. Why? Their interests, expressed as occupational interests, are not compatible.

The Holland vocational preferences model identifies six vocational themes (realistic, investigative, artistic, social, enterprising, conventional) presented in Exhibit 9-3. An individual's occupational personality is expressed as some combination of high and low scores on these six themes. High scores indicate that you enjoy those kinds of activities. Although it is possible to score high or low on all six scales, most people are identified by three dominant scales. The six themes are arranged in the hexagonal structure shown in Exhibit 9-4. This scale model

EXHIBIT 9-3
Holland's General Occupational Themes

Realistic Rugged, robust, practical, prefer to deal with things rather than people; mechanical interests. Best job matches are Agriculture, Nature, Adventure, Military, Mechanical.

Investigative Scientific, task-oriented, prefer abstract problems, prefer to think through problems rather than to act on them, not highly person-oriented, enjoy ambiguity. Corresponding jobs are Science, Mathematics, Medical Science, Medical Service.

Artistic Enjoy creative self-expression, dislike highly structured situations, sensitive, emotional, independent, original. Corresponding jobs are Music/Dramatics, Art, Writing.

Social Concerned with the welfare of others, enjoy developing and teaching others, good in group settings, extroverted, cheerful, popular. Corresponding jobs are Teaching, Social Service, Athletics, Domestic Arts, Religious Activities.

Enterprising Good facility with words, prefer selling or leading, energetic, extroverted, adventurous, enjoy persuasion. Corresponding jobs are Public Speaking, Law/Politics, Merchandising, Sales, Business Management.

Conventional Prefer ordered, numerical work, enjoy large organizations, stable, dependable. Corresponding job is Office Practices.

EXHIBIT 9-4
Structure of Holland's Themes

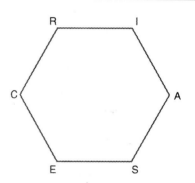

Letters connected by the line indicate reinforcing themes; letters not connected represent opposing themes.

represents the fact that some of the themes are opposing, while others have mutually reinforcing characteristics.

For instance, Realistic and Social are opposite each other in the diagram. A person with a realistic preference wants to work with things, not people. A person with a social preference wants to work with people, no matter what else they do. Therefore, they have opposing preferences about working alone or with others. Investigative and Enterprising are opposing themes, as are Artistic and Conventional preferences.

An example of mutually reinforcing themes is the Social-Enterprising-Conventional (SEC) vocational preference structure. Sally, for example, likes working with people, being successful, and following ordered rules. That combination is perfect for someone willing to climb the ladder in a large bureaucracy. What about Bob? He's Realistic-Investigative-Artistic, preferring solitary work to large groups, asking questions to answering them, and making his own rules instead of following someone else's. How does Bob fit into a large bureaucracy? Some may think his preferred actions label him as a troublemaker. He might fit better in a research lab—both the scientist preference and the research lab environment are characterized by lack of human interruptions and concentration on factual material. That's consistent with the Realistic-Investigative-Artistic profile.

The Schein Anchors

Edgar Schein has identified anchors, or personal value clusters, that may be satisfied or frustrated by work. When the worker holds a particular combination of these personal value clusters (technical-functional competence, managerial competence, security-stability, creativity, and autonomy-independence) and the organization characteristically offers them, that person is "anchored" in that job, organization, or industry.[33] Most people have two or three value clusters that are important to them. If an organization satisfies two out of three, that is considered a stable match. For instance, Donny is a recent college graduate. He wants to use his human resources degree. His father was laid off when his organization downsized last year, and Donny never wants to deal with that type

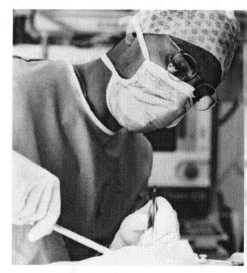

What vocational preferences might this surgeon have? According to Holland, this individual more than likely is investigative (scientific) with an artistic flare. Our preferences make certain careers appear more likely ones that we will enjoy, as well as be more productive in. (Source: Taxi/Getty Images, Inc.)

EXHIBIT 9-5
Characteristics Frequently Associated with Myers-Briggs Types

		Sensing Types S		Intuitive Types N	
		THINKING T	**FEELING F**	**FEELING F**	**THINKING T**
Introverts I	**JUDGING J**	ISTJ Quiet, serious dependable, practical, matter-of-fact. Value traditions and loyalty.	ISFJ Quiet, friendly, responsible, thorough, considerate. Strive to create order and harmony.	INFJ Seek meaning and connection in ideas. Committed to firm values. Organized and decisive in implementing vision.	INTJ Have original minds and great drive for their ideas. Skeptical and independent, have high standards of competence for self and others.
	PERCEIVING P	ISTP Tolerant and flexible. Interested in cause and effect. Value efficiency.	ISFP Quiet, friendly, sensitive. Like own space. Dislike disagreements and conflicts.	INFP Idealistic, loyal to their values. Seek to understand people and help them fulfill their potential.	INTP Seek logical explanations. Theoretical and abstract over social interactions. Skeptical, sometimes critical. Analytical.
Extroverts E	**PERCEIVING P**	ESTP Flexible and tolerant. Focus on here and now. Enjoy material comforts. Learn best by doing.	ESFP Outgoing, friendly. Enjoy working with others. Spontaneous. Learn best by trying a new skill with other people.	ENFP Enthusiastic, imaginative. Want a lot of affirmation. Rely on verbal fluency and ability to improvise.	ENTP Quick, ingenious, stimulating. Adept at generating conceptual possibilities and analyzing them strategically. Bored by routine.
	JUDGING J	ESTJ Practical, realistic, matter-of-fact, decisive. Focus on getting efficient results. Forceful in implementing plans.	ESFJ Warmhearted, cooperative. Want to be appreciated for who they are and for what they contribute.	ENFJ Warm, responsive, responsible. Attuned to needs of others. Sociable, facilitate others, provide inspirational leadership.	ENTJ Frank, decisive, assume leadership. Enjoy long-term planning and goal setting. Forceful in presenting ideas.

Source: Modified and reproduced by special permission of the publisher, Consulting Psychologists Press, Palo Alto, CA 94303 from *Introduction to Type*™, 6th edition by Isabel Briggs Myers. Copyright 1998 by Consulting Psychologists Press. All rights reserved. Further reproduction is prohibited without the publisher's written consent. *Introduction to Type* is a trademark of Consulting Psychologists Press, Inc.

of uncertainty. Schein would describe Donny's anchors as technical competence and security-stability. His current job choices are marketing on a commission basis for a new credit card company, or recruiting for an established and growth-oriented computer firm. Which job should he take? Based on his combination of value clusters, the recruiting job currently appears to better match Donny's preferences.

The Myers-Briggs Typologies

One of the more widely used methods of identifying personalities is the Myers-Briggs Type Indicator (MBTI®).* The MBTI uses four dimensions of personality to identify 16 different personality types based on responses to an approximately 100-item questionnaire (see Exhibit 9-5). More than two and a half million individuals each year in the United States alone take the MBTI.[34] It's used in such companies as Apple Computer, Honda, AT&T, Exxon, 3M, as well as many hospitals, educational institutions, and the U.S. armed forces.

---

*The Myers-Briggs Type Indicator and MBTI are registered trademarks of Consulting Psychology Press, Inc.

WORKPLACE ISSUES

A SPECIAL CASE OF A CAREER: ENTREPRENEURSHIP

Think of someone who is an entrepreneur. Maybe it's someone you know personally or someone you've read about such as Bill Gates of Microsoft, Oprah Winfrey of Harpo Productions, or Larry Ellison of Oracle. How would you describe this person's personality? One of the more researched areas of entrepreneurship has been determining what, if any, psychological characteristics entrepreneurs have in common, what types of personality traits might distinguish them from nonentrepreneurs, and what traits among entrepreneurs might predict who will be successful.

Is there a classic entrepreneurial personality? Although pinpointing specific personality characteristics that all entrepreneurs share is difficult, this hasn't stopped entrepreneurship researchers from searching for common traits.[35] For instance, one list of personality characteristics included the following: high level of motivation, abundance of self-confidence, ability to be involved for the long term, high energy level, persistent problem solver, high degree of initiative, ability to set goals, and moderate risk taker. Another list of characteristics of successful entrepreneurs included high energy level, great persistence, resourcefulness, the desire and ability to be self-directed, and relatively high need for autonomy.[36] A recent development in defining entrepreneurial personality characteristics was the proposed use of a proactive personality scale to predict an individual's likelihood of pursuing entrepreneurial ventures. **Proactive personality** describes individuals more prone to take actions to influence their environment.[37] Obviously, an entrepreneur is likely to exhibit proactivity as he or she searches for opportunities and acts to take advantage of those opportunities. Various items on the proactive personality scale appear good indicators of a person's likelihood of becoming an entrepreneur. These include, for example, education and having an entrepreneurial parent.

The 16 personality types are based on the four dimensions noted in Exhibit 9-5. That is, the MBTI dimensions include extroversion versus introversion (EI), sensing versus intuitive (SN), thinking versus feeling (TF), and judging versus perceiving (JP). The EI dimension measures an individual's orientation toward the inner world of ideas (I) or the external world of the environment (E). The sensing-intuitive dimension indicates an individual's reliance on information gathered from the external world (S) or from the world of ideas (N). Thinking-feeling reflects one's preference of evaluating information in an analytical manner (T) or on the basis of values and beliefs (F). The judging-perceiving index reflects an attitude toward the external world that is either task completion oriented (J) or information seeking (P).[38]

How could the MBTI help managers? Proponents of the instrument believe that it's important to know these personality types because they influence the way people interact and solve problems. For example, if your boss is an intuitor and you are a sensor, you will gather information in different ways. An intuitor prefers gut reactions, whereas a sensor prefers facts. To work well with your boss, you must present more than just facts about a situation and discuss how you feel. The MBTI has been used to help managers match employees with jobs. For instance, a marketing position that requires extensive interaction with outsiders would be best filled by someone who has extroverted tendencies. Also, MBTI has also been found useful in focusing on growth orientations for entrepreneurial types (see Workplace Issues).[39]

proactive personality
Describing those individuals who are more prone to take actions to influence their environment.

ENHANCING YOUR CAREER

Consider managing your career like an entrepreneur managing a small business. Think of yourself as self-employed, even if you work in a large organization. In a world of "free agency," the successful career requires you to maintain flexibility

EXHIBIT 9-6
Suggestions for Managing Your Career

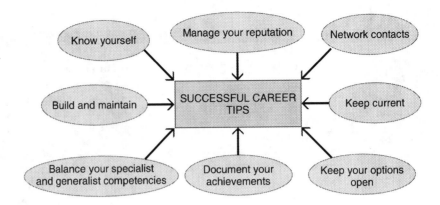

Internships provide a wealth of experience for college students and give a taste of the world of work. This can be crucial in the transition from school to work. (Source: Kei Uesugi/Taxi/Getty Images, Inc.)

and keep skills and knowledge up to date. The following suggestions are consistent with the view that you, and only you, hold primary responsibility for your career (see Exhibit 9-6).

- *Know yourself.* Know your strengths and weaknesses. What talents can you bring to an employer? Personal career planning begins by being honest with yourself (see Learning an HRM Skill, p. 252).
- *Manage your reputation.* Without appearing as a braggart, let others both inside and outside your current organization know about your achievements. Make yourself and your accomplishments visible.[40]
- *Build and maintain network contacts.* In a world of high mobility, you need contacts. Join national and local professional associations, attend conferences, and network at social gatherings. As a student you may want to participate in an internship. Organizations often want individuals who have some experience and who show some initiative. One way of demonstrating these attributes is through an internship. Many universities today not only offer internships as part of their curriculum, they require some type of job experience to fulfill their degree prerequisites. Internships offer you a chance to see what the work is really like, to better understand an organization's culture, and to see if you fit well into the organization. And although no guarantees are given, many organizations use internships as a means of developing their applicant pool—often extending job offers to outstanding interns.
- *Keep current.* Develop specific skills and abilities in high demand. Avoid learning organization-specific skills that don't quickly transfer to other employers.
- *Balance your specialist and generalist competencies.* Stay current within your technical specialty, but also develop general competencies that give you the versatility to react to an ever-changing work environment. Overemphasis in a single functional area or even in a narrow industry can limit your mobility.
- *Document your achievements.* Employers are increasingly looking to what you've accomplished rather than the titles you've held. Seek jobs and assignments that provide increasing challenges and offer objective evidence of your competencies.
- *Keep your options open.* Always have contingency plans prepared that you can call on when needed. You never know when your group will be eliminated, your department downsized, your project canceled, or your company acquired in a takeover. "Hope for the best but be prepared for the worst" may be cliché, but it's still not bad advice.[41]

SUMMARY

(This summary relates to the Learning Outcomes identified on page 231.) After having read this chapter, you can

1. **Explain who is responsible for managing careers.** The responsibility for managing a career belongs to the individual. The organization's role is to provide assistance and information to the employee, but it is not responsible for growing an employee's career.

2. **Describe the term** *career.* A career is a sequence of positions occupied by a person during the course of a lifetime.

3. **Discuss the focus of careers for both organizations and individuals.** Career development from an organizational standpoint involves tracking career paths and developing career ladders. From an individual perspective, career development focuses on assisting individuals in identifying their major career goals and in determining how to achieve these goals.

4. **Describe how career development and employee development differ.** The main distinction between career development and employee development lies in their time frames. Career development focuses on the long-range career effectiveness and success of organizational personnel. Employee development focuses more on immediate and intermediate time frames.

5. **Explain why career development is valuable to organizations.** Career development is valuable to an organization because it (1) ensures needed talent will be available; (2) improves the organization's ability to attract and retain high-talent employees; (3) ensures that minorities and women have opportunities for growth and development; (4) reduces employee frustration; (5) enhances cultural diversity; (6) assists in implementing quality; and (7) promotes organizational goodwill.

6. **Identify the five traditional stages involved in a career.** The five stages in a career are exploration, establishment, mid-career, late-career, and decline.

7. **List the Holland vocational preferences.** The Holland vocational preferences are realistic, investigative, artistic, social, enterprising, and conventional.

8. **Describe the implications of personality typologies and jobs.** Typology focuses on personality dimensions including extroversion-introversion; sensing-intuition; thinking-feeling; and judging-perceiving. These four pairs can be combined into 16 different combination profiles. With this information, job traits personality can be matched to individual personality traits.

9. **Identify several suggestions that can help you manage your career more effectively.** Some suggestions for managing your career include (1) know yourself, (2) manage your reputation, (3) build and maintain network contacts, (4) keep current, (5) balance your specialist and generalist competencies, (6) document your achievements, and (7) keep your options open.

DEMONSTRATING COMPREHENSION: *Questions for Review*

1. What is a career?
2. Contrast employee development with career development. How are they alike? Different?
3. How might a formal career development program be consistent with an organization's affirmative action program?
4. Contrast the external and internal dimensions of a career. Which do you believe is more relevant in determining an employee's work behavior?
5. What are the five traditional career stages? Which of the five is probably least relevant to HRM? Defend your position.
6. Identify the Holland vocational preferences and explain the importance of this model.
7. What is a mentor and how do you go about finding one?

VISUAL SUMMARY

CHAPTER 9: MANAGING CAREERS

1 What Is a Career?

Popular Definitions of Career
- Advancement in a job
- A profession
- Stability in work over time

We define career as a pattern of work-related experiences over one's life.

Career Development—looks at the long-term career success of people in the organization

Employee Development—looks at employee success in the immediate or intermediate time frame

2 Traditional Career Stages

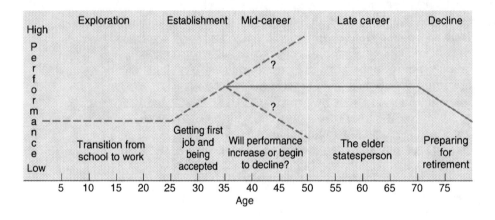

3   Career Choices and Preferences

Holland Vocational Preferences Model
- People have varying occupational preferences
- If you think your job is important, you'll be more productive
- You have more in common with those who share similar interest patterns

Six Vocational Themes
- Realistic (R)
- Investigative (I)
- Artistic (A)
- Social (S)
- Enterprising (E)
- Conventional (C)

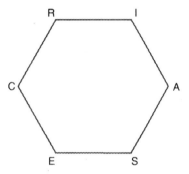

Letters connected by the line indicate reinforcing themes; letters not connected represent opposing themes.

The Myers-Briggs Typologies
  Widely used methods of identifying personalities
16 personality types based on:
EI—extroversion vs. introversion
SN—sensing vs. intuitive
TF—thinking vs. feeling
JP—judging vs. perceiving

4   How Can You Enhance Your Career?

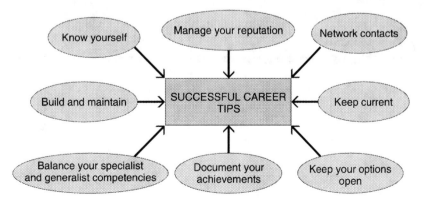

KEY TERMS

career	exploration	preferences	mid-career stage
decline or late	period	model	plateaued mid-
stage	external career	late-career stage	career
establishment	Holland	mentoring or	proactive
period	vocational	coaching	personality

CROSSWORD COMPREHENSION

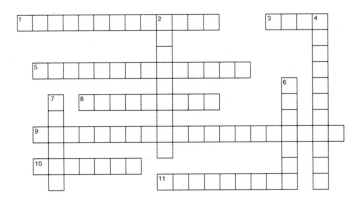

ACROSS

1. a career stage in which one begins to search for work and finds a first job
3. a career stage in which individuals are no longer learning about their jobs nor are expected to outdo previous performance levels
5. attributes related to an occupation's properties or qualities
8. actively guiding another individual
9. describing those individuals who are more prone to take actions to influence their environment
10. the final stage of one's career, usually marked by retirement
11. stagnation of one's career

DOWN

2. a career stage marked by continuous improvement in performance, a leveling off of performance, or the beginning of the deterioration of performance
4. career stage that usually ends in the mid-twenties as one makes the transition from school to work
6. this model represents an individual occupational personality as it relates to vocational themes
7. the sequence of positions that a person has held over his or her life

HRM Workshop

LINKING CONCEPTS TO PRACTICE: Discussion Questions

1. Which career perspective is more relevant to HRM managers—the individual or the organizational? Defend your position.
2. Do you think a person's age and career stage evolve together? Why or why not?
3. Which of the 16 Myers-Briggs typologies do you believe are most consistent with the behaviors needed in (a) a sales position, (b) a computer programmer, and (c) an HRM recruiter? Support your selections.

4. "Women and minorities require more career attention than do white males." Do you agree or disagree with the statement? Why or why not?

5. "Investments in career development do not provide an organization a viable return on its investment. It simply raises employee expectations, which, if not fulfilled, cause employees to leave. Accordingly, the organization has trained employees for its competitors." Take a position in support of this statement, and one against it.

DEVELOPING DIAGNOSTIC AND ANALYTICAL SKILLS

Case Application 9-A: A FUDGE CAREER

What do Brenda Barnes, Geraldine Laybourn, Ellen Marram, Mary Lou Quinlan, and Amy Fudge have in common—besides the very obvious fact that they're all women? Each of these individuals left their jobs in corporate America while they were in their prime. Barnes was the president and CEO of the North American division of PepsiCo; Laybourn was the vice president of Disney/ABC; Marram, the CEO of the Tropicana Beverage Company; Quinlan, the president of N. W. Ayer Advertising Agency; and Fudge was the head of Kraft Foods Dessert and Post division. The big question is why, after years of climbing to the tops of their respective organizations, did these corporate stars just quit? To help find an answer to that question, let's look at the case of Amy Fudge.[42]

After graduating from Simmons College with a bachelor's degree in management and earning an MBA from Harvard, Amy Fudge embarked on a career with General Foods (which later became part of Kraft Foods) as a marketing assistant. Her early career efforts were met with tremendous success. Her performance excelled, propelled by a knack for developing successful marketing campaigns. As a brand manager, she was credited for rekindling the excitement behind Kool-Aid, Log Cabin Syrup, and Stove Top Stuffing. She did this while controlling costs and increasing product quality. For her efforts, senior managers at Kraft rewarded her with a promotion to head of the Dessert and Post division of the company. This division had annual revenues in excess of $5 billion and accounted for more than 15 percent of the entire company's revenues.

After just a year into the job, Fudge stunned everyone. She announced that she was quitting. She was leaving her job—not to raise her children or for a bigger challenge in another organization. Rather, she was quitting so she could spend time on herself. After more than 20 years of working incessantly and infrequently seeing her family, she had had enough. Fudge wanted to go cycling, enjoy her house, and sit on her front deck and read a book. She wanted to meditate, and to have a "normal" life of eating a home-cooked dinner with her husband. For two years she did just that. And like Barnes, Laybourn, Marram, and Quinlan, after her self-imposed sabbatical, she decided to return to the world of work.

In late 2003, Fudge was lured back to corporate America with an opportunity to take the helm of the advertising and communication company Young and Rubicam. A company with revenues of about 40 percent of her previous job, she was taking over an organization that was having serious problems. The past several years, under its previous leadership, the company was neglected. Executive greed was rampant. But more important, the organization was losing customers—so many that it had lost nearly two-thirds of its revenues. Fudge says she is excited by the challenge of turning around Y&R. She feels she can make a difference and build a company that works with independent businesses in an effort to identify problems and implement workable solutions.

While there are some naysayers who don't believe Fudge can come back and be as effective as she once was, she discounts their perceptions. For her, the drive has returned, and she's anxious to use her talents again in a corporate setting.

Questions:

1. Describe what happened in this case to Amy Fudge in terms of career stages.
2. Do you believe that Fudge suffered a mid-life career crisis? Defend your position.
3. What can organizations do to prevent talent like Amy Fudge from leaving their organizations? Explain.

Case Application 9-B: TEAM FUN!

Team Fun

Tony, director of human resources for TEAM FUN!, and Bobby, store manager for the new Florida branch store, are sitting on the beach, sipping a cold one and watching the sun set over the Gulf of Mexico. Tony salutes his bottle to Bobby, "We had a great first week!"

Bobby agrees, "Kenny and Norton couldn't have done it better themselves! They're proud of us, I think."

Tony leans back in his chair, "Great guys. I can't believe they only stayed down here two days before turning us loose on our own. How did they start this? How did they get this way?"

Bobby, Kenny's son-in-law, says, "Gloria [Kenny's daughter] tells a good story. Seems Kenny and Norton have known each other since grade school. They played baseball, football, basketball, stickball. They went fishing, camping, and exploring caves together. They loved all the games. Both had to have other people around to admire them, to be with them. Kenny was happy as long as everyone played. Norton was happy when they won, especially when they won big. They kept in touch through college, marriage (both married their high school sweethearts), and kids. They played on community teams and were big in Little League coaching, stuff like that.

"When they were about 45 years old, they had all the fame and fortune they wanted and decided to give their childhood another try. Kenny left a job as a radio-television marketing and promotions manager. Norton was a structural engineer for an auto manufacturer. They first started TEAM FUN! as a sporting equipment store and used equipment swap for middle-school and high-school teams when their own kids were that age. Gloria remembers getting used softball equipment from the old store."

Tony stares at the water. "Wonder what I'll be doing when I hit the big four-O? I could see myself still at TEAM FUN! I like all the people, and I think people are really important. Sports, fitness, balance, are all part of what is important to me. I'm okay with not a lot of money. What about you?"

Bobby looks at him. "I think I'll own the business by then. I know how it could be more profitable. We could give leaner commissions and cut some of the benefits. I think it could be a lot bigger. Take on the major franchises. I'd like that. Maybe change the name to BOBBY TEAM FUN!"

Questions:

1. Define career and success for Bobby, Tony, Kenny, and Norton.
2. Trace career stages for each of them.
3. What career and employee development activities should Kenny and Norton provide for Bobby and Tony?
4. Identify Holland vocational preferences for Bobby, Tony, Kenny, and Norton.
5. Suggest several career management strategies that Bobby and Tony could utilize.

WORKING WITH A TEAM: *Career Insights*

Imagine that you enter the elevator on your way to an interview for an entry-level job at your first-choice company. Two other individuals are on the elevator, too. As you head to your floor, the elevator stalls, and it will be another 20 minutes before the mechanics can fix the elevator. You and the two other individuals begin to talk, introduce yourselves, and find that each of you is in the building for an interview. You decide to pose questions to one another.

Take turns responding to the following questions, noting similarities and differences in your responses.

- Who do you think is responsible for your career?
- What are your plans to continue your education?

- Why did you pick your chosen career?
- What phase of your career development are you in?
- How would you match what you want out of life and your career? Career goals? Job goals?
- What are your skills, interests, work-related needs, and values?
- What courses do you like best and least? Which are most challenging and most difficult?
- Have you ever had a mentor? Share that experience.

LEARNING AN HRM SKILL: *Making a Career Choice*

About the skill: Career planning can assist you in becoming more knowledgeable of your needs, values, and personal goals through the following three-step, self-assessment process.[43]

1. *Identify and organize your skills, interests, work-related needs, and values.* The best place to begin is by drawing up a profile of your educational record. List each school attended from high school on. What courses do you remember liking most and least? In what courses did you score highest and lowest? In what extracurricular activities did you participate? Did you acquire any specific skills? Have you gained proficiency in other skills? Next, begin to assess your occupational experience. List each job you have held, the organization you worked for, your overall level of satisfaction, what you liked most and least about the job, and why you left. It's important to be honest in covering each of these points.

2. *Convert this information into general career fields and specific job goals.* By completing step **1**, you should now have some insights into your interests and abilities. Now look at how these can convert into organizational settings or fields of endeavor with which you will be a good match. Then become specific and identify distinct job goals. What fields are available? In business? In government? In non-profit organizations? Break your answer down further into

areas such as education, financial, manufacturing, social services, or health services. Identifying areas of interest is usually far easier than pinpointing specific occupations. When you identify a limited set of occupations that interest you, you can start to align these with your abilities and skills. Will certain jobs require you to move? If so, would this be compatible with your geographic preferences? Do you have the educational requirements necessary for the job? If not, what additional schooling will you need? Does the job offer the status and earning potential that you aspire to? What is the long-term outlook for jobs in this field? Does the career suffer from cyclical employment? No job is without its drawbacks—have you seriously considered all the negative aspects? When you have fully answered questions such as these, you should have a relatively short list of specific job goals.

3. *Test your career possibilities against the realities of the organization or the job market.* The final step in this self-assessment process is testing your selection against the realities of the marketplace. Go out and talk with knowledgeable people in the fields, organizations, or jobs you desire. These informational interviews should provide reliable feedback as to the accuracy of your self-assessment and the opportunities in the fields and jobs that interest you.

Enhancing Your Communication Skills

1. Using the material presented in the HRM Skills section, develop a two- to three-page response to your skills, interests, work-related needs, and values.

2. Visit America Online's career and work Web page (on AOL, type key words *career* and *work*). Select careers, and work through the career guidance survey. After completing the survey, write up a two- to three-page analysis of the results you received. End the paper with some insight into what the survey indicated to you.

3. Write a two- to three-page paper on "Where I want to be in 10 years." Describe how you intend to accomplish this and what you'll have to do to increase your chances of attaining this goal.

TEN

Imagine you managed an organization that produced consumer products. Your employees spent countless hours properly designing, producing, and marketing the product. Your product is in every retail store that you had targeted. You are happy that you've met your goal. But have you truly achieved your goal? After some feedback from store owners, you recognize the product is not selling—and you're about to have nearly three-fourths of all the products returned for credit. Appears that your customers don't like what you produced, don't find it usable, and clearly don't see the value of buying it. In such a situation, you'd probably get involved and take some drastic actions. Why, then, when the product is the organization's performance evaluation system, is it ignored?[1]

In a survey of more than 48,000 employees, managers, and CEOs in Canadian organizations, fewer than 15 percent of the employees and just 6 percent of the management team found performance evaluations problematic. These individuals indicated that performance evaluations add no value to the employment relationship or toward organizational goals. About the only redeeming value they had

(*Source:* Justin Pumfrey/Getty Images, Inc.)

was to keep the people in human resources happy! That's because, for the most part, the performance evaluation process did not work well. Managers reported countless hours spent on filling out forms that failed to focus specifically on the individual. Individual accomplishments were often not identified. As such, the feedback session with employees rarely lasted for more than 15 minutes—using the time to describe the form.

Human resources managers, on the other hand, feel the problem is with managers' inability to allow the process to work properly. They indicate that managers don't evaluate employees properly, don't effectively give employees feedback, and simply won't confront poor performance. Conse-

quently everyone is rated average, and outstanding performance is often overlooked. From HR's perspective, it's no wonder employees don't like performance evaluations.

The difficulty is that both sides are correct. There are problems inherent in performance evaluation systems—but they don't need to be so insurmountable. Much of the difficulty comes from the fact that performance evaluation systems are often poorly designed and managers are poorly trained to administer them. Employees, too, often don't understand the rationale behind the performance evaluation process and their importance in the strategic goals of the organization. Properly working performance management systems can be valuable to all stakeholders in the organization, but first they must become part of the organization's culture. For example, in one Canadian organization, the CEO mandated that his vice presidents make the necessary changes to their performance evaluation process. To ensure that they did, the CEO placed 20 percent of each vice president's bonus at stake—meaning that if they failed to implement the organization's performance management process, they would lose 20 percent of their annual bonus. Needless to say, most of the vice presidents saw the wisdom in correcting the performance evaluation process and implemented a review process that was personalized, employee accomplishment–friendly—one that was conducted on a quarterly basis. Only a few failed to make this happen, and as such were penalized financially.

Are performance evaluations good for employers and employees? Properly managed, they are. But making this happen does not occur by accident. It takes a concerted effort by all organizational members—all committed to making the system as effective as it can be!

Establishing the Performance Management System

Learning Outcomes

After reading this chapter, you will be able to

1. Identify the three purposes of performance management systems and whom they serve.
2. Explain the six steps in the appraisal process.
3. Discuss absolute standards in performance management systems.
4. Describe relative standards in performance management systems.
5. Discuss how MBO can be used as an appraisal method.
6. Explain why performance appraisals might be distorted.
7. Identify ways to make performance management systems more effective.
8. Describe the term *360-degree appraisal*.
9. Discuss how performance appraisals may differ in the global village.

INTRODUCTION

Every year, most employees experience an evaluation of their past performance. This may be a five-minute informal discussion between employees and their supervisors or a more elaborate, several-week process involving many specific steps. Employees generally see any such evaluations as having some direct effect on their work lives. They may lead to increased pay, a promotion, or assistance in personal development areas for which the employee needs some training. As a result, any evaluation of employees' work can create an emotionally charged event. Because the performance evaluation is no longer a simple process, it is now more critical to perform one while simultaneously focusing on key job activities. For example, should an employee's body language when interacting with other employees and customers become part of the employee's performance evaluation? How about how well a manager serves as a mentor to her employees? Moreover, should a supervisor's employees have input into their boss's effectiveness at work? Should employee ability to perform tasks in a timely and accurate manner matter in an evaluation of their work? Questions like these cannot be overlooked. If we want to know how well our employees are doing, we must measure their performance—not necessarily an easy task. Many factors go into the performance evaluation process, such as why we evaluate, who should benefit from the evaluation, what type of evaluation we should use, and what problems we might encounter. This chapter seeks answers to these and several other important factors in the performance appraisal process.

Before beginning this chapter, however, recognize that no performance appraisal system is perfect. We have good reasons for completing them properly, but sometimes that simply doesn't happen, perhaps through poor appraisal training or obsolete measures. It could also be the result of the dynamic environment in which employees work. That is, some jobs change so frequently that it's almost impossible to properly define what an employee should do over the next 12 months. As a result, performance appraisals have come under attack.[2]

Regardless of potential problems, one can expect performance management systems to survive in some format. Accordingly, understanding the foundations of performance management systems, the way appraisals might be constructed, as well as the potential problems that one may encounter, benefits anyone involved in contemporary organizations—and helps executives know precisely how well the organization is progressing on meeting its strategic goals.[3]

PERFORMANCE MANAGEMENT SYSTEMS

Performance management systems involve numerous activities, far more than simply reviewing what an employee has done. These systems must fulfill several purposes. Moreover, they are often constrained by difficulties in how they operate. Let's look at these two primary areas.

Purposes of a Performance Management System

Approximately three decades ago, performance evaluations were designed primarily to tell employees how they had done over a period of time and to let them know what pay raise they would receive. This feedback mechanism may have served its purpose then, but today additional factors must be addressed. Specifically, performance evaluations should also address development and documentation concerns.[4]

Performance appraisals must convey to employees how well they have performed on established goals. It's also desirable to have these goals and performance measures mutually set between the employee and the supervisor. Without proper two-way feedback about an employee's effort and its effect on performance, we run the risk of decreasing his

Without proper two-way feedback about an employee's effort and its effect on performance, we run the risk of decreasing his or her motivation.

or her motivation. However, equally important to feedback is the issue of development.[5] By *development,* we are referring to those areas in which an employee has a deficiency or weakness, or an area that simply could be better through effort to enhance performance.[6] For example, suppose a college professor demonstrates extensive knowledge in his or her field and conveys this knowledge to students in an adequate way. Although this individual's performance may be satisfactory, his or her peers may indicate that some improvements could be made. In this case, then, development may include exposure to different teaching methods, such as bringing into the classroom more experiential exercises, real-world applications, Internet applications, case analyses, and so forth.

Finally comes the issue of **documentation.** A performance evaluation system would be remiss if it did not concern itself with the legal aspects of employee performance. Recall in Chapter 3 the discussion about EEO and the need for job-related measures. Those job-related measures must be performance-supported when an HRM decision affects current employees. For instance, suppose a supervisor has decided to terminate an employee. Although the supervisor cites performance matters as the reason for the discharge, a review of this employee's recent performance appraisals indicates that performance was evaluated as satisfactory for the past two review periods. Accordingly, unless this employee's performance significantly decreased (and assuming that proper methods to correct the performance deficiency were performed), personnel records do not support the supervisor's decision. This critique by HRM is absolutely critical to ensure that employees are fairly treated and that the organization is "protected."[7] Additionally, in our discussion of sexual harassment in Chapter 3, we addressed the need for employees to keep copies of past performance appraisals. If retaliation such as termination or poor job assignments occurs for refusing a supervisor's advances, existing documentation can show that the personnel action was inappropriate (see Ethical Issues in HRM).

Because documentation issues are prevalent in today's organizations, HRM must ensure that the evaluation systems used support the legal needs of the organization. However, even though the performance appraisal process is geared to serve the organization, we should also recognize two other important players in the process: employees and their appraisers. Through timely and accurate feedback

documentation
A record of performance appraisal process outcomes.

ETHICAL ISSUES IN HRM

THE INACCURATE PERFORMANCE APPRAISAL

Most individuals recognize the importance of effective performance management systems in an organization. Not only are they necessary for providing feedback to employees and for identifying personal development plans, they serve an important legal purpose. Furthermore, organizations that fail to accurately manage employee performance often find themselves facing difficult times in meeting their organizational goals.

Most individuals would also agree that performance appraisals must meet Equal Employment Opportunity Act requirements. That is, they must be administered in such a way that they result in a fair and equitable treatment for the diversity that exists in the workplace. Undeniably, this is an absolute necessity.[8] But what about those gray areas—instances where an evaluation meets legal requirements but verges on a questionable practice?[9] For example, what if a manager deliberately evaluates a favored employee higher than one he likes less, even though the latter is a better promotional candidate? Likewise, what if the supervisor avoids identifying areas of employee development for individuals, knowing that their likelihood of career advancement is stalemated without better skills?

Supporters of properly functioning performance appraisals point to two vital criteria that managers must bring to the process: sincerity and honesty. Yet no legislative regulations, like EEO laws, enforce such ethical standards. Thus, they may be and frequently are missing from the evaluation process.

Can an organization have an effective performance appraisal process without sincerity and honesty dominating the system? Can organizations develop an ethical evaluation process? Should we expect companies to spend training dollars to achieve this goal? What do you think?

and development we can better serve employees' needs. In doing so, we may also be in a better position to show the effort–performance linkage.

Next, we should keep in mind the needs of the appraiser. If feedback, development, and documentation are to function effectively, appraisers must have a performance system appropriate for their needs—a system that facilitates giving feedback and development information to employees, and one that allows for employee input. For example, if appraisers are required to evaluate their employees using inappropriate performance measures, or to answer questions about employees that have little bearing on the job, the system may not provide the same benefits as one that avoids such negatives. In contrast to evaluations used decades ago, it's acceptable and absolutely necessary for evaluation criteria to differ for some jobs. Tailoring the evaluation process to the job analysis and the organization's and employee's goals is the difference between a satisfactory evaluation system and one that is an integral part of the HRM process.

To create the performance management system we desire, however, we must recognize any difficulties in the process. We must look for ways to either overcome these difficulties or deal with them more effectively. Let's turn our attention to these challenges.

Difficulties in Performance Management Systems

Three constituencies coexist in this process—employees, appraisers, and organizations—and coordinating the needs of each may cause problems. By focusing on the difficulties, we can begin to address them so as to reduce their overall consequence in the process. Let us address two primary categories of difficulties, (1) focus on the individual and (2) focus on the process.

Focus on the Individual Do you remember the last time you received a graded test from a professor and believed that something was marked incorrect that wasn't wrong, or that your answer was too harshly penalized? How did you feel about that? Did you accept the score and leave it at that, or did you question the instructor? Whenever performance evaluations are administered (and tests are one form of performance evaluation), we run into the issue of people seeing eye-to-eye on

DID YOU KNOW?

FUN FACTS ON PERFORMANCE EVALUATIONS

Over the years there's been a lot of information presented about performance evaluations. This ranges from the types of evaluations used to the implications of the evaluation itself. Here are some interesting facts that put performance assessments in perspective.

- More than 90 percent of all U.S. organizations use some form of performance evaluations.
- Once implemented, the evaluation system stays constant for about 4.5 years before any changes are made to the process.
- Nearly three-fourths of all organizations evaluate nearly three-fourths of their employees each year.

- About half of all organizations evaluate employees more than once a year.
- About a third of all organizations use some form of a forced ranking of employees—comparing employees against one another.
- About 25 percent of all organizations use some form of electronic, software-based evaluation systems.
- About three in four employees see a direct link between their performance evaluations and their compensation—although compensation discussions are separated from performance reviews.
- Only one in five employees receive feedback from peers or customers in their performance evaluation process.

Source: "Survey Says," *Training and Development* (October 2003), p. 16; and "Performance Management Systems Are Quickly Becoming More Popular," *HR Focus* (August 2003), p. 8.

the evaluation. Appraising individuals is probably one of the more difficult aspects of a supervisor's job. Why? Because emotions are involved, and sometimes supervisors just don't like to do appraisals. We all think we are performing in an outstanding fashion, but that may be *our* perception. And although a boss recognizes our work is good, it may not be considered outstanding. Accordingly, in evaluating performance, emotions may arise.[10] And if these emotions are not dealt with properly (we'll look at ways to enhance performance evaluations later in this chapter), they can lead to greater conflict. In fact, consider the aforementioned test example, assuming you confronted the professor. Depending on the encounter, especially if it is aggressive, both of you may become defensive.[11] And because of the conflict, nothing but ill feelings may arise. The same applies for appraisers.

A difference on performance outcomes may lead to emotions overcoming both parties, a poor way for evaluations to be handled. Accordingly, our first concern in the process is to remove the emotion difficulty from the process. When emotions stay calm in these meetings, employee satisfaction in the process may increase and may carry over into future job activities, where both the employee and supervisor have opportunities for ongoing feedback in an effort to fulfill job expectations.

Focus on the Process Wherever performance evaluations are conducted, a particular structure must be followed. This structure exists to facilitate documentation that often allows for quantifiable evaluation. Additionally, HRM policies can dictate performance outcomes. For example, if a company ties performance evaluations to pay increases, consider the following potential difficulty: Sometime during spring, managers develop budgets for their units—budgets dictated and approved by upper management. Now, in this budget for the next fiscal year, each manager's salary budget increases by 3 percent. As we enter the new fiscal year, we evaluate our employees. One in particular has done an outstanding job and is awarded a 6 percent raise. What does this do to our budget? To average 3 percent, some employees will receive less than the 3 percent salary increase. Consequently, company policies and procedures may present barriers to a properly functioning appraisal process.[12]

Furthermore, to balance these numbers, an appraiser focuses on negative rather than positive work behaviors of some employees. This can lead to a tendency to search for problems, which can ultimately lead to an emotional encounter. We may also find from the appraiser's perspective some uncertainty about how and what to measure, or how to deal with the employee in the evaluation process. Frequently, appraisers are poorly trained in how to evaluate an employee's performance. This lack of training may lead appraisers to make judgment errors or permit biases to enter into the process. We'll talk more about these problems later.

Because difficulties may arise, we should begin to develop our performance appraisal process so that we can achieve maximum benefit from it. This maximum benefit can translate into employee satisfaction with the process.[13] Such satisfaction is achieved by creating an understanding of the evaluation criteria used, permitting employee participation in the process, and allowing for development needs to be addressed.[14] To begin doing so requires us to initially understand the appraisal process.

Having an effective performance management system in the organization can help reduce confrontations—emotional or otherwise. Everyone needs to recognize that emotions may run high during a performance feedback session. However, a properly designed system and effective implementation (including appraiser training and continuous feedback) will help avoid emotional outbursts like this. (Source: Altrendo Images/Getty Images, Inc.)

PERFORMANCE MANAGEMENT AND EEO

Performance management systems are an integral part of most organizations. Properly developed and implemented performance management processes can help an organization achieve its goals by developing productive employees. The many types of performance management systems, each with its own advantages and disadvantages, require us to be aware of the legal implications that arise.

EEO laws require organizations to have bias-free HRM practices. HRM performance management systems must be objective and job related. That is, they must be reliable and valid! Furthermore, under the Americans with Disabilities Act, performance management systems must also be able to measure "reasonable" performance success. Two factors assist in these matters: (1) The performance appraised must be conducted according to some established intervals, and (2) appraisers must be trained in the process.[15] The reasons for this become crystal clear when you consider that any employee action, such as promotion or termination, must be based on valid data prescribed from the performance management documentation. These objective data often support the legitimacy of employee actions.

Let's turn our attention now to a major component of the performance management system—the appraisal process.

The Appraisal Process

The appraisal process (Exhibit 10-1) begins with establishment of performance standards in accordance with the organization's strategic goals. These should evolve out of the company's strategic direction—and, more specifically, the job analysis and the job description discussed in Chapter 5. These performance standards should also be clear and objective enough to be understood and measured. Too often, standards are articulated in ambiguous phrases that tell us little, such as "a full day's work" or "a good job." What is a full day's work or a good job? A supervisor's expectations of employee work performance must be clear enough in her mind so that she will be able to, at some later date, communicate these expectations to her employees, mutually agree to specific job performance measures, and appraise their performance against these established standards.

Once performance standards are established, it is necessary to communicate these expectations; employees should not have to guess what is expected of them. Too many jobs have vague performance standards, and the problem is compounded when these standards are set in isolation and without employee input. Communication is a two-way street: mere information transfer from supervisor to employee is not communication! The third step in the appraisal process is performance measurement. To determine what actual performance is, we need information about it. We should be concerned with how we measure and what we measure.

Four common sources of information frequently used by managers address how to measure actual performance: personal observation, statistical reports, oral reports, and written reports. Each has its strengths and weaknesses; however, a combination of them increases both the number of input sources and the probability of receiving reliable information. What we measure is probably more critical to the evaluation process than how we measure. Selecting the wrong criteria can produce serious, dysfunctional consequences. And what we measure determines, to

Exhibit 10-1
The Appraisal Process

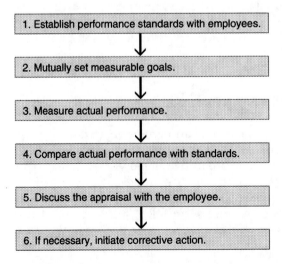

1. Establish performance standards with employees.

2. Mutually set measurable goals.

3. Measure actual performance.

4. Compare actual performance with standards.

5. Discuss the appraisal with the employee.

6. If necessary, initiate corrective action.

a great extent, what people in the organization will attempt to excel at. The criteria we measure must represent performance as it was mutually set in the first two steps of the appraisal process.

The fourth step in the appraisal process is the comparison of actual performance with standards. This step notes deviations between standard performance and actual performance so that we can proceed to the fifth step in the process— discussing the appraisal with the employee. As we mentioned previously, one of the most challenging tasks facing appraisers is to present an accurate assessment to the employee. Appraising performance may touch on one of the most emotionally charged activities—evaluation of another individual's contribution and ability. The impression that employees receive about their assessment has a strong impact on their self-esteem and, importantly, on their subsequent performance. Of course, conveying good news is considerably easier for both the appraiser and the employee than conveying bad news. In this context, the appraisal discussion can have negative as well as positive motivational consequences.

The final step in the appraisal is the identification of corrective action where necessary. Corrective action can be of two types: one is immediate and deals predominantly with symptoms, and the other is basic and delves into causes. Immediate corrective action is often described as "putting out fires," whereas basic corrective action touches the source of deviation and seeks to adjust the difference permanently. Immediate action corrects problems right now and gets us back on track. Basic corrective action asks how and why performance deviated. In some instances, appraisers may rationalize that they lack time to take basic corrective action and therefore must be content to perpetually put out fires. Good supervisors recognize that taking a little time to analyze the problem today may prevent the problem from worsening tomorrow.

APPRAISAL METHODS

The previous section described the appraisal process in general terms. In this section we will look at specific ways in which HRM can actually establish performance standards and devise instruments to measure and appraise an employee's performance. Three approaches exist for doing appraisals: employees can be appraised against (1) absolute standards, (2) relative standards, or (3) outcomes. No one approach is always best; each has its strengths and weaknesses.[16]

Evaluating Absolute Standards

Our first group of appraisal methods uses **absolute standards**. This means that employees are compared to a standard, and their evaluation is independent of any other employee in a work group. This process assesses employee job traits and/or behaviors.[17] Included in this group are the following methods: the critical incident appraisal, the checklist, the graphic rating scale, forced choice, and behaviorally anchored rating scales. Let's look at each of these, focusing on their strengths and weaknesses.

absolute standards
Measuring an employee's performance against established standards.

Critical Incident Appraisal Critical incident appraisal focuses the rater's attention on critical or key behaviors that make the difference between doing a job effectively and doing it ineffectively. The appraiser writes down anecdotes describing employee actions that were especially effective or ineffective. For example, a police sergeant might write the following critical incident about one of her officers: "Brought order to a volatile situation by calmly discussing options with an armed suspect during a hostage situation, which resulted in all hostages being released, and the suspect being apprehended without injury to any individual." Note that with this approach to appraisal, specific behaviors are cited, not vaguely defined individual traits. A behavior-based appraisal such as this should be more valid

critical incident appraisal
A performance evaluation that focuses on key behaviors that differentiate between doing a job effectively or ineffectively.

checklist appraisal
A performance evaluation in which a rater checks off applicable employee attributes.

graphic rating scale
A performance appraisal method that lists traits and a range of performance for each.

How would you evaluate this employee using a graphic rating scale? This employee's supervisor would evaluate the employee based on how well she compared to an established standard on such traits/ behaviors as quantity and quality of work, job knowledge, cooperation, loyalty, dependability, attendance, honesty, integrity, attitudes, and initiative. (Source: Barbara Maurer/Taxi/Getty Images, Inc.)

than trait-based appraisals because it is clearly more job related. It is one thing to say that an employee is "aggressive," "imaginative," or "relaxed," but that does not tell us anything about how well the job is being done. Critical incidents, with their focus on behaviors, judge performance rather than personalities.

The strength of the critical incident method is that it looks at behaviors. Additionally, a list of critical incidents on a given employee provides a rich set of examples from which employees can be shown which of their behaviors are desirable and which ones call for improvement. Its drawbacks are that (1) appraisers must regularly write these incidents down, and doing this on a daily or weekly basis for all employees is time-consuming and burdensome for supervisors; and (2) critical incidents suffer from the same comparison problem found in essays—they do not lend themselves easily to quantification. Comparison and ranking of employees may be difficult.

Checklist Appraisal In the checklist appraisal, the evaluator uses a list of behavioral descriptions and checks off behaviors that apply to the employee. As Exhibit 10-2 illustrates, the evaluator merely goes down the list and checks off "yes" or "no" to each question.

Once the checklist is complete, it is usually evaluated by the HRM staff, not the appraiser completing the checklist. Therefore, the rater does not actually evaluate the employee's performance; he or she merely records it. An HRM analyst scores the checklist, often weighting the factors in relationship to their importance to that specific job. The final evaluation can either return to the appraiser for discussion with the employee, or someone from HRM can provide the feedback.

The checklist appraisal reduces some bias in the evaluation process because the rater and the scorer are different. However, the rater usually can pick up the positive and negative connections in each item—so bias can still be introduced. From a cost standpoint, too, this appraisal method may be inefficient if individualized checklists of items must be prepared for numerous job categories.

Graphic Rating Scale Appraisal One of the oldest and most popular methods of appraisal is the **graphic rating scale**.[18] An example of some rating scale items is shown in Exhibit 10-3. Rating scales can be used to assess factors such as quantity and quality of work, job knowledge, cooperation, loyalty, dependability, attendance, honesty, integrity, attitudes, and initiative. However, this method is most valid when abstract traits like loyalty or integrity are avoided, unless they can be defined in more specific behavioral terms.[19]

To use the graphic rating scale, the assessor goes down the list of factors and notes the point along the scale or continuum that best describes the employee. There are typically five to ten points on the continuum. The challenge in designing the rating scale is to ensure that factors evaluated and scale points are clearly understood and are unambiguous to the rater. Ambiguity introduces bias.

Why are rating scales popular? Although they do not provide the depth of information that essays or critical incidents do, they are less time-consuming to

EXHIBIT 10-2
Sample Checklist Items for Appraising Customer Service Representative

	Yes	No
1. Are supervisor's orders usually followed?	___	___
2. Does the individual approach customers promptly?	___	___
3. Does the individual suggest additional merchandise to customers?	___	___
4. Does the individual keep busy when not serving a customer?	___	___
5. Does the individual lose his or her temper in public?	___	___
6. Does the individual volunteer to help other employees?	___	___

Exhibit 10-3
Sample of Graphic Rating Scale Items and Format

PERFORMANCE FACTOR	PERFORMANCE RATING				
Quality of work is the accuracy, skill, and completeness of work.	☐ Consistently unsatisfactory	☐ Occasionally unsatisfactory	☐ Consistently satisfactory	☐ Sometimes superior	☐ Consistently superior
Quantity of work is the volume of work done in a normal workday.	☐ Consistently unsatisfactory	☐ Occasionally unsatisfactory	☐ Consistently satisfactory	☐ Sometimes superior	☐ Consistently superior
Job knowledge is information pertinent to the job that an individual should have for satisfactory job performance.	☐ Poorly informed about work duties	☐ Occasionally unsatisfactory	☐ Can answer most questions about the job	☐ Understands all phases of the job	☐ Has complete mastery of all phases of the job
Dependability is following directions and company policies without supervision.	☐ Requires constant supervision	☐ Requires occasional follow-up	☐ Usually can be counted on	☐ Requires little supervision	☐ Requires absolute minimum supervision

develop and administer. They also provide a quantitative analysis useful for comparison purposes. Furthermore, in contrast to the checklist, more generalization of items makes possible comparability with other individuals in diverse job categories.

Forced-Choice Appraisal Have you ever completed one of those tests that presumably gives you insights into what kind of career you should pursue? (Questions might be, for example, "Would you rather go to a party with a group of friends or attend a lecture by a well-known political figure?") If so, then you are familiar with the forced-choice format. The **forced-choice appraisal** is a special type of checklist where the rater must choose between two or more statements. Each statement may be favorable or unfavorable. The appraiser's job is to identify which statement is most (or in some cases least) descriptive of the individual being evaluated. For instance, students evaluating their college instructor might have to choose between "(a) keeps up with the schedule identified in the syllabus, (b) lectures with confidence, (c) keeps interest and attention of class, (d) demonstrates how concepts are practically applied in today's organizations, or (e) allows students the opportunity to learn concepts on their own." All the preceding statements could be favorable, but we really don't know. As with the checklist method, to reduce bias, the right answers are unknown to the rater; someone in HRM scores the answers based on the answer key for the job being evaluated. This key should be validated so HRM is in a position to say that individuals with higher scores are better-performing employees.

The major advantage of the forced-choice method is that because the appraiser does not know the "right" answers, it reduces bias and distortion.[20] For example, the appraiser may like a certain employee and intentionally want to give him a favorable evaluation, but this becomes difficult if one is not sure of the preferred response. On the negative side, appraisers tend to dislike this method; many dislike being forced to make distinctions between similar-sounding statements. Raters also may become frustrated with a system in which they do not know what represents a good or poor answer. Consequently, they may try to second-guess the scoring key to align the formal appraisal with their intuitive appraisal.

forced-choice appraisal
A performance evaluation in which the rater must choose between two specific statements about an employee's work behavior.

behaviorally anchored rating scales (BARS)

A performance appraisal technique that generates critical incidents and develops behavioral dimensions of performance. The evaluator appraises behaviors rather than traits.

Behaviorally Anchored Rating Scales An approach that has received considerable attention by academics in past years involves **behaviorally anchored rating scales (BARS)**. These scales combine major elements from the critical incident and adjective rating scale approaches. The appraiser rates the employees based on items along a continuum, but the points are examples of actual behavior on the given job rather than general descriptions or traits. The enthusiasm surrounding BARS grew from the belief that the use of specific behaviors, derived for each job, should produce relatively error-free and reliable ratings. Although this promise has not been fulfilled, it has been argued that this may be partly due to departures from careful methodology in developing the specific scales rather than to inadequacies in the concept. BARS, too, is time-consuming.

Behaviorally anchored rating scales specify definite, observable, and measurable job behavior. Examples of job-related behavior and performance dimensions are generated by asking participants to give specific illustrations of effective and ineffective behavior regarding each performance dimension; these behavioral examples are then translated into appropriate performance dimensions. Those sorted into the dimension for which they were generated are retained. The final group of behavior incidents are then numerically scaled to a level of performance each is perceived to represent. The identified incidents with high rater agreement on performance effectiveness are retained for use as anchors on the performance dimension. The results of these processes are behavioral descriptions such as anticipates, plans, executes, solves immediate problems, carries out orders, or handles emergency situations. Exhibit 10-4 is an example of a BARS for an employee relations specialist's scale.

EXHIBIT 10-4
Sample BARS for an Employee Relations Specialist

Performance dimension scale development under BARS for the dimension "Ability to Absorb and Interpret Policies for an Employee Relations Specialist."
This employee relations specialist

	9 Could be expected to serve as an information source concerning new and changed policies for others in the organization
Could be expected to be aware quickly of program changes and explain these to employees	8
	7 Could be expected to reconcile conflicting policies and procedures correctly to meet HRM goals
Could be expected to recognize the need for additional information to gain a better understanding of policy changes	6
	5 Could be expected to complete various HRM forms correctly after receiving instruction on them
Could be expected to require some help and practice in mastering new policies and procedures	4
	3 Could be expected to know that there is always a problem, but go down many blind alleys before realizing they are wrong
Could be expected to incorrectly interpret guidelines, creating problems for line managers	2
	1 Could be expected to be unable to learn new procedures even after repeated explanations

Source: Reprinted from *Business Horizons* (August 1976), copyright 1976 by the Foundation for the School of Business at Indiana University. Used with permission.

BARS research indicates that, although it is far from perfect, it does tend to reduce rating errors. Possibly its major advantage stems from the dimensions generated, rather than from any particular superiority of behavior over trait anchors.[21] The process of developing behavioral scales is valuable for clarifying to both the employee and the rater which behaviors represent good performance and which don't. Unfortunately, it, too, suffers from the distortions inherent in most rating methods.[22] These distortions will be discussed later in this chapter.

Relative Standards Methods

The second general category of appraisal methods compares individuals against other individuals. These methods are **relative standards** rather than absolute measuring devices. The most popular of the relative methods are group order ranking, individual ranking, and paired comparison (see Workplace Issues).

relative standards
Evaluating an employee's performance by comparing the employee with other employees.

Group Order Ranking Group order ranking requires the evaluator to place employees into a particular classification, such as "top 20 percent." This method, for instance, is often used in recommending students to graduate schools. Evaluators are asked to rank the student in the top 5 percent, the next 5 percent, the next 15 percent, and so forth. But when used by appraisers to evaluate employees, raters deal with all employees in their area. So, for example, if a rater has 20 employees, only 4 can be in the top fifth; and, of course, 4 also must be relegated to the bottom fifth.

The advantage of this group ordering is that it prevents raters from inflating their evaluations so everyone looks good or from forcing the evaluations so everyone is rated near the average—outcomes not unusual with the adjective rating

WORKPLACE ISSUES

FORCED RANKINGS: ARE THEY WORKING?

Forced rankings are one of the fastest-growing trends in performance management systems in corporations. With companies like Ford, General Electric, Hewlett-Packard, Pepsico, Microsoft, and Sun Microsystems using them, forced rankings are now found in about one-third of all organizations. That is, these organizations now rank their employees from best to worst and then use such rankings to determine pay levels as well as in other HRM decisions.

Why the increase in their use? The primary reason is that many executives have become frustrated by managers who rated all their employees above average when in fact they weren't. In addition, these executives wanted to create a system that would increase the organization's competitiveness—one that would reward the very best performers and encourage poor performers to leave. So they turned to forced rankings or what has been called rank and yank by its critics.

One of the better-known forced rankings systems is that of General Electric. Its program is called the 20-70-10 plan. Under this system of evaluation, GE executives force managers to review all professional employees and to identify their top 20 percent, middle 70 percent, and bot-

tom 10 percent. GE then does everything possible to keep and reward the top performers and fires all the bottom performers—the 10 percent. They do so to keep the company moving forward by continually raising the bar of successful performance.

Proponents of forced rankings see such actions as continually improving an organization's effectiveness and a means of improving the organization's workforce. By doing so, the most deserving employees are rewarded most—both momentarily and with career advancement. They also see such systems as growing the best return on investment to shareholders.

Critics, on the other hand, argue that these programs are harsh and arbitrary and create zero-sum games that discourage cooperation and teamwork. It often pits one employee against another and leads to higher rates of turnover. Accordingly, morale suffers, and there is often a great distrust of the organization's leadership—which ultimately increases costs. Critics also say that these programs run counter to the belief held by many individuals that almost any worker is salvageable with proper guidance.

Source: L. Rivenbark, "Forced Ranking," *HR Magazine* (November 2005), p. 131; G. Johnson, "Forced Rankings: The Good, the Bad, and the Alternative," *Training* (May 2004), pp. 24–30; "Why HR Professionals Are Worried About Forced Rankings," *HR Focus* (October 2004), p. 8; "Performance Management Systems Are Quickly Becoming More Popular," *HR Focus* (August 2003), p. 8; and D. Grote, "Forced Ranking," *Executive Excellence* (July 2003), p. 6.

scale. The main disadvantages surface, however, when the number of employees compared is small. At the extreme, if the evaluator is looking at only four employees, all may be excellent, yet the evaluator may be forced to rank them into top quarter, second quarter, third quarter, and low quarter! Theoretically, as the sample size increases, the validity of relative scores as an accurate measure increases, but occasionally the technique is implemented with a small group, utilizing assumptions that apply to large groups.

Another disadvantage, which plagues all relative measures, is the zero-sum game consideration. This means that any change must add up to zero. For example, if 12 employees in a department perform at different levels of effectiveness, by definition, 3 are in the top quarter, 3 are in the second quarter, and so forth. The sixth-best employee, for instance, would be in the second quartile. Ironically, if two of the workers in the third or fourth quartiles leave the department and are not replaced, then our sixth-best employee now falls into the third quarter. Because comparisons are relative, a mediocre employee may score high only because he or she is the "best of the worst." In contrast, an excellent performer matched against "stiff" competition may be evaluated poorly, when in absolute terms his or her performance is outstanding.

individual ranking

Ranking employees' performance from highest to lowest.

Individual Ranking The **individual ranking** method requires the evaluator merely to list employees in order from highest to lowest. In this process, only one employee can be rated "best." If the evaluator is must appraise 30 individuals, this method assumes that the difference between the first and second employee is the same as that between the twenty-first and the twenty-second. Even though some of these employees may be closely grouped, this method typically allows for no ties. In terms of advantages and disadvantages, the individual ranking method carries the same pluses and minuses as group-order ranking. For example, individual ranking may be more manageable in a department of 6 employees than in one where a supervisor must evaluate the 19 employees that report to her.

paired comparison

Ranking individuals' performance by counting the times any one individual is the preferred member when compared with all other employees.

Paired Comparison The **paired comparison** method is calculated by taking the total of $[N(N - 1)]/2$ comparisons. A score is obtained for each employee by simply counting the number of pairs in which the individual is the preferred member. It ranks each individual in relationship to all others on a one-on-one basis. If 10 employees are evaluated, the first person is compared, one by one, with each of the other nine, and the number of times this person is preferred in any of the nine pairs is tabulated. Each of the remaining nine persons, in turn, is compared in the same way, and a ranking is formed by the greatest number of preferred "victories." This method ensures that each employee is compared against every other, but the method can become unwieldy when comparing large numbers of employees.

Using Achieved Outcomes to Evaluate Employees

The third approach to appraisal makes use of achieved performance outcomes. Employees are evaluated on how well they accomplished a specific set of objectives determined as critical in the successful completion of their job. This approach is frequently referred to as goal setting, in many cases, more commonly referred to as **management by objectives (MBO)**. Management by objectives is not new. The concept goes back almost 50 years.[23] Its appeal lies in its emphasis on converting overall objectives into specific objectives for organizational units and individual members.

management by objectives (MBO)

A performance appraisal method that includes mutual objective setting and evaluation based on the attainment of the specific objectives.

MBO makes objectives operational by a process in which they cascade down through the organization. The organization's overall objectives are translated into specific objectives for each succeeding level—divisional, departmental, individual—in the organization.[24] Because lower-unit managers participate in setting their own goals, MBO works from the bottom up as well as from the top down. The result is a hierarchy that links objectives at one level to those at the next level. For the individual employee, MBO provides specific personal performance objectives. Each person, therefore, has an identified specific contribution to make to his or her unit's performance. If all the individuals achieve their goals, the unit will meet its goals. Subsequently, the organization's overall objectives will become a reality.

Common Elements in an MBO Program Four ingredients are common to MBO programs: goal specificity, participative decision making, an explicit time period, and performance feedback. Let's briefly look at each of these.

The objectives in MBO should be concise statements of expected accomplishments. It is not adequate, for example, merely to state a desire to cut costs, improve service, or increase quality.[25] Such desires need to be converted into tangible objectives that can be measured and evaluated—for instance, to cut departmental costs by 8 percent, to improve service by ensuring that all insurance claims are processed within 72 hours of receipt, or to increase quality by keeping returns to less than 0.05 percent of sales.

MBO objectives are not unilaterally set by the boss and assigned to employees, as is characteristic of traditional objective setting. Rather, MBO replaces imposed goals with participatively determined goals. The manager and employee jointly choose the goals and agree on how they will be achieved. Each objective has a concise time, too, in which it is to be completed, typically, three months, six months, or a year.

The final ingredient in an MBO program is continuous feedback on performance and goals. Ideally, ongoing feedback allows individuals to monitor and correct their own actions. This is supplemented by periodic formal appraisal meetings in which superiors and subordinates review progress toward goals and which lead to further feedback.

Does MBO Work? Assessing MBO effectiveness is a complex task. Let's briefly review a growing body of literature on the relationship between goals and performance.[26] If factors such as a person's ability and acceptance of goals are held constant, more difficult goals lead to higher performance. Although individuals with difficult goals achieve them far less often than those who have easy goals, they nevertheless perform at a consistently higher level.

Moreover, studies consistently support the finding that specific, difficult goals produce higher output than no goals or generalized goals such as "do your best." Feedback also favorably affects performance. Feedback lets a person know whether his or her effort is sufficient or needs to increase. It can induce a person to raise his or her goal level after attaining a previous goal and indicate ways to improve performance.

The results cited here are all consistent with MBO's emphasis on specific goals and feedback. MBO implies, rather than explicitly states, that goals must be perceived as feasible. Research on goal setting indicates that MBO is most effective if the goals are difficult enough to require some stretching.

But what about participation? MBO strongly advocates that goals be set participatively. Does the research demonstrate that participatively set goals lead to higher performance than those assigned by a manager? Somewhat surprisingly, research comparing participatively set goals with assigned goals has shown no strong or consistent relationship to performance.[27] When goal difficulty has been held constant, assigned goals frequently do as well as participatively determined goals, contrary to MBO ideology. Therefore, it is not possible to argue for the superiority of participation as MBO proponents do. One major benefit from participation, however, is that it appears to induce individuals to set more difficult goals. Thus, participation may have a positive effect on performance by increasing one's goal aspiration level.

Studies of actual MBO programs confirm that MBO effectively increases employee performance and organizational productivity. One of the more critical components of this effectiveness is top management commitment to the MBO process. When top managers had a high commitment to MBO and were personally involved in its implementation, productivity gains were higher than if this commitment was lacking.[28]

www.wiley.com/college/decenzo
What Would You Do?
EXPERIENCE: Performance Evaluation

MBO's advantage lies in its result-oriented emphasis.

FACTORS THAT CAN DISTORT APPRAISALS

The performance appraisal process and techniques that we have suggested present systems in which the evaluator is free from personal biases, prejudices, and idiosyncrasies. This is defended on the basis that objectivity minimizes potential arbitrary and dysfunctional behavior by the evaluator, which may adversely affect achievement of organizational goals. Thus, our goal should be to use direct performance criteria where possible.

It would be naive to assume, however, that all evaluators impartially interpret and standardize the criteria on which their employees will be appraised. This is particularly true of jobs difficult to program and for which developing hard performance standards is most difficult—if not impossible. These would include, but are certainly not limited to, such jobs as researcher, teacher, engineer, and consultant. In the place of such standards, we can expect appraisers to use nonperformance or subjective criteria against which to evaluate individuals.[29]

A completely error-free performance appraisal is only an ideal we can aim for. In reality, most appraisals fall short, often through one or more actions that can significantly impede objective evaluation. We've briefly described them in Exhibit 10-5.

Leniency Error

leniency error
Performance appraisal distortion caused by evaluating employees against one's own value system.

Every evaluator has his or her own value system that acts as a standard against which appraisals are made. Relative to the true or actual performance an individual exhibits, some evaluators mark high, while others mark low. The former is referred to as positive **leniency error,** and the latter as negative leniency error. When evaluators are positively lenient in their appraisal, an individual's performance becomes overstated. In doing so, the performance is rated higher than it actually should be. Similarly, a negative leniency error understates performance, giving the individual a lower appraisal.

If all individuals in an organization were appraised by the same person, there would be no problem. Any error factor would be applied equally to everyone.[30] The difficulty arises when we have different raters with different leniency errors. For example, assume a situation where Jones and Smith are performing the same job for different supervisors with absolutely identical job performance. If Jones's supervisor tends to err toward positive leniency while Smith's supervisor errs toward negative leniency, we might be confronted with two dramatically different evaluations.

EXHIBIT 10-5
Factors That Distort Appraisals

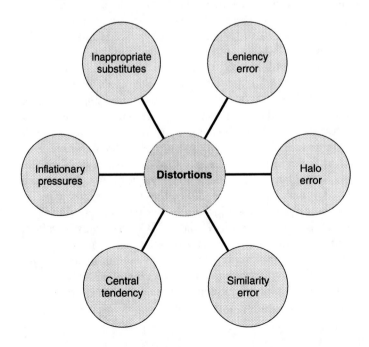

Halo Error

The **halo error** or effect occurs when one is rated either extremely high or extremely low on all factors based on a rating of one or two factors. For example, if an employee tends to be conscientious and dependable, we might become biased toward that individual to the extent that we will rate him or her positively on many desirable attributes.

People who design teaching appraisal forms for college students to fill out in evaluating instructor effectiveness each semester must confront the halo effect. Students tend to rate a faculty member as outstanding on all criteria when they are particularly appreciative of a few things he or she does in the classroom. Similarly, a few bad habits—showing up late for lectures, being slow in returning papers, or assigning an extremely demanding reading requirement—might produce "lousy" ratings across the board.

One method frequently used to deal with the halo error is "reverse wording" evaluation questions so that a favorable answer for, say, question 17 might be 5 on a scale of 1 through 5, and a favorable answer for question 18 might be 1 on a scale of 1 through 5. Structuring questions thus seeks to reduce the halo error by requiring the evaluator to consider each question independently. Another method, where more than one person is evaluated, is to have the evaluator appraise all ratees on each dimension before going on to the next dimension.

halo error
The tendency to let our assessment of an individual on one trait influence our evaluation of that person on other specific traits.

Similarity Error

When evaluators rate other people in the same way that the evaluators perceive themselves, they make a **similarity error.** That is, they project self-perceptions onto others. For example, the evaluator who perceives himself or herself as aggressive may evaluate others by looking for aggressiveness. Those who demonstrate this characteristic tend to benefit, and others who lack it may be penalized.

similarity error
Evaluating employees based on the way an evaluator perceives himself or herself.

Low Appraiser Motivation

If the evaluator knows that a poor appraisal could significantly hurt the employee's future—particularly opportunities for promotion or a salary increase—the evaluator may be reluctant to give a realistic appraisal. Evidence indicates that it is more difficult to obtain accurate appraisals when important rewards depend on the results.

Central Tendency

It is possible that regardless of who the appraiser evaluates and what traits are used, the pattern of evaluation remains the same. Sometimes the evaluator's ability to appraise objectively and accurately has been impeded by a failure to use the extremes of the scale. When this happens, we call the action **central tendency.** Central tendency occurs when a rater refuses to use the two extremes (for instance, outstanding and unacceptable, respectively). Raters prone to the central tendency error continually rate all employees as average. For example, if a supervisor rates all employees as 3 on a scale of 1 to 5, no differentiation among the employees exists. Failure to rate deserving employees as 5 or as 1, as the case warrants it, will only create problems, especially if this information is used for pay increases.

central tendency
The tendency of a rater to give average ratings.

Inflationary Pressures

A middle manager in a large Minnesota-based company could not understand why he had been passed over for promotion. He had seen his file and knew that his average rating by his supervisor was 88. Given his knowledge that the appraisal system defined outstanding performance at 90 or above, good as 80 or above, average as 70 or above, and inadequate performance as anything below 70, he was at a loss to understand why he had not been promoted. The manager's confusion was only somewhat resolved when he found out that the "average" rating for middle managers in his organization was 92. This example addresses a major potential problem in appraisals: inflationary pressures. This, in effect, is a specific case of low differentiation within the upper range of the rating choices.

Inflationary pressures have always existed but appear to have increased as a problem over the past three decades. As "equality" values have grown in importance in our society, as well as fear of retribution from disgruntled employees who fail to achieve excellent appraisals, evaluation has tended to be less rigorous and negative repercussions from the evaluation to be reduced by generally inflating or upgrading appraisals. However, inflating these evaluations has put many organizations in a difficult position when having to defend their personnel action in the case of discharging an employee.

Inappropriate Substitutes for Performance

It is the unusual job that has an absolutely clear performance definition and direct measures for appraising the incumbent. It is more often difficult to find consensus on what is "a good job," and it is even more difficult to produce agreement on what criteria determine performance.[31] Criteria for a salesperson are affected by factors such as economic conditions and actions of competitors—factors outside the salesperson's control. As a result, the appraisal frequently uses substitutes for performance, criteria that supposedly closely approximate performance and act in its place. Many of these substitutes are well chosen and give a good approximation of actual performance. However, the substitutes chosen are not always appropriate. It is not unusual, for example, to find organizations using criteria such as effort, enthusiasm, neatness, positive attitudes, conscientiousness, promptness, and congeniality as substitutes for performance. In some jobs, one or more of these criteria are part of performance. Obviously, enthusiasm does enhance teacher effectiveness; you are more likely to listen to and be motivated by an enthusiastic teacher than by one who is not; increased attentiveness and motivation typically lead to increased learning. But enthusiasm may in no way be relevant to effective performance for many accountants, watch repairers, or copy editors. An appropriate substitute for performance in one job may be totally inappropriate in another.

Attribution Theory

attribution theory

A theory of performance evaluation based on the perception of who is in control of an employee's performance.

In a concept in management literature called **attribution theory,** employee evaluations are directly affected by a "supervisor's perceptions of who is believed to be in control of the employee's performance—the employer or the manager."[32] Attribution theory attempts to differentiate between elements the employee controls (internal) versus those the employee cannot control (external). For example, if an employee fails to finish a project he has had six months to complete, a supervisor may view this negatively if he or she believes that the employee did not manage either the project or his time well (internal control). Conversely, if the project is delayed because top management requested a change in priorities, a supervisor may see the incomplete project in more positive terms (external control).

One research study found support for two key generalizations regarding attribution:[33]

- When appraisers attribute an employee's poor performance to internal control, the judgment is harsher than when the same poor performance is attributed to external factors.
- When an employee performs satisfactorily, appraisers will evaluate the employee more favorably if the performance is attributed to the employee's own efforts than if the performance is attributed to outside forces.

Attribution theory is interesting and sheds new light on rater effects on performance evaluations, but it requires continued study. It does provide much insight on why unbiased performance evaluations are important. An extension of attribution theory relates to *impression management,* which takes into account how the employee influences the relationship with his or her supervisor. That is, where an employee positively impresses his or her supervisor, there is a strong likelihood that the individual's performance rating will be higher.

CREATING MORE EFFECTIVE PERFORMANCE MANAGEMENT SYSTEMS

The fact that evaluators frequently encounter problems with performance appraisals should not lead us to throw up our hands and abandon the concept (see Technology Corner). Performance appraisals can be more effective. In this section, we offer suggestions to be considered individually or in combination (see Exhibit 10-6).

Use Behavior-Based Measures

As we have pointed out, the evidence favors behavior-based measures over those developed around traits. Many traits often related to good performance may, in fact, have little or no performance relationship. Traits such as loyalty, initiative, courage, reliability, and self-expression are intuitively desirable in employees, but are individuals who rate high on those traits higher performers than those who rate low? Of course, we can't definitively answer this question. We know employees sometimes rate high on these characteristics and are poor performers. Yet we can find others who are excellent performers but score poorly on traits such as these. Our conclusion is that traits like loyalty and initiative may be prized by appraisers, but no evidence supports the notion that certain traits will be adequate synonyms for performance in a large cross-section of jobs.

A second weakness in traits is the judgment itself. What is loyalty? When is an employee reliable? What you consider loyalty, we may not. So traits suffer from weak agreement between raters. Behavior-derived measures can deal with both of these objections. Because they deal with specific examples of performance—both good

How would you rate the coaching effectiveness of Chicago White Sox baseball manager Ozzie Guillén? If you evaluate him based on his team's 2005 win-loss record, or getting the White Sox into the postseason playoff for the first time in years, you might come to a positive conclusion. (Source: © AP/Wide World Photos)

TECHNOLOGY CORNER

TECHNOLOGY AND THE EMPLOYEE APPRAISAL

If one was told that technology would be assisting managers in the performance appraisal process, no one would be overly surprised. As we've seen in many organizational activities, computers have made life easier. The managers at UPS can attest to that.

As part of the employee evaluation process, managers are expected to ride along with drivers, assessing them on a variety of metrics—including how drivers adhere to organizational safety practices. In the past, supervisors would ride with the drivers, making notes on what they observed, and then, on returning to their office, write up a report. In many cases, problems arose because supervisors forgot something or waited until much later to write up their report and forgot something vital to the review.

To eliminate this problem, UPS management now equips each supervisor with a personal digital assistant

(PDA). The PDA contains special software developed for UPS that is designed to standardize the appraisal process. In doing so, each supervisor places a checkmark on a list of activities the driver is expected to complete while on the road. The data is then transmitted to the supervisor's computer.

The benefits of such technology are exceptional. Not only are critical elements of the driver's job being evaluated in real time, the software enables supervisors to evaluate all drivers exactly the same. Accordingly, UPS has found that a driver will have an objective evaluation of his or her duties regardless of who is conducting the analysis. This means that evaluations are fair to all drivers and free from bias. As a bonus, areas that are not checked immediately identify those areas of improvement or training that is necessary for a driver.

Documentation, feedback, development—three elements critical to a successful performance management system—all evident in technology-laden activity!

Source: "Online Objectivity," *Training* (July 2004), p. 18.

EXHIBIT 10-6
Toward a More Effective Performance Management System

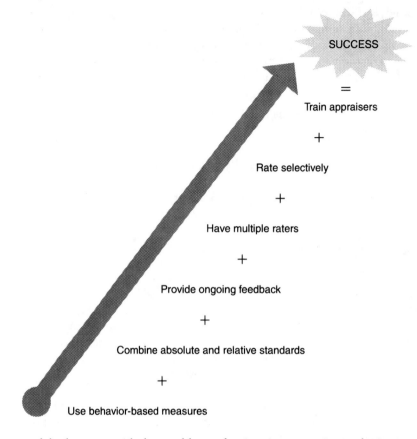

SUCCESS

=

Train appraisers

+

Rate selectively

+

Have multiple raters

+

Provide ongoing feedback

+

Combine absolute and relative standards

+

Use behavior-based measures

and bad—we avoid the problem of using inappropriate substitutes. Additionally, because we are evaluating specific behaviors, we increase the likelihood that two or more evaluators will see the same thing. You might consider a given employee as friendly, while we might perceive her as standoffish. But when asked to rate her in terms of specific behaviors, we might both agree that she "frequently says 'Good morning' to customers," "willingly gives advice or assistance to co-workers," and "always consolidates her cash drawer at the end of her work day."

Combine Absolute and Relative Standards

A major drawback to individual or absolute standards is that they tend to be biased by positive leniency; that is, evaluators lean toward packing their subjects into the high part of the rankings. On the other hand, relative standards suffer when there is little actual variability among the subjects. The obvious solution is to consider using appraisal methods that combine both absolute and relative standards. For example, you might want to use the adjective rating scale and the individual ranking method. This dual method of appraisal, incidentally, has been instituted at some universities to deal with the problem of grade inflation. Students receive an absolute grade—A, B, C, D, or F—and next to it is a relative mark showing how this student ranked in the class. A prospective employer or graduate school admissions committee can look at two students who each received a B in their international finance course and draw considerably different conclusions about each when next to one grade it says "ranked 4th out of 33," while the other "ranked 17th out of 21." Clearly, the latter instructor gave a lot more high grades!

Provide Ongoing Feedback

Several years back, a nationwide motel chain advertised, "The best surprise is no surprise." This phrase clearly applies to performance appraisals. Employees like to know how they are doing. The annual review, where the appraiser shares the employees' evaluations with them, can become a problem, if only because appraisers put them off. This is particularly likely if the appraisal is negative, but the annual review is additionally troublesome if the supervisor "saves up" performance-related information and unloads it during the appraisal review. This creates an extremely trying experience for both evaluator and employee. In such instances, the supervisor may attempt to avoid uncomfortable issues that the employee will likely deny or rationalize.

The solution lies in the appraiser frequently discussing with the employee both expectations and disappointments. Providing the employee with repeated opportunities to discuss performance before any reward or punishment consequences occur will eliminate surprises at the formal annual review. Ongoing feedback should keep the formal sitting-down step from being particularly traumatic for either party. Additionally, ongoing feedback is the critical element in an MBO system that actually works.

Use Multiple Raters

As the number of raters increases, the probability of attaining more accurate information increases.[34] If rater error follows a normal curve, an increase in the number of raters will find the majority clustering about the middle. If a person has had 10 supervisors, 9 of whom rated him or her excellent and 1 poor, then we must investigate what went into that one. Maybe this rater identified an area of weakness needing training or an area to be avoided in future job assignments.[35] Therefore, by moving employees about within the organization to add evaluations, we increase the probability of achieving more valid and reliable evaluations—as well as helping support needed changes. Of course, we assume that the process functions properly and bias-free![36] And let's not forget about the self-rating. Giving employees the opportunity to evaluate themselves and using that information as part of the evaluation process has been shown to increase employee satisfactions.[37]

Use Peer Evaluations Have you ever wondered why a professor asks you to evaluate one another's contributions to a group or team project? The reasoning behind this action is that the professor cannot tell what every member did on the project, only the overall product quality. And at times, that may not be fair to everyone—especially if someone left most of the work up to the remaining group members.

Similarly, supervisors find it difficult to evaluate their employees' performance because they are not observing them every moment of the work day. Unfortunately, without this information, they may not be making an accurate assessment. And if their goal for the performance evaluation is to identify deficient areas and provide constructive feedback to their employees, they do these workers a disservice by not having sufficient data. One of the better means of gathering information is through **peer evaluations**. Peer evaluations are conducted by the employees' co-workers—people explicitly familiar with the behaviors involved in their jobs.

The main advantages of peer evaluation are (1) the tendency for co-workers to offer more constructive insight to each other so that, as a unit, each will improve; and (2) recommendations tend to be more specific regarding job behaviors. Without specificity, constructive measures may be hard to obtain. But caution is in order because these systems, if not handled properly, could lead to increases in halo effects and leniency errors and fear among employees. Thus, along with training our supervisors to properly appraise employee performance, so too must we train peers to evaluate one another.

A slight deviation from peer assessments is a process called the **upward appraisal,** or the reverse review. Used in companies such as Pratt and Whitney, Dow Chemical, CitiCorp, and AT&T, upward appraisals permit employees to offer frank and constructive feedback to their supervisors on such areas as leadership and communication skills.

peer evaluation
A performance assessment in which co-workers provide input into the employee's performance.

upward appraisal
Employees provide frank and constructive feedback to their supervisors.

360-degree appraisals

Performance evaluations in which supervisors, peers, employees, customers, and the like evaluate the individual.

360-Degree Appraisals An appraisal device that seeks performance feedback from such sources as the person being rated, bosses, peers, team members, customers, and suppliers has become popular in organizations.[38] It's called the 360-degree appraisal.[39] It's being used in approximately 90 percent of the Fortune 1,000 firms, which include Otis Elevator, DuPont, Nabisco, Pfizer, ExxonMobil, Cook Children's Health Care System, General Electric, UPS, and Nokia.[40]

Traditional performance evaluations systems may be archaic in today's dynamic organizations.[41] Downsizing has given supervisors greater responsibility and more employees who report directly to them. Accordingly, in some instances, it is almost impossible for supervisors to have extensive job knowledge of each of their employees. Furthermore, the growth of project teams and employee involvement in today's companies places responsibility for evaluation at points at which people are better able to make an accurate assessment (see Workplace Issues).[42]

The 360-degree feedback process also has some positive benefits for development concerns.[43] Many managers simply do not know how their employees view them and their work. For instance, the corporate comptroller for Toronto, Canada, University Health Network was surprised to learn that the financial control system he strengthened over the past year actually seemed too bureaucratic to one of his peers. The feedback allowed the comptroller and peer to discuss the matter, resolve any tension between them, and enhance the internal control system now in place.[44]

Research studies into the effectiveness of 360-degree performance appraisals are generally reporting positive results from more accurate feedback, empowering employees, reducing subjective factors in the evaluation process, and developing leadership in an organization. But 360-degree systems are not without problems. Used improperly, studies do show they can be problematic.[45]

Rate Selectively

It has been suggested that appraisers should rate only in those areas in which they have significant job knowledge. If raters make evaluations on only dimensions they are in a good position to rate, we can increase the inter-rater agreement and make the evaluation a more valid process. This approach also recognizes that different organizational levels often have different orientations toward ratees and observe

WORKPLACE ISSUES

TEAM PERFORMANCE APPRAISALS

Performance evaluation concepts have been developed almost exclusively with individual employees in mind. This reflects the historic belief that individuals are the core building block on which organizations are built.[46] But as we've witnessed, more contemporary organizations are restructuring themselves around teams. How should organizations using teams evaluate performance? Four suggestions have been offered for designing an effective system that supports and improves team performance.[47]

1. Tie team results to organization goals. It's important to find measures that apply to important goals the team should accomplish.

2. Begin with the team's customers and its work process to satisfy customers' needs. The final product the customer receives can be evaluated in terms of the customer's requirements. Transactions between teams can be evaluated based on delivery and quality. And the process steps can be evaluated based on waste and cycle time.

3. Measure both team and individual performance. Define the roles of each team member in terms of accomplishments that support the team's work process. Then assess each member's contributions and the team's overall performance. Remember that individual skills are necessary for team success but are insufficient for good team performance.

4. Train the team to create its own measures. Having the team define its objectives and those of each member ensures everyone understands their role on the team and helps the team develop into a more cohesive unit.

them in different settings. In general, therefore, appraisers should be as close as possible to the organizational level of the individual evaluated. Conversely, the more levels separating the evaluator and employee, the less opportunity the evaluator has to observe the individual's work behavior and, not surprisingly, the greater the possibility for inaccuracies.

The specific application of these concepts makes immediate supervisors or co-workers the major input into the appraisal and lets them evaluate factors they are best qualified to judge. For example, it has been suggested that when professors evaluate secretaries within a university, they use such criteria as judgment, technical competence, and conscientiousness, whereas peers (other secretaries) evaluate, for example, job knowledge, organization, cooperation with co-workers, and responsibility.[48] Such an approach appears both logical and more reliable, because people appraise only those dimensions they are in a good position to judge.

In addition to taking into account the rater's place in the organization or what he or she is allowed to evaluate, selective rating should also consider the characteristics of the rater. If appraisers differ in traits, and if certain of these traits correlate with accurate appraisals and others correlate with inaccurate appraisals, it seems logical to attempt to identify effective raters. Those identified as especially effective could be given sole responsibility for doing appraisals, or greater weight could be given to their observations.

Train Appraisers

If you cannot find good raters, the alternative is to make good raters. Evidence indicates that training appraisers can make them more accurate raters.[49] Common errors such as halo and leniency can be minimized or eliminated when supervisors can practice observing and rating behaviors in workshops. Why should we bother to train these individuals? Because a poor appraisal is worse than no appraisal at all; they can demoralize employees, decrease productivity, and create a legal liability for the company.[50]

INTERNATIONAL PERFORMANCE APPRAISAL

Evaluating employee performance in international environments brings other factors into play. For instance, cultural differences between the parent country and the host country must be considered. Cultural differences between the United States and England are not as great as those between the United States and China, for example. Thus, hostility or friendliness of the cultural environment in which one manages should be considered when appraising employee performance.[51]

Who Performs the Evaluation?

Companies must also consider who will be responsible for the evaluations: the host-country management or the parent-country management. Although local managers would generally be considered a more accurate gauge, they typically evaluate expatriates from their own cultural perspectives and expectations, which may not reflect those of the parent country. For example, a participatory style of management is acceptable in some countries, and in others hierarchical values make it a disgrace to ask employees for ideas. This could vastly alter a supervisor's performance appraisal.

Confusion may arise from the use of parent-country evaluation forms if they are misunderstood, either because the form has been improperly translated or not translated at all, or because the evaluator is uncertain what a particular question means. The home-office management, on the other hand, is often so remote that it may not be fully informed on what is going on in an overseas office. Because they

Are the performance evaluations conducted on Home Depot employees in Mexico different from those conducted on employees in the United States? Logic tells us that evaluations, to be effective, must be adapted to the country in which employees operate. (Source: Tim Boyle/Getty Images)

DID YOU KNOW?

PERFORMANCE METRICS IN CHINA

As you have read through the performance appraisal materials presented in this chapter, one question may arise. That is, are the methods and means of appraising employees in North America similar to those practiced around the globe? There are similarities that may exist among all developed nations, but there are some dramatic differences. Several of these can be found in what is measured. To give you some perspective of this difference, let's look at how U.S. executives and Chinese executives are evaluated. Although the process may be similar, what's different is what is measured.

U.S. Executive Evaluation Focus	Chinese Executive Evaluation Focus
Ability to Do Job	Industriousness (Determination)
Technical Ability	Diligence
Management Skills	Positive Attitude
Cultural Empathy	Compliance with Rules
Adaptability and Flexibility	
Creativity	

What do these differences tell us? They tell us what's important for one to be successful—and if a North American executive is sent to China (or vice versa), how that individual is measured will be different. Accordingly, the expatriate must understand the culture in which he or she will work and adjust work attributes accordingly. For instance, in the United States an executive can be creative—thinking outside the box—for a solution. That same behavior in China is not well regarded, as conformance and compliance with the way things are is the expectation.

Source: J. Shen, "International Performance Appraisals: Policies, Practices and Determinants in the Case of Chinese Multinational Companies," *International Journal of Manpower* Vol. 25, No. 6 (2004), pp. 547–556.

lack access and because one organization may have numerous foreign operations to evaluate, home-office managements often measure performance by quantitative indices, such as profits, market shares, or gross sales. However, "simple" numbers are often quite complex in their calculations, and data are not always comparable. For example, if a company has many operations in South America, it must be aware of the accounting practices in each country. Peru, for instance, counts sales on consignment as firm sales, and Brazil does not. Local import tariffs can also distort pricing schedules, which alter gross sales figures, another often-compared statistic. Even when the measurements are comparable, the comparison country will have an effect. For example, factory productivity levels in Mexico may be below those of similar plants in the United States, but American-owned plant productivity in Mexico may be above that of similar Mexican-owned plants. Depending on where the supervisor's results are compared, different outcomes may occur. Such issues complicate parent-country management performance evaluations by numerical criteria or indices—and can add to the emotional levels in appraisals.

Evaluation Formats

Other issues surround the question of selecting the best format to use in performance appraisals. If we have an overseas operation that includes both parent-country nationals (PCNs) and host-country nationals (HCNs), we must determine if we will use the same forms for all employees. Although most Western countries accept the concept of performance evaluation, some cultures interpret it as a sign of distrust or even an insult to an employee. This complicates a decision to use one instrument such as a graphic rating scale for all employees. On the other hand, using different formats for PCNs and HCNs may create a dual track in the subsidiary, in turn creating other problems.

The evaluation form presents other problems. If there is a universal form for the entire corporation, an organization must determine how it will be translated accurately into the native language of each country. English forms may not be readily understood by local supervisors. For example, clerical and office jobs do not always have identical requirements in all cultures. As a result, some U.S. multinationals may be hesitant about evaluating HCNs and TCNs (third-country nationals). In some countries, notably those that support the communist ideology, all workers are rewarded only when the group performs—with greatly limited punishment or discipline. You'll find this, for example, in the hotel industry in the People's Republic of China. Without the ability to reward good individual performance or to punish poor performance, any motivation to evaluate withers.

SUMMARY

(This summary relates to the Learning Outcomes identified on page 255.)
After having read this chapter, you can

1. **Identify the three purposes of performance management systems and whom they serve.** The three purposes of performance management systems are feedback, development, and documentation. They are designed to support employees, appraisers, and organizations.

2. **Explain the six steps in the appraisal process.** The six-step appraisal process is to (1) establish performance standards with employees, (2) set measurable goals (manager and employee), (3) measure actual performance, (4) compare actual performance with standards, (5) discuss the appraisal with the employee, and (6) if necessary, initiate corrective action.

3. **Discuss absolute standards in performance management systems.** Absolute standards refer to a method in performance management systems whereby employees are measured against company-set performance requirements. Absolute standard evaluation methods involve the essay appraisal, the critical incident approach, the checklist rating, the graphic rating scale, the forced-choice inventory, and the behaviorally anchored rating scale (BARS).

4. **Describe relative standards in performance management systems.** Relative standards refer to a method in performance management systems whereby an employee's performance is compared with that of other employees. Relative standard evaluation methods include group-order ranking, individual ranking, and paired comparisons.

5. **Discuss how MBO can be an appraisal method.** MBO becomes an appraisal method by establishing a specific set of objectives for an employee to achieve and reviewing performance based on how well those objectives have been met.

6. **Explain why performance appraisals might be distorted.** Performance appraisal might be distorted for several reasons, including leniency error, halo error, similarity error, central tendency, low appraiser motivation, inflationary pressures, and inappropriate substitutes for performance.

7. **Identify ways to make performance management systems more effective.** More effective appraisals can be achieved with behavior-based measures, combined absolute and relative ratings, ongoing feedback, multiple raters, selective rating, trained appraisers, peer assessment, and rewards to accurate appraisers.

8. **Describe the term *360-degree appraisal*.** In 360-degree performance appraisals, evaluations are made by oneself, supervisors, employees, team members, customers, suppliers, and the like. In doing so, a complete picture of one's performance can be assessed.

9. **Discuss how performance appraisals may differ in the global village.** Performance management systems used away from the home country may differ in who performs the evaluation and the format used. Cultural difference may dictate that changes in the U.S. performance management system are needed.

VISUAL SUMMARY

CHAPTER 10: ESTABLISHING THE PERFORMANCE MANAGEMENT SYSTEM

1 Performance Management Systems

Purposes
- Feedback
- Development
- Documentation

Difficulties
- Focus on the individual—may become emotional
- Focus on the process—follow a structure that misses some qualitative aspects

Performance Management and EEO

Integral part of most organizations

Must be bias-free

Must measure reasonable performance success

2 Appraisal Process

1. Establish performance standards with employees.

2. Mutually set measurable goals.

3. Measure actual performance.

4. Compare actual performance with standards.

5. Discuss the appraisal with the employee.

6. If necessary, initiate corrective action.

3 Appraisal Methods

One-on-One

Absolute Appraisal Methods
- Critical incident
- Checklist
- Graphic rating scales
- Forced choice
- Behaviorally anchored rating scale

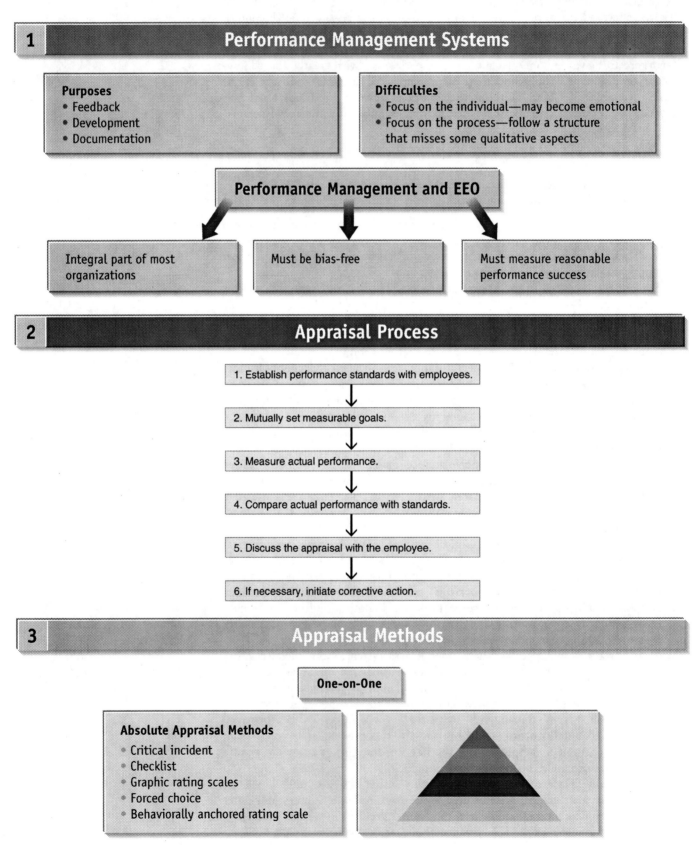

278

3   Appraisal Methods (cont'd)

One-on-Many

Relative Appraisal Methods
- Group order ranking
- Individual ranking
- Paired comparison

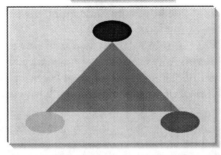

Outcomes-Based or Management by Objective (MBO) Methods

Common elements:
- Goal specificity
- Participating decision making
- Explicit time period
- Performance feedback

4   Factors That Can Distort Appraisals

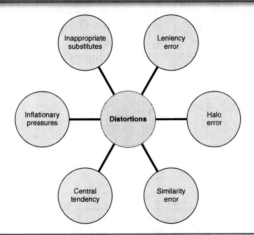

5   Creating More Effective Performance Management Systems

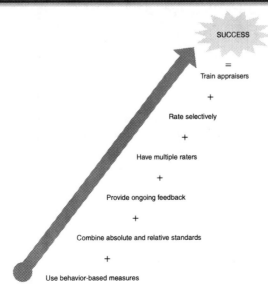

DEMONSTRATING COMPREHENSION: *Questions for Review*

1. To what three purposes can performance appraisal be applied, and whom do they serve?
2. Describe the appraisal process. How should it work?
3. Contrast the advantages and disadvantages of (1) absolute standards and (2) relative standards.
4. What is BARS? Why might BARS be better than trait-oriented measures?
5. Describe MBO, its advantages and disadvantages.
6. What are some major factors that distort performance appraisals?
7. How should performance appraisals change when teams, rather than individuals, are evaluated?
8. What is a 360-degree feedback process? How valid do you believe one to be?
9. Identify ways to make performance evaluations more effective. Do you believe one of the suggestions is of higher priority than the others? Explain.
10. How does the global nature of business affect performance management systems?

KEY TERMS

absolute standards
attribution theory
behaviorally anchored rating scales (BARS)
central tendency
checklist appraisal
critical incident appraisal
documentation
forced-choice appraisal
graphic rating scale
halo error
individual ranking
leniency error
management by objectives (MBO)
paired comparison
peer evaluation
relative standards
similarity error
upward appraisal
360-degree appraisals

CROSSWORD COMPREHENSION

ACROSS

2. a method of performance appraisal that lists traits and a range of performance for each
4. measuring employees' performance by comparing employees to one another

7. performance evaluations in which supervisors, peers, employers, customers, and the like evaluate the individual
9. a performance appraisal method in which the rater must choose between two specific statements about an employee's work behavior
10. performance appraisal error caused by a rater's overuse of average ratings
11. performance appraisal error based on the way an evaluator perceives him- or herself
12. performance appraisal error caused by the tendency to let one's assessment of an individual on one trait influence the evaluation of that person on other traits
13. employees provide frank and constructive feedback to their supervisors
15. a theory of performance evaluation based on the perception of who is in control of an employee's performance
16. a record of performance appraisal outcomes
18. performance appraisal error caused by evaluating employees against one's own value system
19. a method of performance appraisal in which the rater answers yes or no to applicable employee attributes

DOWN

1. ranking employees' performance by counting the times any one individual is the preferred member when viewed with all other employees
3. identifying employee performance from highest to lowest
5. a performance appraisal method that focuses on key behaviors that differentiate between doing the job effectively or not
6. a performance assessment in which co-workers provide input into the employee's performance
8. a performance appraisal method that generates critical incidents and develops behavioral dimensions of performance
14. measuring employees' performance against established standards
17. a performance appraisal method that includes mutual objective setting and evaluation based on the attainment of the specific objectives

HRM WORKSHOP

LINKING CONCEPTS TO PRACTICE: *Discussion Questions*

1. "Performance appraisal should be a multifaceted. Supervisors should evaluate their employees, and employees should be able to evaluate their supervisors. And customers should evaluate them all." Do you agree or disagree with this statement? Discuss.
2. "The higher the position an employee occupies in an organization, the easier it is to appraise his or her performance objectively." Do you agree or disagree with this statement? Why?
3. "Using an invalid performance evaluation instrument is a waste of time." Do you agree or disagree with this statement? Discuss.
4. "Without a supportive culture in an organization, peer evaluations are subject to too many distortions. Accordingly, they should not be widely used." Do you agree or disagree? Defend your position.
5. "Customers feedback needs to be part of every employee's evaluation when that employee has customer contact." Do you agree or disagree? Explain your position.

DEVELOPING DIAGNOSTIC AND ANALYTICAL SKILLS

Case Application 10A: RANK 'EM AND YANK 'EM

Imagine you're the VP of human resources for a Fortune 100 company. You've spent your entire career attempting to enhance the workplace for employees to support their productive work in the organization. While you understand that bottom-line decisions often dominate many of the matters you have to address, you've worked hard to ensure that employees were treated with respect and dignity in all interactions that affected them. You aligned the hiring process to serve the strategic needs of the organization, as well as implementing an effective performance management system. You truly believe in the progress you've made in helping the organization achieve its goals. You simply couldn't imagine doing things differently. But outside pressure could change all of that. It was such pressures that have led upward of 20 percent of all large organizations to adjust their performance management process to what is frequently called rank and yank.[52]

Under such a system, managers are evaluated as a 1, 2, 3, or 4, with 1 being the highest rating and 4 the lowest. In many cases, managers are required to give a 4 rating to the lowest 10 percent of employees each year. Those individuals receiving a rating of 4 for two consecutive years are often severed from the organization. The intent behind this system is that throughout the two-year process, evaluators are to meet frequently with the 4 employees, counseling them, and providing necessary development opportunities.

Employees in organizations that employ such a performance management system often view such a process as unbearable. They view the performance management process as punitive, one in which the organization is attempting to rid itself of higher-paid older workers. In at least one case, Ford Motor Company employees have filed a lawsuit to stop this practice—and prevailed. Ford removed the punitive nature of its evaluation system—and

focused it more on counseling and performance improvement rather than elimination from the organization.

What long-term effect does a performance management system that focuses on rank and yank have on the organization? Only time will tell. One thing we do know, however, is that since the performance management system was eliminated at Ford, nearly 5,000 managers were laid off! One has to wonder if there is any connection between the two.

Questions:

1. What type of evaluation process would you say is being used in this case? Describe the elements to support your position.
2. What effect, if any, do you believe rank and yank evaluation systems have on managers? Do you see these effects as positive or negative? Defend your position.
3. What role does such a system have in distorting performance appraisals?
4. Do you believe there is a connection between the "revised" performance evaluation system and layoffs? Why or why not?

Case Application 10-B: TEAM FUN!

Team Fun

Kenny and Norton, owners of TEAM FUN!, a sporting goods manufacturer and retailer, are hosting their annual management retreat at a hunting lodge in central Canada. This year, the attendees are Tony, director of human resources; Josephine, comptroller; Arlien from marketing, research, and production operations; and the three retail branch store managers, Eric, Joe, and Bobby. They are in day 3 of the hunting, fishing, planning, and evaluating week. Settling into an afternoon of performance appraisal discussions, Tony places soggy agendas in front of them.

Kenny punches Norton in the ribs and says, "Looks like I can catch a 3–4-hour nap this afternoon. Let me know if anyone says anything funny." He turns to Tony, "Sorry about cleaning the fish on these papers of yours. Looked like fish-gut paper to me! Whew. Maybe the smell will keep me awake." The group spent yesterday talking about the successes and failures of each branch for the past year. They talked about each employee, and how that individual helped or hindered overall operations. It was decided to move a few people to new assignments for the coming year.

Tony starts: "Apparently TEAM FUN! has been using a modified MBO process for all of its employees."

Eric, who has run operations since the company was founded, agrees, "Yes, from what you said about MBO, we do. I know I work out with each shift and team goals for each quarter. We usually have five or six goals for each person and group. If all are met, we all get a nice bonus from the profit share plan. If most are met, we get decent raises. One year, no one got raises."

Norton shakes his head, "That was a tough time. We turned it around faster than most, though. And we didn't lay anyone off."

Bobby asks, "What would be good sales goals? My guys set goals like these, for example: Attract 10,000 customers a month by the third month of operation. Keep shrinkage/breakage under 0.5 percent. Have zero customer complaints and returns. Every cash register balances at the end of each shift. All employees speak both Spanish and English."

Tony comments, "Bobby, you were a special case because the south Florida store just opened this year."

Josephine adds, "You all need good financial goals—for each and every employee."

Arlien snaps, "Bobby, you need to sell more. And we need to know what you are promising customers *before* they call to ask me why it's late."

Kenny wakes up and asks, "What about the fun? Do you have goals for fun? Eric, what were you saying about relative and absolute standards for fun that you learned in that supervisor class that Tony sent you and Joe to?"

Tony brightens up and pulls out a chart on absolute rating scales, "Now we're talking!"

Questions:

1. Does TEAM FUN! follow the six-step appraisal process?
2. Is an MBO plan good for the company? What could be done to improve it? Evaluate Bobby's goals according to MBO criteria. Suggest an alternative to their MBO exclusive performance appraisal process.
3. Comment on the overall effectiveness of the performance appraisal process at TEAM FUN!
4. Provide an outline for their discussion on absolute and relative measurement techniques for "fun."

WORKING WITH A TEAM: *The 360-Degree Performance Appraisal*

Supervisors have not adapted as well as desired by management to a change in the appraisal system. As human resource management students, you and your class team have been asked to conduct a 30-minute presentation for 10 to 15 supervisors at the next supervisors' meeting. Develop a 30-minute presentation about the

purposes of the performance management systems, who benefits, and the six basic steps; clarify the difference between relative and absolute standards, with possible distortions; and introduce the 360-degree feedback system.

LEARNING AN HRM SKILL: *Conducting the Performance Evaluation*

About the skill: How does one properly conduct the performance appraisal process? We offer the following steps that can assist in this endeavor.[53]

1. *Prepare for and schedule the appraisal in advance.* Before meeting with employees, perform some preliminary activities. You should at a minimum review employee job descriptions, period goals that may have been set, and performance data on employees you may have. Furthermore, you should schedule the appraisal well in advance to give employees the opportunity to prepare their data, too, for the meeting.

2. *Create a supportive environment to put employees at ease.* Performance appraisals conjure up several emotions. Make every effort to keep employees comfortable during the meeting, such that they are receptive to constructive feedback.

3. *Describe the purpose of the appraisal to employees.* Make sure employees know precisely how the appraisal will be used. Will it have implications for pay increases, or other personnel decisions? If so, make sure employees understand exactly how the appraisal process works and its consequences.

4. *Involve the employee in the appraisal discussion, including a self-evaluation.* Performance appraisals should not be a one-way communication event. Although as supervisor, you may believe that you have to talk more in the meeting, that needn't be the case. Instead, employees should have ample opportunity to discuss their performance, raise questions about the facts you raise, and add their own data/perceptions about their work.[54] One means of ensuring two-way communication is to have employees conduct a self-evaluation. You should actively listen to their assessment. This involvement helps to create an environment of participation.

5. *Focus discussion on work behaviors, not on the employees.* One way of creating emotional difficulties is to attack the employee. Therefore, you should keep your discussion on

the behaviors you've observed. Telling an employee, for instance, that his report stinks does nothing. Indicating that you believe he didn't devote enough time to proofreading the report describes the behavior that may be a problem to you.

6. *Support your evaluation with specific examples.* Specific performance behaviors help clarify to employees the issues you raise. Rather than saying something wasn't good (subjective evaluation), you should be as specific as possible in your explanations. So, for the employee who failed to proof the work, describing that the report had five grammatical mistakes in the first two pages alone would be a specific example.

7. *Give both positive and negative feedback.* Performance appraisals needn't be all negative. Despite a perception that this process focuses on the negative, it should also be used to compliment and recognize good work. Positive, as well as negative, feedback helps employees gain a better understanding of their performance. For example, although the report was not up to the quality you expected, the employee did do the work and completed the report in a timely fashion. That behavior deserves some positive reinforcement.

8. *Ensure that employees understand what was discussed in the appraisal.* At the end of the appraisal, especially where some improvement is warranted, you should ask employees to summarize what you discussed in the meeting. This will help you ensure that you have gotten your information through to the employee.

9. *Generate a development plan.* Most of the performance appraisal revolves around feedback and documentation, but it needs another component. Where development efforts are encouraged, a plan should be developed to describe what is to be done, by when, and what you, the supervisor, will commit to aid in the improvement/enhancement effort.

ENHANCING YOUR COMMUNICATION SKILLS

1. Develop a two- to three-page paper describing the relationship between job analysis and performance evaluations. Cite specific examples where appropriate.

2. Visit the Web site nefried.com/360/360hrmagarticle. html. This article provides data on the pros and cons of using a 360-degree performance appraisal in an organization. Summarize the article and end the paper with your beliefs on

whether 360-degree evaluations should be used in all organizations.

3. Endnote 2 in this chapter refers to several recent articles regarding the potential obsolescence of performance appraisals. Select two of the cited articles, summarize them, and end your report with your analysis and conclusions.

ELEVEN

Imagine you are the human resources manager of a banking operation, and you are looking into a problem in one of your departments. This particular department has 48 employees whose jobs are to process customer checks. Their job requires them to input every customer's check accurately with correct account numbers and dollar amounts in a timely manner. But this is not happening a majority of the time. Incorrect inputting is causing customer satisfaction to decrease. And lateness results in penalties from the federal government bank overseers. Sadly, for Christopher Maurer, executive vice president for human resources at FirstMerit Bank headquartered in Akron, Ohio, this was not his imagination—it was a reality he faced.[1]

The check-proofing department consisted of 48 individuals—all with less than two years of experience in the job. That is, this department has had 100 percent turnover every two years—meaning that department and bank loyalty did not exist, which was creating a problem for FirstMerit. Starting salaries for these employees was approximately

(*Source:* Stockbyte/Getty Images, Inc.)

$9 per hour. Employees and bank officials recognized that the job was monotonous. Employees would spend hours a day typing written amounts on checks into their computers so the checks could be processed. But there was an expectation that although accuracy was paramount, speed was important, too—and employees felt that their pay was not consistent with the expectations of their jobs. Meeting the dual goal of speed and accuracy was something bank officials wanted to achieve, while at

the same time they wanted to find a way to help maintain employee loyalty. After studying the situation, Maurer believed that implementing a pay-for-performance plan would move the organization toward meeting its department goal.

FirstMerit's pay-for-performance program was relatively simple. Relying on the same computers employees were working on, employees would be evaluated on their speed and accuracy. Through an extensive analysis, bank officials determined that the minimum level of acceptable performance would be 10,000 keystrokes an hour. Those who exceeded 10,000 keystrokes an hour would receive extra pay—or pay for performance.

Since this pay-for-performance plan was implemented, the bank has reduced the number of employees in the department from 48 to 27. Of the 27 remaining employees, 1 averages $23 per hour, 9 earn $20 per hour, 13 are in the $15 to $19 per hour range, and 4 are performing at the minimum acceptable level. Overall, 22 of the 27 employees in the department earn in excess of $15 per hour—nearly double the base rate. As a result, employee morale has increased significantly as the performers feel like they are being compensated for their hard work. For the bank, turnover has dropped to zero, as no one has left, nor needed to be hired in the department in more than three years. Customer satisfaction has also increased. And productivity is up, which is remarkable given that the department has had a 44 percent staff reduction. Because of this success, FirstMerit is looking at ways to roll out pay-for-performance systems for other parts of the bank.

Establishing Rewards and Pay Plans

After reading this chapter, you will be able to

1. Explain the various classifications of rewards.

2. Discuss why we call some rewards membership based.

3. Define the goal of compensation administration.

4. Discuss job evaluation and its three basic approaches.

5. Explain the evolution of the final wage structure.

6. Describe competency-based compensation programs.

7. Discuss why executives' salaries are significantly higher than other employees'.

8. Describe the balance-sheet approach to international compensation.

INTRODUCTION

"What's in it for me?" Nearly every individual consciously or unconsciously asks this question before engaging in any behavior. Our knowledge of motivation and people's behavior at work tells us that people do what they do to satisfy needs. Before they do anything, therefore, they look for a payoff or reward.

The most obvious reward employees receive from work is pay. However, rewards also include promotions, desirable work assignments, and a host of other less obvious payoffs—a smile, peer acceptance, work freedom, or a kind word of recognition. We'll spend the majority of this chapter addressing pay as a reward as well as how organizations establish compensation programs.

Among the several ways to classify rewards, we have selected three of the most typical dichotomies: *intrinsic versus extrinsic rewards, financial versus nonfinancial rewards,* and *performance-based versus membership-based rewards.* As you will see, these categories are far from mutually exclusive, yet all share one common thread: they assist in maintaining employee commitment.

Intrinsic versus Extrinsic Rewards

Intrinsic rewards are the personal satisfactions one derives from doing the job. These are self-initiated rewards: pride in one's work, a sense of accomplishment, or enjoying being part of a work team.[2] Job enrichment, for instance (see Workplace Issues), can offer employees intrinsic rewards by making work seem more meaningful. **Extrinsic rewards,** on the other hand, include money, promotions, and benefits. They are external to the job and come from an outside source, mainly management.[3] Consequently, if an employee experiences a sense of achievement or personal growth from a job, we would label such rewards as intrinsic. If the employee receives a salary increase or a write-up in the company magazine, we would label these rewards as extrinsic. The general structure of rewards is summarized in Exhibit 11-1.

intrinsic rewards
Satisfactions derived from the job itself, such as pride in one's work, a feeling of accomplishment, or being part of a team.

extrinsic rewards
Benefits provided by the employer, usually money, promotion, or benefits.

job enrichment
Enhancing jobs by giving employees more opportunity to plan and control their work.

WORKPLACE ISSUES

JOB ENRICHMENT

The most popular structural technique for increasing an employee's reward potential is **job enrichment.** To enrich a job, management allows the worker to assume some of the tasks executed by his or her supervisor. Enrichment requires that workers increase work planning and control, usually with less supervision and more self-evaluation. Job enrichment offers great potential for increasing the internal motivation from doing a job. Motivation grows through increased responsibility, increased employee freedom and independence, tasks organized to allow individuals to complete activities, and feedback with which they can correct their own performance. These factors lead, in part, to a better quality of work life. Furthermore, job-enrichment efforts will succeed only if employees find the enrichment rewarding. If they do not want increased responsibility, for example, then increasing their responsibilities will not have the desired effect. Successful job enrichment, then, is contingent on worker input.

Although a successful job enrichment program increases employee satisfaction and commitment, organizations do not exist solely to create employee satisfaction. They require more direct benefits, as well. Evidence indicates that job enrichment and quality of life programs produce lower absenteeism, reduce turnover costs, and increase employee commitment, but on the critical issue of productivity, evidence is inconclusive or poorly measured. In some situations, job enrichment has increased productivity; in others, productivity has decreased. However, when it decreases, evidence suggests consistently conscientious use of resources and higher quality products or services. In other words, the same input produces higher quality output.

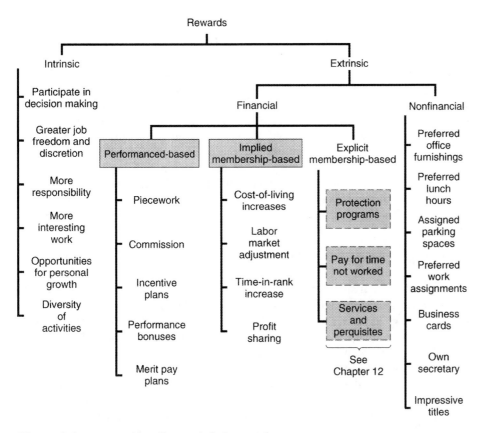

EXHIBIT 11-1
Structure of Rewards

Financial versus Nonfinancial Rewards

Rewards may or may not enhance the employee's financial well-being. Those that do, do so directly—for instance, through wages, bonuses, or profit sharing—or indirectly, through employer-subsidized benefits such as retirement plans, paid vacations, paid sick leaves, and purchase discounts.

Nonfinancial rewards present a smorgasbord of desirable extras for organizations. These do not directly increase the employee's financial position, but rather add attraction to life on the job. We will identify a few of the more general possibilities, but creation of these rewards is limited only by HRM's ingenuity and ability to use them to motivate desirable behavior.

The saying, "One person's food is another person's poison," applies to the entire subject of rewards, but specifically to nonfinancial rewards. What one employee views as "something I've always wanted," another might find relatively useless. Therefore, HRM must take great care in providing the right nonfinancial reward for each person. With proper selection, organizational benefits, by way of increased performance, should be significant.

Some workers, for example, are status conscious. A plush office, a carpeted floor, a large desk, or signed artwork may be just what stimulates them toward top performance. Similarly, status-oriented employees may value an impressive job title, their own business cards, their own administrative assistant, or a well-located parking space with their name clearly painted underneath the "Reserved" sign. Other employees may value opportunities to dress casually while at work or even work in part at home. Such incentives are within the organization's discretion and, carefully used, may enhance performance.

Performance-Based versus Membership-Based Rewards

Organizations allocate rewards based on either performance or membership criteria. HR representatives in many organizations will vigorously argue that their system rewards performance, but you should recognize that this isn't always the case.

Few organizations actually reward employees based on performance—a point we will discuss later in this chapter. Without question, the dominant basis for reward allocations in organizations is membership.

performance-based rewards
Rewards exemplified by the use of commissions, piecework pay plans, incentive systems, group bonuses, or other forms of merit pay.

Performance-based rewards use commissions, piecework pay plans, incentive systems, group bonuses, merit pay, or other forms of pay for performance. *Membership-based rewards,* on the other hand, include cost-of-living increases, benefits, and salary increases attributable to labor-market conditions, seniority or time in rank, credentials (such as a college degree or a graduate diploma), a specialized skill, or future potential (for example, the recent MBA graduate from of a prestigious university). The key point here is that membership-based rewards are generally extended regardless of an individual's, group's, or organization's performance. In any case, performance may be only a minor determinant of rewards, despite academic theories holding that high motivation depends on performance-based rewards.

COMPENSATION ADMINISTRATION

Why do regional managers at Bank of America in Dallas, Texas, earn more than the bank associates? Intuitively, you might say that the regional managers are more skilled and have greater job responsibility, so they should earn more. But how about regional managers who specialize in commercial accounts? Should they make more or less than regional managers who supervise several branch operations? The answers to questions such as these lie in job evaluation.

Job evaluation is the process whereby an organization systematically establishes its compensation program. In this process, jobs are compared to determine each job's appropriate worth within the organization. In this section we discuss the broader topic of compensation, narrow our discussion to job evaluation methods, and conclude with a review of an increasingly controversial topic—executive compensation.

Employees exchange work for rewards. Probably the most important reward, and indeed the most obvious, is money. But not all employees earn the same amount of money. Why? The search for this answer moves us directly into the topic of compensation administration.

compensation administration
The process of managing a company's compensation program.

The goal of **compensation administration** is to design a cost-effective pay structure that will attract, motivate, and retain competent employees.[4] The structure should also appear fair to employees. *Fairness* is a term that frequently arises in the administration of an organization's compensation program. Organizations generally seek to pay the least possible to minimize costs, so fairness means a wage or salary that is adequate for the demands and requirements of the job. Of course, fairness is a two-way street. Employees, too, want fair compensation. As we pointed out in our earlier discussion of motivation, if employees perceive an imbalance in their efforts-rewards ratio to some comparative standard, they will act to correct the inequity. Thus, both employers and employees pursue fairness.

Government Influence on Compensation Administration

In Chapter 3, we described how government policies shape and influence HRM. This influence, however, is unequally felt. For example, collective bargaining and the employee selection process are heavily constrained by government rules and regulations; employment planning and orientation are less so.

Compensation administration falls into the former category. Government policies set minimum wages and benefits that employers must meet, and these policies provide protection for certain groups (see Exhibit 11-2). The laws and regulations we will discuss are highlights only, chosen to help make you aware that government constraints reduce HRM's discretion on compensation decisions. An abundance of laws and regulations define the general parameters within which managers decide what is fair compensation. Let's look at some of these.

Exhibit 11-2
Federal Minimum Wage

Your Rights Under the Fair Labor Standards Act

Federal Minimum Wage

$4.75 per hour
beginning October 1, 1996

$5.15 per hour
beginning September 1, 1997

Employees under 20 years of age may be paid $4.25 per hour during their first 90 consecutive calendar days of employment with an employer.

Certain full-time students, student learners, apprentices, and workers with disabilities may be paid less than the minimum wage under special certificates issued by the Department of Labor.

Tip Credit – Employers of "tipped employees" must pay a cash wage of at least $2.13 per hour if they claim a tip credit against their minimum wage obligation. If an employee's tips combined with the employer's cash wage of at least $2.13 per hour do not equal the minimum hourly wage, the employer must make up the difference. Certain other conditions must also be met.

Overtime Pay

At least $1\frac{1}{2}$ times your regular rate of pay for all hours worked over 40 in a workweek.

Child Labor

An employee must be at least **16** years old to work in most non-farm jobs and at least **18** to work in non-farm jobs declared hazardous by the Secretary of Labor. Youths **14** and **15** years old may work outside school hours in various non-manufacturing, non-mining, non-hazardous jobs under the following conditions:

No more than –
- **3** hours on a school day or **18** hours in a school week;
- **8** hours on a non-school day or **40** hours in a non-school week.

Also, work may not begin before **7 a.m.** or end after **7 p.m.**, except from **June 1** through **Labor Day**, when evening hours are extended to **9 p.m.** Different rules apply in agricultural employment.

Enforcement

The Department of Labor may recover back wages either administratively or through court action, for the employees that have been underpaid in violation of the law. Violations may result in civil or criminal action.

Fines of up to $10,000 per violation may be assessed against employers who violate the child labor provisions of the law and up to $1,000 per violation against employers who willfully or repeatedly violate the minimum wage or overtime pay provisions. This law prohibits discriminating against or discharging workers who file a complaint or participate in any proceedings under the Act.

Note:
- Certain occupations and establishments are exempt from the minimum wage and/or overtime pay provisions.
- Special provisions apply to workers in American Samoa.
- Where state law requires a higher minimum wage, the higher standard applies.

For Additional Information, Contact the Wage and Hour Division office nearest you – listed in your telephone directory under United States Government, Labor Department.

This poster may be viewed on the Internet at this address: http://www.dol.gov/esa/regs/compliance/posters/flsa.htm

The law requires employers to display this poster where employees can readily see it.

U.S. Department of Labor
Employment Standards Administration
Wage and Hour Division
Washington, D.C. 20210

WH Publication 1088
Revised October 1996

Fair Labor Standards Act (FLSA)

Passed in 1938, this act established laws outlining minimum wage, overtime pay, and maximum hour requirements for most U.S. workers.

Fair Labor Standards Act The Fair Labor Standards Act (FLSA), passed in 1938, contained several provisions that affected organizations and their compensation systems. These included issues surrounding minimum wages, overtime pay, record keeping and child labor restrictions. Nearly all organizations, except the smallest businesses, are covered by the FLSA. The act also identified two primary categories of employees: exempt and nonexempt. Exempt employees would include, for instance, those in professional and managerial jobs, although defining these job terms remains in debate.[5] Under the act, jobs categorized as exempt are not required to meet FLSA standards, especially in the area of overtime pay.[6] On the other hand, nonexempt employees receive certain protections under the FLSA. Specifically, employees in these jobs are eligible for premium pay—typically time-and-a-half—when they work more than 40 hours in a week. Moreover, these jobs must be paid at least the minimum wage, which is currently $5.15 per hour.

Both federal and state governments have also enacted laws requiring firms that contract with the government to pay *prevailing wage rates*. In the federal sector, the Secretary of Labor must review industry rates in the specific locality to set a prevailing rate, which becomes the contract minimum prescribed under the Walsh-Healy Act. Under this act, government contractors must also

DID YOU KNOW?

THE MINIMUM WAGE DEBATE

For several years there has been a continuous debate about whether the U.S. federal minimum wage rate should be increased. Proponents and opponents alike have entered into this debate, with both sides emphatically raising their issues. Let's look at both sides of that debate.

Proponents of increasing minimum wage point out that $5.15 per hour is not a livable wage. About 2.5 million workers employed in the United States are paid at this minimum level, representing 3 percent of the workforce. Though 3 percent is not an enormous number, it becomes more noticeable when you consider that about half of those in minimum wage jobs are under the age of 25 and approximately 60 percent are employed in jobs in the service industry. Further complicating this issue is that the federal minimum wage rate has not changed since September 1, 1997, when the minimum wage was raised from $4.75 to its current $5.15.

In the United States, the threshold poverty level for an individual is $9,570. Someone who earns minimum wage will earn approximately $10,712 (40 hours × 52 weeks × $5.15)—thus the individual is barely above the poverty level. But that doesn't take into account the buying power of that income. When factoring inflation into the equation, a $5.15 wage rate in 2005 is equivalent to $4.15 in 1996 constant dollars. That means, in essence, this individual has the buying power of someone earning $8,632 (40 hours × 52 weeks × $4.15). That, in any calculation, puts the individuals below the government defined poverty level. Add a spouse and family to this mix, and the problem only gets worse.

Opponents of increasing the minimum wage rate cite the problems of increasing costs to employers. In a globally competitive marketplace, every cent added to the cost of doing business only drives up the overall costs to the organization—and ultimately erodes competitive opportunities. Although the U.S. minimum wage rate is not the highest among industrialized nations (see Did You Know? page 303), it is significantly higher than many countries that compete with the United States for goods and services. In addition, states have the right to increase the minimum wage in their locations based on market demands. Furthermore, many opponents of the increase cite that the issue is not about wages but about education. There is a direct correlation between one's education level and one's wages. A better-educated, higher skilled worker is more valuable to organizations, and thus market mechanisms increase what an organization is willing to pay for that individual's service.

Clearly there are no easy solutions to this debate. But everyone has an opinion as to whether the federal minimum wage rate should be increased. What's yours?

Sources: "Minimum Wage Among Critical Issues for States," *HR Magazine* (May 2005), p. 34; "Service Jobs Most Likely to Pay Minimum Wage," *Monthly Labor Review* (September 2003), available online at stats.bls.gov/opub/ted/2003/dec/wk1/art03.htm; U.S. Department of labor, Employment Standards Administration Wage and Hour Division, "Minimum Wage Laws in the States—August 2005" (November 22, 2005), available online at www.dol.gov/esa; U.S. Department of Labor, Bureau of Labor Statistics, "Characteristics of Minimum Wage Workers: 2002" (August 8, 2003), available online at stats.bls.gov/cps/monwage2002.htm; InfoPlease, "Federal Minimum Wage Rates, 1995–2005" (2005), available online at www. infoplease.com/ipa/A0774473.html?mail-11-21; and U.S. Department of Labor, Employment Standards Administration Wage and Hour Division, "History of Federal Minimum Wage Rates Under the Fair Labor Standards Act, 1938–1996" (November 22, 2005), available online at www.dol.gov/esa/minwage/chart.htm.

pay time-and-a-half for all work in excess of 8 hours a day or 40 hours a week.

The Civil Rights and Equal Pay Acts

The Civil Rights and the Equal Pay Acts, among other laws, protect employees from discrimination. Just as it is illegal to discriminate in hiring, organizations cannot discriminate in pay on the basis of race, color, creed, age, or sex.

The **Equal Pay Act of 1963** mandates that organizations compensate men and women doing the same job in the organization with the same rate of pay.[7] The Equal Pay Act was designed to lessen the pay gap between male and female pay rates. Despite progress, women in general still earn roughly 75 percent of what their male counterparts earn.[8] Some of this difference is attributable to perceived male- versus female-dominated occupations, but the Equal Pay Act requires employers to eliminate pay differences for the same job. That is, salaries should be established based on skill, responsibility, effort, and working conditions. For example, if an organization is hiring customer service representatives, new employees, irrespective of their sex, must be paid the same initial salary because the attributes for the job are the same. It is important to note that the Equal Pay Act typically affects only initial job salaries. If two workers, one male and one female, perform at different levels during the course of the year, and if performance is rewarded, the act allows that in the next period their pay may be different.

Equal Pay Act of 1963
This act requires equal pay for equal work.

JOB EVALUATION AND THE PAY STRUCTURE

The essence of compensation administration is job evaluation and the establishment of a pay structure. Let's now turn our attention to job evaluation topics and practices.

Job Evaluation

In Chapter 5, we introduced job analysis as the process of describing job duties, authority relationships, skills required, conditions of work, and additional relevant information. We stated that job analysis data could help develop job descriptions and specifications, as well as job evaluations. By job evaluation, we mean using job analysis information to systematically determine the value of each job in relation to all jobs within the organization. In short, job evaluation seeks to rank all jobs in the organization in a hierarchy that reflects the relative worth of each. It's important to note that this is a ranking of jobs, not people. Job evaluation assumes normal job performance by a typical worker. So, in effect, the process ignores individual abilities or performance.

The ranking that results from job evaluation is not an end in itself. It should be used to determine the organization's pay structure. Note that we say *should*; in practice, this is not always the case. External labor market conditions, collective bargaining, and individual skill differences may require a compromise between the job evaluation ranking and the actual pay structure. Yet even when such compromises are necessary, job evaluation can provide an objective standard from which modifications can be made.

Isolating Job Evaluation Criteria

The heart of job evaluation is determining appropriate criteria to arrive at the ranking.[9] It is easy to say that jobs are valued and ranked by their relative job worth, but ambiguity increases when we attempt to state what places one job higher than another in the job structure hierarchy. Most job-evaluation plans use responsibility, skill, effort, and working conditions as major criteria, but each of these, in turn, can be broken down into more specific terms. Skill, for example, is "an observable competence to perform a learned psychomotor act (like keyboarding)."[10] But other criteria can and have been used: supervisory controls, complexity, personal contacts, and the physical demands needed.[11]

You should not expect the criteria to be constant across jobs. Because jobs differ, it is traditional to separate them into common groups. For example, production, clerical, sales, professional, and managerial jobs may be evaluated separately. Treating like groups similarly allows for more valid rankings within categories but still leaves unsettled the importance of criteria between categories. Separation by groups may permit us to say the position of software developer requires more mental effort than that of shipping supervisor, and subsequently receives a higher ranking, but it does not readily resolve whether greater mental effort is necessary for software designers or customer service managers.

Job Evaluation Methods

Three basic methods of job evaluation are currently in use: ordering, classification, and point methods.[12] Let's review each of these.

ordering method

Ranking job worth from highest to lowest.

Ordering Method   The **ordering method** (or ranking method) requires a committee—typically composed of both management and employee representatives—to arrange jobs in a simple rank order, from highest to lowest. No attempt is made to break down the jobs by specific weighted criteria. The committee members merely compare two jobs and judge which one is more important or more difficult to perform. Then they compare another job with the first two, and so on until all the jobs have been evaluated and ranked.

The most obvious limitation to the ordering method is its sheer unmanageability with numerous jobs. Imagine the difficulty of correctly ranking hundreds or thousands of jobs in an organization. Other drawbacks to consider are the method's subjectivity—no definite or consistent standards by which to justify the rankings—and the fact that because jobs are ranked in order, we cannot know the distance between rankings.

classification method

Evaluating jobs based on predetermined job grades.

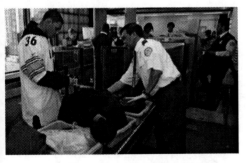

How much should we pay for security? That question may be difficult to answer, but the federal government's classification system tells us that this transportation security screener is paid a minimum salary between $23,600 and $35,400, depending on work location. (Source: © AP/Wide World Photos)

Classification Method   The **classification method** was made popular by the U.S. Civil Service Commission, now the Office of Personnel Management (OPM). The OPM requires that classification grades be established and published in what they call their general schedules. These classifications are created by identifying some common denominator—skills, knowledge, responsibilities—to create distinct classes or grades of jobs. Examples might include shop jobs, clerical jobs, and sales jobs, depending, of course, on the type of jobs the organization requires.

Once the classifications are established, they are ranked in an overall order of importance according to the criteria chosen, and each job is placed in its appropriate classification. This latter action generally requires comparing each position's job description against the classification description and benchmarked jobs. At the OPM, for example, evaluators have classified both a statistician at the Department of Energy and a chemical engineer at the Environmental Protection Agency as positions at the GS-7 grade, an electrician at the Department of the Army and an industrial equipment mechanic at the Military District of Washington as positions at the GS-10 grade.[13]

The classification method shares most of the disadvantages of the ordering approach, plus the difficulty of writing classification descriptions, judging which jobs go where, and dealing with jobs that appear to fall into more than one classification. On the plus side, the classification method has proven itself successful and viable in classifying millions of kinds and levels of civil service jobs.

Point Method The last method we will present breaks down jobs based on various identifiable criteria (such as skill, effort, and responsibility) and allocates points to each of these criteria. Appropriate weights are given, depending on the importance of each criterion to performing the job, points are summed, and jobs with similar point totals are placed in similar pay grades.

An excerpt from a **point method** chart for administrative assistant II positions is shown in Exhibit 11-3. Each job would be evaluated by deciding, for example, the degree of education required to perform the job satisfactorily. The first degree might require the equivalent of skill competencies associated with 10 years of elementary and secondary education; the second degree might require competencies associated with four years of high school; and so forth.

The point method offers the greatest stability of the four approaches presented. Jobs may change over time, but the rating scales established under the point method stay intact. Additionally, the methodology underlying the approach contributes to a minimum of rating error. On the other hand, the point method is complex and therefore costly and time-consuming to develop. The key criteria must be carefully and clearly identified, degrees of factors must be agreed on in terms all raters recognize, the weight of each criterion must be established, and point values must be assigned to degrees. Although it is expensive and time-consuming to both implement and maintain, the point method appears to be the most widely used method. Furthermore, this method can effectively address the comparable worth issue (see Chapter 3).

point method
Breaking down jobs based on identifiable criteria and the degree to which these criteria exist on the job.

Job Class: Administrative Assistant II					
FACTOR	1ST DEGREE	2ND DEGREE	3RD DEGREE	4TH DEGREE	5TH DEGREE
Skill					
1. Education	22	44	66	88	110
2. Problem solving	14	28	42	56	70
Responsibility					
1. Safety of others	5	10	15	20	25
2. Work of others	7	14	21	28	35

3. Problem solving:
This factor examines the types of problems dealt with in your job. Indicate the one level that is most representative of the majority of your job responsibilities.

Degree 1: Performs actions in a set order per written or verbal instruction. Refers problems to supervisor.

Degree 2: Solves routine problems and makes various choices regarding the order in which the work is performed within standard practices. May obtain information from varied sources.

Degree 3: Solves varied problems that require general knowledge of company policies and procedures applicable within area of responsibility. Decisions made based on a choice from established alternatives. Expected to act within standards and established procedures.

Degree 4: Requires analytical judgment, initiative, or innovation in dealing with complex problems or situations. Evaluation not easy because there is little precedent or information may be incomplete.

Degree 5: Plans, delegates, coordinates, and/or implements complex tasks involving new or constantly changing problems or situations. Involves the origination of new technologies or policies for programs or projects. Actions limited only by company policies and budgets.

EXHIBIT 11-3
Excerpts from a Point Method

Source: Material reprinted with permission of The Dartnell Corporation, Chicago, IL 60640.

Establishing the Pay Structure

Once the job evaluation is complete, the data generated become the nucleus of the organization's pay structure. This means establishing pay rates or ranges compatible with the ranks, classifications, or points arrived at through job evaluation.

Any of the three job evaluation methods can provide the necessary input for developing the organization's overall pay structure. Each has its strengths and weaknesses, but because of its wide use, we will use the point method to show how point totals are combined with compensation survey data to form wage curves.

Compensation Surveys Many organizations use surveys to gather factual information on pay practices within specific communities and among firms in their industry. They use this information for comparison purposes. It can tell compensation committees if the organization's wages are in line with those of other employers and, in shortages of individuals to fill certain positions, may help set wage levels. Where does an organization find wage salary data? The U.S. Department of Labor, through its Bureau of Labor Statistics, regularly publishes a vast amount of wage data broken down by geographic area, industry, and occupation. Many industry and employee associations also conduct **compensation surveys** and make their results available. Organizations also can conduct their own surveys, and many large ones do.

It would not be unusual, for instance, for the HRM director at Microsoft in Seattle to regularly share wage data on key positions. This person might identify jobs such as maintenance engineer, electrical engineer, computer programmer, or administrative assistant and share comprehensive descriptions of these jobs with firms in the industry. In addition to the average wage level for a specific job, other information frequently reviewed includes entry-level and maximum wage rates, shift differentials, overtime pay practices, vacation and holiday allowances, the number of pay periods, and the length of the normal work day and work week.

Wage Curves After the compensation committee arrives at point totals from job evaluation and obtains survey data on what comparable organizations are paying for similar jobs, a wage curve can be fitted to the data. An example of a wage curve is shown in Exhibit 11-4. This example assumes use of the point method

compensation surveys
Used to gather factual data on pay practices among firms and companies within specific communities.

EXHIBIT 11-4
A Wage Curve

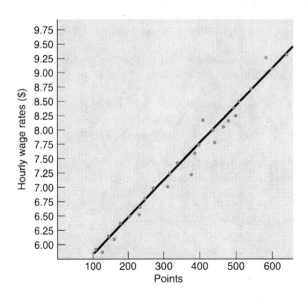

and plots point totals and wage data. A separate wage curve can be constructed based on survey data and compared for discrepancies.

A completed wage curve tells the compensation committee the average relationship between points of established pay grades and wage base rates. Furthermore, it can identify jobs whose pay is out of the trend line. When a job's pay rate is too high, it may be identified as a "red circle" rate. This means that the pay level is frozen or below-average increases are granted until the structure adjusts upward to put the circled rate within the normal range. Of course, a wage rate may be out of line but not red circled. The need to attract or keep individuals with specific skills may require a wage rate outside the normal range, although continuing to attract these individuals, may ultimately upset the internal consistencies supposedly inherent in the wage structure. A wage rate may also be too low. Such undervalued jobs carry a "green-circle" rate, and the company may attempt to grant these jobs above-average pay increases or salary adjustments.

The Wage Structure It is only a short step from plotting a wage curve to developing the organization's **wage structure**. Jobs similar in terms of classes, grades, or points are grouped together. For instance, pay grade 1 may cover the range from 0 to 150 points, pay grade 2 from 151 to 300 points, and so on. As shown in Exhibit 11-5, the result is a logical hierarchy of wages. The more important jobs are paid more; and as individuals assume jobs of greater importance, they rise within the wage hierarchy. Jobs may also be paid in accordance with knowledge- or competency-based pay. We'll return to this topic shortly.

Irrespective of the determinants, notice that each pay grade has a range and that the ranges overlap. Typically, organizations design their wage structures with ranges in each grade to reflect different tenure in positions, as well as levels of performance. Additionally, although most organizations create a degree of overlap between grades, employees who reach the top of their grade can increase their pay only by moving to a higher grade. However, wage structures are adjusted every several years (if not every year), so that employees who top out in their pay grade aren't maxed out forever.

wage structure
A pay scale showing ranges of pay within each grade.

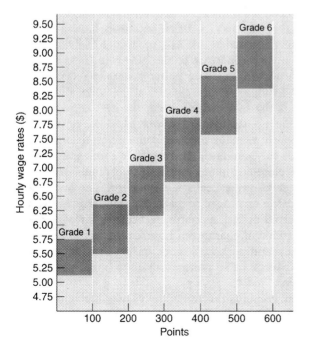

EXHIBIT 11-5
A Sample Wage Structure

A Final Word

No matter how the wage structure is developed, employees must know how the system is derived. Forgetting to keep employees informed, failing to communicate how the process works, will only lead to problems later. In fact, many reports note that how the pay plan is communicated is as important as what is communicated.[14] Accordingly, organizations that want the most from their compensation system will find communicating the process to employees a major leap toward achieving compensation goals.[15]

SPECIAL CASES OF COMPENSATION

As organizations rapidly change in this dynamic world, so, too, do compensation programs. Most notably, organizations are finding that they can no longer increase wage rates by a certain percentage each year (cost-of-living raise) without some comparable increase in performance. Subsequently, more organizations are moving to varied themes of pay for performance. These may include incentive compensation plans, and competency- and team-based compensation. Let's take a closer look at each of these.

Incentive Compensation Plans

In addition to the basic wage structure, organizations sincerely committed to developing a compensation system designed around performance should consider incentive pay. Typically given in addition to—rather than in place of—the basic wage, incentive plans can add a dimension to the wage structure we have previously described.[16] Incentives can be paid based on individual, group, or organization-wide performance—a pay-for-performance concept.

individual incentive plans

Motivation systems based on individual work performance.

merit pay

An increase in pay, usually determined annually.

Individual Incentives Individual incentive plans pay off for individual performances.[17] During the 1990s, these plans were the biggest trend in U.S. compensation administration. Popular approaches included merit pay, piecework plans, time-savings bonuses, and commissions.

One popular and almost universally used incentive system is **merit pay.** Under a merit pay plan, employees who receive merit increases have a sum of money added to their base salary. Somewhat likened to a cost-of-living raise, merit pay differs in that the percentage of increase to the base wage rate is attributable solely to performance. Those who perform better generally receive more merit pay.

Although the merit pay plan is the most widely used, the best-known incentive is undoubtedly piecework. Under a straight *piecework plan,* the employee is typically guaranteed a minimal hourly rate for meeting some preestablished standard output. When output exceeds this standard, the employee earns so much for each piece produced. Differential piece-rate plans establish two rates—one up to standard, and another when the employee exceeds the standard. The latter rate, of course, is higher to encourage the employee to beat the standard. Individual incentives can be based on time saved as well as output generated. As with piecework, the employee can expect a minimal guaranteed hourly rate, but in this case, the bonus is achieved for doing a standard hour's work in less than 60 minutes. Employees who produce an hour's work in 50 minutes obtain a bonus percentage (say, 50 percent) of the labor saved.

Salespeople frequently work on commission. Added to a lower base wage, they earn a percentage of the sales price. On toys, for instance, it may be a hefty 25

How are individuals in the building trades—like this individual installing drywall—compensated? Typically, they receive a rate of pay for each piece they install. The more they install in a day, the more they earn. Accordingly, their pay is up to them. (Source: PhotoDisc/Getty Images, Inc.)

or 30 percent. On sales of multimillion-dollar aircraft or city sewer systems, commissions are frequently 1 percent or less.

Individual incentives work best with clear performance objectives and independent tasks.[18] Otherwise, individual incentives can create dysfunctional competition or encourage workers to cut corners. Co-workers can become the enemy, individuals can create inflated perceptions of their own work while deflating the work of others, and the work environment may become characterized by reduced interaction and communications between employees. And cutting corners may compromise quality and safety.

A potentially negative effect of incentive for performance is that you may "get what you pay for." When incentives are tied to specific goals (only part of the total outcomes expected from a job), people may avoid performing unmeasured, and thus not rewarded, activities in favor of measured, rewarded ones. For example, if your school held a colloquium and brought in a guest speaker, and your instructor decided to take your class, would you go? Your response might be contingent on whether the colloquium was a requirement, the content might be on an exam, and attendance would be taken. If it was just for your information, attending might not be as high a priority. Despite potential negative repercussions from individual incentives in inappropriate situations, they are undoubtedly widespread in practice.

Merit pay, too, has been used as a substitute for cost-of-living raises. Similar to a cost-of-living raise, merit monies accrue permanently to the base salary and become the new base from which to calculate future percentage increases. The problem with merit pay or a cost-of-living system, then, is that pay increases may become expected. But what if the company has a bad year, or employees fail to produce to expectations? Under these traditional systems, workers still expect wage increases. Theoretically, they should give some of their salary back!

Group Incentives Each individual incentive option we describe also can work for groups. That is, two or more employees can be paid for their combined performance. Group incentives make the most sense where employees' tasks are interdependent and thus require cooperation.

group incentive
Motivational plan provided to a group of employees based on the collective work.

Plant-Wide Incentives Plant-wide incentives aim to direct the efforts of all employees toward achieving overall organizational effectiveness. This type of incentive produces rewards for all employees based on organization-wide cost reduction or profit sharing. Kaiser Steel, for example, developed in one of its plants a cost-reduction plan that provides monthly bonuses to employees.[19] The amount of the bonus is determined by computing one-third of all increases in productivity attributable to cost savings as a result of technological change or increased effort. Additionally, Lincoln Electric has had a year-end bonus system for decades, in some years "ranging from a low of 55 percent to a high of 115 percent of annual earnings." The Lincoln Electric plan pays off handsomely when employees beat previous years' performance standards. This bonus is added to the employee's salary, which has made Lincoln Electric workers some of the highest-paid electrical workers in the United Sates.[20]

plant-wide incentive
A motivation system that rewards all facility members based on how well the entire group performed.

One of the best-known organization-wide incentive systems is the **Scanlon Plan**.[21] It seeks cooperation between management and employees through sharing problems, goals, and ideas. (It is interesting to note that many quality circle programs instituted in the 1980s were a direct outgrowth of the Scanlon Plan.) Under Scanlon, each department in the organization has a committee composed of supervisor and employee representatives. Suggestions for labor-saving improvements are funneled to the committee. If accepted, cost savings and productivity gains are shared by all employees, not just the individual who made

Scanlon Plan
An organization-wide incentive program focusing on cooperation between management and employees through sharing problems, goals, and ideas.

IMPROSHARE

An incentive plan that uses a specific mathematical formula for determining employee bonuses.

the suggestion. Typically, about 80 percent of the suggestions prove practical and are adopted.

Another incentive plan that started in the early 1990s is called **IMPROSHARE**. IMPROSHARE, a contraction of Improving Productivity through Sharing, uses a mathematical formula to determine employees' bonuses.[22] For example, if workers save labor costs in producing a product, a predetermined portion of the labor savings goes to the employee.

Profit-sharing plans, or gainsharing plans, are also plant-wide incentives. They allow employees to share in the firm's success by distributing part of the company's profits back to the workers. For instance, Chamberlin Rubber employees receive 75 percent of company profits. In essence, employees become company owners. Profit-sharing plans aim to increase commitment and loyalty to the organization.[23]

All plant-wide incentives suffer from a *dilution effect*. It is hard for employees to see how their efforts affect organization's overall performance. These plans also tend to distribute payoffs at wide intervals; a bonus paid in March 2004 for your efforts in 2003 loses a lot of its reinforcement capabilities. Finally, we should not overlook what happens when organization-wide incentives become both large and recurrent. When this happens, employee often begin to anticipate and expect the bonus. Employees may adjust their spending patterns as if the bonus were a certainty, and the bonus may lose some of its motivating properties. When that happens, it can be perceived as a membership-based reward.

Paying for Performance

pay-for-performance programs

Rewarding employees based on their job performance.

Pay-for-performance programs compensate employees based on a performance measure. Piecework plans, gainsharing, wage incentive plans, profit sharing, and lump sum bonuses are examples of pay-for-performance programs.[24] These forms of pay differ from more traditional compensation plans in that instead of paying an employee for time on the job, pay is adjusted to reflect performance measures that might include individual productivity, team or work group productivity, departmental productivity, or the overall organization's profits for a given period.[25]

Performance-based compensation is probably most compatible with demonstrating to employees a strong relationship between their performance and the rewards they receive.[26] Rewards allocated solely on nonperformance factors—seniority, job title, or across-the-board cost-of-living raises—may encourage employees to reduce their efforts.

Pay-for-performance programs are gaining in popularity in organizations. One survey of 1,000 companies found that almost 80 percent were practicing some form of pay-for-performance for salaried employees.[27] The growing popularity can be explained in terms of both motivation and cost control. From a motivation perspective, conditioning some or all of a worker's pay on performance measures focuses his or her attention and effort on that measure, then reinforces continued effort with rewards. However, if the employee's, team's, or organization's performance declines, so does the reward, thus, encouraging strong efforts and motivation. On the cost-savings side, performance-based bonuses and other incentive rewards avoid the fixed expense of permanent—and often annual—salary increases. Bonuses typically do not accrue to base salary; the amount is not compounded in future years, thus saving the company money.

competency-based compensation

Organizational pay system that rewards skills, knowledge, and behaviors.

A recent extension of the pay-for-performance concept, **competency-based compensation**, is used in such organizations as Amoco Corporation and Champion International.[28] A competency-based compensation program pays and rewards

BAND		SALARY RANGE
Band	VIII:	$150,000–175,000
Band	VII:	85,000–125,000
Band	VI:	70,000–90,000
Band	V:	55,000–80,000
Band	IV:	40,000–60,000
Band	III:	25,000–45,000
Band	II:	20,000–40,000
Band	I:	15,000–25,000

EXHIBIT 11-6
A Sample Banding

Source: Based on the banding compensation program at Coregis Group, Inc., *ACA Journal* (Winter 1995), p. 53.

employees on their skills, knowledge, or behaviors.[29] These competencies may include such behaviors and skills as leadership, problem solving, decision making, or strategic planning. Pay levels reflect the degree of competency. Pay increases in a competency-based system reward growth in personal competencies as well as contributions to the overall organization.[30] Accordingly, an employee's rewards directly reflect his or her ability to contribute to achievement of the organization's goals and objectives.

This is, in essence, a pay scheme based on employees' specific competencies. These may include knowledge of the business and its core values, skills to fulfill these core requirements, and demonstrated employee behaviors. In competency-based pay plans, these preset levels are called **broad-banding**.[31] Among the banding programs documented, some have as few as 4 bands with no salary ranges, and others more than 10 bands and several salary ranges. For example, Exhibit 11-6 shows an eight-band compensation program at Coregis Group. Broad-banding also can help develop wage structures on factors other than skills.

Those who possess competencies within a certain range will be grouped together in a pay category. Pay increases, then, recognize growth in personal competencies, as well as the contribution one makes to the organization. Accordingly, career and pay advancement may not be tied to a promotion per se, but rather to how much more one can contribute to the organization's goals and objectives.

If you are making the connection back to when we discussed the point method of job evaluation, you are reading attentively. However, the point method looked specifically at the job and its worth to the company. Competency-based pay plans assess these points based on the value the employee adds in assisting the organization to achieving its goals. As more organizations move toward competency-based pay plans, HRM will play a critical role. Just as we discussed in Chapter 5, regarding employment planning, once the direction of the organization is established, attracting, developing, motivating, and retaining competent individuals become essential. This will continue to have implications for recruiting, training and development, career development, performance appraisals, as well as pay and reward systems. Not only will HRM ensure that it has the right people at the right place, but it will have assembled a competent team of employees who add significant value to the organization.

broad-banding
Paying employees at preset levels based on their level of competency.

Team-Based Compensation

You've just been handed the course syllabus for a business policy course you're taking this semester, and you quickly glance at how the final grade will be calculated: two tests—a midterm and a final—and a class project. Intrigued, you read further about the class project. You and four other classmates must thoroughly analyze a company's operations. You will make recommendations about the company's financial picture, human resources, product lines, competitive advantage, and strategic direction. The group must turn in a report of no less than 50 pages, double-spaced, and make a 30-minute class presentation about your suggested turnaround. The report and presentation account for 75 percent of the course grade, and each team member will receive the project grade. Not fair? Too much riding on the efforts of others? Welcome to the world of **team-based compensation**.

team-based compensation
Pay based on how well the team performed.

Today's dynamic organizations place much more emphasis on involving employees in most relevant aspects of the job. When organizations group employees into teams and empower them to meet goals, teams reap the benefits of their productive effort. That is, team-based compensation plans are tied to team-based performance.[32]

Under a team-based compensation plan, team members who work on achieving—and in many cases, exceeding—established goals often share equally in the rewards (although, in the truest sense, teams allocate their own rewards). Providing for fair treatment of each team member encourages group cohesiveness.[33] Yet this does not occur overnight. Rather, it requires several key components being in place. For instance, effective teams have a clear purpose and goals. They understand what is expected of them and that their effort is worthwhile.[34] Teams also need the necessary resources to complete their tasks. Because their livelihood may rest on accomplishing their goals, a lack of requisite resources may doom a team effort before it begins. Finally, mutual trust among the team members is critical. They must respect one another, effectively communicate with one another, and treat each member fairly and equitably. Failure here may erect serious obstacles that defeat the sense of purpose group cohesiveness can foster.

EXECUTIVE COMPENSATION PROGRAMS

Executive pay is merely a special case within the topic of compensation, but it does have several twists that deserve special attention. First, the base salaries of executives are almost 300 times higher than those of low-level managers or operative personnel[35]—whether that executive is male or female[36]—and we want to explain why this is so. Second, executives frequently operate under bonus and stock option plans that can dramatically increase their total compensation. A senior executive at Autodesk, Cisco Systems, Occidental Petroleum, or Johnson & Johnson can, in a good year, earn $10 million, $15 million, or more on top of the base salary.[37] We want to briefly look at how such compensations come about and why. Executives also receive perquisites (called perks) or special benefits that others do not. What are these, and how do they impact on executive motivation? These are the topics in this section on compensation.

Salaries of Top Managers

It is well known that executives in the private sector receive considerably higher compensation than their counterparts in the public sector. Mid-level executives regularly earn base salaries of $150,000 to $225,000; the CEO of a billion-dollar corporation can expect a minimum total compensation package in excess of $25 million, and base salaries of $1 million or more are not unusual among senior management of Fortune 100 firms. In 2004, for

ETHICAL ISSUES IN HRM

ARE U.S. EXECUTIVES OVERPAID?

Are we paying U.S. executives too much? Is an average salary in excess of $60 million justifiable? In any debate, there are two sides to the issue. Support for paying this amount is the fact that these executives have tremendous organizational responsibilities. They not only have to manage the organization in today's environment, they must keep it moving into the future. Their jobs are not 9-to-5, but rather 6 to 7 days a week, often 10 to 14 hours a day. If jobs are evaluated on the basis of skills, knowledge, abilities, and responsibilities, executives should be highly paid.[38] Furthermore, there is the issue of motivation and retention.[39] If you want these individuals to succeed and stay with the company, you must provide a compensation package that motivates them to do so. Incentives based on various measures also provide the impetus for them to excel.[40]

On the other hand, most of the research done on executive salaries questions the linkage to performance.[41] Even when profits are down, many executives are paid handsomely. In fact, American company executives are regarded as some of the highest-paid people in the world. Additionally, when performance problems lead to dismissal, some executives are paid phenomenal severance packages. For example, ousted CEOs of Mattel and Conseco were given $50 and $49 million, respectively, as severance pay.[42] U.S. executives make two to five times the salaries of their foreign counterparts—even though some executives in Japan-based organizations perform better. Finally, the U.S. CEOs make more than 500 times as much as the average employee.[43]

Do you believe that U.S. executives are overpaid? What's your opinion?

instance, the average cash compensation (salary plus annual bonus) for the top 48 executives in U.S. corporations was above $8 million.[44] The top 20 of these individuals (CEOs from WellPoint, Danaher, Occidental Petroleum, XTO Energy, and Exxon) averaged more than $100 million in total compensation[45] (including their stock options)—options that enabled William McGuire of UnitedHealth Group, for example, to receive more than $806 million in 2004.[46] Management compensation reflects the market forces of supply and demand.[47] Management superstars, like superstar athletes in professional sports, are wooed with signing bonuses, interest-free loans, performance incentive packages, and guaranteed contracts. Of course, as in the case of athletes, some controversy surrounds the large dollar amounts paid to these executives (see Ethical Issues in HRM).[48]

Supplemental Financial Compensation

In 2004, the average compensation for executives in the Fortune 500 companies in the United States was in the millions. As previously presented, the figure includes their total compensation—base salary plus bonuses and stock options. Bonuses and stock options dramatically increase the total compensation that executives receive. Much of this additional compensation is obtained through a deferred bonus—that is, the executive's bonus is computed on the basis of some formula, usually taking into account increases in sales and profits. This bonus, although earned in the current period, may be distributed over several future periods. Therefore, it is not unusual for an executive to earn a $1 million bonus but have it paid out at $50,000 a year for 20 years. The major purpose of such deferred compensation is to increase the cost to the executive of leaving the organization. In almost all cases, executives who voluntarily terminate their employment must forfeit their deferred bonuses. One of the main reasons why there are so few voluntary resignations among the ranks of senior

How much is an executive worth? At UnitedHealth Group, it's a lot. In 2004, William McGuire received more than $800 million in long-term compensation. This long-term value of his options was in addition to his $10 million salary. (Source: Alberto Incrocci/The Image Bank/Getty Images, Inc.)

management is that these executives would lose hundreds of thousands of dollars in deferred income.

Interestingly, another form of bonus, the *hiring bonus*, has arisen in the past decade, purposely designed to help senior executives defray the loss of deferred income. It is now becoming increasingly popular to pay senior executives a hiring bonus to sweeten the incentive for them to leave their current employer and forfeit their deferred bonuses and pension rights. These bonuses often do provide deferred income to compensate for loss of pension rights.

Stock options also have been a common incentive offered to executives. They generally allow executives to purchase, at some time in the future, a specific amount of the company's stock at a fixed price. Under the assumption that good management will increase the company's profitability and therefore the price of the stock, stock options are viewed as performance-based incentives. It should be pointed out, however, that the use of stock options is heavily influenced by the current status of the tax laws. In recent years, tax reform legislation has taken away some of the tax benefits that could accrue through the issuance of stock options. The success, however, of these changes to curb CEO compensation is limited at best. Deferred pay and supplemental retirement plans appear to be vehicles that skirt around the legalities of tax regulations.[49]

Supplemental Nonfinancial Compensation: Perquisites

Executives are frequently offered a smorgasbord of **perquisites** not offered to other employees. The logic of offering these perks, from the organization's perspective, is to attract and keep good managers and motivate them to work hard in the organization's interest. In addition to the standard benefits offered to all employees (see Chapter 12), some benefits are reserved for privileged executives. Popular perks include the payment of life insurance premiums, club memberships, company automobiles, liberal expense accounts, supplemental disability insurance, supplemental retirement accounts, postretirement consulting contracts, and personal financial, tax, and legal counseling. Some also may be given mortgage assistance.

A popular benefit for top executives that gained popularity in the 1980s and continues today is the **golden parachute**. The golden parachute was designed by top executives as a means of protecting themselves if a merger or hostile takeover occurred. These parachutes typically provide either a severance salary to the departing executive or a guaranteed position in the newly created (merged) operation. The concept here is to provide an incentive for the executive to stay with the company and fight the hostile takeover—rather than leave the organization.

INTERNATIONAL COMPENSATION

Probably one of the most complex functions of international HRM is the design and implementation of an equitable compensation program.[50] The first step in designing an international compensation package is to determine if one policy will apply to all employees or if *parent-country nationals (PCNs), host-country nationals (HCNs),* and *third-country nationals (TCNs)* will be treated differently. Currently, American PCNs and HCNs are commonly treated separately, often also differentiating among types of expatriate assignments (temporary or permanent transfer) or employee status (executive, professional, or technical). It is also necessary to thoroughly understand the statutory requirements of each country to ensure compliance with local laws. International compensation packages in the United States generally use the balance-sheet approach, which considers four factors: base pay, differentials, incentives, and assistance programs.

Base Pay

Ideally, this equals the pay of employees in comparable jobs at home, but the range of pay scales in most countries is far narrower than in the United States. Thus, whereas a middle manager in a U.S. factory might earn $75,000 a year, the same manager in Germany might earn the equivalent of $110,000. However, the U.S. higher-level executive might earn $500,000 and her counterpart in Germany only the equivalent of $150,000. How can human resource managers satisfy the middle manager who earns a third less than the counterpart where he works, while also satisfying the German executive who earns less than her U.S. counterpart?

In addition to fairness among overseas employees, foreign currencies and laws must be considered. Should expatriates be paid in U.S. dollars or the local currency—or a combination of the two? How does the organization deal with changes in currency values? Do restrictions apply to either bringing in or taking out dollars or the local currency? If so, how are savings handled? Should salary increases follow the same standards as those established for domestic employees or local standards? Does the expatriate pay U.S. or foreign income taxes?

Taxation is a major factor in calculating equitable base pay rates. Where substantial differences exist in tax rates—as for instance in Sweden, where income taxes are about 50 percent—will the base pay be adjusted for the actual loss of net income? The U.S. State Department has negotiated agreements with every country to determine where income will be taxed, but the protection of income from foreign tax rates creates new administrative requirements for the organization. Almost all multinational corporations have some tax protection plan so that the expatriate pays no more taxes than if she were in her home country.

If you've just been sent to Bonn, Germany, by your company, your compensation will need adjustment. In the United States, you've been paying nearly $3.00 a gallon for gas, but in Germany, it's about 1.15 Euros per liter, or about $5.50 a gallon in U.S. dollars. That can change a personal budget rather quickly. (Source: © AP/Wide World Photos)

DID YOU KNOW?

COMPENSATION IN THE GLOBAL VILLAGE

Compensation practices in developed countries, though similarities exist, do differ. Below is comparison of minimum wage rates and average work hours per week for Germany, Japan, Sweden, Russia, India, United Kingdom, Singapore, Australia, and the United States.

Country	Minimum Wage Rate Per Hour	Average Work Hours Per Week
Germany	No minimum wage[a]	48
Japan	No minimum wage	40
Sweden	No minimum wage[b]	48
Russia	27.5 rubles[c] ($0.95 USD)	40
India	66 rupees average ($1.14 USD)	48
United Kingdom	£5.85 ($10.30 USD)	44
Singapore	No minimum wage	44
Australia	12.30 AUD ($9.04 USD)	40
United States	$5.15	40

[a]Germany does, however, have bargaining agreements that establish wage floors.
[b]Wage base set through collective bargaining.
[c]Wage rate established in May 2006.

Differentials

The cost of living fluctuates around the world, and the value of the dollar to foreign currencies affects prices. For example, if a gallon of regular unleaded gasoline (in USD) in the United States were $2.25; in England it might be equivalent to $5.83; and in Hong Kong, $6.24. Differentials offset the higher costs of overseas goods, services, and housing. The State Department, which has employees in almost every country in the world, publishes a regularly updated comparison of global costs of living used by most multinational corporations for providing differentials to maintain the standards of living the expatriate would enjoy if he or she were home.[51]

Incentives

Not all employees are willing to leave family, friends, and the comfort of home support systems for long periods of time. Thus, mobility inducements to go on foreign assignments are regularly offered. These may include monetary payments or services, such as housing, car, chauffeur, and other incentives. But companies must decide how a hardship premium should be paid. As a percent of salary? In a lump-sum payment? In home or foreign currency? If foreign housing is provided, what happens to the vacant home back in the United States or to the family housing situation when they eventually return? Incentives require careful planning before, during, and after the overseas assignment.[52]

Assistance Programs

As with any relocation, the overseas transfer requires many expenditures for the employee's family. Some assistance programs commonly offered by multinational corporations include household goods shipping and storage; major appliances; legal clearance for pets and their shipment; home sale/rental protection; automobile protection; temporary living expenses; travel, including prerelocation visits and annual home leaves; special/emergency return leaves; education allowances for children; club memberships (for corporate entertaining); and security (including electronic systems and bodyguards).

Clearly, the design of a compensation system for employees serving overseas is complex and requires enormous administrative expertise, particularly when an organization has expatriates posted in 40 or 50 different countries.

SUMMARY

(This summary relates to the Learning Outcomes identified on page 285.)
After having read this chapter, you can

1. **Explain the various classifications of rewards.** Rewards can be classified as (1) intrinsic or extrinsic, (2) financial or nonfinancial, or (3) performance-based or membership-based.
2. **Discuss why some rewards are considered membership-based.** Some rewards are membership-based because one receives them for belonging to the organization. Employee benefits are an example of membership-based rewards, in that every employee receives them irrespective of performance levels.

3. **Define the goal of compensation administration.** Compensation administration seeks to design a cost-effective pay structure that will not only attract, motivate, and retain competent employees but also seem fair to them.

4. **Discuss job evaluation and its three basic approaches.** Job evaluation systematically determines the value of each job in relation to all jobs within the organization. The three basic approaches to job evaluation are (1) the ordering method, (2) the classification method, and (3) the point method.

5. **Explain the evolution of the final wage structure.** The final wage structure evolves from job evaluation input, compensation survey data, and the creation of wage grades.

6. **Describe competency-based compensation programs.** Competency-based compensation views employees as a competitive advantage in the organization. Compensation systems are established in terms of employee knowledge, skills, and demonstrated behaviors. Possession of these three factors is evaluated and compensated according to a broad-banded salary range established by the organization.

7. **Discuss why executives receive significantly higher salaries than other employees in an organization.** Executive compensation is higher than that of rank-and-file personnel and also includes other financial and nonfinancial benefits not otherwise available to operative employees. This is done to attract and retain executives and motivate them to higher performance levels.

8. **Identify the balance-sheet approach to international compensation.** The balance-sheet approach to international compensation takes into account base pay, differentials, incentives, and assistance programs.

DEMONSTRATING COMPREHENSION: *Questions for Review*

1. Contrast intrinsic and extrinsic rewards.
2. How do financial and nonfinancial rewards differ?
3. What is a membership-based reward? How does it differ from a performance-based reward?
4. What is compensation administration? What does it entail?
5. How do governmental influences affect compensation administration?
6. What is job evaluation? Discuss the three basic methods of job evaluation.
7. What are the advantages and disadvantages of (a) individual incentives, (b) group incentives, and (c) organization wide incentives?
8. What is broad-banding and how does it work?

KEY TERMS

broad-banding	extrinsic rewards	job enrichment	plant-wide
classification method	Fair Labor Standards Act (FLSA)	merit pay	incentives
compensation administration	golden parachute	ordering method	point method
compensation surveys	group incentive	pay-for-performance programs	Scanlon Plan
competency-based compensation	IMPROSHARE	performance-based rewards	team-based compensation
Equal Pay Act of 1963	individual incentive	perquisites	wage structure
	intrinsic rewards		

VISUAL SUMMARY

CHAPTER 11: ESTABLISHING REWARDS AND PAY PLANS

1   Rewards

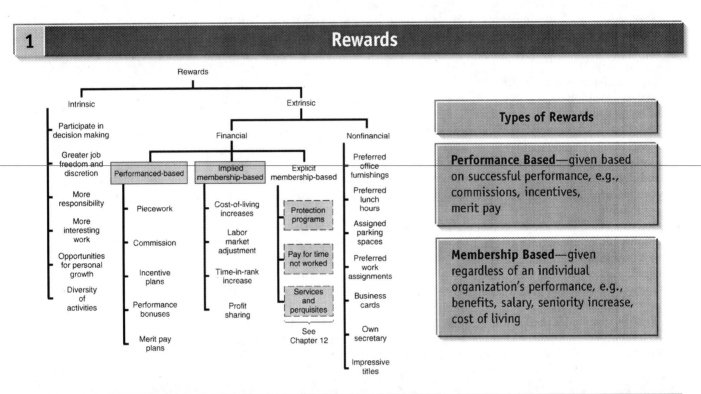

Types of Rewards

Performance Based—given based on successful performance, e.g., commissions, incentives, merit pay

Membership Based—given regardless of an individual organization's performance, e.g., benefits, salary, seniority increase, cost of living

2   What Is Compensation Administration?

Goal—design a cost-effective pay structure that will attract, motivate, and retain competitive employees

The Laws
- **Fair Labor Standards Act (FLSA) of 1938**—minimum wages, overtime pay, record-keeping, child labor restrictions
- **Civil Rights Act**—a compensation system that is bias free
- **Equal Pay Act of 1963**—compensate men and women doing the same job in the organization with the same rate of initial pay

3   Job Evaluation and Pay Structure

Job Evaluation—using job analysis information to determine the relative value of each job in an organization

Methods of Job Evaluation
- Ordering method
- Classification method
- Point method

Pay Structure Components
- Compensation survey
- Wage curves
- Wage structure

306

4   Special Cases of Compensation

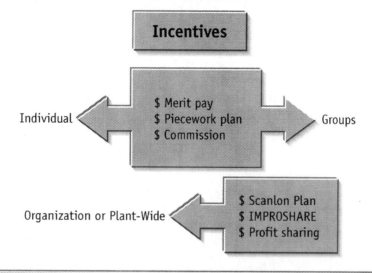

Incentives

Individual ⟵ $ Merit pay / $ Piecework plan / $ Commission ⟶ Groups

Organization or Plant-Wide ⟵ $ Scanlon Plan / $ IMPROSHARE / $ Profit sharing

Pay for Performance
- Paying employees on the basis of some performance measure
- Competency-based compensation—paying and rewarding employees on the basis of skills, knowledge, or behaviors the employees possess

5   Executive Compensation

Are CEOs Overpaid?

Special Financial Compensation
- Stock options
- Perks
- Golden parachute
- Hiring bonus
- Deferred bonuses

$$$

6   International Compensation

Balance-Sheet Approach

Considers:
- Base pay
- Differentials
- Incentives
- Assistance programs

CROSSWORD COMPREHENSION

ACROSS

1. method of job evaluation involving evaluating jobs based on predetermined pay grades
4. a pay scale showing ranges of pay within each grade
7. act requiring equal compensation for equal work
8. paying employees at preset levels based on their level of competency
17. rewards derived from the job itself, such as pride in one's work
18. the process of managing a company's salary and benefits program
19. a financial protection plan for executives in case they are severed from the organization
20. compensation pay based on how well the work group performed
21. attractive benefits, over and above a regular salary, granted to executives
22. an incentive plan that uses a specific mathematical formula for determining employee bonuses

DOWN

2. an organization-wide incentive plan focusing on cooperation between management and employees through sharing problems, goals, ideas
3. an incentive system that rewards all facility members based on how well the entire group performed
5. organizational pay system that rewards skills, knowledge, and behaviors
6. rewarding employees based on their specific job performance
9. method of job evaluation involving ranking jobs from highest to lowest
10. act passed in 1938 establishing minimum wage laws and overtime pay
11. rewards such as commissions, piecework pay plans, or other forms of merit pay

12. instrument used to gather factual data on pay practices among firms
13. rewards provided by the employer, such as money, promotion, or benefits
14. method of job evaluation involving breaking down jobs based on identifiable criteria and the degree to which these criteria exist in a job
15. a motivational compensation plan designed to provide a financial reward to employees based on their collective work
16. enhancing jobs by giving employees more opportunity to plan and control their work

HRM WORKSHOP

LINKING CONCEPTS TO PRACTICE: *Discussion Questions*

1. Would you rather work for an organization where everyone knows what others are earning or an organization where this information is kept secret? Why?
2. "Subjectivity can be successfully removed from the compensation administration process." Build an argument for and against this statement.
3. Team compensation allows some individuals to work harder than others, yet receive the same pay. Do you agree or disagree? Defend your position.

4. "U.S. executives earn every dollar of their pay. People who complain about these people earning millions are just envious that they are not being paid at that level." Build an argument for and against this statement.

DEVELOPING DIAGNOSTIC AND ANALYTICAL SKILLS

Case Application 11-A: IS IT MERIT OR NOT?

Most contemporary organizations are keenly aware of what they need to do to attract and hire the best available talent. Most recognize that employee mobility and competition for the most highly skilled employees make it more difficult to keep outstanding employees. But how companies achieve their compensation goals varies immensely. Take the dichotomy between two organizations—Cisco Systems and AFLAC Insurance.[53] Both of these companies are looking for ways to maximize overall compensation practices and simultaneously increase productivity.

Cisco Systems, the San Jose–based networking company is adding merit pay back into the employee compensation mix, while at the same time increasing base salaries for all employees. Having removed these two compensation practices several years ago, Cisco management believes that doing so will help the company increase its revenue per employee. Cisco currently employs about 27,000 employees in the United States. None of these employees have seen a merit pay increase since 2001. Any pay increases over the past several years have simply gone to those whose pay levels had fallen below market rates and to those who were promoted. Beyond those two categories, salaries remained flat.

At AFLAC, the Columbus, Georgia–based insurance company, past compensation practices focused on keeping base salaries and few (if any) merit increases. Starting salaries were purposefully kept below market wage rates. Employees, however, were given opportunities for significant bonuses and project-by-project cash rewards ranging between $500 and $650. Employees at AFLAC also enjoyed substantial benefits—ranging

from stock purchase plans; tuition reimbursement programs for employees, their children, and grandchildren; and child care on campus. Today, however, AFLAC management is looking for ways to increase pay rates for employees—basing them, however, on pay for performance. The company is focusing on variable pay rates that will reward employees for accomplishments that are consistent with corporate strategic goals—rewards that will be handed out on a monthly basis.

Although it's interesting that both organizations are looking at compensation practices that allow the companies to grow while simultaneously reducing labor costs, each is doing so a bit differently. Cisco is increasing base salaries and looking at annual pay increases. AFLAC, on the other hand, is keeping base pay low and focusing heavily on pay for performance. Are their past compensation practices adversely affecting them? Probably not, as Cisco gets more than 70,000 applications each year and enjoys an industry-low turnover rate of just 4.6 percent annually. AFLAC also receives more than 100 applications for each advertised position—especially in those areas where unemployment rates exceed 6 percent.

Questions:

1. From the material presented in the case, how would you describe the basic compensation philosophy of Cisco and AFLAC, respectively?
2. What factors are affecting the compensation practices of both organizations?
3. If all things were equal, would you prefer to work in a Cisco-type organization where higher base salary and

annual increases (assuming successful performance, of course) dominate, or an AFLAC-type organization where base salaries are lower but incentive pay based on performance can significantly add to your total compensation? Explain your position.

Case Application 11-B: TEAM FUN!

Team Fun

It's day four of the Canadian retreat. Tony's newest topic is rewards and pay plans. He starts: "Edna showed me the salary figures and records for everyone. I can't find any pattern or rationale for how people are paid around here. I think we should work this out."

Kenny sends everyone but Tony and Norton out to find more firewood and looks at Tony. "No one but the four of us know how everyone is paid around here. What were you trying to do? Start a fight?"

Norton adds, "We do fine with the system we have. Why did you think we needed to talk about compensation this week?"

Tony asks tersely, "Would you describe that system for me?"

Kenny starts, "I like a guy, want him to work for us. So, I offer him whatever I made when I was his age. Or what Norton made at his age; especially if it's a technical job, like machine design." Tony groans and holds his head.

Norton adds, "For the pros, though, we talk to them. Find out what pros are getting at other stores to demonstrate and sell the products. We pay that golf guy $10,000 each time he shows up and swings his club around the GREEN." Tony groans and holds his stomach.

Kenny counters, "Well, the pros are special cases, right?" Tony collapses into a chair.

Norton asks, "Tony, you took over setting starting salaries when you got here. What have you been doing?"

Tony says, in a small voice, "Just offering what you offered the last guy in the same job. I couldn't figure out any other pattern. That's why I put compensation on the agenda for this week." Kenny and Norton groan. They all look up as the door opens and Eric comes in with a load of firewood.

Questions

Please review the TEAM FUN! case material at the end of prior chapters before answering these questions.

1. Make lists of TEAM FUN! rewards: extrinsic versus intrinsic; financial versus nonfinancial; performance-based versus membership-based.

2. Evaluate the appropriateness of these rewards for maintaining employee commitment at TEAM FUN! Does the TEAM FUN! compensation system meet the general goals of a compensation system?

3. Make three suggestions to improve the TEAM FUN! compensation system.

4. Identify three features of the compensation system that are excellent for this organization. Would they be suitable for most organizations? What types?

WORKING WITH A TEAM: *Understanding Incentive Plans*

Schedule a 15-minute interview with a compensation specialist in the human resources department of your employer, college, university, hospital, or other organization to ask the following questions. Summarize your results in a one- to two-page report for your class team discussion or class five-minute presentation. You may also want to develop a comparison chart based on your team's results.

1. Could you share a brief job description of a compensation specialist?

2. Do you participate in wage surveys? Can you provide results of a recent survey or samples of types of questions asked?

3. What factors do you consider in developing compensation surveys?

4. What types of plans, if any, does your organization use to provide incentive to employees? How is each plan implemented, and how successful has it been?

LEARNING AN HRM SKILL: *Pay-for-Performance Goal Setting*

About the skill: Employees should have a clear understanding of what they're attempting to accomplish. Furthermore, as a supervisor, you must see that this task is achieved by helping your employees set work goals. This appears to be common sense, but it doesn't always happen. Setting pay-for-performance objectives is a skill that every manager needs to perfect. You can better facilitate this process by following these guidelines:

1. *Identify an employee's key job tasks.* Goal setting begins by defining what you want your employees to accomplish. The best source for this information is each employee's job description.

2. *Establish specific and challenging goals for each key task.* Identify the level of performance expected of each employee. Specify a target for employees to hit. Specify deadlines for each goal to reduce ambiguity, but do not set them arbitrarily. Make them realistic given the tasks to be completed.

3. *Allow employees to actively participate.* Employees who participate in goal setting are more likely to accept the goals. However, it must be sincere participation. That is, employees must perceive that you truly seek their input and are not just going through the motions.

4. *Set priorities.* When you give someone more than one goal, be sure to rank the goals in order of importance. Setting priorities encourages employees to take action and expend effort on each goal in proportion to its importance. Rate

goals for difficulty and importance, not to encourage people to choose easy goals, but so that individuals can receive credit for trying difficult goals, even if they don't fully achieve them.

5. **Build in feedback mechanisms to assess goal progress.** Feedback lets employees know whether their level of effort is sufficient to attain the goal. Feedback should be both self- and supervisor-generated. In either case, feedback should be frequent and recurring.

6. **Link rewards to goal attainment.** It's natural for employees to ask, "What's in it for me?" Linking rewards to achieving goals will help answer that question.

ENHANCING YOUR COMMUNICATION SKILLS

1. Develop a two- to three-page paper on the advantages and disadvantages of competency-based compensation programs. Use specific examples where appropriate.

2. "Some suggest that women executives in major U.S. corporations earn less than their male counterparts." Build an argument that this statement helps confirm the continued existence of the glass ceiling. Next, show how the statement indicates that the glass ceiling has "shattered." End your paper with your conclusion supporting one side of the argument or the other.

3. Working on a team project in class is somewhat similar to working on a team in an organization. Assume your professor gave you the opportunity to develop a "team" reward (grading) procedure for your class project. Indicate what that grading procedure would look like and how you would implement it to maximize the benefits to (a) your learning and (b) your reward.

TWELVE

For several generations of workers, the formula was clear. You worked a number of years with an organization, after which you received your reward—a livable retirement wage based on one's income and years of service. With that retirement came a promise to continue one's health insurance, supplementing one's Medicare coverage offered by the federal government. One's retirement years were times of relaxation, spending the golden years in pursuit of those things that they were interested in and often delayed through years of work. But these promises are no longer valid, and in some cases are simply not being honored in today's organizations. Consider the impact this is having on individuals such as Tim Baker, Kathi Cooper, and James Roberts.[1]

Tim Baker has worked for US Airways for over 19 years. As a pilot, he has seen a lot of changes in the airline industry. Deregulation, competitive pressures, and the like have all led to serious financial problems for the large airline carriers. In an effort to seek relief and avoid bankruptcy, airlines like US Airways have turned to their employees for assistance. One of the areas of interest for the airline was the pilots' pension plan, a lucrative retirement program that had grown so large that US Airways could no longer fund its costs. As a result, the pilots and company officials agreed to turn the retirement problem over to the federal agency that oversees private pension programs and serves as the retirement insurer as a last resort, the Pension Benefit Guarantee Corporation. The net effect for individuals like Tim Baker: his

promise of a six-figure retirement has been broken. Instead he'll receive $28,585 per year.

Kathi Cooper currently works for IBM, where she has spent over 25 years in the company's finance department. As she was reading about the proposed changes company officials were making to their retirement program, she became upset. Her retirement benefits would decrease significantly, and she viewed the change proposals as discriminating against older workers. Furthermore, the company's $7,500 per retiree for health insurance premiums was being discontinued. These were areas that she felt she was promised, entitled to as a long-term IBM employee. Unhappy, she sued. As the case continues, employees at companies like AT&T, Xerox, and Cigna have filed similar suits against their employers based on Cooper's claim.

James Roberts spent his entire work career at Bethlehem Steel, where he worked primarily operating a crane. He frequently worked 6 days a week, 10 hours each day. His job often required him to start work late in the evenings one week and in the wee hours of the morning other weeks. But he did so willingly, as he was committed to his company. At age 53, Roberts retired with a $1,887.75 monthly pension. At the time he was suffering several medical problems but had everything under control with medications—all of which were paid for through the company's health plan. But in 2002, Robert's retirement life changed. When Bethlehem Steel declared bankruptcy, the company's retirement and health insurance

(*Source:* Mark Katzman/Ferguson & Katzman Photography)

Employee Benefits

Learning Outcomes

Affter reading this chapter, you will be able to

1. Discuss why employers offer benefits to their employees.

2. Contrast Social Security, unemployment compensation, and workers' compensation benefits.

3. Identify and describe three major types of health insurance options.

4. Discuss the important implications of the Employee Retirement Income Security Act.

5. Outline and describe major types of retirement programs organizations offer.

6. Explain the reason companies offer vacation benefits to their employees.

7. Describe the purpose of disability insurance programs.

8. List the various types of flexible benefit option programs.

coverage changed dramatically. For Roberts that meant a decrease in his monthly retirement to about $1,250 a month, and he lost his health care coverage. As a result, he must now pay about $450 for his medications—when he can afford it.

Is this the American dream these workers bargained for? Absolutely not. But the solutions to such problems are not easy. It's something that employers, employees, and government officials will need to address. As one individual stated, to fix this "is to leave decades of workers devastated. In the end, someone will have to pay. The only question is who."

INTRODUCTION

employee benefits
Membership-based, nonfinancial rewards offered to attract and keep employees.

When an organization designs its overall compensation program, a critical area of concern is what benefits to provide. Today's workers expect more than just an hourly wage or a salary; they want additional considerations that will enrich their lives. These considerations in an employment setting are called **employee benefits.**

Employee benefits have grown in importance and variety over the past several decades. Once perceived as an added feature, employee benefit administration has transformed itself into a well-thought-out, well-organized package. Ford and Delta, for example, provide every employee with a computer and Internet access for personal use.[2] Employers realize that such benefits affect whether applicants accept their employment offers or, once employed, stay with the organization. Benefits, therefore, are necessary components of an effectively functioning compensation program.

The irony, however, is that although benefits must be offered to attract and retain good workers, benefits as a whole do not directly affect a worker's performance.[3] Benefits are generally membership-based, offered to employees regardless of their performance levels. This does not seem logical business practice, but evidence indicates that inadequate benefits and services for employees contributes to employee dissatisfaction and increased absenteeism and turnover.[4] Accordingly, the greatly negative effect of failing to provide adequate benefits prompts organizations to spend tens of billions of dollars annually to ensure valuable benefits for each worker.

Over the decades, the nature of benefits has changed drastically. Benefits offered in the early 1900s clearly differed from those offered today in focusing on time off from work. The first personnel departments to arrive on the scene emphasized keeping workers "happy and healthy." This meant that their responsibility was to administer such benefits as scheduled vacations, company picnics, and other social activities for workers. Later, around the late 1930s, the practice emerged of having employees complete a sign-up card for some type of health insurance. Those days of simplicity for the organization, unfortunately, are long gone. Federal legislation, labor unions, and the changing workforce have all led to growth in benefit offerings. Today's organizational benefits are more widespread, more creative, and clearly more abundant. As indicated in Exhibit 12-1, employee benefits in the new millennium are designed to ensure value for each worker.

Costs of Providing Employee Benefits

Most of us are aware of inflation and its effect on the wages and salaries of virtually every job in the United States. It seems incredible that just 70 years ago a worker earning $100 a week ranked among the top 10 percent of wage earners in the United States. Although we are aware that hourly wages and monthly salaries have increased in recent years, we often overlook the more rapid growth

Health Insurance		Paid Time Off	
Medical care	53	Holidays	77
Dental	36	Vacations	77
Vision	22	Personal leave	36
Retirement Plans		Funeral leave	68
Defined benefits	21	Jury duty leave	69
Defined contributions	42	Military leave	48
Health Promotion Programs		Sick leave	58
Wellness programs	23	**Miscellaneous**	
Employee assistance	40	Job-related travel assistance	22
Fitness center	13	Educational assistance	49
Family Benefits		Life insurance	52
Child care	14	Short-term disability insurance	40
Long-term care	11	Long-term disability insurance	30
Adoption assistance	9		

EXHIBIT 12-1
Major Employee Benefits (Percent of Employees Participating)

Source: U.S. Department of Labor, U.S. Bureau of Labor Statistics, "National Compensation Survey: Employee Benefits in Private Industry in the United States, March 2005" (2005), pp. 1–32.

in benefits offered to employees. Because the cost of employing workers includes both direct compensation and corresponding benefits and services, the growth in both benefits and services has resulted in dramatic increases in labor costs to organizations. What do these increases mean for employers? From 1980 to 2004, the cost of providing value to each employee increased from $5,560 to nearly $20,000 per year,[5] with the greatest cost increases coming from rising health insurance benefit premiums. Today, benefit and service offerings add nearly 40 percent to an organization's payroll cost,[6] rising costs that more and more companies are trying to control.[7]

Employers have also found that benefits present attractive areas of negotiation when large wage and salary increases are infeasible. For example, if employees were to purchase life insurance on their own, they would have to pay for it with net dollars, that is, with what they have left after paying taxes. If the organization pays for it, the benefit is nontaxable (premiums paid on insurance up to $50,000) for each employee.[8]

Contemporary Benefits Offerings

The number and types of benefits offered have increased dramatically, as have their costs. What has triggered the sweeping changes in benefits offerings that will carry us into the future? The answer to that question lies in part in the demographic composition of the workforce.

Benefits offered to employees reflect many trends in our labor force. As the decades have witnessed drastic changes in educational levels, family status, and employee expectations, benefits have adjusted to meet the needs of the workers.[9] What demographic changes have we seen over the past few decades? Let's explore a few such changes to show why benefits offered today differ from those offered 30 years ago.

Recall from Chapter 1 our discussion of the changing workforce. Let's review this matter with an eye on benefits. As recently as the early 1960s, the workforce was composed of a relatively homogenous group—predominately males. This typical male had a wife who stayed home and cared for their children, necessitating a relatively standard benefit need. That is, most of these workers required a

ETHICAL ISSUES IN HRM

DOMESTIC PARTNER BENEFITS

Health insurance benefits are a traditional offering to employees and their immediate families. However, the definition of *family* has been changing in American society. Living arrangements, either heterosexual or homosexual, differ today from those in any other time in our history. As a result,

many employees are demanding the same opportunities as married counterparts for medical coverage for significant others. Although many companies voluntarily offer domestic benefits to their employees, it is just that—voluntary. Currently, 46 percent of the Fortune 500 offer such benefits.[10] Companies are *not* legally required to do so, and if they do not, they are not acting in a discriminatory manner.

Should companies offer benefits to domestic partners of employees? What is your opinion?

---

domestic partner benefits
Benefits offered to an employee's live-in partner.

legally required benefits
Employee benefits mandated by law.

retirement plan, sick leave, vacation time, and health insurance. Providing these to workers was customary and, for the most part, uncomplicated. However, the typical worker of the early 1960s is rare in today's workforce. Dual-career couples, singles, singles with children, and individuals caring for their parents (elder care) now prevale in the workforce. Equally important is the topic of benefit coverage for a worker's significant other: **domestic partner benefits.** Domestic partner benefits typically include medical, dental, or vision coverage for an employee's live-in partner—whether or not that live-in partner is of the opposite sex (see Ethical Issues in HRM). Nearly half of all Fortune 500 companies offer such benefits.[11]

Today's organizations must satisfy the diverse benefit needs of their employees. Consequently, they adjust benefit programs to reflect a different focus to achieve the goal of "something of value" for each worker. Before we discuss some of those mechanisms, however, it's important to frame what we mean by the term *benefit administration*. Putting together a benefits package involves two issues: (1) what benefits must be offered by law and (2) what benefits and services will make the organization attractive to applicants and current workers. First, we'll explore **legally required benefits.**

LEGALLY REQUIRED BENEFITS

U.S. organizations must provide certain benefits to their employees regardless of whether they want to or not, and they must be provided in a nondiscriminatory manner. With a few exceptions, hiring any employee requires the organization to pay Social Security premiums,[12] unemployment compensation, and workers' compensation (see Diversity Issues in HRM). Additionally, any organization with 50 or more employees must provide family and medical leave. Companies either pay premiums associated with many of these legally required benefits or share costs with employees (as in the case of Social Security) to provide each employee with some basic level of financial protection at retirement or termination or as a result of injury. These benefits also provide a death benefit for dependents in case of a worker's death. Finally, employers must permit employees to take time off from work for certain personal reasons.

The United States, however, is not the only industrialized nation to legally require benefits. Many others, such as Norway, Canada, and China, have them, too. We cannot discuss benefit offerings in each of the industrialized nations, but it's important to understand legally required benefits in the United States. Let's look at each of these.

Social Security

Social Security provides a source of income for American retirees, disabled workers, and surviving dependents of workers who have died. Social Security also provides some health insurance coverage through the federal Medicare program. In 2005, Social Security paid out $518 billion dollar to more than 48 million eligible workers in the United States.[13]

Social Security insurance is financed by employee contributions matched by the employer and computed as a percentage of the employee's earnings. In 2006, for instance, the rate was 12.4 percent (6.2 percent levied on both the employee and the employer) of the worker's earnings up to $94,200 or a maximum levy of $5,840 for each group. Additionally, 2.9 percent is assessed for Medicare on all earned income. Similar to Social Security, employer and employee split this assessment, paying 1.45 percent each in payroll taxes.[14] There is no maximum earnings for the Medicare portion of Social Security.

To be eligible for Social Security, employees must be employed for a minimum of 40 quarters, or 10 years of work.[15] During this work period, employees must have also earned a minimum amount of money each quarter, and for the entire year. In 2005, this amounted to $920 per quarter and $3,680 for the entire year. Prior to 1983, employees became eligible for full benefits at age 65. With revisions to Social Security laws, those born in 1938 and thereafter must wait longer before receiving full retirement benefits.[16]

Keep in mind, however, that Social Security is not intended to be employees' sole source of retirement income. Social Security benefits vary, based on the previous year's inflation, additional earnings, and recipient age. For 2005, the maximum Social Security retirement check was $2,000. Given longer life expectancies, and a desire to maintain one's current standard of living, workers today are expected to supplement Social Security with their own retirement plans. (We'll look at these shortly.) This is true whether or not Social Security will still be around in the year 2031!

Unemployment Compensation

Unemployment compensation laws provide benefits to employees who meet the following conditions: they are without a job, have worked a minimum number of weeks, have applied to their state employment agency for unemployment compensation, have registered for available work, and are willing and able to accept any suitable employment offered them through their state unemployment compensation commission. Unemployment compensation is designed to provide an income to individuals who have lost a job through no fault of their own (for example, layoffs, plant closing). Being fired from a job, however, may result in a loss of unemployment compensation rights.

Funds for paying unemployment compensation come from combined federal and state taxes imposed on the taxable wage base of the employer. At the federal level, the unemployment tax (called FUTA) is 6.2 percent on the first $7,000 of earnings of employees. States that meet federal guidelines are given a 5.4 percent credit, thus reducing the federal unemployment tax to 0.08 percent, or $56 per employee.[17]

State unemployment compensation tax is often a function of a company's unemployment experience; that is, the more an organization lays off employees, the higher its rate. Rates for employers range, for example, from 0.03 to 7.5 percent of state-established wage bases.[18] Eligible unemployed workers receive an amount that varies from state to state but is determined by the worker's previous wage rate and the length of previous employment. Compensation is provided for only a limited period—typically, the base is 26 weeks but may be extended by the state another 26 weeks during times when unemployment runs high.[19]

Unemployment compensation and parallel programs for railroad, federal government, and military employees cover more than 75 percent of the workforce.

Social Security
Retirement, disability, and survivor benefits, paid by the government to the aged, former members of the labor force, the disabled, or their survivors.

unemployment compensation
Employee insurance that provides some income continuation in the event an employee is laid off.

How does this couple manage their retirement? Years ago, some believed that Social Security was the answer. But with life expectancy increasing, financial woes in the Social Security fund, and the like, that's not the case. In fact, Social Security was never meant to be a sole source of retirement funds. Rather, it was to provide additional income for retirees, disabled workers, and surviving dependents of workers who have died. (Source: Christopher Bissell/Stone/Getty Images, Inc.)

DIVERSITY ISSUES IN HRM

WHEN EMPLOYEES ARE CALLED TO ACTIVE DUTY

Military benefits are often overlooked with respect to their importance to employees. Military benefits bridge the gap between one's military pay and one's civilian pay. Under typical conditions, many companies offer military pay to their employees who are members of the National Guard or the armed forces reserves as a means of pay continuity during the employee's two-week annual duty. That is, while reservists or National Guard members are off work during their required training, employers usually make up the difference in their pay. But what if the company does not have a military benefit pay policy? In that case, affected employees can use paid time off (such as vacation) to attend their active duty requirement or take a leave without pay.[20]

In either case, employees on military leave—whether two weeks' annual duty or an extended stay during a call-up as in the Iraqi War—are entitled to all the benefits they would have received had they not been called to active duty. That is, accrued benefits such as vacation and seniority must be given to the "absent" employee. For extended stays on active duty, the employer has the right to hire a temporary replacement, but employees have the right to return to their jobs within 31 days of being released from active duty. All HR actions that might have taken place in their absence (promotion, salary increase, and such) must accrue to the returning military veteran on his or her return.

Major groups excluded include self-employed workers, employees of organizations employing fewer than four individuals, household domestics, farm employees, and state and local government employees. As past recessions have demonstrated, unemployment compensation provides stable spending power throughout the nation. In contrast to the early 1930s, when millions of workers lost their jobs and had no compensatory income, unemployment compensation provides a floor that allows individuals to continue looking for work while receiving assistance through the transitory period from one job to the next.[21]

Workers' Compensation

workers' compensation

Employee insurance that provides income continuation if a worker is injured on the job.

Every state currently has some type of **workers' compensation** to compensate employees (or their families) for death or permanent or total disability resulting from job-related endeavors, irrespective of fault. Federal employees and others working outside the U.S. border are covered by separate legislation. Workers' compensation exists to protect employees' salaries and to attribute the cost for occupational accidents and rehabilitation to the employing organization.[22] This accountability factor considers workers' compensation costs as part of labor expenses incurred in meeting the organization's objectives.

Workers' compensation benefits are based on fixed schedules of minimum and maximum payments. For example, the loss of an index finger may be calculated at $500, or the loss of an entire foot at $5,000. Comprehensive disability payments are computed by considering the employee's current earnings, future earnings, and financial responsibilities.

The entire cost of workers' compensation is borne by the organization. Its rates are set based on the actual history of company accidents, the type of industry and business operation, and the likelihood of accidents occurring. The organization, then, protects itself by covering its risks through insurance. Some states provide an insurance system, voluntary or required, for handling workers' compensation. Some organizations may also cover their workers' compensation risks by purchasing insurance from private insurance companies. Finally, some states allow employers to self-insure. Self-insuring—usually limited to large organizations—requires the employer to maintain a fund from which benefits can be paid.

Most workers' compensation laws stipulate that the injured employee will be compensated by either monetary allocation or payment of medical expenses, or a combination of both. Almost all workers' compensation insurance programs, whether publicly or privately controlled, provide incentives for employers to maintain good safety records. Insurance rates are computed based on the organization's accident experience; hence employers are motivated to keep accident rates low.

Family and Medical Leave Act

The last legally required benefit facing organizations with 50 or more employees is the Family and Medical Leave Act of 1993. Recall from our discussion in Chapter 3 that the FMLA was passed to provide employees the opportunity to take up to 12 weeks of unpaid leave each year for family or medical reasons.

VOLUNTARY BENEFITS

The voluntary benefits offered by an organization are limited only by management's creativity and budget.[23] Exhibit 12-1 (see page 315) illustrates the many different benefits offered—almost all of which carry significant costs to the employer. Some of the most common and critical ones are health insurance, retirement plans, time off from work, and disability and life insurance benefits. We will delay the benefits discussion that deals with health issues, such as employee assistance programs, until the next chapter.

Health Insurance

We all have health-care needs, and most organizations today offer some health insurance coverage to their employees. This coverage has become one of the most important benefits for employees because of the tremendous increases in the cost of health care.[24] In fact, health care costs U.S. businesses more than $450 billion annually—that works out to approximately 13 cents for every dollar in wages spent.[25] This cost is expected to continue to rise.[26] As a result, many organizations, have been looking at a variety of cost-cutting measures, including reducing health care benefits as well as passing certain increased costs on to employees.[27] This may present a difficult situation for both the employer and the employee, although without health insurance almost any family's finances face depletion if a major illness occurs. The purpose of health insurance, then, is to protect the employee and his or her immediate family from the catastrophes of a major illness and to minimize their out-of-pocket expenses for medical care.

Any type of health insurance offered to employees generally provides coverage that can be extended beyond the employee. Specifically, the employee, the spouse, and their children may be covered. Health-care coverage generally focuses on hospital and physician care. It also typically covers major medical expenses. Specific coverages will vary based on the organization's health insurance policy. Generally, three types appear more frequently than others: traditional health-care coverage, health maintenance organizations (HMOs), and preferred provider organizations (PPOs), sometimes referred to as point-of-service (POS) or network plans.[28] All three are designed to provide protection for employees, but each does so in a different way. Interest is also increasing in employer-operated options, such as self-funded insurance. Let's look at each of these various types.

Traditional Health Insurance When health insurance benefits began, decades ago, one type of health insurance was generally offered: the traditional membership program. The cost to the employee, if any, was minimal. This traditional insurance usually was (and is to some extent today) provided through a Blue Cross and Blue Shield Organization.[29] However, it's not uncommon to see traditional health insurance programs being offered by such companies as Cigna or Aetna.

Since its inception in 1929, Blue Cross and Blue Shield (BC/BS) insurance has served as the dominant health-care insurer in the United States. Blue Cross and Blue Shield plans offer special arrangements to members in return for a guarantee that medical services will be provided. **Blue Cross** organizations are concerned with the hospital end of the business. These hospitals contract with Blue Cross to provide hospital services to members and agree to receive reimbursement from the health insurer for their fees. The reimbursement is often paid on a per diem basis for days stayed in the hospital as pays a percentage of the total bill.

The other component of the health insurer is the **Blue Shield** organization. Whereas Blue Cross has special arrangements with the hospitals, Blue Shield signs up doctors to participate in Blue Shield coverage. This participation feature means that a doctor is willing to accept the payment from Blue Shield as payment in full for services rendered. These payments are generally based on *usual, customary, and reasonable* (UCR) fees. The UCR fees reflect physician fees charged in an area.[30]

For many organizations, the costs associated with this "Cadillac" of health insurance plans have become prohibitive. Even passing these costs on to employees has met with little success. Traditional health-care coverage, therefore, is rapidly being replaced by HMOs and PPOs. Traditional insurers such as Blue Cross and Blue Shield, too, have begun to offer other types of health insurance coverage options to employers to help contain rising health-care benefit costs.

Blue Cross

A health insurer concerned with the hospital side of health insurance.

Blue Shield

A health insurer concerned with the provider side of health insurance.

Health Maintenance Organization (HMO)

Provides comprehensive health services for a flat fee.

Health Maintenance Organizations Health Maintenance Organizations (HMOs) strive to provide quality health care at a fixed expense for their members. People's needs have changed, and with these changing needs has come the expectation that they can obtain good health care at a reasonable cost. Traditional coverage does not usually include preventive care. For instance, traditional health insurance coverage would not include visiting a physician for routine baby immunizations or gynecological exams. Accordingly, the costs of such care are borne solely by the employee.

HMOs were created to meet this growing concern and provide the desired services to employees. This creation stemmed from passage of the **Health Maintenance Act of 1973**, which required employers who extended traditional health insurance to their employees to also offer alternative health-care coverage options. HMOs seek efficiencies by keeping health-care costs down, partly by providing preventive care. Approximately 75 percent of all workers in the United States belong to an HMO,[31] although in the early part of the new millennium, HMO membership has been decreasing rapidly.[32]

Exhibit 12-2 is a sample of HMO coverage. The major disadvantage, however, is that HMOs provide full coverage only if clients receive services from selected service centers. Furthermore, being seen outside of the HMO or other services require either permission from the HMO physician or greater out-of-pocket expense. Accordingly, an HMO arrangement significantly limits freedom of health-care choice. This limiting has been one of the greatest concerns expressed regarding HMOs. However, for many, the cost savings far outweigh the imposed restrictions.

Health Maintenance Act of 1973

Established the requirement that companies offering traditional health insurance to its employees must also offer alternative health-care options.

Preferred Provider Organizations (PPOs)

Organization that requires using specific physicians and health-care facilities to contain the rising costs of health care.

Preferred Provider Organizations Preferred Provider Organizations (PPOs) are health-care arrangements where an employer or insurance company has agreements with doctors, hospitals, and other related medical service facilities to provide services for a fixed fee. In return for accepting this fixed fee, the employer or the insurer promises to encourage employees to use their services. The encouragement often results in additional service coverage. PPOs often have lower premiums than traditional health insurance programs. Moreover, insurance companies offering the PPO also provide valuable information to employers.

COVERAGE CONDITIONS	COVERAGE (HMO FACILITY ONLY)
Physician	
Primary care	100% after $15 co-pay
Specialists	100% after $25 co-pay
In-patient care	100% (when preauthorized by plan)
Out-patient care	100% (when preauthorized by plan)
Hospital	100% (when preauthorized by plan)
Surgery	100% (when preauthorized by plan)
Maternity benefits	100% (when preauthorized by plan)
Well-baby care	100% after $15 co-pay
Immunizations	100% (when preauthorized by plan)
Deductibles	
Individual	None
Family	None
Out-of-pocket maximums	
Individual	None
Family	None

EXHIBIT 12-2
Sample Health Maintenance Organization Coverage

Source: State of Maryland, Summary of Benefits for Active & Retired Employees for July 1, 2005–June 30, 2006 (November 2005), pp. 13–20.

Through utilization review procedures, the PPO can provide data to help the employer determine unnecessary plan use. For example, elective surgery often requires preauthorization, which stipulates the approved procedures and hospital stay, if any. These "checks" can act as gatekeepers designed to contain health-care costs (see Exhibit 12-3).

How can a PPO benefit the employee? A PPO can provide much the same service that an HMO provides, and an individual need not use a specific facility—such as a designated hospital. So long as a physician or the medical facility is participating in the health network, the services are covered. The employee who uses a participating physician typically incurs a fixed out-of-pocket expense (defined by the agreement). In those cases, the PPO takes the form of traditional

COVERAGE CONDITIONS	IN NETWORK	OUT OF NETWORK
Physician		
Primary care	100% after $15 co-pay	80% after deductible
Specialists	100% after $25 co-pay	80% after deductible
In-patient care	100%	80% after deductible
Out-patient care	100%	80% after deductible
Hospital	100% for 365 days	80% after deductible
Surgery	100%	80% after deductible
Maternity benefits	100%	80% after deductible
Well-baby care	100% after $15 co-pay	80% after deductible
Immunizations	100%	80% after deductible
Dental coverage		
Diagnostic	Not covered	
Preventive	Not covered	
Deductibles		
Individual	None	$250
Family	None	$500
Out-of-pocket maximums		
Individual	None	$3,000
Family	None	$6,000

EXHIBIT 12-3
Sample Preferred Provider Organization (Point of Service) Coverage

Source: State of Maryland, Summary of Benefits for Active & Retired Employees for July 1, 2005–June 30, 2006 (November 2005), pp. 18–20.

health insurance. However, if an employee decides to go elsewhere for services, the service fee is reimbursed according to specific guidelines.

PPOs attempt to combine the best of both HMOs and traditional insurance. These networks may well be the fastest-growing form of health plans in the United States.[33]

Employer-Operated Coverage Although the types of insurance programs mentioned are the most popular means of health insurance today, many companies are looking for other options to contain rising health-care costs. To this end, some companies have begun reviewing the concept of self-insuring and in many of these instances, using the assistance of a third-party administrator (TPA).[34] One 1980s insurance trend was the formation of self-funded programs. Organizations such as Shell Oil, the State of Maryland, General Motors, Motorola, and General Binding Corporation have ventured into the insurance business to reduce health insurance costs.[35] This insurance plan is customarily established and operated under an arrangement called a *voluntary employees' beneficiary association* (VEBA). In this case, the employer typically establishes a trust fund to pay for the health benefits used.[36] For the most part, this employer trust fund has received favorable treatment from the IRS.

Consolidated Omnibus Budget Reconciliation Act (COBRA)

Provides for continued employee benefits up to three years after an employee leaves a job.

Health Insurance Continuation What happens to an employee's health insurance coverage if that employee leaves the organization or is laid off? The answer to that question lies in the **Consolidated Omnibus Budget Reconciliation Act (COBRA)**. One of the main features established by the COBRA was the continuation of employee benefits for up to three years after the employee leaves the company.[37] COBRA was enacted in 1985 to address an important social issue: employees who were out of work, and more important, no longer had medical insurance. When employees resign or are laid off through no fault of their own, they may continue their health insurance benefits for 18 months, although under certain conditions, the time may be extended to 29 months.[38] The organization must notify affected employees when COBRA benefits are available. Failure to notify in a timely manner can result in sanction and other fines against the organization.[39]

The cost of COBRA is paid solely by the employee. The employer may also charge the employee a small administrative fee for this service. However, COBRA requires employers to offer this benefit through the company's current group health insurance plan, which is at a rate that is typically lower than if the individual had to purchase the insurance himself or herself.[40]

Health Insurance Portability and Accountability Act of 1996 (HIPAA)

Ensures confidentiality of employee health information.

The HIPAA Requirement The **Health Insurance Portability and Accountability Act of 1996 (HIPAA)** deals primarily with health-care entities. This has generally not been a concern for most organizations, but many learned that if they had self-insured health insurance benefit programs, they, too, must comply with HIPAA requirements. Organizations with more than 50 employees and $5 million in revenues[41] had to have in place by April 14, 2003, policies and practices that ensured confidentiality of employee health information. Such organizations cannot release protected health information about an employee without the employee's consent, with regards to benefit plans, health flexible spending plans, employee assistance plans and such (see Chapter 13). Personal health information is any communication that identifies and relates to an employee or dependents' medical conditions, medical care given, enrollment information, premium payments, health status, or current treatments. This issue is also magnified by the concerns over identity theft.[42] For example, let's say you work for a self-insured health insurance organization and one of your employees' dependents has filed for a leave of absence in another organization under the Family and Medical Leave Act for an illness. Your form holds the health insurance information, and the dependent's organization asks you to verify the medical claim. Without written consent of the employee, you cannot release such information. In doing so, you may incur substantial penalties—upward of $100 per day, per violation, up to a maximum of $25,000 annually. It is also interesting to note that a facility that does drug testing for an organization cannot release drug test results to employers without written consent of the person being tested. As a result of HIPAA, organizations need to ensure that they have the proper consent forms in place and signed by the employees before such information is gathered.

RETIREMENT BENEFITS

Retiring from work today does not guarantee a continuation of one's standard of living. Social Security cannot sustain the lifestyle most of us grow accustomed to in our working years. Therefore, we cannot rely on the government as the sole source of our retirement income. Instead, Social Security payments must be just one component of a properly designed retirement system. The other components are retirement monies we may receive from our organization and savings we have amassed over the years. Irrespective of the retirement income vehicles we use, it is important to recognize that retirement plans are highly regulated by the **Employee Retirement Income Security Act (ERISA)** of 1974. Let's take a brief look at ERISA before we discuss the different retirement programs.

Employee Retirement Income Security Act (ERISA)
Law passed in 1974 designed to protect employee retirement benefits.

ERISA was passed to deal with one of the largest problems of the day imposed by private pension plans: employees were not receiving their benefits. Pension plans almost always require a minimum tenure with the organization before the individual has a guaranteed right to pension benefits, regardless of whether they remain with the company. These permanent benefits—or the guarantee of a pension when one retires or leaves the organization—are called **vesting rights**. In years past, employees needed extensive tenure in an organization before they were entitled to their retirement benefits—if they were entitled at all. This meant, for instance, that a 60-year-old employee with 23 years of service who left the company—for whatever reason—would have no right to a pension benefit. ERISA was enacted to prevent such abuses.

Vesting rights guarantee an employee's right to a pension benefit.

vesting rights
The permanent right to pension benefits.

ERISA requires employers who decide to provide a pension or profit-sharing plan to design their retirement program under specific rules. Typically, each plan must convey to employees any information relevant to their retirement. Vesting rights in organizations now typically come after six years of service, and pension programs must be available to all employees over age 21.[43] Employees with fewer than six years of service may receive a prorated portion of their retirement benefit. This shorter vesting period, which came into effect with the 1986 Tax Reform Act, is crucial for employees, especially when one considers that the length of service in companies today is shorter. With this shorter vesting period, employees who leave companies after six years generally can carry their retirement rights with them. That is, ERISA makes pension rights portable.[44]

ERISA also created guidelines for the termination of a pension program. Should an employer voluntarily terminate a pension program, the **Pension Benefit Guaranty Corporation (PBGC)** must be notified. Similarly, the act permits the PBGC, under certain conditions (such as inadequate pension funding), to lay claim on corporate assets—up to 30 percent of net worth—to pay benefits promised to employees. Additionally, when a pension plan is terminated, the PBGC requires the employer to notify workers and retirees of any financial institution that will handle future retirement programs for the organization.[45]

Pension Benefit Guaranty Corporation (PBGC)
The organization that lays claim to corporate assets to pay or fund inadequate pension programs.

Another key aspect of ERISA is its requirement for a company to include a **summary plan description (SPD)**. Summary plan descriptions are designed to inform employees about company benefits in terms the "average" employee can understand.[46] This means that employers must inform employees of the details of their retirement plans, including such items as eligibility requirements and employee rights under ERISA.

Summary Plan Description (SPD)
An ERISA requirement of explaining to employees their pension program and rights.

This employee, and thousands like her, work hard for many years and dream that one day she will retire. ERISA was enacted, with its enforcement arm, the Pension Benefit Guaranty Corporation, to ensure that retirement funds for which someone works hard will in fact be there when retirement comes. (Source: Ryan McVay/Stone/ Getty Images, Inc.)

defined benefit plan

A retirement program that pays retiring employees a fixed retirement income based on average earnings over a period of time.

Finally, it's important to note that another law has had a significant effect on ERISA. This is the 1984 Retirement Equity Act. The Retirement Equity Act decreased plan participation from age 25 to 21 but its main effect was to deal with gender issues in retirement programs. Specifically, women who left the workforce during childbearing years often found themselves penalized in terms of their retirement years of service; retirement was previously determined based on continuous years of service. The Retirement Equity Act also requires plan participants to receive spouse approval before a participant can waive survivor benefits.

Defined Benefit Plans

In decades past, the most popular pension was a **defined benefit plan**. This plan specifies the dollar benefit workers will receive at retirement. The amount typically revolves around some fixed monthly income for life or a variation of a lump-sum cash distribution. The amount and type of the benefit are set, and the company contributes the set amount each year into a trust fund. The amount contributed each year is calculated on an actuarial basis—considering variables such as length of service, how long plan participants are expected to live, their lifetime earnings, and how much return the trust portfolio will receive (for example, 5 percent or 10 percent annually). The pension payout formulas used to determine retirement benefits vary widely.

Over the past two decades, defined benefit plans have received some criticism. Employees have identified a need to receive more retirement benefits and to be permitted to make their own contributions to retirement plans—giving rise to *defined contribution plans.*

Defined Contribution Plans

Defined contribution plans differ from defined benefit plans in at least one important area: no specific dollar benefits are fixed. That is, under a defined contribution plan, each employee has an individual account, to which both the employee and the employer may make contributions.[47] The plan establishes rules for contributions. For example, the Humana defined contribution pension plan allows employees to select both a money purchase plan (described next) and a profit-sharing plan in which the company matches up to 6 percent of salary. In a defined contribution plan, the money is invested and projections are offered as to probable retirement income levels. However, the company is not bound by these projections, and accordingly avoids unfunded pension liability problems. This has made defined contribution plans a popular trend in new qualified retirement planning. Additionally, variations in plan administration frequently allow the employee some selection in the investment choices. For instance, an employee may select bonds for security, common stocks for appreciation and an inflation hedge, or some type of money market fund.

Money Purchase Pension Plan Money purchase pension plans are one type of defined contribution plan. Under this arrangement, the organization commits to deposit annually a fixed amount of money or a percentage of the employee's pay into a fund.[48] IRS regulations, however, permit a maximum 25 percent of worker pay. Money purchase plans have no fixed specific retirement dollar benefits as under a defined benefit plan. Companies do make projections of probable retirement income based on various interest rates, although the company is not bound to the projection.[49]

Profit-Sharing Plans Profit-sharing pension plans are yet another variation of defined contribution plans. Under such a plan, Fisher-Price contributes to a trust fund account an optional percentage of each worker's pay (maximum allowed by law is

15 percent). This, of course, is guided by profit level. The operative word in profit-sharing plans is *optional*. The company is not bound by law to make contributions every year. It should be noted, however, that although employers are not bound by law, the majority of employers feel a moral obligation to make a contribution. Often they will keep to a schedule, even when profits are slim or nonexistent.[50]

Individual Retirement Accounts In the early to mid-1980s, the individual retirement account (IRA) was the darling of retirement planning. The law permitted each worker to defer paying taxes on up to $2,000 of earned income per year ($2,225 for employee and spouse where the spouse did not work) with tax-deferred interest also accumulating on these accounts.[51] This formed a tax shelter for the average person, a good way to build a nest egg. Anyone who had earned income could invest in an IRA. The purpose of an IRA was to make the individual partly responsible for his or her retirement income.

IRAs were popular for the few years they received favorable tax status. However, the Tax Reform Act of 1986 significantly limited IRAs for many workers. To be eligible for deferring income to an IRA, workers now must meet specific conditions, such as not participating in a recognized retirement program at work and falling under limits on the adjusted annual income. Those who do meet the criteria could in 2003 set aside up to $3,000 tax free ($3,500 if age 50 or older). If a spouse is not employed, an equal amount can be set aside for the spouse, too.

Those who don't meet the qualification—such as single individuals earning more than the adjusted annual income level with a company-paid pension—would no longer qualify for a tax deduction from their IRA contribution. The purpose of the tax reform was to focus IRAs on lower-income workers who might not have a retirement program at their place of work or those who deserve to augment the one they have. Others can still make IRA investments, but the contribution is not tax-deductible.

Roth IRAs Effective in 1998, a new version of the IRA was signed into law. This Roth IRA allows an employee to contribute up to $3,000 annually to an account ($3,500 if age 50 and older).[52] However, the money is deposited after taxes. The money then grows tax-free and after the saver reaches a certain age can be withdrawn tax-free. As with the regular IRA, the Roth IRA carries conditions for contribution based on compensation.[53]

401(k)s The Tax Equity and Fiscal Responsibility Act (TEFRA) established capital accumulation programs, more commonly known as 401(k)s or thrift-savings plans. A 401(k) program is named after the IRS tax code section that created it. These programs permit workers to set aside a certain amount of their income on a tax-deferred basis through their employer.[54] In many cases, what differentiated the employer-sponsored 401(k) from an IRA was the amount permissible to set aside and the realization that many companies contributed an amount to the 401(k) on the employee's behalf.[55] This matching feature leads many companies to call their 401(k) a matching-contribution plan, meaning that both the employer and the employee work to create a retirement program. At Starbucks, for example, the company matches 25 to 150 percent of the employees' contributions on their first 4 percent of pay depending on their length of service.[56]

401(k) programs have been popular with employees since their inception, and employees on average contribute approximately 7 percent of their salary before taxes to such programs.[57] Both employers and employees have found advantages to offering capital accumulation plans. The cost of providing retirement income for employees is lower, and employees can supplement their retirement program and often participate in investments. Employees are offered the ease of contributing to their 401(k) through payroll deductions. In some instances, the matching-contribution program may be offered to supplement the employer's

How important are benefits such as the company 401(k) program to Starbucks employees? Most would say very much so. Starbucks matches a particular amount of employees' contributions to their 401(k) program. This, coupled with other HR practices, has resulted in more than 82 percent of Starbucks employees indicating high job satisfaction—and one of the lowest turnover rates in the industry. (Source: © AP/Wide World Photos)

WORKPLACE ISSUES

REVISING THE STOCK OPTION PLAN

Over the past several years there have been many questions raised about how companies treated stock option plans. Especially relevant in publicly traded companies, Financial Accounting Standards Board (FASB) past practices permitted organizations to simply record the intrinsic value of the stock as an expense. For example, assume a company's stock has a market value of $30 per share (that's the cost of a share of stock if someone purchased it). But the market value was not a major concern for organizations or the employees receiving such a benefit. Instead, they were given an option to purchase the stock at a set price at some time in the future. This was called the exercise price. In our example, let's say the exercise price was $18. The intrinsic value of the stock, then, according to the FASB was $12 (the market value minus the exercise value); this intrinsic value ended up on the company's balance sheet as a liability. Accordingly, liabilities were reduced, earnings per share were increased—and actual financial accuracy was questioned. Given some of the public scandals in the early 2000s, the FASB has worked on changing how this transaction is recorded. By 2005, the FASB mandated that stock options must be carried as a liability for the company at market price. Consequently, company earnings are affected.

But not every stock option is treated in a similar fashion. The FASB recognizes that volatility in a stock's price—especially in the technology field—makes it difficult to accurately predict market price. As such, assumptions regarding how a market stock price is determined are permitted (the basis of these assumptions is far beyond the scope of this book). However, a number of public companies are moving away from traditional stock options—deciding, instead, for restricted stock shares or cash bonuses paid out over several years, which in many cases will reflect an actual cost/liability to the company.

Source: "Time to Start Weighing the Option," *Business Week* (January 17, 2005), p. 32; T. V. Eaton and B. P. Prucyk, "No Longer an 'Option:' FASB Mandates How Companies Should Account for Share-Based Compensation," *Journal of Accountancy* (April 2005), pp. 63–68; and J. Marquez, "Firms Replacing Stock Options with Restricted Shares Face a Tough Sell to Employees," *Workforce Management* (September 2005), pp. 71–73.

noncontributory (defined benefit) retirement plan. Additionally, regardless of the mechanics of the program, employers are heavily regulated on offering employees investment advice.

Other Retirement Income Vehicles Although we've described the major retirement plans, we would be remiss not to mention the following retirement vehicles appropriate for selected groups of workers. These are 403(b)s, 457s, simplified employee pension plans (SEPs), Keogh plans, and stock option plans (ESOPs—such as employee stock ownership plans), payroll-based stock ownership plans (PAYSOPs), and tax-benefit-based stock ownership plans (TRASOPs). Exhibit 12-4 provides a summary of several retirement alternatives for certain groups of workers.

EXHIBIT 12-4
Other Retirement Plans

PLAN	ABOUT THE PLAN
403(b)	Designed to be the 401(k) counterpart for educational and nonprofit organizations.
Simplified Employee Pension Plans	Designed for an employer or the self-employed individual. Permits contributions up to 15 percent of net profit or $30,000 (whichever is less).
Keogh Plans	Available to the self-employed, permits contributions of 15 percent of net profit or $30,000 (whichever is less). The main distinction between a Keogh and an SEP lies in the IRS annual report filing requirement.
Stock Option Plans	Individual can purchase company stock through payroll deductions, generally at a discount or at straight market value without broker or commission.
457	Voluntary deferred salary plans for public sector employees.

PAID TIME OFF

Various benefits provide pay for time off from work. The most popular of these are vacation and holiday leave and disability insurance, which includes sick leave and short- and long-term disability programs. Although we'll present these as separate items, some organizations today lump all paid time off into a single "bank." As the time is used, it is charged to one's account whether it is used for vacation, or sick leave.

Vacation and Holiday Leave

After employees have been with an organization for a specified period of time, they usually become eligible for a paid vacation. Common practice is to relate the length of vacation to the length of tenure and job classification in the organization. For example, after six months' service with an organization, an employee may be eligible for one week's vacation; after a year, two weeks; after five years, three weeks; and after ten or more years, four weeks.[58] It is interesting to note

DID YOU KNOW?

BENEFITS AROUND THE GLOBE

Nearly every industrialized nation offers its employees some additional benefits during their employment. This chapter has focused primarily on benefits U.S. employers offer to employees, but how do employees in other countries fare? Let's look at some highlights.

Germany
9 paid holidays
14 weeks paid maternity leave
18 days paid vacation
6 weeks paid sick pay
Mandatory retirement employer and employee contribute 9.75 percent of salary

Japan
15 paid holidays
14 weeks unpaid maternity leave
10–20 days paid vacation (based on seniority)
Pension provided by government

Sweden
12 paid holidays
7 weeks paid maternity leave
25 days paid vacation
14 days paid sick leave
Government-paid pension

Russia
9 paid holidays
70 days paid maternity leave
28 days paid vacation
Sick leave up to 100 percent of pay based on seniority

India
13 paid holidays
12 weeks paid maternity leave
1 day paid vacation for every 20 days worked in the previous year
Government retirement employers and employees contribute 12 percent each

United Kingdom
8 paid holidays
2 weeks paid maternity leave mandatory—may receive 26 additional weeks based on seniority
Up to 28 weeks paid sick leave
Pensions—national insurance plan and private plans

Singapore
10 paid holidays
8 weeks maternity leave
14 days maximum paid vacation (based on seniority)
14 days sick leave
Retirement—employers contribute 13 percent of salary, employees 20 percent

Australia
8 paid holidays
52 weeks unpaid maternity leave
4 weeks paid vacation
2 weeks paid sick leave
Retirement: employers contribute 9 percent of salary; employees 3 percent; government 3 percent

Source: Society of Human Resource Management, "Global HR Library—WorldWatch" (2005), available online at www.shrm.org/ global/library/published/country.

that U.S. workers have shorter vacation periods than many industrialized nations. For example, U.S. workers enjoy on average 15 days of vacation each year, employees in Sweden, Denmark, Austria, and Spain average 30 or more days of vacation each year; and in Japan, it's 25 days.[59]

The rationale behind paid vacation is to provide a break in which employees can refresh themselves. This rationale is important but sometimes overlooked. For example, companies that allow employees to accrue vacation time and sell back to the company any unused vacation days lose sight of the regenerative "battery charging" intent. The cost may be the same to the employer (depending on how long vacation time can be accrued), but employees who do not take a break ultimately may be adversely affected, which can ultimately affect productivity. Moreover, many employees simply cannot completely leave the office behind. Nearly 25 percent of all employees check in with their office daily while on vacation.[60]

Holiday pay is paid time off to observe some special event—federally mandated holidays (such as New Year's Day, Presidents' Day, Martin Luther King Jr.'s Birthday, Memorial Day, Labor Day, Thanksgiving, or Christmas), company-provided holidays (such as Christmas Eve and New Year's Eve), or personal days (days employees can take off for any reason). In the United States, employees average 10 paid holidays per year.[61] Most other countries are similar, with averages of 8 paid holidays in the United Kingdom, 12 in Italy, and 14 in Spain and Portugal.[62]

Disability Insurance Programs

Employees today recognize that salary continuation for injuries and major illnesses is almost more important than life insurance. Most employees face a greater probability of a disabling injury that requires an absence from work of more than 90 days than that they will die before retirement. Programs to address this area of need can be broken down into two broad categories: short-term and long-term disability programs.[63]

Almost all employers offer some type of short-term disability plan. Categories under this heading include the company sick-leave policy, short-term disability programs,[64] state disability laws, and workers' compensation. Each helps replace income in the event of an injury or a short-term illness.[65] For many, this short-term period is defined as six months or less.

One of the most popular types of short-term disability programs is a company's sick-leave plan. Most organizations, such as General Motors and Federal Express, pay their employees on days they do not work because of illness. Sick leave is allocated at a specific number of days a year,[66] often accumulatively. Sick leave costs employers about $2,000 annually per employee in productivity loss.[67] In some organizations, too, the number of days may be expanded relative to years of service with the organization. Each year of employment may entitle the worker to two additional days' sick leave. Regardless of whether sick leave is used, it continues to accumulate (usually up to some maximum number of days). Employees who have been with the company the longest accumulate the most sick-leave credit.

Sick-leave abuse has often been a problem for organizations.[68] The belief, too, that one should amass sick leave for use later in life is quickly diminishing. That belief may have been popular when workers tended to join an organization early in life and retire from that company, but today's mobility renders long-term focus largely meaningless. This is especially alarming when we consider that sick days are not usually transferable to another organization. Thus, the "use them or lose them" concept may only hinder productivity. Recent attempts to combat this potential for sick-leave abuse include financial incentives to individuals who do not fully use their sick leave for the year. Organizations may reward attendance with "well pay." Well pay provides a monetary inducement for workers not to use all of their sick leave, perhaps by buying back unused sick leave, lumping sick-leave days into years of service in calculating retirement benefits, or even having special drawings for those who qualify. Some companies allow workers to donate sick leave to co-workers who have serious illnesses and have exhausted their sick leave.[69] Such incentives intend to serve as a bonus and encourage judicious use of sick time.

When health insurance coverage for prevention fails to prevent major illness, and extended time off work is insufficient for recuperation, employees may need a long-term disability benefits program. Similar to short-term disability, long-term disability programs provide replacement income for an employee who cannot return to work and whose short-term coverage has expired. Long-term disability usually becomes effective after six months. Temporary or permanent long-term disability coverage is in effect in almost all companies. By definition, a temporary disability is one in which an individual cannot perform his or her job duties for the first 24 months after injury or illness. Permanent, long-term disability prevents an individual from performing in any occupation.

The benefits paid to employees are customarily set between 50 and 67 percent, with 60 percent salary replacement the most common. Most plans have a maximum monthly payment of replacement income between 70 and 80 percent of gross pay.[70] This may be as little as $2,000 or greater than $10,000. In most cases, long-term disability payments continue until the individual reaches age 65.[71]

SURVIVOR BENEFITS

Many companies offer life insurance as a benefit to provide protection to the families of employees. Life insurance programs, one of the more popular employee benefits, typically come in two varieties: noncontributory and contributory policies. Our major focus in this context is on the noncontributory variety, which is generally completely employer funded.

Group Term Life Insurance

When a company offers group term life insurance to its employees,[72] the standard policy provides for a death benefit of one to five times their annual rate of pay, with most including a double indemnity provision—that is, should an employee's death result from an accident, the benefit is twice the policy value. About half of all companies provide this coverage.[73]

Death benefits offered usually reflect one's position in the organization. Generally speaking, the more "valuable" an employee is in the organization, the greater the death benefit offered. Those at lower levels of the organization typically receive one to one-and-one-half their annual wage as a benefit, whereas top-level employees may receive as much as three times their salary.

Travel Insurance

Another insurance plan offered to many employees is travel insurance. Policies cover employees' lives in the event of death while traveling on company time. This insurance typically provides a lump-sum payment, from $50,000 to $1 million. Depending on any unique policy provisions, the insurance typically will be paid as long as an employee is conducting business-related activities when the death occurs. For example, if a salesperson's day typically begins by traveling from his or her residence to a client's place of business, coverage begins as soon as this person enters the car. The key element is when death occurs. An employee who normally commutes to work would not be covered under an employer-paid travel insurance benefit if an accident happened on the way.

The Service Side of Benefits

A key component of any benefit package is offering employees something in which they have an interest and that they value.

In addition to the benefits described, organizations offer a wealth of services employees may find desirable. Employees may receive these services at no cost or at a cost shared with the organization.

Services may include such benefits as sponsored social and recreational events, employee assistance programs, credit unions, housing, tuition reimbursement, gym memberships, paid jury duty time, uniforms, military pay, company-paid transportation and parking, free coffee, baby-sitting services or referrals, and even appliance repair services. Companies can be as creative as they like in putting together their benefits program—many today even offer in-house massages for their employees. The crucial point is to provide a package containing benefits in which employees have expressed some interest and perceive some value.

AN INTEGRATIVE PERSPECTIVE ON EMPLOYEE BENEFITS

When an employer considers offering benefits to employees, one of the main considerations is to keep costs down. Traditionally, employers attempted to do this by providing a list of benefits to their employees—whether employees wanted or needed any particular benefit, or used it at all. Rising costs and a desire to let employees choose what they want, led employers to search for alternative measures of benefits administration. The leading alternative to address this concern was the implementation of **flexible benefits**. Although flexible benefits offer greater choices to employees (and might have a motivational effect), we must understand that they are provided mainly to contain benefit costs. The term *flexible benefits* refers to a system whereby employees are presented with a menu of benefits and asked to select, within monetary limits imposed, the employee benefits they desire.[74] Today, almost all major corporations in the United States offer flexible benefits. Three plans are popular: flexible spending accounts, modular plans, and core-plus options (see Exhibit 12-5).

flexible benefits

A benefits program in which employees pick benefits that most meet their needs.

EXHIBIT 12-5
Flexible Benefit Programs

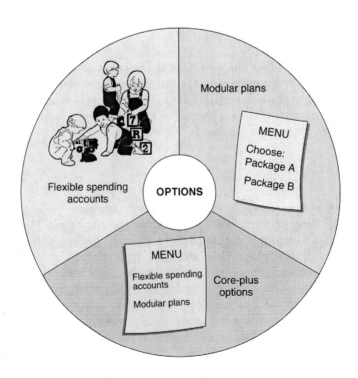

Flexible Spending Accounts

Flexible spending accounts, approved and operated under Section 125 of the Internal Revenue Code (IRC), are special types of flexible benefits that permit employees to set aside up to the dollar amount offered in the plan to pay for particular services.[75] For example, Abbott Laboratories has a flexible benefit plan in which employees pay for such items as health-care and dental premiums under premium accounts.[76] Also, certain medical expenses (deductibles, dental and vision care under a medical reimbursement account and such) and dependent child-care expenses (up to $5,250 in 2005) under a dependent-care reimbursement account can be established. As of 2004, employees can set aside monies in their flexible spending accounts to pay for over-the-counter medications.[77]

By placing a specified amount into a spending account, the employee can pay for these services with monies not included in W-2 income, which can result in lower federal, state, and Social Security tax rates and increase individual spending income. Such accounts also provide Social Security tax savings for the employer. We've presented an example of how using a flexible spending account can result in more take-home pay for an employee (see Exhibit 12-6). Ironically, although the benefits of flexible spending accounts are clearly visible, fewer than 15 percent of all employees actually use them.[78]

Despite tax benefits for employees, workers must understand that flexible spending accounts are heavily regulated. Each account established must operate independently. For instance, money set aside for dependent-care expenses can be used only for that purpose. One cannot decide later to seek reimbursement from one account to pay for services where no account was established or to pay for services from another account because all monies in the designated account have been withdrawn. Additionally, money deposited into these accounts must be spent during the period or forfeited. Unused monies do not revert back to the employee as cash, but typically revert back to the company. This point must be clearly communicated to employees to avoid misconception of the plan requirements.

Modular Plans

The modular plan of flexible benefits is a system whereby employees choose a pre-designed package of benefits. As opposed to selecting cafeteria style, modular plans

	WITHOUT FLEXIBLE ACCOUNT	WITH FLEXIBLE ACCOUNT
Gross Monthly Pay	$2,500	$2,500
Retirement Deduction	−150	−150
Pretax Payroll Deduction	0	−600*
Administrative Fee	0	−5
Taxable Gross Income	$2,350	$1,750
Payroll Taxes	−530	−315
Amount of Paycheck	$1,819	$1,435
After-Tax Expense	−600*	0
Spendable Monthly Pay	$1,219	$1,435
Additional Monthly Income with Flexible Spending Account =		$216
*Assumes an employee is depositing monies monthly in a flexible spending account in the following way:		
Health insurance deduction	$150	
Dental insurance deduction	$20	
Dependent care deduction	$400	
Medical expenses deduction	$30	

EXHIBIT 12-6
An Example of Take-Home Pay (With and Without a Flexible Spending Account)

Source: Based on a similar example presented in South Carolina Budget and Control Board, *2006 Money Plus* (2005), p. 7. Some numbers have been rounded to simplify exhibit.

contain a prearranged package of benefits that are designed to meet particular needs of groups of employees. For example, suppose a company offers its employees two separate modules. Module 1 benefits consist of a life insurance policy at two times annual earnings and HMO health-care insurance (no dental or vision coverage); this policy is provided to all employees at no cost to them. Module 2 benefits consist of a life insurance policy of two times annual earnings, traditional health insurance, and dental and vision coverage. This plan, however, requires a biweekly pretax payroll deduction of $57. Choice does exist, but it is limited to selecting either of the packages in its entirety.

Core-Plus Options Plans

A core-plus options flexible benefits plan exhibits more of a menu selection than the two programs just mentioned. Under this arrangement, employees typically receive coverage of core areas—typically medical coverage, life insurance at one time annual earnings, minimal disability insurance, a 401(k) program, and standard time off from work with pay.[79] These minimum benefits give employees basic coverage from which they can build more extensive packages, and the core-plus option helps keep benefit costs relatively stable.

Under the core-plus plan, employees select other benefits that may range from more extensive coverage of the core plan to spending accounts. Employees generally receive credits to purchase their additional benefits, calculated according to an employee's tenure in the company, salary, and position held. As a rule of thumb, in first-time installations, the credits given equal the amount needed to purchase the identical plan in force before flexible benefits arrived; that is, no employee should be worse off. If the employee decides to select exactly what was previously offered, he or she may purchase such benefits with no added out-of-pocket expenses (co-payments). Payments would now be made before taxes.

SUMMARY

(This summary relates to the Learning Outcomes identified on page 313.)

After having read this chapter, you can

1. **Discuss why employers offer benefits to their employees.** Employers offer benefits to employees to attract and retain them. Benefits are expected by today's workers and must provide meaning and value to the employees.
2. **Contrast Social Security, unemployment compensation, and workers' compensation benefits.** Social Security is an insurance program funded by current employees to provide (1) a minimum level of retirement income, (2) disability income, and (3) survivor benefits. Unemployment compensation provides income continuation to employees who lose a job through no fault of their own. Unemployment compensation typically lasts for 26 weeks. Workers' compensation provides income continuation for employees who are hurt or disabled on the job. Workers' compensation also covers work-related deaths or permanent disabilities. All three are legally required benefits.
3. **Identify and describe three major types of health insurance options.** The three major types of health insurance benefits offered to employees are traditional, health maintenance organizations, and preferred provider organizations. The latter two are designed to provide a fixed out-of-pocket alternative to health-care coverage.
4. **Discuss the important implications of the Employee Retirement Income Security Act.** The Employment Retirement Income Security Act (ERISA) has had a

significant effect on retirement programs. Its primary emphasis is to ensure that employees have a vested right to their retirement monies, that appropriate guidelines are followed in the event of a retirement plan termination, and that employees understand their benefits through the summary plan description.

5. **Outline and describe major types of retirement programs offered by organizations.** The most popular types of retirement benefits offered today are defined benefit pension plans, money purchase pension plans, profit-sharing plans, Social Security, individual retirement accounts, and 401(k)s. For special groups, however, 403(b)s, stock option programs, simplified employee pension plans, and Keogh plans may be used.

6. **Explain the reason companies offer their employees vacation benefits.** The primary reason for a company to provide a vacation benefit is to allow employees a break from work in which they can refresh and reenergize themselves.

7. **Describe the purpose of disability insurance programs.** Disability benefit programs ensure income replacement for employees when a temporary or permanent disability arises from an injury or extended illness (typically originating off the job).

8. **List the various types of flexible benefit option programs.** Flexible benefits programs come in a variety of packages. The most popular versions existing today are flexible spending accounts, modular plans, and core-plus options.

DEMONSTRATING COMPREHENSION: *Questions for Review*

1. Describe why companies provide benefits to their employees. What effect do companies expect benefits will have on employee work behaviors?
2. How does ERISA provide protection for a worker's retirement?
3. Identify and describe four legally required benefits.
4. Describe why an employee might select a PPO health insurance benefit over an HMO.
5. Describe the difference between a defined benefit pension plan and a defined contribution pension plan.
6. Describe the inherent potential for abuse in offering a sick-leave benefit.
7. Describe three types of flexible benefits programs.

KEY TERMS

Blue Shield
Blue Cross
Consolidated Omnibus
  Budget Reconciliation
  Act (COBRA)
defined benefit plan
domestic partner
  benefits
employee benefits
Employee Retirement
  Income Security Act
  (ERISA)

flexible benefits
health maintenance
  organization (HMO)
Health Insurance
  Portability and
  Accountability Act of
  1996 (HIPAA)
Health Maintenance
  Act of 1973
Pension Benefit
  Guaranty Corporation
  (PBGC)

preferred provider
  organization (PPO)
Social Security
summary plan
  description
unemployment
  compensation
vesting rights
workers' compensation

VISUAL SUMMARY

CHAPTER 12: Employee Benefits

1 Costs of Benefits

- Employee benefits cost organizations nearly $20,000 per employee.
- Employee benefits average nearly 40% of the wage dollar.

For example:

Employee wage	$40,000
Benefits	$16,000
Total Employee Cost	$56,000

2 Legally Required Benefits

Most employers are required by law to offer
- Social Security
- Unemployment compensation
- Workers' compensation
- Family and medical leave

3 Voluntary Benefits

Health Insurance
1. Traditional health-care coverage, e.g., Blue Cross, Blue Shield
2. Health Maintenance Organization (HMO)
3. Preferred Provider Organization (PPO)
4. Employer-operated coverage
5. Consolidated Omnibus Budget Reconciliation Act (COBRA)
   - Enacted in 1985
   - Provides health insurance continuation for 18 months on leaving the organization
   - Paid by employee
6. Health Insurance Portability and Accountability Act (HIPAA)
   - Protects patient privacy
   - Personal health information cannot be provided without employee's consent

334

4   Retirement Benefits

Employee Retirement Income Security Act (ERISA) of 1974
- Gives employees vesting rights
- Created Pension Benefit Guaranty Corporation to oversee pension program terminations
- Requires summary plan description, which informs employees about the benefits they receive

Types of Retirement Plans

- Defined benefit plan
- Defined contribution plan
- Money purchase pension plan
- Profit-sharing plan

- Individual retirement account (IRA)
- Roth IRA
- 401(k)
- 403(b)
- 457

- Simplified employee pension plan (SEP)
- Keogh plan
- ESOP
- PAYSOP
- TRASOP

5   Paid Time Off

- **Vacation and Holiday Leave**
- **Disability Insurance**

6   Survivor Benefits

- **Group Term Life Insurance**
- **Travel Insurance**

7   An Integrative Perspective on Employee Benefits

Flexible Spending Accounts allow employees to set aside pretax money to pay for certain benefits.

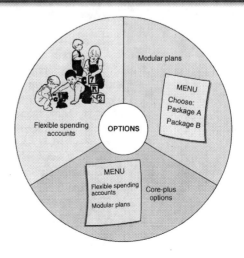

CROSSWORD COMPREHENSION

ACROSS

1. membership-based, nonfinancial rewards offered to attract and keep employees
5. employee insurance that provides income continuation if a worker is injured on the job
8. the permanent right to pension benefits
11. a retirement plan under which the organization commits to annually deposit a fixed amount of money into a retirement fund
15. employee benefits mandated by law
17. the organization that lays claim to corporate assets to pay or fund inadequate pension programs
18. a health insurer concerned with the provider side of health insurance
20. benefits offered to an employee's live-in significant other
21. an organization that provides comprehensive health services for a flat fee
22. a benefit designed to provide a work break in which employees can refresh themselves

DOWN

2. organization that requires using specific physicians and health care facilities to contain the rising costs of health care
3. a requirement of explaining to employees their pension program and rights
4. a retirement plan that pays retiring employees a fixed retirement income based on average earnings over a period of time
6. a benefit to provide protection to the family of an employee who dies
7. a health insurer concerned with the hospital side of health insurance
9. retirement, disability, and survivor benefits paid by the government
10. paid time off to observe some special event such as Thanksgiving or Labor Day
12. compensation that provides some income continuation in the event of an employee layoff
13. a benefits program in which employees pick benefits that most meet their needs
14. act ensuring confidentiality of employee health information
16. a benefit to pay employees who are missing work due to illness
19. law passed in 1974 designed to protect employee retirement benefits

HRM WORKSHOP

LINKING CONCEPTS TO PRACTICE: *Discussion Questions*

1. "Social Security should serve as a foundation for employee retirement programs. Therefore, Congress should explore more extensive revisions to the program to ensure that the next generation of retirees will receive the benefit." Do you agree or disagree with this statement? Explain your response.

2. "Social Security disability and survivor benefits should be the sole responsibility of each employee. A company simply cannot be responsible for the financial welfare of its employees. Additionally, legally required benefits provide some level of worker protection. Therefore, a major means of containing benefit costs should be elimination of disability and survivor benefits." Do you agree or disagree? Explain your response.

3. "Flexible benefits programs are employer inducements to reduce benefits costs. The average employee has neither the ability nor information to make such important choices. Employees should suspect such programs." Do you agree or disagree? Explain your response.

DEVELOPING DIAGNOSTIC AND ANALYTICAL SKILLS

Case Application 12-A: A PERKY WAY TO PRODUCTIVITY

Imagine working in an organization where employee morale is low, turnover is high, and the costs of hiring are astronomical. If that were the case, you'd imagine such affected employers do whatever they can to find, attract, and retain quality employees. But you couple this goal with the reality of the economic picture—you simply cannot throw good money at employees who will jump ship for an extra $1,000. You recognize that statistics say that 41 percent of all employees have no loyalty to their employers and will move on if a better offer comes. What a dilemma!

These issues clearly are a concern for organizations like Motek, Service Net, or Starbucks. But they don't fret over them. That's because they have found that treating employees with respect, and giving them such things as bonuses, rewards for longevity, on-site child care, on-site lunches, and sending employees home with prepared dinners works. Let's look specifically at Motek.[80]

Motek, a Beverly Hills, California, software firm, has a great need for software consultants. Given the nature of their work, continuity of work is crucial. To ensure that employees stay with the organization, company management implemented several company benefits that were designed to meet this goal. For example, employees are offered a company-sponsored lunch each work day. By paying $15 per week, employees are "treated" to lunch

brought in from a different restaurant each day. Given that these software engineers often didn't stop work to have lunch, this perk gives them some needed rest each day from the tedious jobs they perform. Additionally, Motek employees are offered five weeks of paid vacation. They are given a $5,000 bonus to be used on their vacations so long as the vacation consists of three consecutive weeks. Just present the employer with an itinerary for airfare or hotel costs, and the $5,000 is theirs. For those employees who remain with the company for 10 or more years, they are offered a vehicle lease on a Mercedes, Lexus, or BMW of their choice.

Have these benefits worked for Motek? If you translate longevity to morale and loyalty, you'd say they have. Motek has one of the lowest turnover rates in the industry, and their average employee seniority is 13 years.

Questions:

1. Describe the importance of employee benefits as a strategic component of fulfilling the goals of HRM.
2. Explain how Motek is using employee benefits as a motivating tool.
3. Do you believe the incentive benefits such as those offered at Motek can be used in other organizations? Why or why not?

Case Application 12-B: TEAM FUN!

Team Fun

Kenny and Norton, owners of TEAM FUN!, a sporting goods manufacturer and retailer, are sitting with Tony, director of human resources and Edna, compensation and benefits manager. Tony comments, "You mean to tell me that no one has actually retired from TEAM FUN!, and no one asked about the retirement plan before I got here?"

Norton scowls and observes, "You have been the first to bring up a whole lot of issues. And, no. No retirees. No retirement questions. We always had the profit sharing and that tax shelter that Leo set up for us. Everyone does what they want."

Kenny says, "Your mom did, Norton, after she helped us set up that bookkeeping system when we started."

Norton says, "No, she didn't. We never paid her anything but free tickets to all the local pro games, so she didn't really retire."

Tony says, "I'd like to show you how to save some money for health insurance premiums. Offering everyone free full Blue coverage is really expensive. There are some other options. And I think you should consider some money-saving vacation options. I never heard of anyone doing what TEAM FUN! does."

Kenny frowns. "As I recall, the vacation plan was what got you to take your job."

Tony sheepishly grins. "Four weeks to start is incredible. And earmarking one week to try out company products or services with you footing the bill sounded like a dream come true."

Norton nods. "That's what we thought. Anyone who wouldn't see it that way shouldn't work here. Why would you want to change that?"

Edna offers, "I agree that the vacation policy is great. However, we have trouble getting working moms in here. And I think that soccer moms could add a lot to us. We need more family-friendly benefits to really attract them."

Tony jumps in. "Exactly! If we come up with some guidelines to let employees tailor the benefits package to their own circumstances, we will spend benefits dollars more effectively and have a happier workforce."

Kenny frowns. "How could they be any happier?"

"We'd have a more diverse workforce," Tony replies.

"What do you mean, diverse?" asks Norton.

Kenny stands up and stretches and waves Norton over to the door. "Great ideas, Tony. We'll talk more tomorrow. Come on,

Norton. We've got to see the finals of that tournament we watched yesterday."

Questions:

1. As Tony's intern, work up a presentation chart for three major health insurance options. Make a recommendation.
2. How does TEAM FUN!'s vacation package differ from most U.S. companies? Should it be the same? Why or why not?
3. Design a flexible benefits plan for TEAM FUN!
4. Evaluate the retirement policy in light of current human resource practices. Is it effective for this organization?
5. Is TEAM FUN! family friendly? Explain.

WORKING WITH A TEAM: Benefit Selections

Using Exhibit 12-7, determine the mix of benefits that would best fit your needs. After choosing your benefits, form into teams of three to five members and answer the following questions.

1. Explain the reasons for the choices you made. What compelled you to make those specific benefit choices?

2. Compare the benefits you have chosen with those chosen by members of your team. What similarities exist? Differences?
3. Would the benefits you would select five years from now differ from the benefits you selected today? Why or why not?

EXHIBIT 12-7
Sample Flexible Benefit Selection Sheet[a]

Name: Chris Reynolds		Years of Service:	3
Annual Earnings: $38,000		Credits to Spend[b]	6330
Health Care:[c]		**Vacation:[d]**	
HMO	Core	1 week	Core
PPO	3280	2 weeks	730
		3 weeks	1460
Life Insurance:[e]		4 weeks	2190
1 × AE	Core	**Paid Holidays:[f]**	
2 × AE	273	7 days	Core
3 × AE	546		
4 × AE	819	**Personal Days:[g]**	
		1 day	Core
Disability Insurance:		2 days	146
50% AE	Core	3 days	292
55% AE	240		
60% AE	480	**Retirement [401(k)]:**	
65% AE	720	2% match	Core
		3% match	760
Dental Coverage:		4% match	1520
Dental HMO	Core	5% match	2280
Dental PPO	240	6% match	3040

[a]All cost figures represent single employee coverage only, where applicable. For additional family coverages for health insurance, see footnote 3.

[b]All flexible credits are based on 37% of annual salary (AE). Flexible spending credits are those credits available to you to spend on benefits. Credits available for spending is the difference between total flexible credits and costs associated with core coverage. Any amount spent beyond "credits" will be deducted evenly over your 26 biweekly paychecks.

[c]Health-care coverage is based on $283.33 per month for employee coverage only. Add $165 for employee plus one, and $228 for employee plus two or more per month for either coverage.

[d]Vacation costs are calculated at 1/52 of annual salary.

[e]Life insurance is calculated at $.072 per $1,000 of life insurance.

[f]Based on 2,080 hours worked annually and a cost per hour rate.

[g]Based on 2,080 hours worked annually and a cost per hour rate.

LEARNING AN HRM SKILL: *Calculating a Long-Term Disability Payment*

About the skill: Much of the work of a benefits specialist revolves around mathematics and finance calculations.[81] Specific skills are hard to find. However, it is clear that any benefits specialist needs excellent computer skills, especially in spreadsheet applications. To this end, here's a scenario that a benefits specialist may face that lends itself to the use of a spreadsheet application. To practice this skill, place the following information and calculations on a spreadsheet.

Suppose an employee makes $36,000 per year ($3,000 per month). Your organization offers employees a long-term disability (LTD) insurance benefit at 65 percent of earnings, with a monthly cap at $4,000. The company's LTD is also integrated with Social Security disability payments (SSDI) such that no more than 70 percent of salary is covered. The employee has a verifiable illness, is unable to work in any occupation, and has been covered under the company's short-term disability plan for the past six months (the required time before long-term disability starts). To determine this employee's long-term disability payment, you need to know the amount of SSDI monthly payment. Your research reveals that this employee is entitled to $8,400 in SSDI

payments a year ($700 a month). You now have enough data to complete this employee's LTD. After the calculations have been made, you see that this employee, given his circumstances, is eligible for a payment of $500 from SSDI and $900 from the LTD policy. Even though the LTD limit of 65 percent of the employee's salary would be $1,300, the total of LTD integrated with SSDI may not exceed $1,400 (70 percent of monthly salary). Here are the calculations:

- 65% of annual earnings/month = $1,950 ($3,000 × .65)
- 70% of monthly income for integration with Social Security = $2,100 ($3,000 × .70)
- SSDI benefit $8,400/12 = $700/month = $700 (given)
- Proposed total monthly payment without Social Security integration = $2,650 ($1,950 + $700)
- Proposed total monthly payment with Social Security integration = $2,100 (maximum)
- Overage = $550 ($2,650 − $2,100)
- Actual LTD payment = $1,400 ($1,950 − $550)(LTD + overage)

ENHANCING YOUR COMMUNICATION SKILLS

1. Discuss the pros and cons of offering benefits for the sake of being competitive and innovative. In your discussion, address whether you believe it's possible for benefits to become fads.
2. One controversy surrounding benefits administration today is offering domestic partner benefits. Develop a two- to three-page paper arguing (1) why domestic benefits should be offered to organizational members, and (2) why they shouldn't. End the paper with your support of one side or the argument.
3. Visit Social Security's Web site (www.ssa.gov). Research the guidelines established in late 2000 regarding Social Security benefits for the disabled. Write a two- to three-page summary of your findings.

THIRTEEN

During the past several years there has been a lot of emphasis placed on employers to hold mandatory ethics training for their employees. These sessions are supposed to be about helping employees recognize the way to do things properly, distinguish between right and wrong behaviors, and handling those gray areas in the most effective way. The list of companies offering this training reads like a who's who among U.S. corporations. One corporation, Lockheed Martin, however, appears to be the one most identified with it—not because of the precise training but what happened in their training effort.[1]

During the course of the training, one worker stood up in the middle of the mandatory ethics training class and excused himself. He walked out to his car, where he proceeded to heavily arm himself. As he reentered the building he began firing his weapons—shooting six co-workers before turning the gun on himself. All told, this disaster saw seven lives snuffed out.

(*Source:* © AP/Wide World Photos)

In the aftermath, a lot of people began asking questions as to why this happened. We know from government statistics that workplace violence is one of the leading causes of injuries and death in America's workplaces. But do these things just happen out of the blue? The Centers for Disease Control think not—they see this type of activity as a national epidemic. But few organizations (actually only 1 percent of all U.S. organizations) have a policy on antiviolence in their organizations. That's an interesting statistic given that all companies are supposed to provide a safe workplace for employees!

Why the complacency? It's suggested that many company officials believe that workplace violence is a random event—much like violence in society in general is random. But studies dispute this random nature as it applies to the work setting. As a result of research conducted on previous homicides on company premises, one investigator has found that rarely does an individual become spontaneously violent. Instead, such behavior is often the result of escalating behaviors over a period of time. Behaviors that begin with verbal abuse may escalate to verbal threats, property damage, and then the assault. Recognizing this pattern and taking action early is one way the experts suggest that this issue can be reduced.

In the Lockheed Martin plant, the individual responsible for the shooting had made so many violent threats to co-workers that many were afraid to go to work. If some action had been taken against the individual earlier, maybe this disaster could have been averted. Human resource managers must take such threats seriously and have a plan in place to deal with the aggressors. Saying "it couldn't happen to us" will not make this problem go away. The only acceptable action is a concerted effort to address the matter.

Ensuring a Safe and Healthy Work Environment

Learning Outcomes

After reading this chapter, you will be able to

1. Discuss the organizational effect of the Occupational Safety and Health Act.

2. List the Occupational Safety and Health Administration's (OSHA) enforcement priorities.

3. Explain what punitive actions OSHA can impose on an organization.

4. Describe what companies must do to comply with OSHA record-keeping requirements.

5. Identify four contemporary areas for which OSHA is setting standards.

6. Describe the leading causes of safety and health accidents.

7. Explain what companies can do to prevent workplace violence.

8. Define stress and the causes of burnout.

9. Explain how an organization can create a healthy work site.

10. Describe the purposes of employee assistance and wellness programs.

INTRODUCTION

Organization officials have a legal responsibility, if not a moral one, to ensure that the workplace is free from unnecessary hazards and that conditions surrounding the workplace are safe for employees' physical and mental health. Of course, accidents can and do occur, and the severity of them may astound you. Approximately 6,000 work-related deaths and almost 5 million injuries and illnesses are reported each year in the United States.[2] More than 250 million days lost of productive time cost U.S. companies more than $100 billion annually.[3] Heartless as it sounds, employers must be concerned about employees' health and safety if for no other reason than that accidents cost money.

From the turn of the twentieth century through the late 1960s, remarkable progress was made in reducing the rate and severity of job-related accidents and diseases. Yet the most significant piece of legislation in the area of employee health and safety was not enacted until 1970.[4] This law is called the *Occupational Safety and Health Act*. Let's take a closer look at it.

THE OCCUPATIONAL SAFETY AND HEALTH ACT

The passage of the *Occupational Safety and Health Act (OSH Act)* dramatically changed HRM's role in ensuring that physical working conditions meet adequate standards. As the Civil Rights Act altered organizational commitment to affirmative action, the OSH Act has altered organizational health and safety programs.

OSH Act legislation established comprehensive and specific health standards, authorized inspections to ensure the standards are met, empowered the Occupational Safety and Health Administration (OSHA) to police organizations' compliance, and required employers to keep records of illness and injuries and calculate accident ratios. The act applies to almost every U.S. business engaged in interstate commerce. Those organizations not meeting the interstate commerce criteria of the OSH Act are generally covered by state occupational safety and health laws. The safety and health standards the OSH Act established are quite complex. Standards exist for such diverse conditions as noise levels, air impurities, physical protection equipment, the height of toilet partitions, and the correct size of ladders. Furthermore, OSHA researches such areas as repetitive stress (or motion) injuries, problems associated with the eye strain that accompanies video display terminal use, ergonomics, and problems of inadvertent needlesticks in health-care activities. OSHA also develops training and education programs for businesses.

The initial OSH Act standards filled 350 pages in the *Federal Register*, and some annual revisions and interpretations are equally extensive. Nevertheless, employers are responsible for knowing these standards and ensuring compliance with those that apply to them (see Exhibit 13-1).

OSHA Enforcement Priorities

Enforcement of OSHA standards varies depending on the nature of the event and the organization. Typically, OSHA enforces the standards based on a five-item priority listing.[5] These are, in descending priority: imminent danger, serious accidents that have occurred within the past 48 hours, a current employee complaint, inspections of target industries with a high injury ratio, and random inspections.

imminent danger
A condition where an accident is about to occur.

Imminent danger refers to a condition where an accident is about to occur. Although this is given top priority and acts as a preventive measure, imminent danger situations are hard to define. In fact, in some cases, the definition of imminent danger appears to be an accident in progress, and interpretation leaves much to the imagination. For example, suppose you are withdrawing cash at an ATM. As you remove your cash, you are grabbed by an individual who places

EXHIBIT 13-1
OSHA Protection

You Have a Right to a Safe and Healthful Workplace.

IT'S THE LAW!

- You have the right to notify your employer or OSHA about workplace hazards. You may ask OSHA to keep your name confidential.

- You have the right to request an OSHA inspection if you believe that there are unsafe and unhealthful conditions in your workplace. You or your representative may participate in the inspection.

- You can file a complaint with OSHA within 30 days of discrimination by your employer for making safety and health complaints or for exercising your rights under the *OSH Act*.

- You have a right to see OSHA citations issued to your employer. Your employer must post the citations at or near the place of the alleged violation.

- Your employer must correct workplace hazards by the date indicated on the citation and must certify that these hazards have been reduced or eliminated.

- You have the right to copies of your medical records or records of your exposure to toxic and harmful substances or conditions.

- Your employer must post this notice in your workplace.

The *Occupational Safety and Health Act of 1970 (OSH Act)*, P.L. 91-596, assures safe and healthful working conditions for working men and women throughout the Nation. The Occupational Safety and Health Administration, in the U.S. Department of Labor, has the primary responsibility for administering the *OSH Act*. The rights listed here may vary depending on the particular circumstances. To file a complaint, report an emergency, or seek OSHA advice, assistance, or products, call 1-800-321-OSHA or your nearest OSHA office: • Atlanta (404) 562-2300 • Boston (617) 565-9860 • Chicago (312) 353-2220 • Dallas (214) 767-4731 • Denver (303) 844-1600 • Kansas City (816) 426-5861 • New York (212) 337-2378 • Philadelphia (215) 861-4900 • San Francisco (415) 975-4310 • Seattle (206) 553-5930. Teletypewriter (TTY) number is 1-877-889-5627. To file a complaint online or obtain more information on OSHA federal and state programs, visit OSHA's website at **www.osha.gov**. If your workplace is in a state operating under an OSHA-approved plan, your employer must post the required state equivalent of this poster.

1-800-321-OSHA
www.osha.gov

U.S. Department of Labor • Occupational Safety and Health Administration • OSHA 3165

(*Source:* Courtesy US Department of Labor)

a gun in your face and angrily demands your cash. Are you in imminent danger? Of course, most of us would say. But, according to one interpretation, you may not be in "imminent" danger. That state would not exist until the assailant pulled the trigger of the weapon and the bullet was fired. Tragically, by that time it is too late to worry about imminent danger. One's safety has already been threatened.

This has given rise to the priority two category of incidents—those that lead to serious injuries or death. Under the law, an organization must report these serious incidents to the OSHA field office within eight hours of occurrence. This permits the investigators to review the scene and try to determine the cause of the accident.

Priority three incidents, employee complaints, are a major concern for any manager. If an employee sees a violation of OSHA standards, that employee has the right to call OSHA and request an investigation. The worker may even refuse to work on the job in question until OSHA has investigated the complaint. This is especially true when a union is involved. For instance, some union contracts permit workers to legally refuse to work if they believe they are in significant danger. Accordingly, they may stay off the job with pay until OSHA arrives and either finds the complaint invalid or cites the company and mandates compliance.[6]

Next in the priority of enforcement is the inspection of targeted industries.[7] Inspecting each of the several million U.S. workplaces would require several hundred thousand full-time inspectors. OSHA has limited resources, and its budget has been significantly cut in the past. So, to have the largest effect, OSHA began to partner with state health and safety agencies and together direct their attention to those industries with the highest injury rates—industries such as chemical processing, roofing and sheeting metal, meat processing, lumber and wood products, mobile homes and campers, and stevedoring.

A new rule established in 1990 also requires employers who handle hazardous waste (that is, chemicals, medical waste) to follow strict operating procedures; any employer who handles hazardous waste is required to monitor employee exposure, develop and communicate safety plans, and provide necessary protective equipment.

The final OSHA priority is random inspection. Originally, OSHA inspectors were authorized to enter any work area premises, without notice, to ensure that the workplace was in compliance. In 1978, however, the Supreme Court ruled in *Marshall v. Barlow's, Inc.*[8] that employers are not required to let OSHA inspectors enter the premises unless the inspectors have search warrants. This decision does not destroy OSHA's ability to conduct inspections but forces inspectors to justify their choice of inspection sites more rigorously. That is, rather than trying to oversee health and safety standards in all of their jurisdictions, OSHA inspectors often find it easier to justify their actions and obtain search warrants if they appear to be pursuing specific problem areas. But don't let the warrant requirement mislead you into a false sense of security. If needed, an OSHA inspector will obtain the necessary legal document. For example, when inspectors attempted to evaluate work at the Hollywood, Florida, Hotel Diplomat construction site, the general contractor would not let them enter. A few days later, however, the OSHA inspectors returned with warrant in hand.[9]

Attorneys who deal with OSHA suggest that companies cooperate rather than adopt a confrontational stance. Cooperation focuses on permitting the inspection but only after reaching consensus on the inspection process. That's not to say, however, that you may keep inspectors from finding violations. If they are found, inspectors can take the necessary action. Finally, attorneys recommend that any information regarding the company's safety program be discussed with the OSHA inspector, emphasizing how the program is communicated to employees and how it is enforced.

Should an employer believe that the fine levied is unjust or too harsh, the law permits the employer to file an appeal. This appeal is reviewed by the

Marshall v. Barlow's, Inc.
Supreme Court case that stated an employer could refuse an OSHA inspection unless OSHA had a search warrant to enter the premises.

Occupational Safety and Health Review Commission, an independent safety and health board. Although this commission's decisions are generally final, employers may still appeal commission decisions through the federal courts.

Companies should cooperate with OSHA inspections rather than adopt a confrontational stance.

OSHA Record-Keeping Requirements

Under the OSH Act, employers in industries where a high percentage of accidents and injuries occur must maintain safety and health records. It's important to note, however, that organizations exempt from record-keeping requirements—such as universities and retail establishments—still must comply with the law itself; their only exception is the reduction of time spent on maintaining safety records. The basis of record keeping for the OSH Act is the completion of OSHA Form 300 (see Exhibit 13-2).[10] Employers are required to keep these safety records for five years.

In complying with OSHA record-keeping requirements, one issue arises for employers: Just what is a reportable accident or an illness? According to the act, OSHA distinguishes between the two in the following ways: Any work-related illness (no matter how insignificant it may appear) must be reported on Form 300. Injuries, on the other hand, are reported only when they require medical treatment (besides first aid) or involve loss of consciousness, restriction of work or motion, or transfer to another job.

To help employers decide whether an incident should be recorded, OSHA offers a schematic diagram for organizations to follow (see Exhibit 13-3). Using this decision tree, organizational members can decide if, in fact, an event should be recorded. If so, the employer is responsible for recording it under one of three areas: fatality, lost workday cases, or neither fatality nor lost workdays (see Technology Corner). Part of this information is then used to determine an organization's incidence rate. An **incidence rate** reflects the "number of injuries, illnesses, or (lost) workdays related to a common exposure base rate of 100 full-time workers." OSHA uses this rate to determine which industries and organizations are more susceptible to injury. Let's look at the incidence rate formula and use it in an example.

incidence rate
Number of injuries, illnesses, or lost workdays as it relates to a common base of full-time employees.

TECHNOLOGY CORNER

OSHA COMPLIANCE

OSHA reporting got you down? How do you obtain material safety data sheets? Technology can come to the rescue. Below are software packages that can assist you in handling OSHA matters.

Claimzone.com: Claimzone.com (Mountain View Software Corporation, www.mvsc.com/product_stage.html, price varies) is a reporting tool for OSHA matters. This Web-based product can be used to enter, review, and submit to OSHA all first-report injuries. OSHA Form 300 reporting can also be handled with this product.

OSHALOG: Similar to Claimzone, this software can assist an organization in preparing OSHA forms (www.customsafety.com/oshalog.htm).

HazCom: HazCom (Haddock HazCom, www.hazcom.net, price varies) provides its user with hazard communication services such as material safety data sheets, health hazard assessments, and label language recommendations.

EXHIBIT 13-2
OSHA Form 300

346

OSHA's Form 300 (Rev. 01/2004)

Log of Work-Related Injuries and Illnesses

Attention: This form contains information relating to employee health and must be used in a manner that protects the confidentiality of employees to the extent possible while the information is being used for occupational safety and health purposes.

U.S. Department of Labor
Occupational Safety and Health Administration

Year 20____

Form approved OMB no. 1218-0176

You must record information about every work-related death and about every work-related injury or illness that involves loss of consciousness, restricted work activity or job transfer, days away from work, or medical treatment beyond first aid. You must also record significant work-related injuries and illnesses that are diagnosed by a physician or licensed health care professional. You must also record work-related injuries and illnesses that meet any of the specific recording criteria listed in 29 CFR Part 1904.8 through 1904.12. Feel free to use two lines for a single case if you need to. You must complete an injury and illness Incident Report (OSHA Form 301) or equivalent form for each injury or illness recorded on this form. If you're not sure whether a case is recordable, call your local OSHA office for help.

Establishment name _____

City _____ State _____

Identify the person

(A) Case no.	(B) Employee's name	(C) Job title (e.g., Welder)

Describe the case

(D) Date of injury or onset of illness	(E) Where the event occurred (e.g., Loading dock north end)	(F) Describe injury or illness, parts of body affected, and object/substance that directly injured or made person ill (e.g., Second degree burns on right forearm from acetylene torch)
___/___ month/day		
___/___ month/day		
___/___ month/day		
___/___ month/day		
___/___ month/day		
___/___ month/day		
___/___ month/day		
___/___ month/day		
___/___ month/day		
___/___ month/day		
___/___ month/day		
___/___ month/day		
___/___ month/day		

Classify the case

CHECK ONLY ONE box for each case based on the most serious outcome for that case:

Death (G)	Days away from work (H)	Remained at Work — Job transfer or restriction (I)	Remained at Work — Other recordable cases (J)
☐	☐	☐	☐
☐	☐	☐	☐
☐	☐	☐	☐
☐	☐	☐	☐
☐	☐	☐	☐
☐	☐	☐	☐
☐	☐	☐	☐
☐	☐	☐	☐
☐	☐	☐	☐
☐	☐	☐	☐
☐	☐	☐	☐
☐	☐	☐	☐
☐	☐	☐	☐

Page totals ▶

Be sure to transfer these totals to the Summary page (Form 300A) before you post it.

Enter the number of days the injured or ill worker was:

Away from work (K)	On job transfer or restriction (L)
____ days	____ days
____ days	____ days
____ days	____ days
____ days	____ days
____ days	____ days
____ days	____ days
____ days	____ days
____ days	____ days
____ days	____ days
____ days	____ days
____ days	____ days
____ days	____ days
____ days	____ days

Check the injury/ column or choose one type of illness:

(M) Injury (1)	Skin disorder (2)	Respiratory condition (3)	Poisoning (4)	Hearing loss (5)	All other illnesses (6)
☐	☐	☐	☐	☐	☐
☐	☐	☐	☐	☐	☐
☐	☐	☐	☐	☐	☐
☐	☐	☐	☐	☐	☐
☐	☐	☐	☐	☐	☐
☐	☐	☐	☐	☐	☐
☐	☐	☐	☐	☐	☐
☐	☐	☐	☐	☐	☐
☐	☐	☐	☐	☐	☐
☐	☐	☐	☐	☐	☐
☐	☐	☐	☐	☐	☐
☐	☐	☐	☐	☐	☐
☐	☐	☐	☐	☐	☐

Injury (1)	Skin disorder (2)	Respiratory condition (3)	Poisoning (4)	Hearing loss (5)	All other illnesses (6)

Page ____ of ____

Public reporting burden for this collection of information is estimated to average 14 minutes per response, including time to review the instructions, search and gather the data needed, and complete and review the collection of information. Persons are not required to respond to the collection of information unless it displays a currently valid OMB control number. If you have any comments about these estimates or any other aspects of this data collection, contact: US Department of Labor, OSHA Office of Statistical Analysis, Room N-3644, 200 Constitution Avenue, NW, Washington, DC 20210. Do not send the completed forms to this office.

EXHIBIT 13-2
continued

OSHA's Form 300A (Rev. 01/2004)

Summary of Work-Related Injuries and Illnesses

Year 20___

U.S. Department of Labor
Occupational Safety and Health Administration

Form approved OMB no. 1218-0176

All establishments covered by Part 1904 must complete this Summary page, even if no work-related injuries or illnesses occurred during the year. Remember to review the Log to verify that the entries are complete and accurate before completing this summary.

Using the Log, count the individual entries you made for each category. Then write the totals below, making sure you've added the entries from every page of the Log. If you had no cases, write "0."

Employees, former employees, and their representatives have the right to review the OSHA Form 300 in its entirety. They also have limited access to the OSHA Form 301 or its equivalent. See 29 CFR Part 1904.35, in OSHA's recordkeeping rule, for further details on the access provisions for these forms.

Number of Cases

Total number of deaths

_____
(G)

Total number of cases with days away from work

_____
(H)

Total number of cases with job transfer or restriction

_____
(I)

Total number of other recordable cases

_____
(J)

Number of Days

Total number of days away from work

_____
(K)

Total number of days of job transfer or restriction

_____
(L)

Injury and Illness Types

Total number of ...
(M)

(1) Injuries _____

(2) Skin disorders _____

(3) Respiratory conditions _____

(4) Poisonings _____

(5) Hearing loss _____

(6) All other illnesses _____

Establishment information

Your establishment name _____

Street _____

City _____ State _____ ZIP _____

Industry description (e.g., Manufacture of motor truck trailers)
_____

Standard Industrial Classification (SIC), if known (e.g., 3715)
_____

OR

North American Industrial Classification (NAICS), if known (e.g., 336212)
_____

Employment information (If you don't have these figures, see the Worksheet on the back of this page to estimate.)

Annual average number of employees _____

Total hours worked by all employees last year _____

Sign here

Knowingly falsifying this document may result in a fine.

I certify that I have examined this document and that to the best of my knowledge the entries are true, accurate, and complete.

_____   _____
Company executive   Title

(___) ___-____   __/__/__
Phone   Date

Post this Summary page from February 1 to April 30 of the year following the year covered by the form.

Public reporting burden for this collection of information is estimated to average 50 minutes per response, including time to review the instructions, search and gather the data needed, and complete and review the collection of information. Persons are not required to respond to the collection of information unless it displays a currently valid OMB control number. If you have any comments about these estimates or any other aspects of this data collection, contact: US Department of Labor, OSHA Office of Statistical Analysis, Room N-3644, 200 Constitution Avenue, NW, Washington, DC 20210. Do not send the completed forms to this office.

347

EXHIBIT 13-3
Determining Recordability of Case Under OSHA

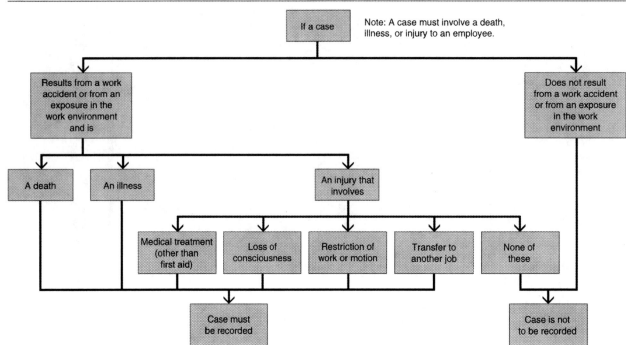

To determine the incidence rate, the formula $(N/EH) \times 200,000$ is used, where

- N is the number of injuries and/or illnesses or lost workdays.
- EH is the total hours worked by all employees during the year.
- 200,000 is the base hour rate equivalent (100 workers × 40 hours per week × 50 weeks per year).

In using the formula and calculating an organization's accident rate, assume we have an organization with 1,800 employees that experienced 195 reported accidents over the past year. We would calculate the incidence rate as follows: $(195/3,600,000) \times 200,000$.[11] The incidence rate, then, is 10.8. The significance of 10.8 depends on several factors. If the organization is in the meatpacking plant industry, where the industry average incidence rate is 14.9, the company is doing well. If, however, they are in the amusement and recreation services industry, where the industry incidence rate is 2.2, 10.8 indicates a major concern.[12]

OSHA Punitive Actions

An OSHA inspector has the right to levy a fine against an organization for noncompliance. Levying the fine is more complicated than described here. An organization that fails to bring a red-flagged item into compliance can be assessed a severe penalty. As originally passed in 1970, the maximum penalty was $10,000 per occurrence per day. However, with the Omnibus Budget Reconciliation Act of 1990, that $10,000 penalty can increase to $70,000 if the violation is severe, willful, and repetitive.[13] Although in its first 20 years questions arose regarding the OSH Act's value to workers' health and safety, such questions appear to be abating. The director of OSHA has made progress in redirecting OSHA's efforts. The agency has increased inspections and has been viewed as taking a tougher stance on workplace health and safety issues. Certain companies have seen what that focus can mean. In 2004, for example, OSHA conducted more than 39,000 inspections and issued more than $85 million in fines.[14] Fines are not levied for safety violations alone. A company that fails to keep its OSH Act records properly can be subjected to stiff penalties. If an employee death occurs, executives in the company can be criminally liable.

OSHA: A Critique

Has the OSH Act worked? The answer is a qualified yes. In fact, the act has had a direct and significant effect on almost every business organization in the United States. Some of the largest organizations have created an additional administrator who is solely responsible for safety. The OSH Act standards have made organizations more aware of health and safety.

Over the next decade, OSHA will continue to concentrate on safety and health violations in organizations and also on problems associated with contemporary organizations, particularly through **National Institute for Occupational Safety and Health (NIOSH)** research and in setting standards in such areas as bloodborne pathogens (see Workplace Issues). Similarly, OSHA continues to explore motor vehicle safety, fitting the work environment to the individual, as well as identifying guidelines for emergency response action.

First, setting standards for bloodborne pathogens is designed to protect individuals, like medical personnel, from becoming infected with such diseases as AIDS and hepatitis. In doing so, OSHA has established guidelines regarding protective

National Institute for Occupational Safety and Health (NIOSH)
The government agency that researches and sets OSHA standards.

WORKPLACE ISSUES

OSHA AND NEEDLESTICKS

As mandated by the Needlestick Safety and Prevention Act, OSHA has revised its bloodborne pathogens standard to clarify the need for employers to select safer needle devices as they become available and to involve employees in identifying and choosing the devices.[15] The updated standard also requires employers to maintain a log of injuries from contaminated sharps. "These changes in the OSHA bloodborne pathogens standard reaffirm our commitment to protecting health care providers who care for us all," said Labor Secretary Alexis M. Herman. "Newer, safer medical devices can reduce the risk of needlesticks and the chance of contracting deadly bloodborne diseases such as AIDS and hepatitis C. Employers need to consult their workers and use the safer devices when possible." According to the Needlestick Act, in March 2000, the Centers for Disease Control and Prevention estimated that selecting safer medical devices could prevent 62 to 88 percent of sharps injuries in hospital settings.

"Our revised bloodborne pathogen standard sets forth clearly the importance of reevaluating needle systems to identify safer devices every year. The new requirement

to record all needlesticks will help employers determine the effectiveness of the devices they use and track how many needlesticks are occurring within their workplaces," said OSHA administrator Charles N. Jeffress.

The revised OSHA bloodborne pathogen standard specifically mandates consideration of safer needle devices as part of the reevaluation of appropriate engineering controls during the annual review of the employer's exposure control plan. It calls for employers to solicit frontline employee input in choosing safer devices. New provisions require employers to establish a log to track needlesticks, rather than recording only those cuts or sticks that actually lead to illness, and to maintain the privacy of employees who have suffered these injuries.

Passed unanimously by Congress and signed by President Clinton in late 2000, the Needlestick Safety and Prevention Act mandated specific revisions of OSHA's bloodborne pathogens standard within six months. The legislation exempted OSHA from certain standard rulemaking requirements so that the changes could be adopted quickly.

The revised bloodborne pathogens standard became effective in April 2001.

Source: National News Release, *USDL: 01–26*, Thursday, January 18, 2001, www.osha.gov/pls/oshaweb/owadisp. show_document?p_table=Federal_Register&p_id-16265.

equipment (such as latex gloves, eye shields), and where a vaccine is available, ensures that exposed workers have access to it. In 2003, OSHA also disseminated information to organizations on the effects and prevention of severe acute respiratory syndrome (SARS), especially for those organizations that had employees traveling in Asia.[16]

Second, chemical processing standards reflect specific guidelines that must be adhered to when employees work with chemicals or other hazardous toxic substances. This requires companies to perform hazard analyses and take any corrective action required. These concerns over chemical hazards led to certain states passing *right-to-know laws*. These laws helped identify hazardous chemicals in the workplace, required employers to inform employees of the chemicals to which they might be exposed, the health risks associated with that exposure, and other policies guiding their use. Although these state laws made progress in providing information regarding workplace toxins, variations arose among them, and some states had no relevant laws at all. To provide some uniformity in protection, OSHA developed the Hazard Communication Standard in 1983. This policy "requires employers to communicate chemical hazards to their employees by labeling containers and by distributing data information provided by the manufacturer" to the employees. (See Exhibit 13-4, *Material Safety Data Sheet*.) In addition, employees exposed to various hazardous chemicals must be trained in their safe handling. As enacted in 1983, this standard applied only to manufacturing industries, but by mid-1989, meeting the requirements of the Hazard Communication Standard became the responsibility of all industries.[17]

The third area, motor vehicle safety, reflects OSHA's interest in addressing problems associated with workers who drive as a substantial part of their job. Nearly half of all worker deaths in any given year are attributed to motor vehicle accidents.[18] Accordingly, OSHA emphasizes substance-abuse testing of drivers, safety equipment, and driver education.

OSHA continues its efforts in studying work environment design, *ergonomics*, as it relates to productive work. OSHA has a Web site (www.osha.gov/SLTC/ergonomics/guidelines.html) that helps organizations understand ergonomics and suggests guidelines. OSHA highlights guidelines, not standards in disguise.[19] We'll revisit ergonomics later in this chapter.

Finally, in cooperation with the Homeland Security Act, OSHA has laid out guideline and practices to assist organizations in emergency preparedness. After the events surrounding September 11, 2001, in the United States—including the terrorists attacks in New York and Washington, DC, and the anthrax scare—OSHA has put together information on how organizations can protect themselves and provides guidance for organizations to develop contingency plans to deal with emergencies.[20]

JOB SAFETY PROGRAMS

If businesses are concerned with efficiency and profits, why would they spend money to create conditions that exceed those required by law? The answer is the profit motive itself. Accident costs can (and for many organizations do) substantially add to the cost of doing business. The direct cost of an accident to an employer shows itself in the organization's worker's compensation premium. This cost, as noted in Chapter 12, is largely determined by the insured's accident history. Indirect costs, which generally far exceed direct costs, also must be borne by the employer. These include wages paid for time lost due to injury, damage to equipment and materials, personnel to investigate and report on accidents, and lost production due to work stoppages and personnel changeover. The impact of these indirect costs can be seen in statistics that describe the costs of accidents for American industry as a whole.

EXHIBIT 13-4
Material Safety Data Sheet

Material Safety Data Sheet

May be used to comply with
OSHA's Hazard Communication Standard,
29 CFR 1910.1200. Standard must be
consulted for specific requirements.

U.S. Department of Labor

Occupational Safety and Health Administration
(Non-Mandatory Form)
Form Approved
OMB No.1218-0072

IDENTITY *(As Used on Label and List)*	Note: Blank spaces are not permitted. If any item is not applicable, or no information is available, the space must be marked to indicate that:

Section I

Manufacturer's Name	Emergency Telephone Number
Address *(Number, Street, City, State, and ZIP Code)*	Telephone Number for Information
	Date Prepared
	Signature of Preparer *(optional)*

Section II — Hazardous Ingredients/Identity Information

Hazardous Components (Specific Chemical Identity; Common Name(s))	OSHA PEL	ACGIH TLV	Other Limits Recommended	% *(optional)*

Section III — Physical/Chemical Characteristics

Boiling Point		Specific Gravity ($H_2O = 1$)	
Vapor Pressure (mm Hg.)		Melting Point	
Vapor Density (AIR = 1)		Evaporation Rate (Butyl Acetate = 1)	
Solubility in Water			
Appearance and Odor			

Section IV — Fire and Explosion Hazard Data

Flash Point (Method Used)	Flammable Limits	LEL	UEL
Extinguishing Media			
Special Fire Fighting Procedures			
Unusual Fire and Explosion Hazards			

(Reproduce locally)

OSHA 174. Sept. 1985

EXHIBIT 13-4
continued

Section V — Reactivity Data

Stability	Unstable		Conditions to Avoid
	Stable		
Incompatibility *(Materials to Avoid)*			
Hazardous Decomposition or Byproducts			
Hazardous Polymerization	May Occur		Conditions to Avoid
	Will Not Occur		

Section VI — Health Hazard Data

Route(s) of Entry:	Inhalation?	Skin?	Ingestion?
Health Hazards *(Acute and Chronic)*			
Carcinogenicity:	NTP?	IARC Monographs?	OSHA Regulated?
Signs and Symptoms of Exposure			
Medical Conditions Generally Aggravated by Exposure			
Emergency and First Aid Procedures			

Section VII — Precautions for Safe Handling and Use

Steps to Be Taken in Case Material Is Released or Spilled
Waste Disposal Method
Precautions to Be Taken in Handling and Storing
Other Precautions

Section VIII — Control Measures

Respiratory Protection *(Specific Type)*			
Ventilation	Local Exhaust	Special	
	Mechanical *(General)*	Other	
Protective Gloves		Eye Protection	
Other Protective Clothing or Equipment			
Work/Hygienic Practices			

*U.S.G.P.O.: 1986-491-529/45775

As we mentioned at the beginning of this chapter, accidents cost employers additional billions of dollars in wages and lost production. The significance of this latter figure grows when we note that this cost is approximately 10 times greater than losses caused by strikes, an issue that historically has received much more attention.

Causes of Accidents

The cause of an accident can be generally classified as either human or environmental. Human causes are directly attributable to human error brought about by carelessness, intoxication, daydreaming, inability to do the job, or other human deficiency. Environmental causes, in contrast, are attributable to the workplace and include the tools, equipment, physical plant, and general work environment. Both of these sources are important, but the human factor is responsible for the vast majority of accidents. No matter how much effort we make to create an accident-free work environment, we can achieve a low accident rate record only by concentrating on the human element.

A main objective of safety engineers is to scrutinize the work environment to locate sources of potential accidents. In addition to such obvious hazards as loose steps or carpets, oil on walkways, or a sharp protrusion on a piece of equipment at eye level, safety engineers will seek those less obvious—like mold or dust particles (see sick building, p. 355). Standards established by OSHA provide an excellent reference to guide the search for potential hazards.

Preventive Measures

What traditional measures can we look to for preventing accidents? The answer lies in education, skills training, engineering, protection devices, and regulation enforcement. We have summarized these in Exhibit 13-5.

Ensuring Job Safety

One way HRM can be assured that rules and regulations are enforced is to develop some type of feedback system such as oral or written reports or periodic walks through the work areas to make observations. Ideally, safety personnel rely on reports from supervisors on the floor and employees in the work areas, and these are supported by the safety inspector's personal observations.

At this height one must be extremely careful. While employers provide all the safety equipment required, sometimes accidents happen. In many cases, the cause is human error. As these window washers know, there's little margin of error before an accident happens. (Source: © AP/Wide World Photos)

www.wiley.com/college/decenzo
What Would You Do?
EXPERIENCE: Workplace Safety

Education	Create safety awareness by posting highly visible signs that proclaim safety slogans, placing accident prevention articles in organization newsletters, or exhibiting a sign proclaiming the number of days the plant has operated without a lost-day accident.
Skills Training	Incorporate accident prevention measures into the learning process.
Engineering	Prevent accidents through both job and equipment design. This may include eliminating factors that promote operator fatigue, boredom, and daydreaming.
Protection	Provide protective equipment where necessary. This may include safety shoes, gloves, hard hats, safety glasses, and noise mufflers. Protection also includes performing preventive maintenance on machinery.
Regulation Enforcement	The best safety rules and regulations will be ineffective in reducing accidents if they are not enforced. Additionally, if such rules are not enforced, the employer may be liable for any injuries that occur.

EXHIBIT 13-5
Accident Prevention Mechanisms

Although safety is everyone's responsibility, it should be part of the organization's culture. Top management must show its commitment to safety by providing resources to purchase safety devices and maintaining equipment. Furthermore, safety should become part of every employee's performance goals. As we mentioned in Chapter 10 on performance evaluations, if something isn't included, there's a tendency to diminish its importance. Holding employees accountable for safety issues by evaluating their performance sends the message that the company is serious about safety.

Another means of promoting safety is to empower action. Some organizations do this through employee groups called *safety committees*. Although chiefly prevalent in unionized settings, these committees serve a vital role in helping the company and its employees implement and maintain a good safety program.

A Safety Issue: Workplace Violence

Inasmuch as we see growing concern for the job safety for our workers, a much greater emphasis today is on increasing violence on the job.[21] No organization is immune, and the problem appears to be growing.[22] An employee leaves the company's sensitivity training seminar and kills several of his co-workers, an upset purchasing manager stabs his boss because they disagreed over how paperwork was to be completed, a disgruntled significant other enters the workplace and shoots his mate, an employee becomes upset over having his wages garnished—incidents like these have become all too prevalent.[23] Consider the following statistics: More than 1,000 employees are murdered, and more than 1 million employees are assaulted on the job each year in more than 300,000 occurrences of workplace violence costing organizations more than $120 billion.[24] Homicide is in the top three causes of work-related deaths in the United States.[25]

More than 1,000 employees are murdered and more than 1 million employees assaulted on the job each year.

Two factors have contributed greatly to this trend—domestic violence and disgruntled employees.[26] The issue for companies, then, is how to prevent on-the-job violence and reduce liability should an unfortunate event occur.[27] Because the circumstances of each incident are different, a specific plan of action for companies is difficult to detail. However, we have several suggestions. First, the organization must develop a plan to deal with the issue. This may mean reviewing all corporate policies to ensure that they do not adversely affect employees. In fact, the many cases where violent individuals caused mayhem in an office setting and didn't commit suicide have had one common factor: these employees were treated with neither respect nor dignity.[28] They were laid off without any warning, or they perceived they were being treated too harshly in the discipline process. Sound HRM practices can help to ensure respect and dignity for employees even in the most difficult issues such as terminations.

Organizations must also train their supervisory personnel to identify troubled employees before problems result in violence.[29] Employee assistance programs (EAPs) can be designed specifically to help these individuals. Rarely does an individual go from being happy to committing some act of violence overnight! Furthermore, if supervisors are better able to spot the types of demonstrated behaviors that may lead to violence, they can remove those who cannot be helped through an EAP before others are harmed.[30] Organizations should also implement stronger security mechanisms.[31] For example, many women killed at work following a domestic dispute die at the hands of someone who didn't belong on company premises. These individuals, as well as violence paraphernalia—guns, knives, and such—must be kept from entering the facilities altogether.[32]

Sadly, no matter how careful the organization, or what attempts at prevention, workplace violence will occur.[33] In those cases, the organization must be prepared to deal with the situation and offer whatever assistance it can to deal with the aftermath.[34]

Scenes like this have become too familiar in the United States. Workplace violence accounts for more than 1,000 murders each year, and more than 1 million employees are assaulted on the job each year. It's an issue that management cannot ignore. (Source: © AP/Wide World Photos)

Maintaining a Healthy Work Environment

Unhealthy work environments are a concern to us all. If workers cannot function properly at their jobs because of constant headaches, watering eyes, breathing difficulties, or fear of exposure to materials that may cause long-term health problems, productivity will decrease. Consequently, creating a healthy work environment is not only proper, it also benefits the employer. Often referred to as **sick buildings**, office environments that contain harmful airborne chemicals, asbestos, or indoor pollution (possibly caused by smoking) that make employees sick, have forced employers to take drastic steps.[35] Many have removed asbestos from their buildings. Links between extended exposure to asbestos and lung cancer have promoted various federal agencies such as the EPA to require companies to remove asbestos altogether or at least seal it so that it cannot escape into the air. But asbestos is not the only culprit! Germs, fungi, mold, and a variety of synthetic pollutants cause problems, too.[36]

sick building
An unhealthy work environment.

Although specific problems and their elimination go beyond the scope of this text, some suggestions for keeping the workplace healthy include[37]

- Make sure workers have enough fresh air. The cost of providing it is peanuts compared with the expense of cleaning up a problem. One simple tactic: unseal vents closed in overzealous efforts to conserve energy.
- Avoid suspect building materials and furnishings. As a general rule, if it stinks, it will emit an odor. Substitute tacks for smelly carpet glue or natural wood for chemically treated plywood.
- Test new buildings for toxins before occupancy. Failure to do so may lead to health problems. Most consultants say that letting a new building sit temporarily vacant allows the worst fumes to dissipate.
- Provide a smoke-free environment. If you don't want to ban smoking entirely, establish an area for smokers that has its own ventilation system.
- Keeping air ducts clean and dry. Water in air ducts is a fertile breeding ground for molds and fungi. Servicing the air ducts periodically can help eliminate growths before they cause harm.
- Paying attention to workers' complaints. Dates and particulars should be recorded by a designated employee. Because employees often are closest to the problems, they are a valuable source of information.

The information presented is important to follow, but one item in particular is noteworthy for us to explore a bit further. This is the smoke-free environment.

The Smoke-Free Environment

Debate is hot over whether smoking should be prohibited in a public place of business, even, say, in a bar, where forbidding smoking could put the establishment out of business. The dangers and health problems associated with smoking have been well documented, and they translate into increased health insurance costs. Furthermore, smokers were found to be absent more than nonsmokers, to lose productivity due to smoke breaks, to damage property with cigarette burns, to require more routine maintenance (ash/butt cleanup), and to create problems for other employees through secondhand-smoke disorders. Smoke-free policies have appeared to control maladies associated with smoking and in conjunction with society's emphasis on wellness.

Although many nonsmokers would prefer a total ban on smoking in the workplace, it may not be the most practical. Employees who smoke may find quitting immediately impossible. The nicotine addiction may prohibit a cold-turkey approach for the most ardent smoker. Accordingly, a total ban on smoking should take a phased-in approach. For example, this gradual process may begin with representative employees helping determine the organization's smoke-free goals and timetables. This means deciding if the organization will ban smoking altogether over a period of time, or if special areas will be designated as smoking rooms. If

ETHICAL ISSUES IN HRM

SAFETY AND HEALTH PROGRAMS

As more organizations go smoke-free, a major question arises. That is, what do the smokers do? If they go outside to smoke, that raises other issues such as lost productivity while employees are outside smoking or cleanup of ashes and butts scattered on the ground. Should smokers have rights? It is well documented that smoking can create health problems. Accordingly, health insurance premiums, as well as other premiums such as life insurance, are significantly higher for those who light up. And in most cases, employers have passed these increased premium costs on to the worker. Companies have developed more stringent policies on smoking, and many have banned smoking on company premises altogether. Clearly, the smoker today is disadvantaged, but how far can that go?

Can an organization refuse to hire someone simply because he or she smokes? Depending on the organization, the job requirements, and the state in which one lives, they might! Even so, employers may take this one step further. Companies may, in fact, be able to terminate an individual for smoking off the job, on an employee's own time. Do you believe companies have the right to dictate what you do outside of work? If an organization can take such action against employees for smoking and justify it on the grounds that it creates a health problem, what about other things we do? Eating too much fatty food can create a health problem, so should we be susceptible to discipline for being caught eating a Big Mac? Some members of the medical community say one or two alcoholic drinks a day may in fact be therapeutic and prevent the onset of certain diseases. Yet alcohol can be damaging to humans. Accordingly, should we be fired for having a glass of wine with dinner or drinking a beer at a sporting event? What do you think? How far should we permit regulating "wellness" in our organizations?

the latter, such rooms must be properly ventilated to keep smoke fumes from permeating other parts of the facility.

Consequently, the organization needs to look at incentives for encouraging people not to smoke (see Ethical Issues in HRM). As mentioned previously, health-care premiums—as well as life insurance policies—for smokers are significantly higher than for nonsmokers. Employers may decide to pay only the nonsmoking premium and pass the additional premium costs on to smokers. Companies also require various options for individuals to seek help. Through assistance programs such as smoking-cessation classes, the organization can show that it is making a deliberate commitment to eliminate the problems associated with smoking in the workplace.

Repetitive Stress Injuries

repetitive stress injuries

Injuries sustained by continuous and repetitive movements of the hand.

musculoskeletal disorders (MSDs)

Continuous-motion disorders caused by repetitive stress injuries.

carpal tunnel syndrome

A repetitive-motion disorder affecting the wrist.

Whenever workers are subjected to a continuous motion like keyboarding, without proper workstation design (seat and keyboard height adjustments), they run the risk of developing **repetitive stress injuries**, or **musculoskeletal disorders** (MSDs). These disorders, which account for nearly 40 percent of annual workplace illnesses from headaches, swollen feet, back pain, or nerve damage, cost U.S. companies several billion dollars annually and account for one-third of all workers' compensation claims.[38] The most frequent site of this disorder is in the wrist (**carpal tunnel syndrome**). It affects more than 40,000 U.S. workers and costs companies more than $60 million annually in health-care claims.[39] Given the magnitude of problems associated with MSDs, OSHA issued its final standards in late 2000 to combat this workplace problem—standards that saved nearly $10 billion from reduced work-related injuries.[40]

One chief means of reducing the potential effects of cumulative trauma disorders for an organization, however, is through the voluntary use of *ergonomics*.[41] Ergonomics involves fitting the work environment to the individual. Reality tells us that every employee is different in shape, size, height, and so forth. Expecting each worker to adjust to standard office furnishings is just not practical. Instead, recognizing and acting on these differences, ergonomics looks at customizing the work environment until it is not only conducive to productive work but keeps the employee healthy.[42]

When we speak of ergonomics, we are primarily addressing two main areas: the "office environment and office furniture."[43] Organizations are reviewing office settings, work environment, and space utilization in an effort to provide more productive atmospheres. This means that new furniture purchased is designed to reduce back strain and fatigue. Properly designed and fitted office equipment, such as Pitney Bowes workstations, can also help reduce repetitive stress injuries.[44] Furthermore, companies are using colors, including mauves and grays, that are more pleasing to the eye, and experimenting with lighting brightness as a means of lessening employee exposure to harmful eyestrain associated with today's video display terminals.

STRESS

Defining Stress

Stress is a dynamic condition in which an individual confronts an opportunity, constraint, or demand related to what he or she desires, and for which the outcome is perceived as both uncertain and important. Stress is a complex issue, so let us look at it more closely. Stress can manifest itself in both positive and negative ways. Stress is said to be positive when the situation offers an opportunity for one to gain something; for example, the psyching up an athlete goes through can be stressful but can lead to maximum performance. When constraints or demands are placed on us, however, stress can become negative.[45] Let us explore these two features—constraints and demands.

Constraints are barriers that keep us from doing what we desire. Purchasing a sports utility vehicle (SUV) may be your desire, but if you cannot afford the $38,000 price, you are constrained from purchasing it. Accordingly, constraints take control of a situation out of your hands. If you cannot afford the SUV, you cannot buy it. Demands, on the other hand, may cause you to give up something you desire. If you wish to go to a movie with friends on Tuesday night but have a major examination Wednesday, the examination may take precedence. Thus, demands preoccupy your time and force you to shift priorities.

Constraints and demands can lead to potential stress. When coupled with uncertainty about the outcome and its importance, potential stress becomes actual stress. Regardless of the situation, if you remove uncertainty or importance, you remove stress. For instance, you may have been constrained from purchasing the SUV because of your budget, but if you just won one in a radio-sponsored contest, the uncertainty element is significantly reduced. Furthermore, if you are auditing a class for no grade, the importance of the major examination is essentially nil. Constraints or demands that affect an important event and leave the outcome unknown add pressure—pressure resulting in stress.

We are not attempting to minimize stress in people's lives, but it is important to recognize that both good and bad personal factors may cause stress. Of course, when you consider the restructuring and other changes occurring in U.S. companies, it is little wonder that stress is so rampant in today's companies. Stress-related problems are costing U.S. corporations nearly $300 billion annually in "lost productivity, increased worker compensation claims, turnover, and health care costs."[46] And stress on the job knows no boundaries.

In Japan, a concept called **karoshi** refers to death from overworking—employees who die after working more than 3,000 hours the previous year—18-plus hours each day with nearly every minute of scheduled out in specific detail. One in six Japanese employees works more than 3,100 hours annually. Upward of 10,000 individuals die each year from heart attack or stroke, and karoshi is listed as their cause of death.[47] Employees in Australia, Germany, and Britain, too, have suffered the ill effects of stress—costing their organizations billions of dollars.[48]

stress
A dynamic condition in which an individual confronts an opportunity, constraint, or demand related to a desire and perceives the outcome both uncertain and important.

Having a really aggravating day? It appears this employee is, too. After significant staffing cutbacks in the organization, she now does the work once handled by three workers. She still has a job, but the job is often overwhelming, causing stress. (Source: Michael Krasowitz/Taxi/Getty Images)

karoshi
A Japanese term meaning death from overworking.

In Japan, upward of 10,000 individuals die annually from being overworked.

EXHIBIT 13-6
Major Stressors

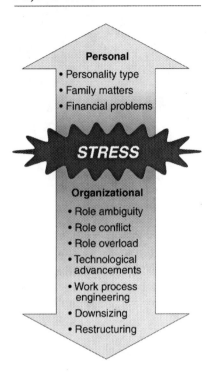

stressor

Something that causes stress in an individual.

role conflicts

Expectations that are difficult to reconcile or achieve.

role overload

When an employee is expected to do more than time permits.

role ambiguity

When an employee is not sure what work to do.

Type A behavior

Personality type characterized by chronic urgency and excessive competitive drive.

Type B behavior

Personality type characterized by lack of either time urgency or impatience.

Common Causes of Stress

Stress can be caused by factors called **stressors**. Causes of stress can be grouped into two major categories: organizational and personal (see Exhibit 13-6).[49] Both directly affect employees and, ultimately, their jobs.

There is no shortage of stressors within any organization.[50] Pressures to avoid errors or complete tasks in a limited time, a demanding supervisor, and unpleasant co-workers are a few examples. Below, we organize stressors into five categories: task, role, and interpersonal demands; organization structure; and organizational leadership.

Task demands relate to an employee's job. They include the design of the person's job (autonomy, task variety, degree of automation), working conditions, and the physical work layout. Work quotas can put pressure on employees when their outcomes are perceived as excessive.[51] The more interdependence between an employee's tasks and the tasks of others, the more potential stress present. *Autonomy*, on the other hand, tends to lessen stress. Jobs where temperatures, noise, or other working conditions are dangerous or undesirable can increase anxiety. So, too, can working in an overcrowded room or in a visible location where interruptions are constant.

Role demands relate to pressures placed on an employee as a function of the particular role he or she plays in the organization. **Role conflicts** create expectations that may be hard to reconcile or satisfy. **Role overload** is experienced when the employee is expected to do more than time permits. **Role ambiguity** is created when role expectations are unclear and the employee is unsure what to do.

Interpersonal demands are pressures created by other employees. Lack of social support from colleagues and poor interpersonal relationships can cause considerable stress, especially among employees with a high social need.

Organization structure can increase stress. Excessive rules and an employee's lack of opportunity to participate in decisions that affect him or her are examples of structural variables that might be potential sources of stress.

Organizational leadership represents the supervisory style of the organization's company officials. Some managers create a culture characterized by tension, fear, and anxiety. They establish unrealistic pressures to perform in the short run, impose excessively tight controls, and routinely fire employees who don't measure up. The effects of this style of leadership flow down through the organization to all employees.

Personal factors that can create stress include family issues, personal economic problems, and inherent personality characteristics. Because employees bring their personal problems to work with them, a manager fully understands employee stress who must first understand these personal factors. Evidence also indicates that employee personality affects susceptibility to stress. The most commonly used descriptions of these personality traits is called *Type A–Type B dichotomy.*

Type A behavior is characterized by a chronic sense of time urgency, excessive competitive drive, and difficulty accepting and enjoying leisure time. The opposite of Type A is **Type B behavior**. Type Bs rarely suffer from time urgency or impatience. Until quite recently, it was believed that Type As were more likely to experience stress on and off the job. A closer analysis of the evidence, however, has produced new conclusions. It has been found only the hostility and anger associated with Type A behavior actually associated with the negative effects of stress. And Type Bs are just as susceptible to these same anxiety-producing elements. Managers must recognize that Type A employees are more likely to show symptoms of stress even if organizational and personal stressors are low.

Symptoms of Stress

What signs indicate that an employee's stress level might be too high? Stress reveals itself in three general ways: physiological, psychological, and behavioral symptoms.

DID YOU KNOW?

EMPLOYEES WASTING TIME AT WORK

For years employers have touted the benefits of computers and technology in their support of enhanced productivity in the organization. But a question remains with regard to technology—that is, do employees use the technology for reasons other than work? For the most part, it appears the answer is yes—and it's called cyberloafing.

Cyberloafing refers to the act of employees using their organization's Internet access during work hours to surf non–job-related Web sites and to send or receive personal emails. The evidence indicates that cyberloafing is consuming a lot of time among workers who have Internet access. Research indicates, for example, that nearly one-fourth of all U.S. employees with Internet access spend at least an hour of each workday visiting sites unrelated to their job. In addition, it is estimated that nearly 40 percent of employees' Internet use at work is for recreational purposes—20 percent of those visiting pornographic Web sites. Cyberloafing is costing U.S. organizations millions of dollars each year.

If the work itself isn't interesting or creates excessive stress, employees are likely to be motivated to do something else. If they have easy access to the Internet, that "something else" is increasingly using the Internet as a diversion. The solution to this problem includes making jobs more interesting to employees, providing formal breaks to overcome monotony, and establishing clear guidelines so employees know what online behaviors are expected. Many employers are also installing Web monitoring software, although there is evidence that such efforts can undermine trust in the organization and adversely affect employee morale.

Source: "Internet Usage Statistics," www.n2h2.com/about/press/usage_stats.php (2004); V. K. G. Lim, "The IT Way of Loafing on the Job: Cyberloafing, Neutralizing, and Organizational Justice," *Journal of Organizational Behavior* (August 2002), pp. 675–694; "Control Your Internet Destiny," www.2watch.com (2005); and M. Conlin, "Workers Surf at Your Own Risk," *Business Week* (June 12, 2000), p. 106.

Most early interest in stress focused on health-related, or *physiological concerns.* This was attributed to the realization that high stress levels result in changes in metabolism, increased heart and breathing rates, increased blood pressure, headaches, and increased risk of heart attacks. Because detecting many of these requires medical training, their immediate and direct relevance to managers is negligible.

Of greater importance to managers are psychological and behavioral symptoms of stress, those that can be witnessed in the person. The *psychological symptoms* appear as increased tension and anxiety, boredom, and procrastination, which can all lead to productivity decreases. So too can *behaviorally related symptoms,* changes in eating habits, increased smoking or substance consumption, rapid speech, or sleep disorders.

Reducing Stress

Reducing stress presents a dilemma for managers.[52] Some stress in organizations is absolutely necessary; without it, workers lack energy. Accordingly, whenever we consider stress reduction, we want to reduce its dysfunctional aspects.

One of the first means of reducing stress is to make sure that employees are properly matched to their jobs—and that they understand the extent of their "authority." Furthermore, letting employees know precisely what is expected of them reduces role conflict and ambiguity. Redesigning jobs can also help ease work overload-related stressors. Employees need input in what affects them: involvement and participation have been found to lessen stress.

You must recognize that no matter what you do to eliminate organizational stressors, some employees will still stress out. You have little or no control over personal factors. You also face an ethical issue when personal factors cause stress. That is, just how far can you intrude on an employee's personal life? To help deal with this issue, many companies have started employee assistance and wellness programs.[53] These employer-offered programs are designed to assist employees in financial planning, legal matters, health, fitness, stress, and similar areas, where employees are having difficulties.

EXHIBIT 13-7
Variables Found to Be Significantly Related to Burnout

ORGANIZATION CHARACTERISTICS	PERCEPTIONS OF ORGANIZATION	PERCEPTIONS OF ROLE	INDIVIDUAL CHARACTERISTICS	OUTCOMES
Caseload	Leadership	Autonomy	Family/friends support	Satisfaction
Formalization	Communication	Job involvement	Sex	Turnover
Turnover rate	Staff support	Being supervised	Age	
Staff size	Peers	Work pressure	Tenure	
	Clarity	Feedback	Ego level	
	Rules and procedures	Accomplishment		
	Innovation	Meaningfulness		
	Administrative support			

Source: Baron Perlman and E. Alan Hartman, "Burnout: Summary and Future Research," *Human Relations,* Vol. 25, No. 4 (1982), p. 294.

A Special Case of Stress: Burnout

burnout

Chronic and long-term stress.

Worker burnout is costing U.S. industry billions of dollars. **Burnout** is a multi-faceted phenomenon, the byproduct of both personal and organizational variables. It can be defined as a function of three concerns: "chronic emotional stress with (a) emotional and/or physical exhaustion, (b) lowered job productivity, and (c) dehumanizing of jobs."[54] Note that none of the three concerns includes long-term boredom. Boredom, often referred to as burnout, is not the same.

Causes and Symptoms of Burnout The factors contributing to burnout can be identified as follows: organization characteristics, perceptions of organization, perceptions of role, individual characteristics, and outcomes.[55] Exhibit 13-7 summarizes these variables. Although they can lead to burnout, their presence does not guarantee that burnout will occur. Much of that outcome is contingent on the individual's capability to work under and handle stress. Because of this contingency, stressful conditions result in a two-phased outcome: the first level is the stress itself and the second level is the problems that arise from its manifestation.

Reducing Burnout Recognizing that stress is a fact of life and must be properly channeled, effective organizations establish procedures for reducing these stress levels before workers burn out. Although no clear-cut remedies are available, we propose four techniques:[56]

1. *Identification.* Analyze the incidence, prevalence, and characteristics of burnout in individuals, work groups, subunits, or organizations.
2. *Prevention.* Attempt to prevent the burnout process before it begins.
3. *Mediation.* Develop procedures for slowing, halting, or reversing the burnout process.
4. *Remediation.* Aid or redirect individuals who are already burned out or are rapidly approaching the end stages of this process.

The key point is to first make accurate identification, and then, and only then, tailor a program to meet that need. The costs associated with burnout lead many companies to implement a full array of programs—including EAPs—to help alleviate the problem. Many of these programs are designed to do two tasks: increase productivity and make the job more pleasant for the worker.

EMPLOYEE ASSISTANCE PROGRAMS

No matter what kind of organization or industry one works in, employees will occasionally have personal problems. Whether the problem relates to job stress or to legal, marital, financial, or health issues, one commonality exists: if an employee experiences a personal problem, sooner or later it will manifest itself at the workplace in terms of lowered productivity, increased absenteeism, or turnover (behavioral symptoms of stress). To help employees deal with these personal problems, more companies are implementing *employee assistance programs (EAPs)*.

A Brief History of EAPs

Thus far, we have discussed the various aspects of HRM designed to create an environment where an employee can be productive. We emphasized finding the right employees to fit the jobs, training them to do the job, then giving them a variety of opportunities to excel. All of this takes considerable time and money. Employees need considerable time to become fully productive—a process that requires the company to invest in its people. As with any investment, the company expects an adequate return. Now, how does this relate to EAPs?

Contemporary **employee assistance programs** (**EAPs**) are extensions of programs that had their start in U.S. companies in the 1940s.[57] Companies such as DuPont, Standard Oil, and Kodak recognized that some employees were experiencing problems with alcohol. Formal programs were implemented on the company's site to educate these workers about the dangers of alcohol and help them overcome their addiction. The rationale for these programs, which still holds today, is returning a productive employee to the job as swiftly as possible. For example, suppose Robert has been with your company for years. Robert was always a solid performer, but lately you notice his performance declining. The quality of his work is diminishing; he has been late three times in the past five weeks, and rumor has it that Robert is having marital problems. You have every right to discipline Robert according to the organization's discipline process, but discipline alone is unlikely to help. Consequently, after a time, you may end up firing him. You'll lose a once-good performer and must fill the position with another—a process that may take 18 months to finally achieve Robert's productivity level. Instead of firing him, you decide to refer Robert to the organization's EAP. This confidential program works with Robert to determine the cause(s) of his problems and seeks to help him overcome them. Although he is meeting frequently at first with the EAP counselor, you notice that after a short period of time, Robert is back on the job—with performance improving.[58] After four months, he is performing at the level prior to when the problem got out of hand. You have your fully productive employee back in 4 months, as opposed to possibly 18 months, had you fired and replaced Robert.

employee assistance programs (EAPs)
Specific programs designed to help employees with personal problems.

EAPs Today

Following their early focus on alcoholic employees, EAPs have ventured into new areas such as adoption counseling, legal assistance, death of a loved one, and child–parent relations.[59] However, one of the most notable areas is the use of EAPs to help control rising health insurance premiums, especially in mental health and substance abuse services.[60]

Organizations do see returns on these investments. U.S. companies spend an estimated almost $1 billion each year on EAP programs. Studies suggest that most companies save from $5 to $16 for every EAP dollar spent.[61] That, for most of us, is a significant return on investment!

No matter how beneficial EAPs may be to an organization, one aspect cannot be taken for granted: employee participation. Employees must see EAPs as worthwhile, designed to help them deal with personal problems.[62] To accept EAPs, employees need to know about the program and understand its confidential nature.[63] Accordingly, they need extensive information regarding how the EAP works, how they can use its services, and its guaranteed confidentiality. Furthermore, supervisors must be properly trained to recognize

Studies suggest that companies save more than $5 for every dollar spent on EAPs.

changes in employee behaviors and to refer them to the EAP in a confidential manner.[64]

Although EAPs can help employees when problems arise, companies have given much support to finding ways to eliminate some factors that may lead to personal problems. In doing so, organizations such as the Adolph Coors Company have promoted wellness programs.

Wellness Programs/Disease Management

wellness programs

Organizational programs designed to keep employees healthy.

In addition to EAPs, many organizations are implementing wellness programs—many designed to help employees avoid certain diseases. A **wellness program** is designed to keep employees healthy.[65] These programs are varied and may focus on smoking cessation, weight control, stress management, physical fitness, nutrition education, high blood pressure control, violence protection, work-team problem intervention, and other issues.[66] Wellness programs can help cut employer health costs and lower absenteeism and turnover by preventing health-related problems.[67]

It is interesting to note that similar to EAPs, wellness programs work only when employees see value in them. This requires top management support—resources and personal use of the programs—or the wrong message may be sent to employees. Second, wellness programs need to serve the family as well as the employees themselves. This not only provides an atmosphere where families can get healthy together, it also reduces possible medical costs for dependents. And finally comes the issue of employee input. Even the best programs, if designed without considering employees' needs, may fail. Organizations need to invite participation by asking employees what they'd use if available. Although many

WORKPLACE ISSUES

THE OBESE NEED NOT APPLY

Almost every organization in the United States recognizes that it's imperative to have healthy employees. Given the significant cost increases in health insurance coverage for employees (see Chapter 12), employers have looked at a number of ways to reduce these ever-increasing financial burdens. Many have implemented wellness/disease-management programs designed to assist employees in maintaining a healthy life. Programs such as exercise, diet, blood pressure control, and smoking cessation can be found in nearly all organizations that offer such assistance to employees. But some other organizations are viewing this a bit differently. Rather than assist employees in preventing such difficulties, they are simply deciding to not hire these employees in the first place. So long as obesity is not attributable to a disability (which would be a potential EEO violation), the organization has every right to do so.

For example, statistics show that the obese have greater health problems, which increase the cost of health insurance to the organization—even more so than smoking or alcohol. And these costs are not just for health insurance premiums but may also include increases in an organization's life and disability insurance, as well as workers compensation. Consequently, obesity is costing U.S. corporations more than $13 billion annually and results in more than 30 million lost productive days at work. Moreover, obesity results in more than 230 restricted work activity days; the obese spend approximately 90 million days in the hospital each year. As such, refusing to hire them is viewed as a cost-cutting matter.

What's your feeling on this issue? Should employers be allowed to "discriminate" against the obese? Why or why not?

Source: See, for example, K. Greco, R. Paul, and B. Pawlecki, "Promoting Healthy Weight: With Obesity on the Rise, Eaps Can Take Advantage of Their Assessment, Referral, and Case Management Skills to Help Employers Keep Healthcare Costs under Control and Encourage Employees to Maintain Healthy Lifestyles," *Journal of Employee Assistance* (December 2004), pp. 14–16; and K. Merx, "The Rising Cost of Fat; Business Is Finding out That Obesity Drives up Costs for More than Just Health Insurance," *Crain's Detroit Business* (September 13, 2004), p. 11.

organization members know that exercise is beneficial, few companies initially addressed how to involve employees. But after finding out that employees would like on-site exercise facilities or aerobics classes, many organizations began appropriate program development.

As wellness programs continue to expand in corporate America, top management support is still intermittent but increasing. Why? Because in finding out how to involve senior executives it was discovered that they, too, wanted a place to go for exercise. Many of these executives receive as perks membership in health clubs. Whether executives or support staff participate in wellness programs or EAPs, U.S. organizations appear to be continuing their efforts to support a healthy work environment. The companies reap a good return on their investments, and thus programs such as EAP and wellness have proven to be win-win opportunities for all involved.[68]

INTERNATIONAL SAFETY AND HEALTH

It is important to know the safety and health environments of each country in which an organization operates. Generally, corporations in Western Europe, Canada, Japan, and the United States put great emphasis on the health and welfare of their employees. However, most businesses in less-developed countries have limited resources and thus cannot establish awareness or protection programs.

Most countries have laws and regulatory agencies that protect workers from hazardous work environments. It is important for American firms to learn the often complex regulations that exist, as well as cultural expectations of the local labor force. Manufacturers, in particular, where myriad potentially hazardous situations exist, must design and establish facilities that meet the expectations of the local employees, not necessarily those of Americans.

International Health Issues

Corporations preparing to send executives on overseas assignments should have a few basic health-related items on every checklist:

- *An up-to-date health certificate.* Often called a "shot book," this is the individual's record of vaccinations against infectious diseases such as cholera, typhoid, and smallpox. Each country has its own vaccination requirements for entry. In addition, the U.S. Department of State Traveler Advisories hotline provides alerts to specific problems with diseases or regions within a country.
- *A general first-aid kit.* This should include all over-the-counter medications such as aspirin and cold and cough remedies that the employee or family members would usually take at home but that might not be available at the overseas drugstore. In addition, any prescription drugs should be packed in twice the quantity expected to be used. In case of an accidental dunking, overheating, or other problem, it is wise to pack the two supplies of drugs separately. It also is advisable to know the generic name—not the U.S. trade name—of any pharmaceutical. Finally, include special items such as disinfectant solutions to treat fresh fruit or vegetables and water-purifying tablets as the sanitation system of the host country warrants.
- *Emergency plans.* On arrival at the foreign destination, employees should check out the local medical and dental facilities and what care can be expected in the host country. This might include evacuation of a sick or injured employee or family member to another city or even another country. For example, expatriates in China often prefer to go to Hong Kong

Anyone who travels outside the United States should visit the U.S. State Department's Travel and Living Abroad Web site. This site provides such valuable information as "Emergencies and Warnings, Living Abroad," and other helpful links that can assist in preparing for foreign travel.

even for regular medical checkups. It is always wise to take along copies of all family members' medical and dental records.

International Safety Issues

Safety for the employee has become increasingly an issue of security, both while traveling and after arrival. Again, the U.S. State Department provides travel alerts and cautions on its Web page.

Safety precautions, however, begin before the overseas journey. Flying first class may be a matter of status and comfort, but experience with skyjacks has shown that it is safer to fly economy class. The goal is to blend into the crowd as much as possible, even if the corporation is willing to pay for greater luxury. Many corporations offer the following advice for traveling executives: blending in includes wearing low-key, appropriate clothing, not carrying obviously expensive luggage, avoiding luggage tags with titles such as "vice president," and, if possible, traveling in small groups. On arrival at the airport, it is advisable to check in at the airline's ticket counter immediately and go through security checkpoints to wait in the less public gate area. The wisdom of this advice has been confirmed in Rome, Athens, and other airport bombings.

Once the expatriate family has landed, the goal remains to blend in. These individuals must acquire some local "savvy" as quickly as possible; in addition to learning the language, they also must adapt to local customs and try to dress in the same style as the local people.

Foremost on many individuals' minds when they go abroad is security. Many corporations now provide electronic safety systems, floodlights, and the like for home and office, as well as bodyguards or armed chauffeurs, but individual alertness is the key factor. Kidnappers often seek potential targets who are valuable to either a government or corporation, with lots of family money or a wealthy sponsor, and they look for an easy opportunity to plan and execute the kidnapping. This last criterion makes it important to avoid set routines for local travel and other behaviors. The employee should take different routes between home and office, and the children should vary their paths to school. The family food shopping should be done at varying times each day or in different markets, if possible. These and other precautions, as well as a constant awareness of one's surroundings, are important for every family member.

SUMMARY

(This summary relates to the Learning Outcomes identified on page 341.)
After having read this chapter you can

1. **Discuss the organizational effect of the Occupational Safety and Health Act.** The Occupational Safety and Health Act (OSH Act) outlines comprehensive and specific safety and health standards.

2. **List Occupational Safety and Health Administration (OSHA) enforcement priorities.** OSHA has an established five-step priority enforcement process consisting of imminent danger, serious accidents, employee complaints, inspection of targeted industries, and random inspections.

3. **Explain what punitive actions OSHA can impose on an organization.** OSHA can fine an organization up to a maximum penalty of $70,000 if the violation is severe, willful, and repetitive. For violations not meeting those criteria, the maximum fine is $7,000. OSHA may, at its discretion, seek criminal or civil charges against an organization's management if they willfully violate health and safety regulations.

4. **Describe what companies must do to comply with OSHA record-keeping requirements.** Companies in selected industries must complete OSHA Form 300 to record job-related accidents, injuries, and illnesses. This information is used to calculate the organization's incidence rate.

5. **Identify four contemporary areas for which OSHA is setting standards.** OSHA is setting standards to protect workers exposed to bloodborne pathogens, chemicals, and other work-related toxins, setting standards for motor vehicle safety, and focusing its attention on ergonomics.

6. **Describe the leading causes of safety and health accidents.** The leading causes of accidents are human or environmental factors.

7. **Explain what companies can do to prevent workplace violence.** A company can help prevent workplace violence by ensuring that its policies are not adversely affecting employees, by developing a plan to deal with the issue, and by training its managers in identifying troubled employees.

8. **Define stress and the causes of burnout.** Stress is a dynamic condition in which an individual is confronted with an opportunity, constraint, or demand for which the outcome appears important and uncertain. Burnout is caused by a combination of emotional and/or physical exhaustion, lower job productivity, or dehumanizing jobs.

9. **Explain how an organization can create a healthy work site.** Creating a healthy work site involves removing any harmful substance, such as asbestos, germs, mold, fungi, cigarette smoke, and so forth, thus limiting employee exposure.

10. **Describe the purposes of employee assistance and wellness programs.** Employee assistance and wellness programs offer employees a variety of services to support mental and physical health, which in turn helps contain organization health-care costs.

DEMONSTRATING COMPREHENSION: *Questions for Review*

1. What are the objectives of the Occupational Safety and Health Act?
2. Describe the priorities of OSHA investigations.
3. Identify three methods of preventing accidents.
4. How are incidence rates calculated? What do the results indicate?
5. What is stress? How can it be positive?
6. Differentiate between physiological, psychological, and behavioral stress symptoms.
7. What can organizations do to help prevent workplace violence?

VISUAL SUMMARY

CHAPTER 13: ENSURING A SAFE AND HEALTHY WORK ENVIRONMENT

1 — The Occupational Safety and Health Act (OSH Act)

Enforcement Priorities
1. Imminent danger
2. Accidents
3. Employee complaints
4. Targeted industries
5. Random inspections

Record-Keeping
Incident Rate = $(N/EH) \times (200,000)$
Where N is the number of injuries/illnesses and EH is the total hours worked by employees in a year. 200,000 is the base hour rate equivalent.

Punitive Action
- $10,000 per occurrence per day, per infraction
- $70,000 if violation is severe, willful, and repetitive

Areas of OSHA Interest
- Bloodborne pathogens standard
- Chemical processing standard
- Motor vehicle safety

2 — Job Safety Programs

Causes of Accidents
- Human factors
  - Error
  - Daydreaming
  - Intoxication
- Environmental factors
  - Tools
  - Physical plant
  - General work environment

Accident Prevention Mechanisms

Education	Create safety awareness by posting highly visible signs that proclaim safety slogans, placing accident prevention articles in organization newsletters, or exhibiting a sign proclaiming the number of days the plant has operated without a lost-day accident.
Skills Training	Incorporate accident prevention measures into the learning process.
Engineering	Prevent accidents through both job and equipment design. This may include eliminating factors that promote operator fatigue, boredom, and daydreaming.
Protection	Provide protective equipment where necessary. This may include safety shoes, gloves, hard hats, safety glasses, and noise mufflers. Protection also includes performing preventive maintenance on machinery.
Regulation Enforcement	The best safety rules and regulations will be ineffective in reducing accidents if they are not enforced. Additionally, if such rules are not enforced, the employer may be liable for any injuries that occur.

Workplace Violence
- More than 1000 people murdered at work each year
- More than 1 million assaulted on job each year
- Domestic violence carrying over into work setting

Prevention
- Sound HRM policies
- Trained supervisors to identify troubled employees
- Building security

366

3   Maintaining a Healthy Work Environment

Sick Buildings—office environments that contain harmful airborne chemicals, asbestos, or indoor pollution

Smoke-Free Environment
- Not permitting smoking on company premise
- Limiting where smoking on a company's premises can occur

Repetitive Stress Injuries
- Account for nearly 40% of annual workplace illnesses, from headaches, swollen feet, back pain, or nerve damage (carpal tunnel)
- Cost U.S. businesses more than $60 million annually

Stress
A dynamic condition in which an individual is confronted with an opportunity, constraint, or demand for which the outcome is both uncertain and important.

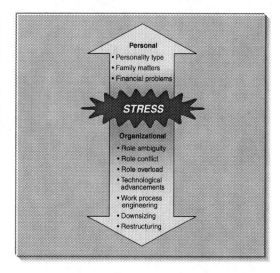

4   Employee Assistance Programs

Employee Assistant Programs—EAP
- Began in the 1940s
- Almost $1 billion spent each year
- Produce up to $16 in benefits for each $1 spent

Wellness Programs
Keep employees healthy
- Smoking cessation
- Weight control
- Stress control
- Physical fitness
- Nutrition education
- High blood pressure control
- Violence protection

8. Describe how EAPs and wellness programs help an organization control rising medical costs.
9. What must an organization do differently with respect to health and safety when operating in another country?

KEY TERMS

burnout
carpal tunnel syndrome
employee assistance programs (EAPs)
imminent danger
incident rate

karoshi
Marshall v. Barlow's, Inc.
musculoskeletal disorders (MSDs)
National Institute for

Occupational Safety and Health (NIOSH)
repetitive stress injuries
role ambiguity
role conflicts

role overload
sick building
stress
Type A behavior
Type B behavior
wellness program

CROSSWORD COMPREHENSION

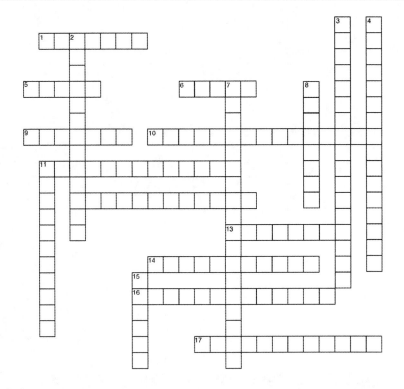

ACROSS

1. a Japanese term meaning death from overworking
5. personality type characterized by chronic urgency and excessive competitive drive
6. personality type characterized by lack of either time urgency or impatience
9. chronic and long-term stress
10. a motion disorder caused by continuous and repetitive movements
11. when an employee is not sure what work to do
12. a repetitive-motion disorder affecting the wrist
13. something that causes stress in an individual
14. an unhealthy work environment/facility
16. a condition where an accident is about to occur
17. the number of injuries, illnesses, or lost workdays as it relates to a common base of full-time employees

DOWN

2. expectations that are difficult to reconcile or achieve
3. injuries sustained by continuous movements of the hand
4. Supreme Court case that stated an employer could refuse an OSHA inspection unless OSHA had a search warrant to enter the premise
7. specific programs designed to help employees with personal problems
8. organizational programs designed to keep employees healthy
11. when an employee is expected to do more than time permits
15. government agency that researches and sets OSHA standards

HRM WORKSHOP

LINKING CONCEPTS TO PRACTICE: *Discussion Questions*

1. "Safety and health practices are good business decisions." Build an argument supporting this statement.
2. "OSHA inspections can become a cat-and-mouse maneuvering activity for organizations. This doesn't serve the interest of the organization, the employees, or OSHA." Do you agree or disagree? Explain your response.
3. "Employers should be concerned with helping employees cope with both job-related stress and off-the-job stress." Do you agree or disagree? Discuss.
4. "Supervisors should know which employees are having troubles and may ultimately cause harm to other employees. When they identify such an individual, they should take some action to ensure that the employee receives assistance before a disaster strikes." Build an argument supporting this statement and one that does not.
5. Some medical experts believe that regular daily exercise results in better health, improved conditioning, and greater tolerance of stressful situations. What would you think about being employed by a company that required you to work out daily on company time? Do you think this would help or hurt the company's recruiting ability? Explain your position.

DEVELOPING DIAGNOSTIC AND ANALYTICAL SKILLS

Case Application 13-A: PROTECTION OSHA-STYLE

Some employers cringe at the thought of OSHA regulations and inspections. These organizations often feel that the regulations are costly to follow, require them to implement practices or procedures that are not needed, and are just plain restrictive. OSHA, on the other hand, sees this differently. If by their actions they can prevent workplace injury or death, then OSHA inspectors feel these inconveniences are worth it. Consider the following:[69]

1. OSHA compliance officers from the El Paso, Texas, District Office made two employees who were working 80 feet above ground stop working until a fall protection system was installed. The workers and the company complied with the request.
2. A construction worker at National Riggers and Erectors is glad such fall protection systems exist. Working in Green Bay, Wisconsin, on the renovation to the Green Bay Packers' football stadium, this worker slipped off a beam while working some six stories above the ground. Through the use of his fall protection gear, he was rescued unharmed and was able to return to work. Not 60 days later, this same system protected a second fall victim at the stadium. Both of these workers undoubtedly would have died from the fall without such protection.
3. Two window washers were left dangling high above the ground after their scaffolding broke. Again their safety equipment prevented them from a certain death—dangling them high above the ground while they awaited rescue.
4. Several workers were ordered off a deteriorating floor at a demolition site in Chicago. The inspector noticed the floor-ing was not stable while workers worked to dismantle part of the floor overhead. Within hours of having the workers removed, the overhead floor caved in—right at the spot where the workers previously stood.
5. An OSHA inspector ordered a worker out of an unshored trench. Barely 30 seconds after the worker left the trench, it collapsed. Had this worker not followed the inspector's order to get out, he surely would have been seriously injured or killed.

Such stories—the successful and the tragic outcomes—occur every day. Unfortunately, headlines are not typically made unless there is some disaster. For OSHA, the success stories are what employee safety is all about—preventing the death or serious injury of all employees!

Questions:

1. What role do OSHA inspections play in preserving safe and healthy work environments? Discuss.
2. "OSHA shouldn't have to inspect every worksite. Employers should act as their own safety inspectors and take action that is warranted." Build an argument supporting this statement, and one opposing this statement.
3. Had any of the five events listed above led to serious injury or death, do you believe the employer was liable? Why or why not? If you believe the employer is liable, do you believe any of these could be construed as willful and severe? Defend your position.

Case Application 13-B: TEAM FUN!

Team Fun

Kenny and Norton, owners of TEAM FUN!, a sporting goods manufacturer and retailer, are meeting with Tony, director of human resources, and Edna, compensation and benefits manager, in the DEN, a casual area with a big-screen TV and sodas and munchies on a side table. Kenny flips on the light. "We can meet here for an hour. No one shows up for break before 9 a.m. Did you see the headlines this morning? I finally figured out what 'postal' means. Wonder why those guys go nuts and shoot each other?"

Norton laughs. "Don't you remember me, before we started TEAM FUN!? I was angry almost all the time. All the stupid politics. Those ridiculous schedules. Everyone stabbing each other in the back to get ahead."

Kenny frowns. "I almost forgot about you. Say, you don't think we need to do anything here for violence, do you? We've got all those bows and arrows, golf clubs. Even baseball bats could be a weapon."

Tony says, "Violence is the last problem I'd expect to find here. You two have made this place very mellow for employees. You let them take play breaks during the day. Schedules and goals are posted publicly. Teams get rewarded for being teams. Customers write in and thank employees by name. Fun is a requirement of every job. You are nearly as friendly as Southwest Airlines."

Edna comments, "I think the wellness program was a natural. Hiring that nutritionist to work at the sports bar fits right in with the gear and the machines. Fit employees are less likely to overreact or burnout."

Norton nods and adds, "Nobody but Bobby ever got stressed or burned out here."

Tony says, "I think Bobby did his own burnout. But the employee assistance program deserves another evaluation."

Kenny stands up. "Okay. Work something up for tomorrow. I want to try out that new paddle boat contraption in the LAGOON. See it down there? Come on, Norton. Grab a couple of sodas and let our HR folks take care of our people."

Questions:

1. Do you agree with Tony's statement about workplace violence? Should TEAM FUN! take further action to prevent workplace violence? Identify the preventive measures already in place.

2. Is Tony too complacent about stress and burnout? Outline for Kenny and Norton any symptoms of stress and burnout that merit notice.

3. What benefits would wellness programs and an employee assistance plan provide TEAM FUN!?

WORKING WITH A TEAM: *Health and Safety*

Your team may wish to role-play this case for the class, then discuss what the supervisor in the scenario should do and how he should respond.

Billy Jo Rhea has been a machinist for Linco Tool and Die, a manufacturer of engine parts for large motors, for 16 years. Lately, more of Billy Jo's parts have been rejected for errors; he seems preoccupied with outside matters—leaving early, asking to take off days beyond sick days allowed. He has missed three work days in two weeks, and Charlie, his supervisor, wondered if he smelled alcohol on his breath after lunch yesterday. Charlie hasn't said anything yet; he doesn't want to invade Billy Jo's privacy. He thinks Billy Jo, who in the past has been cooperative, positive, highly productive, and rarely sick or absent, may just be going through a tough time. Besides, the past month has been difficult because a major shipment required overtime and all machinists have been asked to work 80 to 95 hours a week until the shipment is complete.

At lunch, Charlie overhears an argument between Billy Jo and a co-worker, Terry, each blaming the other for a part being rejected by Quality Assurance. Billy Jo tells Terry to "stay out of his

way and his area," and that "the next time they'll settle it outside," poking him in the chest with his finger. Billy Jo then slams a $250 gauge down on the floor, shouts profanities, and adds, "I don't care if the part falls off or if this place burns to the ground, anymore; I've about had all I can take of you and this place! You know my wife left me for my best friend last week, left me with a two-year-old to raise by myself, and my other kid got expelled for possession. It just doesn't much matter to me what you think, so I'd leave me alone if I were you!" Charlie heads for the human resource office, unsure of how to proceed.

Here are some questions to guide you:

1. What should Charlie do?

2. What advice would you, as the human resource manager, give Charlie?

3. How should Charlie respond to the immediate situation?

4. How can you apply the assessment questions regarding violence to help Charlie and other supervisors handle future situations more effectively?

LEARNING AN HRM SKILL: *Developing Safety Skills*

About the skill: Here are several steps we recommend for developing an organization's safety and health program. Whether or not such programs are chiefly the responsibility of one individual, every supervisor must work to ensure that the work environment is safe for all employees.

1. *Involve management and employees in developing a safety and health plan.* If neither group can see the usefulness and the benefit of such a plan, even the best plan will fail.

2. *Hold someone accountable for implementing the plan.* Plans do not work by themselves. They need someone to champion the cause. This person must have the resources to put the plan in place and also must be accountable for what it's intended to accomplish.

3. *Determine the safety and health requirements for your work site.* Just as each individual is different, so is each workplace. Understanding the specific needs of the facility

will aid in determining what safety and health requirement will be necessary.

4. *Assess workplace hazards in the facility.* Identify potential health and safety problems on the job. Understanding what exists helps you determine preventive measures.

5. *Correct hazards that exist.* Fix or eliminate hazards identified in the investigation. This may mean decreasing the effect of the hazard or controlling it through other means (for example, protective clothing).

6. *Train employees in safety and health techniques.* Make safety and health training mandatory for all employees. Employees should be instructed in how to do their jobs in the safest manner and understand that any protective equipment provided must be used.

7. *Develop the employee mindset that the organization is to be kept hazard-free.* Often employees are the first to witness problems. Establish a means for them to report their findings, including having emergency procedures in place, if necessary. Ensuring that preventive maintenance of equipment follows a recommended schedule can also prevent breakdown of equipment from becoming a hazard.

8. *Continuously update and refine the safety and health program.* Once the program has been implemented, it must continuously be evaluated and necessary changes made. Documenting program progress is necessary for this analysis.

ENHANCING YOUR COMMUNICATION SKILLS

1. Visit OSHA's Web site (www.osha.gov). Locate a news release on an OSHA activity. Provide a two- to three-page summary of the news release, focusing on what OSHA is intending to do, the effect on workers, and the effect on employers.

2. Develop a two- to three-page argument on why sick buildings should be "cured" immediately. Support your position with appropriate documentation.

3. Go to the employee assistance programs provider Interlock's Web site at www.interlock.org. Research the Web site for the following information: What are the components of an EAP, and how does Interlock evaluate an EAP's success? Also identify how Interlock recommends implementing an EAP in an organization. Provide a two- to three-page summary of your findings.

FOURTEEN

What do telephone workers, dockworkers, longshoremen, baseball and hockey players, and the people who employ them have in common? Each over the past few years has found themselves in a labor dispute that resulted in a work stoppage. Not only were there difficulties in reaching an agreement that would keep everyone one the job, but in many cases, the dispute extended into the public arena where spillover effects were witnessed. For example, at issue in the West Coast dockworkers labor dispute was the elimination of some 400 jobs. By eliminating them, management would save over $20 million in wages. But because of the work stoppage, the U.S. economy suffered—estimated at a cost of nearly $10 billion. That's about 500 times the cost of the $20 million dispute. Isn't there anything that can be done to eliminate these effects of a labor dispute—so society doesn't bear the brunt of a labor management dispute? There is one possible answer—it's called the virtual strike—and it's a method that's been successfully used in labor disputes around the globe.[1]

Under the arrangements of a virtual strike, both labor and management put their financial resources at risk. Specifically, rather than work stopping, the wages that would have been paid to employees, as well as the profits that would have been earned by the company, are placed in a special fund. These monies are then held for a period of time. Should an agreement be reached within a specified period of time, the

monies are returned to the respective groups—the employees get their back pay, and employers receive their profits. If, however, a settlement is not reached, the monies are forfeited—and usually donated to some charity. This places the direct effect of a work stoppage on the involved parties. Because work continues, there is no loss of goods or services for the general public, so spillover effects are eliminated. Imagine what comfort that would be when the dispute is between schoolteachers and a Board of Education, or a city and its firefighters or police officers. Rather than reduce or stop these vital public services from being offered, only those directly involved in the labor dispute have something at risk, and the rest of society doesn't get used as a pawn in the process.

Are virtual strikes feasible? They've worked in Italy and Israel, where they've had good results. They've even been witnessed in the United States on a few occasions—which shortened a threatened long strike effort. So they appear to work—and work well.

Though the intent of the virtual strike is to make only those directly involved in a dispute feel the pain, the question is, will they ever catch on in a widespread manner? It's apparent that U.S. labor–management relations often use the public opinion element as a means of influencing one side or the other. Until this strategy is reduced or eliminated, the use of the virtual strike is unlikely to grow significantly. That's too bad for the rest of society that has to suffer in a labor dispute.

(*Source:* © AP/Wide World Photos)

Understanding Labor Relations and Collective Bargaining

Learning Outcomes

After reading this chapter, you will be able to

1. Define the term *unions*.
2. Discuss what effect the Wagner and the Taft-Hartley Acts had on labor–management relations.
3. Identify the significance of Executive Orders 10988 and 11491 and the Civil Service Reform Act of 1978.
4. Describe the union-organizing process.
5. Describe the components of collective bargaining.
6. Identify the steps in the collective-bargaining process.
7. Explain the various types of union security arrangements.
8. Describe the role of a grievance procedure in collective bargaining.
9. Identify the various impasse-resolution techniques.
10. Discuss how sunshine laws affect public-sector collective bargaining.

INTRODUCTION

union

Organization of workers, acting collectively, seeking to protect and promote their mutual interests through collective bargaining.

A **union** is an organization of workers, acting collectively, seeking to promote and protect its mutual interests through collective bargaining. However, before we can examine the activities surrounding the collective bargaining process, it is important to understand the laws that govern the labor–management process, what unions are, and how employees unionize. Although just over 12 percent of the private sector workforce is unionized, the successes and failures of organized labor's activities affect most segments of the workforce in two important ways.[2] First, major industries in the United States—such as automobile manufacturing, communications, construction, as well as all branches of transportation—are unionized, and so unions have a major effect on important sectors of the economy (see Exhibit 14-1). Second, gains made by unions often spill over into other, nonunionized sectors of the economy.[3] So, the wages, hours, and working conditions of nonunion employees at a Linden, New Jersey, lumberyard may be affected by collective bargaining between the United Auto Workers and General Motors at one of the latter's North American assembly plants.

For many managers, HRM practices in a unionized organization consist chiefly of following procedures and policies laid out in the labor contract. This labor contract, agreed to by both management and the labor union, stipulates, in part, the wage rate, hours of work, and terms and conditions of employment for those covered by the negotiated agreement. Decisions about how to select and compensate employees, employee benefits offered, procedures for overtime, and so forth are no longer unilateral prerogatives of management for jobs that fall under the

EXHIBIT 14-1
Union Membership by Industry Classification (Selected)

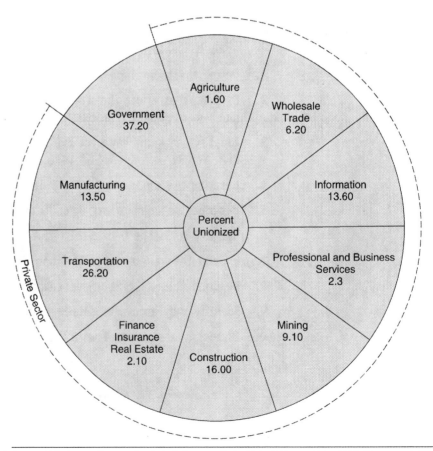

Source: U.S. Census Bureau, *Statistical Abstract of the United States: 2004–2005* (Government Printing Office, 2005), p. 419.

unions' jurisdiction. Such decisions are generally made when the labor contract is negotiated.

The concept of labor relations and the collective-bargaining process may have different meanings to different individuals depending on their experience, background, and so on. We can examine these areas by understanding both the laws that underpin labor-management relationships and why people join unions.

WHY EMPLOYEES JOIN UNIONS

Individuals join unions for reasons as diverse as the people themselves. Just what are they seeking to gain when they join a union? The answer to this question varies—perhaps it is a family history of union membership[4] or an attractive union contract—but the following captures the most common reasons.

Higher Wages and Benefits

The power and strength of numbers sometimes help unions obtain higher wages and benefit packages for their members than employees can negotiate individually.[5] One or two employees walking off the job over a wage dispute is unlikely to significantly affect most businesses, but hundreds of workers going out on strike can temporarily disrupt or even close down a company. Additionally, professional bargainers employed by the union may negotiate more skillfully than any individual could on his or her own behalf.

Greater Job Security

Unions provide their members with a sense of independence from management's power to arbitrarily hire, promote, or fire. The collective-bargaining contract will stipulate rules that apply to all members, thus providing fairer and more uniform treatment.

Influence over Work Rules

Where a union exists, workers can help determine the conditions under which they work and have an effective channel through which they can protest conditions they believe are unfair. Therefore, a union not only represents the worker but also provides rules that define channels in which worker complaints and concerns can be registered. Grievance procedures and rights to third-party arbitration of disputes are examples of practices typically defined and regulated as a result of union efforts.

Compulsory Membership

Many labor agreements contain statements commonly referred to as **union security arrangements**. When one considers the importance of security arrangements to unions—importance related to numbers and guaranteed income—it is no wonder that such emphasis is placed on achieving a union security arrangement that best suits their goals. Such arrangements range from compulsory union membership to giving employees the freedom in choosing to join the union.[6] The various types of union security arrangements—the union shop, the agency shop, and the right-to-work shop, as well as some special provisions under the realm of union security arrangements—are briefly discussed below and summarized in Exhibit 14-2.

The most powerful relationship legally available (except in right-to-work states[7]) to a union is a **union shop**. This arrangement stipulates that employers,

union security arrangements
Labor contract provisions designed to attract and retain dues-paying union members.

union shop
Any nonunion workers, must become dues-paying members within a prescribed period of time.

EXHIBIT 14-2
*Union Security and Related
Provisions*

Union Shop	The strongest of the union security arrangements. Union shops make union membership compulsory. After a given period of time, typically 30 days, a new employee must join the union or be terminated. A union shop guarantees the union dues-paying members. In a right-to-work state, union shops are illegal.
Agency Shop	The second strongest union security arrangement, the agency shop, gives workers the option of joining the union or not; membership is not compulsory. However, because the "gains" made at negotiations will benefit those not joining the union, all workers in the unit must pay union dues. Supreme Court decisions dictate that nonmembers of the union who still pay dues have the right to have their monies used solely for collective-bargaining purposes. Like the union shop, the agency shop is illegal in a right-to-work state.
Open Shop	The weakest form of a union security arrangement is the open shop. In an open shop, workers are free to join a union. If they do, they must stay in the union for the duration of the contract—and pay their dues. Those who do not wish to join the union pay no dues. In an open shop, an escape clause allows a grace time (typically two weeks) in which an individual may quit the union. The open shop is based on the premise of freedom of choice and is the only union security arrangement permitted under right-to-work legislation.
Maintenance of Membership	Because unions must administer their operations, in an open shop, once someone joins the union, they must maintain their union affiliation and pay their dues for the duration of the contract. At the end of the contract, an escape period exists in which those desiring to leave the union may do so.
Dues Checkoff	Dues checkoff involves the employer deducting union dues directly from a union member's paycheck. Under this provision, the employer collects the union dues and forwards a check to the union treasurer. Generally management does not charge an administrative fee for this service.

agency shop

A union security arrangement whereby employees must pay union dues to the certified bargaining unit even if they choose not to join the union.

open shop

Employees are free to join the union or not, and those who decline need not pay union dues.

while free to hire whomever they choose, may retain only union members. That is, all employees hired into positions covered under the terms of a collective-bargaining agreement must, after a specified probationary period of typically 30 to 60 days, join the union or forfeit their jobs.[8]

An agreement that requires nonunion employees to pay the union a sum of money equal to union fees and dues as a condition of continuing employment is referred to as an **agency shop**. This arrangement was designed as a compromise between the union's desire to eliminate the "free rider" and management's desire to make union membership voluntary. In such a case, if for whatever reason workers decide not to join the union (for example, religious beliefs, values), they still must pay dues. Because workers will receive benefits negotiated by the union, they must pay their fair share. However, a 1988 Supreme Court ruling upheld union members' claims that although they are forced to pay union dues, those dues must be specifically used for collective-bargaining purposes only—not for political lobbying.

The least desirable form of union security from a union perspective is the **open shop**, in which joining a union is totally voluntary. Those who do not join are not required to pay union dues or any associated fees. Workers who do join, typically have a maintenance-of-membership clause in the existing contract that dictates certain provisions. Specifically, a **maintenance-of-membership** agreement states that employees who join the union are compelled to remain in the union for the duration of the existing contract. When the contract expires, most such agreements provide an escape clause—a short interval of time, usually 10 days to two weeks—in which employees may choose to withdraw their membership from the union without penalty.

A provision that often exists in union security arrangements is a **dues checkoff**, which occurs when the employer withholds union dues from members' paychecks. Similar to other pay withholdings, the employer collects the dues money and sends it to the union. Employers provide this service, and the union permits them to do so for several reasons. Collecting dues takes time, so a dues checkoff reduces downtime by freeing the shop steward from going around to collect dues. Furthermore, recognizing that union dues are the primary source of union income, knowledge of how much money is in the union treasury can clue management into whether a union is financially strong enough to endure a strike. Given these facts, why would a union agree to such a procedure? The answer lies in guaranteed revenues. By letting management deduct dues from a member's paycheck, the union is assured of receiving their monies. Excuses from members that they don't have their money or will pay next week are eliminated!

Upsets with Management

Among various reasons why employees join a union, we see one common factor: management, especially the first-line supervisor. If employees are upset with the way their supervisor handles problems, upset over how a co-worker has been disciplined, and so on, they are likely to seek help from a union. In fact, it is reasonable to believe that when employees vote to unionize, it's often a vote against their immediate supervisor rather than a vote in support of a particular union.[9]

LABOR LEGISLATION

The legal framework for labor–management relationships has played a crucial role in its development. In this section, therefore, we will discuss major developments in labor law. An exhaustive analysis of these laws and their legal and practical repercussions is not possible within the scope of this book.[10] Instead, we'll focus our discussion on two important laws that have shaped much of the labor relations process. We'll then briefly summarize other laws that have helped shape labor–management activities.

The Wagner Act

The National Labor Relations Act of 1935, commonly referred to as the **Wagner Act,** is the basic bill of rights for unions. This law guarantees workers the right to organize and join unions, to bargain collectively, and to act in concert to pursue their objectives. In terms of labor relations, the Wagner Act specifically requires employers to bargain in good faith over mandatory bargaining issues—wages, hours, and terms and conditions of employment.

The Wagner Act is cited as shifting the pendulum of power to favor unions for the first time in U.S. labor history. This was achieved in part through the establishment of the **National Labor Relations Board (NLRB)**. This administrative body, consisting of five members appointed by the president of the United States, was given the responsibility for determining appropriate bargaining units, conducting elections to determine union representation, and preventing or correcting employer actions that can lead to unfair labor practice charges. The NLRB, however, has only remedial and no punitive powers.

maintenance of membership
Requires an individual who chooses to join a union to remain in the union for the duration of the existing contract.

dues checkoff
Employer withholding of union dues from union members' paychecks.

Unions often display their dissatisfaction with contract negotiations with an economic strike. These workers are showing their solidarity and their displeasure with how negotiations are proceeding. Nearly 500,000 workers were involved in such activities in the first few years of the new millennium. (Source: David McNew/Getty Images News and Sport Services)

Wagner Act
Also known as the National Labor Relations Act of 1935, this act gave employees the right to form and join unions and to engage in collective bargaining.

National Labor Relations Board (NLRB)
Established to administer and interpret the Wagner Act, the NLRB has primary responsibility for conducting union representation elections.

Unfair labor practices (Section 8[a]) include any employer tactics that

- Interfere with, restrain, or coerce employees in the exercise of rights to join unions and to bargain collectively;
- Dominate or interfere with the formation or administration of any labor organization; discriminate against anyone because of union activity;
- Discharge or otherwise discriminate against any employee because he or she filed or gave testimony under the act; and
- Refuse to bargain collectively with the representatives chosen by the employees.

The Wagner Act provided the legal recognition of unions as legitimate interest groups in American society, but many employers opposed its purposes. Some employers, too, failed to live up to the requirements of its provisions. That's because employers recognized that the Wagner Act didn't protect them from unfair union labor practices. Thus, the belief that the balance of power had swung too far to labor's side, and the public outcry stemming from post–World War II strikes, led to passage of the Taft-Hartley Act (Labor-Management Relations Act) in 1947.

The Taft-Hartley Act

Taft-Hartley Act
Amended the Wagner Act by addressing employers' concerns in terms of specifying unfair union labor practices.

The major purpose of the **Taft-Hartley Act** was to amend the Wagner Act by addressing employers' concerns in terms of specifying unfair union labor practices. Under Section 8(b), Taft-Hartley states that it is an unfair labor practice for unions to

- Restrain or coerce employees in joining the union or coerce the employer in selecting bargaining or grievance representatives;
- Discriminate against an employee to whom union membership has been denied or to cause an employer to discriminate against an employee;
- Refuse to bargain collectively;
- Engage in strikes and boycotts for purposes deemed illegal by the act;
- Charge excessive or discriminatory fees or dues under union shop contracts; and
- Obtain compensation for services not performed or not to be performed.

In addition, Taft-Hartley declared illegal one type of union security arrangement: the closed shop. Until Taft-Hartley's passage, the closed shop dominated labor contracts. In closed shops a union controlled the source of labor. Under this arrangement, an individual would join the union, be trained by the union, and sent to work for an employer by the union. In essence, the union acted as the clearinghouse of employees. When an employer needed employees—for whatever duration—the employer would contact the union and request that these employees start work. When the job was completed, and the employer no longer needed the employees, they were sent back to the union. By declaring the closed shop illegal, Taft-Hartley began to shift the pendulum of power away from unions. Furthermore, in doing so, the act enabled states to enact laws that would further reduce compulsory union membership. Taft-Hartley also included provisions that forbade secondary boycotts and gave the president of the United States the power to issue an 80-day cooling-off period when labor–management disputes affect national security. President Bush used this provision in 2002 during the International Longshore and Warehouse Union and the Pacific Maritime Association's labor dispute—the first time the injunction had been used in about 25 years.[11] A *secondary boycott* occurs when a union strikes against Employer A (a primary and legal strike) and then strikes and pickets against Employer B (an employer against which the union has no complaint) because of a relationship that exists between Employers A and B, such as Employer B handling goods made by Employer A. Taft-Hartley also set forth procedures for workers to decertify, or vote out, their union representatives.

Whereas the Wagner Act required only employers to bargain in good faith, Taft-Hartley imposed the same obligation on unions. Although the negotiation process is described later in this chapter, it is important to understand the term *bargaining in good faith*. This does not mean that the parties must reach agreement, but rather that they must come to the bargaining table ready, willing, and able to meet and deal, open to proposals made by the other party, and with the intent to reach a mutually acceptable agreement.

Realizing that unions and employers might not reach agreement and that work stoppages might occur, Taft-Hartley also created the **Federal Mediation and Conciliation Service (FMCS)** as an independent agency separate from the Department of Labor. The FMCS's mission is to send a trained representative to assist in negotiations. Both employer and union have the responsibility to notify the FMCS when other attempts to settle the dispute have failed or contract expiration is pending. An FMCS mediator is not empowered to force parties to reach an agreement, but he or she can use persuasion and other means of diplomacy to help them reach their own resolution of differences. Finally, a fact worth noting was the amendment in 1974 to extend coverage to the health-care industry. This health-care amendment now affords Taft-Hartley coverage to for-profit and nonprofit hospitals, as well as "special provisions for the health care industry, both profit and nonprofit, as to bargaining notice requirements and the right to picket or strike.[12]

Federal Mediation and Conciliation Service (FMCS)
A government agency that assists labor and management in settling disputes.

Other Laws Affecting Labor–Management Relations

The Wagner and Taft-Hartley Acts were the most important laws influencing labor–management relationships in the United States, but other laws, too, are pertinent to our discussion (see Diversity Issues in HRM). Specifically, these are the Railway Labor Act; the Landrum-Griffin Act; Executive Orders 10988 and 11491; the Racketeer Influenced and Corrupt Organizations Act of 1970; and the Civil Service Reform Act of 1978. Let's briefly review the notable aspects of these laws.

DIVERSITY ISSUES IN HRM

UNIONS AND EEO

Although much of the legal discussion thus far in this section has focused specifically on labor legislation, it's important to recognize that many of the laws discussed in Chapter 3 apply to labor organizations as well. For instance, the Equal Pay Act of 1963 requires that wages agreed to during collective bargaining must not be differentiated on the basis of sex. In labor-relations settings, pay may differ only on the basis of skill, responsibility, accountability, seniority, or working conditions.

The Civil Rights Act of 1964 is as relevant to labor organizations as it is to management. Title VII of the act means that not only must unions discontinue any discriminatory practices, they must also actively recruit and give preference to minority group members. For example, if a labor union is located in a geographic area with a large minority population, the union must make an effort to recruit these individuals into the union's apprenticeship programs. This means that unions have to place advertisements where such individuals will be likely to read them, visit schools they attend, and so forth. Failure to take such affirmative action steps may result in a union being found guilty of discrimination.

With regard to the Age Discrimination in Employment Act of 1967, unions cannot mandate retirement of any of their members. They can, as a company, stop contributing to a worker's pension after the individual reaches the age of 70. Additionally, labor unions, in complying with the provisions of the Vocational Rehabilitation Act and the Americans with Disabilities Act, must take affirmative action measures to recruit, employ, and advance all qualified disabled individuals. This means that unions must make reasonable accommodations, like easy-access ramps, for the disabled worker. The same holds true for abiding by the provisions of the Family and Medical Leave Act.

Railway Labor Act

Provided the initial impetus to widespread collective bargaining.

The Railway Labor Act of 1926 The **Railway Labor Act** provided the initial impetus for widespread collective bargaining in the United States.[13] Although the act covers only the transportation industry, it was important because workers in these industries were guaranteed the right to organize, bargain collectively with employers, and establish dispute settlement procedures in the event that no agreement was reached at the bargaining table. This dispute settlement procedure allows congressional and presidential intercession in the event of an impasse.[14]

Landrum-Griffin Act of 1959

Also known as the Labor and Management Reporting and Disclosure Act, this legislation protected union members from possible wrongdoing on the part of their unions. It required all unions to disclose their financial statements.

Landrum-Griffin Act of 1959 The **Landrum-Griffin Act of 1959** (Labor Management Reporting and Disclosure Act) was passed to address the public outcry over misuse of union funds and corruption in the labor movement. This act, like Taft-Hartley, was an amendment to the Wagner Act.[15]

The thrust of the Landrum-Griffin Act is to monitor internal union activity by making officials and those affiliated with unions (for example, union members and trustees) accountable for union funds, elections, and other business and representational matters. Restrictions are also placed on trusteeships imposed by national or international unions, and conduct during a union election is regulated. Much of this act is part of an ongoing effort to prevent corrupt practices and to keep organized crime from gaining control of the labor movement.[16] The mechanisms used to achieve this goal are requirements for filing annual reports to the Department of Labor by unions as organizations and by individuals employed by unions regarding administrative matters: such as their constitutions and bylaws, administrative policies, elected officials, and finances. This information, filed under forms L-M 2, L-M, or L-M 4,[17] is available to the public. Furthermore, Landrum-Griffin allowed all members of a union to vote irrespective of their race, sex, national origin, and so forth. This provision gave union members certain rights unavailable to the general public for another five years until the passage of the Civil Rights Act of 1964. Landrum-Griffin also required that all who voted on union matters would do so in a secret ballot, especially when the vote concerned the election of union officers.

Executive Orders 10988 and 11491 Both of these executive orders deal specifically with labor legislation in the federal sector.[18] In 1962, President Kennedy issued Executive Order 10988, which permitted, for the first time, federal government employees the right to join unions. The order required agency heads to bargain in good faith, defined unfair labor practices, and specified the code of conduct to which labor organizations in the public sector must adhere. Strikes, however, were prohibited.[19]

Although this executive order effectively granted organizing rights to federal employees, areas for improvement were identified, particularly the need for a centralized agency to oversee federal labor relations activities. To address these deficiencies, President Richard Nixon issued Executive Order 11491 in 1969. This executive order made federal labor relations more like those in the private sector and standardized procedures among federal agencies. The order gave the assistant secretary of labor the authority to determine appropriate bargaining units, oversee recognition procedures, rule on unfair labor practices, and enforce standards of conduct on labor relations. It also established the *Federal Labor Relations Council (FLRC)* to supervise implementation of Executive Order 11491 provisions, handle appeals from decisions of the assistant secretary of labor, and rule on questionable issues.

Both of these executive orders were vital in promoting federal-sector unionization. However, if a subsequent administration ever decided not to permit federal-sector unionization, a president would have had only to revoke a prior executive order. To eliminate this possibility, and to remove federal-sector labor relations from direct control of a president, Congress passed the Civil Service Reform Act.

Racketeer Influenced and Corrupt Organizations Act (RICO) of 1970

Although this act has far-reaching tentacles, the **Racketeer Influenced and Corrupt Organizations Act (RICO)** serves a vital purpose in labor relations. RICO's primary emphasis with respect to labor unions is to eliminate any influence exerted on unions by members of organized crime.[20] That is, it is a violation of RICO if "payments or loans are made to employee representatives, labor organizations, or officers and employees of labor organizations,"[21] where such action occurs in the form of "bribery, kickbacks, or extortion."[22] Over the past decade or so, RICO has been used to oust a number of labor officials alleged to have organized crime ties.[23]

Civil Service Reform Act of 1978 Title VII of the **Civil Service Reform Act** established the Federal Labor Relations Authority (FLRA) as an independent agency within the executive branch to carry out the major functions previously performed by the FLRC. The FLRA was given the authority to decide, subject to external review by courts and administrative bodies,[24] union election and unfair labor practice disputes, and appeals from arbitration awards, and to provide leadership in establishing policies and guidance. An additional feature of this act is a broad-scope grievance procedure that can be limited only by the negotiators. Under Executive Order 11491, binding arbitration had been optional. The Civil Service Reform Act of 1978 contains many provisions similar to those of the Wagner Act, with two important differences. First, in the private sector, the scope of bargaining includes wages and benefits and mandatory subjects of bargaining. In the federal sector, wages and benefits are not negotiable—they are set by Congress. Additionally, the Reform Act prohibits negotiations over union security arrangements.

UNIONIZING EMPLOYEES

Employees are unionized after an extensive and sometimes lengthy process called the *organizing campaign*. Exhibit 14-3 contains a simple model of how the process typically flows in the private sector. Let's look at these elements.

Efforts to organize a group of employees may begin by employee representatives requesting a union to visit the employees' organization and solicit members. The union itself might initiate the membership drive, or in some cases, unions use the Internet to promote their benefits to workers. One of the more crucial questions at the beginning of this activity is who is eligible to vote on union representation. For example, in the nursing industry, charge nurses have often been in limbo. Unions claim that these individuals represent patients, like other nurses,

Racketeer Influenced and Corrupt Organizations Act (RICO)
Law passed to eliminate any influence on unions by members of organized crime.

Civil Service Reform Act
Replaced Executive Order 11491 as the basic law governing labor relations for federal employees.

www.wiley.com/college/decenzo
What Would You Do?
EXPERIENCE: Labor Relations

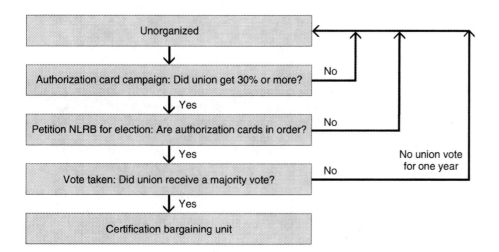

EXHIBIT 14-3
Union Organizing Process

and thus should be part of the bargaining unit. Management, on the other hand, says they exercise independent decision making in guiding the actions of other nurses—actions typical of a supervisor. Thus, management considers them ineligible for the bargaining unit. This debate continues and is the subject of NLRB and court cases.[25]

authorization card

A card signed by prospective union members indicating that they are interested in having a union election held at their work site.

Regardless of who actually belongs in the voting population, as established by the NLRB, the union must secure signed **authorization cards** from at least 30 percent of the employees it wishes to represent. Employees who sign the cards indicate that they wish the particular union to be their representative in negotiating with the employer.

Although a minimum of 30 percent of the potential union members must sign the authorization card prior to an election, unions are seldom interested in bringing to vote situations in which they merely meet the NLRB minimum. After all, to become the certified bargaining unit, the union must be accepted by a majority of those eligible voting workers.[26] Acceptance in this case is determined by secret ballot. This election, held by the NLRB, called a **representation certification (RC)**, can occur only once in 12 months. Thus, the more signatures on the authorization cards, the greater the chances for a victory.

representation certification (RC)

The election process whereby union members vote in a union as their representative.

Even when a sizable proportion of the workers sign authorization cards, the victory is by no means guaranteed. Management rarely is passive during the organization drive (see Workplace Issues). Although laws govern what management can and cannot do, management in an organization may attempt to persuade potential members to vote no. Union organizers realize that such persuasion may work, and thus unions usually require a much higher percentage of authorization cards to increase their odds of obtaining a majority. When that majority vote is received, the NLRB certifies the union and recognizes it as the exclusive bargaining unit. Irrespective of whether the individual in the certified bargaining union voted for or against the union, each worker is covered by the negotiated contract and must abide by its governance. Once a union has been certified, is it there for life?

WORKPLACE ISSUES

THE UNION DRIVE

What can management do when they learn that a union-organizing drive has begun in their organization? Labor laws permit them to defend themselves against the union campaign, but they must do so properly. Here are some guidelines for what to do and what not to do during the organizing drive.[27]

- If your employees ask for your opinion on unionization, respond in a natural manner. For example, "I really have no position on the issue. Do what you think is best."
- You can prohibit union-organizing activities in your workplace during work hours only if they interfere with work operations. This may apply to the organization's e-mail, too.
- You can prohibit outside union organizers from distributing union information in the workplace.

- Employees have the right to distribute union information to other employees during breaks and lunch periods.
- Don't question employees publicly or privately about union-organizing activities—for example, "Are you planning to go to that union rally this weekend?" But if an employee freely tells you about the activities, you may listen.
- Don't spy on employees' union activities, for example, by standing in the cafeteria to see who is distributing pro-union literature.
- Don't make any threats or promises related to the possibility of unionization. For example, "If this union effort succeeds, upper management is seriously thinking about closing down this plant, but if it's defeated, they may push through an immediate wage increase."
- Don't discriminate against any employee who is involved in the unionization effort.
- Be on the lookout for efforts by the union to coerce employees to join its ranks. This activity by unions is an unfair labor practice. If you see this occurring, report it to your boss or to human resources. Your organization may also want to consider filing a complaint against the union with the NLRB.

Certainly not. On some occasions, union members may become so dissatisfied with the union's actions in representing them that they may attempt to turn to another union or return to nonunion status. In either case, the rank-and-file members petition the NLRB to conduct a **representation decertification (RD)**. Once again, if a majority of the members vote the union out, it is gone. However, once the election has been held, no other action can occur for another 12 months. This grace period protects the employer from employees decertifying one union today and certifying another tomorrow.

Finally, and even more rare than an RD, is a representation decertification initiated by management, or RM. The guidelines for the RM are the same as for the RD, except that the employer leads the drive. Although RDs and RMs are ways of decertifying unions, it should be pointed out that most labor agreements bar the use of either decertification election during the term of the contract.

Unions' organizing drives may or may not be successful, but when they do achieve their goal to become the exclusive bargaining agent, the next step is to negotiate the contract. In the next section, we'll look at the specific issues surrounding collective bargaining.

COLLECTIVE BARGAINING

Collective bargaining typically refers to the negotiation, administration, and interpretation of a written agreement between two parties that covers a specific period of time. This agreement, or contract, lays out in specific terms the conditions of employment—that is, what is expected of employees and any limits to management's authority. In the following discussion, we take a somewhat larger perspective and also consider the organizing, certification, and preparation efforts that precede actual negotiation.

Most of us hear or read about collective bargaining only when a contract is about to expire or when negotiations break down. When a railroad contract is about to expire, we may be aware of collective bargaining in the transportation industry. Similarly, teachers' strikes in Cleveland, workers striking Verizon Communications, or baseball players striking against Major League Baseball owners remind us that organized labor deals with management collectively.[28] In fact, collective-bargaining agreements cover about half of all state and local government employees and one-ninth of employees in the private sector. The wages, hours, and working conditions of these unionized employees are negotiated usually for two or three years at a time. Only when these contracts expire and management and the union cannot agree on a new contract are most of us aware that collective bargaining is an important part of HRM.

Objective and Scope of Collective Bargaining

The objective of collective bargaining is to agree on a contract acceptable to management, union representatives, and the union membership. What is covered in this contract? The final agreement will reflect the problems of the particular workplace and industry in which the contract is negotiated.[29]

Irrespective of the specific issues contained in various labor contracts, four issues appear consistently throughout all labor contracts. Three of the four are mandatory bargaining issues, which means that management and the union must negotiate in good faith over these issues. These mandatory issues were defined by the Wagner Act as wages, hours, and terms and conditions of employment. The fourth issue covered in almost all labor contracts is the grievance procedure, which is designed to permit the adjudication of complaints. Before we progress further into collective bargaining, let's inspect our cast of characters.

representation decertification (RD)
The election process whereby union members vote out their union as their representative.

collective bargaining
The negotiation, administration, and interpretation of a written agreement between two parties, at least one of which represents a group that is acting collectively, that covers a specific period of time.

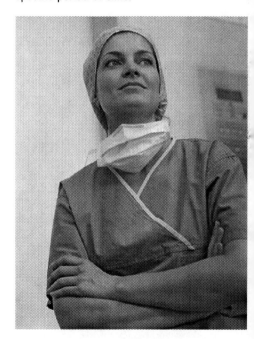

Should this charge nurse be considered part of the bargaining unit? That matter has been the subject of several NLRB and court cases. The unions believe so because the nurse administers patient care. Hospital management sees this individual as a supervisor and ineligible for inclusion to the certified bargaining unit. (Source: Jochen Sand/Digital Vision/Getty Images, Inc.)

Collective-Bargaining Participants

Collective bargaining was described as an activity that takes place between two parties. In this context, the two parties are labor and management. But who represents these two groups? Given our previous discussion, would it be erroneous to add a third party—the government?

Management's representation in collective bargaining talks tends to depend on the size of the organization. In a small firm, for instance, bargaining is probably done by the president. Few small firms have a specialist who deals only with HRM issues; the president of the company often handles this. Larger organizations usually have a sophisticated HRM department with full-time industrial relations experts. In such cases, we can expect management to be represented by the senior manager for industrial relations, corporate executives, and company lawyers—with support provided by legal and economic specialists in wage and salary administration, labor law, benefits, and so forth.

On the union side, we typically expect to see a bargaining team composed of an officer of the local union, local shop stewards, and some representation from the international/national union.[30] Again, as with management, representation is modified to reflect the size of the bargaining unit. If negotiations involve a contract that will cover 50,000 employees at company locations throughout the United States, the team will be dominated by international/national union officers (those most often with a broader perspective of the implication of a contract) with a strong supporting cast of economic and legal experts employed by the union. In a small firm or for local negotiations covering special issues at the plant level for a nationwide organization, bargaining representatives for the union might be the local officers and a few specially elected committee members.

Watching over these two sides is a third party—government. In addition to providing the rules under which management and labor bargain, government provides a watchful eye on the two parties to ensure the rules are followed, and it stands ready to intervene if an agreement on acceptable terms cannot be reached, or if the impasse undermines the nation's well-being.

Negotiation are unlikely to have any other participants, with one exception—financial institutions.[31] Most people are unaware of the financial institution's role in collective bargaining. Although not directly involved in negotiations, these "banks" set limits on the cost of the contract. Exceeding that amount may cause the banks to call in the loans made to the company. This places a ceiling on what management can spend. Although more groups are involved in collective bargaining, our discussion will focus on labor and management. After all, it is the labor and management teams that buckle down and hammer out the contract.

The Collective-Bargaining Process

Let's now consider the actual collective-bargaining process. Exhibit 14-4 contains a simple model of how the process typically flows in the private sector—which includes preparing to negotiate, actual negotiations, and administering the contract after it has been ratified.

Preparing to Negotiate Once a union has been certified as the bargaining unit, both union and management begin the ongoing activity of preparing for negotiations. We refer to this as an *ongoing* activity because ideally it should begin as soon as the previous contract is agreed upon or union certification is achieved. Realistically, it probably begins anywhere from one to six months before the current contract expires. We can consider the preparation for negotiation as composed of three activities: fact gathering, goal setting, and strategy development.

Information is acquired from both internal and external sources. Internal data include grievance and accident records; employee performance reports; overtime

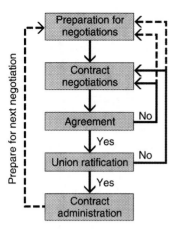

EXHIBIT 14-4
The Collective-Bargaining Process

figures; and reports on transfers, turnover, and absenteeism. External information should include statistics on the current economy, both at local and national levels; economic forecasts for the short and intermediate terms; copies of recently negotiated contracts by the adversary union to determine what issues the union considers important; data on the communities in which the company operates—cost of living, changes in cost of living, terms of recently negotiated labor contracts, and statistics on the labor market—and industry labor statistics to see what terms other organizations, employing similar types of personnel, are negotiating.

With homework done, information in hand, and tentative goals established, both union and management must put together the most difficult part of the bargaining preparation activities, a strategy for negotiations. This includes assessing the other side's power and specific tactics.

Negotiating at the Bargaining Table Negotiation customarily begins with the union delivering to management a list of demands. By presenting many demands, the union creates significant room for trading in later stages of the negotiation; it also disguises the union's real position, leaving management to determine which demands are adamantly sought, which are moderately sought, and which the union is prepared to quickly abandon. A long list of demands, too, often fulfills the internal political needs of the union. By seeming to back numerous wishes of the union's members, union administrators appear to be satisfying the needs of the many factions within the membership.

Both union and management representatives may publicly accentuate their differences, but the real negotiations typically go on behind closed doors. Each party tries to assess the relative priorities of the other's demands, and each begins to combine proposals into viable packages. Next comes the attempt to make management's highest offer approximate the lowest demands that the union is willing to accept. Hence, negotiation is a form of compromise.[32] An oral agreement is eventually converted into a written contract, and negotiation concludes with the union representatives submitting the contract for ratification or approval from rank-and-file members. If the rank-and-file members vote down the contract, negotiations must resume.

Contract Administration Once a contract is agreed on and ratified, it must be administered. Contract administration involves four stages: (1) disseminating the agreements to all union members and managers; (2) implementing the contract; (3) interpreting the contract and grievance resolution; and (4) monitoring activities during the contract period.[33]

Providing information to all concerned requires both parties to ensure that changes in contract language are spelled out. For example, the most obvious would be hourly rate changes; HRM must make sure its payroll system is adjusted to the new rates as set in the contract. Likewise, changes in work rules, hours, and such must be communicated. If both sides agree to something not in existence before, such as mandatory overtime, all must be informed of how it will work. Neither the union nor the company can simply hand a copy of the contract to each organization member and expect it to be understood. It will be necessary to hold meetings to explain the new terms of the agreement.

The next stage of contract administration is ensuring that the agreement is implemented. All communicated changes now take effect, and both sides are expected to comply with the contract terms. One concept to recognize during this phase is *management rights*. Typically, management is guaranteed the right to allocate organizational resources in the most efficient manner; to create reasonable rules; to hire, promote, transfer, and discharge employees; to determine work methods and assign work; to create, eliminate, and classify jobs; to lay off employees when necessary; to close or relocate facilities with a 60-day notice; and to institute technological changes. Of course, good HRM practices suggest that whether the contract requires it or not, management would be wise to notify the union of major decisions that will influence its membership.

Probably the most important element of contract administration relates to spelling out a procedure for handling contractual disputes.[34] Almost all collective-bargaining agreements contain formal procedures for resolving grievances of contract interpretation and application. These contracts have provisions for resolving specific, formally initiated grievances by employees concerning dissatisfaction with job-related issues.

grievance procedure

A complaint-resolving process contained in union contracts.

Grievance procedures are typically designed to resolve grievances as quickly as possible and at the lowest level possible in the organization (see Exhibit 14-5).[35] The first step almost always has the employee attempt to resolve the grievance with his or her immediate supervisor.[36] If it cannot be resolved at this stage, it is typically discussed with the union steward and the supervisor. Failure at this stage usually brings in the individuals from the organization's industrial relations department and the chief union steward. If the grievance still cannot be resolved, the complaint passes to the facilities' manager, who typically discusses it with the

EXHIBIT 14-5
A Sample Grievance Procedure

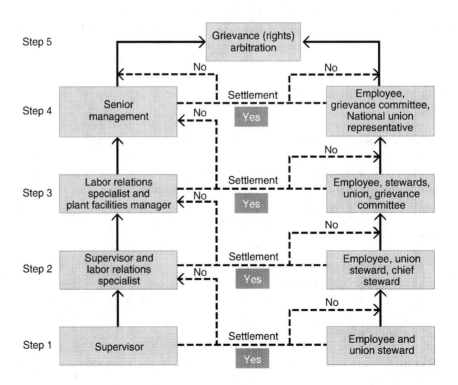

union grievance committee. Unsuccessful efforts at this level give way to the organization's senior management and typically a representative from the national union. Finally, if those efforts are unsuccessful in resolving the grievance, the final step is for the complaint to go to arbitration—called *grievance (rights) arbitration.*

In practice, we find that almost all collective-bargaining agreements provide for grievance (rights) arbitration as the final step to an impasse. Of course, in small organizations these five steps described tend to be condensed, possibly moving from discussing the grievance with the union steward to taking the grievance directly to the organization's senior executive or owner, and then to arbitration, if necessary.

Finally, in our discussion of preparation for negotiations we stated that both company and union gather various data. One of the most bountiful databases for both sides is information kept on a current contract. By monitoring activities, company and union can assess the effectiveness of the current contract, when problem areas or conflicts arose, and what changes might need to be made in subsequent negotiations.[37]

Failure to Reach Agreement

Although contract negotiations aim to achieve an agreement acceptable to all concerned parties, sometimes that goal is not achieved. Negotiations do break down, and an impasse occurs. These events may be triggered by internal issues in the union, the desire to strike against the company, the company's desire to lock out the union, or its knowledge that striking workers can be replaced. Let's explore some of these areas.

Strikes versus Lockouts Negotiations have only two possible preliminary outcomes. First, and obviously preferable, is agreement. The other, lacking any viable solution to the parties' differences, is a strike or a lockout.

There are several types of strikes. The most relevant to contract negotiations is the economic strike. An **economic strike** occurs when the two parties fail to reach a satisfactory agreement before the contract expires. When that deadline passes, the union leadership will typically instruct its members not to work, to leave their jobs.[38] Although in today's legal climate, replacement workers can be hired, no disciplinary action can be taken against workers who participate in economic strike activities (see Ethical Issues in HRM).

Another form of strike is the **wildcat strike**. A wildcat strike generally occurs when workers walk off the job because of something management has done. For example, if a union employee is disciplined for failure to call in sick according to provisions of the contract, fellow union members may walk off the job to demonstrate their dissatisfaction with management action. It is important to note that these strikes happen while a contract is in force—an agreement that usually prohibits such union activity. Consequently, wildcat strikers can be severely disciplined or terminated. In the past, the most powerful weapon unions in the private sector had was the economic strike. By striking, the union was, in essence, withholding labor from the employer, thus causing the employer financial hardships. For instance, U.S. organizations lost more than 4 million workdays to strike activity in 2003.[39] In Canada, it was three-fourths that number.[40]

Today, however, the strike weapon is questioned.[41] Strikes not only are expensive, but public sentiment supporting their use by unions is weak. Management hasn't been sitting by idly, for today it is more inclined to replace striking workers. Although strikes fell to a near record low in 2001, worker dissatisfaction with some management practices may increase strike activity in the years ahead.[42]

In contemporary times, we have also witnessed an increase in management's use of the lockout. A **lockout**, as the name implies, occurs when the organization denies unionized workers access to their jobs during an impasse. A lockout,

economic strike

An impasse that results from labor and management's inability to agree on the wages, hours, and terms and conditions of a new contract.

wildcat strike

An unauthorized and illegal strike that occurs during the terms of an existing contract.

lockout

A situation in labor–management negotiations whereby management prevents union members from returning to work.

Is an economic strike really beneficial to either side? That debate will certainly continue. We do know that such strikes (and lockouts) cause around 4 million lost work days each year. That's a lot of potential productivity, no matter which side of the issue you support. (Source: © AP/Wide World Photos)

ETHICAL ISSUES IN HRM

THE STRIKER REPLACEMENT DILEMMA

Inherent in collective-bargaining negotiations is an opportunity for either side to generate a power base that may sway negotiations in its favor. For example, when labor shortages exist, or when inventories are in short supply, a union strike could have serious ramifications for the company. Likewise, when the situation is reversed, management has the upper hand and could easily lock out the union to achieve its negotiation goals. In fact, both the Wagner and Taft-Hartley Acts saw to it that the playing field was as fair as possible by requiring both sides to negotiate in good faith and permitting impasses if they should be warranted.

For decades, this scenario played itself out over and over again. Timing of a contract's expiration proved critical for both sides. For example, in the coal industry, a contract that expired just before the winter months—when coal is needed in greater supply for heating and electricity—worked to the union's advantage, unless the coal companies stockpiled enough coal to carry them through a lengthy winter strike. This game, although serious to both sides, never appeared anything more than bargaining strategy—one that could show how serious both sides were. And even though a Supreme Court case from 1938, *NLRB v. MacKay Radio*, gave employers the right to hire replacement workers for those engaged in an economic strike, seldom was that used. In fact, often to settle a strike and return to the organization its skilled work force, one stipulation would be to release all replacement workers.

But in the early 1980s, that began to change. When President Ronald Reagan fired striking air traffic controllers and hired their replacements, businesses began to realize the weapon they had at their disposal. As their union-busting attempts materialized, organizations including Caterpillar, the National Football League, and John Deere realized that using replacement workers could be to their advantage. The union members either came back to work on management's terms or they lost their jobs—period.

Undoubtedly, in any strike situation, management has the right to keep its doors open and to keep producing what it sells. That may mean using supervisory personnel in place of striking workers, or in some cases, bringing in replacements. But does a law that permits replacement workers undermine the intent of national labor law? Does it create an unfair advantage for managements that play hardball just to break the union? Should a striker-replacement bill (which would prevent permanent replacement workers from being hired) be passed? Should striking workers' jobs be protected while they exercise their rights under the Wagner Act? What's your opinion?

in some cases, is management's predecessor to hiring replacement workers. In others, it's management's effort to protect their facilities and machinery and other employees at the work site. Although lockouts have been used more frequently over the past decade, their use in the early 2000s has not been successful for some companies. Tight labor markets made finding replacement workers more difficult.[43]

In either case, the strategy is the same. Each side attempts to apply economic pressure on its opponent to sway negotiations in its own direction. And when it works for both negotiations are said to reach an impasse. Impasse-resolution techniques are designed to help such situations.

Impasse-Resolution Techniques When labor and management in the private sector cannot reach a satisfactory agreement themselves, they may need the assistance of an objective third party. This assistance comes in the form of *conciliation and mediation, fact-finding,* or *interest arbitration.*

Conciliation and mediation are two closely related impasse-resolution techniques. Both are techniques whereby a neutral third party attempts to help labor and management resolve their differences. Under conciliation, however, the third party role is to keep negotiations going. In other words, this individual is a go-between—advocating a voluntary means through which both sides can continue negotiating. Mediation goes one step further. The mediator attempts to pull together the common ground that exists and make settlement recommendations for overcoming barriers between the two sides. A mediator's suggestions, however, are only advisory and not binding on either party.

Fact-finding is a technique whereby a neutral third party conducts a hearing to gather evidence from both labor and management. The fact-finder then renders a decision as to how he or she views an appropriate settlement. Similar to mediation, the fact-finder's recommendations are suggestions only—they, too, are not binding on either party.

The final impasse-resolution technique is called **interest arbitration**. Under interest arbitration, generally a panel of three individuals—one neutral and one each from the union and management—hears testimony from both sides. After the hearing, the panel renders a decision on how to settle the current contract negotiation dispute. If all three members of the panel are unanimous in their decision, that decision may be binding on both parties.

Public-sector impasse-resolution techniques show notable differences. For instance, many states that do permit public-sector employee strikes require some form of arbitration. Decisions rendered through arbitration are binding on both parties. Moreover, the public sector uses a particular form of arbitration called *final-offer arbitration,* in which both sides present their recommendations and the arbitrator selects one party's offer in its entirety over the other. Final-offer arbitration makes no attempt to seek compromise.

CRITICAL ISSUES FOR UNIONS TODAY

The declining percentage of unionized workforce throughout the past few decades raises several questions. Why has union membership declined? Can labor and management find a way to work together more harmoniously? Is public-sector unionization different from that in the private sector? And where are unions likely to focus their attention in the next decade? In this section, we'll look at these issues.

Union Membership: Where Have the Members Gone?

The birth of unionization in the United States can be traced back to the late 1700s. Although there was labor strife for about 200 years, not until the passage of the Wagner Act in 1935 did we began to witness significant union gains. In fact, by the early 1940s, union membership in the United States reached its pinnacle of approximately 36 percent of the workforce. Since that time, however, there's been a steady decline (see Exhibit 14-6). Major contributing factors can be identified.

fact-finding
The technique whereby a neutral third party conducts a hearing to gather evidence and testimony from the parties regarding the differences between them.

interest arbitration
An impasse resolution technique used to settle contract negotiation disputes.

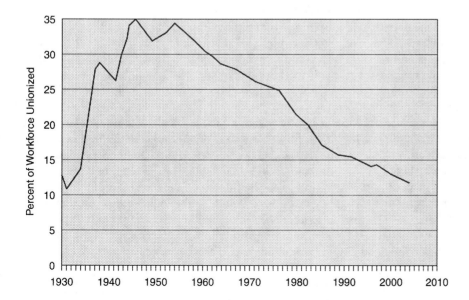

EXHIBIT 14-6
Trends in Union Membership

In the early to mid-1970s, many unionized workers, especially in the private sector, joined the ranks of the middle class as a result of their unions' success at the bargaining table. This often meant that they were more concerned with taxes than with ideological and social issues or with support for legislation that favored the union movement. Furthermore, the private-sector labor movement had difficulty accepting into its ranks public- and federal-sector workers, women, African Americans, and the rising tide of immigrants.

Also, in the 1970s, predictions about the postindustrial age came to pass, and manufacturing was replaced by service as the dominant industry in the American economy. As a consequence, the most rapid employment growth was in wholesale and retail trade, service industries such as high technology, and white-collar jobs. In these areas unions either had not previously focused organizing efforts or were largely unsuccessful for a variety of reasons.

Double-digit inflation, beginning in the mid-1970s, was also a factor. High rates of inflation resulted in the first massive layoffs in both the private and public sectors, which radically diminished the financial resources of numerous unions to represent members and to engage in organizing and political activities. Additionally, the emergence of global competition caught much of American business by surprise. The primary response was to try to restore their financial positions by demanding concessions from workers (concession bargaining) and/or by reducing the workforce. Both of these responses have had an enormous effect on the unions at the workplace. Fueled by these pressures, the latter half of the 1970s ushered in the strongest anti-union movement since the post–World War II era. Outsourcing of production and assembly operations to foreign locations such as the Pacific Rim, Mexico, Brazil, Hong Kong, Taiwan, and parts of Africa originated in the late 1970s.[44]

The 1980s and early 1990s witnessed an even more dramatic decline in union membership and power. Massive layoffs had ripped through the ranks of such unions as the United Automobile Workers (UAW), the United Steelworkers of America (USWA), the United Mine Workers (UMW), the Rubber Workers, and the Communications Workers, so that their numbers were significantly less than at the beginning of the decade. The cumulative effects of factors identified in the 1970s had even harsher consequences during the next 15 years. Union busting and avoidance were no longer sideline issues for management consultants but a thriving and lucrative enterprise in their own right. Worker replacement became a management weapon. If the union would not accept management's best offer, the company simply hired new workers to replace those on strike. The 1980s also witnessed a legislative sentiment that began to turn against unions. In such an environment, the role of the strike took on new meaning. The transition began in 1981, when nationwide attention focused on President Ronald Reagan's firing of illegally striking air traffic controllers. This action sent an important message to employers across the country: the strike is no longer a union weapon but rather a management weapon to push workers out of their jobs in an effort to bust the union and/or to gain concessions from workers that they might not otherwise have given.[45]

The picture for unions in the 1990s was just as bleak. Union-avoidance and -busting tactics, delayering of corporate America, organizations offering fewer jobs, technology advancements, the contingent workforce, replacement workers, and so on, all contributed to a continual decline in membership. From their heyday of almost 36 percent in the early 1940s to their current 12.5 percent in 2004, unions appear not to be the force they once were.[46] But don't count unions out. Stagnant worker wages, health insurance cutbacks, and the like, are making union philosophies more amenable to employees.[47] Unions are also changing some of their organizing tactics, and public sentiment might be changing to support and sympathize with union causes (see Workplace Issues). Unions have also posted some major victories, such as winning elections at AT&T Cellular. Unions have found

WORKPLACE ISSUES

THE UNION SUMMER

Borrowing a page from many private sector organizations looking to find good talent, the AFL-CIO began a program in 1996 called the Union Summer Program. The Union Summer program is a five-week internship to help interested college students learn skills for union-organizing activities. It's proven a good training ground for individuals who may have an interest in working for a union, as well as a "sourcing" activity for unions to find qualified talent.

The Union Summer Program seeks to bring together individuals "committed to uniting workers, students, and community activists to bring about social justice through workplace and community organizing".[48] During the summer internship, these interns work in a variety of activities that typically take place during an organizing campaign. For example, interns may interview potential union members to find out what they believe needs to be changed in their work setting. They may also assist the union and potential members with organizing picket lines, as well as educating community members on workers' rights issues.

Since its inception, the program has had several thousand summer interns.

recruiting members in the service sectors—with a fair amount of success in Las Vegas, as well as with university graduate students—rewarding.[49]

Labor–Management Cooperation

Historically, the relationship between labor and management was built on conflict. The interests of labor and management were seen as basically at odds—each treating the other as the opposition. But times have somewhat changed. Management has become increasingly aware that successful efforts to increase productivity, improve quality, and lower costs require employee involvement and commitment. Similarly, some labor unions have recognized that they can help their members more by cooperating with management rather than fighting them.

Past U.S. labor laws, passed in an era of mistrust and antagonism between labor and management, were initially a barrier to both parties becoming cooperative partners.[50] As a case in point, the National Labor Relations Act was passed to encourage collective bargaining and to balance workers' power against that of management. That legislation also sought to eliminate the then-widespread practice of firms setting up company unions for the sole purpose of undermining efforts of outside unions organizing their employees. The law prohibited employers from creating or supporting a "labor organization." Furthermore, the National Labor Relations Board ruled in the Electromation case that it was an unfair labor practice for the employer to set up employee committees "to impose its own unilateral form of bargaining on employees." Furthermore, Electromation's actions were also viewed as a means of thwarting a Teamsters Union organizing campaign that began in its Elkhart, Indiana, plant. Certain implications of the Electromation case and a broader NLRB interpretation in the Crown Cork and Seal case indicated that companies could have such programs as quality circle, quality of work life, and other employee involvement programs legal under federal labor laws.

Although this issue had been the subject of congressional debate, the current legal environment doesn't prohibit employee-involvement programs in the United States. Rather, to comply with the law, management must give employee-involvement programs independence. That is, when such programs become dominated by management, they're likely to be interpreted as groups that perform some functions of labor unions but are controlled by management. Actions that would indicate that an employee-involvement program is not dominated by management might include choosing program members through secret-ballot elections, giving program members wide latitude in deciding what issues to deal with, permitting members to meet apart from management, and specifying that program members are not susceptible to dissolution by management whim. The key theme labor laws convey is that where employee-involvement programs are introduced, members must have the power to make decisions and act independently of management.

Public-Sector Unionization

Unionizing government employees, either in the federal sector or in state, county, and municipal jurisdictions, has proven lucrative for unions.[51] Significant gains have been made in these sectors, as unions increased membership from 11 percent in 1970 to nearly 37 percent in 2004.[52] In fact, these white-collar unionized jobs account for nearly one-half of all union membership.[53] But labor relations in the government sector differs from its private-sector counterpart. For example, in the federal sector, wages are nonnegotiable. Likewise, compulsory membership in unions is prohibited. At the state, county, and local levels, laws must be passed to grant employees in any jurisdiction the right to unionize—and more important, the right to strike. Yet probably the most notable difference lies in determining "who's the boss."

In a private company, management is the employer. This, however, is not the case in government sectors. Instead, a president, a governor, a mayor, a county executive, and so forth is responsible for the government's budget. These *elected* officials have fiduciary responsibilities to their citizenry. Who, then, "owns" the government? The people, of course. Accordingly, unionized employees in the public sector actually negotiate against themselves as taxpayers. And even if some agreement is reached, the negotiated contract cannot be binding, even though the union members support it, until some legislative body has approved it.

Finally, because these negotiations are a concern to the general public, citizens have the right to know what is going on. This is handled through *sunshine laws*.[54] These laws require parties in public-sector labor relations to make public their negotiations; that is, contract negotiations are open to the public. This freedom of information is based on the premise that the public-sector negotiations directly affect all taxpayers and thus should provide direct information regarding what is occurring. However, although information is important, sunshine laws have been questioned by labor-relations personnel. They contend that what the public may see or hear during open negotiations may ultimately differ from the final contract, and public members who do not understand what happens in negotiations, may gain a false sense of negotiation outcomes.

Unionizing the Nontraditional Employee

The strength of unionization in years past resided in the manufacturing industries of the U.S. economy. Steel, tires, automobiles, and transportation were major industries that dominated every aspect of American life—and the world. In each of these industries ran a common element: the presence of unions. Over the past few decades, however, the United States has changed gears. Once a manufacturing giant, the United States has become a service economy. Unfortunately for unions, the service sector previously had not been one of their targeted areas for organizing employees. That, too, is changing, as unions survival depends on reaching out and fulfilling the needs of nontraditional employees. Nontraditional employees could be classified as anyone not in the manufacturing and related industries. Such people include government workers, nurses, secretaries, professional

DID YOU KNOW?

IS THERE ADDITION BY SUBTRACTION?

Throughout the past several decades, the percent of the workforce unionized has continually declined. A lot of reasons have been cited for the decline, but one question that needs to be asked is, has labor contributed in any way to their own decline? Have their strategies for growing union membership been properly set and executed? Have they reached out to all potential union members? If you listen to several union chieftains, they believe the answer to these questions is no—and this internal strife is a problem for organized labor.

For example, at its convention in July 2005, the AFL-CIO was hit with a major blow. Two of the nation's largest unions—the Teamsters and the Service Employees International Union—along with five other unions, broke away from the AFL-CIO. Their reason: they believe the AFL-CIO just wasn't paying enough attention to the kind of workers that these unions represent. Attempting to unionize more service-type employees, these renegade unions feel they can reach out in a way that the AFL-CIO could not—organizing many of today's working poor. If they are successful, they could increase pay and benefit levels to these workers, similar to what unions did in the 1930s for those employees in the smokestack industries.

A calculated gamble? Of course. Only time will tell if the strategy works.

Source: A. Bernstein and J. Weber, "So Long, AFL-CIO. Now What," *Business Week* (August 8, 2005), p. 35.

and technical employees, dot-com employees, and even some management members. Most notably, unions such as the United Food and Commercial Workers have targeted companies including Wal-Mart, Target, and K-mart as excellent union-organizing grounds.[55]

As the world of work continues to radically evolve, it is safe to assume that unions will target an even broader group of employees. The same causes that unions sold 50 years ago to interest people in the union cause—wages, benefits, job security, and a say in how employees are treated at work—are the same concerns of employees as we enter the early years of the new millennium. Restructuring, delayering, and the dejobbing of corporate America have forced affected workers to pay closer attention to what the unions promise. For the health-care professionals, for example, who voted to be represented by unions, this has resulted in job security and wages and benefits above their nonunion counterparts.[56] And with the recent problems experienced by workers at technology companies as many of these upstart organizations began shedding thousands of employees, unions are targeting the high-tech field for their next organizing emphasis.[57]

Is history repeating itself? Only time will tell. But remember, the decline in union membership—especially in the traditional industries in the 1970s—was brought about in part by people achieving their middle-class status. As organizational changes threaten this social class rank, we have every reason to believe that workers will present a unified, mutual front to the employer. In some cases, that is best achieved through union activities.

INTERNATIONAL LABOR RELATIONS

Labor relations practices, and the percent of the workforce unionized, differ in every country (see Exhibit 14-7). Nowhere is employee representation exactly like that in the United States. In almost every case, relationships among management, employees, and unions (or other administrative bodies) are the result of long histories. The business approach to unionism, or emphasizing economic objectives, is uniquely American. In Europe, Latin America, and elsewhere, unions have often evolved out of a class struggle, resulting in labor as a political party. The Japanese Confederation of Shipbuilding and Engineering Workers' Union only recently began dropping its "class struggle" rhetoric and slogans to pursue a "partnership"

EXHIBIT 14-7
Unionization Around the World

COUNTRY	PERCENT UNIONIZED
Sweden	80.0
Belgium	53.0
Canada	33.0
Germany	32.0
Mexico	30.0
United Kingdom	26.0
Singapore	22.0
Japan	18.0
Spain	17.0
United States	12.5
France	10.0

Source: Society of Human Resource Management "Global HR WorldWatch" (2005), available online at www.shrm.org/global/worldwatch; and U.S. Department of Labor, Bureau of Labor Statistics, "Union Members Summary" (January 27, 2005); available online at www.bls.gov.

with management. The basic difference in perspective sometimes makes it difficult for U.S. expatriates to understand how the labor-relations process works because even the same term may have different meanings. For example, in the United States, "collective bargaining" implies negotiations between a labor union and management. In Sweden and Germany, it refers to negotiations between the employers' organization and a trade union for the entire industry. Furthermore, arbitration in the United States usually refers to the settlement of individual contractual disputes, whereas in Australia arbitration is part of the contract bargaining process.

Not only does each country have a different history of unionism, each government has its own view of its role in the labor-relations process.[58] This role is often reflected in the types and nature of the regulations in force. The U.S. government generally takes a hands-off approach toward intervention in labor–management matters but the Australian government, to which the labor movement has strong ties, is inclined to be more involved. Thus, not only must the multinational corporate industrial relations office be familiar with the separate laws of each country, it also must be familiar with the environment in which those statutes are implemented. Understanding international labor relations is vital to an organization's strategic planning. Unions affect wage levels, which in turn affect competitiveness in both labor and product markets. Unions and labor laws may limit employment-level flexibility through security clauses that tightly control layoffs and terminations (or redundancies). This is especially true in such countries as England, France, Germany, Japan, and Australia, where various laws place severe restrictions on employers.

Differing Perspectives Toward Labor Relations

If labor relations can affect the organization's strategic planning initiatives, it is necessary to consider the issue of headquarters' involvement in host-country international union relations. The organization must assess whether the labor-relations function should be controlled globally from the parent country, or whether it would be more advantageous for each host country to administer its own operation. There is no simple means of making this assessment; frequently, the decision reflects the relationship of the product market at home to that of the overseas product market. For instance, when domestic sales are larger than those overseas, the organization is more likely to regard the foreign office as an extension of the domestic operations. This is true for many U.S. multinational organizations because the home market is so vast. Thus, American firms have been more inclined to keep labor relations centrally located at corporate headquarters. Many European countries, by contrast, have small home markets with comparatively larger

Unions can be found in most industrialized nations in the world. Workers around the world have found it useful to collectively fight for better wages, benefits, and working conditions. (*Source:* © AP/Wide World Photos)

international operations; thus, they are more inclined to adapt to host-country standards and have the labor-relations function decentralized.

Another divergence among multinational companies in their labor relations is the national attitude toward unions. Generally, American multinational corporations view unions negatively at home and try to avoid workforce unionization. Europeans, on the other hand, have had greater experience with unions, are accustomed to a larger proportion of the workforce being unionized, and are more accepting of the unionization of their own workers. In Japan, as in other parts of Asia, unions are often closely identified with an organization.

The European Community

The European Community brings together a dozen or more individual labor relations systems. For both the member nations and other countries doing business in Europe, such as the United States and Japan, it is important to understand the dynamics of what will necessarily be a dramatically changing labor environment.

Legislation about workers' rights is continually developing, which has far-ranging implications for all employers. The French and Germans lean toward strong worker representation in labor policy, reflecting their cultural histories, but the United Kingdom and Denmark oppose it. Many basic questions remain regarding implementation of the free trade of labor across national boundaries. For example, with the increase in production that accompanies the opening of this market, workers and their union representatives will want their fair share. And what is this fair share? For starters, European unions want a maternity package that provides 80 percent of salary for a 14-week period. They are also seeking premium pay for night work, full benefits for workers employed more than eight hours a week, participation on companies' boards of directors, and an increase in the minimum wage level to two-thirds of each country's average manufacturing wage. Some of these inducements will be difficult to obtain, but companies doing business overseas must be aware of what is happening in pending labor legislation and fully understand and comply with the host country's laws and customs.

SUMMARY

(This summary relates to the Learning Outcomes identified on page 373.)
After having read this chapter you can

1. **Define the term _unions_.** A union is an organization of workers, acting collectively, seeking to promote and protect their mutual interests through collective bargaining.
2. **Discuss the effects of the Wagner and the Taft-Hartley Acts on labor-management relations.** The Wagner (National Labor Relations) Act of 1935 and the Taft-Hartley (Labor-Management Relations) Act of 1947 represent the most direct legislation affecting collective bargaining. The Wagner Act gave unions the freedom to exist and identified employer unfair labor practices. Taft-Hartley balanced the power between unions and management by identifying union unfair labor practices.
3. **Identify the significance of Executive Orders 10988 and 11491 and the Civil Service Reform Act of 1978.** Executive Orders 10988 and 11491 paved the way for labor relations to exist in the federal sector. Additionally, Executive Order 11491 made federal labor relations similar to its private-sector counterpart. The Civil Service Reform Act of 1978 removed federal-sector labor relations from under the jurisdiction of the president and established a forum for its continued operation.

VISUAL SUMMARY

Chapter 14: Understanding Labor Relations and Collective Bargaining

1 — Why Do Employees Join Unions?

Union—an organization of workers seeking to promote its interests through collective bargaining

Interests Include
- Higher wages
- Greater job security
- Influence work rules
- Compulsory membership—union shop, agency shop, open shop
- Being upset with management

2 — Labor Legislation

Railway Labor Act (1929)
- Initial impetus for collective bargaining
- Covers transportation industry only

Landrum-Griffin Act (1959)
- Passed to address misuse of union fund and corruption
- Requires financial forms by unions

1920   1930   1940   1950   1960   1970   2000   Present

Wagner Act (1935)
- Union bill of rights
- Unfair labor practices by companies
- Established NLRB

Taft-Hartley (1947)
- Amended Wagner Act
- Unfair labor practices by unions
- Created FMCS

3 — How Are Employees Unionized?

Unorganized

Authorization card campaign: Did union get 30% or more? — No

Yes

Petition NLRB for election: Are authorization cards in order? — No

Yes

Vote taken: Did union receive a majority vote? — No

No union vote for one year

Yes

Certification bargaining unit

4 Collective Bargaining

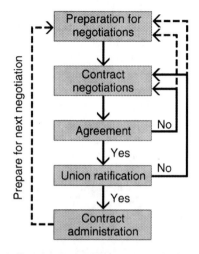

Collective Bargaining—negotiation, administration, and interpretation of a written agreement between labor and management

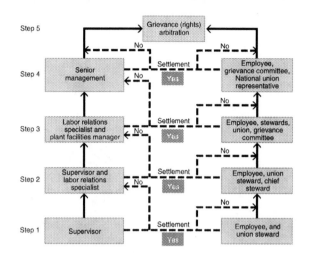

Grievance Procedure—designed to resolve employee complaints as quickly as possible

---

Strike vs. Lockout

Economic strike occurs when two parties cannot reach a satisfactory agreement before a contract expires. **Lockout** occurs when the organization denies unionized workers access to their jobs.

---

5 International Labor Relations

Country	Percent Unionized
Sweden	80.0
Belgium	53.0
Canada	33.0
Germany	32.0
Mexico	30.0
United Kingdom	26.0
Singapore	22.0
Japan	18.0
Spain	17.0
United States	12.5
France	10.0

Source: Society of Human Resource Management "Global HR WorldWatch" (2005), available online at www.shrm.org/global/worldwatch; and U.S. Department of Labor, Bureau of Labor Statistics, "Union Members Summary" (January 27, 2005); available online at www.bls.gov.

4. **Describe the union-organizing process.** The union-organizing process officially begins with the completion of an authorization. If the required percentage of potential union members show their intent to vote on a union by signing the authorization card, the NLRB will hold an election. If 50 percent plus one of those voting vote for the union, then the union is certified to be the bargaining unit.

5. **Describe the components of collective bargaining.** Collective bargaining typically refers to the negotiation, administration, and interpretation of a written agreement between two parties that covers a specific period of time.

6. **Identify the steps in the collective-bargaining process.** The collective-bargaining process is comprised of the following steps: preparation for negotiations, negotiations, and contract administration.

7. **Explain the various types of union security arrangements.** The various union security arrangements are the closed shop (made illegal by the Taft-Hartley Act); the union shop, which requires compulsory union membership; the agency shop, which requires compulsory union dues; and the open shop, which enforces workers' freedom of choice to select union membership or not.

8. **Describe the role of a grievance procedure in collective bargaining.** The grievance procedure provides a formal mechanism in labor contracts for resolving issues over the interpretation and application of a contract.

9. **Identify the various impasse-resolution techniques.** The most popular impasse-resolution techniques include mediation (a neutral third party informally attempts to bring the parties to agreement); fact-finding (a neutral third party conducts a hearing to gather evidence from both sides); and interest arbitration (a panel of individuals hears testimony from both sides and renders a decision).

10. **Discuss how sunshine laws affect public-sector collective bargaining.** Sunshine laws require parties in the public sector to make their collective-bargaining negotiations open to the public.

DEMONSTRATING COMPREHENSION: *Questions for Review*

1. What is a union and why do they exist?
2. What three pieces of legislation have been most important in defining the rights of management and unions?
3. What is the process for establishing a union as the legal collective-bargaining representative for employees?
4. Why is compulsory union membership so important to unions?
5. Where are unionizing efforts focused today?
6. What is collective bargaining? How widely is it practiced?
7. Describe the collective bargaining process.
8. What is the objective of collective bargaining?
9. Why do a union's initial demands tend to be long and extravagant?

KEY TERMS

agency shop	dues checkoff	grievance	maintenance of
authorization	economic strike	procedure	membership
card	fact finder	interest	National Labor
Civil Service	Federal	arbitration	Relations Board
Reform Act	Mediation and	Landrum-Griffin	(NLRB)
collective	Conciliation	Act of 1959	open shop
bargaining	Service (FMCS)	lockout	

Racketeer
  Influenced and
  Corrupt
  Organizations
  Act (RICO)

Railway Labor
  Act
representation
  certification
  (RC)

representation
  decertification
  (RD)
Taft-Hartley Act
union

union security
  arrangements
union shop
Wagner Act
wildcat strike

CROSSWORD COMPREHENSION

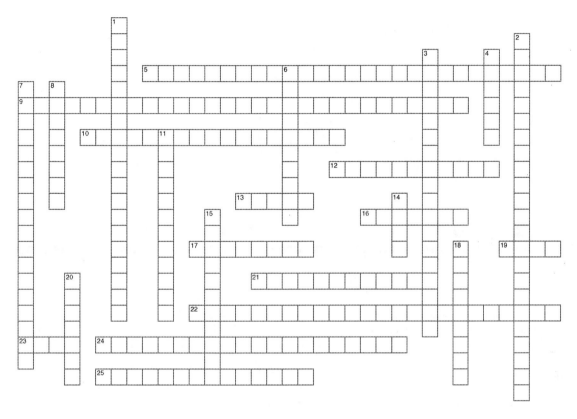

ACROSS

5. the election process whereby union members vote in a union as their representative
9. the election process whereby union members vote out their union as their representative
10. the document signed by prospective union members indicating that they are interested in having a union represent them
12. act addressing employers' concerns in terms of specifying unfair labor union practices
13. an organization of workers acting collectively, seeking to promote their mutual interests
16. a type of strike that is unauthorized and illegal during the terms of an existing contract
17. a type of strike that results from labor and management's inability to agree on a new contract
19. government agency that assists labor and management in settling disputes
21. employer withholding of union dues from union members' paychecks
22. labor contract provisions designed to attract and retain dues-paying union members
23. legislation passed to eliminate any influence on unions by members of organized crime
24. the negotiation, administration, and interpretation of a written agreement between labor and management
25. legislation that protected union members from possible wrongdoing on the part of their unions and required all unions to disclose their financial statements

DOWN

1. an impasse-resolution technique used to settle contract negotiation disputes
2. requires an individual who chooses to join a union to remain in the union for the duration of the existing contract
3. act that replaced Executive Order 11491 as the basic law governing labor relations for federal employees
4. this act gave employees the right to form and join unions and engage in collective bargaining
6. an arrangement whereby employees must pay union dues to the union even if they chose not to join the union
7. a complaint-resolving process contained in union contracts
8. an arrangement whereby employees are free to join the union or not, and those who decline need not pay union dues
11. act providing the initial impetus to widespread collective bargaining
14. established to administrate and interpret the Wagner Act and conducts union representation elections
15. the technique whereby a neutral third party conducts a hearing to gather evidence about differences that exist between the two parties
18. an arrangement whereby any nonunion workers must become dues paying members within a prescribed period of time
20. a situation whereby management prevents union members from returning to work

HRM WORKSHOP

LINKING CONCEPTS TO PRACTICE: *Discussion Questions*

1. "All that is required for successful labor–management relations is common sense, sound business judgment, and good listening skills." Do you agree or disagree with this statement? Explain.
2. Given your career aspirations, might you join a union? Why or why not? Explain.
3. "An employer might not want to stifle a union-organizing effort. In fact, an employer might want to encourage his employees to join a union." Do you agree or disagree with this statement? Explain your position.
4. "If management treats employees well, pays them a fair wage, communicates with them, and ensures that they have a safe and healthy work environment, there is no need for a union." Do you agree or disagree with the statement? Explain your position.

DEVELOPING DIAGNOSTIC AND ANALYTICAL SKILLS

Case Application 14-A: HOCKEY ON ICE

The sporting world anxiously awaited the midnight deadline of the pending work stoppage by the National Hockey Players Association and the team owners. For years these two groups had worked out their differences. Although previous negotiations had traditionally been hard fought, no one really anticipated what would happen in February 2005. On February 16, negotiations reached a total standstill—and the remainder of the 2005 hockey season was canceled. Hockey's Stanley Cup championship would not occur—only the second time in its history this had happened—and not since 1919.[59] In past negotiations, one almost expected some disputes and some strong words between the owners and the players association. But no one expected negotiations to fall apart like they did this time. Ironically, the season was lost over an issue that amounted to about $6.5 million. That is, at issue was a salary cap. The owners wanted a salary cap at $42.5 million, and the players wanted it set at $49 million per team. The owners felt this was needed because of failing markets in certain areas of the country. To assist in this issue, the players were willing to take a 24 percent pay cut to keep the season alive. But the owners held steadfast on the salary cap. Rather than recognizing that team and league revenues in smaller markets were problematic—and possibly eliminating some of the more financially strapped franchises—the owners issued a take-it-or-leave-it ultimatum to the players association.

Ironically the $42 million salary cap was not a true number. Just before the season was canceled, the hockey commissioner indicated that he was willing to consider a counteroffer by the players union—and could see a compromise somewhere in the $45 million ballpark. But the union executive director wanted none of the compromise and declined—opting instead to take the "leave it" part of the ultimatum.

Questions:

1. What role do personalities and emotions play in labor–management negotiations? Discuss.
2. How could more cooperation between the players union and the owners averted canceling the remainder of the 2005 hockey season? Be specific in your response.
3. What are the risks associated with take-it-or-leave-it ultimatums? Do you believe this is an effective negotiations strategy? Why or why not?

Case Application 14-B: TEAM FUN!

Team Fun

Kenny and Norton, owners of TEAM FUN!, a sporting goods manufacturer and retailer are kayaking in the LAGOON, their water-gear area. Kenny splashes Norton. "Did you see the paper this morning?" Norton shakes his head no as Kenny continues. "I bet I know why Keith was talking about changing operations at his company and finding out how happy all his employees are. Those guys voted in a union. Honest. Front page of the business section." (Keith is one of their longtime competitors.)

Norton frowns. "Why would they go union? He's a great guy. Tony found out that they pay better than we do. Say, do we need to worry about a union here?" (Tony is director of human resources for TEAM FUN!.)

Kenny reassures him, "No worries here. Besides, they have to let us know ahead of time if they are having a 'certification vote.' I think he said two years, or maybe that's two months, before they organize one. We can go talk to all the employees if you want. Next month's picnic doesn't have a topic yet. We'll ask Tony as soon as he shows up. You'll never catch me in a union."

"We were in a union before," says Norton. "Remember that food processing plant in Texas where we shoveled frozen peas into boxcars? We paid dues, filed grease bandages, the whole bit. It was a closed shop."

Kenny: "My fingers got frostbit there. I never paid dues. And, I thought I was bribing that guy not to tell when we came in late. I never had a closet for any of my stuff. That place wasn't anything like TEAM FUN! Ask Tony what he thinks about a union. Did you ever figure out why they called the complaint procedure a 'greased bandage?'"

Norton snorts, "I'll fire him if he thinks it's a good idea."

Kenny smiles. "We can just fire all of them if they think it's a good idea."

Questions:

1. How accurate is Kenny's description of the union organizing process? Give details.
2. Explain to Norton the union activities he remembers from their Texas job.
3. Is TEAM FUN! likely to organize?
4. Should the organization resist or encourage such activities?

WORKING WITH A TEAM: *Handling a Grievance*

Break into teams of three. This role-play requires one person to play the role of the HR director (Chris), another to play the role of the employee (Pat), and a third to play the role of the union steward (C.J.).

Each team member should read the following scenario and the excerpt from the union contract and then role-play a meeting in Chris's office. This role-play should take no more than 15 minutes.

Scenario: The head of security for your company has recently been focusing attention on the removal of illegal substances from the company's workplace. One morning last week, a guard suspected the possession of a controlled substance by an employee, Pat. The guard noticed Pat placing a bag in a personal locker and subsequently searched the locker. The guard found a variety of pills, some of which he thought were nonprescription types. As Pat was leaving work for the day, the security guard stopped Pat with a request for Pat to empty the contents of the bag being carried. Pat was not told why the request was being made. Pat refused to honor the request and stormed out of the door, leaving the company's premises. Pat was terminated the next morning by the boss for refusing to obey the legitimate order of a building security guard. Feeling as if they were unable to address the issue satisfactorily with Pat's supervisor, Pat and C.J. have set up this meeting with Chris.

Chris has just gone into a meeting with Pat and C.J. Chris wishes to enforce Pat's supervisor's decision to terminate Pat and justify the reason for it. C.J. and Pat, on the other hand, claim this action is a violation of the union contract.

Relevant Contract Language: The following is excerpted from the labor agreement: An employee who fails to maintain proper standards of conduct at all times, or who violates any of the following rules, shall be subject to disciplinary action.

Rule 4: Bringing illegal substances, firearms, or intoxicating liquors onto company premises, using or possessing these on company property, or reporting to work under the influence of a substance is strictly prohibited.

Rule 11: Refusal to follow supervisory orders or acting in any way insubordinate to any company agent is strictly prohibited.

Role for Chris: To handle this grievance, listen to the employee's complaint, investigate the facts as best you can, make your decision, and explain it clearly.

LEARNING AN HRM SKILL: *Negotiation Skills*

About the skill: The essence of effective negotiation can be summarized in the following six recommendations.[60]

1. *Research your opponent.* Acquire as much information as you can about your opponent's interests and goals. What people must he or she appease? What is his or her strategy? This information will help you better understand your opponent's behavior, predict his or her responses to your offers, and frame solutions in terms of his or her interests.
2. *Begin with a positive overture.* Research shows that concessions tend to be reciprocated and lead to agreements. As a result, begin bargaining with a positive overture—perhaps a small concession—and then reciprocate your opponent's concessions.
3. *Address problems, not personalities.* Concentrate on the negotiation issues, not on the personal characteristics of your opponent. When negotiations become tough, avoid the tendency to attack your opponent. You disagree with your opponent's ideas or position, not him or her personally. Separate the people from the problem and don't personalize differences.
4. *Pay little attention to initial offers.* Treat an initial offer as merely a point of departure. Everyone needs an initial position, and initial positions tend to be extreme and idealistic. Treat them as such.
5. *Emphasize win-win solutions.* If conditions are supportive, look for an integrative solution. Frame options in terms of your opponent's interests and look for solutions that allow your opponent, as well as you, to declare a victory.
6. *Be open to accepting third-party assistance.* When stalemates are reached, consider the use of a neutral third party—a mediator, an arbitrator, or a conciliator. Mediators can help parties come to an agreement, but they don't impose a settlement. Arbitrators hear both sides of the dispute, then impose a solution. Conciliators are more informal and act as a communication conduit, passing information between the parties, interpreting messages, and clarifying misunderstandings.

ENHANCING YOUR COMMUNICATION SKILLS

1. In a two- to three-page report, discuss the pros, cons, and class perceptions of what it is/would be like to work in a unionized environment. Would you consider working in such an environment? Why or why not?
2. Visit the AFL-CIO's Web site (www.aflcio.com). Research and summarize two current union issues the AFL-CIO is working on/supporting legislation for. End your report with your support for or against the union perspective.
3. Investigate how the Racketeer Influenced and Corrupt Organizations Act (RICO) has been used in the past five years to attack corrupt practices in labor unions. Cite specific examples found in your research.

Endnotes

Chapter One: Strategic Implications of a Dynamic HRM Environment

1. K. Kelleher, "66,207,896 Bottles of Beer on the Wall," *Business 2.0* (February 2004). Available online at www.business20.com.
2. Ibid.
3. See for example, "The Forbes 500s" (March 26, 2002), pp. 48–55.
4. C. Y. Chen, "The World's Most Admired Companies 2002," *Fortune* (March 4, 2002), pp. 91–93; N. Stein, "Global Most Admired: The World's Most Admired Companies," *Fortune* (October 2, 2000), p. 182; "Global Most Admired: And the Winners Are . . ." *Fortune* (October 2, 2000), pp. 191–194; and K. Capell, H. Dawley, W. Zellner, and K. N. Anhalt, "Wal-Mart's Not-So-Secret British Weapon," *Business Week* (January 14, 2000), p. 132.
5. A multinational corporation has significant operations in two or more countries. A transnational corporation maintains significant operations in two or more countries simultaneously and gives each the decision-making authority to operate in the local country.
6. For a more comprehensive coverage of the cultural dimension, see Geert Hofstede, *Cultural Consequences: International Differences in Work-Related Values* (Beverly Hills, CA: Sage Publications, 1980).
7. Material in this section is adapted from S. D. Trujillo, "The Third Wave," *Executive Excellence* (January 202), p. 19; R. W. Rice, "The World of Work in 2010," *CMA Management* (December 2001/January 2002), pp. 38–41; "The Third Wave of Revolution," *Monthly Labor Review* (February 2001), p. 59; and A. Toffler, *The Third Wave* (New York: Bantam Books, 1981).
8. B. Goldberg, "Contrarian Thoughts About Older Workers," *Financial Executive* (January/February 2002), p. 28; A. L. Liput, "Workforce 2000: Legal Issues in a Diverse Workforce," *Human Resource Professional* (May/June 2000), pp. 19–21; J. Laabs, "Strategic HR Won't Come Easily," *Workforce* (January 2000), pp. 52–56; and S. J. Wells, "A Female Executive Is Hard to Find," *HR Magazine* (June 2001), pp. 40–49.
9. M. Conlin, M. Mandel, M. Arndt, and W. Zellner, "Suddenly It's the Big Freeze," *Business Week* (April 16, 2001), pp. 38–39; B. Blackstone and R. Christie, "Top Economic Index Declines as Growth Continues, Though at More Modest Pace," *Wall Street Journal* (March 23, 2001), p. A-2; "Strategic Value Configuration Logics and the 'New' Economy: A Service Economy Revolution," *International Journal of Service Industry Management* (January 2001), p. 70; and "Time for Change," *Business Asia* (March 6, 2001), pp. 1–3.
10. B. B. Hughes, "Global Social Transformation: The Sweet Spot, the Steady Slog, and the Systemic Shift," *Economic Development and Cultural Change* (January 2001), pp. 423–458; C. R. Greer, "E-Voice: How Information Technology Is Shaping Life Within Unions," *Journal of Labor Research* (Spring 2002), pp. 215–235; R. A. Miller, "The Four Horsemen of Downsizing and the Tower of Babel," *Journal of Business Ethics* (January 2001), pp. 147–151; R. L. Schott, "The Origins of Bureaucracy: An Anthropological Perspective," *International Journal of Public Administration* (January 2000), pp. 53–78; and J. Cross and T. O'Driscoll, "Workflow Learning Gets Real: Welcome to an Era in Which Learning Fuses with Real-Time Work. The Convergence Is Ushering in a Whole New Era," *Training* (February 2005), pp. 30–34.
11. "Telecommuting: Managing Off-Site Staff for Small Business," *Canadian Manager* (Spring 2002), p. 27; and A. Fisher, "How Telecommuters Can Stay Connected," *Fortune* (May 30, 2005), p. 142.
12. R. M. Kesner, "Running Information Services as a Business: Managing IS Commitments Within the Enterprise," *Information Strategy* (Summer 2002), pp. 15–35; and "Telework Seen as Helpful to Employers, yet Full-Time Arrangements Are Rare," *HR Focus* (June 2005), p. 8.
13. For an interesting perspective on this issue, see D. Zweig and J. Webster, "Where Is the Line Between Benign and Invasive? An Examination of Psychological Barriers to the Acceptance of Awareness Monitoring Systems," *Journal of Organizational Behavior* (August 2002), pp. 602–634.
14. J. Jusko, "A Watchful Eye," *Industry Week* (May 7, 2001), p. 9; and "Big Brother Boss," *U.S. News and World Report* (April 30, 2001), p. 12.
15. T. George and E. Colkin, "Spring Cleaning for University Tech Offerings," *Information Week* (April 22, 2002), pp. 88–90.
16. H. F. Gale Jr., T. R. Wojan, and J. C. Olmsted, "Skills, Flexible Manufacturing Technology, and Work Organization," *Industrial Relations* (January 2002), pp. 48–79.
17. M. A. Verespej, "Inappropriate Internet Surfing," *Industry Week* (February 7, 2000), pp. 59–64.
18. Ibid.
19. Ibid., p. 51.
20. Ibid.
21. O. C. Richard, "Racial Diversity, Business Strategy, and Firm Performance: A Resource-Based View," *Academy of Management Journal* (April 2000), pp. 164–177; and M. Lien, "Workforce Diversity: Opportunities in the Melting Pot," *Occupational Outlook Quarterly* (Summer 2004), pp. 28–37.
22. A. S. Wellner, "Tapping a Silver Mine," *HR Magazine* (March 2002), pp. 26–32; and Neal Thompson, "American Work Force Is Seeing More Gray," *Baltimore Sun* (October 8, 2000), pp. A1; A13.
23. See Society of Human Resource Management, "What Are Some Strategies for Recruiting and Retaining a Diverse Workforce?" *Workplace Diversity Initiative* (September 29, 2000), pp. 1–3.
24. B. Leonard, "Not All Training Programs Have Felt the Full Squeeze of Corporate Belt-Tightening," *HR Magazine*

(April 2002), p. 25; R. Koonce, "Redefining Diversity," *Training and Development* (December 2001), pp. 22–33; and T. Colling, "Institutional Theory and the Cross-Cultural Transfer of Employment Policy: The Case of Workforce Diversity in US Multinationals," *Journal of International Business Studies* (May 2005), pp. 304–321.

25. B. Benham, "Get Your Share," *Working Woman* (April 2001), pp. 54–58.

26. See also L. Grensing-Pophal, "A Balancing Act on Diversity Audits," *HR Magazine* (November 2001), pp. 87–95; T. Minton-Eversole, "Coke Also Reviews Benefits Program During Its Diversity Analysis," *HR News* (December 2001), p. 4; and J. T. Childs Jr., "Managing Workforce Diversity at IBM: A Global HR Topic That Has Arrived," *Human Resource Management* (Spring 2005), pp. 73–77.

27. L. Grensing-Pophal, "Reaching for Diversity," *HR Magazine* (May 2002), pp. 53–56.

28. See, for instance, "Friends of the Family: 100 Best Companies for Working Mothers—16th Annual Survey," *Working Mother* (October 2001), pp. 60–148; and S. D. Brown, "Head of the Class," *Black Enterprise* (May 2002), pp. 39–44.

29. See, for instance, P. Cappelli, J. Constantine, and C. Chadwick, "It Pays to Value Family: Work and Family Trade-Offs Reconsidered," *Industrial Relations* (April 2000), pp. 175–198; M. A. Verespej, "Balancing Act," *Industry Week* (May 15, 2000), pp. 81–85; and R. C. Barnett and D. T. Hall, "How to Use Reduced Hours to Win the War for Talent," *Organizational Dynamics* (March 2001), p. 42.

30. See, for instance, L. Belkin, "From Dress-Down Friday to Dress-Down Life," *New York Times* (June 22, 2003), p. 1; and E. Tahminicioglu, "By Telecommuting, the Disabled Get a Key to the Office, and a Job," *New York Times* (July 20, 2003), p. 1.

31. M. Conlin, "The New Debate over Working Moms," *Business Week* (November 18, 2000), pp. 102–103.

32. "The New World of Work: Flexibility Is the Watchword," *Business Week* (January 10, 2000), p. 36.

33. See, for example, "U.S. Employers Polish Image to Woo a Demanding New Generation," *Manpower Argus* (February 2000), p. 2.

34. L. L. Martins, K. B. Eddleston, and J. F. Veiga, "Moderators of the Relationship Between Work-Family Conflict and Career Satisfaction," *Academy of Management Journal* (May 2002), pp. 399–409; and L. Carlson, "Work-Life Benefits Don't Guarantee Work-Life Balance: Having a Work-Life Benefits Program Isn't Enough: You Must Be Sure That Executives and Managers Are Walking the Talk," *Employee Benefits News* (August 1, 2005), pp. 1–2.

35. D. Eisenberg, "The Coming Job Boom," *Time* (May 6, 2002), pp. 40–44.

36. D. Eisenberg, "Firms Brace for Worker Shortage," *Time* (May 6, 2002), p. 44.

37. N. Grossman, "Shrinking the Work Force in an Economic Slowdown," *Compensation and Benefits Management* (Spring 2002), pp. 12–23.

38. "Human Resources," *Business Asia* (March 11, 2002), pp. 6–8; D. Michaels, "British Airways to Cut More Jobs and Routes to Address Losses," *Wall Street Journal* (February 14, 2002), p. A-15; and T. Waddel, "Contracting Out—Is In," *New Zealand Management* (November 2000), p. 92.

39. L. M. Gossett, "The Long-Term Impact of Short-Term Workers," *Management Communication Quarterly* (August 2001), pp. 115–120.

40. For an interesting background perspective of contingent workers, see S. F. Befort, "Revisiting the Black Hole of Workplace Regulation: A Historical and Comparative Perspective of Contingent Work," *Berkeley Journal of Employment and Labor Law* (Summer 2003), pp. 153–178.

41. See, for instance, B. A. Lautsch, "Uncovering and Explaining Variance in the Features and Outcomes of Contingent Work," *Industrial and Labor Relations Review* (October 2002), pp. 23–44.

42. See K. J. Bannan, "Breakaway (A Special Report)—Getting Help—Together: By Bundling Job-Recruiting Efforts, Small Firms Seek Attention—and Leverage," *Wall Street Journal* (April 23, 2001), p. A-12.

43. A. Gabor, "He Made America Think About Quality," *Fortune* (October 30, 2000), pp. 292–293.

44. See, for example, J. McElroy, "Six Lessons for Ford," *Ward's Auto World* (December 2001), p. 17.

45. "Continuous Improvement: Ten Essential Criteria," *Measuring Business Excellence* (January 2002), p. 49.

46. "Winning with Kaizen," *IIE Solutions* (April 2002), p. 10.

47. J. A. M. Coyle-Shapiro, "Changing Employee Attitudes: The Independent Effects of TQM and Profit Sharing on Continuous Improvement Orientation," *Journal of Applied Behavioral Science* (March 2002), pp. 57–77.

48. M. Budman, "Jim Champy Puts His 'X' on Reengineering," *Across the Board* (March/April 2002), pp. 15–16.

49. S. A. DiPiazza, "Ethics in Action," *Executive Excellence* (January 2002), pp. 15–16.

50. "Coming Clean," *Money* (May 2002), p. 33.

51. B. R. Gaumnitz and J. C. Lere, "Contents of Codes of Ethics of Professional Business Organizations in the United States," *Journal of Business Ethics* (January 2002), pp. 35–49; and C. C. Verschoor, "Benchmarking Ethics and Compliance Programs," *Strategic Finance* (August 2005), pp. 17–19.

52. M. M. Clark, "Corporate Ethics Programs Make a Difference, But Not the Only Difference," *HR Magazine* (July 2003), p. 36; and T. F. Shea, "Employees' Report Card on Supervisors' Ethics: No Improvement," *HR Magazine* (April 2002), p. 29.

53. See also "Angels in the Boardroom," *Business Week* (July 7, 2003), p. 12; and A. G. Peace, J. Weber, K. S. Hartzel, and J. Nightingale, "Ethical Issues in eBusiness: A Proposal for Creating the eBusiness Principles," *Business and Society Review* (Spring 2002), pp. 41–60.

54. Case based on "Work/Life Balance at Baxter" (2005), available online at www.baxter.com/about_baxter/sustainability/our_people/work_life/sub/background.html; and M. Arndt, "How Does Harry Do It?" *Business Week* (July 22, 2002), pp. 66–67.

Chapter Two: Fundamentals of HRM

1. No specific date is identified regarding the "birth" of personnel departments, but the generally accepted inception of personnel was in the early 1900s in the BF Goodrich Company. Early personnel departments were often seen as performing relatively unimportant activities. In fact, the personnel department was often viewed as an "employee graveyard"—a place to send employees who were past their prime and couldn't do much damage.

2. B. Roberts, "Side-by-Side," *HR Magazine* (March 2004), pp. 52–57; B. Becker, "Measuring HR?" *HR Magazine* (December 2003), pp. 57–61; S. Bates, "The Metrics Maze," *HR Magazine* (December 2003), pp. 52–55; and R. J. Grossman, "Forging a Partnership," *HR Magazine* (April 2003), pp. 40–46; and R. J. Grossman, "Holding Back Bankruptcy," *HR Magazine* (May 2003), pp. 45–52.

3. S. Bates, "Super HR Manufacturing Plants Outperform Others, Survey Finds," *HR News,* available online at www.shrm.org/hrnews (June 8, 2004); and B. Roberts, "Count on Business Value," *HR Magazine* (August 2002), pp. 65–72; and J. Dung, B. Menguc, and J. Benson, "The Impact of Human Resource Management on Export Performance of Chinese Manufacturing Enterprises," *Thunderbird International Business Review* (July–August 2003), pp. 409–429.

4. See, for instance, Nancy Wong Bryan, "HR by the Numbers," *Workforce* (June 2000), pp. 94–104.

5. Substantial criticism of the Hawthorne studies regarding the conclusions they drew has in no way diminished the significance of opinions they represent in the development of the HRM field.

6. Arnold Packer, "Getting to Know the Employee of the Future," *Training and Development* (August 2000), pp. 39–43.

7. "Strategic HR—Aligning Human Resources with Corporate Goals," *Management Services* (August 2000), p. 5; and Jennifer Laabs, "Strategic HR Won 't Come Easily," *Workforce* (January 2000), pp. 52–56.

8. Bill Leonard, "Investment in HR Reaps Benefits," *HR Magazine* (June 2000), p. 22.

9. See, for example, S. Bates, "Most Workers Only Moderately Engaged, Study Finds," *HR News* (August 14, 2003), p. 1.

10. See, for example, Richard Henderson, *Compensation Management in a Knowledge-Based World,* 9th ed. (Upper Saddle River, NJ: Prentice Hall, 2003).

11. G. A. Stevens and J. Burley, "Piloting the Rocket of Radical Innovation: Selecting the Right People for the Right Roles Dramatically Improves the Effectiveness of New Business Development," *Research-Technology Management* (March–April 2003), pp. 16–26.

12. "Money Still Talks When It Comes to Retention," *Workforce* (September 2000), p. 30.

13. See, for instance, Edward L. Powers, "Employee Loyalty in the New Millennium," *SAM Advanced Management Journal* (Summer 2000), pp. 4–8.

14. Carla Johnson, ". . . and Other Duties as Assigned," *HR Magazine* (February 2000), pp. 66–72.

15. Information based on Society for Human Resource Management, "HR Basics 2000" (October 2000).

16. As we will show in Chapter 5, during a period of downsizing, the employment department may also handle layoffs.

17. It should be noted that compensation and benefits may be, in fact, two separate departments. However, for reading flow, we will consider the department as a combined, singular unit.

18. See, for example, Karen S. Whelan-Berry and Judith R. Gordon, "Strengthening Human Resource Strategies: Insights from the Experiences of Mid-Career Professional Women," *Human Resource Planning* (January 2000), pp. 27–37; and "Flexible Benefits: Beyond the New Regulations," *Employee Benefit Plan Review* (June 2000), pp. 43–45.

19. Perquisites, or perks, are special offerings accorded to senior managers in an attempt to attract and retain the best managers possible.

20. See G. Roper, "Managing Employee Relations," *HR Magazine* (May 2005), pp. 101–104; and J. A. Segal, "Labor Pains for Union-Free Employers: Don't Be Caught Unaware of Nonunion Employees' Labor Law Rights," *HR Magazine* (March 2004), pp. 113–118.

21. Mark C. Johike and Dale F. Duhan, "Supervisor Communication Practices and Service Job Outcomes," *Journal of Service Research* (November 2000), p. 154.

22. See, for instance, Lin Grensing-Pophal, "Follow Me," *HR Magazine* (February 2000), pp. 36–41.

23. Mike Hoffman, "Breaking Up the Kitchen Cabinet," *Inc.* (January 30, 2001), pp. 101–102.

24. "Employee Relations," *HR Magazine* (February 2003), p. 127; and L. A. Weatherly, "HR Technology, Leveraging the Shift to Self-Service—It's Time to Go Strategic," available online at www.shrm.org/research/quarterly/2005/0305RQuart_essay.asp (March 2005).

25. Samuel F. Del Brocco and Robert W. Sprague, "Getting Your Supervisors and Managers in the Right Team," *Employment Relations Today* (Autumn 2000), pp. 13–27.

26. Watson Wyatt Worldwide, "Effective Recruiting Tied to Stronger Financial Performance," available online at www.watsonwyatt.com/news/press.asp?id=14959 (2005).

27. Ibid.

28. Strategic business units, or market-driven units, operate as independent entities in an organization with their own set of strategies and mission.

29. C. Horn, "HR: Down the Line," *Personnel Today* (October 23, 2001), p. 1.

30. Bill Leonard, "Organizations Benefit from Sharing HR Services," *HR Magazine* (February 2000), p. 32.

31. Bob Cecil, "Shared Services: Moving Beyond Success," *Strategic Finance* (April 2000), pp. 64–68.

32. "HR Outsourcing Is Not All About the Money," *HR Magazine* (April 2003), p. 14; and S. Bates, "Facing the Future," *HR Magazine* (July 2002), p. 30.

33. D. Nilsen, B. Kowske, and K. Anthony, "Managing Globally," *HR Magazine* (August 2005), pp. 111–115.

34. Sarah Cuthill, "Cross-Cultural Training: A Critical Step in Ensuring the Success of International Assignments," *Human Resource Management* (Summer Fall 2000), pp. 239–250.

35. "International Transfers: Making Relocation Offers Employees Can't Refuse," *SHRM Information Center* (April 2000), pp. 1–6.

36. See, for instance, Maria Antonia del Rio, "Expatriate Tax: Understanding the Spanish System," *Benefits and Compensation* (July–August 2000), pp. 27–30.

37. "Coming Clean," *Money* (May 2002), p. 33.

38. Based on J. A. Segal, "The Joy of Uncooking," *HR Magazine* (November 2002), p. 53.

39. Ibid.

40. C. Hirschman, "Someone to Listen: Ombuds Can Offer Employees a Confidential, Discrete Way to Handle Problems—But Setup and Communication Are Crucial to Making this Role Work Properly," *HR Magazine* (January 2003), pp. 46–52.

41. B. McConnel, "Executives, HR Must Set Moral Compass, Says Ethics Group," *HR News* (www.shrm.org/hrnews.published/archives/CMS.003406.asp), August 19, 2003.

42. This case is based on P. J. Sauer, "Open-Door Management," *Inc.* (June 2003), p. 44; and online company information available at www.techtarget.com/html/ab_index.htm (2005).

43. *Human Resource Certification Institute,* See *PHR, SPHR, GPHR Handbook* (Alexandria, VA: HRCI, Society for Human Resource Management, 2005).

CHAPTER THREE: EQUAL EMPLOYMENT OPPORTUNITY

1. A. Craigwell, "Hire Calling," *Fortune* Small Business (May 2005), available online at www.fortune.com/fortune/smallbusiness/managing/articles/0,15114,1048512,00.html; and Diversity Services Web site (2005), www.diversity-services.com.

2. Human Rights Campaign, "Statewide Anti-Discrimination Laws and Policies" (July 2005), available online at www.hrc.org/Template.cfm?Section=Your_Community&Template=/ContentManagement/ContentDisplay.cfm&ContentID=14821.

3. See, for instance, ReligiousTolerance.org, "Governments Which Have Recognized Same Sex Relationships" (2003), available online at www.religioustolerance.org/hom_mar4.htm.

4. L. Turner, "Wal-Mart Changes Policy to Protect Gays," *Arkansas Business* (July 7, 2003), p. 10; "Policies Toward Gays," *Workforce Week* (September 1–6, 2003), p. 3; and J. Cook, C. McGann, and C. Pope, "Microsoft Now Backs Gay Rights Bills," *Seattle-Post Intelligencer Reports* (May 7, 2005), available online at seattlepi.nwsource.com/business/223353_msftgay07.html.

5. Cases filed under this act could be heard by a jury. Such opportunity was unavailable under the Civil Rights Act of 1964.

6. Under the Civil Rights Act of 1964, the only remedy is back pay.

7. *Patterson v. McLean Credit Union*, 87 U.S. Supreme Court, 107 (1989).

8. Another stipulation is receiving $50,000 or more of government monies. Thus, a two-person operation that has a government contract for more than $50,000 is bound by Title VII. J. Gill, "Gender Issues," *Inc. Magazine* (April 2005), pp. 38–40.

9. *Washington Metropolitan Police Department v. Davis*, 422 U.S. Supreme Court, 229 (1976).

10. The EEOA of 1972 amended Title VII in several ways, including expanding the definition of employer to include state and local government agencies and educational institutions, reducing the minimum number of employees in private sector organizations from 25 to 15; and giving more power to the EEOC to file suit against alleged violators of Title VII.

11. R. Roosevelt Thomas Jr., "From Affirmative Action to Affirming Diversity," *Harvard Business Review* (March–April 1990), p. 107.

12. See, for instance, Harry Holzer and David Neumark, "Assessing Affirmative Action," *Journal of Economic Literature* (September 2000), pp. 483–568; and Robert J. Grossman, "Is Diversity Working?" *HR Magazine* (March 2000), pp. 46–50.

13. See, for example, Bill McConnell, "Stay or No Stay, EEO's Here to Stay," *Broadcasting & Cable* (April 17, 2000), p. 22; and Arthur A. Fletcher, "Business and Race: Only Halfway There," *Fortune* (March 6, 2000), pp. F-76–F-78.

14. Adverse impact refers to an employment practice that results in a disparate selection, promotion, or firing of a class of protected group members, whereas adverse treatment affects one or more individuals. M. M. Clark, "Court: Workers Can Sue for Unintentional Age Bias," *HR Magazine* (May 2005), p. 29; and A. L. Rupe, "Legal Gender Bending," *Workforce Management* (May 2005), pp. 12–14.

15. ADEA is afforded to all individuals age 40 and older employed in organizations with 20 or more employees.

16. Executive and high policy-making employees may still be required to retire. Three conditions must be met, however: they are at least 65 years of age, will receive a substantial pension from the organization, and have been in this executive or high policy-making position for the previous two years.

17. See *Price v. Maryland Casualty Co.*, 561 F.2d 609, 612 (C.A. 5th Cir., 1977).

18. The U.S. Equal Employment Opportunity Commission, "Facts About Age Discrimination" (www.eeoc.gov/facts/age.html, 2003).

19. This act defines a disability as any condition that curtails one or more major life activities for an individual.

20. Stephen P. Sonnenberg, "Mental Disabilities in the Workplace," *Workforce* (June 2000), pp. 142–146.

21. "Accommodation Will Be the Next ADA Issue," *HR Focus* (March 2000), p. 2.

22. An undue hardship under the Americans with Disabilities Act refers to a situation in which an organization, in making accommodations, would incur significant expenses or difficulties that would severely impact the organization's finances or its operations.

23. Employees covered under the FMLA are individuals who have worked for an employer for at least 1,250 hours in the previous 12-month period.

24. The Department of Labor has defined just what does and does not count toward the 50-employee threshold. Specifically, temporary employees and those on permanent layoff do not count toward the 50 minimum. Furthermore, under certain circumstances, and in compliance with company policy, the employee or the employer may substitute paid personal leave or accrued vacation time for the unpaid leave. The paid-leave portion of the act, however, has several limitations and qualifiers. See also "DOL Regs Requiring Designation of FMLA Leave Are Invalid," *HR Focus* (September 2000), p. 2; and "FMLA Miles Measured by Driving Distance," *HR Magazine* (July 2005), p. 109.

25. U.S. Department of Labor. "Fact Sheet #28. The Family and Medical Leave Act of 1993" (www.dol.gov/esa/regs/compliance/main.htm, 2003); and A. Bernstein, "The Fight Brewing over Family Leave," *Business Week* (June 13, 2005), pp. 62–63.

26. Bill Leonard, "FMLA Does Create Hardships for Employers," *HR Magazine* (August 2000), p. 28; and Milton Zall, "The Family and Medical Leave Act: An Employer Perspective," *Strategic Finance* (February 2000), pp. 46–50.

27. For example, with 15–100 employees, the maximum damage award is $50,000; 101–200 employees, $100,000; 201–500 employees, $200,000; and more than 500 employees, $300,000. See Barbara Gutek, "Workplace Sexual Harassment Law: Principles, Landmark Developments, and Framework for Effective Risk Management," *Personnel Psychology* (Autumn 2000), p. 746.

28. *Connecticut v. Teal*, U.S. Supreme Court, 102, Docket No. 2525 (1982).

29. We must note here that the 4/5ths rule, as established, does not recognize specific individuals' requirements; that is, a minority could be any group. For example, when airlines hired only females as flight attendants, males were the minority.

30. *McDonnell-Douglas Corp. v. Green*, 411 U.S. 792, 80 (U.S. 1973).

31. Such a case is frequently referred to as a prima facie case. These cases have enough evidence to support the charge, and will be considered sufficient unless refuted by the organization.

32. *McDonnell-Douglas Corp. v. Green*, 411 U.S. 792, 80 (U.S. 1973).

33. Jillian B. Berman, "Defining the 'Essence of the Business': An Analysis of Title VII's Privacy Controls After Johnson Controls," *University of Chicago Law Review* (Summer 2000), p. 749.

34. Reasonable accommodation here is a difficult area not to support. If through the use of personal leave an individual can be accommodated, then no BFOQ exists. Also, the courts may view how an enterprise treats traditional Christian holidays in viewing reasonable accommodation. See Tracey I. Levy, "Religion in the Workplace," *Management Review* (February 2000), pp. 38–40.

35. See, for example, Karen C. Cash, George R. Gray, and Sally A. Rood, "A Framework for Accommodating Religion and Spirituality in the Workplace: Executive Commentary," *Academy of Management Executive* (August 2000), pp. 124–134.

36. "FedEx Faces Lawsuit Citing Religious Bias Against an Ex-Driver," *Wall Street Journal* (March 20, 2000), p. B-17.

37. D. D. Hatch, J. E. Hall, and M. T. Miklave, "New EEOC Guidance on National-Origin Discrimination," *Workforce* (April 2003), p. 76.

38. A disparate impact occurs when an HRM practice eliminates a group of individuals from job considerations. Disparate treatment exists when an HRM practice eliminates an individual from employment consideration.

39. *Albemarle Paper Company v. Moody*, 422 U.S. Supreme Court (U.S. 1975).

40. *Wards Cove Packing Co., Inc., v. Atonio*, U.S. Supreme Court, Docket No. 87-1387, June 5, 1989.

41. *Bakke v. Regents of the University of California*, 438 U.S. 265 (1978).

42. *United Steelworkers of America v. Weber*, 99 S. CT. 2721 (1979).

43. *Firefighters Local 1784 v. Stotts*, 467 Supreme Court, 561 (1984).

44. *Wyant v. Jackson Board of Education*, 106 Supreme Court, 842 (1986).

45. D. D. Hatch, J. E. Hall, and M. T. Miklave, "New EEOC Guidance on National-Origin Discrimination," *Workforce* (April 2003), p. 76.

46. See, for instance, U.S. Equal Employment Opportunity Commission, "EEOC Reaches Landmark 'English-Only' Settlement: Chicago Manufacturer to Pay Over $190,000 to Hispanic Workers," www.eeoc.gov/press/9-1-00.html (September 1, 2000), pp. 1–2; and Lisa Girion, "13 Phone Operators Win Record $709,284 in English-Only Suit," *Los Angeles Times* (September 20, 2000), p. C-1.

47. It is important to note that individuals are not required to file charges against the organization through the EEOC. They may, at their discretion, use a state agency (such as a human rights commission) or proceed on their own. However, the outcomes of these other avenues are not binding to the EEOC. Additionally, charges may be filed by the individual, his or her representative (for example, union), or the EEOC itself.

48. We'll look at the Equal Pay Act in Chapter 11 as it relates to compensation plans.

49. Under the Americans with Disabilities Act, the EEOC enforces Titles I and V of the act.

50. In *EEOC v. Commercial Office Products*, U.S. Supreme Court Docket No. 86-1696 (1988), the Court ruled that if a work-sharing arrangement exists between the EEOC and a state or local agency, the time limit increases to 300 days.

51. Adapted from the 1981 *Guidebook to Fair Employment Practices*, pp. 123–161; unpublished manuscript by Stanley Mazaroff, Esquire, "A Management Guide to Responding to a Charge of Discrimination Filed with the EEOC" (Baltimore, MD: Venable, Baetjer, and Howard, Attorneys-at-Law, 1994), p. 1. It should also be noted that the EEOC automatically refers all claims to the appropriate state agency. If, however, the state agency defers back to the EEOC, it will proceed with the case. See also Maria Greco Danaher, "EEOC Allowed to Pursue Discrimination Claim on Behalf of Pregnant Nurse," *HR News* (October 2000), p. 6.

52. U.S. Equal Employment Opportunity Commission, "Charge Statistics: FY 1992 Through FY 2002" (www.eeoc.gov/stats/charges.html, 2003).

53. Bureau of National Affairs, "EEOC Identifies Enforcement Strategies and Priorities Covering the Next Five Years," *Daily Labor Report* (September 2000), pp. 1–3; and J. Bravin, "For This First-Grader, Cutting Red Tape Just Wouldn't Be Fair Play," *Wall Street Journal* (July 13, 2000), p. B-1.

54. Bureau of National Affairs, "EEOC Identifies Enforcement Strategies and Priorities Covering the Next Five Years," *Daily Labor Report* (September 2000), pp. 1–3.

55. Under Section 503 of the Vocational Rehabilitation Act, those organizations that have a contract or subcontract in the amount of $2,500 must have affirmative action plans to hire the disabled. For the Vietnam Veterans Readjustment Act, the amount is $10,000.

56. See Equal Employment Opportunity Commission, "Sexual Harassment Charges: EOC & FEPAs Combined: FY 1992–FY 2004" (2005), available online at www.eeoc.gov/stats/harass.html.

57. Norman F. Foy, "Sexual Harassment Can Threaten Your Bottom Line," *Strategic Finance* (August 2000), pp. 56–57.

58. "Federal Monitors Find Illinois Mitsubishi Unit Eradicating Harassment," *Wall Street Journal* (September 7, 2000), p. A-8.

59. Liberty J. Munson, Charles Hulin, and Fritz Drasgow, "Longitudinal Analysis of Dispositional Influences and Sexual Harassment: Effects on Job and Psychological Outcomes," *Personnel Psychology* (Spring 2000), p. 21.

60. See, for instance, Gerald L. Maatman Jr., "A Global View of Sexual Harassment," *HR Magazine* (July 2000), pp. 151–158.

61. "*Nichols v. Azteca Restaurant Enterprises*," *Harvard Law Review* (May 2002), p. 2074; Adam Jack Morrell, "Non-Employee Harassment," *Legal Report* (January–February 2000), p. 1.

62. While the male gender was referred to here, it is important to note that sexual harassment may involve either sex sexually harassing another or the same sex harassing another individual. (See, for instance, *Oncale v. Sundowner Offshore Service, Inc.*, 118 S. Ct. 998.)

63. See also M. Rotundo, D. H. Nguyen, and P. R. Sackett, "A Meta-Analytic Review of Gender Differences in Perceptions of Sexual Harassment," *Journal of Applied Psychology* (October 2001), pp. 914–922.

64. Richard L. Wiener and Linda E. Hurt, "How Do People Evaluate Social Sexual Conduct at Work? A Psychological Model," *Journal of Applied Psychology* (February 2000), p. 75.

65. *Meritor Savings Bank v. Vinson*, U.S. Supreme Court 106, Docket No. 2399 (1986).

66. Robert D. Lee and Paul S. Greenlaw, "Employer Liability for Employee Sexual Harassment: A Judicial Policy-Making Study," *Public Administration Review* (March/April 2000), p. 127.

67. Ibid.

68. "You and DuPont: Diversity," DuPont Company Documents (1999–2000), www.dupont.com/careers/you/diverse.html; and "DuPont Announces 2000 Dr. Martin Luther King, Jr., Days of Celebration," DuPont Company Documents (January 11, 2000), www.dupont.com/corp/whats-news/releases/00/001111.html.

69. It should be noted here that under Title VII and the Civil Rights Act of 1991, the maximum award under the federal act is $300,000. However, many cases are tried under state laws that permit unlimited punitive damages.

70. J. W. Janove, "Sexual Harassment and the Big Three Surprises," *HR Magazine* (November 2001), pp. 123–130; and L. A. Baar and J. Baar, "Harassment Case Proceeds Despite Failure to Report," *HR Magazine* (June 2005), p. 159.

71. In addition to the Ellerth case, a second Supreme Court ruling in 1998 (*Faragher v. City of Boca Raton*) reinforced similar areas of employer liability in terms of sexual harassment charges. See, for example, J. W. Janove, "The Faragher/Ellerth Decision Tree," *HR Magazine* (September 2003), pp. 149–155; W. L. Kosanovich, J. L. Rosenberg, and L. Swanson, "Preventing and Correcting Sexual Harassment: A Guide to the Ellerth/Faragher Affirmative Defense," *Employee Relations Law Journal* (Summer 2002), pp. 79–99; and Milton Zall, "Workplace Harassment and Employer Liability," *Fleet Equipment* (January 2000), p. B-1. See also, "Ruling Allows Defense in Harassment Cases," *HR Magazine* (August 2004), p. 30.

72. See, for instance, Peter W. Dorfman, Anthony T. Cobb, and Roxanne Cox, "Investigations of Sexual Harassment Allegations: Legal Means Fair—Or Does It?" *Human Resource Management* (Spring 2000), pp. 33–39.

73. A. Gross-Shaefer, R. Florsheim, and J. Pannetier, "The Swinging Pendulum: Moving from Sexual Harassment to Respectful Workplace Relationships," *Employee Relations Law Journal* (Fall 2003), pp. 50–70.

74. G. P. Panaro, "Investigation of Harassment Can Give Rise to Negligence Claim," *Fair Employment Practices Guidelines* (June 2003), pp. 1–3.

75. See, for example, G. F. Dreher, "Breaking the Glass Ceiling: The Effect of Sex Ratios and Work-Life Programs on Female Leadership at the Top," *Human Relations* (May 2003), pp. 541–563; and Cornell University School of Industrial and Labor Relations, Glass Ceiling Commission, "About the Glass Ceiling," *Glass Ceiling Commission* (2000), pp. 1–2.

76. L. Karamally, "Where Are the Women," *Workforce Management* (June 2004), p. 50.

77. C. James, "Breaking Glass," *Far Eastern Economic Review* (September 28, 2000), p. 26.

78. "Federal Investigation into Coca-Cola Shifts to Pay-Bias Concerns," *Wall Street Journal* (June 16, 2000), p. B-8.

79. C. M. Solomon, "Cracks in the Glass Ceiling," *Workforce* (September 2000), pp. 86–94.

80. "Women Rise in Workplace But Wage Gap Continues," *Wall Street Journal* (April 25, 2000), p. A-12.

81. A. Hughes, "More Work, Less Pay: Study Shows the Corporate Glass Ceiling Is Still Intact," *Black Enterprise* (December 2002), p. 32.

82. This case is based on the U.S. Equal Employment Opportunity Commission, *Federal Express to Pay Over $3.2 Million to Female Truck Driver for Sex Discrimination, Retaliation* (February 25, 2004). Available online at www.eeoc.gov; and S. P. Duffy, "$3.2M Verdict Against FedEx for Sex Harassment," *Law.com* (February 27, 2004); available online at www.law.com/jsp/article.jsp?id=1076428422471.

83. 1-false; 2-true; 3-false; 4-true; 5-true; 6-true; 7-true; 8-true; 9-true; and 10-false.

CHAPTER FOUR: EMPLOYEE RIGHTS AND HR COMMUNICATIONS

1. Opening vignette based on S. Shellenbarger, "Workplace Romances Encounter Obstacles," *Wall Street Journal* (February 20, 2004), available online at www.contracostatimes.com/mld/cctimes/business/7998950.htm?template=contentModules.

2. G. R. Simpson, "U.S. Web Sites Violate Rules, GAO Maintains," *Wall Street Journal* (September 12, 2000), p. A-12.

3. This act applies to all private-sector organizations except those organizations the Secretary of labor deems too small (e.g., family-owned businesses). M. Heller, "Court Ruling that Employers' Integrity Test Violated ADA Could Open Door to Litigation," *Workforce Management* (September 2005), pp. 74–77.

4. See, for example, J. Ghannam, "Truth Be Told," *ABA Journal* (September 2000), p. 17; and M. K. Zachary, "Labor Law for Supervisors: Union Campaigns Prove Sensitive for Supervisory Employees," *Supervision* (May 2000), pp. 23–26.

5. However, when they are job related (required of someone who has fiduciary responsibilities in an organization), they may be used.

6. Of course, an organization could do these things. If it did, however, it could be in violation of WARN and subjected to the penalties imposed under the act. M. M. Clark, "Employers Fail to Give Required Notice in Majority of Mass Layoffs and Closures," *HR Magazine* (December 2003), p. 34.

7. Worker Adjustment and Retraining Notification Act, Public Law 100-379.

8. C. J. DeGroff, "Desperate Measures: Invoking WARN's Unforeseeable Business Circumstances," *Employee Relations Law Journal* (Winter 2002), pp. 55–74; and "Plant Closing Falls Within Exception," *Fair Employment Practices Guidelines* (February 1, 2003), p. 3.

9. U.S. Department of Labor, "Employment Law Guide: Plant Closings and Mass Layoffs," 29 USC § 2101 et seq.20 CFR 639 (www.dol.gov/dol/compliance/comp-warn.htm, 2003).

10. K. R. Collins, "Identifying and Treating Employee Substance Abuse Problems," www.shrm.org/hrresources/whitepapers_published/CMS_000187.asp (September 8, 2003).

11. K. Blumberg, "Critical Components of Workplace Drug Testing," *SHRM White Paper* (July 2004), available online at www.shrm.org/hrresources/whitepapers_published/CMS_009212.asp.

12. N. Koch, "No More Drug Free Urine Sold Here," *Philadelphia Enquirer* (August 7, 2002), p. A-1.

13. "Fewer Employers Are Currently Conducting Psych and Drug Tests," *HR Focus* (October 2000), p. 78. It is important to note that drug testing may be constrained by collective bargaining agreements or state laws.

14. D. R. Comer, "Employees' Attitude Toward Fitness-for-Duty Testing," *Journal of Managerial Issues* (Spring 2000), p. 61.

15. J. A. Segal, "Searching for Answers," *HR Magazine* (March 2002), [Available on-line at http://www.shrm.org/hrmagazine/articles/0302/0302legal.asp].

16. K. Kunsman, "Oral Fluid Testing Arrives," *Occupational Health and Safety* (April 2000), pp. 28–34.

17. See, for instance, "What Honesty Tests Reveal," Human Resource Department Management Report, (February 2002), p. 8.

18. B. Eisenberg and L. Johnson, "Being Honest About Being Dishonest," SHRM White Paper (March 2001). Available on-line at http://www.shrm.org/hrresources/whitepapers_published/CMS_000397.asp.

19. See, for example, M. E. Paronto, D. M. Truxillo, T. N. Bauer, and M. C. Leo, "Drug Testing, Drug Treatment, and Marijuana Use: A Fairness Perspective," *Journal of Applied Psychology* (December 2002), pp. 1159–1167; and H. J. Bernardin and D. K. Cooke, "Validity of an Honesty Test in Predicting Theft Among Convenience Store Employees," *Academy of Management Journal*, vol. 38, no. 5 (Fall 1993), pp. 1097–1108.

20. See also M. J. Gundlach, S. C. Douglas, and M. J. Martinko, "The Decision to Blow the Whistle: A Social Information Processing Framework," *Academy of Management Review* (January 2003), pp. 107–124.

21. D. A. Keary, "The Skinny on Sarbanes-Oxley," *SHRM Home* (May 16, 2003). Available on-line at http://www.shrm.org/hrnews_published/archives/CMS_004557.asp#P-4_0.

22. For an interesting overview of this topic, see D. Zweig and J. Webster, "Where Is the Line Between Benign and Invasive? An Examination of Psychological Barriers to the Acceptance of Awareness Monitoring Systems," *Journal of Organizational Behavior* (August 2002), pp. 605–634; and B. Helm, "Software that Knows Your Every Move; It's Called Worklenz, and It Can Be a Powerful Management Tool for Tracking Projects and People," *Business Week Online* (September 2004), available online at www.businessweek.com/technology/content/sep2004/te20040923_0520_tc024.htm.

23. "Brain Food: Workplace Rights," *Management Today* (August 4, 2003), p. 17.

24. "GAO Investigates On-the-Job Computer Monitoring," *Fair Employment Practices Guidelines* (February 1, 2003), pp. 1–3.

25. "Electronic Monitoring," *Society of Human Resource Management: Government Affairs* (September 2000), pp. 1–3.

26. M. France and D. K. Berman, "Big Brother Calling," *Business Week* (September 25, 2000), pp. 92–98.

27. M. A. Verespej, "Internet Surfing," *Industry Week* (February 7, 2000), pp. 59–64; and L. M. Bernardi, "The Internet at Work: An Employment Danger Zone," *Canadian Manager* (Summer 2000), pp. 17–18.

28. See M. Broad, "Clear Guidance Needed for Internet and E-Mail Abuse," *Personnel Today* (October 8, 2002), p. 2.

29. N. L. Torres, "I Spy . . . Workplace Surveillance Is Coming to Small and Mid-size Businesses," *Entrepreneur* (August 2003), p. 20.

30. See, for example, C. A. Pierce, H. Aquinis, and S. K. R. Adams, "Effects of a Dissolved Workplace Romance and Rater Characteristics of Responses to a Sexual Harassment Accusation," *Academy of Management Journal* (October 2000), pp. 869–884; C. A. Pierce and H. Aquinis, "A Framework for Investigating the Link Between Workplace Romance and Sexual Harassment," *Group and Organization Management* (June 2001), pp. 206–230; C. C. Cleggett, "How Do I Love Thee? Let Me Check Our Consensual Relationship Contract," *Daily Record* (July 22, 2000), p. 1; J. Greenwald, "Office Romances May Court Trouble," *Business Insurance* (February 14, 2000), p. 3; and B. P. Sunoo, "Flirting: Red Flag or Lost Art?" *Workforce* (June 2000), pp. 128–133.

31. "HR Managers/Executives Worry About Workplace Romance," *Human Resource Department Management Report* (April 2002), p. 8; and S. Armour, "Cupid Finds Work as Office Romance No Longer Taboo," *USA Today* (February 11, 2003), p. 1B.

32. "Workplace Romance Works Out Well for Many People, Poll Shows," *Seattle Times/Knight Ridder/Tribune Business News* (February 14, 2003), p. A1; and C. A. Pierce, B. J. Broberg, J. R. McClure, and H. Aquinis, "Responding to Sexual Harassment Complaints: Effects of a Dissolved Workplace Romance on Decision Making Standards," *Organizational Behavior & Human Processes* (September 2004), pp. 66–82.

33. Ibid.

34. G. N. Powell, "Workplace Romances Between Senior-Level Executives and Lower-Level Employees: An Issue of Work Disruption and Gender," *Human Relations* (November 2001), pp. 519–545.

35. *Payne v. Western and Atlantic Railroad Co.*, 812 Tenn. 507 (1884). See also C. Hirschman, Off Duty, Out of Work," *HR Magazine* (February 2003), pp. 51–52.

36. Ibid; and D. Seligman, "The Right to Fire," *Forbes* (November 10, 2003), p. 126.

37. P. Falcone, "Fire My Assistant Now!" *HR Magazine* (May 2002), pp. 27–35; T. M. Shaughnessy, "How State Exceptions to Employment-at-Will Affect Wages," *Journal of Labor Research* (Summer 2003), pp. 447–457; D. A. Ballam, "Employment-at-Will: The Impending Death of a Doctrine," *American Business Law Journal* (Summer 2000), pp. 653–687; and R. M. Howie and L. A. Shapero, "Lifestyle Discrimination Statutes: A Dangerous Erosion of At-will Employment, a Passing Fad, or Both?" *Employee Relations Law Journal* (Summer 2005), pp. 21–38.

38. Adapted from Carroll R. Daugherty, *Enterprise Wire Co.* 46 LA 359 (1966).

39. For a complete overview of this topic, see J. J. Moran, *Employment Law*, 2nd ed. (Upper Saddle River, NJ: Prentice Hall, 2002). See also M. Heller. "A Return to At-Will Employment" *Workforce* (May 2001), p. 42.

40. *Toussaint v. Blue Cross and Blue Shield of Michigan*, 408 Michigan, 529, 292 N.W. 2d 880 (1980).

41. *Fortune v. National Cash Register*, 364 373 Massachusetts 91, 36 N.E. 2d 1251 (1977).

42. S. Bahls and J. E. Bahls, "Fire Proof," *Entrepreneur* (July 2002), p. 70.

43. W. Cottringer, "The ABC's of Employee Discipline," *Supervision* (April 2003), pp. 5–8.

44. "In Disciplining or Firing, Know the Infractions," *HR Briefing* (June 1, 2003), p. 5.

45. Robert McGarvey, "Lords of Discipline," *Entrepreneur* (January 2000), pp. 127–129.

46. "You Be the Judge," *HR Briefing* (March 1, 2002), p. 4; G. A. Bielous, "Five Worst Disciplinary Mistakes (and How To Avoid Them)," *Supervision* (February 2005), pp. 16–18.

47. See, for instance, G. A. Bielous, "Five Worst Disciplinary Mistakes (and How to Avoid Them)," *Supervision* (March 2003), pp. 16–19.

48. B. Schaefer, "Weingarten Rights Clarified for Now," *SHRM Online* (April 22, 2005), available online at www.shrm.org.

49. It is true that two other disciplinary actions may be used—pay cuts or demotion —but they are rare.

50. See J. C. Connor, "Disarming Terminated Employees," *HR Magazine* (January 2000), pp. 113–116.

51. C. Cash and G. R. Gray, "A Framework for Accommodating Religion and Spirituality in the Workplace," *Academy of Management Executive*, vol. 14, no. 3 (August 2000), p. 124.

52. D. P. Ashmos and D. Duchon, "Spirituality at Work: A Conceptualization and Measure," *Journal of Management Inquiry* (June 2000), p. 139.

53. A. A. Mohamed, J. Wisnieski, M. Askar, and I. Syed, "Towards a Theory of Spirituality in the Workplace," *Competitiveness Review*, vol. 14, no. 1, (Winter–Fall 2004), pp. 102–107.

54. See I. A. Mitroff and E. A. Denton, *A Spiritual Audit of Corporate America: A Hard Look at Spirituality, Religion, and Values in the Workplace* (San Francisco, CA: Jossey-Bass, 1999); J. Milliman, J. Ferguson, D. Trickett, and B. Condemi, "Spirit and Community at Southwest Airlines: An Investigation of a Spiritual Values-Based Model," *Journal of Organizational Change Management*, vol. 12, no. 3 (1999), pp. 221–233; E. H. Burack, "Spirituality in the Workplace," *Journal of Organizational Change Management*, vol. 12, no. 3 (1999), pp. 280–291; and F. Wagner-Marsh and J. Conley, "The Fourth Wave: The Spirituality-Based Firm," *Journal of Organizational Change Management*, vol. 12, no. 3 (1999); pp. 292–302.

55. M. Conlin, "Religion in the Workplace: The Growing Presence of Spirituality in Corporate America," *Business Week* (November 1, 1999), pp. 151–158; and P. Paul, "A Holier Holiday Season," *American Demographics* (December 2001), pp. 41–45.

56. For a thorough review of the benefits of workplace spirituality, see J. Marques, S. Dhiman, and R. King, "Spirituality in the Workplace: Developing an Integral Model and a Comprehensive Definition," *Journal of American Academy of Business* (September 2005), pp. 81–92. See also Conlin, "Religion in the Workplace," p. 153, C. P. Neck and J. F. Milliman, "Thought Leadership: Finding Spiritual Fulfillment in Organizational Life," *Journal of Managerial Psychology*, vol. 9, no. 8 (1984), p. 9; D. W. McCormick, "Spirituality and Management," *Journal of Managerial Psychology*, vol. 9, no. 6 (1994), p. 5; E. Brandt, "Corporate Pioneers Explore Spirituality Peace," *HR Magazine* (April 1996), p. 82; P. Leigh, "The New Spirit at Work," *Training and Development* (February 1997), p. 193; and J. Milliman, A. Czaplewski, and J. Ferguson, "An Exploratory Empirical Assessment of the Relationship Between Spirituality and Employee Work Attitudes," paper

presented at the National Academy of Management Meeting, Washington, D.C. (August 2001).

57. See, for instance, J. Marques, "HR's Crucial Role in the Establishment of Spirituality in the Workplace," *Journal of American Academy of Business* (September 2005), pp. 27–31.

58. M. Scott, "7 Pitfalls for Managers When Handling Poor Performers and How to Overcome Them," *Manage* (February 2000), pp. 12–13.

59. Ibid.

60. S. F. Del Brocco and R. W. Sprague, "Getting Your Supervisors and Managers in the Right Team," *Employment Relations Today* (Autumn 2000), pp. 13–27; and D. L. Barrette, "What's New," *HR Magazine* (November 2000), pp. 185–188.

61. D. L. Barrette, "What's New," *HR Magazine* (November 2000), pp. 185–188.

62. "Virtual HR," *Business Europe* (March 8, 2000), p. 1; "The Payoffs of Self-Service HR Are Significant," *HR Focus* (January 2001), p. 10; and D. L. Prucino and C. M. Rice, "Point-and-Click Personnel Policies: State Laws May Affect Electronic Employee Handbooks," *Employment Relations Today* (Autumn 2000), p. 111.

63. See, for example, R. R. Panko, *Business Data Networks and Communications*, 4th ed. (Upper Saddle River, NJ: Prentice Hall, 2003).

64. "Virtual Paper Cuts," *Workforce* (July 2000), pp. 16–18.

65. J. Rohwer, "Today, Tokyo, Tomorrow the World," *Fortune* (September 18, 2000), pp. 140–152; and S. Rosenbush and

E. Einhorn, "The Talking Internet," *Business Week* (May 1, 2000), pp. 174–188.

66. See, for instance, A. Cohen, "Wireless Summer," *Time* (May 29, 2000), pp. 58–65; and K. Hafner, "For the Well Connected, All the World's an Office," *New York Times* (March 30, 2000), p. D1.

67. T. E. Weber, "Worried Your E-Mail May Offend the Boss? Just Check It for Chilis," *Wall Street Journal* (September 25, 2000), p. B-1.

68. E. S. Hendriks, "Do More Than Open Doors," *HR Magazine* (June 2000), p. 171.

69. L. Grensing-Pophal, "Talk to Me," *HR Magazine* (March 2000), p. 66.

70. "Forging New Employee Relationships via E-HR," *HR Focus* (December 2000), p. 13.

71. Case is based on C. Hirschman, "Off Duty, Out of Work," *HR Magazine* (February 2003). Available online at www.shrm.org/hrmagazine/articles/0203/0203 hirschman.asp.

72. Adapted from S. P. Robbins and P. L. Hunsaker, *Training in Interpersonal Skills*, 3rd ed. (Upper Saddle River, NJ: Prentice Hall, 2003), chapter 5; Commerce Clearing House, "The Do's and Don'ts of Confronting a Troubled Employee," *Topical Law Reports* (Chicago, IL: Commerce Clearing House, October 1990), pp. 4359–4360; G. D. Cook, "Employee Counseling Session," *Supervision* (August 1989), p. 3; and A. E. Schuartz, "Counseling the Marginal Performer," *Management Solutions* (March 1988), p. 30.

CHAPTER FIVE: HUMAN RESOURCE PLANNING AND JOB ANALYSIS

1. L. Lavelle, "How to Groom the Next Boss," *Business Week* (May 10, 2004), pp. 93–94.

2. See "The 2002 SOTA/P Report Draws the Map for Achieving Customer Satisfaction Through the Integration of HR Practices and Policy with Business Strategy," *Human Resource Planning* (March 2002), p. COV3; and B. Roberts, "Pick Employees' Brains," *HR Magazine* (February 2000), p. 175.

3. "What Do CEOs Want from the HR Department?" *Human Resource Department Management Report* (December 2002), p. 1.

4. P. M. Wright, D. L. Smart, and G. C. McMahan, "Matches Between Human Resources and Strategy Among NCAA Basketball Teams," *Academy of Management Journal*, Vol. 38, No. 4 (Winter 1995), pp. 1052–1074; and M. J. Plevel, S. Nells, F. Lane, and R. S. Schuler, "AT&T Global Business Communications Systems: Linking HR with Business Strategy," *Organizational Dynamics* (1994), pp. 59–71.

5. G. Kesler, "Four Steps to Building an HR Agenda for Growth: HR Strategy Revisited," *Human Resource Planning* (September 2000), p. 24.

6. As previous users have concurred, although strategic planning cannot be oversimplified in a two-page discussion, a quick overview is in order. With respect to the strategic nature of business, we recommend, for a comprehensive review of strategic planning, T. Whelan and J. D. Hunger, *Strategic Management and Business Policy* (Upper Saddle River, NJ: Prentice Hall, 2004).

7. G. Sutton, "Manager's Journal—Faddish Business: Cubicles Do Not a Utopia Make," *Wall Street Journal* (January 7, 2002), p. A-24.

8. "A Restatement of Purpose," *Fast Company* (October 2001), p. 2.

9. Home Depot Annual Report, 2002. Available online at ir.homedepot.com/reports.cfm.

10. Established goals are a function of various factors. The economy, government influences, market maturity, technological advances, company image, location, and other such issues will factor into the analysis.

11. See, for example, L. Lavelle, "The Case of the Corporate Spy," *Business Week* (November 26, 2001), pp. 56–58; C. Britton, "Deconstructing Advertising: What Your Competitor's Advertising Can Tell You About Their Strategy," *Competitive Intelligence* (January/February 2002), pp. 15–19; and L. Smith, "Business Intelligence Progress in Jeopardy," *Information Week* (March 4, 2002), p. 74.

12. S. Greenbard, "New Heights in Business Intelligence," *Business Finance* (March 2002), pp. 41–46; K. A. Zimmermann, "The Democratization of Business Intelligence," *KN World* (May 2002), pp. 20–21; and C. Britton, "Deconstructing Advertising: What Your Competitor's Advertising Can Tell You About Their Strategy," *Competitive Intelligence* (January/February 2002), pp. 15–19.

13. L. Weathersby, "Take This Job and ***** It," *Fortune* (January 7, 2002), p. 122.

14. See C. Lachnit, "A People Strategy That Spans the Globe: Human Resources Is Key to the Success of a Company That Is 'Only World Famous in Denmark,'" *Workforce* (June 2003), p. 76.

15. See also D. Cadrain, "Put Success Insight: Show Employees the Link Between Their Jobs and Company Goals, and Then Reward Them for Helping Your Firm Hit the Mark," *HR Magazine* (May 2003), pp. 84–90.

16. J. Sullivan, "Getting Managers to Own Retention," *HR Magazine* (Winter 2000), pp. 25–29.

17. B. Patterson and S. Lindsey, "Mining the Gold," *HR Magazine* (September 2003), pp. 131–136; and "HRIS for the HR Professional: What You Need to Know," *HR Focus* (June 2005), pp. 10–11.

18. See, for example, J. Meade, "One-Stop HRIS Strong on Reports," *HR Magazine* (March 2000), pp. 137–139; and J. Meade, "Affordable HRIS Strong on Benefits," *HR Magazine* (April 2000), pp. 132–134.

19. "What Are the Top HRIS Issues in 2003?" *HR Focus* (May 2003), p. 3; and E. Sherman, "Use Technology to Stay in SOX Compliance," *HR Magazine* (May 2005), pp. 95–99.

20. J. Meade, "Web-Based HRIS Meets Multiple Needs," *HR Magazine* (August 2000), pp. 129–133.

21. "How Employers Save on HRIS Costs," *HR Focus* (December 2002), p. 10.

22. J. Meade, "New Functions Upgrade a Familiar Product," *HR Magazine* (January 2000), pp. 105–108.

23. Ibid.

24. P. L. Moore and D. Brady, "Running the House That Jack Built," *Business Week* (October 2, 2000), pp. 130–131.

25. "Exclusive Survey: HR Has Many Ideas . . . But Little Support for Succession Preparation," *HR Focus* (July 2003), p. S-1. See also Y. Zhang and N. Rajagopalan," *Academy of Management Journal* (June 2003), pp. 327–339; and L. Daniel, "Checking the Exits," *HR Magazine* (April 2005), pp. 101–103.

26. "Succession Planning: Competency-Based Programs Boost Morale 25%," *PR Newswire* (August 6, 2003). Available online at www.cuttingedgeinfo.com; and J. Jusko, "Nurturing Leaders: Manufacturers Lead in Developing Future Executives," Industry Week (June 2005), p. 18.

27. K. Ellis, "Making Waves: With a Leadership Crisis on the Horizon, Organizations Are Looking Within to Build Talent Pools of Their Own," *Training* (June 2003), pp. 16–22; and J. Jusko, "Unplanned Future: Private Company CEOs Give Little Thought to Succession Planning," *Industry Week* (March 2005), p. 20.

28. "How Intel Melds Talent Management with Succession," *HR Focus* (July 2003), p. S-2; and "Companies Taking Succession Planning More Seriously," *HR Briefing* (March 15, 2003), p. 8.

29. "Layoffs: Consider Other Options Before Reducing Full-Time Staff," *Fair Employment Practice Guidelines* (April 15, 2003), pp. 1–3; and C. Huff, "With Flextime, Less Can Be More," *Workforce Management* (May 2005), pp. 65–70.

30. See R. Henderson, *Compensation Management in a Knowledge-Based World*, 9th ed. (Englewood Cliffs, NJ: Prentice Hall, 2003).

31. D. M. Truxillo, M. E. Paronto, M. Collins, and J. L. Sulzer, "Effects of Subject Matter Expert Viewpoint on Job Analysis Results," *Public Personnel Management* (Spring 2004), p. 33.

32. S. A. Fine, *Functional Job Analysis Scales: A Desk Aid, No. 7* (Kalamazoo, MI: W.E. Upjohn Institute for Employment Research, 1973).

33. See R. Henderson, *Compensation Management in a Knowledge-Based World*, 9th ed. (Englewood Cliffs, NJ: Prentice Hall, 2003).

34. See also C. Joinson, "Refocusing Job Description," *HR Magazine* (January 2001), pp. 65–70.

35. Adapted from "TeamFuel Raises $5.5 Million to Challenge Fuel Procurement Supply Chain," www.teamfuel.com/corporate/index.html (September 15, 2003), p. 1; "The Top 500 Women-Owned Businesses," *Working Woman* (June 1999), pp. 52–54; S. Cook, "Learning Needs Analysis: Part 6—Assessing the Job," *Training Journal* (June 2005), pp. 64–67; and E. J. Felsberg, "Conducting Job Analyses and Drafting Lawful Job Descriptions Under the Americans with Disabilities Act," *Employment Relations Act* (Fall 2004), pp. 91–93.

36. Case is based on information provided in J. Greene, "Troubling Exits at Microsoft," *Business Week* (September 26, 2005), pp. 99–108.

Chapter Six: Recruiting

1. V. Powers, "Finding Workers Who Fit," *Business 2.0* (November 2004), p. 74; and information on the company Web site, www.containerstore.com.

2. See also "Recruitment at Southern Company Reflects Demographic Shift in U.S.," *Fortune* (June 11, 2001), p. S-15.

3. T. Chapelle, "Merrill Rolls Out New Recruiting Deals," *On Wall Street* (September 1, 2003), p. 1.

4. R. Levering and M. Moskowitz, "100 Best Companies to Work For," *Fortune* (January 20, 2003). Available online at www.fortune.com/fortune/subs/article/0,15114,404352,00.html.

5. See, for instance, "Executive Hires and Compensation: Performance Rules," *HR Focus* (July 2003), p. 1.

6. Vignettes adapted from CCH Business Owner's Toolkit, "Case Study—Discrimination in Ads," SOHO Guidebook, www.lycos.com/business/cch/guidebook.html?1pv_=_1&docNumber_=_P05-0683] (2000), pp. 1–4.

7. J. Britt, "Alumni Networks Can Cut Recruiting Costs, Boost Employer's Image," *HR Magazine* (February 2002), pp. 25–26.

8. See, for instance, S. Cuthill, "Guest Column: Managing HR Across International Borders," *Compensation and Benefits* (Summer 2000), pp. 43–45; and "Global Recruiting," *Practical Accountant* (October 2000), p. 6.

9. "Ensure You Don't Make a Bad Expat Investment," *Personnel Today* (August 19, 2003), p. 15.

10. See, for example, J. A. Volkmar, "Context and Control in Foreign Subsidiaries: Making a Case for the Host Country National Manager," *Journal of Leadership and Organizational Studies* (Summer 2003), pp. 93–106.

11. M. N. Martinez, "The Headhunter Within," *HR Magazine* (August 2001), pp. 48–55; "Employee Referral Programs: Highly Qualified New Hires Who Stick Around," *Canadian HR Reporter* (June 4, 2001), p. 21; and C. Lachnit, "Employee Referral Saves Time, Saves Money, Delivers Quality," *Workforce* (June 2001), pp. 66–72.

12. J. Dash, "Filling Slots with Inside Referrals," *Computerworld* (July 10, 2000), p. 35.

13. B. McDonnell, "Companies Lure Job Seekers in New Ways," *HR News* (April 2002), p. 1.

14. "Recruitsoft Selected by Hewlett Packard to Optimize Global Recruiting," *Canadian Corporate News* (December 13, 2000), p. 1.

15. "Even CEOs Use the Internet for Recruiting," *HR Magazine* (March 2003), p. 14; Michelle Neely Martinez, "Get Job Seekers to Come to You," *HR Magazine* (August 2000), pp. 42–52; M. Frase-Blunt, "Make a Good First Impression," *HR Magazine* (April 2004), pp. 81–86; D. Robb, "Career Portals Boost Online Recruiting," *HR Magazine* (April 2004), pp. 111–115; and J. Marshall, "Don't Rely Exclusively on Internet Recruiting," *HR Magazine* (November 2003).

16. D. Brown, "Unwanted Online Jobseekers Swamp HR Staff," *Canadian HR Reporter* (April 5, 2004), pp. 1–2.

17. A. A. Mohamed, "The Legality of Key Word Search as a Personnel Selection Tool," *Employee Relations*, Vol. 5, No. 5 (2002), pp. 516–522.

18. Martinez, "Get Job Seekers," p. 50.
19. See, for example, Bill Leonard, "Online and Overwhelmed," *HR Magazine* (August 2000), pp. 37–42; Pat Curry, "Log On for Recruits," *Industry Week* (October 16, 2000), pp. 46–54; Rachel Emma Silverman, "Your Career Matters: Raiding Talent via the Web—Personal Pages, Firms's Sites Are Troves of Information for Shrewd Headhunters," *Wall Street Journal* (October 3, 2000), p. B-1; Michelle Neely Martinez, "Get Job Seekers to Come to You," *HR Magazine* (August 2000), pp. 45–52; and P. A. Hausdorf and D. E. Duncan, "Firm Size and Internet Recruiting in Canada: A Preliminary Investigation," *Journal of Small Business Management* (July 2004), pp. 325–334; and "Hot Internet Recruiting Sites," *HR Focus* (February 2004), p. 8.
20. M. Zall, "Internet Recruiting," *Strategic Finance* (June 2000), p. 66; S. L. Thomas and K. Ray, "Recruiting and the Web: High-Tech Hiring," *Business Horizons* (May–June 2000), p. 43; and S. Bates, "Even CEOs Use the Internet for Recruiting," *HR Magazine* (March 2003), p. 14.
21. M. Whitford, "Hi-Tech HR, Hotel," *Hotel and Motel Management* (October 16, 2000), p. 49.
22. C. Wilde, "Recruiters Discover Diverse Value in Web Sites," *Informationweek* (February 7, 2000), p. 144.
23. See also A. E. Schultz, "Beware the Legal Risks of Hiring Temps: When Hiring Stalls and Stops, It 's Tempting to Hire Contingent Workers. To Avoid a Microsoft-sized Lawsuit, Understand the Critical Legal Issues Involving Temporary Workers," *Workforce* (October 2002), pp. 50–58.
24. "How Well Are You Treating Your Temporary Workers?" *HR Briefing* (January 15, 2003), pp. 6–8; and M. Frase-Blunt, "A Recruiting Spigot," *HR Magazine* (April 2003), pp. 71–79.
25. D. Fenn, "Respect Your Elders," *Inc.* (September 2003), pp. 29–30.
26. Reasons cited by the American Association of Retired Persons include the need to make money, to obtain health insurance coverage, to develop skills, to use time more productively, to feel useful, to make new friends, to provide some structure to daily lives, or to have a sense of achievement.
27. "8 Interview Questions for Older Workers to Anticipate," *AARP Bulletin* (September 2002). Available online at www.aarp.org/bulletin/yourmoney/Articles/0905_sidebar_4.html. Also see Robert Half International Inc., (2005), www.rhii.com.
28. Caution is warranted regarding for whom an individual works. Although the employee usually is the leasing company's responsibility. Under certain circumstances, like long-term duration of the lease, the acquiring organization may be the employer of record. The leasing company may only handle HRM-associated paperwork.
29. C. Hirschman, "For PEOs, Business Is Booming," *HR Magazine* (February 2000), pp. 23–28.
30. The U.S. Equal Employment Opportunity Commission, *Best Practices Presented by Companies in Recruitment and Hiring* (February 28, 2002).
31. See, for instance, K. Maher, "The Jungle," *Wall Street Journal* (August 19, 2003), p. B8.
32. "Job-Hunting Professionals Rank Networking Over Internet," *HR Magazine* (May 2002), p. 25.
33. J. Meade, "Where Did They Go?" *HR Magazine* (September 2000), pp. 81–84, and "Manage Hiring Steps with Web-Based Aid," *HR Magazine* (February 2000), pp. 121–124; and Track It Solutions, "!Trak It Applicant" (2005), available online at www.applicant-tracking-software.com/index.html.
34. J. Meade, "Recruiting Software Can Streamline Hiring Process," *HR Magazine* (September 2001), pp. 139–140.
35. Case is based on J. H. Coplan, "Se Habla Temp," *Business Week Small Business* (April 2, 2001), p. 42; and Priority Staffing Solutions (2005), available online at www.prioritystaff.com/index.html.
36. This skill vignette is based on information provided in CCC Business Owner's Toolkit, "Information To Include in Job Ads," *SOHO Guidebook* (2003), p. 1. Available online at www.toolkit.cch.com/text/P05_0673.asp.

CHAPTER SEVEN: FOUNDATIONS OF SELECTION

1. Opening vignette based on "Mistakes and Problems: Things Not to Do in an Interview," *Pagewise* (2005), available online at www.pagewise.com/things-do-interview.htm; "What Are Some Applicants Thinking," *HR Briefing* (January 15, 2003), p. 5; H. Delozalek, "Behavioral Blunders," *Training* (January 2003), p. 1; and "Interview Blunders Can Close the Door," *Westchester County Business Journal* (December 16, 2002), p. 17.
2. This story was influenced by an example in Arthur Sloan, *Personnel: Managing Human Resources* (Englewood Cliffs, NJ: Prentice Hall, 1983), p. 127.
3. See I. Kotlyar and L. Karakowsky, "If Recruitment Means Building Trust, Where Does Technology Fit In?" *Canadian HR Reporter* (October 7, 2002), p. 21.
4. See Matthew T. Miklave and A. Jonathan Trafimow, "Ask Them If They Were Fired, But Not When They Graduated," *Workforce* (August 2000), pp. 90–93. See also "About Us," Pinpoint Networks, (www.pinpoint.com/aboutUs/profile.html), 2003.
5. Y. Y. Chung, "The Validity of Biographical Inventories for the Selection of Salespeople," *International Journal of Management* (September 2001), p. 322.
6. See, for instance, S. R. Kaak, H. S. Field, W. F. Giles, and D. R. Norris, "The Weighted Application Blank," *Cornell Hotel and Restaurant Administration Quarterly* (April 1998), pp. 18–24. The seven items were not specifically identified so that the competitive edge the hotel had in hiring practices would not be weakened.
7. K. Tyler, "Put Applicants' Skills to the Test," *HR Magazine* (January 2000), p. 75.
8. See, for example, J. H. Prager, "Nasty or Nice: 56-Question Quiz," *Wall Street Journal* (February 22, 2000), p. A-4.
9. G. Nicholsen, "Screen and Glean: Good Screening and Background Checks Help Make the Right Match for Every Open Position," *Workforce* (October 2000), pp. 70, 72.
10. S. Bates, "Personality Counts," *HR Magazine* (February 2002), pp. 27–34.
11. See F. Lievens, "Trying to Understand the Different Pieces of the Construct Validity Puzzle of Assessment Centers: An Examination of Assessor and Assessee Effects: *Journal of Applied Psychology* (August 2002), pp. 675–687; and D. J. Schleicher, B. T. Mayes, D. V. Day, and R. F. Riggio, "A New Frame of Reference Training: Enhancing the Construct of Validity of Assessment Centers" *Journal of Applied Psychology* (August 2002), pp. 735–747.
12. "Mind Your P's and Q's," *Successful Meetings* (February 2000), p. 33.
13. J. Blau, "At Nokia Temperament Is a Core Competency," *Research Technology Management* (July/August 2003), p. 6; and R. A. Posthuma, F. P. Morgeson, and M. A. Campion,

"Beyond Employment Interview Validity: A Comprehensive Narrative Review of Recent Research and Trends Over Time," *Personnel Psychology* (Spring 2002), pp. 1–80.

14. "Job Interviews Reveal Trouble Later On," *HR Briefing* (January 15, 2003), p. 8.

15. For an interesting look into the applicant's reaction to the interview, see C. B. Goldberg, "Applicant Reactions to the Employment Interview: A Look at Demographic Similarity and Social Identity Theory," *Journal of Business Research* (August 2003), pp. 561–672.

16. "It's Not Your Grandfather's Hiring Interview," *Supervision* (May 2003), pp. 21–23.

17. For a thorough review of the literature on interview effectiveness, see R. A. Posthuma, F. P. Morgeson, and M. A. Campion, "Beyond Employment Interview Validity: A Comprehensive Review of Recent Research and Trends Over Time," *Personnel Psychology* (Spring 2002). pp. 1–82; and F. L. Schmidt and T. D. Zimmerman, "A Counterintuitive Hypothesis About Employment Interview Validity and Some Supporting Evidence," *Journal of Applied Psychology* (June 2004), pp. 553–561.

18. W. Poundstone, "Beware the Interview Inquisition," *Harvard Business Review* (May 2003), pp. 18–19; and T. Raz, "How Would You Design Bill Gates's Bathroom?" *Inc.* (May 2003), p. 29.

19. "Focus on Ethics Includes Honest Interviews," *HR Briefing* (April 1, 2003), p. 7.

20. See, for instance, "Recruitment: Job Seekers Take Offense at Interview Blinders," *Personnel Today* (July 1, 2003), p. 3. See also M. Knudstrup, S. L. Segrest, and A. E. Hurley, "The Use of Mental Imagery in the Simulated Employment Interview Situation," *Journal of Managerial Psychology* (June 2003), pp. 573–591.

21. For a more detailed discussion of impression management, see N. L. Vasilopoulos, R. R. Reilly, and J. A. Leaman, "The Influences of Job Familiarity and Impression Management on Self-Report Measure Scales and Response Latencies," *Journal of Applied Psychology* (February 2000), pp. 50–64; and D. R. Pawlowski and J. Hollwitz, "Work Values, Cognitive Strategies, and Applicant Reactions in a Structured Pre-Employment Interview for Ethical Integrity," *Journal of Business Communication* (January 2000), pp. 58–76.

22. J. Silvester, F. M. Anderson-Gough, N. R. Anderson, and A. R. Mohamed, "Locus of Control, Attributions and Impression Management in the Selection Interview," *Journal of Occupational and Organizational Psychology* (March 2002), pp. 59–77; and L. G. Otting, "Don't Rush to Judgement," *HRT Magazine* (January 2004), pp. 95–98.

23. C. H. Middendorf and T. H. Macan, "Note-Taking in the Employment Interview: Effects on Recall and Judgment," *Journal of Applied Psychology* (April 2002), pp. 293–304.

24. A. Phillips and R. L. Dipboye, "Correlation Tests of Predictions from a Process Model of the Interview," *Journal of Applied Psychology*, Vol. 74 (1989), pp. 41–52; M. Ronald Buckley and R. W. Edner, "B. M. Springbett and the Notion of the 'Snap Decision' in the Interview," *Journal of Management*, Vol. 14, No. 1 (March 1988), pp. 59–67.

25. See P. J. Taylor and B. Small, "Asking Applicants What They Would Do Versus What They Did Do: A Meta-Analysis Comparison of Situation and Past Behavior Employment Interview Questions," *Journal of Occupational and Organizational Psychology* (September 2002), pp. 277–294; J. Merritt, "Improve at the Interview," *Business Week* (February 3, 2003), p. 63; S. D. Mauer, "A Practitioner-Based Analysis of Interviewer Job Expertise and Scale Format as Contextual Factors in Situational Interviews," *Personnel Psychology* (Summer 2002), pp. 307–328; and J. M. Barclay, "Improving Selection Interviews

with Structure: Organizations' Use of Behavioural Interviews," *Personnel Review*, Vol. 30, Issue 1 (2001), pp. 81–95; K. Tyler, "Train for Smarter Hiring," *HR Magazine* (May 2005), pp. 89–93; A. C. Poe, "Graduate Work," *HR Magazine* (October 2003), pp. 95–100; "Using Behavioral Interviewing to Help You Hire the Best of the Best," *HR Focus* (August 2004), p. 5.

26. J. Merrit, "Improve at the Interview," p. 63, and P. J. Taylor and B. Small, "Asking Applicants What They Would Do Versus What They Did Do."

27. See, for instance, R. Buda, "The Interactive Effect of Message Framing, Presentation Order, and Source Credibility on Recruitment Practices," *International Journal of Management* (June 2003), pp. 156–164.

28. Y. Ganzach, A. Pazy, Y. Ohayun, and E. Brainin, "Social Exchange and Organizational Commitment: Decision-Making Training for Job Choice as an Alternative to the Realistic Job Preview," *Personnel Psychology* (Autumn 2002), pp. 613–638.

29. For an interesting discussion on this topic, see P. G. Irving and J. E. Meyer, "On Using Residual Differences Scores in the Measurement of Congruence: The Case of Met Expectations Research," *Personnel Psychology* (Spring 1999), pp. 85–95; and R. D. Bretz Jr., and T. A. Judge, "Realistic Job Previews: A Test of Adverse Self-Selection Hypothesis," *Journal of Applied Psychology* (April 1998), pp. 330–337.

30. S. Bates, "Tight-Knit Reference Checks Rise," *HR News* (February 2002), pp. 1, 4; V. Tsang, "No More Excuses," *CHRR Report on Recruitment and Staffing* (May 23, 2005), available online at www.hrreporter.com; "Liar, Liar, Pants on Fire," *HR Magazine* (September 2005), p. 16; "Cost of Poor People Management Is High," *HR Magazine* (August 2004), p. 18; and J. George and K. Marett, "The Truth About Lies," *HR Magazine* (May 2004), pp. 87–91.

31. C. Garvey, "Outsourcing Background Checks," *HR Magazine* (March 2001), pp. 95–103.

32. M. Mayer, "Background Checks in Focus," *HR Magazine* (January 2002), pp. 59–62; J. H. Maxwell, "Of Resumes and Rap Sheets," *Inc.* (June 13, 2000), p. 94; and C. Mason-Draffen, "Resume Lies Are on the Rise," *Baltimore Sun* (June 10, 2004) available online at www.baltimoresun.com/business; and P. Babcock, "Spotting Lies," *HR Magazine* (October 2003), pp. 46–52.

33. M. N. Le and B. H. Kleiner, "Understanding and Preventing Negligent Hiring," *Management Research News,* Vol. 23, No. 7/8 (2000), pp. 53–56.

34. E. Zimmerman, "A Subtle Reference Trap for Unwary Employers," *Workforce* (April 2003), p. 22; and A. G. Schaefer, R. Quinones, and M. Kanny, "Open References Policies: Minimizing the Risk of Litigation," *Labor Law Journal* (Summer 2000), pp. 106–117.

35. D. Lacy, S. Jackson, and A. St. Martin, "References, Cafeteria Changes, Smokers," *HR Magazine* (April 2003), p. 37.

36. See, for example, S. L. Rynes, R. D. Bretz, and B. Gerhart, "The Importance of Recruitment in Job Choice: A Different Way of Looking," *Personnel Psychology*, Vol. 44, No. 3 (Autumn 1991), pp. 487–521.

37. For an interesting review of self-managed team behavior when evaluating one another, see C. P. Neck, M. L. Connerly, C. A. Zuniga, and S. Goel, "Family Therapy Meets Self-Managing Teams: Explaining Self-Managing Team Performance Through Team Member Perception," *Journal of Applied Behavioral Science* (June 1999), pp. 245–259; G. A. Neuman, S. H. Wagner, and N. D. Christiansen, "The Relationship Between Work Team Personality Composition and the Job Performance of Teams," *Group & Organization Management* (March 1999), pp. 28–45; and V. U. Druskat and S. B. Wolff, "Effects and Timing of Developmental Peer Appraisals in Self-Managing Work Groups," *Journal of Applied Psychology* (February 1999), pp. 58–74.

38. M. Frase-Blunt, "Peering Into an Interview" *HR Magazine* (December 2001), pp. 71–77.

39. See C. Hymowitz, "In the Lead: How to Avoid Hiring the Prima Donnas Who Hate Teamwork," *Wall Street Journal* (February 15, 2000), p. B-1.

40. As one previous reviewer correctly pointed out, there are several methods of determining reliability. These include equivalent form, test-retest method, and internal consistency forms of reliability. Their discussion, however, goes well beyond the scope of this text. "Reliability vs. Validity: When a Company Overstresses the Former, the Opportunity to Exploit Design to Create Something New and Better Can Easily Be Missed," *Business Week Online* (September 2005), p. 1.

41. See, for example, R. E. Riggio, *Introduction to Industrial/Organizational Psychology*, 4th ed. (Upper Saddle River, NJ: Prentice Hall, 2003).

42. For an interesting perspective on the use of construct validity, see J. M. Hunthausen, D. M. Truxillo, T. N. Bauer, and L. B. Hammer, "A Field Study Frame of Reference Effects on Personality Test Validity," *Journal of Applied Psychology* (June 2003), pp. 545–552; C. C. Hoffman, L. M. Holden, and K. Gale, "So Many Jobs, So Little 'N': Applying Expanded Validation Models to Support Generalization of Cognitive Test Validity," *Personnel Psychology* (Winter 2000), p. 955; and L. Van Dyne and J. A. LePine, "Helping and Voice Extra-Role Behaviors: Evidence of Construct and Predictive Validity," *Academy of Management Journal* (February 1998), pp. 108–119.

43. A limitation of concurrent validity is the possibility of restricting the range of scores in testing current employees. This occurs because current employees may have been in the upper range of applicants. Those not hired were undesirable for some reason. Therefore, these scores theoretically should represent only the top portion of previous applicant scores. W. Arthur, E. A. Day, T. L. Mcnelly, and P. S. Edens, "A Meta-Analysis of the Criterion-Related Validity of Assessment Center Dimensions," *Personnel Psychology* (Spring 2003), pp. 125–154.

44. A specific correlation coefficient for validation purposes is nearly impossible to pinpoint. Many variables will enter into the picture, such as the sample size, the power of the test, and what is measured. However, for EEO purposes, correlation coefficients must indicate a situation where the results are predictive of performance greater than one where chance alone dictated the outcomes.

45. Cut scores are determined through a sets of mathematical formulas—namely, a regression analysis and the equation of a line. We refer you to any good introductory statistics text for a reminder of how these formulas operate.

46. F. L. Schmidt and J. E. Hunter, "Developing a General Solution to the Problem of Validity Generalization," *Journal of Applied Psychology*, Vol. 62, No. 5 (October 1977), pp. 529–539.

47. See, for instance, C. O. and D. A. Harrison, "Meta-Analysis, Level of Analysis, and Best Estimates of Population Correlations: Cautions for Interpreting Meta-Analytic Results in Organizational Behavior," *Journal of Applied Psychology* (April 1999), pp. 260–270; C. C. Hoffman, "Generalizing Physical Ability Test Validity: A Case Study Using Test Transportability, Validity Generalization, and Construct-Related Validation Evidence," *Personnel Psychology* (Winter 1999), pp. 1019–1041; and N. S. Raju, T. V. Anselmi, J. S. Goodman, and A. Thomas, "The Effect of Correlated Artifacts and True Validity on the Accuracy of Parameter Estimation in Validity Generalization," *Personnel Psychology* (Summer 1998), pp. 453–465.

48. See F. L. Oswald, S. Saad, and P. R. Sackett, "The Homogeneity Assumption in Differential Prediction Analysis: Does it Really Matter?" *Journal of Applied Psychology* (August 2000), p. 536; J. N. Farrell and M. A. McDaniel, "The Stability of Validity Coefficients Over Time: Ackerman's (1988) Model and the General Aptitude Test Battery," *Journal of Applied Psychology* (February 2001), p. 60; P. R. Jeanneret and M. H. Strong, "Linking O*Net Job Analysis Information to Job Requirement Predictors: An O*Net Application," *Personnel Psychology* (Summer 2003), p. 465; and F. L. Schmidt, K. Pearlman, J. E. Hunter, and H. R. Hirsh, "Forty Questions About Validity Generalization and Meta-Analysis," *Personnel Psychology*, Vol. 38, No. 4 (Winter 1985), pp. 697–822.

49. M. T. Brannick, "Implications of Empirical Bayes Meta-Analysis for Test Validation," *Journal of Applied Psychology* (June 2001), p. 468.

50. See, for instance, I. F. H. Wong and L. Phooi-Ching, "Chinese Cultural Values and Performance at Job Interviews: A Singapore Perspective," *Business Communication Quarterly* (March 2000), pp. 9–22.

51. Michael A. O'Neil, "How to Implement Relationship Management Strategies," *Supervision* (July 2000), p. 3.

52. A. Kristof-Brown, M. R. Barrick, and M. Franke, "Applicant Impression Management: Dispositional Influences and Consequences for Recruiter Perceptions of Fit and Similarity," *Journal of Management* (January 2002), pp. 27–46.

53. See, for example, K. J. Dunham, "Career Journal: The Jungle," *Wall Street Journal* (May 21, 2002), p. B-10.

54. P. L. Lail, and K. D. Kale, "Post-Offer Medical Exam Was Premature," *HR Magazine* (June 2005), p. 163.

Chapter Eight: Socializing, Orienting, and Developing Employees

1. Opening vignette based on J. Alserver, "English to Go: Chipotle Puts Language Classes on the Menu to Build Employee Loyalty," *Business 2.0* (March 2005), p. 56.

2. "FedEx Gets to the Heart of Turnover," *Work and Family* (May 2002), p. 4.

3. For a thorough review of this topic, see C. M. Riordan, E. W. Weatherly, R. J. Vandenberg, and R. M. Self, "The Effects of Pre-Entry Experiences and Socialization Tactics on Newcomer Attitudes and Turnover," *Journal of Managerial Issues* (Summer 2001), pp. 159–173.

4. See, for example, S. L. Robinson and Elizabeth Wolfe, "The Development of Psychological Contract Breech Violation: A Longitudinal Study," *Journal of Organizational Behavior* (August 2000), pp. 525–546.

5. J. Van Maanen and E. H. Schein, "Career Development," in J. R. Hackman and J. L. Suttle (eds.), *Improving Life at Work* (Santa Monica, CA: Goodyear, 1977), pp. 58–62. See also J. P. Wanous, A. E. Reichers, and S. D. Malik, "Organizational Socialization and Group Development," *Academy of Management Review*, Vol. 9 (1992), pp. 670–683.

6. D. C. Feldman, "The Multiple Socialization of Organization Members," *Academy of Management Review* (April 1981), p. 310.

7. For a thorough discussion of these issues, see J. A. Chatman, "Matching People and Organizations: Selection and Socialization in Public Accounting Firms," *Administrative Science Quarterly* (September 1991), pp. 459–485.

8. For example, see G. Blau, "Early-Career Job Factors Influencing the Professional Commitment of Medical Technologies," *Academy of Management Journal* (December 1999), pp. 687–699; and C. R. Wanberg, "Unwrapping the Organizational Entry Process: Disentangling Multiple Antecedents and

Their Pathways to Adjustment," *Journal of Applied Psychology* (October 2003), pp. 779–794.

9. See T. J. Fogarty, "Socialization and Organizational Outcomes in Large Public Accounting Firms," *Journal of Managerial Issues* (Spring 2000), pp. 13–33. See also T. Y. Kim, D. M. Cable, and S. P. Kim, "Socialization Tactics, Employee Proactivity, and Person-Organization Fit," *Journal of Applied Psychology* (March 2005), pp. 232–241.

10. See, for instance, T. G. Reio Jr., and A.Wiswell, "Field Investigations of the Relationship Among Adult Curiosity, Workplace Learning, and Job Performance," *Human Resource Development Quarterly* (Spring 2000), p. 5.

11. M. Messmer, "Orientation Programs Can Be Key to Employee Retention," *Strategic Finance* (February 2000), pp. 12–14; and H. J. Klein and N. A.Weaver, "The Effectiveness of an Organizational-Level Orientation Training Program in the Socialization of New Hires," *Personnel Psychology* (Spring 2000), pp. 47–60.

12. C. Garvey, "The Whirlwind of a New Job," *HR Magazine* (June 2001), pp. 110–117; and C. A. Hacker, "New Employee Orientation: Make It Pay Dividends for Years to Come," *Information Systems Management* (Winter 2004), pp. 89–92.

13. See, for example, R. L. Robbins, "Orientation: Necessity or Nightmare?" *Supervision* (October 2002), pp. 8–10.

14. "American Family Insurance Takes Employee Orientation Online," *Human Resource Department Management Report* (February 2002), p. 9. See also C. W. Autry and A. R. Wheeler, "Post-Hire Human Resource Management Practices and Person-Organization Fit: A Study of Blue-Collar Employees," *Journal of Managerial Issues* (Spring 2005), pp. 58–77.

15. L. Mallak, "Understanding and Changing Your Organization's Culture," *Industrial Management* (March/April 2001), pp. 18–24.

16. W. W. Jones and N. Macris, "Where Am I and Where Do I Go from Here?" *Planning* (June 2000), pp. 18–21.

17. See S. P. Robbins, *Business Today: The New World of Business* (New York: Harcourt, 2001), pp. 317–318.

18. M. Boyle, "Just Right," *Fortune* (June 10, 2002), pp. 207–208; and T. Davis and M. Landa, "The Story of Mary? How 'Organization Culture' Can Erode Bottom-Line Profitability," *Canadian Manager* (Winter 2000), pp. 14–17.

19. See, for example, S. Hicks, "Successful Orientation Programs," *Training and Development* (April 2000), pp. 59–60.

20. C. Garvey, "The Whirlwind of a New Job," p. 117.

21. P. Harris, "Outsourced Learning: A New Market Emerges: The Lure of Cost-Savings and Other Incentives Are Prompting More Organizations to Outsource Their Entire Learning Function, or Large Portions of It. But Trainers Shouldn't Feel Threatened, Say Insiders, They Figure That Within 10 Years, Half of Them Will Be Working for Outsourcing Partners," *Training and Development* (September 2003), pp. 30–39.

22. See, for instance, E. G. Tripp, "Aging Aircraft and Coming Regulations Political and Media Pressures Have Encouraged the FAA to Expand Its Pursuit of Real and Perceived Problems of Older Aircraft and their Systems. Operators Will Pay," *Business and Commercial Aviation* (March 2001), pp. 68–75.

23. C. S. Duncan, J. D. Selby-Lucas, and W. Swart, "Linking Organizational Goals and Objectives to Employee Performance: A Quantitative Perspective," *Journal of American Academy of Business* (March 2002), pp. 314–318; and "Goal Seekers," *Training Magazine* (September 7, 2005), p. 12.

24. "You Don't Always Get What You Pay For," *Training and Development* (June 2003), p. 6; and T. Galvin, "The 2002 Training Top 100," *Training* (March 2002), pp. 20–29.

25. "Are Your Training Programs Legal Time Bombs," *HR Focus* (July 2000), pp. 6–7.

26. R. Langlois, "Fairmont Hotels: Business Strategy Starts with People," *Canadian HR Reporter* (November 5, 2001), p. 19; and "Line Manager Skills Top List of Learning Needs," *Personnel Today* (May 24, 2005), p. 46.

27. See K. Ellis, "Top Training Strategies: New Twists on Familiar Ideas," *Training* (August 2003), pp. 30–36.

28. See, for instance, "6 Ways to Transform Your 'See-Level' Employees Into Leaders," *Human Resource Department Management Report* (September 2003), p. 5.

29. B. Pfau and I. Kay, "HR: Playing the Training Game and Losing," *HR Magazine* (August 2002), pp. 49–53.

30. See D. Forman, "Eleven Common-Sense Learning Principles: Lessons from Experience, Sages, and Each Other," *Training and Development* (September 2003), pp. 39–47.

31. K. Ellis, "Making Waves: With a Leadership Crisis on the Horizon, Organizations Are Looking Within to Build Talent Pools of Their Own," *Training* (June 2003), pp. 16–22; and "The Changing Face of Talent Management," *HR Focus* (May 2003), p. 1.

32. H. Dolezalek, "Pretending to Learn: Training Professionals Are Using Games and Simulations in Complex Ways to Help Employees Understand Business Concepts and Uncover Millions in Cost Savings," *Training* (July–August 2003), pp. 20–26.

33. T. Kelly and W. Olson, "The Advisability of Outdoor Training: Caveat Emptor," *Review of Business* (Spring-Summer 2000), p. 4; and S. D. Williams, T. S. Graham, and B. Baker, "Evaluating Outdoor Experimental Training for Leadership and Team Building," *Journal of Management Development* (January 2003), pp. 45–59.

34. "Brazil: Outdoor Training Increases in Brazil," *South American Business Information* (September 26, 2001), p. 1.

35. S. Hicks, "What Is Organization Development?" *Training and Development* (August 2000), p. 65.

36. R. Morgan, "Employers Must Prepare Staff for Change in Uncertain Times," *HR Briefing* (May 15, 2003), pp. 2–4.

37. The idea for these metaphors came from P. Vaill, *Managing as a Performing Art: New Ideas for a World of Chaotic Change* (San Francisco: Jossey-Bass, 1989).

38. K. Lewin, *Field Theory in Social Science* (New York: Harper & Row, 1951).

39. R. E. Levasseur, "People Skills: Change Management Tools—Lewin's Change Model," *Interfaces* (August 2001), pp. 71–74.

40. See, for instance, C. R. Leana and B. Barry, "Stability and Change as Simultaneous Experiences in Organizational Life," *Academy of Management Review* (October 2000), pp. 753–759.

41. A. Mudio, "GM Has a New Model for Change," *Fast Company* (December 2000), pp. 62–64.

42. A. E. Christopher, G. F. Worley, "Reflections on the Future of Organization Development" *Journal of Applied Behavioral Science* (March 2003), pp. 97–115; H. Hornstein, "Organizational Development and Change Management: Don't Throw the Baby Out with the Bath Water," *Journal of Applied Behavioral Science* (June 2001), pp. 223–227; and Sabrina Hicks, "What Is Organization Development?" *Training and Development* (August 2000), p. 65.

43. M. J. Austin, "Introducing Organizational Development (OD) Practices into a Country Human Service Agency," *Administration in Social Work* (Winter 2001), p. 63.

44. See, for instance, H. B. Jones, "Magic, Meaning, and Leadership: Weber's Model and the Empirical Literature," *Human Relations* (June 2001), p. 753.

45. Gib Akin and Ian Palmer, "Putting Metaphors to Work for a Change in Organizations," *Organizational Dynamics* (Winter 2000), pp. 67–79.

46. J. Grieves, "Skills, Values or Impression Management? Organizational Change and the Social Processes of Leadership, Change Agent Practice, and Process Consultation," *Journal of Management Development* (May 2000), p. 407.

47. M. McMaster, "Team Building Tips," *Sales and Marketing Management* (January 2002), p. 140; and "How To: Executive Team Building," *Training and Development* (January 2002), p. 16.

48. B. Raabe and T. A. Beehr, "Formal Mentoring Versus Supervisor and Co-Worker Relationships: Differences in Perceptions and Impact," *Journal of Organizational Behavior* (May 2003), pp. 271–294.

49. Initial work on the learning organization is credited to P. M. Senge, *The Fifth Discipline: The Art and Practice* (New York: Doubleday, 1990); C Kontoghiorghes, S. M. Awbre, and P. L. Feurig, "Examining the Relationship Between Learning Organization Characteristics and Change Adaptation, Innovation, and Organizational Performance," *Human Resource Development Quarterly* (Summer 2005), pp. 185–212; and P. Tosey, "The Hunting of the Learning Organization: A Paradoxical Journey," *Management Learning* (September 2005), pp. 335–353.

50. "Or Do You?" *Training and Development* (June 2003), p. 6.

51. M. Dalahoussaye, "Show Me the Results," *Training* (March 2002), p. 28.

52. "How to Measure 'Softer' Results," *HR Focus* (April 2001), pp. 5–7; and A. Putra, "Evaluating Training Programs: An Exploratory Study of Transfer of Learning Onto the Job at Hotel A and Hotel B, Sydney, Australia," *Journal of Hospitality and Tourism Management* (April 2004), pp. 77–87.

53. See, for example, D. L. Gay and T. J. LaBonte, "Demystifying Performance: Getting Started: This Conclusion to Article 1 (May) Spells Out How to Build Confidence and Credibility," *Training and Development* (July 2003), pp. 40–451; and R. E. Catalano and D. L. Kirkpatrick, "Evaluating Training Programs—The State of the Art," *Training and Development Journal* (May 1968), pp. 2–9. See also "Why a Stakeholder Approach to Evaluating Training," *Advances in Developing Human Resources*, Vol. 7, No. 1 (2005), pp. 121–134. For another perspective, see D. L. Bradford and W. W. Burke, "Introduction: Is OD in Crisis?" *Journal of Applied Behavioral Science* (December 2004), pp. 369–373.

54. M. A. Shaffer and D. A. Harrison, "Forgotten Partners of International Assignments: Developments and Test of a Model of Spouse Adjustment," *Journal of Applied Psychology* (April 2001), p. 238.

55. J. Selmer, "The Preference for Pre-Departure or Post-Arrival Cross-Cultural Training: An Exploratory Approach," *Journal of Managerial Psychology* (January 2001), p. 50; N. Zakaria, "The Effects of Cross-Cultural Training on the Acculturation Process of the Global Workforce," *International Journal of Manpower* (June 2000), pp. 492–511; and F. Lievens, E. Van Keer, M. M. Harris, and C. Bisqueret, "Predicting Cross-Cultural Training Performance: The Validity of Personality, Cognitive Ability, and Dimensions Measured by an Assessment Center and a Behavior Description Interview," *Journal of Applied Psychology* (June 2003), pp. 76–89.

56. See, for example, D. M. Eschbach, G. E. Parker, and P. A. Stoeberl, "American Repatriate Employees' Retrospective Assessments of the Effects of Cross-Cultural Training on the Adaptation to International Assignments," *International Journal of Human Resource Management* (March 2001), p. 270. See also S. Taylor and N. K. Napier, "An American Woman in Turkey: Adventures Unexpected and Knowledge Unplanned," *Human Resource Management* (Winter 2001), pp. 347–365; and R. C. May, S. M. Puffer, and D. J. McCarthy, "Transferring Management Knowledge to Russia: A Culturally Based Approach," *Journal of Management Executive* (May 2005), pp. 24–35.

57. See, for instance, A. Yan, G. Zhu, and D. T. Hall, "International Assignments for Career Building: A Model of Agency Relationships and Psychological Contracts," *Academy of Management Review* (July 2002), pp. 373–392; and D. Beadles, "An American Expat View," *Training and Development* (July 2001), p. 76.

58. L. Lavelle, "For UPS Managers, a School of Hard Knocks," *Business Week* (July 22, 2002), pp. 58–59; UPS, "Community Internship Program" (2005), available online at http://www.community.ups.com/diversity/workplace/intern.html.

CHAPTER NINE: MANAGING CAREERS

1. Opening vignette based on B. Dalbey, "Job Changes after 40 Don't Have to Be Frightening," *Business Record (Des Moines)*, September 19, 2005, pp. 24–25.

2. L. T. Eby, M. Butts, and A. Lockwood, "Predictors of Success in the Era of the Boundaryless Career," *Journal of Organizational Behavior* (September 2003), pp. 689–709.

3. D. C. Feldman and C. R. Leana, "What Ever Happened to Laid-Off Executives?: A Study of Re-employment Challenges After Downsizing," *Organizational Dynamics* (Summer 2000), pp. 64–75.

4. K. Heim, "With Layoffs up and Stock Prices Down at High-Tech Firms, Unions Step up Their Quest for Power in the New Economy," *San Jose Mercury News* (December 28, 2000), p. A-1.

5. See "Career Development Ranks Among the Most Demanded Content Areas Across Industries Worldwide," *Training and Development* (September 2003), p. 18. See also P. Kaihla, "How to Land Your Dream Job," *Business 2.0* (November 2004), pp. 103–108.

6. D. T. Hall, *Careers in Organizations* (Santa Monica, CA: Goodyear Publishing, 1976); and J. Van Maanen and E. H. Schein, "Career Development," in J. R. Hackman and J. L. Suttle (eds.), *Improving Life at Work: Behavioral Sciences Approaches to Organizational Change* (Santa Monica, CA: Goodyear Publishing, 1977), pp. 341–355.

7. J. H. Greenhaus, *Career Management* (New York: Dryden Press, 1987), p. 6.

8. See, for instance, R. MacLean, "My Start-Up, Myself," *Inc.* (October 17, 2000), pp. 210–211. See also J. Goodman and S. Hansen, "Career Development and Guidance Programs Across Cultures: The Gap Between Policies and Practices," *Career Development Quarterly* (September 2005), pp. 57–65.

9. D. Cyr, "Life at the Top," *Working Mother* (March 2000), p. 75.

10. "Career Development: Employers Urged to Act to Retain Key Workers," *Personnel Today* (January 28, 2003), p. 7. See also J. Sturges, N. Conway, D. Guest, and A. Liefooghe, "Managing the Career Deal: The Psychological Contract as a Framework for Understanding Career Management, Organizational Commitment, and Work Behavior," *Journal of Organizational Behavior* (November 2005), p. 821. See also R. Van Esbroeck, E. L. Herr, and M. L. Savickas, "Introduction to the Special Issue: Global Perspectives on Vocational Guidance," *Career Development Quarterly* (September 2005), pp. 8–11.

11. K. O'Sullivan, "Why You're Hiring All Wrong," *Inc.* (February 2002), p. 86.

12. Van Maanen and Schein, p. 343.

13. Ibid.; D. T. Hall, *Careers in Organizations* (Santa Monica, CA: Goodyear Publishing, 1976); and M. London and S. A. Stumpf, *Managing Careers* (Reading, MA: Addison Wesley, 1982).

14. Greenhaus, *Career Management*, p. 6.

15. B. Morris, "So You're a Player: Do You Need a Coach?" *Fortune* (February 21, 2000), pp. 144–154.

16. J. J. Sosik and V. M. Godshalk, "Leadership Styles, Mentoring Functions Received, and Job-Related Stress: A Conceptual Model and Preliminary Study," *Journal of Organizational Behavior* (June 2000), p. 365; and K. Tyler, "Find Your Mentor," *HR Magazine* (March 2004), pp. 89–93.

17. B. R. Ragins, J. L. Cotton, and J. S. Miller, "Marginal Mentoring: The Effects of Type of Mentor, Quality of Relationship, and Program Design on Work and Career Attitudes," *Academy of Management Journal* (December 2000), pp. 1177–1194.

18. See A. C. Poe, "Establish Positive Mentor Relationships," *HR Magazine* (February 2002), pp. 62–69; and H. Van Emmerik, S. G. Baugh, and M. C. Euwena, "Who Wants to Be a Mentor? An Examination of Attitudinal, Instrumental, and Social Motivation Components," *Career Development International*, Vol. 10, No. 4 (2005), pp. 310–326.

19. C. Daniels, "Women vs. Wal-Mart," *Fortune* (July 7, 2003). Article available online.

20. See, for example, J. J. Columbo and W. B. Werther Jr., *Strategic Career Coaching for an Uncertain World*," *Business Horizons* (July–August 2003), pp. 33–39; and S. Overman, "Mentors Without Borders," *HR Magazine* (March 2004), pp. 83–86.

21. T. D. Allen and L. T. Eby, "Relationship Effectiveness for Mentors: Factors Associated with Learning and Quality," *Journal of Management* (July–August 2003), pp. 469–487.

22. T. D. Allen and L. M. Finkelstein, "Beyond Mentoring: Alternative Sources and Functions of Development Support," *Career Development Quarterly* (June 2003), pp. 346–356; and L. M. Finkelstein, T. D. Allen, and L. A. Rhoton, "An Examination of the Role of Age in Mentoring Relationships," *Group and Organization Management* (June 2003), pp. 249–281.

23. B. Raabe and R. A. Beehr, "Formal Mentoring Versus Supervisory and Coworker Relationships: Differences in Perceptions and Impact," *Journal of Organizational Behavior* (May 2003), pp. 271–294.

24. For an interesting perspective on this matter, see S. J. Armstrong, C. W. Allinson, and J. Hayes, "Formal Mentoring Systems: An Examination of the Effects of Mentor/Protege Cognitive Styles on the Mentoring Process," *Journal of Management Studies* (December 2002), pp. 1111–1127.

25. C. M. Solomon, "Cracks in the Glass Ceiling," *Workforce* (September 2000), p. 86.

26. J. A. Segal, "Mirror-Image Mentoring," *HR Magazine* (March 2000), pp. 157–165. For another view on this topic, see T. Allen, M. L. Poteet, and J. E. A. Russell, "Protege Selection by Mentors: What Makes the Difference?" *Journal of Organizational Behavior* (May 2000), pp. 271–282.

27. J. A. Segal, p. 158.

28. See M. C. Higgins, L. Trotter, S. L. Ablon, S. Pearson, and M. Mohan, "What Should C. J. Do?" *Harvard Business Review* (November–December 2000), pp. 43–52; J. Hutchins, "Getting to Know You," *Workforce* (November 2000), pp. 44–48; R. Sharpe, "As Leaders, Women Rule," *Business Week* (November 20, 2000), pp. 74–84; C. Benabou and R. Benabou, "Establishing a Formal Mentoring Program for Organizational Success," *National Productivity Review* (Autumn 2000), pp. 1–8; and D. Zeilinski, "Mentoring Up," *Training* (October 2000), pp. 136–140.

29. See, for example, D. E. Super, *The Psychology of Careers* (New York: Harper & Row, 1957); E. Schein, *Career Dynamics: Matching Individual and Organizational Needs* (Reading, MA: Addison Wesley, 1978); and D. J. Levinson, C. N. Darrow, E. B. Klein, M. H. Levinson, and B. McKee, *A Man's Life* (New York: Knopf, 1978). Also see C. P. Chen, "Integrating Perspectives in Career Development Theory and Practice," *Career Development Quarterly* (March 2003), pp. 203–217.

30. See M. Messmer, "Moving Beyond a Career Plateau," *National Public Accountant* (September 2000), pp. 20–21; and J. Blenkinsopp and K. Zdunczyk, "Making Sense of Mistakes in Managerial Careers," *Career Development International*, Vol. 10, No. 5 (2005), pp. 356–359.

31. D. E. Super, "A Life-Span Life Space Approach to Career Development," *Journal of Vocational Behavior*, Vol. 16 (Spring 1980), pp. 282–298.

32. J. Holland, *Making Vocational Choices*, 2nd ed. (Englewood Cliffs, NJ: Prentice Hall, 1986).

33 For an interesting discussion of Schein anchors, see E. H. Schein, "Career Anchors Revisited: Implications for Career Development in the 21st Century," *Academy of Management Journal*, Vol. 10, No. 1 (January 1996), pp. 80–88; and D. C. Feldman and M. C. Bolino, "Career Patterns of the Self-Employed: Career Motivations and Career Outcomes," *Journal of Small Business Management* (July 2000), pp. 53–67.

34. See, for example, J. Michael, "Using the Myers-Briggs Type Indicator as a Tool for Leadership Development? Apply with Caution," *Journal of Leadership and Organizational Studies*," (Summer 2003), pp. 68–82; R. Badham, V. Morrigan, W. Rifkin, and M. Zanko, "The Use of Personality Typing in Organizational Change, Discourse, Emotions, and the Reflective Subject," *Human Relations* (February 2003), pp. 211–235; and D. P. Shuit, "At 60, Myers-Briggs Is Still Sorting Out and Identifying People's Types; Demand for the Venerable Personality Test Remains Strong, Even Though the World Has Changed," *Workforce Management* (December 2003), pp. 72–73.

35. P. B. Robinson, D. V. Simpson, J. C. Huefner, and H. K. Hunt, "An Attitude Approach to the Prediction of Entrepreneurship," *Entrepreneurship Theory and Practice* (Summer 1991), pp. 13–31.

36. B. M. Davis, "Role of Venture Capital in the Economic Renaissance of an Area," in R. D. Hisrich (ed.), *Intrapreneurship, Intrapreneurship, and Venture Capital* (Lexington, MA: Lexington Books, 1986), pp. 107–118.

37. J. M. Crant, "The Proactive Personality Scale as a Predictor of Entrepreneurial Intentions," *Journal of Small Business Management* (July 1996), pp. 42–49; J. D. Kammeyer-Mueller and C. R. Wanberg, "Unwrapping the Organizational Entry Process: Disentangling Multiple Antecedents and Their Pathways to Adjustment," *Journal of Applied Psychology* (October 2003), pp. 779–794; J. A. Thompson, "Proactive Personality and Job Performance: A Social Capital Perspective," *Journal of Applied Psychology* (September 2005), pp. 1011–1017; and D. G. Allen, K. P. Weeks, and K. R. Moffitt, "Turnover Intentions and Voluntary Turnover: The Moderating Roles of Self-Monitoring, Locus of Control, Proactive Personality, and Risk Aversion," *Journal of Applied Psychology* (September 2005), pp. 980–990.

38. Consulting Psychologists Press, *Myers-Briggs Type Indicator*® *(MBTI*®*)*, wwwl.cpp.com/products/mbti/index.asp (2000); R. B. Kennedy and D. A. Kennedy, "Using the Myers-Briggs Type Indicator® in Career Counseling," *Journal of Employment Counseling* (March 2004), pp. 38–44; and J. Sample, "The Myers-Briggs Type Indicator and OD: Implications for Practice From Research," *Organization Development Journal* (Spring 2004), pp. 67–75.

39. P. Moran, "Personality Characteristics and Growth-Orientation of the Small Business Owner Manager," *Journal of Managerial Psychology* (July 2000), p. 651; and M. Higgs, "Is There a Relationship Between the Myers-Briggs Type Indicator and Emotional Intelligence?" *Journal of Managerial Psychology* (September-October, 2001), pp. 488–513.

40. S. J. Henderson, "Follow Your Bliss: A Process for Career Happiness," *Journal of Counseling and Development* (Summer 2000), pp. 305–315; S. Bing, "How to Succeed in Business," *Fortune* (May 1, 2000), p. 81; J. S. Lublin, "Cover

Letters Get You in the Door, So Be Sure Not to Dash Them Off," *Wall Street Journal* (April 6, 2004), p. B-1; and J. Kador and B. Caulfield, "A Resume That Shows Them the Super-You," *Business 2.0* (April 2004), p. 134.

41. See also M. Ligos, "Turning Down a Transfer Can Freeze a Career," *New York Times* (September 28, 2003), p. B-8.

42. Case is based on D. Brady, "Act II," *Business Week* (March 29, 2004), pp. 72–82.

43. I. R. Schwartz, "Self-Assessment and Career Planning: Matching Individuals and Organizational Goals," *Personnel* (January-February 1979), p. 48.

CHAPTER TEN: ESTABLISHING THE PERFORMANCE MANAGEMENT SYSTEM

1. Based on D. Brown, "Performance Management Systems Need Fixing: Survey," *Canadian HR Reporter* (April 11, 2005); available online at www.hrreporter.com.

2. For some interesting articles on this subject, see B. Nelson, "Are Performance Appraisals Obsolete?" *Compensation and Benefits Review* (May–June 2000), pp. 39–42; J. A. Segal, "86 Your Performance Process?" *HR Magazine* (October 2000), pp. 199–206; D. Grote, "Performance Evaluations: Is It Time for a Makeover?" *HR Focus* (November 2000), pp. 6–7; M. Schrage, "How the Bell Curve Cheats You," *Fortune* (February 21, 2000), p. 296; "HR Execs Dissatisfied with Their Performance Appraisal Systems," *HR Focus* (January 2000), p. 2; and L. Grensing-Pophal, "Motivate Managers to Review Performance," *HR Magazine* (March 2001), pp. 44–48.

3. K. J. Hatten and S. R. Rosenthal, "Why- and How-To Systemize Performance Measurement," *Journal of Organizational Excellence* (Autumn 2001), pp. 59–74.

4. We would like to recognize Dr. Peter F. Norlin, an organizational consultant specializing in performance management systems, for providing the framework terminology for purposes, who is served, and inherent difficulties. See also A. Kleingerd, H. Van Tuijl, and J. A. Algera, "Participation in the Design of Performance Management Systems: A Quasi Experiential Field Study," *Journal of Organizational Behavior* (November 2004), pp. 831–851.

5. H. Levinson, "Management by Whose Objectives? *Harvard Business Review* (January 2003), pp. 107–110; and M. D. Cannon and R. Witherspoon, "Actionable Feedback: Unlocking the Power of Learning and Performance," *Academy of Management Executive* (May 2005), pp. 120–134.

6. See also "Companies Appraise to Improve Development," *Personnel Today* (February 25, 2003), p. 51.

7. C. Joinson, "Making Sure Employees Measure Up," *HR Magazine* (March 2001), pp. 36–41.

8. T. Juncaj, "Do Appraisals Work?" *Quality Progress* (November 2002), pp. 45–50.

9. See, for example, M. Brown and J. Benson, "Rated to Exhaustion? Reaction to Performance Appraisal Process," *Industrial Relations Journal* (March 2003), pp. 67–81; and B. Erdogan, M. L. Kraimer, and R. C. Liden, "Procedural Justice as a Two-Dimensional Construct: An Examination in the Performance Appraisal Context," *Journal of Applied Behavioral Science* (June 2001), pp. 205–223.

10. H. M. Findley, K. W. Mossholder, and W. F. Giles, "Performance Appraisal Process and System Facets: Relationships with Contextual Performance," *Journal of Applied Psychology* (August 2000), pp. 634–640.

11. See, for example, S. Wilmer, "The Dark Side of 360-Degree Feedback," *Training and Development* (September 2002), pp. 37–44.

12. See, for instance, M. S. Taylor, S. S. Masterson, M. K. Renard, and K. B. Tracy, "Managers' Reactions to Procedurally Just Performance Management Systems," *Academy of Management Journal* (October 1998), pp. 568–678.

13. S. S. K. La, M. S. M. Yik, and J. Schaubroeck, "Responses to Formal Performance Appraisal Feedback: The Role of

Negative Affectivity," *Journal of Applied Psychology* (February 2002), pp. 192–202.

14. See Barry R. Nathan, Allan M. Mohrman Jr., and John Milliman, "Interpersonal Relations as a Context for the Effects of Appraisal Interviews on Performance and Satisfaction: A Longitudinal Study," *Academy of Management Journal* (June 1991), pp. 352–363.

15. D. C. Martin, K. M. Bartol, and P. E. Kehoe, "The Legal Ramifications of Performance Appraisal: The Growing Significance," *Public Personnel Management* (Fall 2000), pp. 379–406.

16. Readers might find the following article of interest: J. Park and J. K. S. Chong, "A Comparison of Absolute and Relative Performance Appraisal Systems," *International Journal of Management* (September 2000), pp. 423–429.

17. For an overview of appraisal methods, see A.Tziner, C. Joanis, and K. R. Murphy, "A Comparison of Three Methods of Performance Appraisal with Regard to Goal Properties, Goal Perception, and Ratee Satisfaction," *Group and Organization Management* (June 2000), pp. 175–191; and G. J. Yun, L. M. Donahue, D. M. Dudley, and L. A. McFarland, "Rater Personality, Rating Format, and Social Context: Implications for Performance Appraisal Ratings," *International Journal of Selection and Assessment* (June 2005), p. 97.

18. See R. I. Henderson, *Compensation Management in a Knowledge-Based World*, 9th ed. (Upper Saddle River, NJ: Prentice Hall, 2003), Ch. 13.

19. A. Tziner and R. Kopelman, "Effects of Rating Format on Goal-Setting: A Field Experiment," *Journal of Applied Psychology* (May 1988), p. 323.

20. M. L. Tenopyr, "Artificial Reliability of Forced-Choice Scales," *Journal of Applied Psychology* (November 1988), pp. 750–751.

21. See, for example, A. Tziner, C. Joanis, and K. R. Murphy, "A Comparison of Three Methods of Performance Appraisal with Regard to Goal Properties, Goal Perception, and Ratee Satisfaction," *Group and Organization Management* (June 2000), pp. 175–190; K. R. Murphy and V. A. Pardaffy, "Bias in Behaviorally Anchored Rating Scales: Global or Scale Specific," *Journal of Applied Psychology* (April 1989), pp. 343–346; and M. J. Piotrowski, J. L. Barnes-Farrell, and F. H. Esris, "Behaviorally Anchored Bias: A Replication and Extension of Murphy and Constans," *Journal of Applied Psychology* (October 1988), pp. 827–828.

22. A. Tziner, C. Joanis, and K. R. Murphy, "A Comparison of Three Methods of Performance Appraisal with Regard to Goal Properties, Goal Perception, and Ratee Satisfaction," *Group and Organization Management* (June 2000), pp. 175–190; and R. B. Kaiser, and R. E. Kaplan, "Overlooking Overkill? Beyond the 1-to-5 Rating Scale," *Human Resource Planning*, Vol. 28, No. 3 (2005), pp. 7–11.

23. The concept of management by objectives is generally attributed to Peter F. Drucker, *The Practice of Management* (New York: Harper & Row, 1954). See also J. F. Castellano and H. A. Roehm, "The Problem with Managing by Objectives and Results," *Quality Progress* (March 2001), pp. 39–46; J. Loehr and T. Schwartz, "The Making of a Corporate Athlete,"

Harvard Business Review (January 2001), pp. 120–128; and A. J. Vogl, "Drucker, of Course," *Across the Board* (November/December 2000), p. 1.

24. M. Green, J. Garrity, and B. Lyons, "Pitney Bowes Calls for New Metrics," *Strategic Finance* (May 2002), pp. 30–35.

25. See, for example, I. M. Jawahar and G. Salegna, "Adapting Performance Appraisal Systems for a Quality Driven Environment," *Compensation and Benefits Review* (January–February 2003), pp. 64–71.

26. See, for example, E. A. Locke, "Toward a Theory of Task Motivation and Incentives," *Organizational Behavior and Human Performance* (May 1968), pp. 157–189; E. A. Locke, K. N. Shaw, L. M. Saari, and G. P. Latham, "Goal Setting and Task Performance: 1969–1980," *Psychological Bulletin* (July 1981) pp. 12–52; E. A. Locke and G. P. Latham, *A Theory of Goal Setting and Task Performance,* (Upper Saddle River, NJ: Prentice Hall, 1990); P. Ward and M. Carnes, "Effects of Posting Self-Set Goals on Collegiate Football Players' Skill Execution During Practice and Games," *Journal of Applied Behavioral Analysis* (Spring 2002), pp. 1–12; D. W. Ray, "Productivity and Profitability," *Executive Excellence* (October 2001), p. 14; D. Archer, "Evaluating Your Managed System '" *CMA Management* (January 2000), pp. 12–14; and H. Levinson, "Management by Whose Objectives?" *Harvard Business Review* (January 2003), p. 107.

27. T. D. Ludwig and E. S. Geller, "Intervening to Improve the Safety of Delivery Drivers: A Systematic Behavioral Approach," *Journal of Organizational Behavior Management* (April 4, 2000), pp. 11–24; P. Latham and L. M. Saari, "The Effects of Holding Goal Difficulty Constant on Assigned and Participatively Set Goals," *Academy of Management Journal* (March 1979), pp. 163–168; M. Erez, P. C. Earley, and C. L. Hulin, "The Impact of Participation on Goal Acceptance and Performance: A Two Step Model," *Academy of Management Journal* (March 1985), pp. 50–66; and G. P. Latham, M. Erez, and E. A. Locke, "Resolving Scientific Disputes by the Joint Design of Crucial Experiments by the Antagonists: Application to the Erez Latham Dispute Regarding Participation in Goal Setting," *Journal of Applied Psychology* (November 1988), pp. 753–772.

28. See, for instance, J. R. Crow, "Crashing with the Nose Up: Building a Cooperative Work Environment," *Journal for Quality and Participation* (Spring 2002), pp. 45–50; and E. C. Hollensbe and J. P. Guthrie, "Group Pay-for-Performance Plans: The Role of Spontaneous Goal Setting," *Academy of Management Review* (October 2000), pp. 864–972.

29. See E. McMullen, J. Chrisman, and K. Vesper, "Some Problems in Using Subjective Measures of Effectiveness to Evaluate Entrepreneurial Assistance Programs," *Entrepreneurship Theory and Practice* (Fall 2001), pp. 37–55. See also K. Tyler, "Performance Art," *HR Magazine* (August 2005), pp. 58–63; and R. F. Martell and D. P. Evans, "Source-Monitoring Training: Toward Reducing Rater Expectancy Effects in Behavioral Measurements," *Journal of Applied Psychology* (September 2005), pp. 956–963.

30. For an interesting discussion of leniency errors, see J. S. Kane, H. J. Bernardin, P. Villanova, and J. Peyrefitte, "Stability of Rater Leniency: Three Studies," *Academy of Management Journal*, Vol. 38, No. 4 (November 1995), pp. 1036–1051.

31. "Performance Appraisal Consistency is a Rare and Wonderful Thing," *Pay for Performance Report* (December 2002), p. 8.

32. D. Kipnis, K. Price, S. Schmidt, and C. Stitt, "Why Do I Like Thee: Is It Your Performance or My Orders?" *Journal of Applied Psychology* (June 1981), pp. 324–328. See also P. A. Heslin, D. Vande Walle, and G. P. Latham, "The Effect of Implicit Person Theory on Performance Appraisals," *Journal of Applied Psychology* (September 2005), pp. 842–856.

33. Ibid.

34. An assumption has been made here. That is, these raters have specific performance knowledge of the employee. Otherwise, more information may not be more *accurate* information. For example, if the raters are from various levels in the organization's hierarchy, these individuals may not have an accurate picture of the employee's performance; thus, quality of information may decrease. See also C. Fletcher and C. Baldry, "A Study of Individual Differences and Self-Awareness in the Context of Multi-Source Feedback," *Journal of Occupational and Organizational Psychology* (September 2000), pp. 303–319.

35. See, for example, H. R. Rothstein, "Interrater Reliability of Job Performance Ratings: Growth to Asymptote Level with Increasing Opportunity to Observe," *Journal of Applied Psychology* (June 1990), pp. 322–327. See also M. D. Zalesny, "Rater Confidence and Social Influence in Performance Appraisals," *Journal of Applied Psychology* (June 1990), pp. 274–289.

36. For an interesting perspective on aspects to avoid when using multiple raters, see A. H. Church, S. G. Rogelberg, and J. Waclawski, "Since When Is No News Good News? The Relationship Between Performance and Response Rates in Multi-rater Feedback," *Personnel Psychology* (Summer 2000), pp. 435–451; and E. J. Inderrieden, R. E. Allen, and T. J. Keaveny, "Managerial Discretion in the Use of Self-Ratings in an Appraisal System: The Antecedents and Consequence," *Journal of Managerial Issues* (Winter 2004), pp. 460–483.

37. J. S. Miller, "Self-Monitoring and Performance Appraisal Satisfaction: An Exploratory Field Study," *Human Resource Management* (Winter 2001), pp. 321–333.

38. "Feedback, Feedback Everywhere . . . But How Effective Is the 360-Degree Approach?" *Training Strategies for Tomorrow* (November/December 2002), pp. 19–23. See also B. I. J. M. Van Der Heiden and A. H. J. Nijhof, "The Value of Subjectivity: Problems and Prospects for 360-Degree Appraisal System," *International Journal of Human Resource Management* (May 2004), pp. 493–511.

39. J. F. Brett and L. E. Atwater, "360-Degree Feedback: Accuracy, Reactions, and Perceptions of Usefulness," *Journal of Applied Psychology* (October 2001), pp. 930–942; and P. Googe, "How to Link 360 Degree Feedback and Appraisal," *People Management* (January 27, 2005), pp. 46–47.

40. M. Debrayen and S. Brutus, "Learning from Others' 360-Degree Experiences," *Canadian HR Reporter* (February 10, 2003), pp. 18–20. See also "Performance Appraisals," *Business Europe* (April 3, 2002), p. 3.

41. M. A. Peiperl, "Getting 360 Feedback Right," *Harvard Business Review* (January 2001), pp. 142–147.

42. T. J. Maurer, D. R. D. Mitchell, and F. G. Barbeite, "Predictors of Attitudes Toward a 360-Degree Feedback System and Involvement in Post-Feedback Management Development Activity," *Journal of Occupational and Organizational Psychology* (March 2002), pp. 87–107.

43. A. Evans, "From Every Angle," *Training* (September 2001), p. 22.

44. P. Kamen, "The Way That You Use It: Full Circle Can Build Better Organizations with the Right Approach," *CMA Management* (April 2003), pp. 10–13.

45. J. F. Brett and L. E. Atwater, "360-Degree Feedback: Accuracy, Reactions, and Perceptions of Usefulness," *Journal of Applied Psychology* (October 2001), p. 930; M. Kennett, "First Class Coach," *Management Today* (December 2001), p. 84; and T. A. Beehr, L. Ivanitsjaya, C. P. Hansen, D. Erofeev, and D. M. Gudanowski, "Evaluation of 360-Degree Feedback Ratings: Relationships with Each Other and with Performance and Selection Predictors," *Journal of Organizational Behavior* (November 2001), pp. 775–788. For an opposing view on the

benefits of 360-degree feedback, see B. Pfau, I. Kay, K. M. Nowack, and J. Ghorpade, "Does 360-Degree Feedback Negatively Affect Company Performance," *HR Magazine* (June 2002), pp. 54–60.

46. Stephen P. Robbins, *Organizational Behavior*, 10th ed. (Upper Saddle River, NJ: Prentice Hall, 2004), p. 494.

47. J. Day, "Simple, Strong Team Ratings," *HR Magazine* (September 2000), pp. 159–161.

48. W. C. Borman, "The Rating of Individuals in Organizations: An Alternative Approach," *Organizational Behavior and Human Performance* (August 1974), pp. 105–124.

49. C. P. Neck, G. L. Stewart, C. C. Manz, "Thought Self-Leadership as a Framework for Enhancing the Performance of Performance Appraisers," *Journal of Applied Behavior Science* (September 1995).

50. See S. J. Reinke, "Does the Form Really Matter?" *Review of Public Personnel Administration* (March 2003), pp. 23–38.

51. For an opposing view on the need to adjust performance evaluations based on location, see S. C. Borkowski, "International Managerial Performance Evaluations: A Five-Country Comparison," *Journal of International Business Studies* (Fall 1999), pp. 533–545; J. Shen, "Effective International Performance Appraisals: Easily Said, Hard to Do," *Compensation and Benefits Review* (July–August 2005), pp. 70–79;

R. Piekkari, E. Vaara, J. Tienari, and R. Santti, "Integration or Disintegration? Human Resource Implications of a Common Corporate Language Decision in a Cross-Border Merger," *International Journal of Human Resource Management* (March 2005), p. 330; and H. A. Shih, Y. H. Chiang, and I. S. Kim, "Expatriate Performance Management from MNEs of Different National Origins," *International Journal of Manpower*, Vol. 26, No. 2 (2005), pp. 157–178.

52. Case based on L. Rivenbark, "Forced Ranking," *HR Magazine* (November 2005), p. 131; G. Johnson, "Forced Ranking: The Good, the Bad, and the Alternative," *Training* (May 2004), pp. 24–30; and D. Sears, "The Rise and Fall of Rank and Yank," *Information Strategy* (Spring 2003), p. 6. The case was also influenced by D. Kiley and D. Jones, "Ford Alters Worker Evaluation Process," *USA Today* (July 11, 2001), p. 1-B; and "The Changing Employment Picture," *WashingtonPost.com* (July 25, 2002), available online at www.washingtonpost.com.

53. See also Paula Peters, "7 Tips for Delivering Performance Feedback," *Supervision* (May 2000), pp. 12–14.

54. See W. R. Boswell and J. W. Boudreau, "Employee Satisfaction with Performance Appraisals and Appraisers: The Role of Perceived Appraisal Use," *Human Resource Development Quarterly* (Fall 2000), pp. 283–299.

CHAPTER ELEVEN: ESTABLISHING REWARDS AND PAY PLANS

1. Based on A. Dalton, "Pay-for-Performance Plan Helps Shrink Bank's Turnover," *Workforce Management* (2005), available online at www.workforce.com/archive/article/24/02/86.php?ht=.

2. See, for example, C. Ginther, "Incentive Programs that Really Work," *HR Magazine* (August, 2000), pp. 117–120; A. Drach-Zahavy, "The Proficiency Trap: How to Balance Enriched Job Designs and the Team's Need for Support," *Journal of Organizational Behavior* (December 2004), pp. 980–997. See also D. R. May, R. L. Gilson, and L. M. Harter, "The Psychological Conditions of Meaningfulness, Safety, and Availability and the Engagement of Human Spirit at Work," *Journal of Occupational and Organizational Psychology* (March 2004), pp. 11–37.

3. "Dissatisfaction with Salary Review," *Report on Salary Surveys* (June 2002), p. 8.

4. See, for example, D. W. Organ, "What Pay Can and Can't Do," *Business Horizons* (September, 2003), p. 1.

5. B. McConnell, "Survey Finds Companies in the Dark About FLSA Changes," *SHRM Home* (August 18, 2003), p. 1.

6. B. McConnell, "SHRM Members Speak Out About FLSA Changes," *HR Magazine* (October 2003), pp. 135–137.

7. D. M. Lawrence, "The Equal Pay Act: Overview and Update," *Employee Rights Quarterly* (Winter, 2003), pp. 26–40.

8. "The Equal Pay Act Celebrates 40 Years, But Some Say Its Progress Has Been Slow," *Knight Ridder/Tribune Business News* (June 13, 2003), p. 1; "Closing the Pay Gap," *Business Week* (August 28, 2000), p. 38; L. Chavez, "Comparable Worth," *Wall Street Journal* (August 24, 2005), p. A-10; and "Salary Gender Gap Keeps Growing," *Canadian HR Reporter* (August 31, 2005), available online at www.hrreporter.com.

9. C. Banks, "How to Recognize, Avoid Errors in the Job Evaluation Rating Process," *Canadian HR Reporter* (February 24, 2003), pp. 17–19; M. J. Ducharme, P. Singh, and M. Podolsky, "Exploring the Links Between Performance Appraisals and Pay Satisfaction," *Compensation and Benefits Review* (September–October 2005), pp. 46–52; and S. Watson, "Is Job Evaluation Making a Comeback—Or Did It Never Go Away?" *Benefits and Compensation International* (June 2005), pp. 8–13.

10. J. J. Martocchio, *Strategic Compensation: A Human Resource Management Approach*, 3rd ed. (Upper Saddle River, NJ: Prentice Hall, 2004), p. 202.

11. Ibid.

12. For a thorough discussion of various methods of determining the pay structure, see Martocchio, Part III, "Design a Compensation Systems."

13. Office of Personnel Management, November 8, 2003. Available on-line at www.opm.gov.

14. T. Satterfield, "Speaking of Pay," *HR Magazine* (March, 2003), pp. 99–101.

15. L. Greensing-Pophal, "Communication Pays Off," *HR Magazine* (May 2003), pp. 77–82.

16. See D. Lewin, "Incentive Compensation in the Public Sector: Evidence and Potential," *Journal of Labor Research* (Fall 2003), pp. 597–621; and S. J. Wells, "No Results, No Raise," *HR Magazine* (May 2005), pp. 77–80.

17. "Companies More Cautious Over Pay Practices," *Benefits and Compensation International* (September 2002), p. 34.

18. For an interesting article on this topic, see L .R. Gomez-Mejia, T. M. Welbourne, and R. M. Wiseman, "The Role of Risk Sharing and Risk Taking Under Gainsharing," *Academy of Management Review* (July 2000), pp. 492–507.

19. H. Stieglitz, "The Kaiser Steel Union Sharing Plan," *National Industrial Conference Board Studies in Personnel Policy*, no. 187 (New York: 1963).

20. See www.lincolnelectric.com/corporate/career/default.asp (Lincoln Electric, 2003).

21. R. J. Long, "Gainsharing and Power: Lessons from Six Scanlon Plans," *Industrial & Labor Relations Review* (April 2000), pp. 533–535.

22. Martocchio, p. 148.

23. M. A. Verespej, "Sharing in Success," *Industry Week* (September 4, 2000), p. 9; and "Why Gainsharing Works Even Better Today than in the Past," *HR Focus* (April 2000), pp. 3–5.

24. See, for example, J. Wells, "Stock Incentives Remain Preferred Compensation Option," *HR News* (September 2000), p. 17; and K. Kroll, "Benefits: Paying for Performance," *Inc.*

(November 2004), p. 46. See also J. Bowley and D. A. Link, "Supporting Pay for Performance with the Right Technology," *Compensation and Benefits Review* (September–October 2005), pp. 36–41.

25. D. Cadrain, "Put Success in Sight," *HR Magazine* (May 2003), pp. 85–92; and Jeffrey Pfeiffer, "Sins of Commission," *Business 2.0* (May 2004), p. 56.

26. T. J. Hackett and D. G. McDermott, "Seven Steps to Successful Performance-Based Rewards," *HR Focus* (September 2000), pp. 11–13; "PFP Plans Tied to Lower Health Costs," *HR Focus* (September 2005), p. 12; and D. Adler, "P4P in Maine: Local Pilot Teaches Global Lessons," *Employee Benefits News* (October 1, 2005), p. 1.

27. "Performance-Based Pay Plans," *HR Magazine* (June 2004), p. 22.

28. D. J. Cira and E. R. Benjamin, "Competency-Based Pay: A Concept in Evolution," *Compensation and Benefits Review* (September–October 1998), pp. 22; R. Long, "Paying for Knowledge: Does it Pay?" *Canadian HR Reporter* (March 28, 2005), available online at www.hrreporter.com.

29. "Competency-Based Pay Programs: Too Hard to Live With or the Right Stuff?" *Pay for Performance Report* (May 2002), p. 6; and R. K. Zingheim and J. R. Schuster, "The Next Decade for Pay and Rewards," *Compensation and Benefits Review* (January–February 2005), pp. 26–32.

30. K. Ellis, "Developing for Dollars," *Training* (May 2003), pp. 34–39.

31. "Is Broadbanding an Administrative Nightmare Worse than That of Any Grading System?" *Pay for Performance Report* (August 2002), p. 8.

32. See, for example, N. Katz, "Getting the Most out of Your Team," *Harvard Business Review* (September 2001), p. 22.

33. J. McAdams, "The Essential Role of Rewarding Teams and Teamwork," *Compensation & Benefits Management* (Autumn 2000), pp. 15–27.

34. "Team Compensation: Compensation Is the Hot Button of Teaming: Learn How to Do It Right," *On Wall Street* (October 1, 2003), p. 1.

35. D. P. Shuitt, "Pay Unchecked," *Workforce Management* (October 2003), pp. 28–33.

36. W. F. Bowlin, C. J. Renner, and J. M. Rives, "A DEA Study of Gender Equity in Executive Compensation," *Journal of Operations Research Society* (July 2003), pp. 751–758.

37. "Business Week 50 Executive Compensation," *Business Week* (April 4, 2005), available online at www.businessweek.com; and Society of Human Resource Management, "CEO Pay in 2004, Overall Company Performance Closely Tied," *HR News Briefs* (April 14, 2005), p. 2, available online at www.shrm.org/hrnews.

38. See, for example, G. Colvin, "The Great CEO Pay Heist," *Fortune* (June 25, 2001), pp. 64–70; L. Lavelle, "The Artificial

Sweetener in CEO Pay," *Business Week* (March 26, 2001), p. 53.

39. "Executive Hires and Compensations: Performance Rules," *HR Focus* (July 2003), p. 1.

40. M. A. Carpenter and W. G. Sanders, "Top Management Team Compensation: The Missing Link Between CEO Pay and Firm Performance," *Strategic Management Journal* (April 2002), pp. 367–376.

41. H. B. Herring, "At the Top, Pay and Performance Are Often Far Apart," *New York Times* (August 17, 2003), p. B-9.

42. L. Lavelle, "CEO Pay: Nothing Succeeds Like Failure," *Business Week* (September 11, 2000), p. 48.

43. A. Tobias, "Are They Worth It?" *Parade Magazine* (March 3, 2002), p. 9.

44. "Business Week 50 Executive Compensation."

45. Ibid.

46. Ibid.

47. E. Krell, "Getting a Grip on Executive Compensation," *Workforce* (February 2003), pp. 30–33. S. Bates, "Shifts Seen in Executive Compensation," *HR Magazine* (June 2003), p. 14.

48. See, for example, S. Bates, "Piecing Together Executive Compensation," *HR Magazine* (May 2002), pp. 60–68.

49. Ibid. Under IRS regulations, beginning in 1994, annual salaries paid to a company's five top officers in a publicly held firm are not tax deductible if the salaries are over $1 million. Most companies have simply ignored this new ruling, while others are deferring the excess income for these executives until retirement.

50. For further reading on international compensation, see K. B. Lowe, J. Millman, H. DeCeiri, and P. J. Dowling, "International Compensation Practices: A Ten-Country Comparative Analysis," *Human Resource Management* (Spring 2002), pp. 45–67; "How Do Your Peers Handle International Compensation and Benefits? *HR Focus* (July 2001), p. S-4; E. Ng, "Executive Pay in Asia—The Stock Option Game," *Benefits & Compensation International* (September 2000), pp. 3–6; S. Overman, "In Sync," *HR Magazine* (March 2000), pp. 25–27; C. Reynolds, "Global Compensation and Benefits in Transition," *Compensation and Benefits Review* (January–February 2000), pp. 28–38; and J. E. Richard, "Global Executive Compensation: A Look at the Future," *Compensation and Benefits Review* (May–June 2000), pp. 35–38.

51. U.S. Bureau of Public Affairs, Department of State (2003), www.state.gov.

52. H. Adrion, "Rewarding the International Executive Using Stock Options: Part 2," *Benefits & Compensation International* (December 2000), pp. 13–128.

53. Case is based on F. Hansen, "A New Way to Pay," *Workforce Management* (October 24, 2005), pp. 33–40.

CHAPTER TWELVE: EMPLOYEE BENEFITS

1. Based on N. Byrnes, "The Benefits Trap," *Business Week* (July 19, 2004), pp. 64–72.

2. K. Kerwin, P. Burrows, and D. Foust, "Workers of the World Log On," *Business Week* (February 21, 2001), p. 52.

3. C. Ryan, "Employee Retention —What Can the Benefits Professional Do?" *Employee Benefits Journal* (December 2000), p. 18.

4. F. Herzberg, *Work and the Nature of Man* (New York: World, 1966).

5. E. Jones, "An Overview of Employee Benefits," *Occupational Outlook Quarterly* (Summer 2005), pp. 12–21.

6. Society for Human Resource Management, *2005 Benefits: Survey Report* (June 2005), p. 2.

7. S. Armour, "Companies Chisel Away at Workers' Benefits," *USA Today* (November 18, 2002), p. 2B.

8. This assumes that the insurance policy is part of a group term plan. If it were a single policy, other than term insurance, or if the plan discriminated in favor of the more highly paid employees, the entire benefit would be taxable. See E. E. Vollmar, "Group Term Life Insurance," *Employee Benefits Journal* (June 2000), pp. 36–41.

9. As discussed in Chapter 3, government regulations had a major impact on the increases in employee benefits. It is equally important to note that management practices and labor unions also have affected benefit offerings.

10. "More Employers Offer Benefits to Workers' Domestic Partners," *HR Focus* (September 2005), p. 12; S. Moon, "Making a Business Case for Domestic Partner Benefits," *Employee Benefit News* (July 1, 2005), p. 1; and "How HR Is Addressing Domestic Partner Benefits," *HR Focus* (July 2004), p. S-1.

11. See, for instance, "Gay Rights Group Reports More Employers Offer Health Coverage for Domestic Partners," *BNA Daily Report* (September 26, 2000), p. 1; and K. I. Mills, "GLBT Employees Make Gains in Workplaces Nationwide," *Diversity Factor* (Fall 2000), pp. 8–11.

12. *Social Security* here refers to FICA taxes for Old Age, Survivors, and Disability Insurance (OASDI).

13. ssa.gov/pressoffice/basicfact.htm.

14. Based on the passage of the Omnibus Budget Reconciliation Act of 1993, the 2.9 percent Medicare portion no longer has a salary cap. Also, for diehard Social Security fans, Social Security taxes are actually divided into three parts: OASDI; HI [hospital insurance (Medicare)]; and FUTA [Federal Unemployment Tax]. OASDI and HI are combined together to form the FICA taxes deducted from employees' pay and matched by the employer. See, for example, T. Herman, "A Special Summary and Forecast of Federal and State Tax Developments," *Wall Street Journal* (October 25, 2000), p. A-1.

15. Those born after 1929 need 40 credits. Those born before 1929 need fewer than 40 credits—one less credit for each year they were born prior to 1929 (for example, if born in 1928, 39 credits; 1927, 38 credits; and so forth).

16. ssa.gov/policy/docs/quickfacts.

17. See U.S. Department of Labor, Employment and Training Administration, "Unemployment Insurance Tax Topic," (2003), p. 1. Available online at workforcesecurity.doleta.gov/uitaxtopic.asp.

18. Wage bases for unemployment insurance vary. Some states follow the federal $7,000 base, while others vary, to a maximum of $30,200 in Hawaii.

19. See, for instance, U.S. Department of Labor, Office of Workforce Security, "Unemployment Compensation" (April 2002), workforcesecurity.doleta.gov/unemploy/pdf/partnership.

20. "When Duty Calls," *Entrepreneur* (March 2000), p. 127.

21. Although unemployment benefits are federally mandated, problems still can occur. Tremendous layoffs in the latter part of 1990 and early 1991, led some states to deplete their unemployment funds. Accordingly, in states including Connecticut, Massachusetts, Ohio, Michigan, Arkansas, West Virginia, and Missouri, rates charged to employers increased.

22. R. Ceniceros, "Rising Rates Have Employers Looking for Ways to Cut Costs," *Business Insurance* (October 16, 2000), pp. 3–6.

23. See, for instance, J. Romeu, "Worldwide Business Trends Create New Leverage for Voluntary Benefits," *Employee Benefits Journal* (December 2000), p. 24; B. Liddick, "Voluntary Benefits Go by the Wayside Amid an Uncertain Economy," *Workforce Management* (April 2005), pp. 68–69; and D. Woolf, "Voluntary Benefits Can Beef up Total Rewards," *Canadian HR Reporter* (February 14, 2005), available online at www.hrreporter.com.

24. "What Benefit Is Most Important to Your Employees?" *HR Focus* (December 2000), p. 11; K Gurchiek, "Health Benefit Cost Rise Is Lowest Since 1999," *HR Magazine* (July 2005), p. 38; and J. Sahadi, "Healthcare Costs Spike Again," *CNN Money* (September 14, 2005), available online at money.cnn.com/2005/09/13/pf/insurance/kaiser_study/index.htm?cnn=yes.

25. Employee Benefit Research Institute, "Employer Spending on Benefits" (May 2004), p. 1.

26. "What Are Your Priorities for 2001?" *HR Focus* (January 2001), p. 7.

27. B. Gossage, "Tabling Benefits," *Inc.* (June 2003), pp. 46–48; P. Mizra, "Workers May Be Willing to Pay for More Benefits Than They Get," *HR Magazine* (April 2002), p. 26.

28. Point-of-service or network plans are often a variation of preferred provider organizations. The main distinction typically lies in the degree of choice permitted. For example, under preferred provide coverage, a subscriber can see any physician who participates. In a point-of-service (POS) or network, possible physicians may be more limited. Constraints placed on choosing a physician are less than those imposed by an HMO. See also "Maximize Your Benefits: A Guide for All Employees," *Employee Benefits Journal* (December 2000), p. 53.

29. Blue Cross and Blue Shield is the most widely known organization for traditional insurance, but not the only one. Mutual of Omaha, New York Life, Aetna, and other commercial insurance companies offer health-care coverage that models the BC/BS plan.

30. It is important to understand the difference between two terms widely used in Blue Shield contracts: *non-pars* and *participating physicians*. A non-par, or nonparticipating physician, will not accept Blue Shield payments as payment in full for services rendered. This means that any costs incurred above the repayment schedule set by the health insurer are the responsibility of the patient. Participating physicians, as the term implies, agree to accept Blue Shield payments as payments in full for services rendered.

31. D. R. Henderson, "Sure, Visit Your Doctor, Take Your Medicine, But Who Will Pay for It?" *Wall Street Journal* (January 8, 2001), p. A-30. See also "HMO-PPO Medicare-Medicaid Digest for 2002," *Medical Benefits* (February 28, 2003), pp. 1–3.

32. "HMOs Lose 3 Million Enrollees in 2001," *Health Care Strategic Management* (January 2003), p. 13.

33. "PPOs Growing in Popularity Among Patients: Enrollment Jumps 12% in Three Years," *Health Care Strategic Management* (December 2000), p. 12.

34. See G. Gunsauley, "Creative Solutions: Third-Party Administrators Offer Novel Ideas and Aggressive Benefit Designs to Help Plan Sponsors Cope with Surging Health Coverage Costs," *Employee Benefit News* (September 1, 2003), p. 1; and J. Greene, "Employers Look to Direct Contracting to Save Money, Improve Health Care Quality," available online at www.shrm.org/hrnews (April 16, 2003); "TPA Business for Self-Funded Plans Stable in 1999," *Employee Benefit Plan Review* (July 2000), pp. 12–14; R. Sychangco and A. Babcock, "To Self-Insure or Not, That Is the Question," *Canadian HR Reporter* (April 25, 2005), available online at www.hrreporter.com.

35. J. Greene, "Employers Look to Direct Contracting to Save Money, Improve Health Care Quality"; L. Cohn, P. Eliopoulos and A. Weintraub, "What Comes After Managed Care?" *Business Week* (October 23, 2000), pp. 149–156; B. Shutan, "High-Touch Service Spurs TPA Growth," *Employee Benefit News* (September 1, 2005), p. 1.

36. It also should be noted that in some self-funding cases, organizations seek assistance from another company commonly referred to as a *third-party administrator* (TPA). The TPA's role is simply to process health-care forms.

37. When employees have been terminated or their hours reduced, coverage time is 18 months (possibly extended to 29 months if qualifying dependents are covered).

38. The additional 11 months (19–29 months of coverage) were available to those disabled prior to receiving COBRA benefits.

Under the Health Insurance Portability and Accountability Act of 1996, effective January 1, 1997, the 11-month extension is possible for any individual who becomes disabled within the first 60 days of COBRA coverage.

39. "Avoid Delivery Problems with COBRA Notices," *HR Briefing* (June 1, 2003), pp. 2–4.

40. It may also be interesting to note that in early 2003, an IRS ruling mandated that continuation of medical coverage is required in the case of a divorce. The organization must, then, make health insurances coverage available to the divorced spouse as of the date of the divorce. See "Spouse Gets COBRA at the Time of Divorce," *HR Focus* (March 2003), p. 2.

41. Organizations with less than $5 million in revenues had until April 2004 to comply with the HIPAA requirements.

42. See "12 Steps to Ensure Your HR Department Meets HIPAA's April 14 Date," *Human Resource Department Management Report* (February 2003), p. 7; M. Kolton, M. Costa, and D. B. Spanier, "The Effect of HIPAA Privacy Rules on Personal Medical Records," *Journal of Compensation and Benefits* (July–August 2002), pp. 5–16; J. Plavner, "A Regulatory Surprise," *HR Magazine* (May 2003), pp. 127–131; J. A. Brislin, "HIPAA Privacy Rules and Compliance with Federal and State Employment Laws: The Participant Authorization Form," *Employee Benefits Journal* (March 2003), p. 51–64; M. Verespej, "HR Should Set High Standards on Privacy," *HR Magazine* (August 2005), p. 32; K. Gurchiek and M. Verespej, "HIPAA Violation Liability Narrowed," *HR Magazine* (July 2005), p. 36; and B. D. Annulis, "Identity Theft Case Creates HIPAA Concerns for Hospitals," *Health Care Strategic Management* (January 2005), pp. 11–12.

43. The Retirement Equity Act of 1984 and the Tax Reform Act of 1986 modified participation ages, minimum vesting age, and vesting rights, requiring full vesting after five years, partial vesting after three years, and seven-year full vesting with plan years beginning after December 1, 1988. Companies with a retirement plan year prior to that date were not required to go to the new lower vesting rules until December 1, 1989. It is also important to note, as will be discussed later in the chapter, that any monies contributed by employees toward their retirement are immediately 100 percent vested.

44. Portability of pension rights is a complex issue beyond the scope of this book. However, depending on the company, employees may receive a permanent right to their monies, receiving a pension from the organization at retirement age or receive a check that allows them to reinvest those monies on their own.

45. L. Bivins, "Pension Treasure," *Wall Street Journal* (June 5, 2000), p. A-4.

46. P. G. Lester, "A Checklist for Disability Plan Design," *Compensation and Benefits Review* (September–October 2000), pp. 59–61.

47. R. M. McCaffery, *Employee Benefit Programs: A Total Compensation Perspective* (Boston, MA: PWS-Kent Publishing, 1992), p. 131.

48. Ibid., p. 142.

49. The Economic Growth and Tax Relief Reconciliation Act of 2001 (EGRTRRA) included several changes that may minimize the benefits of companies offering money purchase plans. Those changes go well beyond the scope of this book. See A. L. Cavanaugh, "The Money Purchase Plan," *Journal of Pension Benefits* (Autumn 2001), pp. 43–49.

50. Profit-sharing plans require profits before a contribution can be made. When the period shows no profits, no contributions need be made. The only partial exception is that contributions can be made in a year in which there are no profits if there are accumulated profits from prior years. However, should this occur, further restrictions apply. See also J. Marquez, "Firms

Replacing Stock Options with Restricted Shares Face a Tough Sell to Employees," *Workforce Management* (September 2005), pp. 71–73.

51. J. VandeHei and D. Rogers, "House Approves Plan to Raise Limits on IRAs," *Wall Street Journal* (September 20, 2000), p. A-4.

52. C. M. Cropper, "What to Do with a Ravaged IRA: Try Changing It to a ROTH," *Business Week* (December 16, 2002), p. 140.

53. See A. P. Curatola, "Roth IRAs Revisited," *Strategic Finance* (December 2000), pp. 18–20.

54. J. Cleaver, "They Want Their 401(k)s," *Workforce* (December 2000), p. 62.

55. Many companies offering matching contribution features to their 401(k) programs limit the amount of their contribution. Typically, their matching amount is set as one-half of the amount the employee contributes, with a 3 percent maximum. Thus, an employee setting aside 4 percent of his or her salary will have a 2 percent match, with up to 3 percent for a 6 percent deduction.

56. M. Hammers, "Starbucks Is Pleasing Employees and Pouring Profits," *Workforce Management* (October 2003), pp. 58–59.

57. B. Leonard, "Workers' Contributions to 401(k)s Average Nearly 7 Percent of Salary," *HR Magazine* (December 2001), p. 25.

58. See, for instance, "Survey Updates National Norms for Bonuses, Paid Leave, and Vacation Days," *Report on Salary Surveys* (June 2003), p. 1.

59. Based on information provided by Economic Policy Institute World Almanac, 2001.

60. K. Gurchiek, "Vacationing Workers Find It Hard To Let Go," *HR Magazine* (August 2005), p. 30.

61. "Survey Updates National Norms for Bonuses, Paid Leave, and Vacation Days," *Report on Salary Surveys* (June 2003), p. 1, Table 2.

62. Based on articles found on HRM.Guide.com.uk, "3-Million Not Entitled to Easter Bank Holiday," (April 16, 2003); and "Call for More Public Holidays (May 3, 2002), www.hrmguide.co.uk/rewards/public_holidays.htm.

63. "Absence Makes the Workplace Grow Poorer," *Fair Employment Practices Guidelines* (April 15, 2003), p. 8.

64. Short-term disability programs may be provided through commercial carriers or through self-funding arrangements. The more popular of the two is purchased coverage.

65. Before we proceed, an important piece of federal legislation warrants mentioning. Based on the 1978 Pregnancy Discrimination Act, employers that offer short-term disability insurance to their employees must include pregnancy as part of the policy's coverage. This means that in whatever capacity employers cover disabilities such as an extended illness, coverage for disability due to pregnancy must be the same (see Chapter 3).

66. The number of sick days offered to employees generally varies according to their position in the organization and their length of service. Many organizations require a waiting period, approximately six months, before sick leave kicks in.

67. K. M. Blassingame, "Firms Press to Quantify Control Presenteeism," *Medical Benefits* (February 28, 2003), p. 10.

68. See, for example, S. Armour, "Faced With Less Time Off, Workers Take More," *USA Today* (October 29, 2002), p. 1A.

69. P. Robinson, "Bank Launches Pooled Sick Leave Plan," *Australian Business Intelligence* (November 12, 2003), p. 1.

70. The 70 to 80 percent of replacement income stems from the tax-free nature of some payments. (Payments from an employer LTD are generally taxable; the amount received from LTD based on employee-paid premiums is not taxable income.) If long-term payments were not reduced, it is conceivable that an employee receiving LTD and government

disability payments could have a greater income than when working. This logic defeats the purpose of the program.

71. Some disability plans pay benefits for different periods if the disability relates to illness rather than injury.

72. Depending on company policy, there may be a time lag before a new employee's insurance policy takes effect. Waiting periods, when used, typically last about six months. Additionally, eligibility periods may be waived for management personnel.

73. "Flexible Benefits: Research," *Employee Benefits Journal* (September 4, 2003), p. PS-15.

74. J. J. Meyer, "The Future of Flexible Benefit Plans," *Employee Benefits Journal* (June 2000), pp. 3–7.

75. J. A. Fraser, "Stretching Your Benefits Dollar," *Inc.* (March 2000), pp. 123–126.

76. See, for instance, "Survey Recounts Benefits Offerings for State Employees," *Employee Benefit Plan Review* (September 2000), pp. 34–36.

77. B. Kiviat, "Save More on Drugs," *Time* (October 13, 2003), p. 94.

78. C. Gunsauley, "Tax Advantages Fail to Promote Flexible Spending Accounts," *Employee Benefit News* (September 15, 2002), p. 1; and "TPAs Stay in the Game as Rules Keep Changing," *Employee Benefit News* (September 15, 2002), p. 1.

79. McCaffery, p. 197.

80. Case is based on S. Hirsh, "Perks Help Keep Workers Happy," *Baltimore Sun* (July 11, 2004), available online at www.baltimoresun.com.

81. This example was directly influenced by a similar example given in J. S. Rosenbloom and G. V. Hallman, *Employee Benefits Planning*, 3rd ed. (Englewood Cliffs, NJ: Prentice Hall, 1991), p. 225. See also J. S. Rosenbloom, *Handbook of Employee Benefits Design, Funding, and Administration*, 4th ed. (New York: McGraw-Hill Professional Book Group, 1996). Actual benefits under SSDI vary according to family status, average annual income, and the consumer price index. Therefore, SSDI given in this example is only an estimate.

Chapter Thirteen: Ensuring a Safe and Healthy Work Environment

1. Based on A. Fisher, "How to Prevent Violence at Work," *Fortune* (February 21, 2005), p. 42.

2. U.S. Department of Labor, Occupational Safety and Health Administration, "OSHA Facts," (2005). Available online at www.osha.gov/as/opa/oshafacts.html.

3. U.S. Bureau of the Census, *Statistical Abstracts of the United States, 2005* (Washington, DC: Government Printing Office, 2005), p. 416.

4. The Occupational Safety and Health Act was amended in 1998.

5. "What to Expect if OSHA Comes Knocking," *Safety Compliance Letter* (August 15, 2003), pp. 5–6.

6. In the Supreme Court case of *Whirlpool Corporation v. Marshall* [445 U.S. 1(1980)], employees may refuse to work if they perceive doing so can cause serious injury. This case has weakened termination for insubordination when the refusal stems from a safety or health issue. This refusal was further clarified in *Gateway Coal v. United Mine Workers* [94 S. Ct. 641(1981)], where a three-part test was developed. This was where (1) the refusal is reasonable; (2) the employee was unsuccessful in getting the problem fixed; and (3) normal organizational channels to address the problem haven't worked.

7. "OSHA Targets 3,200 Workplaces for Surprise Inspections," *Safety Compliance Letter* (July 1, 2003), p. 4.

8. *Marshall v. Barlow, Inc.*, 436 U.S., 307 (1978).

9. "OSHA Inspection Delay Is Legal," *ENR* (May 3, 1999), p. 21.

10. C. S. Kline, "Recordkeeping Review: OSHA's Revised Rule Has Simplified Injury and Illness Reporting," *Industrial Safety and Hygiene News* (December 2002), pp. 22–23.

11. The number 3,600,000 is determined as follows: 1,800 employees, working 40-hour weeks, for 50 weeks a year [1,800 × 40 × 50]. U.S. Department of Labor, Occupational Safety and Health Administration, *OSHA Facts–December 2004* (2004), pp. 1–5. Available online at www.osha.gov. It's also important to note that in addition to Federal inspections, state inspectors conducted nearly another 58,000 inspections in 2004, bringing the total of inspections by Federal and State inspectors to nearly 100,000 per year.

12. U.S. Bureau of the Census, *Statistical Abstracts of the United States, 2005* (Washington, DC: Government Printing Office, 2005), p. 417.

13. For willful violation the minimum penalty is $5,000; other fines levied for violations other than those willful and repetitive carry a $7,000 maximum. R. Ilaw, "When OSHA Comes Knocking: Give 'Em the Facts, Just the Facts," *Industrial Safety and Hygiene News* (September 2005), pp. 50–51.

14. U.S. Department of Labor, Occupational Safety and Health Administration, "OSHA Facts," (2003). Available online at www.osha.gov/as/opa/oshafacts.html; and "OSHA $100,000 Club Safety Citations," *Occupational Hazards* (October 2005), p. 62.

15. J. Gambardello "OSHA Issues Safety and Health Information Bulletin on Disposal of Contaminated Needles and Blood Tube Holders," *America's Intelligence Wire* (October 16, 2003), p. 1.

16. U.S. Department of Labor, Occupational Safety and Health Administration, "Information Regarding Severe Acute Respiratory Syndrome (SARS)" (May 30, 2003).

17. See U.S. Department of Labor, Occupational Safety and Health Administration, *Hazard Communication Guidelines for Compliance* (Washington, DC: Government Printing Office, 2000); "OSHA Clarifies Hazard Communications Rule: Places Responsibility on Employer," *Paint & Coatings Industry* (September 2005), p. 10; and S. G. Minter, "Will OSHA Act to Improve MSDS: Twenty Years Since MSDSs entered the Safety Mainstream, Critics Say They Too Often Are Confusing and Unreliable," *Occupational Hazards* (September 2003), p. 8.

18. U.S. Bureau of the Census, *Statistical Abstracts of the United States, 2002* (Washington, DC: Government Printing Office, 2002), p. 409.

19. S. Bates, "Industry Ergonomic Guidelines 'Not Standards in Disguise,' OSHA Official Says," *HR News* (September 2003), p. 34.

20. U.S. Department of Labor, Occupational Safety and Health Administration, "OSHA Emergency Preparedness," www.osha-slc.gov/SLTC/emergencypreparedness/index.html (2003); and M.Totty and C. Hymowitz, "Workplace Security (A Special Report): How Vulnerable Are You? The Latest Ways to Protect Your Employees, Facilities, and Information," *Wall Street Journal* (September 29, 2003), p. R-1.

21. J. Dietz, S. L. Robinson, R. Folger, R. A. Baron, and M. Schultz, "The Impact of Community Violence and an Organization's Procedural Justice Climate on Workplace Aggression," *Academy of Management Journal* (June 2003), pp. 317–327.

22. D. Costello, "Stressed Out: Can Workplace Stress Get Worse?—Incidents of 'Desk Rage' Disrupt America's Offices—Long Hours, Cramped Quarters Produce Some Short Fuses; Flinging Phones at the Wall," *Wall Street Journal* (January 16, 2001), p. B-1.

23. See, for example, "Fatal Workplace Violence Claims 13 Lives," *Occupational Hazards* (August 2003), pp. 14–15.

24. S. V. Magyar Jr., "Preventing Workplace Violence," *Occupational Health and Safety* (June 2003), p. 64; D. Cadrain, ". . . And Stay Out," *HR Magazine* (August 2002), p. 83; and K. Gurchiek, "Workplace Violence on the Upswing," *HR Magazine* (July 2005), pp. 27–28.

25. "Study: Lights, Nosolo Workers Help Reduce Homicides," *Occupational Hazards* (April 2002), p. 17; U.S. Department of Labor, Occupational Safety and Health Administration, *Workplace Violence* (Washington, DC: Government Printing Office, 2002), p. 1; L. Miller, K. Caldwell, and L. C. Lawson, "When Work Equals Life: The Next State of Workplace Violence," *HR Magazine* (December 2000), pp. 178–180; and K. Gurchiek, "Workplace Violence on the Upswing," p. 27.

26. P. A. Paziotopoulos, "Workplace Domestic Violence," *Law and Order* (August 2003), p. 104; and M. Lynch, "Go Ask Alice," *Security Management* (December 2000), pp. 68–73.

27. T. Anderson, "Training for Tense Times," *Security Management* (March 2002), pp. 68–75.

28. See P. M. Buhler, "Workplace Civility: Has It Fallen by the Wayside?" *Supervision* (April 2003), pp. 20–22.

29. "How Can HR Help Address the Threat of Workplace Violence," *HR Focus* (October 2003), p. 8; L. Stack, "Employees Behaving Badly," *HR Magazine* (October 2003), pp. 111–115; "The Most Effective Tool Against Workplace Violence," *HR Focus* (February 2003), p. 11; and "How to Predict and Prevent Workplace Violence," *HR Focus* (April 2005), pp. 10–11.

30. P. Falcone, "Dealing with Employees in Crisis: Use this Blueprint for Proactive Management Intervention," *HR Magazine* (May 2003), pp. 117–122; and "How Can HR Help Address the Threat of Workplace Violence?" *HR Focus* (October 2003), p. 8. For another insight into this matter, see E. Roche, "Do Something—He's About to Snap," *Harvard Business Review* (July 2003), pp. 23–30.

31. See S. G. Minter, "Prevention to Solution to Workplace Violence," *Occupational Hazards* (August 2003), p. 22; L. R. Chavez, "10 Things Healthy Organizations Do to Prevent Workplace Violence," *Occupational Hazards* (August 2003), p. 22; and "Is Your Lobby Ripe for Violence?" *HR Focus* (September 2003), p. 5.

32. R. J. Grossman, "Bulletproof Practices," *HR Magazine* (November 2002), pp. 34–42.

33. J. I. Pasek, "Crisis Management for HR," *HR Magazine* (August 2002), p. 111.

34. Paul Temple, "Real Danger and 'Postal' Myth," *Workforce* (October 2000), p. 8.

35. "Sick Building Syndrome: A New Territory for Liability," *HR Briefing* (March 1, 2002), pp. 6–7.

36. A. Underwood, "A Hidden Health Hazard," *Newsweek* (December 4, 2000), p. 74; and M. Conlin and J. Carey, "Is Your Office Killing You?" *Business Week* (June 5, 2000), pp. 114–128.

37. See Conlin and Carey, "Is Your Office Killing You?"; and R. Schneider, "Sick Buildings Threaten Health of Those Who Inhabit Them," *Indianapolis Star* (September 23, 2000).

38. U.S. Department of Labor, "Ergonomics: The Study of Work," *OSHA 3125* (Washington, DC: Government Printing Office, 2000), p. 4.

39. K. J. DiLuigi, "Help for the Overworked Wrist," *Occupational Hazards* (October 2000), pp. 99–101.

40. "OSHA Issues Final Ergonomics Standards," *Healthcare Financial Management* (January, 2001), p. 9; G. Flynn, "Now is the Time to Prepare for OSHA's Sweeping New Ergonomic Standard," *Workforce* (May 2001), pp. 76–77; C. Haddad, "OSHA New Regs Will Ease the Pain—For Everybody," *Business Week* (December 4, 2000), pp. 90–91; and Y. J. Dreazen, "Ergonomic Rules Are the First in a Wave of Late Regulations," *Wall Street Journal* (November 14, 2000), p. A-41. For another view on these standards, see P. Kuntz, "What a Pain: Proposed OSHA Rules for Workplace Injuries Make Companies Ache—Agency Stretches Data to Fit Burgeoning Mission; Cost of Compliance Debated—Looking for 10 Pallbearers," *Wall Street Journal* (September 18, 2000), p. A-1.

41. See, for example, S. Bates, "Industry Ergonomic Guidelines 'Not Standards in Disguise,' OSHA Official Says," *HR Magazine* (September 2003), p. 34.

42. See Occupational Safety and Health Administration, *OSHA's Ergonomics Enforcement Plan* (Government Printing Office, March 6, 2003).

43. U.S. Department of Labor, "Ergonomics: The Study of Work," *OSHA 3125* (Washington, DC: Government Printing Office, 2000), p. 1; and R. Kaletsky, "Beyond Musculoskeletal Disorders: Subtle Aspects of Ergonomics," *Safety Compliance Letter* (November 2005), pp. 4–5.

44. F. M. Spina, "Ergonomically Correct," *Risk Management* (December 2000), pp. 39–41; and L. Eig and J. Landis, MSDs and the Workplace: EA Professionals Can Work with Ergonomists to Identify Jobs and Workstations That Place Employees at Risk for Musculoskeletal Disorders," *Journal of Employee Assistance* (September 2004), pp. 12–14.

45. "HR Execs Polled About Stress," *Work and Family Newsbrief* (May 2002), pp. 2–4.

46. William Atkinson, "When Stress Won't Go Away," *HR Magazine* (December 2000), p. 104.

47. "Japan Asks If It Works Too Hard," *Christian Science Monitor (Tokyo)* (April 6, 2000), p. 4. See also "When Heartache May Bring on a Heart Attack," *Business Week* (May 6, 2002), p. 97.

48. "Managers Fail to Tackle Rising Stress," *Personnel Today* (June 25, 2002), p. 10; and "Downtime: the Workers' Reaction to Workplace Stress," *Australasian Business Intelligence* (June 27, 2002), p. 1008.

49. For some interesting reading on organizational stress, see Elaine Wethington, "Theories of Organizational Stress," *Administrative Science Quarterly* (September 2000), p. 640; and T. Beehr, "Consistency of Implications of Three Role Stressors Across Four Countries," *Journal of Organizational Behavior* (August 2005), pp. 467–487.

50. K. Tyler, "Cut the Stress," *HR Magazine* (May 2003), pp. 101–106.

51. See, for example, "Stressed Out: Extreme Job Stress: Survivors' Tales," *Wall Street Journal* (January 17, 2001), p. B-1; M. C. Bolino and W. H. Turnley, "The Personal Costs of Citizenship Behavior: The Relationship Between Individual Initiative and Role Overload, Job Stress, and Work-Family Conflict," *Journal of Applied Psychology* (July 2005), pp. 740–748; and "Stressed Out," *Training* (December 2004), p. 16.

52. N. Merrick, "Boxing Clever: Reducing Stress," *Employee Benefits* (March 2000), p. 34; "Stress Steals Two Weeks a Year," *Work & Family Newsbrief* (April 2005), p. 5.

53. "Employee Assistance Programs," *HR Magazine* (May 2003), p. 143.

54. N. Schutte, S. Toppinen, R. Kalimo, and W. Schaufeli, "The Factorial Validity of the Maslach Burnout Inventory—General Survey (MBI–GS) Across Occupational Groups and Nations," *Journal of Occupational and Organizational Psychology* (March 2000), pp. 3–66.

55. See, for instance, S. Vanheule, A. Lievrouw, and P. Verhaeghe, "Burnout and Intersubjectivity: A Psychoanalytical Study from a Lacanian Perspective," *Human Relations* (March 2003), pp. 321–339; and D. Wise, "Employee Burnout Taking Major Toll on Productivity," *Los Angeles Times* (July 9, 2001), p. 29.

56. See, for instance, S. Bates, "Expert: Don't Overlook Employee Burnout," *HR Magazine* (August 2003), p. 14.

57. "EAPs: They're Well Intentioned, But Also Risky," *HR Briefing* (May 1, 2002), pp. 2–3; and Fay Hansen, "Employee Assistance Programs (EAPs) Grow and Expand Their Reach," *Compensation and Benefits Review* (March/April 2000), p. 13.

58. Employee rights legislation mandates that any activity in an EAP remains confidential. This means records of who is visiting the EAP, the problems, and intervention, must be maintained separately from other personnel records. Also, HIPAA regulations (see Chapter 12) may also mandate confidentiality of EAP activities.

59. "EAPs with the Most," *Managing Benefits Plans* (March 2003), p. 8; and K. Tyler, "Helping Employees Cope with Grief," *HR Magazine* (September 2003), pp. 55–58. "EEOC Considers EAPs a 'Best' Practice," *HR Briefing* (April 1, 2003), p. 5.

60. F. Phillips, "Employee Assistance Programs: A New Way to Control Health Care Costs," *Employee Benefit Plan Review* (August 2003), pp. 22–24.

61. William Atkinson, "Wellness, Employee Assistance Programs: Investments, Not Costs," *Bobbin* (May 2000), pp. 42–48.

62. K. Lee, "EAP Diversity Detracts from Original Focus, Some Say," *Employee Benefits News* (July 1, 2003), p. 1.

63. K. M. Quinley, "EAPs: A Benefit That Can Trim Your Disability and Absenteeism Costs," *Compensation and Benefits Report* (February 2003), pp. 6–7.

64. "EAPs Flounder Without Manager Support," *Canadian HR Reporter* (June 2, 2003), p. 7.

65. J. Useem, "The New Company Town," *Fortune* (January 10, 2000), pp. 62–70; N. Moeller-Roy, "Helping Employees Make Informed Decisions: By Having Employee Health as an Asset to Be Managed, Employers Can Use Health Promotion and Wellness Programs to Instill Healthy Behaviors Among Workers and Encourage Them to Make Smarter Health Choices," *Journal of Employee Assistance* (October 2005), pp. 24–25; and "More Companies Commit to Wellness Plans, Despite Little Hard Data on Results," *HR Focus* (April 2005), pp. S1–S3.

66. See, for instance, M. Derer, "Corporate Benefits Take Aim Against Obesity," *USA Today* (September 1, 2003), p. A1; P. Petesch, "Workplace Fitness or Workplace Fits?" *HR Magazine* (July 2001), pp. 137–140; and J. L. Barlament, "Disease Management: Legal Implications," *Benefits and Compensation Digest* (November 2005), pp. 32–36.

67. Carolyn Petersen, "Value of Complementary Care Rises, But Poses Challenges," *Managed HealthCare* (November 2000), pp. 47–48; T. Anderson, "Employers Boost Financial Incentives for Disease Management," *Employee Benefit News* (October 1, 2005), p. 1; and "43% of Companies Have Adopted 'Formal' Disease-Management/Wellness Programs," *Managing Benefits Plans* (August 2005), p. 9.

68. K. Sweeney, "Wellness Programs Must Be Properly Constructed and Marketed for Maximum Return on Investment," *Employee Benefit News* (March 1, 2005), p. 1.

69. Vignettes for this case were found at the U.S. Department of Labor, Occupational Safety and Health Administration, "Making a Positive Difference: OSHA Saves Lives," (November 27, 2005), available online at www.osha.gov/as/opa/oshasaveslives.html.

Chapter Fourteen: Understanding Labor Relations and Collective Bargaining

1. Based on R. J. Burnette, "Walking Out on Wages," *Workforce Management* (August 2005), pp. 12–13.

2. AFL-CIO, "Union Membership by Industry" (2003). Available online at www.aflcio.org/aboutunions/joinunions/whyjoin/uniondifference/uniondiff11.cfm.

3. D. B. Klaff and R. G. Ehrenberg, "Collective Bargaining and Staff Salaries in American Colleges and Universities," *Industrial and Labor Relations Review* (October 2003), pp. 92–104.

4. J. Bladen, and S. Machin, "Cross-Generation Correlations of Union Status for Young People in Britain," *British Journal of Industrial Relations* (September 2003), p. 391; and R. J. Grossman, "Unions Follow Suit," *HR Magazine* (May 2005), pp. 47–51.

5. See AFL-CIO, "Unions Raise Wages—Especially for Minorities and Women," www.aflcio.org/uniondifference/uniondiff4.htm, from U.S. Department of Labor, Employment and Earnings (January 2001).

6. Readers should recognize that although the closed shop (compulsory union membership before one is hired) was declared illegal by the Taft-Hartley Act, a modified form still exists today. That quasi-closed shop arrangement is called the *hiring hall* and is found predominantly in the construction and printing industries. However, a hiring hall is not a form of union security because it must assist all members despite their union affiliation. Additionally, the hiring hall must establish procedures for referrals that are nondiscriminatory.

7. Currently, 22 of 50 states are right-to-work states. These are Alabama, Arizona, Arkansas, Florida, Georgia, Idaho, Iowa, Kansas, Louisiana, Mississippi, Nebraska, Nevada, North Carolina, North Dakota, Oklahoma, South Carolina, South Dakota, Tennessee, Texas, Utah, Virginia, and Wyoming. See "South Carolina Reaffirms Right-to-Work Status," *Labor Relations Bulletin* (October 2002), p. 8.

8. There are, however, exceptions to this in the construction industry.

9. See, for instance, M. Romano, "Hospital Accused of Iron-Fist Tactics," *Modern Hospital* (January 8, 2001), p. 16.

10. For a comprehensive review of labor laws, see B. Feldacker, *Labor Law Guide to Labor Law*, 4th ed. (Upper Saddle River, NJ: Prentice Hall, 2000).

11. L. Stein, "Ports of Call," *U.S. News and World Report* (October 21, 2002), p. 14.

12. B. Feldacker, *Labor Law Guide to Labor Law*, 4th ed., p. 5.

13. The Railway Labor Act created the National Mediation Board, which works on matters of recognition, dispute resolution, and unfair labor practices in the railroad and airline industries only. The National Railroad Adjustment Board was also part of the Railway Labor Act, and this body arbitrated disputes between railroads and unions.

14. W. Zellner and M. Arndt, "Concession at the Bargaining Table, Too," *Business Week* (March 19, 2001), p. 46.

15. It is also important to note that the Wagner Act was also amended in 1974 with the Health Care Amendments. This amendment brought both nonprofit hospitals and health-care organizations under the jurisdiction of the Wagner Act.

16. M. J. Goldberg, "An Overview and Assessment of the Law Regulating Internal Union Affairs," *Journal of Labor Research* (Winter 2000), pp. 15–36.

17. L-M 2 reports are required of unions that have revenues of $200,000 or more and those in trusteeship. L-M 3 reports are a simplified annual report, which may be filed by unions with total revenues of less than $200,000, and if the union is not in trusteeship. L-M 4 is an abbreviated form and may be used by unions with less than $10,000 in total annual revenues, and if the union is not in trusteeship. These reports are due within 90 days after the end of the union's fiscal year. See union-reports. dol.gov/olmsWeb/docs/simanreprt.html.

18. It must be noted that when one discusses government labor relations, two categories emerge. One is the federal sector, the other the public sector. In a brief discussion of government labor relations, the focus is on the federal sector due to its federal legislation. However, one must realize that state or municipal statutes do define practices for labor–management relationships for state, county, and municipal workers (typically police officers, fire fighters, and teachers). Because these laws differ in the many jurisdictions, it goes beyond the scope of this text to attempt to clarify each jurisdiction's laws.

19. Although government employees often face a no-strike clause, with the exception of the air traffic controllers case, such restrictions are generally ineffective. Working to rules, "blue flues," and recorded sanitation, nursing, and teacher strikes across this country support the contention that a no-strike clause is weak.

20. United States Code Annotated, Title 18, Section 1961 (St. Paul, MN: West Publishing, 1984), p. 6.

21. Ibid., p. 228.

22. United States Code Annotated, Title 29, Section 186 (St. Paul, MN: West Publishing, 1978), p. 17.

23. U.S. Department of Labor, Office of the Inspector General, *Semiannual Report to the Congress April 1, 2002–September 30, 2002* (Washington, DC: Government Printing Office, 2002).

24. Only pure grievance awards can be solely determined by the FLRA.

25. M. M. Clark, "NLRB Still Unsure How 'To Define' Supervisor," *HR Magazine* (September 2003), pp. 23–24; J. E. Lyncheski and R. J. Andrykovitch, "Who's a Supervisor?" *HR Magazine* (September 2001), pp. 159–168; and D. Foust, "The Ground War at FedEx," *Business Week* (November 28, 2005), pp. 42–43.

26. Elections may not be the only means of unionizing. In cases where a company has refused to recognize a union because of a past unfair labor practice, the NLRB may certify a union without a vote.

27. Adapted from S. P. Robbins and D. A. DeCenzo, *Supervision Today*, 4th ed. (Upper Saddle River, NJ: Prentice Hall, 2004), p. 434; M. K. Zachary, "Labor Law for Supervisors: Union Campaigns Prove Sensitive for Supervisory Employees," *Supervision* (May 2000), pp. 23–26; S. Greenhouse, "A Potent, Illegal Weapon Against Unions: Employers Know It Costs Them to Fire Organizers," *New York Times* (October 24, 2000), p. A-10; and J. E. Lyncheski and L. D. Heller, "Cyber Speech Cops," *HR Magazine* (January 2001), pp. 145–150.

28. See, for instance, S. Greenhouse, "Two Sides Differ on State of Talks of Verizon Pact," *New York Times* (August 6, 2003), p. C1.

29. D. C. Bok and J. T. Dunlop, "Collective Bargaining in the United States: An Overview," in W. Clay Hammer and Frank L. Schmidt (eds.), *Contemporary Problems in Personnel* (Chicago: St. Clair Press, 1997), p. 383.

30. An international union, in this context, refers to a national union in the United States that has local unions in Canada.

31. If we take into account public-sector collective bargaining, we have another exception—the public. The taxpaying, voting public can influence elected officials to act in certain ways during negotiations.

32. D. Hakim, "Tough Times Force U.A.W. to Employ New Strategy," *New York Times* (September 17, 2003), p. C1.

33. M. H. Bowers and D. A. DeCenzo, *Essentials of Labor Relations* (Englewood Cliffs, NJ: Prentice Hall, 1992), p. 101.

34. For a thorough explanation of the grievance procedure, see ibid., pp. 109–114.

35. See also M. I. Lurie, "The 8 Essential Steps in Grievance Processing," *Dispute Resolution Journal* (November 1999), pp. 61–65.

36. Adapted from P. Stephen Robbins and David A. DeCenzo, *Supervision Today*, 4th ed. (Upper Saddle River, NJ: Prentice Hall, 2004), p. 438.

37. S. Shellenbarger, "Companies Are Finding Real Payoffs in Aiding Employee Satisfaction," *Wall Street Journal* (October 11, 2000), p. B-1.

38. To be accurate, a strike vote is generally held at the local union level in which the members authorize their union leadership to call the strike.

39. U.S. Department of Labor, *Statistical Abstracts of the United States: 2004–2005* (Washington, DC: Government Printing Office, 2005), p. 419; and U.S. Department of Labor, Bureau of Labor Statistics, "Work Stoppages" (April 8, 2005), available online at www.bls.gov.news.release.

40. "Is Workplace Strife Looming?" *University of Toronto News Digest* (July 23, 2005), available online at www.news.utoronto. ca/inthenews/archives/2005_07_24.html.

41. C. Tejada, "Labor Talks Turn into Marathons; Wary of Economic Climate, Unions, Businesses Strive to Avoid Strikes, Lockouts," *Wall Street Journal* (August 22, 2003), p. A3.

42. "Business Brief—Kaiser Aluminum Corp.: United Steelworkers Finalize Labor Pact, Ending Lockout," *Wall Street Journal* (September 19, 2000), p. C-19.

43. K. Helliker, "Grocery Lockout: Food for Thought on Labor's Power—Union Mostly Prevails in Kansas After Replacement Workers Prove Hard to Attract," *Wall Street Journal* (June 30, 2000), p. A-2.

44. Outsourcing in this context refers to a situation where work is taken away from unionized workers in a company and given to nonunionized employees in a separate location.

45. It is also interesting to point out that President Clinton lifted the ban on hiring air traffic controllers who had been fired by President Reagan. Any air traffic controller fired by Reagan was not eligible to work again for the Federal Aviation Administration—the agency that hires air controllers. The removal of the ban came on August 12, 1993.

46. "Union Membership," *Monthly Labor Review* (February 2005), p. 2; and U.S. Department of Labor, Bureau of Labor Statistics, "Union Members Summary" (January 27, 2005), available online at www.bls.gov/news.release/union2. nr0.htm.

47. AFL-CIO, "Trends in Union Membership" (2003), available online at www.aflcio.org.

48. This Workplace Issues vignette is based on AFL-CIO, "Union Summer Q & A" (2005), available online at www.aflcio.org/ aboutunions/unionsummer/qapage.cfm.

49. C. Tejada, "Graduate Students at Private Universities Have Right to Unionize, Agency Rules," *Wall Street Journal* (November 2, 2000), p. B-22; and A. Bernstein, "Big Labor's Day of Reckoning," *Business Week* (March 7, 2005), pp. 65–66.

50. This section based on G. R. King, "New Guidelines From the National Labor Relations Board Regarding Participative Management Initiatives and Employee Committee," *SHRM Legal Report* (August 2001).

51. R. C. Kearney, "Patterns of Union Decline and Growth: An Organizational Ecology Perspective," *Journal of Labor Research* (Fall 2003), p. 561.

52. U.S. Department of Labor, *Statistical Abstracts of the United States: 2004–2005* (Washington, DC: Government Printing Office, 2005), p. 419.

53. M. M. Clark, "AFL-CIO Not Just Blue-Collar Stronghold, Report Says," SHRM Home (September 8, 2003), available online at www.shrm.org/hrnews.

54. Sunshine laws exist in 11 states: Alaska, California, Delaware, Florida, Idaho, Iowa, Minnesota, Texas, Ohio, Vermont, and Wisconsin. In addition, Indiana, Kansas, Maryland, Montana, and Tennessee have laws regarding the openness of the collective-bargaining process.

55. W. Zellner and A. Bernstein, "Up Against the Wal-Mart," *Business Week* (March 13, 2000), pp. 76–78.

56. U.S. Department of Labor, *Employment and Earnings* (January 2001), and AFL-CIO, www.aflcio.org/uniondifference/uniondiff5.htm.

57. K. Pfleger, "Unions Active in High-Tech Fields," *Editor and Publisher* (January 29, 2001), p. 1; A. Bernstein and R. Hof, "A Union for Amazon," *Business Week* (December 4, 2000), p. 86; and A. Bernstein and J. Weber, "So Long, AFL-CIO. Now What?" *Business Week* (August 8, 2005), p. 35.

58. See, for example, R. Harbridge, R. May, and G. Thickett, "The Current State of Play: Collective Bargaining and Union Membership Under the Employment Relations Act of 2000," *New Zealand Journal of Industrial Relations* (September 2003), p. 140.

59. Based on J. Greene, "Into the Penalty Box—Permanently," *Business Week* (February 17, 2005), available online at www.businessweek.com.

60. Based on R. Fisher and W. Ury, *Getting to Yes: Negotiating Agreement Without Giving In* (Boston: Houghton Mifflin, 1981); J. A. Wall Jr., and M. W. Blum, "Negotiations," *Journal of Management* (June 1991), pp. 295–96; M. H. Bazerman and M. A. Neale, *Negotiating Rationally* (New York: Free Press, 1992); David A. DeCenzo and Stephen P. Robbins, *Fundamentals of Management,* 5th ed. (Upper Saddle River, NJ: Prentice Hall, 2006), pp. 413–416.

Glossary

absolute standards Measuring an employee's performance against established standards.

adverse (disparate) impact A consequence of an employment practice that results in a greater rejection rate for a minority group than for the majority group in the occupation.

adverse (disparate) treatment An employment situation where protected group members receive treatment different from other employees in matters such as performance evaluations, and promotions.

affirmative action A practice in organizations that goes beyond discontinuance of discriminatory practices to include actively seeking, hiring, and promoting minority group members and women.

Age Discrimination in Employment Act (ADEA) This act prohibits arbitrary age discrimination, particularly among those over age 40.

agency shop A union security arrangement whereby employees must pay union dues to the certified bargaining unit even if they choose not to join the union.

Albemarle Paper Company v. Moody Supreme Court case that clarified the requirements for using and validating tests in selection processes.

Americans with Disabilities Act of 1990 Extends EEO coverage to include most forms of disability, requires employers to make reasonable accommodations, and eliminates post–job-offer medical exams.

application form Company-specific employment form used to generate specific information the company wants.

assessment center A facility where performance simulation tests are administered. These include a series of exercises used for selection, development, and performance appraisals.

attribution theory A theory of performance evaluation based on the perception of who is in control of an employee's performance.

authorization card A card signed by prospective union members indicating that they are interested in having a union election held at their work site.

baby boomers Individuals born between 1946 and 1965.

background investigation The process of verifying information job candidates provide.

behavioral interview Observing job candidates not only for what they say but how they behave.

behaviorally anchored rating scales (BARS) A performance appraisal technique that generates critical incidents and develops behavioral dimensions of performance. The evaluator appraises behaviors rather than traits.

blind-box ad An advertisement that does not identify the advertising organization.

Blue Cross A health insurer concerned with the hospital side of health insurance.

Blue Shield A health insurer concerned with the provider side of health insurance.

bona fide occupational qualification (BFOQ) Job requirements that are "reasonably necessary to meet the normal operations of that business or enterprise."

broad-banding Paying employees at preset levels based on their level of competency.

burnout Chronic and long-term stress.

career The sequence of positions a person holds over his or her life.

carpal tunnel syndrome A repetitive-motion disorder affecting the wrist.

central tendency The tendency of a rater to give average ratings.

change agent Individual responsible for fostering the change effort and assisting employees in adapting to changes.

checklist appraisal A performance evaluation in which a rater checks off applicable employee attributes.

Civil Rights Act of 1866 Federal law that prohibited discrimination based on race.

Civil Rights Act of 1991 Employment discrimination law that nullified selected Supreme Court decisions. Reinstated burden of proof by the employer, and allowed for punitive and compensatory damage through jury trials.

Civil Service Reform Act Replaced Executive Order 11491 as the basic law governing labor relations for federal employees.

classification method Evaluating jobs based on predetermined job grades.

code of ethics A formal document that states an organization's primary values and the ethical rules it expects organizational members to follow.

collective bargaining The negotiation, administration, and interpretation of a written agreement between two parties, at least one of which represents a group that is acting collectively, that covers a specific period of time.

communications programs HRM programs designed to provide information to employees.

comparable worth Equal pay for jobs similar in skills, responsibility, working conditions, and effort.

compensation administration The process of managing a company's compensation program.

compensation surveys Used to gather factual data on pay practices among firms and companies within specific communities.

competency-based compensation Organizational pay system that rewards skills, knowledge, and behaviors.

complaint procedure A formalized procedure in an organization through which an employee seeks to resolve a work problem.

comprehensive interview A selection device used to obtain in-depth information about a candidate.

comprehensive selection Applying all steps in the selection process before rendering a decision about a job candidate.

concurrent validity Validating tests by using current employees as the study group.

conditional job offer A tentative job offer that becomes permanent after certain conditions are met.

Consolidated Omnibus Budget Reconciliation Act (COBRA) Provides for continued employee benefits up to three years after an employee leaves a job.

constraints on recruiting efforts Factors that can limit recruiting outcomes.

construct validity The degree to which a particular trait relates to successful job performance, as in IQ tests.

content validity The degree to which test content, as a sample, represents all situations that could have been included, such as a typing test for a clerk typist.

contingent workforce The part-time, temporary, and contract workers used by organizations to fill peak staffing needs or perform work not done by core employees.

continuous improvement Organizational commitment to constantly improving quality of products or services.

controlling Management function concerned with monitoring activities to ensure goals are met.

core competency Organizational strengths that represent unique skills or resources.

core employees An organization's full-time employee population.

criterion-related validity The degree to which a particular selection device accurately predicts the important elements of work behavior, as in the relationship between a test score and job performance.

critical incident appraisal A performance evaluation that focuses on key behaviors that differentiate between doing a job effectively or ineffectively.

cut score A scoring point below which applicants are rejected.

decline or late stage The final stage in one's career, usually marked by retirement.

defined benefit plan A retirement program that pays retiring employees a fixed retirement income based on average earnings over a period of time.

diary method A job analysis method requiring job incumbents to record their daily activities.

discipline A condition in the organization when employees conduct themselves in accordance with the organization's rules and standards of acceptable behavior.

dismissal A disciplinary action that results in the termination of an employee.

documentation A record of performance appraisal process outcomes.

domestic-partner benefits Benefits offered to an employee's live-in partner.

downsizing An activity in an organization aim at creating greater efficiency by eliminating certain jobs.

Drug-Free Workplace Act of 1988 Requires specific government-related groups to ensure that their workplace is drug free.

drug testing The process of testing applicants/employees to determine if they are using illicit substances.

dues checkoff Employer withholding of union dues from union members' paychecks.

economic strike An impasse that results from labor and management's inability to agree on the wages, hours, and terms and conditions of a new contract.

employee assistance programs (EAPs) Specific programs designed to help employees with personal problems.

employee benefits Membership-based, nonfinancial rewards offered to attract and keep employees.

employee counseling A process whereby employees are guided in overcoming performance problems.

employee development Future-oriented training that focuses on employee personal growth.

employee handbook A booklet describing important aspects of employment an employee needs to know.

employee monitoring An activity whereby the company keeps informed of its employees' activities.

employee referral A recommendation from a current employee regarding a job applicant.

employee relations function Activities in HRM concerned with effective communications among organizational members.

Employee Retirement Income Security Act (ERISA) Law passed in 1974 designed to protect employee retirement benefits.

employee training Present-oriented training that focuses on individuals' current jobs.

employment-at-will doctrine Nineteenth-century common law that permitted employers to discipline or discharge employees at their discretion.

encounter stage The socialization stage where individuals confront the possible dichotomy between their organizational expectations and reality.

Equal Employment Opportunity Act (EEOA) Granted enforcement powers to the Equal Employment Opportunity Commission.

Equal Employment Opportunity Commission (EEOC) The arm of the federal government empowered to handle discrimination in employment cases.

Equal Pay Act of 1963 This act requires equal pay for equal work.

establishment period A career stage in which one begins to search for work and finds a first job.

ethics A set of rules or principles that defines right and wrong conduct.

executive search firm Private employment agency specializing in middle- and top-management placements.

expatriate An individual who lives and works in a country of which he or she is not a citizen.

exploration period A career stage that usually ends in the mid-twenties as one makes the transition from school to work.

external career Attributes related to an occupation's properties or qualities.

extrinsic rewards Benefits provided by the employer, usually money, promotion, or benefits.

fact-finding A neutral third-party individual who conducts a hearing to gather evidence and testimony from the parties regarding the differences between them.

Fair Credit Reporting Act of 1971 Requires an employer to notify job candidates of its intent to check into their credit.

Fair Labor Standards Act (FLSA) Passed in 1938, this act established laws outlining minimum wage, overtime pay, and maximum hour requirements for most U.S. workers.

Family and Medical Leave Act of 1993 Federal legislation that provides employees up to 12 weeks of unpaid leave each year to care for family members, or for their own medical reasons.

Federal Mediation and Conciliation Service (FMCS) A government agency that assists labor and management in settling disputes.

flexible benefits A benefits program in which employees pick benefits that most meet their needs.

forced-choice appraisal A performance evaluation in which the rater must choose between two specific statements about an employee's work behavior.

4/5ths rule A rough indicator of discrimination, this rule requires that the number of minority members a company hires must equal at least 80 percent of the majority members in the population hired.

glass ceiling The invisible barrier that blocks females and minorities from ascending into upper levels of an organization.

global village A concept in which telecommunication and transportation technologies have effectively reduced time and distance effects to produce a single worldwide economic community.

golden parachute A financial protection plan for executives in case they are severed from the organization.

graphic rating scale A performance appraisal method that lists traits and a range of performance for each.

grievance procedure A complaint-resolving process contained in union contracts.

Griggs v. Duke Power Company Landmark Supreme Court decision stating that tests must fairly measure the knowledge or skills required for a job.

group incentive Motivational plan provided to a group of employees based on the collective work.

group interview method Meeting with a number of employees to collectively determine what their jobs entail.

halo error The tendency to let our assessment of an individual on one trait influence our evaluation of that person on other specific traits.

Hawthorne studies A series of studies that provided new insights into group behavior.

Health Insurance Portability and Accountability Act of 1996 (HIPAA) Ensures confidentiality of employee health information.

Health Maintenance Act of 1973 Established the requirement that companies offering traditional health insurance to its employees must also offer alternative health-care options.

Health Maintenance Organization (HMO) Provides comprehensive health services for a flat fee.

Holland vocational preferences model Represents an individual occupational personality as it relates to vocational themes.

honesty test A specialized question-and-answer test designed to assess one's honesty.

host-country national (HCN) A citizen of the host country hired by an organization based in another country.

hot-stove rule Discipline, like the consequences of touching a hot stove, should be immediate, provide ample warning, be consistent, and be impersonal.

human resource information system (HRIS) A computerized system that assists in the processing of HRM information.

human resource planning Process of determining an organization's human resource needs.

imminent danger A condition where an accident is about to occur.

implied employment contract Any organizational guarantee or promise about job security.

impression management Influencing performance evaluations by portraying an image desired by the appraiser.

IMPROSHARE An incentive plan that uses a specific mathematical formula for determining employee bonuses.

incidence rate Number of injuries, illnesses, or lost workdays as it relates to a common base of full-time employees.

individual incentive plans Motivation systems based on individual work performance.

individual interview method Meeting with an employee to determine what his or her job entails.

individual ranking Ranking employees' performance from highest to lowest.

initial screening The first step in the selection process whereby job inquiries are sorted.

interest arbitration An impasse resolution technique used to settle contract negotiation disputes.

intergroup development Helping members of various groups become a cohesive team.

internal search A promotion-from-within concept.

intrinsic rewards Satisfactions derived from the job itself, such as pride in one's work, a feeling of accomplishment, or being part of a team.

job analysis Provides information about jobs currently being done and the knowledge, skills, and abilities that individuals need to perform the jobs adequately.

job description A statement indicating what a job entails.

job enrichment Enhancing jobs by giving employees more opportunity to plan and control their work.

job evaluation Specifies the relative value of each job in the organization.

job morphing Readjusting skills to match job requirements.

job rotation Moving employees horizontally or vertically to expand their skills, knowledge, or abilities.

job specification Statements indicating the minimal acceptable qualifications incumbents must possess to successfully perform the essential elements of their jobs.

kaizen The Japanese term for an organization's commitment to continuous improvement.

karoshi A Japanese term meaning death from overworking.

knowledge workers Individuals whose jobs are designed around the acquisition and application of information.

Landrum-Griffin Act of 1959 Also known as the Labor and Management Reporting and Disclosure Act, this legislation protected union members from possible wrongdoing on the part of their unions. It required all unions to disclose their financial statements.

late-career stage A career stage in which individuals are no longer learning about their jobs nor expected to outdo levels of performance from previous years.

leading Management function concerned with directing the work of others.

learning organization An organization that values continued learning and believes a competitive advantage can be derived from it.

leased employees Individuals hired by one firm and sent to work in another for a specific time.

legally required benefits Employee benefits mandated by law.

leniency error Performance appraisal distortion caused by evaluating employees against one's own value system.

lockout A situation in labor–management negotiations whereby management prevents union members from returning to work.

maintenance function Activities in HRM concerned with maintaining employees' commitment and loyalty to the organization.

maintenance of membership Requires an individual who chooses to join a union to remain in the union for the duration of the existing contract.

management The process of efficiently completing activities with and through other people.

management by objectives (MBO) A performance appraisal method that includes mutual objective setting and evaluation based on the attainment of the specific objectives.

management thought Early theories of management that promoted today's HRM operations.

Marshall v. Barlow's, Inc. Supreme Court case that stated an employer could refuse an OSHA inspection unless OSHA had a search warrant to enter the premises.

McDonnell-Douglas Corp. v. Green Supreme Court case that led to a four-part test used to determine if discrimination has occurred.

medical/physical exam An examination to determine an applicant's physical fitness for essential job performance.

mentoring or coaching Actively guiding another individual.

merit pay An increase in pay, usually determined annually.

metamorphosis stage The socialization stage during which the new employee must work out inconsistencies discovered during the encounter stage.

mid-career stage A career stage marked by continuous improvement in performance, leveling off in performance, or beginning deterioration of performance.

mission statement A brief statement of the reason an organization is in business.

motivation function Activities in HRM concerned with helping employees exert at high energy levels.

multinational corporations (MNCs) Corporations with significant operations in more than one country.

musculoskeletal disorders (MSDs) Continuous-motion disorders caused by repetitive stress injuries.

National Institute for Occupational Safety and Health (NIOSH) The government agency that researches and sets OSHA standards.

National Labor Relations Board (NLRB) Established to administer and interpret the Wagner Act, the NLRB has primary responsibility for conducting union representation elections.

observation method A job analysis technique in which data are gathered by watching employees work.

open shop Employees are free to join the union or not, and those who decline need not pay union dues.

ordering method Ranking job worth from highest to lowest.

organization culture The system of sharing meaning within the organization that determines how employees act.

organization development (OD) The part of HRM that addresses systemwide change in the organization.

organizing A management function that deals with determining what jobs are to be done, by whom, where decisions are to be made, and how to group employees.

orientation Activities that introduce new employees to the organization and their work units.

outsourcing Sending work outside the organization to be done by individuals not employed full-time with the organization.

paired comparison Ranking individuals' performance by counting the times any one individual is the preferred member when compared with all other employees.

pay-for-performance programs Rewarding employees based on their job performance.

peer evaluation A performance assessment in which co-workers provide input into the employee's performance.

Pension Benefit Guaranty Corporation (PBGC) The organization that lays claim to corporate assets to pay or fund inadequate pension programs.

performance-based rewards Rewards exemplified by the use of commissions, piecework pay plans, incentive systems, group bonuses, or other forms of merit pay.

performance simulation tests Work sampling and assessment centers evaluate abilities in actual job activities.

perquisites Attractive benefits, over and above a regular salary, granted to executives, "perks."

planning A management function focusing on setting organizational goals and objectives.

plant-wide incentive A motivation system that rewards all facility members based on how well the entire group performed.

plateaued mid-career Stagnation in one's current job.

point method Breaking down jobs based on identifiable criteria and the degree to which these criteria exist on the job.

Polygraph Protection Act of 1988 Prohibits the use of lie detectors in screening all job applicants.

Position Analysis Questionnaire (PAQ) A job analysis technique that rates jobs on elements in six activity categories.

post-training performance method Evaluating training programs based on how well employees can perform their jobs after training.

prearrival stage This socialization process stage recognizes that individuals arrive in an organization with a set of organizational values, attitudes, and expectations.

predictive validity Validating tests by using prospective applicants as the study group.

Pregnancy Discrimination Act of 1978 Law prohibiting discrimination based on pregnancy.

Preferred Provider Organizations (PPOs) Organization that requires using specific physicians and health-care facilities to contain the rising costs of health care.

pre–post-training performance method Evaluating training programs based on the difference in performance before and after training.

pre–post-training performance with control group method Evaluating training by comparing pre- and post-training results with untrained individuals.

Privacy Act of 1974 Requires federal government agencies to make available information in an individual's personnel file.

proactive personality Describing those individuals who are more prone to take actions to influence their environment.

qualified privilege The ability for organizations to speak candidly to one another about employees.

quality management Organizational commitment to continuous process of improvement that expands the definition of *customer* to include everyone involved in the organization.

Racketeer Influenced and Corruption Organizations Act (RICO) Law passed to elimnate any influence on unions by members of organized crime.

Railway Labor Act Provided the initial impetus to widespread collective bargaining.

realistic job preview (RJP) A selection device that allows job candidates to learn negative as well as positive information about the job and organization.

reasonable accommodations Providing the necessary technology to enable affected individuals to do a job.

recruiting The process of seeking souring for job candidates.

relative standards Evaluating an employee's performance by comparing the employee with other employees.

reliability A selection device's consistency of measurement.

repetitive stress injuries Injuries sustained by continuous and repetitive movements of the hand.

replacement chart HRM organizational charts indicating positions that may become vacant in the near future and the individuals who may fill the vacancies.

representation certification (RC) The election process whereby union members vote in a union as their representative.

representation decertification (RD) The election process whereby union members vote out their union as their representative.

reverse discrimination A claim made by white males that minority candidates are given preferential treatment in employment decisions.

rightsizing Linking employee needs to organizational strategy.

role ambiguity When an employee is not sure what work to do.

role conflicts Expectations that are difficult to reconcile or achieve.

role overload When an employee is expected to do more than time permits.

Scanlon Plan An organization-wide incentive program focusing on cooperation between management and employees through sharing problems, goals, and ideas.

scientific management A set of principles designed to enhance worker productivity.

sexual harassment Anything of a sexual nature that creates a condition of employment, an employment consequence, or a hostile or offensive environment.

shared services Sharing HRM activities among geographically dispersed divisions.

sick building An unhealthy work environment.

similarity error Evaluating employees based on the way an evaluator perceives himself or herself.

simulation Any artificial environment that attempts to closely mirror an actual condition.

Social Security Retirement, disability, and survivor benefits, paid by the government to the aged, former members of the labor force, the disabled, or their survivors.

socialization A process of adaption that takes place as individuals attempt to learn the values and norms of work roles.

staffing function Activities in HRM concerned with seeking and hiring qualified employees.

strengths An organization's best attributes and abilities.

stress A dynamic condition in which an individual confronts an opportunity, constraint, or demand related to a desire and perceives the outcome as both uncertain and important.

structured questionnaire method A specifically designed questionnaire on which employees rate tasks they perform in their jobs.

suggestion program A process that allows employees to tell management how they perceive the organization is doing.

summary plan description (SPD) An ERISA requirement of explaining to employees their pension program and rights.

survey feedback Assessment of employees' perceptions and attitudes regarding their jobs and organization.

suspension A period of time off from work as a result of a disciplinary process.

SWOT analysis A process for determining an organization's strengths, weaknesses, opportunities, and threats.

Taft-Hartley Act Amended the Wagner Act by addressing employers' concerns in terms of specifying unfair union labor practices.

team-based compensation Pay based on how well the team performed.

technical conference method A job analysis technique that involves extensive input from the employee's supervisor.

technology Any equipment, tools, or operating methods designed to make work more efficient.

Title VII The most prominent piece of legislation regarding HRM, it states the illegalality of discriminating against individuals based on race, religion, color, sex, or national origin.

360-degree appraisals Performance evaluations in which supervisors, peers, employees, customers, and the like evaluate the individual.

training and development function Activities in HRM concerned with assisting employees to develop up-to-date skills, knowledge, and abilities.

Type A behavior Personality type characterized by chronic urgency and excessive competitive drive.

Type B behavior Personality type characterized by lack of either time urgency or impatience.

unemployment compensation Employee insurance that provides some income continuation in the event an employee is laid off.

union Organization of workers, acting collectively, seeking to protect and promote their mutual interests through collective bargaining.

union security arrangements Labor contract provisions designed to attract and retain dues-paying union members.

union shop Any nonunion workers must become dues-paying members within a prescribed period of time.

upward appraisal Employees provide frank and constructive feedback to their supervisors.

validity The proven relationship of a selection device to relevant criterion.

vesting rights The permanent right to pension benefits.

wage structure A pay scale showing ranges of pay within each grade.

Wagner Act Also known as the National Labor Relations Act of 1935, this act gave employees the right to form and join unions and to engage in collective bargaining.

Wards Cove Packing Company v. Atonio A notable Supreme Court case that had the effect of potentially undermining two decades of gains made in equal employment opportunities.

weaknesses Resources an organization lacks or activities it does poorly.

websumés Web pages that are used as résumés.

weighted application form A special type of application form that uses relevant applicant information to determine the likelihood of job success.

wellness programs Organizational programs designed to keep employees healthy.

whistle-blowing A situation in which an employee notifies authorities of wrongdoing in an organization.

wildcat strike An unauthorized and illegal strike that occurs during the terms of an existing contract.

work process engineering Radical, quantum change in an organization.

work sampling A selection device requiring the job applicant to actually perform a small segment of the job.

Worker Adjustment and Retraining Notification (WARN) Act of 1988 Specifies for employers notification requirements when closing down a plant or laying off large numbers of workers.

workers' compensation Employee insurance that provides income continuation if a worker is injured on the job.

workforce diversity The varied personal characteristics that make the workforce heterogeneous.

workplace romance A personal relationship that develops at work.

workplace spirituality The recognition that people have an inner life that nourishes and is nourished by meaningful work that takes place in the context of an organizational community.

written verbal warning Temporary record that a verbal reprimand has been given to an employee.

written warning First formal step of the disciplinary process.

Company Index

Subject Index